Experiencing Cities

Mark Hutter

Rowan University

Boston   New York   San Francisco
Mexico City   Montreal   Toronto   London   Madrid   Munich   Paris
Hong Kong   Singapore   Tokyo   Cape Town   Sydney

Senior Series Editor: *Jeff Lasser*
Series Editorial Assistant: *Erikka Adams*
Senior Marketing Manager: *Kelly May*
Production Supervisor: *Beth Houston*
Composition Buyer: *Linda Cox*
Manufacturing Buyer: *JoAnne Sweeney*
Editorial Production Service and Electronic Composition: *Elm Street Publishing Services, Inc.*
Photo Researcher: *Naomi Rudov*
Cover Administrator: *Joel Gendron*

For related titles and support materials, visit our online catalog at www.ablongman.com.

Between the time website information is gathered and then published, it is not unusual for some sites to have closed. Also, the transcription of URLs can result in typographical errors. The publisher would appreciate notification where these errors occur so that they may be corrected in subsequent editions.

Library of Congress Cataloging-in-Publication Data

Hutter, Mark
    Experiencing cities/Mark Hutter.
        p. cm.
    Includes bibliographical references and index.
    ISBN 0-205-27451-X
    1. Sociology, Urban. 2. Cities and towns. I. Title.

HT151.H89 2007
307.76—dc22   2006050658

Printed in the United States of America

10 9 8 7 6 5 4 3 2 1   10 09 08 07 06

To my parents who taught me to love city life
and
To my wife who shares my love of city life
and
To our children who provide domicile space in DC and NYC

Contents

15 *Baseball as Urban Drama* 371

PART SEVEN • *The Urban World* 391

16 *The Suburbanization of America* 393

17 *Social Capital and Healthy Places* 423

Preface

This book serves as a reflection of both my academic interests in urban sociology and my life-long passion for experiencing city life. As a card-carrying symbolic interactionist, I have particular concerns for understanding interaction dynamics in a wide range of urban and suburban contexts. My deep academic roots in Chicago School Sociology helped inform and let me appreciate the variety of urban structures and processes and their effect on the everyday lives of people living in cities. This book, however, extends the Chicago School perspective by minimizing its urban ecology underpinnings and reintegrating it with a social psychological perspective derived from symbolic interaction incorporated into a macrolevel examination of social organization, social change, social stratification and power in the urban context that is informed by a political economic perspective.

From my earliest memories, family and interpersonal life were integrated with community life within the geographical boundaries of the city. Yet, I was also constantly enamored with leaving my neighborhood and going to "the city" first with my parents and later with my friends or just alone and witnessing what my friend and colleague, Lyn H. Lofland, refers to as "a world of strangers." I, too, was "a walker in the city," as so aptly phrased by Alfred Kazin, and delighted in the sounds and sights of "downtown's" myriad urban activities.

I utilize a systematic urban social psychological perspective derived from symbolic interactionism and informed by political economy that encourages better appreciation of the variety of urban structures and processes and their effect on the everyday lives of people living in both urban and suburban areas. I am concerned about helping students understand the nature and detail of how people experience and give meaning to their lives as urbanites and suburbanites.

This book discusses demographic, social, economic, and political trends in the stability and change of American cities and in the larger metropolitan areas of ever-changing suburbia. This discussion will be informed by attention to the discipline's academic commitment to integrate issues of gender, race, ethnicity, and class into the urban studies curriculum.

This book also seeks to benefit through the utilization of interdisciplinary urban studies particularly through the incorporation of urban geography, urban history, urban literature, and urban art and architectural history. This book features conceptualizations from allied disciplines that reflect areas of convergence with sociology to understand how people experience city life.

What goes into an urban sociology text is to a large extent a matter of judgment. I seek to balance theoretical concerns with descriptive accounts. I sought to produce an informative, interrelated, set of topics that examines, from several perspectives, the urban experience. I believe that this thoughtful topical selection will be especially relevant not only to teachers of urban sociology, but other urbanists who might also find this text useful in enhancing class lectures and discussions. Moreover, I wish this book to be especially beneficial to the students undertaking the sociological examination of urban life that will also enhance their understanding of experiencing cities.

Acknowledgments

This book is the result of a life-long love and fascination with city life. I consider myself so lucky to be able to integrate my experiencing of cities with my academic career. I was most fortunate my mentors at Brooklyn College and the University of Minnesota that included Sidney Aronson, Peter L. Berger, Sylvia Fava, Reuben Hill, Alfred McClung Lee, Audrey Myers, Gregory P. Stone, and Murray Straus provided the theoretical and methodological know-how to foster my own academic understanding of the sociological imagination. My friends and colleagues who share my love of cities and the understanding of them include James R. Abbott, Bernice Braid, Kathy Charmaz, Jay Chaskes, Minna Doskow, Michael Farrell, Frank Falk, David Franks, Mary Gallant, Norman Goodman, Marilyn Goodman, Richard Juliani, David Karp, Irene Levin, Lyn H. Lofland, Patrick Luck, Marianna Luck, DeMond Miller, Melinda Milligan, John Myers, Robert Perinbanayagam, Wilhelmina Perry, Helen Searing, Tony Sommo, Jan Trost, William Yoels, Flora Dorsey Young, and Margaret Zahn. The many students in my courses, especially "Social Psychology of City Life," "Urban Sociology," "Suburban Studies," "Self and Society," and "Sociology of the Family," both provided a sounding board for my ideas and helped mold and sharpen my thinking.

I have had the most wonderful opportunities to participate in interdisciplinary institutes and seminars that helped sharpen and shape my interdisciplinary urban studies perspective. Over the years I have been involved in a number of National Endowment of the Humanities Institutes and Seminars. The directors were Avrom Fleishmann at Johns Hopkins University; Kenneth T. Jackson at Columbia University; Olivier Zunz at the University of Virginia; Townsend Luddington, Joy Kasson, and John Kasson at the University of North Carolina; and William Brumfield (Tulane University) and James C. Curtis (University of Missouri) who conducted their institute in Moscow, Russia; and Robert Bruegmann at the University of Illinois at Chicago. In addition, I have benefited through participation as an Andrew Mellon Fellow: Humanities Seminars for Visiting Scholars at New York University, David M. Reimers, seminar director; and at Rutgers University as a participant in a humanities grant from the New Jersey Department of Higher Education with Virginia Yans-McLaughlin, Project Director. As a participant in the New Jersey State College Fellowship Program at Princeton University under the directorship of Theodore K. Rabb, I attended seminars with John Darley and Georges Teyssot. I am indebted to these individuals and fellow participants for broadening my conceptual lens in understanding the city experience.

My years of involvement in the Society for the Study of Symbolic Interaction, in Alpha Kappa Delta, the International Sociology Honor Society, and in the National Collegiate Honors Council and the North-East Region National Collegiate Honors Council benefited me immeasurably in terms of friendship, colleagueship, and scholarship. My association with faculty and students who were involved in the Bantivoglio Honors Program and in the Department of Sociology enhanced my understanding of the wonders and joys of the academic profession. The Bantivoglio Honors Program's program assistants, Janice Stokes and Francesca McClay and Marianne McCulley, the administrative assistant in the Department of Sociology, were most helpful, supportive, and sympathetic as I vainly tried to balance my various obligations, duties, and responsibilities. Over the years, Rowan University has provided me with research grants that have permitted me the extra time that was vitally needed to work on this project. I would also like to thank the reviewers of this text, William Cross, Illinois College, and Peter Venturelli, Valparaiso University.

I thank my editors at Allyn and Bacon, Jeff Lasser, Karen Hanson, and earlier Sarah Dunbar Kelbaugh for their support of this project. The production team under the supervision of Beth Houston and Eric Arima, the project editor at Elm Street Publishing Services, Inc., was of immeasurable help and most able.

My wife, sweet Lorraine, and our children, Daniel and Elizabeth, all share a common love of city life. Living in the Philadelphia metropolitan area and in the Northeast Corridor of the United States has allowed me to visit many cities very frequently. Further, having children who live in Washington, DC and New York City provides the added incentive to not only see them often but also to appreciate their views of city life and to share with them their city experiences . . . to a certain degree.

MARK HUTTER

Part I

Historical Developments

1

Introduction to Experiencing Cities

The contemporary world is becoming more urban. The twenty-first century marks the first time in history that almost half of the world's inhabitant's live in cities. This is remarkable given that just 200 years ago the vast majority of people lived in rural areas. Today, all industrial nations have become overwhelmingly urbanized, and in the world the processes of urbanization are accelerating rapidly.

The Urban World

The urban population growth is accelerating at a rate of two and a half times faster than it is in rural areas. As of the summer of 2006, approximately 3 billion people (48 percent of the human population) live in urban areas; the 50 percent mark will likely be reached by 2007. At that time, for the first time in history the world will have more urban dwellers than rural ones (*World Urbanization Projects* 2004). By the year 2030 urban areas are expected to be home to more than 6 out of 10 people living on this planet. This is astonishing given that just 250 years ago, only one country—England—could describe itself as an urban society, in which the majority of its people lived in cities and not on farms or in villages.

The pedestrian "dance" in a world of strangers.

The demographer Kingsley Davis (1955) highlights the fact that cities are a recent phenomenon as compared to other aspects of human society and culture:

> Compared to most other aspects of society—e.g., language, religion, stratifaction, or the family—cities appeared only yesterday, and urbanization, meaning that a sizable proportion of the population lives in cities, has developed only in the last few moments of man's existence. (Davis 1955: 429)

The processes of urbanization are accelerating rapidly all over the world. In 1800, only 3 percent of the world's population lived in cities (Hauser and Schnore 1965). In 1950, 29 percent of the world's population lived in cities; in 1975, that figure rose to 37 percent and was approaching 50 percent (47 percent) at the turn of the twenty-first century. By the year 2030, that figure is projected to rise to 61 percent (Torrey 2004). In 1995, 78 percent of the developed countries and 40 percent of the developing countries had urban populations (Statistical Abstracts 1997). According to projections, the less developed areas of the world (Africa, Asia, Latin America, and Oceania) will all have more than 50 percent of their populations living in cities by the year 2030 (Torrey 2004). Today, more than 421 cities, many of which did not even exist two hundred years ago, have populations of 1 million or more (Brinkhoff 2004). Barbara Boyle Torrey (2004), writing for the Population Research Bureau, observes that the most striking examples of the urbanization of the world are the megacities of 10 million or more people.

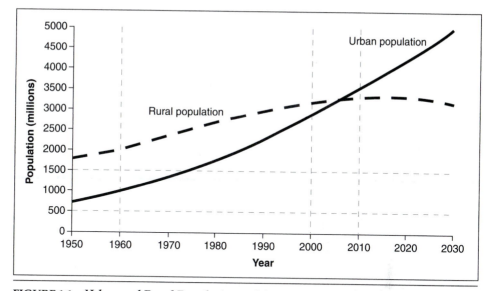

FIGURE 1.1 *Urban and Rural Populations of the World: 1950–2030.*

Source: United Nations Department of Economic and Social Affairs/Population Division. 2004. *World Urbanization Prospects: The 2003 Revision.* New York: United Nations.

In 1950 only two (New York City and Tokyo) existed. The number doubled to four in 1975 with the addition of Shanghai and Mexico City. In 2003 there were 20 megacities, and the United Nations estimates that by 2015 there will be 22 (United Nations 2004).

This rapid growth in the urbanization of the world is startling given the patterns of population growth and the rates of urbanization prior to the twentieth century. Only within the time span of the last two hundred years, concurrent with the Industrial Revolution, has a sizable proportion of the human population lived in cities. Indeed, at the time when cities are believed to have first emerged, approximately 7,000 to 10,000 years ago, there were only about 5 million human beings on the face of this planet, about the same number that currently live in Chicago (Davis 1955). Advances in agriculture associated with the movement away from the nomadic hunting and gathering economy led to accelerated population growth. From the period when cities emerged until 1 AD the worldwide population was about 250 million. It took only about 1,650 years for the population to double to one-half billion, and in a mere 200 years (AD 1850) it doubled again. Then, in a time span of only 80 years—from 1850 to 1930—the population increased to 2 billion. By 1975, 45 years later, the population again doubled to approximately 4 billion people. By the end of the twentieth century the world's population reached 6 billion. By the year 2030 the United Nations (United Nations 2004) predicts that 8 billion people will be living on this planet. Most of the population growth will occur in the poorest and least developed countries located in

TABLE 1.1   *Population of Urban Agglomerations with 10 Million Inhabitants or More: 1950, 1975, 2003, and 2015 (millions)*

	1950		1975		2003		2015	
	Urban Agglomeration	Population	Urban Agglomeration	Population	Urban Agglomeration	Population	Urban Agglomeration	Population
1	New York, USA[1]	12.3	Tokyo, Japan	26.6	Tokyo, Japan	35.0	Tokyo, Japan	36.2
2	Tokyo, Japan	11.3	New York, USA[1]	15.9	Mexico City, Mexico	18.7	Mumbai (Bombay), India	22.6
3			Shanghai, China	11.4	New York, USA[1]	18.3	Delhi, India	20.9
4			Mexico City, Mexico	10.7	São Paulo, Brazil	17.9	Mexico City, Mexico	20.6
5					Mumbai (Bombay), India	17.4	São Paulo, Brazil	20.0
6					Delhi, India	14.1	New York, USA[1]	19.7
7					Calcutta, India	13.8	Dhaka, Bangladesh	17.9
8					Buenos Aires, Argentina	13.0	Jakarta, Indonesia	17.5
9					Shanghai, China	12.8	Lagos, Nigeria	17.0
10					Jakarta, Indonesia	12.3	Calcutta, India	16.8
11					Los Angeles, USA[2]	12.0	Karachi, Pakistan	16.2
12					Dhaka, Bangladesh	11.6	Buenos Aires, Argentina	14.6
13					Osaka-Kobe, Japan	11.2	Cairo, Egypt	13.1
14					Rio de Janeiro, Brazil	11.2	Los Angeles, USA[2]	12.9
15					Karachi, Pakistan	11.1	Shanghai, China	12.7
16					Beijing, China	10.8	Metro Manila, Philippines	12.6
17					Cairo, Egypt	10.8	Rio de Janeiro, Brazil	12.4
18					Moscow, Russian Federation	10.5	Osaka-Kobe, Japan	11.4
19					Metro Manila, Philippines	10.4	Istanbul, Turkey	11.3
20					Lagos, Nigeria	10.1	Beijing, China	11.1
21							Moscow, Russian Federation	10.9
22							Paris, France	10.0

[1] Refers to the New York–Newark urbanized areas.

[2] Refers to the Los Angeles–Long Beach–Santa Ana urbanized area.

Source: United Nations Department of Economic and Social Affairs/Population Division. 2004. *World Urbanization Prospects: The 2003 Revision.* New York: United Nations.

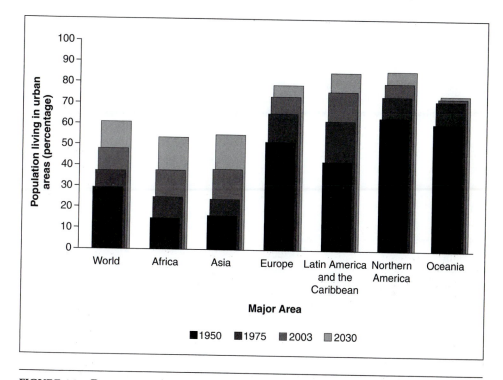

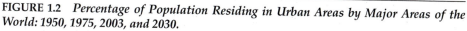

FIGURE 1.2 *Percentage of Population Residing in Urban Areas by Major Areas of the World: 1950, 1975, 2003, and 2030.*

Source: United Nations Department of Economic and Social Affairs/Population Division. 2004. *World Urbanization Prospects: The 2003 Revision.* New York: United Nations.

Africa, southern Asia, and Latin America. Further, almost all of that growth is expected to reside in the urban areas of the less-developed regions of the world.

The last half of the twentieth century saw an urban population explosion never seen before in the history of the world. The first urban revolution began about 10,000 years ago, with the origin and development of cities. It was followed by the second urban revolution nearly 11,800 years later (1800 AD), which was brought about by the Industrial Revolution—led by Western capitalism first in England, Germany, and France, and later the United States and then through European colonization of almost the entire world. From our current perspective, the beginning of the twentieth-first century, we can see the globalization of urbanization patterns that began in earnest after World War II. Indeed, a third urbanization revolution is occurring, characterized by massive urban growth in non-Western cities and, in effect, the urbanization of the entire world.

In 1950, five years after World War II, the list of the 15 largest cities in the world was dominated by Western cities, with New York City being the largest metropolitan area in the world. Also on that list were London, United Kingdom; Paris, France; Moscow, Russian Federation; Essen (Rhein-Ruhr North), Germany;

TABLE 1.2   *Milestones in World Total and Urban Populations*

Type of Data	World Population (billions)	Year When Reached	Number of Years It Took to Increase by One Billion	Urban Population (billions)	Year When Reached	Number of Years It Took to Increase by One Billion
Estimates	1	1804		1	1960	
	2	1927	123	2	1985	25
	3	1960	33			
	4	1974	14			
	5	1987	13			
	6	1999	12			
Medium projection variant	7	2012	13	3	2002	17
	8	2028	16	4	2017	15
	8.1	2030		4.9	2030	

Source: United Nations Department of Economic and Social Affairs/Population Division. 2004. *World Urbanization Prospects: The 2003 Revision.* New York: United Nations.

Chicago, United States of America; Los Angeles, United States of America; Milan, Italy; and Berlin, Germany. According to United Nations data (United Nations 2004), in 2000 only two United States cities, New York City and Los Angeles, remained on that list, and they ranked third and tenth, respectively. In 2015, New York City is projected to slip to sixth, and Los Angeles, to the next-to-lowest ranked of the 15 most populous cities. Among those cities from non-Western countries expected on that list are eight cities from Asia [Tokyo, Mumbai (Bombay), Delhi, Dhaka, Jakarta, Calcutta, Karachi, and Shanghai]; four from Central and South America (Mexico City, Sao Paulo, Buenos Aires, and Rio de Janeiro); and two from Africa (Lagos and Cairo). *No* European city is projected to be on the list.

This book will examine the effects of *urbanization, urban growth,* and *urban transition* on the lives of city dwellers—*urbanism. Urbanization* is defined as the expansion of a city or metropolitan area. More specifically it refers to the proportion of the total population that lives in urban locales, including cities and towns, and to the proportional increase of this urban population over its rural counterparts. *Urban growth* refers to the rate that an urban population or area increases over a given period of time relative to its initial size at the start of that period. *Urban transition* refers to the redistribution of population from a predominantly rural, agricultural world to a predominantly urban, nonagricultural world. *Urbanism* is defined as the social and psychological consequences that urbanization, urban growth, and the urban transition have on an urban population. It refers to the behaviors and social patterns anchored by norms, values, and customs of people living in cities.

What are the key factors for such urban population growth? What are the economic, political, social, and environmental global interconnections? What are the consequences of such extremely rapid urban population growth on city dwellers in the longer established cities of the West and for the newer cities rapidly developing in other parts of the world? How has it affected human life? How do people experience cities?

Civilization and Cities

The growth of cities has long been associated with the idea of human progress and with an underlying belief that equates cities with *civilization. Civilization* is often defined as a highly developed society and culture. Accompanying that definition is the belief that the center of civilization is the city. The words *civilization* and *city* are etymologically linked. Indeed, the very word, *civilization*, has its etymological roots in the Latin word for city, *civitas*. The origin of the word *city* comes from the Latin word *civitas* that refers to both the city and its inhabitants—*citizens*. The word *urban* is itself a derivative of the Latin word *urbs*, which refers to the physical structures or buildings—the built environment—that make up a city. Of particular emphasis is the belief that while the built environment composed of buildings, bridges, and roads makes up the physical structure of the city, it's the interactions and relationships among city dwellers that make up the community.

One of the most prominent urbanologists of the twentieth century, Lewis Mumford (1938) puts forth the fundamental importance of cities and the articulation of human culture:

> The city, as one finds it in history, is the point of maximum concentration for the power and culture of a community . . . The city is the form and symbol of an integrated social relationship: it is the seat of the temple, the market, the hall of justice, the academy of learning. Here in the city the goods of civilization are multiplied and manifolded; here is where human experience is transformed into viable signs, symbols, patterns of conduct, systems of order. Here is where the issues of civilization are focused: here, too, ritual passes on occasion into the active drama of a fully differentiated and self-conscious society. (Mumford 1938:3)

The etymological origin of the word *civilization* from *civitas* is a reflection of the belief that human culture emerges from city life. The city has played an historical role in the transformation of culture and is the setting in which new states of mind come into being. I follow the definition put forth by a former teacher, Sylvia Fava, and her associate Noel Gist that the term "civilization" refers "to a complex social system that involves its participants in a different set of interaction than do noncivilized societies" (Gist and Fava 1974: 3).

"City air makes men free" (Stadt luft macht frei) is a medieval adage referring to the right of a serf to become a free person after one year and one day in a city (Clapp 1984: 11). This adage has taken on wider meaning in recognizing that cities are influential in broadening one's thoughts and ideas from the parochial control of smaller rural communities. Park and Burgess in their seminal *Introduction to the Science of Sociology* state:

> The old adage which describes the city as the natural environment of the free man still holds as far as the individual man finds in the chances, the diversity of tasks, and in the vast unconscious co-operation of city life, the opportunity to choose his own vocation and develop his peculiar individual talents. (Park and Burgess 1970/1921:352)

The dominant concern of this book is the impact of the city on the human experience. Kingsley Davis (1909–1997), one of the most preeminent sociologists of the twentieth century, remarked that in the course of world history urban developments represent fundamental change in "the whole pattern of social life . . . . and affect every aspect of existence" (1955:429).

In this book we will examine how people experience cities in their everyday lives. However, in order to have a microlevel understanding of what is referred to as the "social psychology of city life," we must have a basic understanding of the macrolevel character of a city—how a city is shaped by political, economic, and social and cultural institutions.

Microlevel Sociology and Macrolevel Sociology and Experiencing Cities

There are some sociologists who focus on how people perceive and interact in the built environment of the city—a *microlevel* approach. Microlevel sociology focuses on the pattern of interactional dynamics especially as they impact on individuals in a social setting. Other sociologists focus on the economic and political institutions and how they impact on and are reflected in land-use patterns of the built environment of the city—a *macrolevel* approach. Macrolevel sociology focuses on the interrelationships of structures and organizations of a society. The interplay between economic and political factors and, to a lesser extent, social and cultural factors is investigated to see how they impact on those structures and organizations.

In this book, the microsociological approach of *symbolic interactionism* has strongly influenced my intellectual orientation to the study of city life. Symbolic interactionism is the study of how people use shared symbols to define and give meaning to their environment and make sense of their world. Included within this perspective are concerns with constructions of identity, socialization, and interactional patterns. Most importantly, however, the macrosociological approach put forth by *urban political economy* has also had a strong impact on this analysis. Urban political economy examines historical changes brought about by political and economic institutions on large-scale structures and features of the city—social class, specialization of functions, divisions of labor, power and authority—and how they impact on land-use patterns and the built environment.

I seek to demonstrate how the experience of cities becomes manifest through the reciprocal influence of both microlevel factors and macrolevel factors.

The macrolevel approach to the study of microlevel interactional patterns tends to see those patterns as being determined by large-scale structural features of society or the cultural and value systems. There is little analysis, or recognition, of the way that people can be creative in their interaction with others. For the most part, social interaction is seen as being determined by social norms and mores, secular laws and sacred religion, economics and class, and societal imposed consciousness and ideology. In contrast, the microlevel approach emphasizes the emergent creative aspects of individuals and the nondetermined emergent quality of social interaction. The proper study of social interaction patterns can only be accomplished through the examination of the meanings and ways that symbols, structures, and organization are perceived by individuals and how different individuals often come to interpret interaction differently. Unfortunately, the reciprocal affects that macrolevel factors and microlevel factors have on individuals, structures, and organizations are often downplayed or not recognized.

Sociology as a discipline arose in the nineteenth century as a consequence of dramatic changes in European societies as they saw their nonindustrial and rural communities change as a consequence of the Industrial Revolution and rapid urbanization. Sociologists who took a microlevel perspective focused on the change from rural society to urban society and how that change impacted on people's mentality and the interactional patterns they had with family, neighbors, friends, and strangers. Sociologists who took a macrolevel perspective focused on the way institutions in the society were changing as a consequence of the movement away from an agricultural-based rural economy to an industrial-manufacturing economy. Migration patterns from the countryside into the city, emerging economic and class structures and institutions, and the dynamics of urban growth patterns were of central concern. In a later chapter, I will focus on the political and economic factors that gave rise to industrialization and urbanization and eventually to today's urban world. Now, I want to spell out in more detail the symbolic interaction perspective and its utility in studying how people experience cities.

Symbolic Interactionism and the Study of City Life

This book is anchored in the theoretical perspective of symbolic interaction. Symbolic interaction is a social psychological perspective that begins with the basic premise that people are active interpreters of their environment. Further, they respond to their environment on the basis of their interpretations of that environment. The objective conditions of that environment are seen to influence behavior through the interpretive process, and behavior is not seen to be simply a mechanical or automatic response to the environment. George Herbert Mead (1863–1931), a philosopher at the University of Chicago, taught a very popular course in social psychology. Lecture notes compiled by students who attended that class were posthumously published as *Mind, Self and Society*. This book (Mead 1934) articulated the theoretical premises of what has become known as symbolic interactionism.

Herbert Blumer (1900–1987), a student of Mead's, set forth the basic tenet of symbolic interaction that applies to the study of the city. Blumer taught the Social Psychology course after Mead no longer was able to do so. For the next 25 years and for a similar period of time at the University of California at Berkeley, Blumer, who coined the term *symbolic interaction*, was the key influential figure for the development of the perspective.

Blumer outlines three basic premises that relate to the importance of meaning in human action, the source of meaning, and the role of meaning in interpretation:

1. Human beings act toward things on the basis of the meanings that the things have for them.
2. The meanings of things arise out of the social interactions one has with his or her fellows.
3. These meanings are handled or modified through an interpretive process used by persons in dealing with the objects or situations that they encounter. (Blumer 1969: 2)

Karp, Stone, and Yoels (1977) in their seminal book, *Being Urban,* succinctly summarize how the symbolic interaction perspective is applied to the study of the built environment of the community and the city:

> The perspective of symbolic interaction is based on the uncomplicated idea that the social world is composed of acting, thinking, reacting, and interpreting human beings in interaction with one another. Persons are not merely puppets pushed around by forces over which they have no control. As symbolic interactionists we hold a picture of social life in which persons are the architects of their worlds. Reality is, then, socially constructed and to understand human behavior we must inquire into those processes through which persons do construct and transform their social worlds . . . For those who accept the validity of these premises, the major concern of any social psychological treatment is to establish the relationship between the meanings persons attach to their environments and the consequences of these "definitions of the situation" for their behavior. (Karp, Stone, and Yoels 1977: vi)

Symbolic interactionists believe that environmental space, whether a building, a street, a neighborhood, or a city, should not be perceived solely in terms of its physical structure or characteristics. Rather, it should also be seen in terms of the symbolic meaning it has for people. This perspective, while recognizing that meanings will vary by social, political, cultural, educational, religious, and economic factors, does not focus on or fully integrate how these factors come into play in the ability to define social reality. People and groups in positions of power can influence the social construction of reality through their ability to influence and control norms and values. I will have more to say about conceptual limitation in later chapters. For now, I want to look at the basic premises of symbolic interaction and how it orients thinking about the built environment and the experiencing of cities. I will examine the thinking of four major sociologists, whose viewpoints scan the twentieth century—W. I. Thomas, Robert E. Park, Anselm Strauss, and Lyn H. Lofland.

W. I. Thomas: The Definition of the Situation

To reiterate, a basic premise of symbolic interaction is that an individual's response to someone's behavior is based on the *meaning* that is attached to that behavior. The question remains on how these "meanings" are derived. Typically, these meanings reflect the norms and values of the dominant culture as learned through socialization experiences. The meanings attached to people's actions are shaped by our interactions with them within the context of the larger society. Berger and Luckmann (1966) take this perspective to the next level and observe that reality itself can be seen as being socially constructed from social interactions. "Reality" is thus shaped by perceptions, evaluations, and definitions that emerge out of participation in ongoing social interactional processes.

W. I. Thomas (1863–1947) was an influential sociologists who was at the University of Chicago in the early part of the twentieth century. Thomas focused on the importance of the interactive dependence of individuals and social life and culture. He probably is best known for his term (1923) "the definition of the situation" that appeared in *The Unadjusted Girl*. By this term he meant that before an individual acts, he or she ascertains, examines, and deliberates. In a 1928 book, *The Child in America*, his famous theorem appears (Thomas and Thomas 1928: 572): "If men define situations as real, they are real in their consequences." His assertion is that human behavior is ultimately subjective. He observed that people respond not only to the objective features of a situation but also to the meaning that the situation has for them. A key component of social interaction is people's interpretation or definitions of others' behavior in given situations.

To understand human behavior we need to know how people define reality. Thomas believed that a person's actions were based on his or her "definition of the situation." He further noted that how a person defines a situation may differ from the definitions provided by the society and may reflect those of the group(s) s/he belonged to. Building on this conceptualization, Karp, Stone, and Yoels (1977) assert that the *interpretations* that people have of their objective social statuses, attributes, and group affiliations may have greater impact on their behavior and their sense of identification as urbanites: "A sense of community may reside in a person's feelings of identification with a city. Such identification cannot be appreciated by simply documenting urbanites' structural position" (Karp, Stone, and Yoels 1977: 78).

In his most influential work, *The Polish Peasant in Europe and America,* written with Florian Znaniecki (1882–1958), Thomas examined Polish immigrants in Chicago in the early part of the twentieth century. This work has been recognized by such prominent contemporary theorists as Lewis Coser (1977) as being one of the major landmarks of early American sociological research. It utilized a biographical approach to understanding the transnational study of migration. Thomas and Znaniecki's focus was on the adjustment of Polish rural peasant immigrants to urban big-city Chicago. They used a vast assortment of personal life history documents including case histories, letters to or from immigrants to America, archives from a Polish newspaper, and documents from Polish-American parishes and organizations. It has become popular sociological folklore that Thomas's interest in personal documents was spurred by his being nearly hit by trash thrown out of a window that contained a personal letter written by a Polish immigrant women.

Thomas and Znaniecki were interested in detailing the connections between individuals' definition of the situation and their family and community affiliations and backgrounds. In one example, they note that a group of young uneducated men who were subjugated to horrible working conditions in mills and factories felt that it might be easier to rob banks. They speculate that these men's misperceptions of the difficulty of actually achieving a successful bank robbery could have resulted in very negative results. Kornblum and Julian (1998:13) who utilize this example conclude: "Thus from the interactionist perspective an individual or group's definition of the situation is central to understanding the actions of that individual or group."

The significance of Thomas and Znaneicki's *The Polish Peasant* is demonstrating the importance of the social environment for individuals' understanding of their lives and circumstances and how through such understandings individuals can impact and change their environment. Andrew Abbott (1999: 208) in his assessment of the work of Thomas and Znaneicki states that this work "showed how the complexities of the social environment worked themselves out in individual lives and then rebounded through the individuals to reshape the environment and institutions. The relation of individual and society was thus itself reconceptualized as one of mutual contexts for each other."

Robert E. Park: The City as a State of Mind

Robert E. Park (1864–1944) was influenced by the work of Georg Simmel, whom he studied with in Germany. Simmel's formulations emphasized the necessity to study the social psychological effects that city life has on its inhabitants rather than to study the city totally as a physical environment. In his influential essay, "The Metropolis and Mental Life," Simmel (1995) raises the ideas that the city values rationality more than emotionality (the head rather than the heart), and emphasizes the importance of the money economy, impersonality, punctuality, and a blasé attitude. These values, in turn, lead to an emphasis on personal freedom unique to city life. In his opening remarks in his important essay, "The City: Suggestions for the Investigation of Human Behavior in the Urban Environment," (1925/1967), Robert Park states a basic premise of symbolic interaction thought on the nature of urban imagery and urban identification that the city is a "state of mind":

> The city is . . . a state of mind, a body of customs and traditions, and of the organized attitudes and sentiments that inhere in these customs and are transmitted with the tradition. The city is not, in other words, merely a physical mechanism and an artificial construction. It is involved in the vital processes of the people who compose it. (Park 1925/1966)

Park's statement emphasized symbolic and psychological adjustments to the social organization of urban life influenced by shared sentiments and values. Park saw the city as a product of the participation and communication of its inhabitants and not simply as a physical artifact or a collection of people. He was particularly interested in the urban conditions that resulted in the breakdown of human communication and interaction that ultimately led to the decline of the primary group, the breakdown of the community, and to social disorganization. Park utilized Charles Horton Cooley's concept of primary group—a group in which face-face association and cooperation predominated—to articulate this view. "It is probably the breaking down of local attachments and the weakening of the restraints and inhibitions of the primary group, under the influence of the urban environment, which are largely responsible for the increase of vice and crime in great cities" (Park 1966/1925: 25).

However, Park also employed an ecological model of city life. The following quote indicates how he saw the interconnectedness between ecology and social psychology: "The city is rooted in the habits and customs of the people who inhabit it. The consequence is that the city possesses *moral* as well as a *physical organization*, and these two mutually interact in characteristic ways to mold and modify one another" (italics added) (Park 1966/1925: 4). This reference to "physical organization" reflects Park's interest in urban ecology.

The ecological model borrowed terms from biology and environmental ecology and is concerned with the interrelationships between people and their spatial setting and physical environment. Park utilized the ideas by ecologists who studied plant and animal communities to examine city life and urban land use patterns. The ecological model gradually dominated his theoretical orientation. The cultural model, with its concern for the social psychological and cultural emphasis in the study of city life, took on secondary importance and significance. I will have more to say about the ecological perspective and its usage in urban sociology with particular focus on the Chicago School and Burgess's concentric zone hypothesis in a later chapter. For now, let's bookmark it, and look at the next influential urbanist social psycholgist, Anselm Strauss.

Anselm L. Strauss: *Images of the City*

Anselm L. Strauss (1917–1996) was a student of Herbert Blumer. In his *Images of American Cities* (1961) Strauss sets forth his intellectual agenda. "It is a framework of a social psychologist—which in this instance means a joining of sociological, psychological, and historical perspectives" (1961: x). His particular concern is the examination of American imagery with focus on the "spatial and temporal aspects of that imagery." That is, he is concerned with the "meaning" that the city has for its inhabitants. By "urban imagery" Strauss is referring to the symbolization of the city.

With the historian R. Richard Wohl (Wohl and Strauss 1958), Strauss first picks up on the theme articulated by Park that the city is "a state of mind." They comment on the nature of urban imagery and urban identification by informing us that given objects of the city become symbolically representative of the city as a whole. Thus the New York skyline, San Francisco's Golden Gate Bridge, and the French Quarter of New Orleans became the identification symbol of the given city and serve as a source of personal identification for the inhabitants. They point out how the spatial complexity and the social diversity of a city often become integrated by the use of "sentimental" history in selected landscapes such as the Water Tower in Chicago or Telegraph Hill in San Francisco. They build on this observation by arguing that an invariable characteristic of city life is that in order to "see" the city people must employ certain stylized and symbolic objects.

> The city, then, sets problems of meaning. The streets, the people, the buildings, the changing scenes do not come already labelled. They require explanation and interpretation. (Wohl and Strauss 1958:527)

In his perceptive monograph, *Images of the American City*, Strauss (1961) builds on his essay with Wohl. He observed that people know best ("see") those parts of a city that they are intimately involved in—where they go to school, where they shop, where they work, and where they meet their friends. In Strauss's words:

> The various kinds of urban perspectives held by the residents of a city are constructed from spatial representations resulting from membership in particular social worlds (1961: 67).

For Strauss, then, the images that a person has of the city are based on relationships. Images can be seen as a spatial consequence of the different types of social relationship that people have with each other in different places. Strauss examined how the physical reality of cities is interpreted through the "images" that people have of the cities. The *feelings* that people have of cities impact on how they perceive and act toward them.

Strauss also placed these images in an historical context. He believed that these images do not come out of the blue but are conceptualized through an understanding of the rapid historical transformation of rural America to an urban society. Of essential interest to Strauss was how this social change was observed and felt by its citizens. By getting an understanding of how people "saw" the city, one would get a better understanding of how they experienced it. "What Americans see and have seen in their towns, and what they say and have said about them, can tell us a great deal about how they lived in them, how they have felt about, how they have managed to cope with the problems raised by the conditions of life there" (Strauss 1961: viii).

Strauss examined the writings of Americans on the different viewpoints that were held of rural, regional, and urban life, on the processes and consequences of rapid urbanization, on the attraction and fear manifested toward cities. He investigated through this examination of the writings on American cities why some viewed the city as exciting and friendly, while others viewed it with fear and dread. Lyn Lofland (2003) in her assessment of Strauss observes that Strauss was not only interested in recording the symbolic representations historically attached to American cities, but also their consequences. "He wanted to grasp the form and themes of those representations in their own right, but he also viewed them as phenomenon with serious consequences for other areas of social life; that is, he was interested in mapping the symbols and in tracing their uses and abuses" (Lofland (2003:946).

Gist and Fava (1979: 583) point out that Strauss's emphasis on the "subjective side of American urbanization" is not fully developed in urban sociology. They concur with Strauss on the importance of understanding the sentiments and symbols attached to cities. They argue that emotional and symbolic representations of cities color not only the attitudes that people have toward cities but often have social policy implications. They further observe that the study of the American city has often been subjugated to an anti-urban bias reflecting a deep-seated preference for the rural way of life. Through the twentieth century and into the twenty-first century this bias continues with the "ideal" way of life being lived in the suburbs. This viewpoint has led to dire consequences for American cities and is one factor that helps explain the predominance of suburbs in contemporary society. This theme will be extensively examined in later parts of this book. As Lofland emphasizes (2003) Strauss's concern with mapping city symbolic representations and tracing their uses and abuses is a continuing concern of symbolic interactionists and is reflected in this book as well.

Lyn Lofland: The World of Strangers and the Public Realm

Lyn H. Lofland (1938–) is a self-defined "unashamed cityphile" (quoted in Perry, Abbott, and Hutter 1997). She has spent most of her academic career at the University of California–Davis building on the conceptual framework of symbolic interaction and its utility to study urban life. Lofland has articulated a view of the "city as a world of strangers" and on the critical importance of the "public realm" as the "quintessential social territory" (1973, 2000). The importance of Lofland's work rests on her emphasis and analysis of the *public realm*—social-psychological space, often associated with cities, that contains streets, plazas, parks, bus stations, downtown bars, and coffee shops and is inhabited by people who don't know each other.

> A crucial dynamic of the public realm emerges from the fact that not only do many of the inhabitants not "know" one another in the biographical sense, they often also do not "know" one another in the cultural sense. The public realm is populated not only by persons who have not met but often, as well, by persons who do not share "symbolic worlds." (Lofland 1998: 8)

In *A World of Strangers: Order and Action in Public Space* (1973), Lofland proposes that entering the world of strangers is the peculiar, distinctive urban experience—being "a stranger in the midst of strangers." Lofland cogently argued for the salience of the public domain: "To cope with the city is among other things, to cope with strangers [and] . . . The locus of the city as a world of strangers resides in the city's public space" (1973: x).

Lofland historically analyzed the various techniques utilized by urban dwellers to create social-psychological order in the city. She argued that both appearance and location provided cues to the identity of strangers in the public realm. She observes that the trend of urban history is the movement from appearantial order to spatial order in her study of the preindustrial city, the early industrial city, and the modern city. The investigation of contemporary urban public behavior was a wonderful display of a symbolic interactionist's skills in studying interactional processes in that world of strangers.

In *The Public Realm*, Lofland (1998) fully articulates her analysis of the city by focusing on the "city's quintessential social territory." It is here, in the public space of parks, plazas, and streets that a special form of social life is articulated and gives the city its special character. Lofland, working with a fellow symbolic interactionist, Spencer Cahill, in an edited collection of papers on the "community of the streets (Cahill and Lofland 1994) observes that even in reference to "the streets," which carries with it "the ideas of alienation, asociality, and unrelieved anonymity"—viable and important patterns of social life exist and flourish (Cahill and Lofland 1994: xiv). Lofland examines the characteristics of the public realm by looking at the underlying patterns and principles of its normative system, the relational web of participants, places, and temporality and location.

In *The Public Realm*, Lofland (1998) puts forth a devastating critique of the anti-urban bias toward the public realm, the emotional and behavioral forms that this bias takes as particularly guided by a belief in the glorification of privatism and the fear and loathing of public life. By *privatism*, Lofland means the "personalistic and individualistic" lifestyle choice whereby people move their activity out of the public realm where "some things that humans used to do outside their private spaces in the presence of their neighbors, their acquaintances, or strangers, they do exclusively or mostly or increasingly inside their private space in the presence—if of anyone at all—of intimates (1998: 143–144). She adds a caustic look at architectural power (evident in "the fortressing of America" and gated communities) guided by this anti-urban anti-public–realm perspective. This bias has severely distorted the conceptual lens in viewing city life, and Lofland analyzes its consequences. In turn, this conceptual distortion is shown by Lofland to have consequences on how individuals develop their "definitions of the situation":

> As we know from innumerable microsociological studies, definitions of the situation bring macrophenomena to the microlevel; they link such large-scale entities as ideologies with the cognitive and emotional processes of individual human actors. That is, as they go about trying to make sense of the situations in which they find themselves, humans are relying not only on "clues" currently available to them, nor only on their past experiences, nor only on a combination of the two. They are also drawing upon the lore of their social group: upon the cultural, political, and other "stories" that their "people" tell about various objects. And, . . . many of these stories about settlements that Anglo-American people now tell and have told for many years are strongly antiurban. (Lofland 1998: 169)

Lofland has been acutely aware of the importance of macrolevel analysis to both the understanding and the context of how political and economic inequality is articulated in the everyday world of stranger interaction patterns. But she takes issue with those who would study the city solely in terms of it as a site for social disorganization or as a dependent variable susceptible to national and international economic and political forces. She asserts the need to extend urban analyses to include the study of social organizational forms of city life, the nature of the urban community as the site for communal sentiments, and, most important, the unique dimension of the social-psychological urban environment. It is in her investigation of the public realm, a realm inhabited, for the most part, by strangers, that Lofland makes an outstanding contribution to symbolic interaction. Rather than focus on the individual, the unit of analysis for Lofland is the nature of the interactional patterns that develops among strangers in everyday circumstances in the public realm.

Experiencing Cities through Symbolic Interactionism

In this chapter I have introduced the theoretical perspective of symbolic interaction that anchors my intellectual understanding of city life. In an analysis of the contributions, utility, and limitations of symbolic interaction tied to urban sociology, Perry, Abbott, and Hutter (1997: 60) describe two specific analytical interests of urban interactionists—"behaviors and relations in urban places (or *the place approach*) and role identities of special categories of urbanites (or *the people approach*)," and suggest a third, the *urban imagery approach.*

The place approach focused on the refutation of the "community lost" theme in urban sociology. A long-standing theme in urban sociology centers on the urbanization and the growth of cities brought about by the Industrial Revolution, which led to the disappearance of communities based on primary relationships of family, which, in turn, led to the disappearance in the city of kinship, neighbors, and friends. Research studies begun in the 1950s and 1960s "rediscovered the community." This research led to a new assumption in the discipline that urban settings do not necessarily work against community viability. Another line of inquiry about "urban place" is that there are settings in the city, away from home and work, in which people can gather voluntarily and informally, and, if so desired, on a regular basis. A third line of inquiry is the focus of the public sphere as the site for meaningful social interactions that are qualitatively different from the social relationships that exist in the private setting of the home or in the community.

The urban people approach has a basic theme of the search for "meaningful" identity in the urban context and a concomitant notion of "incompleteness" (Perry, Abbot, and Hutter 1997: 75). Here the examination is of "regulars" in urban scenes such as bars and coffee houses. Also attention is given to those with stigmatized and/or vulnerable identities such as minorities, females, and homeless persons. Another focus of inquiry is on the importance of place identity—the power of symbol construction and manipulation—to affect community mobilization in the face of challenges from those who wish to impose alternative conceptualizations and land-use patterns. Others, who utilize the urban people approach to focus on the salience of the city to evoke the "good life," cite social diversity, openness, tolerance, and personal freedom as appealing dimensions of city life.

A third approach touched on by Perry, Abbott, and Hutter (1997) is on urban imagery. They observe that few interactionists, aside from Anselm L. Strauss, have chosen to investigate, on the one hand, the interactional dynamics that lie at the center of urban imagery, and on the other hand, the degree to which imagery acts as an independent variable in shaping urban life itself. Here, the work of urbanologists, including Lewis Mumford (1961) and Kevin Lynch (1960), who have investigated the dynamics of urban imagery is of interest. Lynch's work is on how urbanites construct cognitive maps that reflect urbanites' images or sense of the city. This approach is based on the perspective that different individuals and groups invest different meanings to city spaces and carry different pictures of the city in their heads. Therefore, it is important to analyze these mental maps along with objective environment (Perry, Abbott, and Hutter 1973: 84).

Perry, Abbott, and Hutter (1997) conclude that symbolic interactionism should be more highly visible in influencing the direction of work in urban sociology. They call for the development of more research and issue initiatives and observe that revitalization should occur through broadening the conceptual framework by looking "within the broader sociological discipline and across disciplines" (Perry, Abbott, and Hutter 1997: 85).

Before we begin our discussion of cities in the chapters that follow, I would like to present a brief autobiographical sketch of my own earliest city experiences to shed some light on my theoretical perspective.

Growing Up in the City: A Personal Odyssey

> Dere's No Guy livin' dat knows Brooklyn t'roo an' t'roo, because it'd take a guy a lifetime just to find his way around duh goddam town.
> (Wolfe 1940: 128)

I was born on a small island in the North Atlantic and raised on another. On my home island, the major transportation system that moved people from one island to the other had directional designations on the train stations that proclaimed—"From the City" and "To the City." "The City" referred to an extremely dense commercial, financial, manufacturing, cultural, and entertainment metropolitan area. The island, not considered part of "the city," was noted for its residential communities and for being a "borough of churches." And, especially during the time that I was "growing up," it was famous for its professional baseball team and for the colorful accent and speech of its inhabitants.

The people in my neighborhood were divided into two major ethnic groups. Visually, they seemed to be indistinguishable; both had swarthy features and were very verbal and very demonstrative. When speaking, members of one group gestured in; the other gestured out. And both held strong traditions regarding the importance of communal membership and of family and kinship ties. Indeed, the

The author at bat right before he hit a three-sewer home run in Bensonhurst, Brooklyn, New York City about 1962. Photo is courtesy of Mel Lippmann.

respective emphasis given to in-group solidarity led to a situation in which these two groups lived side-by-side but with parallel institutions, most of which they did not share with the other. The result was that while the neighborhood was spatially integrated, it was culturally, institutionally, and socially segregated.

As you may have surmised, the two islands referred to above are Manhattan and Long Island, respectively. [The part of Long Island that I was raised in was Brooklyn. New York City is composed of five boroughs—Manhattan, Richmond, Brooklyn, Queens, and the Bronx. New York City is situated on three Islands—Manhattan, Staten Island (Richmond), and Long Island (Brooklyn and Queens)—with the Bronx being the only borough on the "mainland" of the United States. Brooklyn and Queens share Long Island with two counties, Nassau and Suffolk, which are not incorporated into New York City.] The community in Brooklyn that I called home was Bensonhurst, and the two ethnic groups were Italians and Jews.

When I was young I witnessed the building of the Verrazano Bridge, which became the longest suspension bridge in the world at that time. The bridge would link Brooklyn and Staten Island and would spell the end of the automobile ferry service between these two boroughs of New York City. This had special meaning for me in that my parents had a business on Staten Island, and I would accompany my dad on Saturday mornings to that business via the ferry. We would drive to the ferry via the Belt Parkway. During the busy summer months, the wait for cars to board that ferry would often take up to two hours. The bridge would end all that and open the least populated borough of NYC to suburban growth within the city. I wondered what that growth would mean for the island, for the people who lived there, and, more specifically, for my parent's business.

From my home to the bridge, I would bike along the shore esplanade adjacent to the Belt Parkway, which was built, like the Verrazano Bridge, through the efforts of Robert Moses, whose many projects transformed NYC. When traffic wasn't too heavy the Belt allowed a fairly quick trip to the Battery Tunnel and the bridges that linked Brooklyn to Manhattan. Going east, in the other direction, the Belt led one to the beaches of Coney Island, Queens, and the suburbs, where Joel, my best friend, moved with his parents and sister in the mid-fifties. The park at Bay Parkway had a children's playground and shaded seating areas that were separated from the esplanade, tennis courts, and baseball fields by the parkway. What this meant, in effect, is that young children and their parents (usually their mothers) and older people used one segment of the park, while teenagers and more active adults used the other. It was not uncommon for fights to break out among the unsupervised teenagers, and it was for that reason that many parents preferred that their children play either on the side of the park where there were no ball fields and where they could be watched, or not use the park at all and play in the streets by their homes where there were always "eyes on the street."

Thomas Wolfe (1940) in his short story, "Only The Dead Know Brooklyn," which first appeared in the *New Yorker* in 1935, tells of a man who wants to take a train to "Bensenhoist" because he likes the sound of the name. He asks the narrator, and other fellow traingoers, for directions. The narrator ends his account of conversations and musings with a concluding reflection:

> Jesus! What a nut *he* was! I wondeh what eveh happened to 'm, anyway! I wondeh if someone knocked him on duh head, or if he's still wanderin' aroun' in duh subway in duh middle of duh night with his little map! Duh poor guy! Say, I've got to laugh, at dat, when I t'ink about him! Maybe he's found out by now dat he'll neveh live long enough to know duh whole of Brooklyn. It'd take a guy a lifetime to know Brooklyn t'roo an' t'roo. An' even den, you wouldn't know it all. (Wolfe 1940: 128)

Well, 50 plus years later, and hopefully with much more living in my lifetime to go, I continue to learn more about my childhood neighborhood and about Brooklyn, New York City, and other cities both in the United States and worldwide. Now that I am an older and perhaps wiser, or certainly a more knowledgeable individual, I think that I can answer some of the questions that I asked so many years ago. I always wondered why the park on Bay Parkway was designed as it was and what affect the parkway and the bridge had and would have on the people who used it. I did not fully understand why there was such an interpersonal and institutional separation between the two ethnic groups that shared the same neighborhood and that seemed so much the same. I wished to know more about the history of my city and wished to understand more about its dynamic character. This dynamism—epitomized by the move of the beloved baseball team, the Brooklyn Dodgers, to Los Angeles, and on a more personal level, the movement of friends and family to the suburbs—indicated that nothing remains the same and that change is constant.

In later life, as a sociologist and a symbolic interactionist I would develop the theoretical perspective that provided the insights to many of these questions. In this book I would like to share my perspective to enable you to better understand cities and to inform your own experience of them. In this book, I hope that you will learn a little more about your own "Bensenhoist" and that you will gain a broad understanding of how cities are experienced.

2

The Emergence of Cities

This chapter is about the origins of cities: why they occurred, where they occurred, and when they occurred. Of particular interest is the effect that cities had on their inhabitants. Our story begins in Africa 75,000 years ago. In 2004, two startling archaeological findings were made in Africa. The first was the discovery of two ostrich eggshell beads, believed to be about 70,000 years old, from an archaeological dig site in the Serengeti National Park in Tanzania. The other find was in a coastal area in South Africa. The find consisted of 30 seashells that were perforated in a similar manner to suggest that they were used as beads and thus would be evidence of the use of jewelry from a human ancestor nearly 75,000 years ago. If in fact these ostrich eggshells and seashells were used as jewelry, they would provide concrete evidence of symbolic thinking in ancient humans—30,000 years earlier than previously thought. These findings may provide some answers to the debate whether modern behavior evolved gradually, or whether there was a sudden "creative emergence" about 45,000 years ago. The account that follows is based on two 2004 articles by Hillary Mayell in *National Geographic News*.

The contemporary archaeological belief is that anatomically modern humans first emerged in Africa about 120,000 years ago. Yet, the archaeological evidence that has been found over a very large geographic area seems to indicate that the first forms of modern behavior emerged about 45,000 years ago. At that time there were waves of human migration from Africa that ultimately resulted in human presence throughout the world. In Europe the evidence includes cave paintings, jewelry, specialized tools, and elaborate burial rituals that date from 40,000 years ago.

Two questions are raised by these facts. The first is why is there no archaeological evidence from the period between 120,000 years ago to 45,000 years that would demonstrate that these anatomically modern humans had the ability for creative thought. The second is how and under what circumstances "modern" humans came into being. Two points of view have been articulated. The first postulates a culture-lag point of view. Proponents of this theory believe that while anatomically modern humans emerged 120,000 years ago, technological and cultural change were fostered only when there was a sudden genetic change, a "creative explosion" possibly precipitated by population density. The migration from Africa may have resulted in cultural change in Europe as a consequence of the competition between them and Neanderthals, who did not exist in Africa. This would be about 45,000 years ago. According to this view then, modern behavior may have emerged suddenly. The second position is that modern behavior evolved gradually in tandem with anatomical modernity.

The second point of view argues that "behavioral modernity" gradually evolved in Africa. While the capability for creative thought was there it wasn't expressed. The lack of archaeological evidence in Africa is a reflection of the fact that very little archeological work was done there. By contrast, European archaeological sites have been extensively studied for many decades. The very recent discovery in two different sites of shell "jewelry" in Africa 70,000 to 75,000 years ago provides support for this view. In addition, Mayell (2004a) reports that 28 bone tools and thousands of pieces of ocher—a mineral that is often used to create paint for body decoration and cave painting—were found in a cave in South Africa. These artifacts were dated at about 70,000 years of age. Some pieces of ocher were marked with abstract lines suggestive of artistic expression.

The important significance of jewelry is that it is a form of produced art that is universally accepted as an indicator of symbolic thinking. Citing the beliefs of anthropologists and archaeologists, Mayell states that bead making is considered evidence of symbolic thinking because it has little to do with survival. "Other traits thought of as 'modern' include the ability to plan ahead, innovate technologically, establish social and trade networks, create art, and adapt to changing conditions and environments" (Mayell 2004a).

Christopher Henshilwood is the director of the archaeological site where these beads were found. He is also affiliated with the University of Bergen in Norway and the State University of New York. Henshilwood argues that these beads, whether they are a form of jewelry to identify oneself or a designation of group status or group membership or relationship, are strongly suggestive of the existence of language. He points out: "What the beads might symbolize is unknown, but it does imply that there had to be some means of communicating meaning, which plausibly is language. Everyone knew what it meant, just as today if you're wearing Gucci sunglasses or a diamond tennis bracelet, there's a message being put out" (Henshilwood quoted in Mayell 2004). John Bower, an archaeologist and paleonthropologist at the University of California–Davis who is involved in the archaeological digs in Tanzania, asserts, "Beads are tangible evidence of a concept of self. You're not going to decorate yourself if you have no concept of self" (Bower quoted in Mayell 2004a).

The discovery of these beads provides strong evidence that humans as symbolic beings emerged 75,000 years ago, 30,000 years earlier than previously thought. If that is indeed the case, then the population that began the great human migration were already humans. Christopher Henshilwood concludes:

> "The beads add to a growing pile of evidence that humans acquired a suite of "modern" skills much earlier than previously thought. There's more and more evidence that they could fish and hunt large mammals, and that they were making fine bone tools. When our ancestors left Africa, they were already modern, already thinking and behaving in many senses the way we do today. (Mayell 2004a)

There has been debate whether the oyster eggshells and the perforated seashells were used as beads and jewelry as Henshilwood claims. Richard Klein, an anthropologist at Stanford University, is also working extensively at archaeological dig sites in South Africa. Klein is a believer in the theory that modern humans emerged quite rapidly around 45,000 years ago. He postulates that there was a genetic change in the brain that allowed for the use of language. He believes that ostrich-shell beads such as those found at the Serengeti site would certainly be evidence of a fully modern mind. But the problem is in establishing correct dates. In regard to the seashells, he questions whether the holes were created by humans or by gulls or were done much later. In the later case, the shells would be just another example of a later deposit of an archaeological artifact that has slumped into older layers. Henshilwood postulates that the people who made the jewelry 75,000 years ago were coastal people and may have lived under environmental circumstances that would have given them the opportunity to create jewelry. He conjectures that other human ancestors may have lived under environmentally unfavorable conditions where they would not have the surplus time for such activity. He explains the "creative explosion" of 45,000 years ago as a consequence of new environmental and social changes. These changes could have included population increases or consequences of meeting the challenges posed by confrontation with other human species like Neanderthals, who while not present in Africa were present in Europe for several hundred thousand years.

John Bower supports the position that human creativity evolved over a long period of time. He states that there is archaeological evidence that conceivably could reflect "modern" behavior. He concludes that the concept of "modern" may indeed be a vague concept that does not reflect human evolution.

> I hate the use of the word "modern". Modern behavior is talking on the telephone. Clearly that's not what humans were doing a hundred thousand years ago. Emerging evidence suggests that aspects of human technology are now strung out way back in time . . . . long before the creative explosion of 40,000 to 45,000 years ago. I'm inclined to think we should get rid of the whole concept of "modern behavior." (Bower quoted in Mayell 2004a)

One can only conclude that it is still uncertain whether indeed there was a "creative explosion" brought about by anatomical changes in the brain or climatic or environmental changes or social changes or a combination of these factors. But both sides of the argument agree that by 45,000 years ago, humans as we are today lived on our planet. However, the fact remains that humans did not begin living in large settlements until between 7,000 and 10,000 years ago. That is, there is a time span of 35,000 years when humans did not live in any type of settlement that can even approach our definition of what a city is. Why humans didn't form large settlements and why cities finally emerged will now be investigated.

The Origin of Cities

What happened in history regarding the origin and development of cities will forever be shrouded in mystery. At best, we can reasonably speculate on the factors and events occurring in that long ago time that led people to band together into permanent settlements, settlements with a sufficiently large and dense population that we can label them as cities. Our tentativeness reflects the fact that written historical records occurred thousands of years after the first cities appeared and that the archaeological evidence is fragmentary and limited. The noted sociologist and demographer, the late Kingsley Davis (1955), observes that the role of cities in antiquity may be exaggerated by archaeological enthusiasm that may tend to call a city any digging that reveals a few streets and a public building or two. The urbanologist Lewis Mumford echoes a similar view:

> No ancient town has yet been completely excavated and some of the most ancient which might reveal much, still continue in existence as dwelling places, smugly immune to the excavator's spade . . . . five thousand years of urban history and perhaps as many of proto-urban history are spread over a few score of only partly explored sites. The great urban landmarks, Ur, Nippur, Uruk, Thebes, Heliopolis, Assur, Ninevah, Babylon, cover a span of three thousand years whose vast emptiness we cannot hope to fill with a handful of monuments and a few hundred pages of written records (1961:55).

Given this warning, archaeologists are in some agreement that the first cities developed independently in Mesopotamia (the area which is now southern Iraq), in Egypt, in the Indus River Valley (now Pakistan), in the Yellow River basin in China, in the valley of Mexico, in the jungles of Guatemala and Honduras, and in the coastlands of Peru (Daniel 1968). These seven civilizations arose in markedly different epochs. Mesopotamia, Egypt, and India, the three oldest, are considered "dead" cultures from which Western civilizations emerged. Despite being more recent (about 600 AD) than Chinese civilization, the three Meso-American cultures—Mexican (Aztec), Central American (Mayan), and Peruvian (Inca)—are also "dead" cultures. They were obliterated at their respective stages of development and decline by the Spanish conquistadors in a brief, but brutal, 15-year period between 1519 and 1533. This destruction was so complete that virtually little is known of them today. China, the remaining original civilization, is the only "living" one. It originated in Shang (the yellow

River Basin) in the late third millennium BC, and its culture has remained intact to the present day.

The overriding consensus is that two requirements had to be met for the birth of urban settlements. The first was that there would be a sufficient surplus of food and other necessities to allow some people to live in settlements where they would not need to be concerned about producing their own food and where they could depend upon others to supply their food and other needs. The second was that there would exist a form of social organization that would guarantee that the produced surplus would be distributed to those in need of it. It could not be limited to a form based on the family and kinship, for it would require the surplus to be distributed to people who lived apart from the producers. This social organization would have to be one in which groups would have reciprocal ties, loyalties, and obligations to groups other than the family and kin.

The Agricultural Revolution

Humans for most of their 500,000 years of existence were nomadic wanderers existing on naturally occurring foodstuffs in the form of berries, fruits, roots, and nuts with supplementary intakes of meat and fish. This hunting and gathering economy provided the sole source of livelihood for humans for nearly 98 percent of the time that they have spent on this planet. The period from about 500,000 BC to 10,000 BC has been called the Paleolithic or Old Stone Age by archaeologists; geologists name this period the Pleistocene or Ice Age.

During several times in the Pleistocene epoch, vast glacial ice sheets covered, receded, and then covered again all of Antarctica, large parts of Europe, North America, and South America, and small parts of Asia. To illustrate the extent of these ice sheets one can draw a line stretching across Cape Cod, through Long Island, New Jersey, and Pennsylvania, along the lines of the Ohio and Missouri rivers to North Dakota, and through Montana, Idaho, and Washington to the Pacific. Similarly, in Europe ice sheets covered Scandinavia, Finland, northwest Russia, Northern Germany, and the British Isles. Pleistocene mammals included the mastodon, the mammoth, saber tooth carnivores, the giant sloth, and armadillos. Humans did not attain their modern physical and mental characteristics until near the end of this epoch, around 40,000 BC, which further handicapped their development. The climatic and geological conditions of the Pleistocene epoch imposed a limit on the population as well as on the economy. The predominant social unit was made up of small nomadic clan groups containing families who constantly had to move to fresh sources of food. They had to carry their meager possessions with them, and they lived in crude and temporary shelters.

The highly influential Australian-born archaeologist V. Gordon Childe observed in his popular treatises *Man Makes Himself* (1936) and *What Happened in History* (1942) that the hunting and gathering societies found in isolated jungles of Malaya and Central Africa, in the deserts of northwestern Australia and South Africa, and in the Arctic regions have a similar hunting and gathering economy.

However, he cautions that one must not make the mistake of equating the similarities of economies with social and cultural similarities. "Although these contemporary societies all have a Stone Age economy, that does not justify the assumption that Stone Age men, living in Europe or the Near East 6,000 or 20,000 years ago, observed the same sort of social and ritual rules, entertained the same beliefs, or organized their family relationships along the same lines as modern peoples on a comparable level of economic development" (Childe 1951:42).

The end of the Pleistocene epoch around 9,000 BC brought about climatic changes that allowed people to begin to live in settled communities. Under very favorable environmental conditions, most notably in the alluvial valleys of the Nile, the Tigres-Euphrates, and the Indus, people began to raise crops and domesticate animals. The economy was transformed into one that was able to produce a food surplus that allowed for permanent settlements. In addition, technological achievements in a wide variety of fields, including transportation, architecture, pottery, textiles, and metallurgy, permitted the growth of concentrated populations. These technological achievements included, in agriculture, the invention or improvement of stone tools, including axes, hoes, sickles, and blades. The ox-drawn plow and the wheeled cart were invented, as were pottery for the cooking and storing of foods, and, later, weaving. These concentrated populations could transport needed goods, clear fields effectively, and store surplus commodities. Taken together, these innovations combined with a benign geography brought about a productive agricultural economy that in Kingsley Davis's words helped "to make possible the 'sine qua non' of urban existence, the concentration in one place of people who do not grow their own food" (1955:430).

This innovative period has been called the Neolithic (New Stone Age) Revolution or the Agricultural Revolution. However, I have omitted one crucial component that characterizes this time period: without it urban settlements could not have come into existence. As Davis has pointed out, high agricultural productivity does not require that the cultivators share their surplus with others. It is conceivable that the cultivators could simply increase their numbers to the extent that they produce just enough to sustain themselves. This key factor was a more complex form of social organization.

> The rise of towns and cities therefore required, in addition to highly favorable agricultural conditions, a form of social organization in which certain strata could appropriate for themselves part of the produce grown by the cultivators. Such strata—religious and governing officials, traders, and artisans—could live in towns, because their power over goods did not depend on their presence on the land as such. They could thus realize the advantages of town living, which gave them additional power over the cultivators. (Davis 1955:430)

The Urban Revolution

The key to what V. Gordon Childe (1950) has called the "urban revolution" was the development of a whole series of new institutions that could secure, store, and distribute the accumulated food surplus. Childe summarizes the major distinctive properties that distinguish early cities from other forms of human settlements. Taken together, these ten enumerated traits account for the uniqueness of the early cities. They are:

1. Larger and more densely populated permanent settlements.
2. Social classes of nonagricultural specialists including craftsmen, transport workers, merchants, officials, and priests.
3. A system of taxation and capital accumulation to gods or kings who concentrated the surplus.
4. Monumental public buildings such as temples and palaces that not only distinguish the city from the village but also serve as a symbol of the concentrated surplus.
5. A ruling class composed of priests, civil and military leaders, and officials who absorbed, accumulated, and organized the surplus.
6. The invention of systems of recording and exact sciences. For example, arithmetic, geometry, and astronomy are necessary for prediction, measurement, and standardization.
7. The invention of a written language, with established writing techniques. This assures the elaboration of the aforementioned exact and predictive sciences.
8. Specialists in artistic expression, i.e., sculptors, painters, seal engravers that are supported by the concentrated surplus.
9. A system of long-distance trade of raw materials needed for industry or religion.
10. A social organization based on residence rather than kinship for community membership.

Reviewing the above discussion of the key factors that led to the "urban revolution," four broad categories can be identified. These categories, which urban ecologists who study urban growth patterns like to describe as the "ecological complex," are population, organization, environment, and technology. The urban ecologist Otis Dudley Duncan (1982) suggests that they can be referred to by the acronym "POET." "Population" would refer to the totality of people functioning as a collectivity. In this case it would refer to the increase of population resulting from the agricultural surplus. "Organization" refers to the social structure that enables the population to function in this social environment. Here we would be referring to the increased division of labor and the development of a ruling strata containing religious and governing officials. The "environment" contains the ecological landscape. In the case of the emerging towns and settlements it would refer to the favorable geographical climate, such as found in the Tigris-Euphrates valley, that would allow the development of an agricultural surplus. The last category, "technology," refers to all the materials, tools, and techniques that helped increase food production, storage, and distribution.

Childe's thesis was largely based on the archaeological evidence found in the cities located in the Tigris-Euphrates region of Mesopotamia, today's Iraq, and parts of Syria. This was the Sumerian civilization, and one of its largest and richest cities was called "Uruk."

Sumerian Cities

In the Old Testament, these words appear in the eleventh chapter of the Book of Genesis:

> And it came to pass, as they journeyed from the east, that they found a plain in the land of Shinar, and they dwelt there. And they said to one another, "Go to, let us make brick and burn them thoroughly." And they had brick for stone and slime had they for mortar. And they said "Go to, let us build a city and a tower, whose top may reach unto heaven, and let us make a name, lest we be scattered abroad upon the face of the whole earth.

This passage refers to the Tower of Babel that was located in the land of Shinar. It is also called Sumer, and its people were called Sumerians. The ancient Hebrews wrote this account of the origins of one of the earliest and oldest civilizations around 800 BC. The existence of the Sumerian civilization is corroborated by extensive archaeological evidence that was first discovered in the nineteenth century. New discoveries continue to this very day.

The Sumerian civilization existed from about 3500 BC to about 1800 BC. It was composed of a number of city-states with Uruk being one of the most influential. Sumerian cities were relatively small compared to today's standards. They ranged

A man and a child stand in the ruins of the ancient Sumerian city of Uruk, Iraq.

in size from about 5,000 to 25,000 inhabitants, with Uruk, one of the largest, having a population between 40,000 and 50,000 inhabitants.

The cities were surrounded by brick walls and were heavily fortified. City centers were dominated by temples and pyramidical towers called "ziggurats." Ziggurats were the most prominent feature of the urban landscape, befitting the fact that cities were theocracies ruled by the priestly class. The central enclosure contained the high priests's residences, courts, monasteries and convents, workshops, administrative offices, and support facilities that included granaries, stables, and sheds.

Outside the temple complex resided the artisans the scribes, the domestic servants, and other retainers of the ruling class. Streets were narrow and meandered, following the original trails similar to those of oasis towns in contemporary northern Africa (Hawley 1981). Housing of two or three stories was dense and congested. Each house was built around an inner court with blank walls facing the street. The development of this form of courtyard housing was in response to potential street dangers. In addition to defensive precaution, this form of housing shielded the house from the noise and dirt of the congested streets and insured domestic privacy. It has its present-day counterparts in the inward-looking patio house types found in such affluent row home communities as Society Hill in Philadelphia.

The Sumerian marketplaces, located outside the city walls by the river harbor, were the site of intercity and interregional trade. Initially, there was a negligible amount of domestic internal trade. As the agricultural surplus developed—with the crucial aid of such cultural advances as writing and record keeping, systems of numbers, chronological accounting and astronomical calculations, and law and administrative procedures—considerable trade developed. This trade was carried over considerable distances following caravan routes and river courses.

Trade, in turn, led to the dissemination of cultural advances to other city-states. A. Leo Oppenheim (1964) in his informative book, *Ancient Mesopotamia: Portrait of a Dead Civilization*, also advances the argument that warfare and conquest along with trade played an important role in the advancement of culture. As city-states were conquered, freed, and reconquered, new ideas and information were introduced to the interacting city-states. Conquered wealth and surplus would also allow for the creation of great works of art in sculpture, painting, architecture, and drama, glorifying the city while also culturally advancing it. One significant example of a great work of art is the *Epic of Gilgamesh.*

The *Epic of Gilgamesh* is at least 1,500 years older than Homer's *The Illiad* and *The Odyssey.* The clay tablets that contained the epic were found in the mid-nineteenth century in Mesopotamia. Soon after, they were deciphered at the British Museum in London. Probably what was most astonishing about the epic was that it contains an account of The Flood that predates the biblical story of Noah by over 750 years!

The epic is an heroic account of the life of Gilgamesh, a king of Uruk, who lived in 2700 BC. Uruk, known as Warka in modern Arabic and as Erech in the Bible, flourished from about 3500 BC to 2300 BC and was of greatest importance at about 2800 BC. Its defensive perimeters consisted of a double wall some 6 miles in length that was strengthened by nearly a thousand semicircular bastions. A temple complex that consisted of a group of splendid temples and other monumental buildings occupied the center of the city. This temple complex was called the "Eanna" (Lampl 1968). It had a population of between 40,000 and 50,000 inhabitants.

The walls of the city of Uruk and its temple complex, the Eanna, have been immortalized in the heroic *Epic of Gilgamesh:*

> *Of ramparted Uruk the wall he built.*
> *Of hallowed Eanna, the pure sanctuary.*
> *Behold its outer wall, whose cornice is like copper.*
> *Peer at the inner wall, which none can equal!*
> *Seize upon the threshold which is of old!*
> *Draw near to Eanna the dwelling of Ishtar*
> *Which no future king, no man, can equal*
> *Go up and walk on the walls of Uruk,*
> *Inspect the base terrace, examining the brickwork:*
> *Is it not brickwork of burnt brick?*
> *Did not the "Seven Sages" lay its foundation.*

The epic relates Gilgamesh's adventures in his fruitless quest for immortality and of his friendship with Enkidu, the wild man of the hills. In his wanderings, Gilgamesh encounters Utnapishtim, an elderly man metamorphosed into a god. Utnapishtan tells the story of the great flood and how the gods commanded him to build an ark that could contain the seeds of all living things. After sailing for days and nights through storms the ark comes to rest on a mountain top. After the rains end and the weather clears, Utnapishtan and all the ship's inhabitants find a home in the fertile valley between the rivers.

In addition to the astonishing *Epic of Gilgamesh,* a vast number of tablets were discovered. The majority of them contained text on commercial and administrative matters, business archives, lists, and inventories. In addition, there are literary works of various kinds that include poems, proverbs, and essays.

Trade Theory and the Origin of Cities

Mid-twentieth century archaeological excavations, excavations that were made after Childe's influential work was completed, have led scientists to question his theories on the origin of cities. Ancient Jericho was first discovered in the mid-nineteenth century. However important new discoveries about Jericho in the 1950s and about a heretofore-unknown city in Turkey that archaeologists have called "Catal Huyuk" (pronounced Chatal Hooyook) soon after have challenged the thesis that civilization and cities first emerged in Mesopotamia. These discoveries have also led archaeologists to question Childe's view that trade followed cities as cities followed agriculture (Hamblin 1973). Jane Jacobs (1969) developed one of the most controversial of these theories. Let's first look at the archaeological evidence found in Ancient Jericho and in Catal Huyuk and then we'll examine Jacobs's theory.

"Joshua fit the battle of Jericho and the walls came tumbling down." These popular folk song lyrics are based on an Old Testament story. Biblical scholars date the battle of Jericho between the Israelites and the inhabitants of that city to about 1500 BC. However, the works of the archaeologist Kathleen Kenyon at Jericho in the 1950s has established that Jericho was in existence for more than 6,000 years before the historic battle occurred. Further, remnants of a series of walls and other artifacts indicate that the city was settled, abandoned, and resettled by a number of different peoples over this time period. Kenyon (1970) believes that as early as 8000 BC the city had formidable defenses and an evolved administration that assumed an urban character.

The ruins of Jericho contained traces of foreign goods (like seashells), hematite (an iron-oxide mineral valued for its red color), and obsidian (a grayish black volcanic glass that can be carved into razor sharp tools or elaborate ritual objects)—evidence that it was a center of trade. These objects provide evidence that a considerable amount of trade must have existed between Jericho, which had access to valuable minerals such as salt from the nearby Dead Sea, and its distant neighbors.

Catal Huyuk, the name given to a city that was discovered in modern Turkey, is estimated to be at least 8,500 years old. It covers 32 acres that could house at least 6,000 people. Archaeological evidence indicates that it was a trade center and a religious center. The excavations of Catal Huyuk began in the early 1960s.

Aerial view of archaeological site at Catal Huyuk.

The city's discoverer, the British archaeologist, James Mellaart (1967), beautifully describes and illustrates its discovered glories in his book, *Catal Huyuk*.

The city was located on a mound, and the houses and shrines were clustered around a courtyard. These houses were constructed without doorways so that to enter one had to descend from the roof. This construction served as a defensive measure. Among the objects discovered included women's jewelry, intricately carved weapons, and sculpted figurines. The walls were decorated with representational and abstract wall paintings, which depicted scenes of bulls, people, and cattle. In one room there was a mural of a diving vulture assailing a headless man. Mellaart interprets this as a symbol of the cleansing of dead people to permit burial in shrines or in homes of relatives.

Mellaart addresses the fundamental question of what accounts for the richness of this city. His answer, trade, is based on the fact that Catal Huyuk lies in a geographical region rich in obsidian. Obsidian, a volcanic produced natural glass, is a valuable mineral that has great utility, as it can be carved into knives, mirrors, razors, jewelry, etc. Excavations throughout the Middle East find evidences of obsidian from the region of Catal Huyuk. Also found in the ruins of Catal Huyuk are such foreign materials as seashells from the Mediterranean Sea, almost 100 miles to the south; fine flint from Syria to the east; and foreign nuts and fruit seeds. In addition, skeletal remains of two distinct racial types of humans were found in the excavations of Catal Huyuk. One was of European stock; the other was Asian. This would indicate that trade existed among different peoples over long distances.

Does the archaeological evidence found in Jericho and in Catal Huyuk warrant the conclusion that these settlements were in fact cities? While there is some disagreement among social scientists, the general consensus is that, despite the lack of evidence of writing, both seem to fit Childe's criteria of a city. This being the case, then, the origins of cities moves back in time from the Sumerian cities of 3500 BC to the middle eastern cities of Jericho and Catal Huyuk, which are about twice as old. The significance of this lies in the fact that trade, rather than the production of an agricultural surplus, may be the key factor in the development of cities. This view has been most forcibly argued by Jane Jacobs. In her book, *The Economy of Cities* (1969), asserts Jacobs that agriculture and animal husbandry arose in cities rather than as an essential rural prerequisite for the development of cities. Her thesis is largely based on Mellaart's discovery of Catal Huyuk on the Anatolian Plateau of today's Turkey and the importance of obsidian as an essential industrial material that was traded in that part of the world. She invents an imaginary city, "New Obsidian," that is based on Catal Huyuk, to develop her argument.

New Obsidian is a pre-agricultural city of hunters in which a grain culture and the domestication of animals could have developed. New Obsidian is depicted as a center for the trade of obsidian. Its inhabitants, who initially number about 2,000, mine obsidian, and as trade develops they become skillful in crafting it into desirable objects. A system of trade develops in which traders bring bartered goods, including foodstuffs, from other regions into New Obsidian. These imported grains and animals mixed with the local food resources, and those that proved most durable and hardy survived and flourished in the adopted New Obsidian region. Trade, then, stimulated agricultural and husbandry development. As trade developed, food production flourished. Agriculture, then, was invented in order to stimulate and develop trade. Thus, according to Jacobs's thesis, urban primacy accounts for the development of agriculture rather than agricultural primacy accounting for the development of cities:

> The traders of New Obsidian, when they go off on their trips, take along New Obsidian food to sustain themselves. Sometimes they bring back a strange animal, or a bit of promising foreign seed. And the traders of other little cities who come to New Obsidian sometimes take back food with them and tell what they seen in the metropolis. Thus, the first spread of the new grains and animals is from city to city. The rural world is still a world in which wild food and other wild things are hunted and gathered. The cultivation of plants and animals is, as yet, only city work. It is duplicated, as yet, only by other city people, not by the hunters of ordinary settlements.
>   . . . it was not agriculture then, for all its importance, that was the salient invention, or occurrence if you will, of the Neolithic Age. Rather it was the fact of sustained, interdependent, creative city economies that made possible many new kinds of work, agriculture among them. (Jacobs 1969: 31, 36)

Jacobs's theory is based primarily on the ruins of Jericho and Catal Huyuk and the discovery of non-native materials found in them. These included minerals and food grains. In addition, the discovery of foreign items such as obsidian in the ruins of ancient settlements throughout the Middle East provides further support for this view. However, a significant number of social scientists (cf. Morris, 1979) take issue with Jacobs's theory.

The architect and town planner A.E.J. Morris (1979), in his book, *History of Urban Form,* raises three questions regarding Jacobs's conclusions. First, Jacobs conjectures that New Obsidian's population of 2,000 were city dwellers largely engaged in the mining, crafting, and trading of obsidian. To sustain this population it would require a surrounding support area of 2,000 square miles (a circle radius of approximately 80 miles) to provide the necessary foodstuffs. This would be relatively impossible given the primitive technology available at that time; wheeled transportation was not invented until 5,000 years later. Second, it would have been impossible for New Obsidian to store sufficient amounts of killed animals in the absence of curing techniques. Third, extensive trading activity would have been very difficult without some kind of permanent recording system. Yet, as far as is known, writing was not invented until several millennia had past. Morris concludes, "The 'dogma of agricultural primacy' is not seriously challenged by New Obsidian" (1979:304).

The controversy regarding the origin of the city still continues. One strongly suspects that this issue will never be resolved. The fragmentary nature of the archaeological evidence precludes a definitive settlement. However, some scholars, particularly sociologists, take a different tact in examining this issue. Based on sociological perspectives, they argue for the importance of cultural and social organizational factors to account for the creation and development of cities. This approach depends less on archaeological evidence and more on sociological theories of the nature of human societies. Further, archaeological artifacts, albeit flimsy, provide additional data to help generate these theories. The next section of this chapter will be devoted to the sociological point of view, which also speculates on why the same social and cultural factors that led to the appearance and development of early urban settlements also were the major contributing factors that limited their growth and ultimately led to their decline.

Social and Cultural Factors and the Emergence, Development, and Decline of Early Cities

I met a traveler from an antique land
Who said: Two vast and trunkless legs of stone
stand in the desert . . . Near them, on the sand,
Half sunk, a shattered visage lies, whose frown,
And wrinkled lip, and sneer of cold command,
Tell them its sculptor well those passions read

American baseball players on world tour in 1889 climbing on the Sphinx in Egypt.

Which yet survive, stamped on these lifeless things,
The hand that mocked them, and the heart they fed:
And on the pedestal these words appear:
"My name is Ozymandias, king of kings:
Look on my works, ye mighty, and despair!"
Nothing beside remains. Round the decay
Of that colossal wreck, boundless and bare
The lone and level sands stretch far away.

(Shelley 1968)

This stirring poem, *Ozymandias*, written by Percy Bysshe Shelley (1792–1822) in 1817 captures the essence of the concerns. It dramatizes the importance of social and cultural factors for the origin, development, and decline of the early cities. I'll begin with a brief opening comment on the importance of religion in early cities.

Religion in Early Cities

You may recall that James Mellaart in his excavations of Catal Huyuk unearthed a shrine containing the bizarre drawings of vultures descending upon headless men. Mellaart attributes religious meaning to these drawings. His opinion reflects a long-held view in sociology that religion serves as a cohesive element that gives people a collective sense of community.

In 1864, Fustel de Coulanges (1830–1899), a French scholar, wrote a classic account of Grecian and Roman cities in the earliest stages of their history. *The Ancient City* (1864/1956) is a study of the religious and civil institutions of ancient Greece and Rome. It sought to demonstrate that religion was the basis of and dominated every aspect of ancient Greek and Roman city life. Coulanges wrote before the archaeological record of these societies confirmed his view and before anthropological data on nonliterate societies did likewise.

In the twentieth century, the urbanologist, Lewis Mumford (1961:7) speculates, "The city of the dead antedates the city of the living." By this he means that the fear of the unknown and of death led paleolithic humans to gather together to pay homage to the dead and to reaffirm their bonds of social solidarity. "Early man's respect for the dead, itself an expression of fascination with his powerful images of daylight fantasy and nightly dream, perhaps had an even greater role than more practical needs in causing him to seek a fixed meeting place and eventually a continuous settlement" (Mumford 1961: 6–7).

I would not go as far as Mumford's speculation that religion may have served as vital a role in the origin and nature of the city as did agricultural surplus, trade, and technology. Nor do I assert that Mumford fails to recognize these other major contributing factors, for he does. What Mumford's analysis does do is highlight the importance of social and cultural factors as a crucial element in the appearance of early cities.

I follow the lead of urbanologists like Mumford, Robert McC. Adams (1960, 1966), Kingsley Davis (1955), and Gideon Sjoberg (1960), who reason that the rise of towns and cities require, in addition to favorable agricultural conditions, a form of social structure and organization in which certain social classes would appropriate for themselves part of the agricultural surplus. This strata of religious and governing officials, traders, and artisans comprised social and political structures that demanded additional production to maintain themselves in cities without the necessity to produce it themselves. According to this perspective, the urban revolution was a decisive cultural and social change whose "essential element was a whole series of new institutions and the vastly greater size and complexity of the social unit, rather than basic innovations in subsistence" (Adams 1960: 154).

What this analysis provides is a focus on the interactive effects of agricultural and technological advances with changes in social and organizational structures. They constantly feed back upon each other. An integral aspect of this viewpoint is the underlying power aspect between those who live in the towns and cities and are dependent upon those who work the land. To assure a steady supply of productive goods and to secure, concentrate, and distribute them, the emerging urban elite had to develop new social organizational forms, specialized roles and divisions of labor, and an elaboration of the social structure of the society. These included differentiated socioeconomic classes on the basis of power, status, and wealth; military, political, and administrative elites; and economic networks of tribute, trade, and redistribution (Adams 1966).

The rise of cities can be seen in terms of power between those who lived in the city and those who lived on the land, with the former seeking to dominate the later to assure their continued existence. Ironically, then, agriculture made the city possible, but urban social structure, organization, and culture made the city dominant.

The result was early cities like those in Mesopotamia that had a distinctive social organization compared to prior neolithic villages. Early city dwellers had primary loyalty to the city, not to their kinship groups or clans. Power over the surrounding countryside was in the hands of the city elite. Religious and political institutions in the city served as the basis of social order supplementing and in many cases replacing the family and kinship groups. Finally, the freeing of people from the everyday chores of food production and manual work allowed for cultural inventiveness that included the building of monumental temples and structures; large-scale irrigation canals; the invention of writing; the elaboration of arithmetic, algebra, and astronomy; the composing of literature; and the creation of masterful sculpture and art. The result is that the urban revolution can be seen as a social and cultural revolution as well as a technological one that resulted in the transformation of Neolithic human society in a fundamental and radical manner.

The general consensus among scholars on the emergence of the earliest cities is based on the above innovations that date toward the end of the fourth millennium BC. They generally discount the neolithic communities that were in existence for 3,000 years prior to this time. The cities of Mesopotamia and Egypt around 3,000 BC and in India a thousand years later are called "true" cities by Kingsley Davis. By this later date, 2,000 BC, cities existed throughout the Middle

East with Memphis (Cairo) being the largest with a population of perhaps 100,000 (Chandler and Fox 1974). However, the majority of urban settlements were of much smaller size, with populations that vary from 4,000 to 15,000 being more common.

Further, by the year 1,000 BC the cities in the Middle East region went into decline and eclipse. Cities emerged later in Greece and Rome. V. Gordon Childe (1951) comments on this by suggesting that cities are not always a stimulant of economic and social growth and advance. He explains the arrested growth of the Babylonian and Egyptian cities by noting the internal contradictions within them.

These contradictions stem from the concentration of power and wealth in the hands of the relatively small but powerful urban elite. He argues that the specialized craftsmen and laborers were relegated to lower-class status by the created ruling class of pharaohs, kings, and temple priests, and their relatives and favorites. Once in power, they discouraged rational science, which might work against their magical and religious claims of ascendancy. They also had few incentives to encourage invention. They controlled unlimited reserves of labor and thus did not need labor-saving devices such as improvements in harnessing the power of animals, or of sail, or of metal tools. Instead, the lower classes were treated virtually as beasts of burden. The unproductive insulation and excessive power of the religious and political elite led to stagnation in agriculture and technology (Childe 1951). Kingsley Davis (1955) concurs:

> Agriculture was so cumbersome, static, and labor-intensive that it took many cultivators to support one man in the city. The ox-drawn plow, the wooden plowshare, inundation irrigation, stone hoes, sickles, and axes were instruments of production, to be sure, but clumsy ones . . . The technology of transport was as labor-intensive as that of agriculture. The only means of conveying bulky goods for mass consumption was by boat and though sails had been invented, the sailboat was so inefficient that rowing was still necessary. The oxcart, with its solid wheels and rigidly attached axle, the pack animal, and the human burden-bearer were all short-distance means of transport, the only exception being the camel caravan. Long-distance transport was reserved largely for goods which had high value and small bulk—i.e., goods for the elite—which could not maintain a large urban population. The size of the early cities was therefore limited by the amount of food, fibers, and other bulky materials that could be obtained from the immediate hinterland by labor-intensive-methods, a severe limitation which the Greek cities of a later period, small as they remained, nevertheless had to escape before they could attain their full size. (1955: 431)

To these factors Davis adds political and military limitations. The early cities were constantly threatened and conquered by neighboring settlements and by nomadic bands, resulting in cities that were constantly besieged, overrun, conquered, and devastated only to be rebuilt and eventually overwhelmed in turn by new invaders and conquerors. The accumulated wealth found in cities and their dependence upon the countryside beyond their fortifications made them vulnerable targets and subject to constant danger and outside attack.

William Howells (1963), on the basis of archaeological evidence, describes the constant warfare among various Sumerian city-states until their inevitable defeat by Saigon from the north. Saigon's empire in turn was conquered and destroyed by the inhabitants of Gutium from the more distant Zagros Mountains. The result was continuous political instability and discontinuity of these earliest cities that contributed to their growth limitations.

In 2005, a major archaeological discovery highlights the importance and impact of warfare on the rise and fall of early cities. In northeastern Syria, archaeologists who were part of a research team from the Oriental Institute at the University of Chicago working with the Department of Antiquities in Syria reported on the excavation of a war zone located in the ancient city of Hamoukar. From the architectural remains that have been excavated there is powerful evidence that a large-scale battle of organized warfare occurred that pitted warriors of northern and southern cultures in ancient Mesopotamia around 3,500 BC (Wilford 2005).

Abdel-Razzaq Moaz, who is Syria's deputy minister of culture, and Guillermo Algaze, an archaeologist at the University of California–San Diego, have both commented on the significance of the archaeological finding to the *New York Times* (Wilford 2005). Dr. Moaz believes that the Hamoukar site illuminates the understanding of the rise of ancient cities. Dr. Algaze, who was not involved in the exploration, believes that this new evidence of warfare helps tell the story of ancient Mesopotamia and the factors involved in the southern expansion. Other archaeologists see the battle as a conflict in which "growing cities in the south sought raw materials such as wood, stone and metals" (Wilford 2005:A28). The significance of this architectural find is that it demonstrates the importance warfare had in the rise and fall of ancient cities. In this case, it reveals the importance of a northern cultural city in Mesopotamia—Hamoukar—and its collapse as a consequence of the rise of southern culture and its subsequent domination of the region. This discovery and earlier excavations at this site now provide strong evidence that in this northern region, cities developed independently of the better-known early southern cities such as Uruk. It was through major conflicts as well as through the spread of culture and colonization that southern culture became dominant in ancient Mesopotamia.

One important side effect of warfare and political instability and discontinuity is the cultural diffusion of urban culture. As the city-state expands into outlying regions, the sphere of urbanization widens. The urban outposts of Greek city-states and of Rome are evidence of this. The various Greek city-states set up colonies throughout the Mediterranean region. The spread of the Roman Empire through military conquest into northwestern and central Europe led to the rise of cities in Gaul and Britain. However, the risk, as history has taught us, is that such expansion opens the city-state to itself being invaded and overrun. This is the case of what happened to the Sumerian cities. Howell reports that the constant rise and fall of Sumerian cities and empires results in "diffusing its culture over a wider and wider area, and finally attracting the barbarians on the fringes, who come in with nothing to lose, use the weapons of the civilized to conquer them, and end by becoming part of the civilized realm themselves" (1963: 321).

Other factors that hindered urban growth were primitive sanitation facilities and the lack of scientific medicine. This kept urban mortality rates high and prevented significant growth. The tie of the peasant to the land and the need for a large population to be involved in cultivation minimized growth through rural-urban migration. The absence of manufacturing, the traditionalism and religiosity of all classes, and the bureaucratic control of the peasantry all contributed to the hampered experimentation and technological and economic advances (Davis 1955:432).

Finally, in addition to social and cultural organizational limitations and weaknesses, and vulnerability to raids and conquests, these early cities were particularly affected by natural disasters such as famine, floods, and diseases, as well as by plagues that killed both people and livestock.

All these factors placed severe limitations on size and explain why the early cities were quite small in terms of contemporary comparisons. It is considered highly unlikely that even the largest concentrations of Mesopotamia, India, or Egypt ever numbered more than 200,000 inhabitants, no more than 1 percent of the total population for the world as a whole and little more for the region in which they originated.

To conclude this discussion on the origins of cities I share the view of the archaeologists who caution us to temper our theories in light of the flimsy and fragmentary quality of the prehistorical evidence. As V. Gordon Childe states "almost every statement in prehistory should be qualified by the phrase 'On the evidence available today the balance of probability favors the view that' . . ." (1951: Preface).

Given this caveat, I may conclude that *on the evidence available today the balance of probability favors the view that* the development of agricultural surpluses was a result of major ecological changes that occurred soon after the end of the great ice ages around 10,000 BC. These surpluses developed in conjunction with dramatic changes in the social and cultural organizations of human societies. These included the development of complex social structures and organizations characterized by specialization and differentiations of labor and a hierarchical power structure. These factors interacted in the first cities and led to what has been called the "urban revolution."

3

The Industrial Revolution and the Rise of Urban Sociology

All that is solid melts into air.

—Karl Marx

The intervening time span, between the origin and decline of the earliest cities and the onset of the Industrial Revolution, was one in which the demographic character of cities remained essentially the same. The earliest cities had populations of less than 10,000 people with the possible exception of the ancient city of Ur, whose population may have reached 40,000. The Roman Empire and its capital city, Rome (all roads lead to Rome), may have attained a population between 350,000 to 600,000 people. Some of the central and South American cities of the Mayan, Aztec, and Inca civilizations may have attained a size of 200,000. But, relatively speaking, for more than a thousand years cities remained virtually small. Between 800 AD and 1600 AD very few cities in the world had populations of more than 150,000 people.

Similarly dependent upon the production of an agricultural surplus by workers in the surrounding countryside people throughout the world lived relatively the same. There was limited specialization and a minimal division of labor. Large cities were not possible until both the cities and rural agriculture became

43

industrialized. Their size limitation was a consequence of both the small amount of surplus food produced by the rural population and by the inability to efficiently move that surplus to urban areas. Changes in the population size of cities would become possible only when the technology of food production made it possible for larger numbers of people to be supported by the same number of agricultural workers. The larger the agricultural surplus that could be produced, the larger the urban population that could be supported.

It was with the coming of the Industrial Revolution that significant changes were being implemented that significantly changed the size, density, structure, and composition of cities. England, the country that was in the forefront of the Industrial Revolution, had only 106 towns with populations of more than 5,000 in 1800. However, things changed dramatically in the ensuing 100 years. By 1891, there were 622 towns of this or greater, with a total population of nearly 20 million people (Hosken 1985, cited in Bryjak and Soroka 2001). London, the largest city in the world in 1800, saw its population soar from a then incredible 861,000 to nearly 6.5 million by the year 1900. Similarly, other European cities that also were experiencing industrialization during the nineteenth century were experiencing rapid growth. From 1800 to 1900 Paris went from nearly 550,000 to 3,330,000; Berlin from 172,000 to 2,324,000; Vienna from 231,000 to 1,662,000. Smaller cities such as Amsterdam, Hamburg, Madrid, and Rome also saw their populations more than double in size (Chandler and Harris 1974).

The Industrial Revolution affected cities in the United State slightly later than it did in Europe. Citing U.S. Census figures Macionis and Parrillo (2004) report that in 1790, shortly after the American Revolution, the previous colonial cities of New York, Philadelphia, Boston, Baltimore, and Charleston all had populations under 50,000. New York was the largest city with a little over 44,000 inhabitants; Philadelphia had slightly more than 33,000. The total urban population was

TABLE 3.1 *Population of Selected European Cities, 1700–1998 (in thousands)*

City	1700	1800	1900	2006
Amsterdam	172	201	510	729
Berlin	—	172	2,424	3,387
Hamburg	70	130	895	1,705
Lisbon	188	237	363	563
London	550	861	6,480	7,074
Madrid	110	169	539	2,824
Naples	207	430	563	1,047
Paris	530	547	3,330	2,152
Rome	149	153	487	2,649
Vienna	105	231	1,662	1,540

Source: Adapted from T. Chandler and G. Fox, *3000 Years of Urban History* (New York: Academic Press, 1974); 2006 *City Mayors: The 500 largest European Cities,* http://www.citymayors.com/features/euro_cities1/htm Retrieved from Internet January 31, 2006.

TABLE 3.2   *Population of the 10 Largest Urban Places in the United States: 1790*

Rank	Place	Population
1	New York (city), NY	33,131
2	Philadelphia (city), PA	28,522
3	Boston (town), MA	18,320
4	Charleston (city), SC	16,359
5	Baltimore (town), MD	13,503
6	Northern Liberties (township), PA	9,913
7	Salem (town), MA	7,921
8	Newport (town), RI	6,716
9	Providence (town), RI	6,380
10t	Marblehead (town), MA	5,661
10t	Southwark (district), PA	5,661

Population of the 10 Largest Urban Places in the United States: 1870

Rank	Place	Population
1	New York (city), NY	942,292
2	Philadelphia (city), PA	674,022
3	Brooklyn (city), NY	396,099
4	St. Louis (city), MO	310,864
5	Chicago (city), IL	298,977
6	Baltimore (city), MD	267,354
7	Boston (city), MA	250,526
8	Cincinnati (city), OH	216,239
9	New Orleans (city), LA	191,418
10	San Francisco (city), CA	149,473

Source: U.S. Bureau of the Census Internet Release date: June 15, 1998.

202,000—only 5.1 percent of the total American population. By 1870, a little bit more than one quarter (25.7) percent (9,902,000 people) of the population lived in cities. New York City, the largest city, had nearly 1,000,000 inhabitants, with Philadelphia, the second largest city, having 674,022 urban dwellers.

The rapid urbanization of nineteenth-century European and American cities was a consequent of both technological and social innovations stemming from the Industrial Revolution. Technological advances in production, including the steam engine, the spinning jenny, the cotton gin, and the automatic weaving machine, made the mass production of goods possible. Transportation innovations, especially the steam-driven railroad, road improvements, and inland canals, made the quick movement of products feasible. Technological innovations in agriculture, including new machinery to harvest crops as well as scientific innovations in crop rotations and animal breeding, allowed for heightened production.

However, it was the social, cultural, political, and economic changes that accompanied industrialization that led to and was reinforced by rapid urbanization. The impact on people living during this time period of accelerating change captured the attention and the imagination of social scientists. It is now time to turn attention to the consequences of industrialization and urbanization.

The Industrial Revolution and Nineteenth-Century European Cities

European societies during the nineteenth century underwent massive changes. The old social order anchored in kinship, the village, the community, religion, and old regimes were attacked and fell to the twin forces of industrialism and revolutionary democracy. The sweeping changes had particular effect on the individual, the family, and the community. There was a dramatic increase in such conditions as poverty, child labor, desertions, prostitution, illegitimacy, and women abuse. These conditions were particularly evident in the newly emerging industrial cities. The vivid writings of a novelist such as Charles Dickens in *Oliver Twist and Hard Times* provide startling portraits of a harsh new way of life.

Hansom cabs in Regent Circus (later Oxford Circus), London. Late 19th century.

The Industrial Revolution dramatically changed the nature of economic and social life. The factory system developed, and, with its development, there was a transformation from home industries in rural areas to factories in towns and cities of Europe and America. Rural people were lured by the novelty of city life and the prospects of greater economic opportunity.

The Industrial Revolution shattered the domestic economy centered in the household. Looking at mid-eighteenth-century England, we are best able to observe its impact. England was primarily rural, with men and women largely engaged in some form of domestic industry. This activity occurred within the home. In the cities, women as well as men were involved in some form of trade, frequently serving as partners in joint work activities. The agrarian revolution at the end of the eighteenth century saw the lessening of the necessity for productive work at home. Industrial development deprived women of their involvement in the older domestic industries and trades:

> *If you go into a loom-shop, where there's three or four pairs of looms,*
> *They are all standing empty, encumbrances of the rooms;*
> *And if you ask the reason why, the older mother will tell you plain*
> *My daughters have forsaken them, and gone to weave by steam (J. Harland,* Ballads and Songs of Lancashire, *1865. Cited in Thompson, 1963:308)*

Family members were absorbed into the new economy as wage earners. This led to the differentiation between work and the home. E. P. Thompson, the English historian, in his *The Making of the English Working Class* (1963) comprehensively examines the changes occurring in people's ways of life between 1780 and 1832. In the following passage, he contrasts the differences between two economies:

> Women became more dependent upon the employer or the labour market, and they looked back to a "golden" period in which home earnings from spinning, poultry and the like could be gained around their own door. In good times the domestic economy supported a way of life centred upon the home, in which inner whims and compulsions were more obvious than external discipline. Each stage in industrial differentiation and specialisation struck also at the family economy, disturbing customary relations between man and wife, parents and children, and differentiating more sharply between "work" and "life." It was to be a full hundred years before this differentiation was to bring returns, in the form of labour-saving devices, back into the working woman's home. Meanwhile, the family was roughly torn apart each morning by the factory bell. (Thompson 1963:416)

England became the first and prime example of the new society. In 1801 London with 861,000 inhabitants, was the only city with a population over 100,000. By 1900 its population had soared to nearly 6.5 million people. In the great midlands, such cities as Birmingham, Leeds, Manchester, and Sheffield emerged. Manchester, which was probably the first industrial city in history, saw its population shoot up from some 70,000 people in 1801 to over 225,000 by 1830 and to slightly over 300,000 by 1850. In these new industrial cities, large amounts of labor, raw materials, and capital were centered.

Neil J. Smelser (1959) describes the effects on the family of the mechanization of spinning and weaving in the cotton industry. The domestic economy of the preindustrial family disappeared. The rural- and village-based family system no longer served as a productive unit. The domestic economy had enabled the family to combine economic activities with the supervision and training of its children; the development of the factory system led to a major change in the division of labor in family roles.

Patriarchal authority was weakened with urbanization. Previously, in rural and village families, fathers reigned supreme; they were knowledgeable in economic skills and were able to train their children. The great diversity of city life rendered this socialization function relatively useless. The rapid change in industrial technology and the innumerable forms of work necessitated a more formal institutional setting—the school—to help raise the children. Partially in response to the changing family situation, the British passed legislation to aid children. Separated from parental supervision, working children were highly exploited. Laws came into existence to regulate the amount of time children were allowed to work and their working conditions. The law also required that children attend school. These legal changes reflected the change in the family situation in the urban setting; families were no longer available or able to watch constantly over their children.

The separation of work from the home had important implications for family members. Increasingly, the man became the sole provider for the family, and the women and children developed a life comprised solely of concerns centered around the family, the home, and the school. Their contacts with the outside world diminished, and they were removed from community involvements. The family's withdrawal from the community was tinged by its hostile attitude toward the surrounding city. The city was depicted as a sprawling and planless development bereft of meaningful community and neighborhood relationships. The tremendous movement of a large population into the industrial centers provided little opportunity for the family to form deep or lasting ties with neighbors. Instead, the family viewed their neighbors with suspicion and weariness. Exaggerated beliefs developed on the prevalence of urban poverty, crime, and disorganization.

Manchester: The Shock City of the Mid-Nineteenth Century

Asa Briggs (1970), the British social historian, introduces the term *shock city* to refer to a city in a given historical period that had symbolic significance reflecting both awe at spectacular growth and technical progress and also deep concerns about emerging economic, political, and social problems. Manchester, England, was the shock city of the Industrial Revolution. In 1775 Manchester had a population of 24,000. In 1801, the year of the first official census, its population had more than doubled to 70,000. By the middle of the century, the population had soared to over 250,000 people in the city itself—a tenfold increase in 75 years.

The working class districts of nineteenth-century Manchester, England were characterized by deplorable living conditions. Even after 100 years the slum conditions of Manchester still prevailed.

In the 1840s it represented an incomprehensible new standard of urban life that radically differed from both the urban as well as the rural past. Lewis Mumford dramatically describes this new urban phenomenon and what it might foretell for the future:

> Considering this new urban area on its lowest physical terms, without reference to its social facilities or its culture, it is plain that never before in human history had such vast masses of people lived in such a savagely deteriorated environment, ugly in form, debased in content. The galley slaves of the Orient, the wretched prisoners in the Athenian silver mines, the depressed proletariat in the insulae of Rome—these classes had known, no doubt, a comparable foulness; but never before had human blight so universally been accepted as normal: normal and inevitable. (1961: 474)

Manchester became the site for visitation by scholars who sought to study the city to better understand it and what it portended for other cities and its inhabitants in the emerging industrial urban society. These visitors included Alexis

De Tocqueville and Friedrich Engels. They described and made assessments that reflected both the wonder and fear for the future that Manchester represented. The French conservative intellectual thinker and probably the most astute travel observer of the nineteenth century, Alexis de Tocqueville (1805–1859), wrote the following after a visit to Manchester, England:

> From this foul drain the greatest stream of human industry flows out to fertilize the whole world. From this filthy sewer pure gold flows. Here humanity attains the most complete development and its most brutish, here civilization works its miracles and civilized man is turned almost into a savage. (Cited in Nisbet 1966:29)

De Tocqueville's illuminating comments, "From this filthy sewer pure gold flows," is a concise summary of the ambivalence that many felt about the emerging industrial city that Manchester examplified. Briggs observes that there was no consensus on the implications, both moral and social, of the emerging Victorian industrial cities. He notes the disagreements:

> In the most general terms, on the one side was fear—fear of a change in the pattern of social relationships associated with change in the scale of the city; fear of the emergence and of the mounting pressure of new social forces which were difficult to interpret, even more difficult to control; fear about the capacity of society to deal quickly enough with urgent social problems before the social fabric was torn apart. On the other side was pride—pride in achievement through self help and, through self help, in economic growth; pride in local success through rivalry with other places, not only in the tokens of wealth and in the symbols of prestige but also in the means of control—mileage of sewers, number of water-taps or water-closets, number of school places or of policeman. (Briggs 1976: 85)

The essence of the new certainty of uncertainty was perhaps captured best in Marx and Engels's phrase: "All that is solid melts into air."

> All fixed, fast-frozen relations, with their train of ancient and venerable prejudices and opinions are swept away, all new formed ones become antiquated before they can ossify. All that is solid melts into air, all that is holy is profaned. (Karl Marx and Friedrich Engels, *The Communist Manifesto*, 1848)

Friedrich Engels (1820–1905) was a young man when his father sent him from their home in Barmen near Dusseldorf, Germany, to Manchester in 1842. His mission was to complete his business education by studying the operation of the cotton mills that would prove useful to the operation of the prosperous family business in Germany. What he learned changed his life and his ideas. With his life-long collaborator, Karl Marx, their Communist philosophy impacted and continues to impact the lives of millions of people.

While ostensibly apprenticed to his father's business firm in Manchester, Engels's worldview became centered on his sympathies to the working classes and his Communist perspective. The result was his recording in the most graphic language the "conditions of the working class in England." Engels delineated the macro-structure of the city. His detailed presentation of the spatial distribution of factories, businesses and residential areas, and the spatial segregation of the classes anticipated the focus on urban spatial distribution of the Chicago School's urban ecology perspective.

According to Engels's communist perspective, the street patterns, the geographic centrality of the business district, the class-segregated spatial distribution of residences, and the layout of transit thoroughfares were reflections of the capitalistic economic consequence of the Industrial Revolution. He provided a vivid description of the working conditions of the laboring classes, the very long hours of daily work extended over a six-day week, and the extremely low subsistence wages that were paid. The houses of the poor were located in the worst areas of the city and did not benefit from even the most rudimentary sanitation systems. Many were located on the banks of the Ilk River. The river served more as an open sewer and the deposit site of raw sewage and the wastes of slaughtered animals. The conditions of the more affluent were most appreciably better, and their residential areas were far removed from the filth, smells, and noise pollution of the dwelling areas of the poor. In Engels's words:

> Manchester contains, at its heart, a rather extended commercial district . . . consisting almost wholly of offices and warehouses. Nearly the whole district is abandoned by dwellers, and is lonely and deserted at night; only watchmen and policemen traverse its narrow lanes with their dark lanterns. This district is cut through by certain main thoroughfares upon which the vast traffic concentrates, and in which the ground level is lined with brilliant shops. In these streets the upper floors are occupied, here and there, and there is a good deal of life upon them until late at night. (Engels 1999: 57–58)

Engels continues by describing the residentially segregated communities of the upper and middle bourgeoisie located in the outskirts of the city, communities ranging from fine and comfortable houses to villas with gardens located on hills with breezy winds. Omnibuses are available to take these affluent residents to the central business district without seeing or being seen by the poorer classes:

> And, the finest part of this arrangement is this, that the members of the monied aristocracy can take the shortest road through the middle of all the labouring districts to their places of business, without ever seeing that they are in the midst of the grimy misery that lurks to the right and the left. For the thoroughfares leading from the Exchange in all directions out of the city are lined, on both sides, with an almost unbroken series of shops, and are so kept in the hands of the middle and lower bourgeoisie, which out of self interest, care for a decent and cleanly external appearance and *can* care for it. True, these shops bear some relation to the districts which lie behind them, and are more elegant in the commercial and residential quarters than when they hide grimy working-men's dwellings; but they suffice to conceal from the eyes of the wealthy men and women of strong stomachs and weak nerves the misery and grime which form the complement of their wealth. (Engels 1999: 58)

Engels's description of the horrible living conditions of the working class, his "reading of the illegible," to use Steven Marcus's (1973, 1974) memorable phrase, are astonishing in their vivid portrayal of those conditions.

> Right and left a multitude of covered passages lead from the main street into numerous courts, and he who turns a thither gets into a filth and disgusting grime, the equal of which is not to be found—especially in the courts, which lead down to the Irk, and which contains unqualifiedly the most horrible dwellings which I have yet beheld. In one of these courts there stands directly at the entrance, at the end of the covered passage, a privy without a door, so dirty that the inhabitants can pass into and out of the court only by passing through foul pools of stagnant urine and excrement. (Engels 1999: 60–61)
>
> The view from this bridge, mercifully concealed from smaller mortals by a parapet as high as a man, is characteristic for the whole district. At the bottom flows, or rather stagnates, the Irk, a narrow, coal-black, foul smelling stream, full of debris and refuse, which it deposits on the shallower right bank. In dry weather, a long string of the most disgusting, blackish-green slime pools are left standing on the bank, from the depths of which bubbles of miasmatic gas constantly arise and give forth a stench unendurable even on the bridge 40 or 50 feet above the surface of the stream. (Engels 1999: 62)

In summary, what Engels achieved was a depiction of an industrial city whose savagery was reflected not only in the working conditions of the poor, but in the actual physical layout of the city, in its built environment.

> It is Manchester itself in its negated and estranged existence. This chaos of alleys, courts, hovels, filth—and human beings—is not a chaos at all. Every fragment of disarray, every inconvenience, every scrap of human suffering has a meaning. Each of these is inversely and ineradicably related to the life of the middle classes, to the work performed in the factories, and to the structure of the city as a whole. (Marcus 1973: 272)

The Ideal Type: Community and Interpersonal Relationships

The profound shift in the basis of social organization that attended the growth of nineteenth-century European cities had far-reaching consequences for institutional and personal life. The twentieth century theoretician Robert N. Nisbet (1966) observes that the rise of sociological analysis in that century focused on this shift and what was seen as the changing nature of the "social bond."

Nisbet observed that the nineteenth century was marked by pervasive disharmony and disorder. He argues that the history of the modern epoch can best be understood in terms of massive changes that have taken place in the larger contexts of human association. These are changes in allegiances to institutions in the location of social functions, in the relationship of men and women and the norms of culture, and, above all, in the source of diffusion of political power. He believes that the contemporary problem of intermediate association in state, industry, and community has its roots in certain conflicts of authority and function that have been notable aspects of the social history of modern Europe.

Nisbet believes that the fundamental change in the nature of the social bond became the focal point of nineteenth-century sociology. The urbanists Karp, Stone, and Yoels (1977) build on Nisbet's analysis. They recognize this "fundamental transformation" in the nature of the social bond. However, they add that it is important to "recognize that the nature of a social bond between persons is continuously in a state of transformation" (Karp, Stone, and Yoels 1977: 8). Thus, rather than think of preindustrial and industrial social relationships as being static entities we must think of them in process terms that are constantly in a state of transformation. Given that proviso, let us turn our attention to the development of the construct of the *ideal type* by European sociologists as a procedure to account for and explain historical changes in Western societies—from agriculture-based economies to industrialization-based ones. This sociological construct sought to delineate how and why life in cities differed from that found in rural areas.

The ideal type is a conceptual construct used in the analysis of social phenomena. The techniques for its use were fully elaborated and articulated by the German sociologist Max Weber (1949) in the early twentieth century. But it was an implicit technique used by nineteenth-century sociologists as well. The ideal type is constructed from observation of the characteristics of the social phenomena under investigation, but it is not intended to correspond exactly to any single case; rather, it designates the hypothetical characteristics of a "pure" or "ideal" case. The ideal type, then, does not imply evaluation or approval of the phenomena being studied. The ideal type characterizes a social phenomenon by emphasizing its essential characteristics. It is an analytically constructed model.

The ideal type does not conform to reality, being an abstraction that hypothesizes certain qualities or characteristics of the social phenomena under study. For example, an ideal type is constructed on the characteristics of cities. No cities would actually conform in an absolute sense to this ideal type, but the construct is useful in that it provides a focus point, a frame of reference, for the study of a given city.

Social scientists have found ideal types highly useful as analytical tools. These types make possible a conceptualization of social phenomena and facilitate cross-cultural and historical comparison among them. They aid in locating factors of social change in societies and enable the comparative investigation of institutions, such as the city, over time and space. Yet they have severe limitations. In this chapter, some ideal types of communities will be examined in terms of relevancy in the study of urbanization and processes of urbanism. Our focus is on the ideal type as it conceived of changes in interpersonal relationships, with particular emphasis on personal, family, and work relationships, and community involvements.

The dominant sociological view was that the perceived chaotic world of the city was countered by the family turning in onto itself. A strong emotional transformation characterizes the nineteenth century. The emotional bonds that individuals held for the community, the village, and the extended family were transformed into the development of an exclusive emotional attachment to nuclear family members. With the work world seen as hostile and precarious, the family took on an image as a place of refuge. The home was seen as a place that provided security and safety from a cruel, harsh, and unpredictable industrial urban society.

This anti-urban state of mind was echoed in the works of nineteenth-century social scientists. The revulsion toward the city and the bemoaning of the loss of an idealized past led sociologists to develop contrasting models of city life versus rural life. The city became identified with social disorganization, alienation, and the loss of community and meaningful relationships. The newly emerging urban world was typified by competition, conflict, and contractual relationships. In comparison, the small village and the rural community were seen as the antithesis of the urban world and were based on cooperation, integration, and kinship relationships. They were romanticized for their orderliness, noncompetitiveness, and meaningfulness of personal relationships.

Robert A. Nisbet (1966) observes that both radicals and conservatives viewed the past with nostalgia and the urban present with distaste. Although the radicals eventually embraced the city, seeing in it the hope for the revolutionary future, they too were aghast at the social conditions existing in the emerging industrial cities of the nineteenth century. Friedrich Engels, as was seen earlier, was a romantic radical who was appalled by the urban prospect:

> We know well enough that [the] isolation of the individual . . . is everywhere the fundamental principle of modern society. But nowhere is this selfish egotism as blatantly evident as in the frantic bustle of the great city. (Engels cited in Nisbet 1966:29)

One is struck by the similarity of Engels's view with that of the conservative Alexis de Tocqueville (1805–1859), cited earlier in this chapter.

The Ideal Type: Rural and City Life

Let us now look at some of the famous and influential typologies that were developed during this period. These typologies often took the form of dichotomies or polar opposites and have often been reinterpreted by more contemporary theorists as continua that emphasize a range of variation. The key theorists are Henry Sumner Maine, Ferdinand Tönnies, Emile Durkheim, and Max Weber.

Henry Sumner Maine and Ferdinand Tönnies

Henry Sumner Maine's (1862/1960) distinction of "status to contract" society was one of the earliest of such typologies. Maine postulated that *status societies* are characterized by group relations that are anchored in tradition. Tradition, in turn, determines the rights and obligations of individuals. The individual's status was fixed by his or her family and kinship system, which served as the foundation of social organization. The movement to *contract* relations was fostered by urbanization, with kinship bonds becoming less strong. With the ascendancy of the state, civil law replaced traditional customs in enforcing and regulating social obedience and social control. Maine argued that with the increased power of the state, the influence of the family over the individual would decline and women's social status, which was extremely low in status communities, would rise and familism would decline. The essence of Maine's argument was that the powers, privileges, and duties that were once vested in the family had shifted to the national state. Concomitantly, people's social relationships, which were based on their *status*, shifted to individually agreed *contracts*.

Farmers loading hay on to a wagon in a field in Whitby, England overlooking the North Sea. Nineteenth century.

Maine's work had great influence on his nineteenth century contemporaries. Ferdinand Tönnies (1855–1936), who wrote *Gemeinschaft und Gesellschaft [Community and Society,]* (1887/1963), has been an inspirational source for students of community analysis to the present day. *Gemeinschaft and Gesellschaft* are ideal types and refer to the nature of social relationships, basic social groups, and institutions.

Gemeinschaft (community) relationships are intimate, traditional, enduring, and based on informal relations determined by *who* the individual is in the community as opposed to *what* he or she has done—in sociological parlance, ascriptive status rather than achieved status. The culture of the community is homogeneous, and the moral custodians are the family and the church. For Tönnies, there are three central aspects of *Gemeinschaft:* kinship, neighborhood, and friendship. These institutions serve as the foundation for social life and activities.

Gesellschaft (society association) refers to the large scale, contractual, impersonal relationships that Tönnies saw emerging in industrializing and urbanizing Europe in the late nineteenth century. *Gesellschaft* includes business-oriented relations based on rational calculations geared to instrumental ends. Personal relationships are subordinate. In the *Gesellschaft*, family groups and institutions no longer serve as the basis of social life; rather, such societies are organized around work relationships and bureaucratic institutions.

Tönnies was antagonistic to the growth of individualism. He believed that acute individualism led to egotistic, self-willed individuals who sought friends only as means and ends to self-interested gains. He decried the involvement of women in the labor force and feared the loss of their involvement in the family. Likewise, he saw the destructive effects of child labor on the family. Basically a conservative, Tönnies cites Karl Marx in documenting the ill effects of child labor. Taken together, these changes are seen as destroying the fabric of traditional society and the solidarity of its people. The young no longer internalize old values and attitudes, and the intertwining rights and obligations that bound the traditional community together are weakened and gradually dissolve. The family itself becomes subordinated to personal interests. "The family becomes an accidental form for the satisfaction of natural needs, neighborhood and friendship are supplanted by special interest groups and conventional society life" (Tönnies 1887/1963:168).

In summary, Tönnies's depiction of the *Gesellschaft* is strikingly similar to that of Karl Marx. But unlike Marx, who sought future revolutionary changes, Tönnies yearned for the return of the romantic past described in his ideal typification of the *Gemeinschaft*. In Table 3.3, a schematic representation of Tönnies' societal types is delineated.

TABLE 3.3   *Summary of the Contrasts Between Gemeinschaft and Gesellschaft*

	Societal Types	
Social Characteristic	*Gemeinschaft*	*Gesellschaft*
Dominant social relationships	Fellowship Kinship Neighborliness	Exchange Rational calculations
Central institutions	Family law Extended kin group	State Capitalistic economy
The individual in the social order	Self	Person
Characteristic from of wealth	Land	Money
Type of law	Family law	Law of contract
Ordering of institutions	Family life Rural village life Town life	City life Rational life Cosmopolitan life
Type of social control	Concord Folkways and mores Religion	Convention Legislation Public opinion

Emile Durkheim

Emile Durkheim (1855–1917) also distinguished the nature of social relationships with these two contrasting types of social orders. His ideal type constructs represent two contrasting bases of social integration. Durkheim's doctoral dissertation, *The Division of Labor in Society,* was published in 1893. He compared societies based on *mechanical solidarity* with societies based on *organic solidarity* in regard to social integration. Mechanical solidarity describes the form of social cohesion that exists in small-scale societies that have a minimal division of labor. The type of relationships that link members of such small, stable communities are characterized as being overlapping and interrelated; they are cohesive because of shared bonds and habits. Social unity, Durkheim said, is mechanical and automatic in that the parts of the society are interchangeable. Close friendship and kinship groups are typical of mechanical solidarity in that they are secured by personal, stable, and emotional attachments.

In contrast, societies based on organic solidarity, which Durkheim believed was emerging in Europe, were founded on increased specialization and the division of labor. Organic solidarity-type relationships are impersonal, transient, fragmented, and rational. The source of societal unity is the interdependence of specialized and highly individualized members and the complementary diversity of their positions and life experiences. In relationships marked by organic solidarity one does not relate as a whole individual, but one relates to those qualities that are relevant to the particular function one is performing in relation to others. Durkheim associated the shift in these two types of solidarities, from mechanical to organic, as resulting from the increased size and density of population, the ease and rapidity of communication, and especially the increased division of labor. All of these factors are linked with the rise of industrialization and the growth of cities.

In some ways Durkheim mirrors the conservatism of Maine and Tönnies. In *The Division of Labor in Society* as well as in his other works, notably *Suicide* (1897/1951), Durkheim argues that the cohesive and stabilizing forces of European society are disintegrating. The destructive forces of industrialization, secularization, and revolution, account for alienation, anomie (normlessness), and the isolation of modern urban life. Indeed, in his *The Elementary Forms of Religious Life* (1912), Durkheim viewed collective consciousness as arising out of the individual's participation in the communal life. The origins of man's conceptualization of the universe and the categories of knowledge, he said, stem from this communal perspective. It is no wonder, then, that Durkheim reflects the concern of his contemporaries, both sociologists and laypeople, about the problems inherent in the modern industrial urban society.

Yet Durkheim differs from Tönnies and Maine in a notable way. In his analysis of organic solidarity, Durkheim observes the increased importance of specialization of function and division of labor as the basis of an emerging form of social unity based on mutual interdependence that is likened to the different parts of a living organism. In this type of society, where so many people are dissimilar to each other, civil law is restitutive and is contractual with legally defined penalties and punishment, unlike mechanical solidarity society, where law is repressive and based on motives of revenge and violence. He does caution, however, that there must be a shared moral basis that underlies contractual relationships. Organic solidarity is basic to a society that is undergoing social change associated with rapid growth of the population, increased size and diversity, ease and rapidity of communication, and increasing specialization and division of labor. Thus, Durkheim's typology from mechanical solidarity to organic solidarity is seen as accompanying the change toward an urban society.

In conclusion, the ideal type was developed to contrast the emerging industrial city with the preindustrial rural and village community. This typological approach was often tinged with an anti-urban bias that distorted both the analyses of these sociologists and the many subsequent analyses of the city. Further, since typologies were too broadly based and too vague, rather than aiding in the analysis of urban patterns, they often led to obfuscation and distortion. Finally, the typologies failed to deal with the wide range of variations within cities as well as with cross cultural and historical variations.

Max Weber

Max Weber (1864–1920) in his classic work on the rise of urbanism, *Die Stadt* (1921) [translated as *The City* (1958) by Martindale and Neuwirth], sought to overcome ahistorical and noncomparative analyses of the city. He extended the typology through an examination of cities across historical periods and city cultures. Weber sought to outline the basic characteristics of the urban community, which would include the underlying elements of the European city. Weber identifies these elements:

> To constitute a full urban community, a settlement must display a relative predominance of trade-commercial relations with the settlement as a whole displaying the following features: (1) a fortification; (2) a market; (3) a court of its own and at least partially autonomous law; (4) a related form of association, and (5) at least partial autonomy and autocephaly, thus also an administration by authorities in the election of whom the burgheres particpated. (Weber 1958: 80–81)

Weber's typology centered on the distinction between "traditional society" based on ascriptive status and "legal-rational society" based on the superiority of authority and on formalized rules and depersonalized bureaucratic principals. Weber follows the line of thinking of Tönnies. He sees European cities moving away from patriarchalism and brotherhood that was characteristic of medieval society. Weber sees this as a process of "rationalization" that parallels Tönnies concept of the *gesellschaft*. Tönnies sees medieval societies as moving away from their communal base toward an individualistic, capitalistic modern society; Weber sees this transformation as the result of "rationalization" based on acts of efficiency and the amount of return. Rationality is now seen as a central principle of modernity.

As the sociologist Richard Sennett (1969) points out, Weber's definition of the city approximates the term *cosmopolitan*. A cosmopolitan settlement is one that permits a variety of lifestyles and the coexistence of different types of people.

Weber transposed this definition to the nature of the city itself: the city is that social form which permits the greatest degree of individuality and uniqueness in each of its actual occurrences in the world. To define the city is not to describe one style of life, but one set of social structures that can produce a multitude of concretely different styles of life. The city is therefore the set of social structures that encourage social individuality and innovation, and is thus the instrument of historical change. (Sennett 1969: 6)

Weber saw the city as having three defining characteristics: a city was a market settlement, a political administrative center, and a community where urban dwellers had duties, rights, and status of their association. Weber, then, linked the economic and political components of urban life with its community aspects. This linkage was not picked up, as we shall see, by the Chicago School, which developed the predominant theoretical perspective on city life. Nor did the Chicago School pick up on Weber's emphasis on the multidimensionality of city life or on his belief that the city, in its encouragement of social individuality and innovation, is also the major instrument of historical change.

Finally, I would like to point out that Weber was also familiar with the work of Georg Simmel. Like Simmel, Weber noted the influence that the urban economy had on transforming occupations into professions, and be observed that the city dweller's mind had little time for reflection and was crowded by impressions (Martindale and Neuwirth 1958). I would like to now turn to an examination of Simmel's essay, "Metropolis and Mental Life, which detailed the perceived impact of the city on the urban psyche.

Simmel: Metropolis and Mental Life

Georg Simmel (1868–1918) was a prominent German sociologist in the early part of the twentieth century. His masterful essay, "Metropolis and Mental Life" (1903/1995), has been extremely influential in framing the sociological discussion of the social psychology of city life. He argued that urban life produced a unique form of consciousness, a distinct metropolitan personality that was caused by the conditions under which people lived. The two predominant conditions were the intensity of the nervous stimuli in the city, and the pervasiveness of the economic market on people's relationships. Urban consciousness was characterized by intellectuality—the individual reacts with his head, not his heart—rationality, anonymity, and "sophistication."

For Simmel, the metropolitan personality was a product of both the characteristics of the physical structure of the city and the economic characteristics of the society that consisted of its money economy and its specialized division of labor. Money becomes the measure of all things, including people. And the measurement is made through a calculating rational eye.

Simmel argued that the size, density, and complexity of urban life resulted in the fact that the individual, during the course of a day, would come into contact with vast numbers of people. Think here of an individual standing on a busy downtown street corner watching literally thousands of people passing by hourly. The urban dweller can only become acquainted with a very few, and even here these relationships are often superficial. The development of a blasé attitude and of tolerance can be seen as a protective reaction to the multitude of stimuli characteristic of urban life.

Simmel articulates the theme of freedom and loneliness that has been picked up by so many social scientists [cf. Erich Fromm (1941), *Escape from Freedom;* David Riesman (1950), *The Lonely Crowd*]. Simmel observes that a characteristic of the urban way of life is the diminished obligations that individuals have to social groups and the sometimes petty and prejudicial views individuals hold toward others. City life is seen to cause the separateness of the individual from the social group, which can result in greater personal and spiritual development and intellectual and affectional freedom. The result is a liberating effect as a consequence of these urban opportunities for individualism and autonomy. However, such freedom is seen to carry a stiff price . . . . loneliness: "It is obviously only the obverse of this freedom that, under certain circumstances, one never feels as lonely and deserted as in this metropolitan crush of persons" (Simmel 1995:40).

In his analysis of the paradoxical intertwining of freedom and loneliness, Simmel hits on a theme that becomes echoed in American urban sociology as particularly represented by the Chicago School. Simmel's work was influential on the thinking of the Chicago School and was introduced to American sociology by Robert Park, who studied under Simmel in Germany. Park and his associates at Chicago, most notably Louis Wirth, in their analytical construction of city life point to social disorganization as a major manifestation of its inherent deconstruction. The work of the Chicago School will be examined in the next chapter of this book.

Part II

Disciplinary Perspectives

4

Chicago School: Urbanism and Urban Ecology

Arthur Schlessinger, in his reinterpretation of American history and Turner's frontier thesis, *The Rise of the City, 1878–98* (1933), emphasizes the importance of the industrial city in defining American society.

> It was the city rather than the unpeopled wilderness that was beginning to dazzle the imagination of the nation. The framer, once the pride of America, was descending from his lofty estate, too readily accepting the city's scornful estimate of him as a "rube" and a "hayseed". "We must face the inevitable," Josiah Strong exclaimed; "the new civilization is certain to be urban, and the problem of the twentieth century will be in the city." (Schlessinger 1933 cited in Briggs 1970: 82)

Chicago: The Shock City of the Early Twentieth Century

During the early twentieth century, the city that captured the American imagination was Chicago. Earlier in this book, I pointed out how Asa Briggs (1970; 1976) introduced the term *shock city* to refer to a city in a given historical period that had symbolic significance reflecting both awe at spectacular growth and technical progress, while also raising deep concerns about emerging economic, political, and social problems. Manchester, England, was the shock city of the emerging cities of the Industrial Revolution. Chicago, in the beginning of the twentieth century, became the shock city of the later stages of the Industrial Revolution.

In 1850 there were six American cities with more than 100,000 inhabitants. From the largest to the smallest these were: New York, Baltimore, Philadelphia, Boston, New Orleans, and Cincinnati. Over the next 50 years, the total population of the United States jumped from 23 million to 76 million, largely as a result of immigration from Europe. In 1900 the three largest American cities were New York, Chicago, and Philadelphia, all with over 1,000,000 inhabitants. Boston, Baltimore, and St. Louis had populations over 500,000. Cities with populations of a quarter of a million people included Cincinnati and New Orleans, as well as the emerging cities of the midwest: Cleveland, Buffalo, Pittsburgh, Detroit, and Milwaukee. San Francisco and Washington, D.C., rounded out the list.

Chicago epitomizes the phenomenal population growth of American cities; in 1860, its population was 112,000; by the turn of the century (1900), its population

Under the elevated train in the "Loop," Downtown Chicago. Photo by author.

was over 1.5 million; and it proceeded to grow at a rate of over 500,000 for each of the next three decades, culminating in a population of over 3.5 million by 1930.

Chicago best personifies the "shock city" of that time period, not only because of the rapidity of its growth—it was the fastest growing city in the United States and perhaps the world, especially after the Great Fire of 1871—but because it was a major metropolis that contained a diversified population from both rural America and from Eastern and Southern Europe and elsewhere. Students of urban life were enthralled at the commercial development of its central business district, the Loop, with its distinctive and innovative skyscrapers. The city's use of modern technology put it in the forefront of both horizontal growth, through its expansive rail and trolley systems, and vertical growth, made possible by the use of electricity, the telephone, and the elevator. The Columbian World Exhibition ("The White City") held in that city in 1893 provided increased international attention on the realities and the possible futures of the emerging American industrial city.

The Beaux Arts grandeur of the Chicago Theater on State Street, that great street, the "Loop," Downtown Chicago. Photo by author.

The Chicago School and Social Disorganization

As Maurice Stein (1964) has stated, Chicago's growth statistics can give but a suggestion as to what it means in human terms to live in a city whose population swells at such a rapid rate. The unprecedented demands for the development of municipal services—street and transportation systems, sanitary water supplies, garbage disposal and sewage systems, fire and police protection, schools, libraries, parks, playgrounds, and so on—must have been overwhelming. Further complicating the situation was the fact that the new urban population was comprised predominantly of an influx of European immigrants (who had little familiarity with American customs and language) and migrants from rural America, groups unfamiliar with and unaccustomed to city life and each other. For these reasons, Chicago can be considered the shock city of the early twentieth century, as Manchester was in the mid-nineteenth century.

Anchoring the southern end of Chicago's Magnificent Mile are three architectural marvels—the Wrigley Building, the Medinah Athletic Club (now the Hotel Inter-Continental Chicago), and the Tribune Tower—all built in the 1920s. Photo by author.

Chicago during the first half of the twentieth century was a cauldron of social change. It was also the site where American sociology began to flourish at the University of Chicago and its "Chicago School." The University of Chicago's intellectual activities can be best understood within the historical context of the growth of urban America in general, and of Chicago in particular, in the second half of the nineteenth century and into the twentieth. It is not surprising, given the momentous and unplanned changes taking place in American cities during this period, that social scientists emphasized the negative and opposed the positive qualities of urban life. They focused on social disorganization and its consequences—alienation, anomie, social isolation, juvenile delinquency, crime, mental illness, suicide, child abuse, separation, and divorce—as inherent characteristics of urban life. "Small wonder that the Chicago sociologists focused on the absence of established institutional patterns in so many regions of the city, stressing that the neighborhoods grew and changed so rapidly that sometimes the only constant feature appeared to be mobility . . . and why 'disorganization' accompanied 'mobility'" (Stein 1964: 16).

The Chicago School of Sociology was composed of such important sociologists as Robert E. Park, Ernest W. Burgess, Louis Wirth, E. Franklin Frazier, W. I. Thomas, and Florian Znaniecki at the University of Chicago. It also contained reform-minded researchers, led by Jane Addams, who gathered at Hull House, a neighborhood center and independent social agency designed to not only understand the nature of city life but to improve the lives of the immigrant populations that lived in the surrounding community. The Chicago School contributed much to the development and establishment of American sociology. As the Italian sociologist, Marco d'Eramo (2002) has recently pointed out, "And just as sociology began in Chicago, it began by studying Chicago." Under the influence of the chair of the department at the University of Chicago, students were encouraged to go out and experience the city. Park's famous admonition to graduate students is worth noting:

> You have been told to go grubbing in the library, thereby accumulating a mass of notes and a liberal coating of grime. You have been told to choose problems wherever you can find musty stacks of routine records based on trivial schedules prepared by tired bureaucrats and filled out by reluctant applicants for aid or fussy do-gooders or indifferent clerks. This is called "getting your hands dirty in real research." Those who counsel you are wise and honorable; the reasons they offer are of great value. But one more thing is needful: first hand observation. Go and sit in the lounges of the luxury hotels and on the doorsteps of the flophouses; sit on the Gold Coast settees and on the slum shakedowns; sit in the Orchestra Hall and in the Star and Garter Burlesk. In short, gentlemen, go get the seat of your pants dirty in real research. (Park quoted in Bulmer 1984).

The Chicago School of Sociology also had two major theoretical components. One was the development of a conceptual perspective that sought to develop a scientific description of urban forms and processes. The idea of ecology, the scientific study of the relationships between organisms and their environment, was adapted to the study of the city—*urban ecology*. The second component, *urbanism*, was essentially a social psychology of city life. It sought to understand the nature of human associations in the urban setting.

In the study of *urbanism*, the Chicago School elaborated a distinct contrast between urban and rural life that followed the ideal types put forth by European sociology predecessors. The intent of this and the next chapter is to examine the two underlying theoretical perspectives of the Chicago School—urban ecology and urbanism. It is necessary to understand where "their heads were coming from" to fully comprehend their discussion of the urban community. In this chapter I will first discuss the *urbanism* of the Chicago School and how its critics responded to this perspective. Then, I will focus on the urban ecology model put forth by the Chicago School and how its critics responded to it. To begin the discussion of *urbanism* let's start with the contributions of the founder of the Chicago School, Robert Ezra Park.

Robert E. Park: Urbanism

Robert Park, the founder of the Chicago School, was a journalist who studied in Germany with Georg Simmel. Park linked his interest in journalistic knowledge with a study of urban sociology. Simmel's formulations emphasized the city as a state of mind rather than as merely a physical environment. In his influential essay, "The Metropolis and Mental Life," Simmel raises the idea that the city values rationality more than emotionality (the head rather than the heart) and emphasizes the importance of the money economy, impersonality, punctuality, and a blasé attitude. These values, in turn, lead to an emphasis on personal freedom unique to city life. Park articulated that view in his seminal statement:

> The city is . . . a state of mind, a body of customs and traditions, and of the organized attitudes and sentiments that inhere in these customs and are transmitted with the tradition. The city is not, in other words, merely a physical mechanism and an artificial construction. It is involved in the vital processes of the people who compose it (Park 1925/1966).

Park saw the city as a product of the participation and communication of its inhabitants and not simply as a physical artifact or a collection of people. He was particularly interested in the urban conditions that resulted in the breakdown of human communication and interaction, which ultimately led to the decline of the primary group, the breakdown of the community, and to social disorganization. Park utilized Charles Horton Cooley's concept of primary group—a group in which face-face association and cooperation predominated—to articulate this view. "It is probably the breaking down of local attachments and the weakening of the restraints and inhibitions of the primary group, under the influence of the urban environment, which are largely responsible for the increase of vice and crime in great cities" (Park 1966/1925: 25).

In Park's theoretical model, the city is organized on two interconnected levels, the "biotic" and the "cultural." The biotic refers to biological and environmental factors and forces, including competition, invasion, and succession, which determine land use. The biotic level became associated with the perspective called *urban ecology*. The cultural level refers to symbolic and psychological adjustments and to the social organization of urban life influenced by shared sentiments and values. The cultural level became associated with the *symbolic interaction* perspective and what has become known as the *sociocultural perspective*.

In Park's thinking on local communities it is the cultural model that predominates: "The city is rooted in the habits and customs of the people who inhabit it. The consequence is that the city possesses *moral* as well as a physical organization, and these two mutually interact in characteristic ways to mold and modify one another" (italics added) (Park 1966/1925: 4).

The cultural model emphasized symbolic and psychological adjustments and the social organization of urban life influenced by shared sentiments and values. However, the cultural model, with it its concern for the social-psychological and cultural emphasis in the study of city life, was subsumed by the ecological model. As he developed his ideas, Park was more and more influenced by the ecological model. But for now, let us complete our examination of the Chicago School and its ideas regarding urbanism.

The Chicago School and Urbanism

For sociology, the changing nature of the social bond was a fundamental issue in the study of the city. The attention of nineteenth-century sociologists, such as Maine, Tönnies, Durkheim, Weber, and Simmel, was on contrasting the differences in the types of community that characterized the emerging urban industrial society with that of the rural society—the world that was lost. Rural life was seen to be composed of orderly social relationships anchored by the social institutions of family, neighbors, and the church. In contrast, life in the city was seen to be one of individual isolation and social relationships anchored in what you are, not who you are.

The commonalities in the theoretical orientations of the above sociologists were integrated in the Chicago School's conceptualization of *urbanism*. The culminating statement was articulated in Louis Wirth's seminal essay, "Urbanism as a Way of Life," published in 1938. In this chapter we will examine the Chicago School's ideas about the nature of the urban dweller, the community, and city life.

The Chicago School developed a distinct contrast between urban and rural life; proponents saw traditional patterns of life being broken down by debilitating urban forces, resulting in social disorganization within the family and negative impacts on the community and the individual.

Yet, the Chicago School also saw and recognized the importance of the large number of urban enclaves that were found in the city. In Robert Park's terms he observed that the city was *a mosaic of little worlds* (1966/1916). [Louis Wirth (1938) in his seminal essay, "Urbanism as a Way of Life," referred to the city as *a mosaic of social worlds*.] These small communities located in the large city are relatively isolated from each other, and thus the great diversity (heterogeneity) of the city is complemented by local neighborhoods that are characterized by patterns of segregation. Further it's this pattern of residential segregation that allows for the development of patterns of social order among these mosaics of social worlds.

In Park's terms:

> The processes of segregation establish moral distances which make the city a mosaic of little worlds which touch but do not interpenetrate. This makes it possible for individuals to pass quickly and easily from one moral milieu to another and encourages the fascinating but dangerous experiment of living at the same time in several contiguous, but otherwise widely separate, worlds. (Park, 1966/1916:40).

Thus two somewhat contradictory points of view emerged from the Chicago School perspective. One view builds on the notion of the city as impersonal, segmented, and secondary. It often emphasized that the city brings about the destruction of communities, families, and ultimately individuals who are befallen to the psychological fears of loneliness, alienation, and anomie. The other view observes that the city is a mosaic of social worlds that, while segregated from each other, includes patterns of social order that exhibit a spirit of tolerance. The Chicago School thus had two views of the city. One was the perceived "social disorganization" of communities; the other was the perception of the existence of an underlying social organization contained in these urban enclaves. But these communities ultimately are seen to collapse under the influence of assimilation to the broader societal cultural values.

Louis Wirth: Urbanism as a Way of Life

Louis Wirth (1897–1952) wrote the culminating statement that developed the contrast between rural and urban ways of life. Wirth was a sociology student at the University of Chicago who also taught in the sociology department at the University of Chicago until his untimely sudden death in 1952. It was in 1938 that he published his seminal essay, "Urbanism as a Way of Life." This essay was the most influential statement on urbanism that came out of the Chicago School.

Wirth argued that cities were characterized by a distinctive pattern of behavior that he called *urbanism*. Three critical factors were the determinants of urbanism: size, density, and heterogeneity (diversity) of the population. The consequences of these three variables were the relative absence of personal relationships; the depersonalization and segmentation of human relations, characterized by anonymity, superficiality, and transitoriness; and the breakdown of social structures and increased mobility, instability, and insecurity.

TABLE 4.1 *Louis Wirth's Sociological Definition of the City in Relation to Size, Density, and Heterogeneity*

A Schematic Version

PERMANENCE

SIZE
An increase in the number of inhabitants of a settlement beyond a certain limit brings about changes in the relations of people and changes in the character of the community

> Greater the number of people interacting, greater the potential differentiation
>
> Dependence upon a greater number of people, lesser dependence on particular persons
>
> Association with more people, knowledge of a smaller proportion, and of these, less intimate knowledge
>
> More secondary rather than primary contacts; that is, increase in contacts which are face to face, yet impersonal, superficial, transitory, and segmental
>
> More freedom from the personal and emotional control of intimate groups
>
> Association in a large number of groups, on individual allegiance to a single group

DENSITY
Reinforces the effect of size in diversifying men and their activities, and in increasing the structural complexity of the society

> Tendency to differentiation and specialization
>
> Separation of residence from work place
>
> Functional specialization of areas—segregation of functions
>
> Segregation of people: city becomes a mosaic of social worlds

HETEROGENEITY
Cities products of migration of peoples of diverse origin

Heterogeneity of origin matched by heterogeneity of occupations

Differentiation and specialization reinforces heterogeneity

> Without common background and common activities premium is placed on visual recognition: the uniform becomes symbolic of the role
>
> No common set of values, no common ethical system to sustain them: money tends to become measure of all things for which there are no common standards
>
> Formal controls as opposed to informal controls. Necessity for adhering to predictable routines. Clock and the traffic signal symbolic of the basis of the social order
>
> Economic basis: mass production of goods, possible only with the standardization of processes and products
>
> Standardization of goods and facilities in terms of the average
>
> Adjustment of educational, recreational, and cultural services to mass requirements
>
> In politics success of mass appeals—growth of mass movements

Source: Eshref Shevky and Wendell Bell. *Social Area Analysis*. Stanford Sociological Series #1 (Stanford, CA, Stanford University Press, 1955), pp. 7–8. As reproduced in Noel Gist and Sylvia Fava. *Urban Society*, 6th ed. (New York: Thomas Y. Crowell, 1974).

Wirth summarizes his view of the influence of the city on the people who live there in the following statement: "The distinctive features of the urban mode of life have often been described sociologically as consisting of the substitution of secondary for primary contacts, the weakening of the bonds of kinship, and the declining social significance of the family, the disappearance of the neighborhood, and the undermining of the traditional basis of social solidarity" (Wirth 1938b: 21–22).

In Wirth's opinion, the development of secondary relationships downplays the significance of primary group involvements. The reduction of involvements with neighbors and friends and the weakening of kinship and family ties all serve to weaken social bonds in local communities. Thus, the work of Wirth, like that of his European predecessors who developed typologies on the urban-rural dichotomization of society, shared a common orientation—a negative view of the impact of the city and urban life on individuals, the family, and the neighborhood. Wirth's position has been referred to as "determinist theory" (Fischer, 1976). That is, the causal variables of "size, density, and heterogeneity" determine both community and psychological outcomes. The future is bleak for a community with diminished fundamental social bonds, and the individual is doomed to feelings of alienation and anomie.

Wirth's determinist theory has undergone extensive criticism. This criticism takes the form of a "compositional theory" (cf. Fischer 1976: 32–36). Compositionalist theorists argue that it is the composition of groups of people who populate a city that influence their respective "urban way of life." Thus it is a person's age, ethnicity, and stage in the life cycle and economic circumstance that dictates his or her urbanism.

Compositionalists emphasize the importance of the composition of the population—class, stage in the life cycle, and lifestyle orientations—in determining the impact of urbanism on individuals and groups. They downplay the importance of the urban environment in determining urban relationships. These theorists advocate that there is no *one* urban way of life, but many depending on population characteristics.

Compositionalists can be seen as building on an important aspect of Chicago School analysis, which describes the city as a "mosaic of social worlds." As Fischer (1984: 33) observes, these worlds are described as sites of extended kinship ties, ethnicity, neighborhood, lifestyles. Wirth has been taken to task for his emphasizing the anomic and alienating character of the city without reference to the viable communities discussed by Park, Zorbaugh, Burgess, and other members of the Chicago School. Indeed, Wirth, himself, in his 1925 doctoral dissertation that was later published as *The Ghetto* (1928), vividly described Chicago's Jewish ghetto. Yet he does not make reference to "social world" in his definition of the city as put forth in his seminal essay. Further, in his own personal life, Wirth experienced the city in a way that he deemed not possible. His colleague Everett Hughes observed: "Louis used to say all those things about how the city is impersonal—while living with a whole clan of kin and friends on a very personal basis" (quoted in Kasarda and Janowitz 1974: 338).

Gans: Urbanism and Suburbanism as Ways of Life

Herbert Gans is a major compositionalist who has made a significant challenge to determinist theory. Gans argues that there is a myriad of urban adaptation processes and to speak of "urbanism" in the singular as *a way of life* is misleading and wrong. The title of his (1962b) influential article, "Urbanism and Suburbanism as Ways of Life," puts forth his basic argument.

Herbert Gans's (1962b) work has been a very influential statement of the compositional theory position. Gans takes issue with Louis Wirth's "Urbanism as a Way of Life." Gans makes the following points: (1) Wirth's urbanites do not represent a picture of urban men and women but rather depict the depersonalized and atomized members of mass society—they are representative of society, not of the city; (2) residents of the outer city tend to exhibit lifestyles more characteristic of suburbia than of the inner city; and (3) Wirth's description of the urban way of life fits best the transient areas of the inner city—but here too it is best to view the inner city as providing a diversity of ways of life rather than a single way of life. In short, Gans argues that the ways of life of the city are not simply explained as the product of the size, density, and heterogeneity of their settlement. Rather, the ways of city life are better explained in terms of social class and stages in the life cycle.

Gans builds on urban differences and postulates that there are at least five urban ways of life that characterize the downtown areas and vary depending on

Orchard Street on the Lower East Side of New York City. Photo by author.

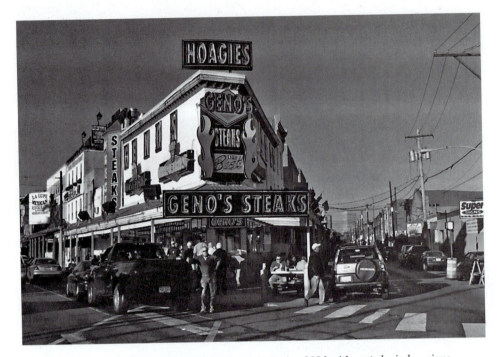

Geno's Steaks in South Philly made national news in Spring 2006 with posted window signs admonishing patrons to speak English when ordering its famous cheese steaks. This was perceived by the many immigrants who now live in the area as a reflection of anti-immigration sentiment. Ironically, the owner of Geno's is himself a son of Italian immigrants whose parents had limited knowledge of English. Photo by author.

the basis of social class and the stages in the family life cycle. Gans uses the following classifications:

1. Cosmopolites
2. The unmarried or childless
3. Ethnic villages
4. The deprived
5. The trapped and downwardly mobile

This schema incorporates compositional elements such as economic factors (cosmopolites and the deprived, trapped), cultural factors (urban villagers), and stages in the life cycle (singles and married but childless).

The cosmopolites place a high value on the cultural facilities located in the center of the city. They tend to be composed of artistically inclined persons, such as writers, artists, intellectuals, and professionals. A large proportion of inner-city dwellers are unmarried or, if married, childless. This group is composed of the affluent and the powerful members of the city. The less-affluent cosmopolites may move to suburban areas to raise their children while attempting to maintain kinship and primary-group relationships and resist the encroachment of other ethnic or racial groups.

Members of the deprived population find themselves in the city through no choice of their own. This group is composed of the very poor, the emotionally disturbed or otherwise handicapped, broken families, and—in significant number—the nonwhite poor who are forced to live in dilapidated housing and blighted neighborhoods because of racial discrimination and an economic housing marketplace that relegated them to the worst areas of the city.

The fifth and final group are composed of trapped people who stay behind in the city as a result of downward mobility. They cannot afford to move out of a neighborhood when it changes; they cannot compete economically for good housing. Aged persons living on fixed incomes and families that do not have a stable economic income fall into this category.

Gans goes on to describe a sixth urban way of life that is characteristic of individuals and families who live in the outer regions of the city or in the suburbs. He describes the relationship between neighbors as *quasi primary*, "Whatever the intensity or frequency of these relationships, the interaction is more intimate than a secondary contact, but more guarded than a primary one" (Gans 1962b: 634).

Cosmopolites, professionals who are single or cohabitating and those who are married but childless, live in the city by choice. The city does not have the social disorganizational character described by earlier theorists. Those living in the outer areas of the city or in suburbia have a middle-class way of life: they tend to live in single-family dwellings; more of them are married; they have higher income; and they hold more white-collar positions than their inner-city counterparts.

Among the city resident groups described by Gans, the ethnic working-class villages are the most highly integrated and tend to resemble small-town homogeneous communities more than they resemble Wirth's depiction of urbanism. Far from being depersonalized, isolated, and socially disorganized, ethnic, or urban, villagers (the terms are interchangeable) put an emphasis "on kinship and the primary group, the lack of anonymity and secondary-group contacts, the weakness of formal organization, and the suspicion of anything and anyone outside their neighborhood" (Gans 1962b: 630).

The poor, and those trapped in the poverty areas of the city, have no choice in where to live. For them, at least at first appearance, the city seems to be associated with all the characteristics of social disorganization vividly depicted earlier. Their family system also seems to take on all the negative characteristics of the family described by the social disorganization and alienation theories of urban life. But as we shall see in a later chapter, their family life structures and processes are much more complicated than supposed.

In summary, the differences between the determinist theory of Wirth and the compositional theory of Gans rest on different beliefs about how the city affects small groups. Wirth's determinist theory believes that the ecological factors of size, density, and heterogeneity severely disrupt the "mosaic of social worlds," ultimately undermining the social bonds based on kinship, family, neighborhood, and friends. Compositionalists, like Gans, take a different view. For them the urban enclaves that have developed shield the residents from the impact of the alienating city, "and that urbanism thus has no serious, *direct* effects on groups of individuals" (Fischer 1976:35).

Indeed Gans explains differences in the *ways* of life of urban and suburban dwellers not only in terms of urbanism or the differences in family, peer, neighborhood, and church involvements, but also in political economy terms:

> Characteristics do not explain the causes of behavior, rather, they are clues to socially created and culturally defined roles, choices, and demands. A causal analysis must trace them back to the larger, social, economic, and political systems which determine the situations in which roles are played and the cultural content of choices and demands, as well as the opportunities for their achievement. (Gans 1962b: 641)

Gans further argues that the urban economy cannot be solely understood through an examination of ecological processes at the local and regional level. Rather it is necessary to also understand the role played by national economic and social systems and their impact on regional and local ways of life.

Claude Fischer's Subcultural Theory

The urban sociologist Claude Fischer (1975, 1976) takes issue with both the determinist theory and the compositional theory and postulates his own theoretical approach that he labels as *subcultural theory* (Fischer 1975, 1976). This theory has become very influential in understanding the variations in urbanism patterns.

It is only in large cities that a "critical mass" exists that can support a street lined with specialized ethnic restaurants; East Village, New York City. Photo by author.

In Fischer's assessment, he agrees with the compositionalists that Wirth underestimated the importance of compositional factors in influencing the urban way of life. Fischer is critical of Wirth's belief that the city can only destroy social groups. Rather, he observes that urbanism can, in effect, strengthen given groups. For it is in the city that a large number of people can gather who share similar interests and values and who can form subcultures. In a similar manner, Fischer is critical of compositional theory for its failure to acknowledge the impact of size, density, and heterogeneity on urban life.

In essence, Fischer postulates that the ecological variables of size, density, and heterogeneity do have an effect on social life. However, unlike Wirth, he argues that these effects can create, intensify, and strengthen social groups and that they do not necessarily break them down. Instead, community size and density helps create diverse subcultures, based on shared interests—whether it be in a stage of the life cycle or ethnicity. He cites as examples college students and Chinese Americans, who thrive when in contact and involvement within their respective groups. Similarly, other subgroups develop thriving social communities, such as groups based on shared economic interests and stage in the life cycle, like *Yuppies* (young urban professionals); those based on shared cultural and personal values, like the gay and lesbian communities in Greenwich Village in New York or the Castro district in San Francisco; artists and bohemians, such as those living in Soho in New York; and new racial and ethnic groups, such as Cubans in Little Havana in Miami, or Russian-Jews in Little Odessa in Brooklyn.

These subcultures are able to develop because the size, density, and heterogeneity of cities mean that people with shared interest can find each other and develop community ties, forming additional mosaics of little worlds. Fischer speaks of *critical mass* as a defining factor, since only cities can attract enough people of a given subculture. This *critical mass* makes it likely that enough people who share similar values and interests can get together. There are not enough of these people in the small towns to form these subcultures. For example, devotees of classical guitar may not be in sufficient *numbers* to form a specialized subculture in a small town but do not have that problem in a large city. Thus like-minded people can meet and develop a community in a city and do not necessarily experience feelings of alienation and anomie. Only in large cities can one speak of a "favorite fill-in-the blank ethnic restaurant"; small towns cannot support a variety of such "exotic" eateries. "Thus urbanism has unique consequences, including the production of 'deviance,' but not because it destroys social worlds—as determinists argue—but more often because it creates them" (Fischer 1976:36–37).

The Chicago School's view of urbanism was essentially linked to its conceptual framework of urban ecology.

The Chicago School and Urban Ecology

Ecology is the branch of biology dealing with the relations and interactions between organisms and the environment. *Human ecology* is a sociological analytical framework that is concerned with the spacing and interdependence of humans with institutions and the environment. It looks at the influence of the physical environment and its impact on people's lives,—for example, how mountains impede human settlements, or how rivers serve as both conduits for transportation and as barriers. Human ecology also focuses on how humans can impact the environment; for example, how air-conditioning allowed for the development of cities in very hot geographical regions such as the Southwest. *Urban ecology* focuses on ecological processes as they affect urban settlements.

Urban ecology was associated with, and was articulated by, the Chicago School beginning in 1915, under the auspices of Robert Park and his colleagues and students at the University of Chicago. Urban ecology influenced and shaped the direction of American urban sociology through most of the twentieth century. Park found the analogy with plant ecology fitting and elaborated on the utility for urban studies of such concepts as *dominance, symbiosis, invasion,* and *succession.* The urban ecological model emphasized analogical, biological, and environmental factors and forces that determined land use patterns of urban communities.

It was the concept of *competition* that Park saw as the key concept in terms of understanding land use patterns—the competition for space. Here the reference was to economic competition with biologic competition its counterpart. In the city, the strongest economic group would compete and win and control the prime locations, and others would have to adjust. *Competition* was a fundamental ecological process that explained community structure. This competition resulted in the *segregation* of communities into *natural areas.* Competition and segregation did not result in static communities, but through ecological processes of *invasion* and *succession* there was a constant change of land use patterns. The contraction and expansion of the central business district through market forces and the changing ethnic composition of communities as one ethnic group succeeded another captured the attention of ecologists.

The urban eologists saw the organization and physical layout of the city as developing with a life of its own. A Chicago School student-colleague of Robert Park, Harvey Zorbaugh (1926), in his seminal work, *The Gold Coast and the Slum,* presents this view:

> The city is curiously resistant to the fiats of man. Like the Robot, created by man, it goes its own way indifferent to the will of its creator . . . It becomes apparent that the city has a natural organization that must be taken into account. (Zorbaugh 1926:188)

Thus the city was viewed not as artifact of human creation but as a natural phenomenon.

Ernest Burgess and the Concentric Zone Hypothesis

Probably the most famous articulation of the urban ecological position was by Ernest Burgess (1886–1966) in his examination of the processes that underlie the growth of cities. Burgess was another of the key University of Chicago faculty members who defined sociology in early twentieth-century America. He spent most of his career there, and his influence extended to the sociological study of the family as well as urban sociology. With Park, he coauthored the famous textbook, *Introduction to the Science of Sociology,* which was first published in 1921 by the University of Chicago and which later went into multiple editions. His *concentric zone hypothesis* played a pivotal role in the articulation of urban ecology. Illustrated by an ecological map of mid-1920s Chicago, the concentric zone hypothesis is seen to apply to other American cities as well. The diversity of cities was simplified into a regularized circular pattern of concentric zones, each with certain distinguishing characteristics.

Burgess observes that these zones are idealized concepts; they will be modified by such natural physical barriers as rivers, lakes, and hills, and by man-made lines of transportation such as train lines and automobile highways. Indeed, his example, the concentric zonal arrangement of Chicago, is severely modified by its location on the shore line of Lake Michigan, which cuts through the center of the five circles and gives the city an ecological pattern of five hemispheric zones.

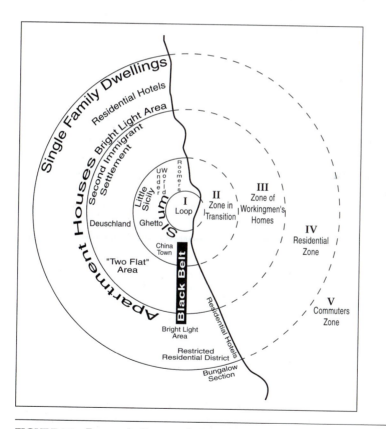

FIGURE 4.1 *Burgess's Concentric Zone Diagram of the City.*

Reprinted from Ernest W. Burgess. 1925/1966. "The Growth of the City An Introduction to a Research Project." P. 55 in Robert E. Park, Ernest W. Burgess and Roderick D. McKenzie. *The City.* Pp. 47–62. Chicago: University of Chicago Press.

The city is visualized as consisting of five concentric zones, each larger than the one before it, and all with a common center. Burgess's argument is that economic competition will ultimately decide how the land found in these five zones is utilized. The first or inner zone comprises the "central business district" (CBD). It is in this area that land values are the highest and where there is a concentration of office skyscrapers, department stores, banks, and recreational and service facilities such as hotels, hotels, restaurants, and theaters. The most desirable pieces of land obtained are by those who can pay the most. It is these types of businesses and services that extract the maximum profit and which therefore can pay the highest prices for land and for the taxes that inevitable follow. In Chicago, this area is known as the "Loop," in recognition of the elevated train lines that loop around the downtown area from the outer suburbs. It is the area of the city with the highest mobility of population, with people commuting in and out of it during the course of the day and evening.

The zone surrounding the central business district is referred to as the "zone in transition." It is so named because it is susceptible to the expansion of business, industrial, and commercial interests. It is a "natural" area that has developed as a direct consequence of economic speculation. If the land is ultimately more valuable than the buildings that currently occupy the space, why spend money in repairing them? As a result, this area has the city's oldest structures, many in deteriorated condition. Those who reside there are people who have no other options. The transition zone contains petty criminals, prostitutes, and the "down and out" living in rooming houses. This area also contains marginal minority groups denied better housing. In Chicago, in the middle 1920s, the transitional area contained the Jewish ghetto, the Italian Little Sicily, and parts of the Black Belt of recently arrived rural African Americans. Often the zone of transition also has a self-contained area of affluent housing. In Chicago this area is called the "gold coast."

The third zone is called the "zone of workingmen's homes." It is an area that includes settlements of the children of immigrants. It contains better housing than that in the zone of transition, but falls short of the residential districts of the middle classes in the next zone. Settlement patterns reflect not only economic factors but a desire to live in close proximity to nearby factories. Burgess's reference to "Deutschland" in his concentric zone diagram of the city refers to the settlement of upwardly mobile Jews seeking to emulate the affluent German Jews who preceded their Eastern European counterparts in coming to the United States.

The fourth zone, or the "residential zone," contains "better" residences. It is a middle-class area of nice apartments and substantial private dwellings with spacious yards and gardens. Populating the zone are professional people, owners of small businesses, managerial groups, and white-collar employees. Also contained in this zone are residential hotels. Burgess observes that in this zone "satellite Loops," also known as local business districts, duplicate, to a smaller degree, some of those services found in the central business district.

The fifth zone, the "commuter's zone," rings the city. This is the area of suburbs located either in the political boundaries of the city or immediately outside of it in small satellite towns. The commuter's zone is economically dependent upon the city, and many of its inhabitants commute to the city to work. The communities in this zone are often referred to as "bedroom" suburbs.

Often, the Burgess model is erroneously depicted as a static entity; the focus is on the ahistorical nature of city layouts. However, Burgess recognized the processes of expansion of the city and in particular of the central business district in his discussion of the development of other business districts.

> The Chicago of yesterday, an agglomeration of country towns and immigrant colonies, is undergoing a process of reorganization into a centralized decentralized system of local communities coalescing into sub-business areas visibly or invisibly dominated by the central business district. The actual process of what may be called centralized decentralization are now being studied in the development of the chain store, which is only one illustration of the change in the basis of the urban organization. (Burgess 1966/1925:52)

Burgess's conceptualization of a *centralized decentralization* argues that as the city grows, other nuclei form on smaller scales that reproduce to some degree the characteristics of the city's central core. Burgess's insight has been under appreciated. In discussions of Burgess's concentric zone hypothesis, the discussion of processes of urban growth often shifts to a discussion of Homer Hoyt and of Ullman and Harris, who build on the ecological model laid down by Burgess and reflect the historical changes that were occurring in urban development. But it is important to note that Burgess did see this historical development, although it is not reflected in his concentric zone schema.

Before we discuss the works of Hoyt and Harris and Ullman, it will be wise to place their theoretical formulations in an historical perspective. In a well-received book, the noted urban historian Robert Fogelson (Fogelson 2001) presents a fascinating account of downtowns in *Downtown: The Rise and Fall of Downtown, 1880–1950*.

Fogelson traces the rise and fall of downtowns in urban America from 1880–1950. His historical research sheds new light on the importance of both *intercity* rivalries and, as important if not more so, on *intracity* rivalries. *Intracity* rivalries were responsible for the shift where the downtown business district reigned supreme to the development of outlying business districts, and the downtown became one of many, albeit the most significant, areas—therefore earning its title as the *central* business district. Fogelson historically traces through the late nineteenth and early twentieth centuries the use and development of subway systems and the battle over the development of skyscrapers. These developments are seen in political and economic terms that reflect intracity rivalries. The attempts to handle the emerging traffic congestion and parking problems generated by the rise of automobile usage through the invention of parking meters, parking lots, and traffic lights provides further evidence of these conflicts. Of utmost importance Fogelson documents the importance of the battle among business people, property owners, and real-estate developers who had different economic interests in different sections of the city and its surroundings and how they played out in urban land-use patterns. His analysis implicitly questions the validity of the urban ecologist's viewpoint that there was a "natural" order for urban form and growth patterns.

Modifications of the Concentric Zone Hypothesis: Hoyt's Sector Model, Harris and Ullman's Multiple Nuclei Model, and Shevky and Bell's Social Area Analysis

The two most cited early efforts to modify Burgess's ecological model were undertaken by Homer Hoyt (1939) and by Harris and Ullman (1945). Their efforts were followed by the ecology model that Shevky and Bell called *social area analysis*. Let's examine each in turn. Hoyt, an urban land economist, argues for "sectoral patterns"

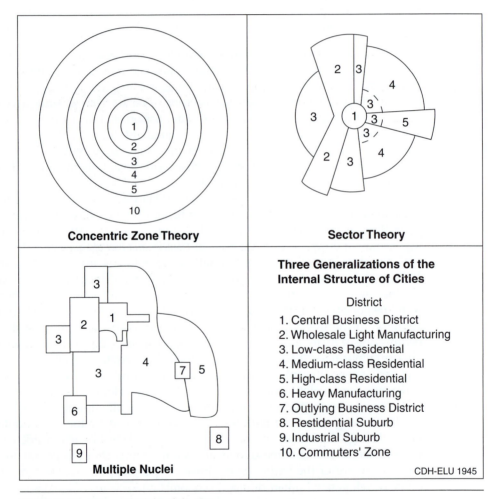

Concentric Zone Theory

Sector Theory

Multiple Nuclei

Three Generalizations of the Internal Structure of Cities

District

1. Central Business District
2. Wholesale Light Manufacturing
3. Low-class Residential
4. Medium-class Residential
5. High-class Residential
6. Heavy Manufacturing
7. Outlying Business District
8. Restidential Suburb
9. Industrial Suburb
10. Commuters' Zone

CDH-ELU 1945

FIGURE 4.2   *Three Models of the City.*

Reprinted from Chauncy D. Harris and Edward L. Ullman, "The Nature of Cities." *The Annals*, Vol. 242 (November 1945): 7–17.

of urbanization based on geographical terrain such as hills and rivers and shipping and transportation lines. For example, an industrial area might develop along a river or in close proximity to a railroad line or a major highway.

Hoyt further adds an historical dimension to his analysis. Unlike Burgess, who focused primarily on Chicago, Hoyt based his conclusions on the spatial configuration of 142 United States cities over three time periods, 1900, 1915, and 1936, Hoyt's *sector model*, like Burgess's model, emphasized the importance of the central business district. But he modified Burgess by postulating the existence of urban zones that were pie- or wedge-shaped sectors radiating out of the CBD to the periphery. Hoyt also focused attention on the importance on the residential patterns of the upper class in determining spatial organization. They often took advantage of "prestige" terrains, for example, hilltops (Boston's Beacon Hill), waterfronts (Chicago's Gold Coast), or convenient locations along transportation lines to downtown (Philadelphia's Main Line). The placement of middle-class and lower-class residential areas are relegated to the remaining space.

A second revisionist model of urban ecology was developed by the urban ecologists and geographers Chauncey Harris and Edward Ullman (1945). Taking issue with Hoyt's emphasis on residential patterns, Harris and Ullman developed a *multiple nuclei model* of urban land use. Their examination of cities emphasized the development of numerous centers based on specific urban activities or needs. Thus, they take issue with both the concentric zone hypothesis and the sector model. They see the American city of the early twentieth century in a process of *decentralized* growth and moving to a multicentered urban pattern. For example, in their analysis of retail districts, they observe that these districts were initially located in downtowns. But over the years, as the city experienced growth and migration of its populace, outlining retail districts developed. In a similar manner, manufacturing sites were located on large plots of land adjacent to convenient transportation venues. Nuclei, then, develop around a center of diversified activities that could include manufacturing, retailing, and education. Harris and Ullman emphasize the importance of such factors as urban growth, geographical terrain, and transportation. Further, and most interesting, they see this decentralization taking different shapes depending on the historical and cultural circumstances, as well as on the economic and ecological situations of a given city. The significant breakthrough in Harris and Ullman's analysis is this attention given to such additional factors as history and culture in influencing urban land use.

In summary, while, the ecological models developed by Burgess, Hoyt, and Harris and Ullman do, to some degree, take notice of historical and cultural factors in determining urban land use, essentially their models continue to reflect ecological deterministic thinking. Further, they all focus solely on the early twentieth century and the land-use patterns of cities in the United States. This was a unique time period characterized by rapid industrial and population growth and migration of vast numbers of immigrants from Eastern and Southern Europe and of poor whites and blacks from the rural south. They did not utilize comparative perspectives; they did not examine cities in other societies and cultures and in other historical periods.

A final variation of the ecological model, developed by Shevky and Bell (1955), builds on the ecological models developed by Burgess, Hoyt, and Harris and Ullman. *Social area analysis,* as they call it, attempts to articulate the dimensions of urban life that are responsible for the spatial distribution found in American cities. Three intersecting indices are identified: family patterns (number of children, working mothers, and residence types); social class and status (income, education, and occupation); and race and ethnicity. Using these indexes, Shevky and Bell examined the San Francisco, Bay area and found variations in residential patterns that conformed to their indices. Minority neighborhoods were located in specific areas of Oakland, Richmond, and San Francisco, outside of the central business districts. Wealthy families lived in communities in relatively close proximity to cultural attractions found in downtown areas. The middle class with school-age children were located in areas containing large apartment houses or increasingly in single family suburban houses with good schools.

Essentially, however, Shevky and Bell's analysis is an extension of urban ecology. They do not fundamentally question the underlying ecological premises. A major work that examined the ecological position of the Chicago School and found it wanting was by Walter Firey. His research made a major contribution to symbolic interactionism and its study of city life.

Walter Firey: Sentiment and Symbolism as Ecological Variables

In the late 1930s and early 1940s, Walter Firey examined land-use patterns in Boston to test Burgess's concentric zone hypothesis. Firey outlined what he saw as the basic shortcomings of the urban ecology approach. He argued that people respond not solely to the physical environment but to conceptions of that environment. One can only understand the environment in the context of sentiment and symbolization of that environment. People don't simply respond to space but rather to the symbolization of that space.

Firey criticized the human ecologists for not stressing the moral or cultural side of society but instead focusing on the physical nature of the environment itself to determine urban spatial patterning. Firey argued that two social psychological factors—sentiment and symbolism—were also at work in addition to economic competition in determining land use. Sentiment and symbolism, in fact, can supersede other considerations and can result in noneconomic, "nonrational" use of land. They therefore must be considered as important cultural factors influencing locational processes and must be seen as additional ecological variables.

To demonstrate, Firey selects four areas of Boston whose spatial identity is not determined by ecological variables. These places, the Boston Commons, the Burial Grounds, Beacon Hill, and the North End, provide illustrative examples of the power of the cultural heritage, sentiment, and symbolism attached to conceptualizations of space. People's usage of these places reflects the cultural importance placed on them.

Firey looked at the upper-class community of Beacon Hill; the working-class Italian American enclave of North Boston; and the park-like Boston Commons and

Swan boats in Public Garden, downtown Boston.

the Old Revolutionary War era public burial grounds, both located in downtown Boston. Firey's research, to my mind, is a more salient critique of Burgess's ecological conceptualization than either Hoyt's or Harris and Ullman's modifications of the concentric zonal model, which are fundamentally based on the belief of the primacy of ecological economic determinism. Burgess and his modifiers fail to recognize the importance of sociocultural variables, including sentiment and symbolism, in determining land-use patterns. Firey's research emphasizes the power of place, the importance of social-psychological factors, and the emotional attachments and enduring connections between social groups and specific communities.

For social psychologists, a major criticism of the Burgess concentric zone hypothesis and urban ecology is that they fail to take into consideration that humans, unlike other animals, have developed a complex culture. This culture influences decision making regarding how one sees, interprets, and uses one's environment. Rather than simply reacting to one's environment, people act on it through social choices. Burgess's concentric zone hypothesis and urban ecology rely too much on impersonal forces, such as competition, in their explanations of land-use patterns. Walter Firey developed a counterargument that sentiments, symbolism, and other "nonrational" elements are often of decisive importance in the choice of specific locations. Firey states that Burgess's deterministic view is based on "a denial that social values, ideals, or purposes can significantly influence the use of land" (1947:1).

Firey's study of location choices in central Boston indicated that two social-psychological factors, symbols, and sentiments were at work in influencing land-use patterns. In addition, to competition, "Space . . . also (has) an additional property, *viz.*, that of being at times a symbol for certain cultural values that have become associated with a certain spatial area. Locational activities are not only economizing agents but may also bear sentiments which can significantly influence the locational process."

Firey applies Burgess's concentric zone model to Boston. He found, in the zone of transition adjacent to the central business district, three anomalies that cannot be explained by Burgess's ecological theory. The Boston Common, several colonial burial sites, and historic churches and meetinghouses are located there. The Boston Common has socially evolved into a 48 acre park setting located in the downtown business area. Rather than respond with their heads instead of their hearts, as Simmel suggested, Bostonian's responded with their hearts, and these historical landmarks remain in the "heart" of downtown, even though its not economically rational for them to takeup such valuable real estate.

Sentiment and symbolism can also be seen as determining factors in regard to residential preferences. Beacon Hill is directly adjacent to the CBD. At the time that Firey was doing his research, it was a once fashionable, upper-class residential area falling into hard times. Many of the large houses were being converted into rooming houses, and wealthy residents were leaving for the new upscale community of Back Bay. However, a sufficient number of residents remained, and along with an influx of affluent people who moved into the area, Beacon Hill turned things around, remaining an upper-class, relatively low-density residential area today.

Sentimental and symbolic attachments are not restricted to historic or upper-class residential areas. The North End of Boston was the site for a flourishing immigrant Italian working class community. Even when those families had the economic means to move to more upscale residential areas with greater housing amenities, many chose to remain in the traditional ethnic enclave. Extended family connections; intensive involvements with neighbors and community institutions, including the church; and localized retail shopping—all helped to cater to the ethnic needs and desires of these families, assuring them this homogenous community was preferable to moving to more heterogeneous areas that would be social psychologically less satisfying. Firey concludes:

> In all these examples, we find a symbol-sentiment relationship which has exerted a significant influence upon land use. Nor should it be thought that such phenomenon are mere ecological "sports." Many other older American cities present similar locational characteristics . . . . (1945: 146)

Symbolic Interactionism and City Life: Summary Statement

Ecology, with its emphasis on the individual's direct and immediate relationship with the physical environment, is seen by symbolic interactionists as a gross distortion of the social nature of human beings. Urban ecology has no room for social psychology. It does not see that people symbolically transform their environment. People respond to conceptions of the physical world not the actual world. People don't react to space itself but to the symbolization of space. In *Being Urban*, the symbolic interactionists Karp, Stone, and Yoels express this view in the following way:

> It is the sentiment attached to urban areas: it is the whole range of meanings attached to urban areas . . . that essentially determines the shape and social organization of cities . . . Unless we consider the use, the meaning, the symbolic significance, and frequently the sentiments and emotions attached to various features of the city's topology, we shall incorrectly understand patterns of interaction in the city, and by definition, therefore, incompletely understand the city's social organization" (Karp, Stone, and Yoels 1977:74).

A second criticism of the ecological conception of the city stems from the first. There is an overemphasis on spatial patterning without sufficient attention to the nature of social interaction between persons that transcends specified geographical boundaries. Symbolic interactionists seek to redefine the community in terms of human communication and the interactive process as opposed to a territorial basis for community. This leads to the notion of "symbolic" urban communities illustrated by the fact that persons in a desire to overcome the impersonal rationality of the contemporary urban city seek alternatives to provide them with sources of personalization, identity, and community involvement.

The failure of much of urban ecology to see the emerging primary relationships and processes of urban identification stems in part from its ahistorical anti-urban bias and its enbracement of urban ecology as its prime conceptual framework. Such a view does not account for the changing meaning of the city over time. Urban social relations, like all human interactions, are in a continual state of change, transition, or process. The community is alive. The city is not a concrete, static object. The city must be seen as a symbolic entity, with its inhabitants active participants in its construction. Further, the spatial and symbolic arrangements often reflect power arrangements that reflect the need of those in power to maintain control.

Symbolic interactionism, however, did not fully integrate the study of power arrangements into its analysis of city life. It was the development of the perspective of *political economy* that focused on power and economics as crucial factors that influenced how life in the city was played out on the streets, neighborhoods, and business districts of the city. I will pick up on the discussion of political economy in a later chapter of this book. The next chapter will discuss the city through the disciplinary perspective of urban planning.

5

Urban Planning

The Spanish-born American philosopher George Santayana (1863–1932) said that those who don't study the past are forced to repeat it. By the same token, while we live in the present our actions are influenced both by our past experiences and by our views of the future. Geographers, sociologists, architects, and planners are all in agreement that while the physical environment is not the sole determinant of our behavior in the world, it certainly influences and constrains our actions. In the context of the city and its built environment, there is a shared belief that a city's shape and form not only influence social action but also are a reflection of society's values and culture. The belief is not of physical or environmental determinism but rather a realization of the interactive effects of environment, values, and behavior.

This being the case, of particular interest is the work of city planners and visionaries and their views of how the future city should be constructed. Their conceptualizations of future cities are reflections not only of how specific aspects of the built environment will affect people but also, on a more general level, of their underlying worldview and value system.

Leonard Reissman (1970) in his examination of the "urban process" observes the contribution of the visionary, the planner, toward the sociology of the city. The subtext of the visionary's plans centers on underlying ideas about the nature of the city, which provide important information about the urban environment. The complexity of that environment is often realized by the limitations and naivete of the planning schema. For example, Reissman notes that visionaries often fail to fully acknowledge the importance of human motivations and human needs in their planning schemas. The assumption that all people prefer to live in small communities and want to get back to nature is not an established fact, and visionaries should not assume that it is. The sociologist's knowledge of social values and social norms would be of great benefit to the visionary. But, Reissman also observes, sociologists often allow their own unwarranted assumptions and naivete bias their work. The anti-urban bias that was inherent in many of the theories of the early urban sociologists, as well as a personal nostalgia for a return to a rural way of life, clouded their judgment of the city.

Reissman argues that an evaluation of the works of visionaries may prove useful to understanding the underlying values that lie at the core of city life. "The study of utopias are sociologically relevant not because of an interest in utopias, but because of an interest in the reasons why they fail. A morbid conclusion, perhaps, but true" (Reissman 1970: 68).

To overcome the perceived problems of the city and to realize the potential for the betterment of city life, planners offered a number of myriad proposals. While differing radically, the various proposals and visionary plans provided guidelines that were influential in determining urban development policies. In this chapter we will study some of the major visionary proposals on what the future of the city should be: Daniel Burnham's the City Beautiful Movement; Ebenezer Howard's idea of the Garden City in the late nineteenth and early twentieth century; the Radiant City model of Le Corbusier; and Frank Lloyd Wright's conception of Broadacre City. In this chapter I will outline the achievements of these perspectives and will begin to spell out their inherent and fundamental problems. This analysis will continue to the next chapter when we will investigate the effects of urban planning on social policies within the context of our understanding of the social psychology of city life.

As we study the foundations of modern planning and its affects on urban form and community development, we will examine the work of four pivotal urban planners: Daniel Burnham, Ebenezer Howard, Frank Lloyd Wright, and Le Corbusier. We begin this chapter by looking at Daniel Burnham's advocacy of the building of monumental cities—*the City Beautiful*—which glorified the achievement of industrial capitalism and its generation of civic pride and which had the support of governmental municipalities. This discussion will be followed by an examination of the ideas of Howard, Wright, and Le Corbusier.

We chose Howard, Wright, and Le Corbusier based on the insights of Robert Fishman, who in his major work, *Urban Utopias in the Twentieth Century* (1982), observed that all three urban visionaries had a passionate hatred for the grimy industrial cities of the late nineteenth and early twentieth centuries. Yet their shared dislike manifested in three quite divergent utopian visions. Ebenezer Howard created the concept of the "garden city," a *gemeinschaft*-like town that had the positive attributes of both the city and the countryside. Wright's *Broadacre City* personified the ultimate suburb that reflected Jeffersonian agrarian individualism while extolling the automobile. Le Corbusier's *Radiant City*, which was the city as skyscraper but without city streets, glorified modern technology in the building of mass-scaled vertical buildings. In this chapter, we will also examine the work of Robert Moses and Edmund Bacon, two urban planners that were instrumental in the redevelopment of New York City and Philadelphia, respectively. The chapter concludes with an examination of the perspective of Jane Jacobs, who argued vigorously against much of the underlying philosophies of urban planning. I begin with a look at the 1893 Columbian Exposition, the *White City*, where the City Beautiful movement came into being.

Burnham and the City Beautiful

> *Make no little plans, they have no magic to stir men's blood.*
> Daniel Burnham (1846–1912)

The dawn of the twentieth century was seen as the beginning of the age of the city. Industrialization and commercial growth marked the unprecedented growth of cities. Further, the labor-saving mechanization of agriculture required fewer people to work the farms and allowed for the further growth of cities. In 1870 approximately 60 percent of the American labor force worked on farms; by 1900 that figure was reduced to 37 percent (Hine 1979). Urbanization seemed to be the "inevitable wave of the future" (Teaford 1986: 1). While some saw this future in a positive manner more viewed it with acrimony and alarm. The problems of the city were seen to far outweigh the promises. The urban historian Jon Teaford, catalogs these problems:

> Most Americans at the turn of the century also agreed, however, that the city was the overriding problem of the present and the future. With its striking contrasts between wealth and poverty, its debilitating congestion, its ethnic diversity, and its crime and vice, the city was the nation's greatest social problem. (Teaford 1986:2)

Sir Peter Hall (2002) has observed that the 1890s were years of intense introspection in urban America. The nation's social reformers and planners viewed the increased growth of the city with its myriad problems as the site for the development of cities that could surpass any that were built before.

The social historian Carl Smith (1994) investigated cataclysmic events in Chicago, the "shock" city of the late nineteenth century, and their perceived linkage to social disorder and social reality. He studies the great Chicago Fire of 1871; the Haymarket bombing of 1876, and the subsequent "anarchist" trial; and the model town of Pullman and its labor strike. These events and the public's perception of them are seen to be highly influential in shaping America's view of the "dangerous" city. Smith argues that many people saw social and cultural disorder as an inevitable consequence of urban growth and social change. To combat the threat of the emerging city and its "alien" population of immigrants and migrants, many felt that "the best thing to do with the city was to remake it, or at least reduce its influence on the rest of the country" (Smith 1994: 261).

> Most suggestions on how to do this in one way or another involved programs to slow or even reverse the movement of population to American's urban centers, whether from rural America or abroad. Besides restricting immigration, one of the most popular "solutions" offered . . . was the old proposal that the discontented and unstable urban population should be sent out onto the vast bosom of the American countryside, where, in harmony with the land these unproductive and disorderly city-dwellers would be transformed into solid and responsible citizens. (Smith 1994: 261)

In the early twentieth century, during what has been called the Progressive era, city governments established city planning departments that were initially charged with developing immediate solutions to everyday infrastructure problems, including road congestion, air pollution, and substandard housing. In some cases, municipalities developed long-range and comprehensive plans for urban development and for rebuilding their cities. The problems of American cities were particularly acute, as much of the growth of those cities occurred with no comprehensive plan. Further, the sudden quickness of that growth, especially with governments working with a de facto, laissez-faire economic policy that pretty much allowed business and industrial concerns free reign, led to many problems in both the physical and social environment.

Social reformers saw the necessity to solve urban problems, which included various forms of social disorganization such as high rates of crime, juvenile delinquency, and dislocated families. The built environment was in shambles: inadequate housing, filthy streets, inadequate sewage systems, air pollution, and severe traffic congestion. Inadequate health care and high mortality rates were the norm. Urban planners and visionaries saw the necessity to overcome the deficiencies of the unplanned city, with models for new cities that would reflect a better way of life for its inhabitants. Many of the urban visionaries felt that the only plan for the urban future would be a reworking of the economic and political structures of the city.

During the second half of the nineteenth century, large landscaped parks, like New York's Central Park, were created as part of an overall plan to not only beautify cities but to also encourage the development of civic interest and pride. Those who frequented this newly designed public realm would also be instructed through example—by witnessing how the upper classes, with their decorum and orderliness, used the park. By the end of the century landscape architecture merged with the civic-oriented professions of architecture and planning to create the City Beautiful movement. The basic goal was to improve life within cities by enhancing civic design. Paul Boyer (1978), the urban historian, asserts that the fundamental premise of the City Beautiful movement was the conviction that the creation of monumental buildings, boulevards, and civic centers as part of an attractive and livable urban environment would improve the moral condition and generate civic loyalty of the urban populace. In turn, it would increase civic responsibility in the urban community. Further this surge of civic loyalty "would retard or even reverse the decay of social and moral cohesiveness which seemed so inevitable a concomitant of the rise of cities" (Boyer 1978:284).

An inherent bond was seen to exist between a city's physical appearance and its moral state. "The challenge was heightened by the paucity of landmarks, traditions, and civic symbols in most American cities. . . . Where were the American Arcs de Triomphe, Piazzas San Marco, or Trafalgar Squares?" (Boyer 1978: 262). The City Beautiful movement sought to change the built environment of the city to stimulate civic idealism and pride.

Initially, the City Beautiful movement saw the necessity for municipal improvements. This took the form of beautifying existing streets through trash pickups; the planting of trees, plants, and shrubberies; and betterment projects, including the curtailment or elimination of factory pollution and the construction of underground telephone and electricity lines. Eventually, the movement saw the necessity for more comprehensive city planning.

The City Beautiful movement had as its leader Daniel H. Burnham, a prominent Chicago architect who, with his partner John Root, designed some of the classic early skyscrapers, including the Reliance Building in Chicago and the Flatiron Building in New York City. Burnham was the moving force behind the City Beautiful movement. His city planning admonition to fellow architects and planners was put forth in *The Plan for Chicago* (1909):

> Make no little plans. They have no magic to stir men's blood and probably will not be realized. Make big plans; aim high in hope and work, remembering that a noble, logical diagram once rewarded will never die, but long after we are gone will be a living thing, asserting itself with ever-growing insistency. Remember that our sons and grandsons are going to do things that would stagger us. Let your watchword be order and your beacon beauty. (Burnham quoted in Hall 2002: 188)

Burnham and other influential architects of the late nineteenth century, including the architectural firm of McKim, Mead, and White, believed that the true source of civic beauty was the Renaissance and Baroque cityscapes based on the classicism of ancient Greece and Rome. For American architecture to achieve international greatness and recognition they believed that it must borrow and build on the achievements of the neoclassical great monuments of Europe.

Burnham was inspired by the boulevards and promenades of Haussmann's reconstruction of Paris under Napolean III, by the classical architecture of Rome, and by the construction of the Ringstrasse of Vienna, with its electric streetcars built to encircle the city and its broad boulevards containing new monumental buildings. He envisioned a city of wide, tree-lined streets and avenues that would focus on civic buildings. Civic buildings, city halls, theaters, libraries, and museums built in the classical style would reflect the progress of human civilization in general and of modern industrial America in specific.

The impetus for the implementation of their ideal city, the *White City*, was the Columbian Exposition of 1893 in Chicago. Burnham and his architectural compatriots had their opportunity to build the ideal city, albeit a temporary one, with this

Pedestrians on bridge at the "White City," Columbian Exposition, Chicago, Illinois, 1893.

world's fair. The federal government granted Chicago the right to commemorate the four hundredth anniversary of Columbus's voyage to the western hemisphere. Chicago after the devastating fire of 1871 was in the forefront of architectural achievement and was becoming the personification of the new American city. The Columbian Exposition "came to symbolize the rise of the city in American life" (Glaab and Brown 1983: 260).

The White City, as it came to be called because of the white color of its buildings and monuments, was constructed very quickly of lath and plastic. It followed a Beaux-Art European neoclassical architectural plan. It was a plan that ironically ignored the contemporary architectural innovations of such architects as Louis Sullivan. Sullivan's Transportation Building, which adhered to his "form follows function" dictum of modern architectural design, was the notable exception. The layout of the grounds was characterized by grand vistas and magnificent landscaping. The buildings that lined its boulevards, its majestic pools ornamented with gargantuan sculptures and statues, were designed to replicate Greek and Roman temples or Renaissance grand structures.

The White City sought to give a positive preview to what was possible in the future city. Its use of telephones and electric transportation systems and its dramatic electrical lighting of the fairgrounds during the evenings was in stark contrast to the contemporary industrial city. This promise of a clean, orderly, and urbane city was in sharp contrast to cities impacted by the economic difficulties that the country was experiencing at the same time. The United States was in a steep economic depression with its attendant unemployment and strikes during the seven-month period of the Chicago fair.

Millions of people, the official attendance was more than 27 million, visited the White City and were awed by its splendor and entertained by its midway. The midway included all sorts of popular exhibits, including quasi-anthropological exhibits of "primitive and exotic" people, the belly-dancer "Little Egypt," and its Ferris Wheel, which provided a thrilling bird's-eye sweeping view of the fairgrounds. Most importantly, the White City provided a dramatic sense of the possibilities of city planning, heightening the desire for civic improvements and the appropriate civic character that cities might become. The urban social historian Roy Lubove states: "The ephemeral White City stimulated a mood of dissatisfaction with the 'awful monotony of ugliness' which reigned in the real cities where people lived and worked. This mood the City Beautiful translated into a quest for communities planned as works of art" (1967: 10). The historians Glaab and Brown (1983) share a similar positive assessment: "The symbolic value of the magnificent fair can hardly be overstated: it encouraged people to think about their cities as artifacts, and to believe that with sufficient effort and imagination they could be reshaped nearer to images of civilized living" (1983: 261).

The White City was the prototype for the monumental neoclassical architectuaral style that became characteristic of the City Beautiful movement in its efforts at civic improvement. The City Beautiful movement flourished through the first two decades of the twentieth century. It was the inspiration for the construction of monumental public buildings. New York's Municipal Hall is a prime example, as were civic centers such as the one in San Francisco. In some instances it generated projects that embraced a broader city scope. In 1900, several of the White City architectural teams were involved in the creation of the mall between the Capitol and the Potomac River as part of an overall plan to beautify Washington, D.C. Burnham's 1909 plan for Chicago shaped the development of not only downtown areas but the city as a whole for the next 50 years and is considered a landmark in urban planning. Burnham's plan was to create a "well-ordered, convenient, and unified city" (Burnham, cited in Chudacoff and Smith 2000: 199). The emphasis was on a harmonious and ordered city:

> Chicago in common with other cities realizes that the time has come to bring order out of chaos incident to rapid growth, and especially to the influx of people of many nationalities without common traditions or habits of life. (Burnham quoted in Teaford 1986: 42)

Burnham's plan called for the redevelopment of the entire Chicago area. It specified a metropolitan system of parks and boulevards, including a 20-mile lakeside park along the shore of Lake Michigan. A grandiose civic center was planned, a new railroad terminal was to be built, and an east–west boulevard was to be constructed. Many of its proposals were accepted, including the construction of the lakefront park. However, while the expansiveness of the project led to the cancellation of some of its more elaborate proposals, most of the proposed constructions were eventually built. As Chudacoff and Smith observe: "Its scope and innovation aroused national fascination" (2000: 199–200).

In Philadelphia, the Benjamin Franklin Parkway, a wide boulevard, was created through the destruction of a dense and overcrowded neighborhood. The Parkway extended from the huge Victorian city hall, which was crowned by the statue of William Penn, to the Philadelphia Art Museum, which stood on top of a hill with a sweeping view of center city. (For those familiar with the movie *Rocky* it was on its steps that the "heroic" boxer climbed triumphed.)

Ultimately, however, the City Beautiful movement was destined to have limited importance. Its most significant contribution was the incorporation of the landscape city park movement into twentieth-century planning. While it did provide the impetus for a number of civic improvements it did not address itself to more fundamental urban problems, including providing for the needs of all a city's citizens.

The urban geographer Edward Relph provides a concise assessment of Burnham and the City Beautiful movement:

> For all Burnham's rhetoric his was just an aesthetic movement characterized by a sort of localized benevolent capitalist authoritarianism. After the first flush of enthusiasm city governments had neither the inclination nor the funds to carry out pretty master plans, especially while there were pressing needs for social reform, for the improvement of basic living conditions, for paving roads and for the installation of sewerage systems. (Relph 1987: 55)

A more important planning agenda than the City Beautiful movement and one that would have profound social implications for contemporary urban form came from the Garden City movement, which had its origins in England and in its prophet, Ebenezer Howard.

Ebenezer Howard: The Garden City Movement

Ebenezer Howard proposed what was to be known as the Garden City movement in his 1898 book, *Tomorrow! A Peaceful Path to Real Reform* (later re-named and well known as *Garden Cities of Tomorrow* [1902/1965]). At the time that he wrote the book, which would prove so influential for urban planning, Howard was not an architect or a planner but a shorthand stenographer in the London courts. Howard was reacting against the modern industrial city, which he believed had many inherent problems, including an appalling physical environment with overcrowded housing. He was deeply disturbed by the divisions between the rich and the poor who lived in these cities. The overcrowded conditions were the result of the increasing number of people who moved to the city for economic opportunities and jobs. The biggest cities would continue to grow because they continued to generate the most jobs. Echoing Simmel, he also alluded to the social-psychological character of city life—the "isolation of crowds" (Howard 1996: 347)

The private ownership of land was held responsible for exorbitant property values in center cities, and that led to the development of outer city sprawl. The surrounding countryside, while having a much better physical environment with open fields and fresh air, did not have the economic foundation—too little jobs—or viable social amenities. Howard was motivated to answer the question on how to merge the benefits of city life with those of the countryside so that people could enjoy both without suffering the disadvantages of either.

To remedy the situation, Howard proposed the establishment of autonomous garden cities in rural areas, reflecting the nineteenth-century British tradition of community planning. These garden cities would combine the attractive qualities of both city and rural life without suffering the negative consequences of these two other forms of settlement. Howard's plan was to sustain "a healthy, natural, and economic combination of town and country life" by balancing city and countryside, industry and agriculture, and work and leisure" (Howard (see Figure 5.1) 1898/1956: 51). Howard's schema of the three magnets conveys his objective.

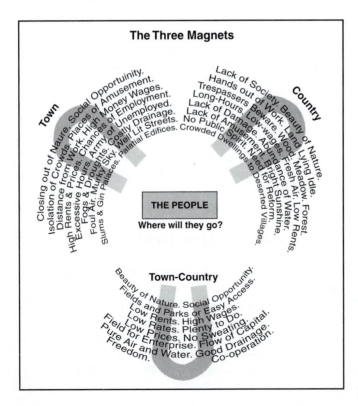

FIGURE 5.1 *Ebenezer Howard's The Three Magnets*

Source: Ebenezer Howard. 1898. *Tomorrow! A Peaceful Path to Real Reform. London: Swann Sonnenschein.*

Hall and Ward observe that while the famous diagram of the three magnets reflects dated language and archaic style (the figures are hand-drawn with Victorian lettering by Howard), "it is a brilliant encapsulation of the virtues and vices of the late Victorian English city and English countryside" (1998: 18).

In Howard's "Three Magnets" diagram, the respective appeal of the town magnet and countryside magnet presented is contrasted with the proposed new town–country magnet, which combines the urban benefits of employment and entertainment with the rural ones of healthy and spacious living.

> There are in reality not only, as is so constantly assumed, two alternatives—town life and country life—but a third alternative, in which all the advantages of the most active and energetic town life, with all the beauty and delight of the country, may be secured in perfect combination; and the certainty of being able to live this life will be the magnet which will produce the effect for which we are all striving—the spontaneous movement of the people from our crowded cities to the bosom of our kindly mother earth, at once the source of life, of happiness, of wealth, and of power. (Howard 1898: 7 quoted in Hall and Ward 1998: 19)

Howard's proposed Garden Cities were based on principles of cooperative ownership. A company would hold the land for the common good and would thus control real-estate speculation; any increases of property values would be to the benefit of the community as a whole. Howard's plans were to control growth to a maximum of 30,000 people who lived in neighborhood centers (wards) of 5,000, with each ward in essence being a small town or community. The garden cities would be self-sufficient, possessing their own industrial base, local businesses, schools, and shops, as well as other community amenities. A permanent greenbelt would be located within walking distances of all inhabitants. This greenbelt would serve two functions: it would allow people to enjoy the benefits of open space, and it would also prevent the cities from taking the land over for further growth. Housing within the wards would vary in design, some having common gardens and cooperative kitchens. All would be located on tree-lined avenues.

Howard saw the cities as being anchored by two cohesive forces located in the city's public realm (Fishman 1982). Howard proposed a "Central Park" located in the center of the town that would provide recreational opportunities, including a large park area and theaters. The "Crystal Palace," an arcade adjacent to the park, would be the site for the sale of manufactured goods and other forms of shopping. The Central Park would also be the location for the second cohesive force, "civic pride." It would be here—with the city's town hall, library, museum, concert and lecture halls, and hospital—that "the highest values of the community are brought together—culture, philanthropy, health, and mutual cooperation" (Fishman 1982: 44).

As a garden city prospered, new towns would be formed instead of expanding or further congesting existing ones. In time, the towns were conceived of as components of cities—cluster cities—that would enable residents to move freely within the network of component towns and stay within easy distance to the surrounding countryside. The individual garden city would become part of a much larger cluster of garden cities around a central city, all interconnected and sharing leisure facilities and services.

Howard's ideas on the creation of new towns to meet all of people's needs were instrumental in forming the Garden City movement. In England, Howard himself was very influential in the establishment of two English garden cities, Letchworth (1902) and Welwyn Garden City (1920). Both turned out to be more practical garden suburbs than the utopian garden city envisioned by Howard. They were to have a profound worldwide impact on the thinking about urban planning and were the stimulus for a city planning movement.

Roy Lubove (1967) observes that the underlying principles of the Garden City movement are as follows:

1. urban decentralization;
2. the establishment of cities limited in size, but possessing a balanced agricultural-industrial economy;
3. use of a surrounding greenbelt to help limit size, and to serve as an agricultural-recreational area;
4. cooperative landholding to insure that the community rather than private individuals benefited from appreciation of land values;
5. the economic and social advantages of large-scale planning.(Lubove 1967: 11)

In the United States, Howard's ideas influenced a number of planners and architects. For the most part, they never fully articulated a new conception of community. Instead his ideas were reflected in the development of what variously became called as "garden villages," "garden suburbs," and "garden homes" after 1910 (Glaab and Brown 1983). A more comprehensive attempt to bring Howard's garden city to the United States was attempted by the planners of Radburn, New Jersey, in the late 1920s and by the greenbelt towns in the 1930s.

Radburn, New Jersey, and the Greenbelt Town of the 1930s

In 1928–29, just prior to the Great Depression, the American architects Clarence Stein and Henry Wright created Radburn, New Jersey, a town that gained national attention as a "town for the motor age" (Jackson 1985: 162). Stein felt that "Dinosaur" cities like New York and Chicago were outdated as a consequence of modern technology. These cities required vast amounts of financial expenditures for transit and utility systems. They were overly congested and required intensive land utilization that resulted in highly inflated property values. An endless spiral of speculative real estate investments led to more intensive land use and even more congestion (Lubove 1967).

The alternative was seen in the concept of the "regional city" proposed by Stein and Wright and their associates of the Regional Planning Association of

America (RPAA). The RPAA was organized in 1923 and saw the application of their ideas in Radburn, New Jersey. This model town, located in suburban northeastern New Jersey, 17 miles from New York City, with a projected size of 28,000 people, was conceived following Howard's guidelines. However, unlike Howard, who was a champion of social integration, Radburn was designated as a community for the more affluent; in addition, restrictive covenants prohibited the selling of houses to Jews and to African Americans. Its advocates were bowing to the pressures for privacy, exclusivity, and safety and protection that were so prevalent then and that became increasingly an inherent characteristic of post–World War II suburbia.

This "town for the motor age" was designed to minimize the requirement for automobiles. Automobiles were relegated to main arterial streets that were on the periphery, thus enabling the separation of pedestrian and vehicle traffic. People were able to wander through the local parks and pathways without worry of traffic, and underpasses were built under major streets. "Superblocks" were created covering 23 acres with shared parklands. The planning designs of Radburn, which included the separation of main streets from cul-de sacs, local parkways, and rural-like settings and houses, became features of subsequent suburban development plans. Unfortunately, the depression of the 1930s prevented the full development of this planned community. However, as the historian Jon Teaford assesses, "Although only a portion of the community was completed according to original plans, the scheme excited many professional planners and influenced their work. Moreover, the Radburn project was indicative of the growing concern for minimizing the discomfort and dangers posed by the automobile" (1986: 68). Radburn also became the inspiration for a series of new towns that would be undertaken by the federal government during the Great Depression.

In the 1930s, the federal government was influenced by the beliefs of sociologists and urban planners that the unimpeded growth of cities would only foster social disorganization and depersonalization. The government also sought to regulate and control unplanned urban sprawl by implementing a Resettlement Administration that would alleviate both the need for affordable housing and provide employment for thousands of workers who lost their jobs during the depression. Headed by Rexford Guy Tugwell, the Resettlement Administration had intellectual affinity to the Garden State ideals of Ebenezer Howard, which "included a belief in planning as a device to implement a broader social and economic restructuring of society" (Schuman and Sklar 1996: 437).

The remedy for overcoming the evils of city life would be the building of 3,000 planned suburban communities set in permanent green parks, "greenbelt cities," outside major cities. The initial plans of the greenbelt program called for the building of 25 towns of limited size containing about 10,000 people. Conveniently located near employment opportunities, they would also provide pleasant surroundings for their inhabitants. At the same time, they would relieve slum congestion, provide low-cost housing, and foster community cohesion (Chudacoff and Smith 2005). The underlying policy behind this plan was stated by Rexford G. Tugwill, a government official under the Roosevelt administration: "My idea is to go just outside centers of population, pick up cheap land, build a whole community and entice people into it. Then go back into the city and tear down whole slums and make parks of them" (quoted in Chudacoff 1975).

However, only three "Greenbelt Cities" were actually built. They provided work for between 20,000 and 30,000 people (Schuman and Sklar 1996). These towns—Greenbelt, Maryland, on the countryside outside of Washington D.C.; Greenhills, Ohio, on farmland near Cincinnati; and Greendale, Wisconsin, 3 miles southeast of Milwaukee—contained many of the design elements of the Garden State movement, including the use of "superblocks" and a "greenbelt" of undeveloped land surrounding the community. Depression budgetary concern, pressure from private real-estate developers who were fearful of the economic consequences to their industry, and governmental supporters who viewed this community planning project as socialistic led to the abandonment of government garden city planning initiatives. After these three towns were built, the Resettlement Administration was abolished, and after World War II Congress authorized the sale of greenbelt land and buildings to nonprofit organizations with sale preferences to existing residents and returning veterans (Chudacoff and Smith 2005; Schuman and Sklar 1996).

The Three Magnets Revisited

Sir Peter Hall (2002), the eminent English urban historian and critic, in his important intellectual history of urban planning, *Cities of Tomorrow*, feels that it is vital to understand Ebenezer Howard more as a social visionary than as a urban physical planner. He says of Howard and his Garden City followers, including those in England and the United States as elsewhere, that their "vision . . . was not merely of an alternative built form, but of an alternative society, neither capitalist nor bureaucratic-socialistic: a society based on voluntary co-operation among men and women, working and living in small self-governing commonwealths" (Hall 2002: 3).

Hall and Colin Ward (1998) in their assessment of the legacy of Ebenezer Howard and the Garden City movement update Howard's "three magnets" schematic. A hundred years after Howard, they examine the startling differences in the nature of the "town" and of the "country" magnets found in England. In Figure 5.2, Howard's Three Magnets schematic of advantages and disadvantages is reformulated by Hall and Ward to reflect contemporary conditions.

The town is now seen to have taken on some of the negative attributes associated with the county of a hundred years ago. It is now the site for dying industries with the resultant substantial loss of jobs and a high rate of unemployment. Competition from abroad, as a consequence of the global economy, has resulted in many industrial jobs going elsewhere. Cities have become the centers for global informational services. The consequences are a new form of inequality with higher educated and skilled jobholders found in the city and a large number of low educated individuals who can't find less-skilled jobs. A new form of pollution

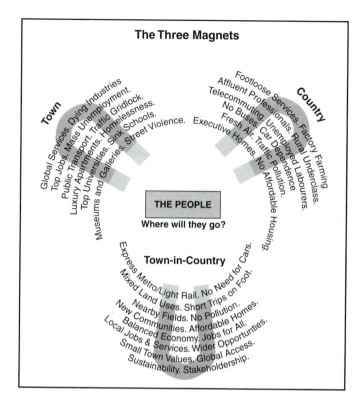

The Three Magnets

Town

Global Services. Dying Industries. Top Jobs. Mass Unemployment. Public Transport. Traffic Gridlock. Luxury Apartments. Homelessness. Top Universities. Sink Schools. Museums and Galleries. Street Violence.

Country

Footloose Services. Factory Farming. Affluent Professionals. Rural Underclass. Telecommuting. Unemployed Labourers. No Buses. Car Dependence. Fresh Air. Traffic Pollution. Executive Homes. No Affordable Housing.

THE PEOPLE

Where will they go?

Town-in-Country

Express Metro/Light Rail. No Need for Cars. Mixed Land Uses. Short Trips on Foot. Nearby Fields. No Pollution. New Communities. Affordable Homes. Balanced Economy. Jobs for All. Local Jobs & Services. Wider Opportunities. Small Town Values. Global Access. Sustainability. Stakeholdership.

FIGURE 5.2
Ebenezer Howard's The Three Magnets Revisited. The Three Magnets, 1898. Howard's famous statement of advantages and disadvantages, rephrased for the conditions of the 1990s. The town has been sanitised and the country has been given urban technology, but both still suffer problems; and, still, towns set in the country offer on optimal lifestyle. Source: Peter Hall.

Source: Peter Hall and Colin Ward. 1998. *Sociable Cities: The Legacy of Ebenezer Howard.* New York: John Wiley & Sons.

has emerged; the industrial fog resulting from the containments of coal burning have been replaced by photochemical smog. Traffic remains congested but now from automobiles and trucks rather than from horse-drawn carriages and wagons. Remaining as a constant is the perception of the town as a deprived, crime-ridden, and problematic place not fit to raise children a place with inadequate schools and where desire to move elsewhere for a better life is always present (Hall and Ward 1998).

Hall and Ward observe that the countryside has been transformed as well. Improvements in technology and transportation, particularly electricity and the automobile, provide opportunities. The telephone, e-mail, and fax enhance communication. Further lifestyle improvements, including central heating, television and the video recorder, and the Internet have turned the home into a center for entertainment and instruction—inconceivable in Howard's time. Hall and Ward conclude that "The remarkable fact is that over the intervening century, we have turned the English countryside into a version of Howard's town-country on a vast scale" (1998: 105).

Hall and Ward report that in the last 50 years there has been a re-population of the English countryside. The British government, particularly after World War II, saw the necessity for the building of new housing and communities to replace the destruction caused by that war and to alleviate the population pressures of its metropolitan centers, particularly London. The 1946 New Towns Act of England was created, which became a keystone of long-term government policy for the development of new cities. More than 35 new towns were built following some of the guiding garden cities principles. Government policies coincided with many of the views of the populace regarding new housing and communities.

People's migration to these new towns has been fostered by both "push and pull" factors. They have been both "pushed by what they saw as the bad things about living in the cities—the familiar litany, however exaggerated of bad schools, crime, danger, poor environment—and pulled by their relative absence in the small towns and the villages" (Hall and Ward 1998: 105). However, Hall and Ward do report some important differences in the contemporary "town-country" magnet that do not reflect Howard's vision. The growth has been in the more rural areas of England and not in the new-town districts. More importantly, Howard would have been most displeased that the growth process has been economically and socially restrictive and exclusive. Lower income groups have remained in the cities, often residing in ghettoized public housing estates (projects). Further, Howard would have been disturbed by the dependence on the automobile and the necessity to travel long distances to work and to entertainment.

Wright's Broadacre City

> "The outcome of the cities will depend on the race between the automobile and the elevator, and anyone who bets on the elevator is crazy."
> (Wright 1974)

Frank Lloyd Wright (1867–1959) was probably the greatest American architect of the twentieth century. He had very opinioned ideas about the industrial city, about what should be done to remedy its perceived fundamental deficiencies and what was necessary to keep the agrarian way of life viable. He likened the large industrial city as the cross-section of some "fibrous tumour" and the symbol of the exploitation of humankind. His ideas were formulated in the late nineteenth and early twentieth century when the United States was undergoing its dramatic transformation from a more rural to a highly industrial urban society. However, the principles of homesteading and the tradition of the good life being anchored on working the land still held romantic sway.

Wright's answer was *Broadacre City*, a concept that reflected his emphasis on individualism and his love of nature. Wright echoed Thomas Jefferson's view that true democracy can only be achieved when everyone is a landowner. He sought the integration of the city into the countryside and the development of a decentralized city that stressed agrarian living anchored in the family. Wright's Broadacre City personified the ultimate suburb, which reflected Jeffersonian agrarian individualism. Modern technology and especially electricity and the automobile would make it possible.

Wright rejected what he perceived as the unnatural and inhumane urban environment. He put the blame of the evilness of the city on the capitalist economy and its stress on land rent, money, and profit, and on government and bureaucracy (Reissman 1970). Wright's solutions were an end to the high-density industrial city, a return to the land and honest labor, and living in the dispersed city of the future under the guidelines of Jeffersonian democracy.

> Infinite possibilities exist to make of the city a place suitable for the free man in which freedom can thrive and the soul of man grow, a City of cities that democracy would approve and so desperately needs. . . . Yes, and in that vision of decentralization and reintegration lies our natural twentieth dawn. Of such is the nature of the democracy free men honestly call the new freedom. (Wright 1938: 193 quoted in Reissman 1970: 60)

Wright's Broadacre City was appropriately named, as it reflected his "prairie school" of horizontal design. It was an ultra-low density city that called for a completely decentralized grid-system of plots of land, each plot being about one acre in size. Modern technology and especially electricity and the automobile would make it possible. Small farms, industries, and schools would be dispersed over the landscape. Housing would be designed for individual families and would represent the basic economic unit of his society. People would work on their farms and would also work part-time in the small factories and industries or the shops and offices that dot the landscape. Sir Peter Hall sees Broadacre City as a culmination of not only Wright's philosophy but of Wright's "weav(ing) together almost every significant strain of American urban—more precisely, anti-urban thinking" (2002: 312). Wright's model combined the individualistic views of Jeffersonian thought with the new technological forces to "re-create in America a nation of free independent farmers and proprietors: 'Edison and Ford would resurrect Jefferson'" (Hall 2002: 312, citing and quoting Fishman 1982: 123).

The houses that Wright proposed also reflected a horizontal layout. These "Usonian" houses were the forerunners of suburban ranch-style houses, which emphasized open space and a functional design appropriate for modern life. "Automobilization" would make Wright's suburban "sprawl" ideal city viable in the future because people would no longer need to live in close proximity to each other in urban centers. The automobile on superhighways would allow for travel over long distances freely and quickly. As Wright puts it, this new sprawling city could now be located "nowhere yet everywhere" (cited in Stern 1986).

Wright's ideal city rejects the traditional urban community in favor of a dispersed landscape of independent house-owning families living private lives. As Stephen V. Ward notes, city planners in the 1930s were weary of Wright's abandonment of urban communities. Yet, Wright anticipated a view of suburban dispersal that would be shared by many Americans after World War II (Ward 2002). However, the overall design so desired by Wright would not be realized in that suburban and exurban sprawl that characterizes much of the contemporary landscape.

Broadacre City was also Wright's response to the Radiant City proposals of Le Corbusier (discussed next). Rather than build *up*, he sought to build *out*; this view was epitomized by his opinion of the contrasting growth potentials of the elevator and the automobile in the quote that opened this section of the chapter. Yet, near the end of his career, and possibly with tongue-in-cheek, he proposed the building of a mile-high skyscraper in recognition of the fact that the continuous growth of the population would ultimately impact on what earlier appeared to be limitless land supply.

Talieson West, Wright's home and office complex built in 1937–38 in the Arizona desert at Maricopa Mesa, Paradise Valley, was itself the victim of urban sprawl. Wright carefully selected the site, located about 10 miles from downtown Phoenix, with great care and forethought, thinking that suburban expansion would never affect him. It was built on a hill with sweeping vistas. However, rapidly developing Phoenix constructed pylons that carried electricity to its outer reaches and marred the view of the landscape. Wright sued the city to prevent the inevitable—and lost. The architectural critic Herbert Muschamp found great irony in this:

> Didn't the Adventurer in Wright want to roar with laughter at the thought that the greatest architect of all time had made possible the conversion of America's natural paradise to an asphalt continent of Holiday Inns, Tastee-Freeze stands, automobile graveyards, billboards, smog, tract housing, mortgaged and franchised from coast to coast? (Muschamp quoted in Hall 2002: 315)

Le Corbusier: Cities Without Streets

The Skyscrapers of New York are Too Small.

(Le Corbusier 1947)

This startling proclamation was made by Le Corbusier (1887–1965). Charles-Edward Jeanneret was a famous Swiss-born French architect who spent most of his professional years in Paris practicing under the pseudonym "Le Corbusier." In 1930 Le Corbusier visited New York. Based on his observations he believed that there were too many skyscrapers in New York and that they were packed too closely together. Further he was especially angered by the busyness of New York's streets. The New York urbanist Marshall Berman (1999) observes that while Le Corbusier said he loved New York's skyscrapers he despised the way they were linked to the street:

> Streets were his special obsession: they made him foam at the mouth. Again and again his writings declared in effect, *"We must kill the street!"* Against modern urban street life, he would celebrate "a titanic renaissance of a new phenomenon, TRAFFIC! Cars, cars, fast, fast!" He would clear all the streets and reorganize space into endless rows of great concrete-and-glass slabs, each one a separate world with its own underground garage; the slabs would be linked to each other by broad highways, each slab "a factory for producing traffic," landscaped with plenty of trees and grass. He called his new model "the tower in the park" (Berman 1999: 537)

Le Corbusier's less ambitious plans for the development of buildings surrounded by parklands is shown in this photo. However, his more elaborate plans for the rebuilding of cities—the Radiant City—composed of residential and business high-rise towers connected by roadways and sit in park-like settings is reflected in the Futurama *exhibition presented by General Motors at the New York's World Fair of 1939–1940. See photo on page 108.*

Le Corbusier was reacting to his own experience in Paris and what he saw as a similar situation in New York. Downtown areas of cities were highly congested. Business offices were adjacent to slum areas racked with filth and centers of disease. Ground transportation often found itself gridlocked. The key for Le Corbusier was his famous paradox: the centers of cities must be decongested by increasing their density (Hall 2002). This paradox would be resolved by building high skyscrapers over a small part of the total ground area. These skyscrapers would be surrounded by green open space linked to one another by a rapid speed underground and elevated transportation system. To accomplish this vision, Le Corbusier proposed the demolition of congested downtowns and their replacement by what he subsequently called the "Radiant City" (Le Corbusier 1967).

In a word, the city was seen as being chaotic and congested. Most significantly, Le Corbusier believed that the city was encumbered by its historical past, with its unplanned growth and its failure to adapt to the conditions of a new modern age. Le Corbusier's model of the Radiant City (Ville Radieuse) called for the elimination of both the historical city and the pedestrian-oriented street in the new modern city:

> It is the street of the pedestrian of a thousand years ago, it is a relic of the centuries: it is a non-functioning, an obsolete organ. The street wears us out. It is altogether disgusting! Why, then, does it still exist? (quoted in Gold 1998: 48)

Le Corbusier's vision of the city is represented in his Plan Voisin for Paris designed in 1925. His "city" is comprised of 60-story uniformly designed office buildings set in open space and linked to surrounding standardized residential apartment houses with high-speed transportation routes. The total population would be 3 million people. Le Corbusier superimposed his plan on the rundown Right Bank center of Paris. He proposed to tear down the historic quarters of Paris while preserving only a few central monuments. Buildings located there were viewed as obsolete and unsanitary. The various functions that the historic core had provided would now be contained in standardized uniform structures. His plan, therefore, was to obliterate the historical city with all its variety and complexity. The immediate response of Parisians was shock and dismay. Le Corbusier was seen as a "barbarian" who would substitute a cold, sterile, and lifeless city in place of their beloved Paris.

The architectural historian Ada Louise Huxtable (2004) believes that if the 1925 Plan Voisin had been carried out, the result would have been a disaster. "Seductive in the context of a decade infused with a belief in the perfectability of society through radical renewal, the plan would have replaced the intimate, event-filled humanity and historic and cultural diversity of one of the richest urban accretions in the world with a scaleless limbo of relentlessly imposed order and epic sterility" (Huxtable 2004:200).

Lewis Mumford (1975) observes that the impact of Le Corbusier's work was his ability to integrate two dominating conceptions of early twentieth century architecture and city planning. The first was the utilization of bureaucratization and standardization toward modern technology to develop a machine-made environment. The second was to offset the building of dense high-rise skyscraper cities with the utmost utilization of wide-open space to provide sunlight, views, and areas of green.

While Mumford recognizes the contribution of Le Corbusier, in a scathing criticism he argues that three main misconceptions are prevalent in his work. The first mistake is the overvaluation placed on the bureaucratization ideas of standardization, regimentation, and centralized control. To Le Corbusier skyscrapers were of extravagant heights because they were technologically feasible. They could be placed over vast areas of open space because modern transportation systems could temporally shrink distance. But they would still be spatially isolated with no common public gathering grounds for people.

The second mistake was in Le Corbusier's "contempt for historic and traditional forms" that ignored the historical "past in all its cultural richness and variety" (Mumford 1975: 119, 117). Le Corbusier's image was to remove the past from the city. His was a city of ahistorical design that had no cultural core with the past; the city he created was a cultural vacuum that overemphasized the present without allowing it to benefit from the errors of the past and threatening with destruction whatever permanent values the present might create. Mumford refers to this error as the "disposable urban container" (1975:120).

The third mistake was the extravagant use of open space conceived as sites for parks. Mumford felt that the parks were, by and large, sterile sites that ignored the variety of human needs and the complexities of human associations, as vividly pointed out in Jane Jacobs's classic, *The Death and Life of Great American Cities*. Le Corbusier wanted to avoid the worse cases of overcrowding witnessed in urban slums. But by distancing activities through extreme spatial segregation Le Corbusier destroyed the essence of human character. While he created visual open spaces of views and greenery he forgot the nonvisual purposes of functional open spaces—"for meeting and conversation, for the play of children, for gardening, for games for promenades, for the courting of lovers, for outdoor relaxation" (Mumford 1975:120).

Mumford concludes that this model of the "city in a park" fails because its aesthetic monotony reflects social regimentation, uniformity, and conformity. "Neither high-rise structures, vertical transportation, spatial segregation, multiple expressways and subway, or wholesale parking space will serve to produce a community that can take advantage of all the facilities modern civilization offers and work them into an integrated urban form" (Mumford 1975: 120). It is necessary to recognize the diversity of the human community with its freedom, family intimacy, and spontaneous and creative use of the physical environment.

Le Corbusier built few buildings, let alone the cities that he envisioned. Yet, he was one of the most highly influential architects and urban planners of the twentieth century. He himself was partially responsible for Chandigath, a regional capital in the Punjab region of India. The urban design does not reflect the cultural heritage of India nor is it applicable to the environmental climate. Successful buildings such as Punjab University are underutilized and are surrounded by slums in which people live without electricity and heat.

Brasilia, the futuristic capital of Brazil, was built by his students in the 1950s and follows Corbusierian principles. Brasilia startlingly juxtaposes modern buildings and highways with the Brazilian *favela*, or squatter settlements, growing unabated in its periphery.

Le Corbusier was part of the modernist movement in early twentieth-century architecture. He and fellow architects such as Walter Gropius and Mies Van der Rohe disdained the traditional city characterized by nonuniformity in its urban layouts and the diversity of structures in its built environment, which reflected different historical periods in its growth. Their architecture was at first scorned and ridiculed but became the basis of an international design that set the standard for what the modern office building and skyscraper should look like. Shorn of any ornamentation, the modern skyscraper, with its stripped form and functionality, became the standard for post–World War II American cities. Further, Le Corbusier's vision of the city of the future consisting of high-rise towers connected by roadways became the model for urban redevelopment programs in the post–World War II United States. The mass housing of the urban poor in "projects" became the standard.

Futurama: General Motors and the 1939–40 New York World's Fair

At the New York World's Fair in 1939, General Motors had an exhibit that many consider the highlight of the fair. In its Highways and Horizons building, General Motors constructed a miniaturized scale model of a United States of the future—the United States of 1960. *Futurama* was designed under the direction of

General Motors's Futurama model of the city of the future exhibited at the New York World's Fair of 1939–1940 was highly influenced by Le Corbusier.

Norman Bel Geddes, a very prominent industrial designer, and was built under the supervision of George Wittbold. The scale model consisted of a half-million individually designed buildings and houses; thousands of miles of multilane highways; more than a million trees and shrubs of eighteen species; rivers, lakes and streams; mountains; bridges; industrial centers; college and resort towns; great towering cities; and 50,000 scale model vehicles. A moving conveyor comprised of 552 chairs had a capacity of transporting 2,150 people per hour, or a total of approximately 28,000 people a day through this 35,000 square-foot multilevel third of a mile exhibition area (General Motors 1939; General Motors 1940). From an aerial perspective, the viewer saw the future city of towers and highways inspired by Le Corbusier vision.

What captures ones attention is the depiction of the city of the future—a miniaturized realization of the LeCorbusierian radiant city and the integral role that General Motors foresees for the automobile in that future. In the introduction to the *Futurama* brochure, Alfred P. Sloan, the chairman of General Motors, articulates the view that the progress of civilization is tied to advancements in transportation. The success of future communities rests on the development of better and more efficient ways of moving people and materials. In another promotional brochure, this view is also expressed: "The 'Futurama' is presented not as a detailed forecast of what the highways of the future may be, but rather as a dramatic illustration of how, through continued progress in highway design and construction, the usefulness of the motor car may be still further expanded and the industry's contributions to prosperity and better living be increased" (General Motors 1939).

The following is the text of the voiceover narration heard as one proceeded on the conveyer passed the city of tomorrow:

> In 1940 this American city actually existed. Its population then was approximately a million persons. Today—in 1960—it is much larger, divided into three units, residential, commercial and industrial. Nine miles out from the city is a vast airport.

Here is an American city replanned around a highly developed modern traffic system, and, even though this is 1960, the system as yet is not complete. Whenever, possible the rights of way of these express city thoroughfares have been so routed as to displace outmoded business sections and undesirable slum areas. (General Motors 1940)

World War II began in September 1939, the same year that the World's Fair opened. The fair continued on schedule for another year. The total fair attendance exceeded 45 million people. It was not until after the war that the vision of *Futurama* became the sought-for reality for American cities and suburbs.

David Gelernter (1995) has written a fascinating account of the World's Fair. He points out that the political analyst Walter Lippmann wrote one of the most quoted contemporary citations on the World's Fair. Lippmann wrote on the *Futurama* exhibit and discussed the role of private enterprise in the building of the future America. "GM has spent a small fortune to convince the American public that if it wishes to enjoy the full benefit of private enterprise in motor manufacturing, it will have to rebuild its cities and highways by public enterprise" (Lippmann quoted in Gelernter 1995: 362). Lippmann's comment became part of a larger debate on the role that the automobile in general and GM's influence in particular played on the building of post–World War II America and on urban renewal, interstate highways, and suburbia.

Part of the debate was on the extent of an interstate highway system—what Geddes called a *transcontinental* superhighway—and on the role the highway system would play in that future. Some, including Robert Moses, who was New York's Park Commissioner and who was the driving force in the building of highway systems that served the city, felt no need for transcontinental superhighways. *Futurama*, in a very real sense, however, became the prototype for the urban reconstruction of New York, and ultimately for innumerable city planners and their design plan for many American cities, especially after World War II. The historian Max Page observes that, "Not only Le Corbusier but also New York's city builders and imaginers, its developers and preservationists, had come to believe that the remaking of the city was not only desirable but possible—and perhaps inevitable" (1999:19).

Robert Moses: The Power Broker—New York City and Portland, Oregon

Robert Moses (1988–1981) epitomized governmental involvement in the development of the twentieth-century American city. He was an urban planner and city builder whose influence from the 1920s through the 1960s was instrumental not only in defining the greater New York City metropolitan area but much of urban America. While he never held elected office, Moses wielded unprecedented power through a series of interlocking appointive positions, such as the head of the Long Island Parks Commission, the Triborough Bridge Authority, the New York City Planning Commission, and the mayor's Slum Committee. Among his achievements

The New York City Opera, Lincoln Center, New York City. The site of Lincoln Center was previously occupied by "slum" housing. This demolished neighborhood was where West Side Story *was filmed. Photo by author.*

were the Long Island Expressway, the Triborough and Verrazano Bridges that link the boroughs of New York City with interconnecting highways, the Lincoln Center for the Performing Arts, and the World's Fair of 1963–64.

Through his urban renewal projects, this highway engineer and city planner transformed New York City. The Long Island Expressway, built in the 1930s, opened the then-rural areas of Long Island for the middle classes in New York City. Initially, it provided access to the beaches of Long Island: Jones Beach, a massive seashore park, was a most impressive accomplishment. This early, crowning achievement allowed the middle-class, provided they had cars, to venture to a magnificent beach environment and escape the summer heat and discomfort of the city. The highway systems played an important role in suburban development and the ultimate exodus of much of New York City's middle class to suburbia.

However, his controversial Cross–Bronx expressway, built in the late 1950s and early 1960s, destroyed not "slum" areas but a viable economically stable urban village. Sixty thousand people, mostly working class and middle-class Jews as well as Blacks, Italian-Americans, and Irish-Americans, were legally evicted from their homes. The controversy that developed in the destruction of this community for a highway system ultimately was the beginning of the end of the massive urban renewal and urban highway-building period in New York City. Marshall

Berman, a political scientist and urbanist, witnessed the shattering of his neighborhood by the building of the Cross–Bronx Expressway from his personal vantage point as a boy growing up in the Bronx. He comments: "Thus depopulated, economically depleted, emotionally shattered—as bad as the physical damage had been the inner wounds were worse—the Bronx was ripe for all the dreaded spirals of urban blight" (1988: 293).

In an article that appeared in the *New York Times,* Alan Feuer (2002) reports that the East Tremont and Morris Heights neighborhoods never recovered from the construction of the Cross–Bronx Expressway, which split their communities. Furthermore, residents now suffer filth and nausea from the polluting effects of hydrocarbon fumes. While some still argue that the highway was a vital necessity for the commerce highway link of traffic from Long Island and New England through the Bronx to New Jersey and points west, the highway has proven to be a traffic nightmare. It has earned the reputation of being one of the most "savage" roads in New York City. Hampered by poor lighting, poor drainage, poor ramps, and poor lines of sight, it still carries nearly 180,000 vehicles a day. In 2000, the last year when statistics were available, there were 2,622 accidents of, which 5 were fatal (Feuer 2002).

Robert Moses's influence extended beyond New York City to many other American cities as well. A case in point is Portland, Oregon. In 1943, Robert Moses visited Portland and recommended the construction of highways and the elimination of ethnic neighborhoods on the southside for the sake of urban renewal. His plans, endorsed by the city government, were entitled "Freeway City" and were quickly implemented. The major highway that was built, "Harbor Drive," followed the river bank and replaced what may have been the largest concentration of cast-iron buildings outside of the SoHo district of New York City (Breen and Rigby 2004). The results of Moses's urban renewal plans was the virtual destruction of a number of ethnic neighborhoods that were replaced by an unattractive auditorium, middle-income nondescript housing, and office towers, and the dissembling of a once-vital urban downtown area.

It was not until the 1970s that Portland began the urban redevelopment projects that have revitalized the downtown. These redevelopments include the building of a light-rail transit system that is integrated with an extensive bus system, providing a fare-free zone downtown, and redesigned one-way streets used by these buses. The resultant light automobile traffic downtown has helped transform it into an attractive area conducive for walking. A pedestrian-friendly downtown characterized by both parks and stores has overturned the "Moses-bred direction Portland had been taking since World War II" (Breen and Rigby 2004:177). Riverwalk parks on both sides of the Willamette have been created to provide additional urban amenities. Immediately adjacent to downtown is the Pearl District, containing condominium residential units, art galleries, restaurants, and Powell's Book Store. Powell's, a unique, nonchain bookstore massive inside with an irregularly laid-out floor plan spread over a one-block area, has become both an oasis for the city populace and also a major tourist attraction. The Pearl District was created by both 30-year olds and by members of the older baby-boom generation, who are attracted to the "gritty character of the neighbor-hood" (Breen and Rigby 2004:180).

An examination of Robert Moses's projects reveals his intellectual align-ment with the Radiant City ideas of Le Corbusier. Le Corbusier and Moses have been described as loving the abstract public interest but as disdaining people (Campbell and Fainstein 1996). William H. Whyte refers to their ideas on the city as *anti-cities:*

> Everybody, it would seem, is for the rebuilding of our cities . . . with a unity of approach that is remarkable . . . But this is not the same thing as *liking* cities . . . Most of the rebuilding underway . . . . is being designed by people who don't like cities. They do not merely dislike the noise and the dirt and the congestion, they dislike the city's variety and concentration, its tension, its hustle and bustle . . . . The results are not cities within cities, but *anti-cities* [italics added] (Whyte cited in Burns et al. 1999: 494)

Their version of the city is often referred to as the city of highways and tow-ers, and towers in the park. The towers, separated by park areas, are divided by highways instead of traditional streets. Such cities are devoid of the street and the myriad ways of street life.

Edmund N. Bacon: The Redevelopment of Philadelphia

> Philadelphia: "the worst, most backward, stupid city that I ever heard of . . . . That come hell or high water, I would devote my life's blood to making Philadelphia as good as I can".
>
> (Edmund N. Bacon quoted in Salisbury and Boasburg 2005:A5)

Edmund N. Bacon (1919–2005) was one of the most prominent urban planners in the twentieth century—Philadelphia's counterpart to New York City's Robert Moses. His prominence was reflected in his picture being on the cover of *Time* magazine in 1964 in a featured story on urban renewal. (His other claim to fame is that he is the father of the actor Kevin Bacon.) Bacon, however, did not have the same political and economic clout in Philadelphia as Moses, who had control of hundreds of millions of dollars, had in New York City. Bacon served as the execu-tive director of the City Planning Commission from 1949 to 1970, a very influential position but without power to bring about change on its own. Yet, the modern Philadelphia cityscape was a result of his personal urban vision, his tenacity, and the support he received from powerful reform-minded politicians, most notably two of Philadelphia's post–WWII mayors, progressives Joseph Clark and Richard-son Dillworth (Hine 1989; 1999).

Inga Saffron (2005), the architecture critic of the *Philadelphia Inquirer*, points out that Bacon grew up in a city characterized by crowded slums, horse-drawn vehicles, and fetid sewers. He was influenced by the urban planners of his day,

A "Yuppie" couple in Society Hill shopping area, Philadelphia, PA.

including Le Corbusier. Saffron comments, "Like Le Corbusier and other socially progressive modernists of his time, Bacon was committed to bringing order, hygiene, open space, and twentieth-century automotive technology to dense, dark, industrial-era cities" (2005: 1).

Similarly to Robert Moses and Le Corbusier, Bacon saw the necessity of the automobile as a key urban transportation medium. To that end, he misguidedly advocated the demolition of a busy retail street, South Street, in favor of a cross-town expressway that would have linked the Schuylkill and Delaware interstate expressways. The resultant political protest prevented this from occurring. As a consequence, South Street, famous in song as a place where "hippies" meet, today is a vibrant commercial shopping area composed primarily of locally owned stores that cater to a wide variety of customers.

Penn Center was an urban project that showed the influence of Le Corbuserian twentieth-century urban planning. As originally conceived by Bacon, this high-rise office building complex would include many shops and restaurants. It was a replacement for a railroad yard with a huge stone viaduct, known as the *Chinese Wall,* that blockaded Center City from the Schuylkill to City Hall. The resultant Penn Center is a vast improvement over the Chinese Wall, and it ushered in a wave of downtown renewal. Unfortunately, many of Bacon's conceptual ideas for

Penn Center were not actualized, instead bowing to economic expediency, and many urban amenities were discarded in favor of more office space. Its design flaws, including the failure to incorporate a pedestrian-friendly thoroughfare, has turned it into a rather sterile complex of office buildings.

Bacon was also influential in the building of a huge suburban mall-like shopping center called the Gallery in downtown Philadelphia. It has been a partial economic success, but it reflects more of suburban mall thinking than it does at getting at the character of urban downtown shopping. Virtually no use is made of the street; stores are turned into a multilevel mall of privatized retail space. Yet the Gallery is linked to the new Convention Center and serves as the terminus for railway links to the rest of the city.

However, what sets Bacon apart from Robert Moses and other urban planners in the post–World War II period is his image of the experienced city. The prevalent viewpoint of urban planners was that the best way to save old communities, "slum" communities, was to destroy them and replace them through urban renewal projects. Bacon had another vision: "Slum clearance was the architects' delight, . . . It was considered a liberal enlightened policy, but of course it was foolish" (quoted in Hine 1989:1H). Bacon was responsible for the rehabilitation of Society Hill, an historic neighborhood in Philadelphia, at a time when innovative renovations of such neighborhoods did not occur.

A dilapidated section of the city, Society Hill contained a wholesale fruit-and-vegetable-market as well as structurally sound historical—many Colonial era— row homes. Bacon rejected federal monies that were used to level such historic areas in other cities. Bacon saw Society Hill as salvageable. The wholesale food exchange was moved elsewhere; built in its place were three high-rise apartment buildings designed by I. M. Pei that became the homes of affluent residents. The adjacent housing, most of it in deplorable condition, was selectively rehabilitated through local government programs that encouraged urban homesteading. The Victorian structures were demolished and replaced by colonial-style buildings; the colonial buildings were rebuilt. This gives Society Hill a somewhat arrested colonial appearance that does not reflect its actual architectural history (Saffron 2005).

More importantly, influenced by an earlier visit to Shanghai, China, Bacon designed a winding network of small, mid-block pedestrian walkways and vest pocket parks for Society Hill. Thomas Hine, a former architecture critic for the *Philadelphia Inquirer,* assessed the effectiveness of Bacon's plans: "Not only did this system produce some delightful, intimate spaces; it also helped convince people about to invest money in Society Hill that there was public support for creating a uniquely desirable neighborhood" (1999:88). Today, Society Hill is a very affluent community and a constant reminder of old Philadelphia as a premier "walking city." Further, it has impacted on the revitalization overflow of nearby residential areas.

Bacon was also a long-time and leading advocate of the "gentlemen's agreement" that no structure in Philadelphia would be taller than Billy Penn's hat on the statue of William Penn atop Philadelphia's massive Victorian city hall. The result of this agreement was that Philadelphia, while being one of the most populated cities in the United States, had a center city that did not have a high central business district population density. To walk in Center City Philadelphia even during "rush hour" one never feels the overwhelming sense of vast crowds. In the 1980s and in subsequent years, the city has built taller buildings than City Hall—most notably One Liberty Place and Two Liberty Place—skyscrapers designed by Helmut Jahn of Houston, which was experiencing a recession. However, these skyscrapers do not overwhelm the skyline; City Hall still is prominent and the downtown character of the city remains intact.

Bacon designed Dillwirth Plaza and Love Park, adjacent to City Hall. Love Park has attracted skateboarders who find the concrete layout of the park most suitable. It is a paramount example of how people can redefine and reinterpret the built environment and use it in ways that the builders never anticipated. In the early 2000s, the mayor's office sought to ban skateboarding on the grounds that it would adversely affect other park users. Bacon, at the time in his 90s, donned a helmet and briefly skateboarded in the park in a celebrated appearance televised on every local newscast. This media event proved an effective vehicle to show his disdain for the banning as unjust and unwise. He declared: "Show me a skateboarder who killed a little old lady and I'll reconsider." His advocacy of skateboarding was a vivid demonstration of both his often cantankerous demeanor but more important his belief in the importance of the built environment as a reflection of the needs of the urban populace.

In 1989, Bacon summarized his career in this way to Thomas Hine:

> I think Philadelphia has been a marvelous taskmaster. It has accepted my gifts and it has rejected them. I'm grateful for what it has accepted and just as grateful for what it rejected. (Hine 1989:16H)

Inga Saffron in her assessment of Bacon's impact on modern Philadelphia reflects the contrary opinions that are shared by many:

> It is ironic that Bacon's greatest projects—Society Hill, Penn Center, the Gallery— are flawed. It's one of the things that makes it so infuriatingly hard to evaluate his historic legacy. He was imperfect, but it is hard to imagine what Philadelphia would be like without those imperfections. (Saffron 2005:2)

Jane Jacobs: **The Death and Life of Great American Cities**

Jane Jacobs (1916–2006) was a social activist residing in the Greenwich Village section of New York City in the 1950s and 1960s. She became the leading voice in both the theoretical fight against the Le Corbuserian view of the city and the practical fight against modern urban planning and the urban renewal plans of Robert Moses. In her profoundly influential masterpiece, *The Death and Life of Great American Cities* (1961), Jacobs sought to demolish the intellectual foundation of urban renewal practices while at the same time advocate the virtues of small-scale

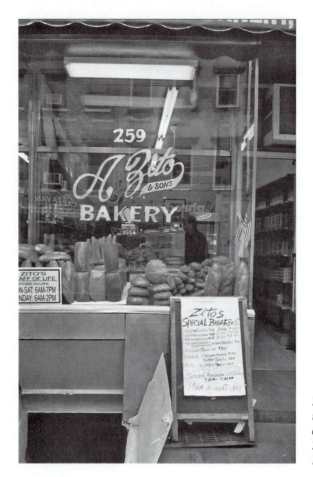

Zito's bakery was a local landmark in Greenwhich Village through most of the twentieth century. It closed in 2005 much to the dismay of residents. Photo by author.

diverse communities like Greenwich Village. She vehemently argued against the destruction of high-density, mixed-use neighborhoods that integrated small stores and businesses with residences. She emphasized the importance of diversified mixed-income and mixed-race communities as being vital components for a lively urban environment. Their replacement by segregated housing communities for the affluent and high-rise, low-income projects for the poor was seen as ultimately being a colossal failure for a viable urban way of life. The later would become the sites of crime, delinquency, and general social hopelessness. She argues that these large-scale projects built with billions of dollars of government funds don't result in the "rebuilding" of cities; they result instead to the "sacking" of them:

> Low-income projects that become worse centers of delinquency, vandalism and general social hopelessness than the slums they were supposed to replace. Middle-income housing projects which are truly marvels of dullness and regimentation,

sealed against any buoyancy or vitality of city life. Luxury housing projects that mitigate their insanity, or try to, with a vapid vulgarity. Cultural centers that are unable to support a good bookstore. Civic centers that are avoided by everyone but bums, who have fewer choices of loitering place than others. Commercial centers that are lackluster imitations of standardized suburban chain-store shopping. Promenades that go from no place to nowhere and have no promenadors. Expressways that eviscerate great cities. This is not the rebuilding of cities. This is the sacking of cities. (Jacobs 1961: 4)

Her book is concerned with the effects of spatial patterns and the built environment on the quality of social life in the city. Jacobs's importance lies in convincing us that city culture depends on the relationship between personal interaction and public space. She examines different parts of the city with particular focus on the spontaneous interaction patterns that characterized unplanned high-density, mixed-use neighborhoods with the planned utilization of urban spaces such as high-density segregated projects. She examines variations in the social texture of different neighborhoods. Jacobs is concerned with the small-scale diverse and mixed neighborhoods of the city and is fundamentally antagonistic to the large-scale government imposed expressways, huge housing projects, or equally huge downtown redevelopments. The essential quality of urban life is seen in its diversity, which is played out in local neighborhoods. Jacobs also argued that there are other virtues to small-scale diversity, such as the watching eyes in mixed neighborhoods restraining crime. In this context we can see parallels between Jacobs's advocacy of the small neighborhood and William H. Whyte's (1988) advocacy of the use of small parks and of the crowded use of streets in the public sphere. Both argue on the importance of diversity as an essential quality of city life.

Jacobs's fundamental problem with the Le Corbusierian view of the city is that it seeks through social planning to dictate how people would live in the "radiant city." It denies the fact that individuals don't simply react to their environment. Rather, people act on their environment and redefine it in appropriate ways for their personal benefit. Thinking of my experience growing up in the Bensonhurst community in Brooklyn and the various street games that children played, the truth of this point is evident. Boys, playing stickball or punchball, redefined the manhole cover ("sewer") in the middle of the street as home plate and the one further down the block as second base. First and third bases were the tires of parked vehicles. Girls transformed the sidewalk squares into games of "hit the penny" and "potsy." The front steps (stoops) of row houses became places for people to congregate or for children to play innumerable games like stoopball. Roofs served as "tar beaches." Neighborhood stores were sites for people to meet and exchange gossip as well as to shop. Streets were seen as linkages to neighborhoods and not simply as a conduit to get through neighborhoods to some distant place. Robert Moses and other urban practitioners and "master builders" failed to see the viability of life in the areas that he defines as slums. Jacobs was a leading antagonist in the battle against Robert Moses, who sought the construction of an expressway through the destruction of the heart of Chinatown, SOHO, and Greenwich Village.

Marshall Berman (1988) in his account of the destruction of the Bronx community by the Cross–Bronx expressway drew on the ideas of Jane Jacobs. He notes that Jane Jacobs's city is a world of small neighborhoods characterized by personal relationships and involvements with family, friends, neighbors, storekeepers, and even with the familiar strangers who one encounters over periods of time on the public streets. He believes that Jacobs's view of the city is a feminist reflection based on her experiences.

> She writes out of an intensely lived domesticity . . . She knows her neighborhood in such precise twenty-four hour detail because she has been around it all day, in ways that most women are normally around all day, especially when they become mothers, but hardly any men ever . . . She knows all the shopkeepers, and the vast informal social network they maintain, because it is her responsibility to take care of her household affairs. She portrays the ecology and phenomenology of the sidewalks with uncanny fidelity and sensitivity, because she has spent years piloting children (first in carriages and strollers, then on roller skates and bikes) through these troubled waters, while balancing heavy shopping bags, talking to neighbors and trying to keep hold of her life. Much of her intellectual authority springs from her perfect grasp of the structures and processes of everyday life. She makes her readers feel that women know what it is like to live in cities, street by street, day by day, far better than the men who plan and build them. (Berman 1988: 322).

Berman observes that Jacobs never uses expressions such as 'feminism" and "women's rights"; writing in the early 1960s those words were not yet in vogue. Nevertheless, her perspective on the city was in the forefront of the later feminist movement that sought to "rehabilitate the domestic worlds, 'hidden from history,' which women had created and sustained for themselves through the ages" (Berman 1988: 322). Berman shares Jacobs's view that the city and its local neighborhoods of family, home, and street involvements and relationships were being destroyed by what Berman calls the "expressway world" advocated by Robert Moses and Le Corbusier. Berman's praise of Jacobs is based on their shared vision of the importance of cities composed of small neighborhoods and local ties:

> Jacobs is celebrating the family and the block . . . : her ideal street is full of strangers passing through, of people of many different classes, ethnic groups, ages, beliefs, and lifestyles; her ideal family is one in which women go out to work, men spend a great deal of time at home, both parents work in small and easily manageable units close to home, so that children can discover and grow into a world where there are two sexes and where work plays a central role in everyday life. (Berman 1988:322)

Jacobs's (1961) critique of urban planners is a sweeping indictment of all forms of decentralized planning. Her amalgamation term, *Radiant Garden City Beautiful*, attacks the underlying ideologies common to all. All are seen as being fearful of the unplanned emergent quality of city life. All the models have as their core a desire for control and manipulation of people. Rather than let people live their lives, they have developed various utopian models of what city life should be like. Jacobs argues for the diversity of city life taking place in high-density neighborhoods.

Mixed land use of residences and small businesses require a constant use of city streets throughout the day, and this contributes to the vitality of the community:

> From beginning to end, from Howard and Burnham to the latest amendment on urban-renewal law, the entire concoction is irrelevant to the workings of cities. Unstudied, unrespected, cities have served as sacrificial victims. (Jacobs 1961: 25).

Conclusion

In summary, the works of Le Corbusier, Howard, and Wright have been most influential in the thinking on the nature of the city, the suburb, and on new town planning. Le Corbusier was instrumental in shaping urban planning in post–World War II America. His ideas translated into urban renewal policies, particularly in the construction of high-rise, high-density public housing projects. Robert Moses was the major practitioner of Le Corbuserian ideas on the nature of the city. He proved to be a highly articulate spokesperson and influenced city planning throughout major American cities.

New town planning in the twentieth century has been influenced by two underlying theories (Calthorpe 1994). One was the Garden City movement, first elaborated by Ebenezer Howard. The second was the modernist approach, developed by Le Corbusier and by Frank Lloyd Wright. Howard's vision was that of a small town of around 30,000 inhabitants surrounded by a greenbelt. It was seen to combine the best of country and town living. The vision followed the traditional urban pattern dominated by civic spaces and surrounded by village-scale centers. During the Depression, both Le Corbusier and Wright developed town plans that called for the segregation of spatial uses, including specified areas for industry, residences, and all buildings separated from pedestrian-oriented streets. Both adherred to the fundamental Modernist principles of "segregation of use, love for the auto and dominance of private and public space" (Calthorpe 1994: xv).

The architectural historian William J. R. Curtis (1996), in his summation of Le Corbusier and Wright, observes that both reacted to the problems of their time period by believing in the power of architecture to re-link individuals and societies into a new form of natural order and a new form of civilization. They were mistaken:

> Both Frank Lloyd Wright and Le Corbusier regarded themselves as latter-day versions of the philospher-king, who enshrines the constitution of a perfect society in the form of an ideal city. Despite obvious differences between their respective urban models, they addressed similar questions: how to overcome the schisms resulting from the division of labour, how to employ the machine yet maintain a sense of wholeness socially and visually, how to reintegrate man and "nature" . . . . The dusty model of Broadacre city and the fading drawings of the Ville Radieuse remained the property of their creators: two individualist artist-thinkers who optimistically, but mistakenly, imagined that architectural form could fashion a new integrated civilization. (Curtis 1996: 327)

6

Urban Political Economy, The New Urban Sociology, and The Power of Place

In this chapter I continue the discussion of urbanism and urban ecology by focusing on the theoretical perspective of *urban political economy,* also known as the *new urban sociology.* This perspective will be discussed within the context of how space is socially constructed in the city.

Two major criticisms dominate contemporary discussion of the ecological model of the Chicago School. One stems from the viewpoint of the *urban political economy perspective*, which argues that the ecological approach underplays the importance of political and economic factors that have guided urban growth. This perspective, developed in the late 1960s and early 1970s as a reaction to the urban turmoil that was occurring in the United States, put forth a radically different notion of urban land use. Proponents of this viewpoint felt that the ecological perspective was inadequate to fully explain or to have predicted urban land use (cf. Gottdiener and Feagin 1988; Smith 1988). This *urban political economy* model has become a dominant perspective in contemporary urban sociology.

The other perspective emphasizes the importance of *social psychological* factors in understanding the urban experience. This viewpoint has its origins, in part, from a social psychological orientation that stems from the symbolic interaction perspective developed by such scholars as George Herbert Mead and his student, Herbert Blumer, in the 1920s and 1930s. It argues that the ecological model failed to fully appreciate or give importance to social psychological factors. Social psychological factors place emphasis on how individuals and groups do not simply react to their environment but rather act on the meaning that that environment has for them. The symbolic investigation of the meaning of space in the urban setting was the focus of the work of those steeped in the social psychological perspective, which came to be known as symbolic interaction and which was the anchoring orientation of Anselm Strauss and his study of urban imagery. I discussed symbolic interactionism in the introductory chapter and critiqued the Chicago School's view of urban ecology and urbanism in Chapter Four. The focus of this chapter is on *urban political economy.*

Urban Political Economy

The two theoretical components of the Chicago School, urban ecology and urbanism, faced a crisis situation in the 1960s. The crisis stemmed from a number of different causes, including the impact of government policies on American cities during the Great Depression of the 1930s and after World War II in 1945. Increasingly the federal government was setting policies regarding housing, highway development, and urban redevelopment, which impacted on urban structures and dynamics. The ecological assumption that "natural forces" and open free market competition were the causes of urban patterns was not viable in the face of governmental intervention policies.

The development of post–World War II suburbia while urban central cities were stagnating or undergoing decline was not predicted or understood within the urban ecology paradigm and its concentric zone model. Similarly, the increased racial polarization of American cities and the development and persistence of racially segregated poverty areas was unexplainable. The continued movements of white ethnic minority populations from inner-city to outer-city areas conformed to the concentric zone hypothesis but the increased segregation of poor African Americans in inner-city ghettos could not be explained.

The urban riots generated by poor African Americans in the Watts section of Los Angeles, in Newark, in Philadelphia, in Washington D.C., and in other cities were a reaction to their continued living under poverty conditions. As the sociologist John Walton (1986) has observed, anger, rather than feelings of alienation or anomie, motivated people's actions. City centers were deteriorating into sprawling ghettos of poverty and were not becoming zones of transition as hypothesized by Ernest Burgess in his concentric zone model. Social "disorganization" was a consequence of poverty, which in turn was a result of racial and class inequality, and not a consequence of size, density, or heterogeneity, as postulated by Wirth.

In the 1970s the urban crisis continued. There was an urban housing crisis, an oil crisis, and inflationary pressures with a concomitant decline in people's standards of living. While people in all areas of the United States felt these economic pressures, the problem was most acute in American cities. The Marxian perspective, which focused on class issues, seemed to be a more pertinent perspective to use to examine urban ills than an ecological model.

World urbanization developments, especially in so-called third world or underdeveloped nations, were very different from the historical urban patterns of development of urban cities in the industrial developed nations of Europe, the United States, and Canada. As articulated in Wirth's ideas of universal urban patterns as presented in "Urbanism as a Way of Life," the failure of urban ecology to account for the different urban growth patterns in poor underdeveloped nations also led the search for a new urban theoretical framework.

As the political-economic sociologist Joe Feagin (1999) has observed, ecological theories often assume that "the land-patterning is impersonal and unconscious, even biotic or subcultural" (134). Citing Walter Firey (1947: 17), Feagin states that the underlying ecological assumptions are of a "'spontaneous, natural stability and order' in the layout of cities" (Feagin: 134). These assumptions, however, could not explain what was happening to cities in the United States in particular as well as in cities around the world. The inadequacy of the formulations of the Chicago School to either predict or explain the urban crisis or understand non-Western urban growth patterns led to a search for a new paradigm for explanation. This new framework was *urban political economy*.

The political economic model begins with a basic premise: the growth and development and the decline and fall of cities do not occur simply by happenstance. Social, economic, and political factors are key factors, and the city must be understood within the context of social structures and processes of change that benefit some at the expense of others. The model is based on a Marxian orientation. Karl Marx, while never developing a theory of urbanism, applied his perspective to the city by observing that it was the site for workplace struggles of class conflict and capitalist accumulation.

As was discussed in an earlier chapter, urban ecology developed a model of urban land use and urban growth based on "natural" ecological processes of invasion and succession. Robert Park found the analogy with plant ecology fitting and elaborated on the utility for urban studies of such concepts as dominance, symbiosis, invasion, and succession. The relations between people and their environment was seen in a similar manner as the interactions between plants and animals in their surroundings.

It was the concept of competition that Park saw as the key concept in terms of the competition for space. Here the reference was to economic competition, with biologic competition its counterpart. In the city, the strongest economic group would compete and win and control the prime locations, while others would have to adjust. But, as elaborated, urban ecology focused more on the "biotic" than the "social or economic" competition.

Urban political economy takes issue with this view and poses a different model of spatial use based on social conflict and anchored in Marxian thought. Manual Castells states this position succinctly: "Space has always been connected to the state" (Castells 1983: 317). Castells (1979, 1983) argues that land-use patterns and urban development can always be seen in terms of who benefits and who loses. He takes issue with urban ecology, which conceptualizes urban social organization as being less dependent on class relations and social data than on natural, spatial, technological, and biological data. Such a model is seen to play into the hands of the ruling power elite.

David Harvey (1973), the Marxist geographer, observes that modern conceptualizations of the city are still intellectually dependent on the assessments of both Friedrich Engels in his view of Manchester and of Robert Park and his examination of Chicago. In assessing the two perspectives (speaking to geographers but his assessment can be extended to sociologists as well), he stated: "it seems a pity that contemporary geographers have looked to Burgess and Park rather than to Engels for their inspiration" (1973: 133). Commenting on the similarity of Engels's description of Manchester and its land-use patterns and Burgess's concentric zone hypothesis, Harvey says:

> The line of approach adopted by Engels in 1844 was and still is far more consistent with hard economic and social realities than was the essentially cultural approach of Park and Burgess. In fact with certain obvious modifications, Engels description could easily be made to fit the contemporary American city (concentric zoning with good transport facilities for the affluent who live on the outskirt, sheltering of commuters into the city from seeing the grime and misery which is the complement of wealth, etc.). . . . The social solidarity which Engels noted was not generated by any superordinate "moral order." Instead the miseries of the city were an inevitable concomitant to an evil and avaricious capitalist system. Social solidarity was enforced through the operation of the market exchange system. (Harvey 1973: 133)

Harvey (1973, 1985) applied a Marxian political economic perspective to an examination of the spatialization of social conflicts, focusing on class-based struggles with governmental imposed space usages. Harvey puts forth the idea that space is not simply a physical phenomenon, something "out there" that impacts on people, but rather people give a cultural interpretation to space. Space becomes defined in a social sense. This viewpoint is very similar to that of symbolic interactionists who put forth the belief that individuals don't simply react to their environment, but interpret that environment and give it meaning. In the broadest sense, than, reality is not something out there, but is socially constructed. Where Harvey goes beyond symbolic interactionism is his specification on the usage of physical space as being determined by the social construction of symbols that are a result of manipulation by economic and political interests. Rejecting urban ecology, he asserts that space should be seen as a scarce resource that is distributed not by natural ecological processes, but rather by outcomes based on economic and political conflict and competitive processes. In the constant struggle for profit accumulations, capitalist forces impact on political and economic decision-making processes, which often result in social conflict, class struggle, and spatial development. Harvey's perspective emphasizes the importance of profit as a key factor in the determination of the physical form of the built environment of cities.

David Harvey's Baltimore

Applying this perspective to the growth and development of American cities David Harvey sees growth and development as a consequence of the capitalist desire to maximize profits through land-usage patterns. Harvey had personally witnessed changes in Baltimore, Maryland, through being on the faculty at Johns Hopkins University. Harvey (1973, 1985) believes that the constant physical transformation of that city is a reflection of the desire for profit and future capital accumulation and the means by which people of economic power had the wherewithall to build and rebuild the physical environment. Harvey (1973: 137) goes further than most social scientists in his belief that is essential to go beyond a *description* of the built environment to take an *advocacy* position; he believes it is necessary to bring desirable physical change based on a "socially controlled urban land market and socialized control of the housing sector" rather than on the "competitive bidding for land use." His (2000) descriptive analysis describes the transformation of Baltimore from an industrial city to a deindustrialized city, with the loss of most of its manufacturing jobs and the subsequent ghettoization

A water taxi docks at Baltimore's Inner Harbor. The Harborplace is the site of many tourists attractions including a national aquarium and a science center.

of its poor, to its emergence as a major tourist destination with reputably more visitors than Disneyland, as a consequence of the rebuilding of the Inner Harbor with shopping pavilions, a national aquarium, a science museum, baseball and football stadiums, and hotels.

Harvey (2000) observes how despite the "Developers' utopia: Baltimore's Inner Harbor renewal," the city of Baltimore is now much more of a "mess" than when he first moved to Baltimore in 1969. He reports that there are now more vacant and abandoned houses, more homeless, and more working poor. Inequalities of both opportunities and standards of life are growing. Public schools are failing to educate their students. The disparities between the poor and the rich are everywhere: chronic poverty and signs of social distress are visible side-by-side with some of the finest medical and public health facilities in the world. Life expectancy of the poor is among the lowest in the nation and is similar to that found in the poorest countries of the world. The affluent, both black and white, are continuing to leave the city. He reports that the "private-public partnership" to invest in the downtown and in the Inner Harbor renewal transformed the harbor area into an "urban spectacle as a commodity" (Harvey 2000: 144). However, the "feeding of the downtown monster"—his reference to the government's subsidies for the building of the Inner Harbor shopping and restaurant pavilions, tourist attractions, downtown hotels, convention center, the baseball stadium for the Baltimore Orioles, and a football stadium for the relocated Cleveland Browns [renamed the Baltimore Ravens]—often meant that "the public takes the risks and the private takes the profit" (Harvey 2000: 141). Yet, the city puts forth the rhetoric that all is well:

> In the midst of all this spiraling inequality, thriving corporate and big money interests (including the media) promote their own brand of identity politics, with multiple manifestations of political correctness. Their central message, repeated over and over, is that any challenge to the glories of the free market (preferably cornered, monopolized, and state subsidized in practice) is to be mercilessly put down or mocked out of existence. The power of these ideas lies, I suspect, at the core of our current sense of helplessness. (Harvey 2000: 154)

In a recent land-use funding battle in Baltimore, Harvey's theoretical perspective continues to be illuminating in understanding the underlying issues in the redevelopment conflict. In 2005, the *New York Times* (Gately 2005) reported on two contrasting sites in Baltimore. The first is a block located in a blighted community in East Baltimore, located two miles from the second site, a planned hotel in the Inner Harbor tourist area. The city of Baltimore is planning to build a $305 million upscale hotel that would connect with the Convention Center, which is owned by the city. Protesting are residents and leaders of the East Baltimore community, who are angry over the perceived reneging of an agreement by the city to spend $50 million to aid in the redevelopment of their community. The pastor, Rev. Douglas Miles, the co-chairman of the advocacy group Baltimoreans United in Leadership Development (BUILD), sees the conflict as symbolizing two different cities: "It's a tale of two cities and two visions—one uptown, one downtown, one doing extremely well, one struggling to survive" (quoted in Gately 2005: A12).

City officials state that the reason the $50 million is not slated for East Baltimore is because of the failure of that community to present a feasible redevelopment plan. They support the building of the hotel with government funds as necessary to stay competitive and successfully compete in the convention tourist business. They further argue that it would be a profit maker for the city, even though private hotel corporations have refused to invest their own monies fearing that the venture would turn out unprofitable. Critics contend that with declining tourist and convention business it is inappropriate and foolhardy to build this hotel. More importantly they feel that the city should not be in the hotel business but rather they should invest their financial resources in the rebuilding of poor neighborhoods, which contain more than 16,000 vacant or abandoned dwellings. In a walking tour of the neighborhood, pastors point to the abandonment of buildings, debris in alleys, and to a graffitied wall memorializing the names of two dozen victims of violence

A city councilman, Keiffer Mitchell, is proposing a referendum to let voters decide on whether the city should build the hotel: "I have a hard time explaining to my constituents that the city wants to invest $305 million to build and operate a hotel downtown, and we're fighting for crumbs" (quoted in Gately 2005: A12). Gately reports that Mitchell supports his position by "seeing a direct connection between blight and the sad cycle of violence, poverty and despair in a city where half of those who start public high schools never finish, where the homicide rate last year was five times greater than that of New York City and where health officials suggest that almost one in 10 people are drug addicts" (Gately 2005: A2).

From Chicago to LA: The LA School

Just as Chicago could be considered as the "shock city" of the early twentieth century, Los Angeles can be considered the "shock city" of the late twentieth century. Los Angeles, the second largest city in the United States with a population of approximately 4 million, has a metropolitan area of more than 4,000 square miles. The megalopolis area of Southern California, which contains the five counties of Los Angeles, Orange, Riverside, San Bernardino, and Ventura, has a population of more than 16 million people (Dear 2002).

Just as Chicago has absorbed a huge immigration population into its growing metropolis, so too does Los Angeles serve as a concentration center for immigrants. Since 1965 vast populations of immigrants from Central and South America and Asia have dramatically changed the ethnic composition of this city. From being a predominantly white or "Anglo" city, LA now has 80 percent of its population almost equally divided between non-Hispanic whites and Hispanics; the remaining 20 percent are almost equally divided between African Americans and Asians. The election of its first Hispanic mayor in 2005 symbolically reflects the changing demographic patterns.

Los Angeles is not only the second largest city in the United States, but it is a "world" city whose global economic system plays a central role in the international economic system of Pacific Rim nations. The economy is postindustrial, based on diversified manufacturing sectors and information and financial based services. The urban geographer Edward Soja (1992: 150), based at the University of California—Los Angeles, points out that ". . . perhaps more than any other place Los Angeles is *everywhere* . . . being global in the fullest senses of the word." In addition to its political-economic importance, he points out the global ideological importance of LA based on its influential motion picture industry. Equally important is its prominence in the United States.

> Everywhere seems also to be *in* Los Angeles. To it flows the bulk of the transportation trade of the United States of America, a cargo which currently surpasses that of the smaller ocean to the east. Global currents of people, information, and ideas accompany the trade. Once dubbed Iowa's seaport, today Los Angeles has become an entrepôt [warehouse] to the world, a true pivot of the four quarters, a congeries of East and West. And from the teeming shores of every quarter has poured a pool of cultures so diverse that contemporary Los Angeles re-presents the world in urban microcosms, reproducing in situ the customs and ceremonies, the conflicts and confrontations of a hundred homelands. (Soja 2002: 151)

Unlike Chicago, with its concentric zone pattern so graphically depicted by Ernest Burgess and vividly described by Harvey Zorbaugh (*The Gold Coast and the Slum*), LA's spatial patterns are economically decentralized, its ethnic populations are dispersed, and culturally diverse patterns are scattered throughout the metropolitan area. A number of influential social scientists working in LA, most notably Michael Dear (2002), Mike Davis (1990, 1992, 1998), and Edward Soja (2002), have articulated an urban theoretical perspective that opposes the urban ecological perspective proposed by the Chicago School and that articulates a view of the city that reflects an urban political-economy orientation. They argue that postmodern cities like Los Angeles are based on political-economic factors rather than on the Chicago School's urban ecological model, and that these cities should be seen as the analytical paradigm for the investigation of the urban future.

Michael Dear, a University of Southern California geographer, reports that he and fellow regional colleagues "assert that Southern California is an unusual amalgam—a polycentric, polyglot, polycultural pastiche that is deeply involved in rewriting American urbanism" (Dear 2002: 6). The patterns of urban change are seen as being so radical that they call for the development of a different analytical framework. Dear observes that "the consequent epistemological difficulties are manifest in the problem of naming the present condition, witness the use of such terms as *post-modernity, hyper-modernity,* and *super-modernity*" (Dear 2002: 6). Dear cites his intellectual colleague, Ed Soja, as being one of the first scholars to see Los Angeles as "the prototype of late twentieth-century postmodern geographies":

> What better place can there be to illustrate and synthesize the dynamics of capitalist spatialization? In so many ways, Los Angeles is the place where "it all comes together" . . . one might call the sprawling urban region . . . a prototopos, a paradigmatic place; or . . . a mesocosm, an ordered world in which the micro and the macro, the idiographic and the nomothetic, the concrete and the abstract, can be seen simultaneously in an articulated and interactive combination. (Soja 1989:191 quoted in Dear 2002: 11)

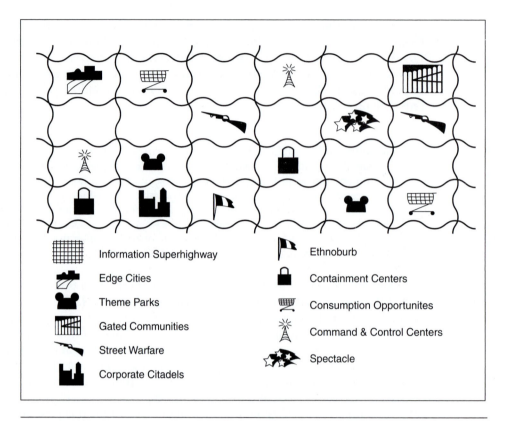

FIGURE 6.1   *Keno Capitalism: A Model of Postmodern Urban Structure.*

Reprinted from Michael J. Dear and Steven Flusty, 1998. "Postmodern Urbanism," in *Annals of the American Association of Geographers,* Vol. 88, No. 1, pp. 50–72. Copyright by Blackwell Publishers.

Dear (2002) proceeds to outline the new urban spatial arrangements that contrast contemporary Los Angeles with the concentric zonal arrangement of early twentieth-century Chicago. He and his colleague Steven Flusty (Dear and Flusty 1998; Dear 2002) coin the term "Keno capitalism" to describe the lotto-like decision-making process influencing land-use patterns in postmodern cities like Los Angeles. They reject ecological land-use patterns based on center-driven agglomeration economies, such as the Chicago School's emphasis on concentric circles, in favor of a seemingly randomized land-use pattern that reflects contemporary technological, transportation, and communication conditions. These conditions have resulted in key urban changes that they label as *edge cities, privatopias, cultures of heteropolis, city as theme park, fortified city, interdictory spaces, historical geographies of restructuring, Fordist versus Post-Fordist regimes of accumulation and regulation, globalization, and politics of nature.*

Edge Cities

Joel Garreau, a *Washington Post* reporter, coined the term *edge cities* to refer to a cluster of commercial, residential, and retail activity anchored by a regional mall located at the intersection of an urban beltway, a hub-and-spoke lateral road, and often a major interstate (1991). Los Angeles is seen as the "great-granddaddy" of edge cities. The underlying conditions that lead to the emergence of edge cities are the dominating presence of the automobile; accommodating roads and parking facilities; the communications revolution; and the entry of large numbers of women into the labor force.

Privatopia

Privatopias, more familiarly referred to as *gated communities,* have become the quintessential residential form. They are often walled and gated communities that are private housing developments governed by a common-interest association or homeowners association. They have often been criticized as a "secession of the successful" that has altered concepts of citizenship to one in which "one's duties consist of satisfying one's obligations to private property" (McKenzie 1994: 196 quoted in Dear 2002: 18). Dear and Flusty (1998) view them as essentially being undemocratic and anti-community because they are based on exclusion, control, and nonparticipation in the larger surrounding municipality.

Culture of Heteropolis

The ethnic diversity and the rise of minority populations in Los Angeles and Southern California is a defining social-cultural characteristic. Dear and his colleague Charles Jencks see this as a key to LA's emergent urbanism: "Los Angeles is a combination of enclaves with high identity, and multi-enclaves with mixed identity, and, taken as a whole, it is perhaps the most heterogeneous city in the world" (Jencks 1993:32 quoted in Dear 2002: 18). Los Angeles is seen to differ from other cities in that its ethnic populations have size and vigor and underlying cultural dynamics have led to the development of ethnic adaptation fusions in the areas of music, food, architecture, and new art forms. The downside of LA's and Southern California's heteropolis is socioeconomic polarization, racism, inequality, homelessness, and social unrest (Dear 2002).

City as Theme Park

LA as a "dreamscape" is personified by its movie industry and most popularly by Disneyland. The urban critic Michael Sorkin (1992) describes the "city as theme park" as characterized by places that are synthetic and simulations of real places. The resultant built environment does not reflect any architectural style or historical period—it is both any place and no place. The "phoniness of place" combined with modern telecommunications technology results in a lack of community and a sense of connectivity. "The phone and modem have rendered the street irrelevant, and the new city threatens an 'unimagined sameness' characterized by the loosening of ties to any specific space, rising levels of surveillance, manipulation, and segregation, and the city as theme park" (Dear 2002:19).

Fortified City

LA and Southern California are sometimes depicted as *dystopias,* similar to the city shown in the film *Blade Runner.* Dear cites the work of Mike Davis (1992), who views the city as a fortress. The class and ethnic polarization of LA has led the affluent to seek ways to "protect" themselves from "others." The result is a transformation of the physical form of the city into fortified and segregated commercial and residential areas and the diminishing of public space. Davis describes this urban phenomena in Los Angeles as culminating "on the hard edge of postmodernity (1992:155 quoted in Dear 2002:19). Gated residential developments and shopping malls are fortified, and high-tech policing methods are employed for the sake of security. The outcome for Dear is that "in the consequent carceral city, the working poor and destitute are spatially sequestered on the mean streets, and excluded from the affluent forbidden cities through security by design" (2002:19).

Interdictory Spaces

Mike Davis (1990, 1992, 1992a, 1992b, 1998) depicts Los Angeles as a fortress characterized by "the militarization of city life" and spatially organized by an *ecology of fear.* Davis builds on the Chicago School's human ecology model. Davis observes Ernest Burgess's model of a big-city human ecology of concentric zones organized according to "biological" forces of concentration, segregation, invasion, and succession. Davis remaps that ecological urban structure by taking it into the future. He preserves the ecological determinants of income, land value, class, and race and adds *fear* as a decisive new factor.

Elaborating on Davis's concept of fortress urbanism, Steven Flusty (1994) and later Dear and Flusty (1998) develop the term *interdictory spaces* to describe the application of modern security technology to a variety of suppression and surveillance techniques used for the *entire* city. The result is a city that has a built environment composed of fortress-style high-rise buildings, guarded residential complexes, gated communities, and a police force utilizing profiling and harassment techniques to control and "keep-in-their-place" undesirables.

Historical Geographies of Restructuring

Dear (2002) cites the important contribution of Edward Soja (1996) in articulating six kinds of restructuring that serve to define the contemporary urban process in this region. *Exopolis* is a massive simulation of what a city should be. Soja sees Orange County as the prime example, exhibiting a "scamscape"—a theme park noted for the bankruptcy of its county government, the home of mail-fraud operations, and savings and loan failures. The other five forms are summarized by Dear as follows:

> Soja lists: *Flexcities,* associated with the transition to post-Fordism, especially deindustrialization and the rise of the information economy; and *Cosmopolis,* referring to the globalization of Los Angeles both in terms of its emergent world city status

and its internal multicultural diversification. According to Soja, peripheralization, post-Fordism, and globalization together define the experience of urban restructuring in Los Angeles. Three specific geographies are consequent upon these dynamics: *Spintered Labyrinth,* which describes the extreme forms of social, economic, and political polarization characteristic of the postmodern city; *Carceral City,* referring to the new "incendiary urban geography" brought about by the amalgam of violence and police surveillance; and *Simcities,* the term Soja uses to describe the new ways of seeing the city that are emerging from the study of Los Angeles—a kind of epistemological restructuring that foregrounds a postmodern perspective. (Dear 2002:20–21)

Fordist versus Post-Fordist Regimes of Accumulation and Regulation

Here Dear (2002) is referring to the transition from an era of mass production (Fordist) and the cities of industrial capitalism, including Detroit, Chicago, and Pittsburgh, to an era based on a form of small-size, small-batch industrial production (Post-Fordist). In Los Angeles, post-Fordist production takes the form of labor-intensive crafts such as garments and jewelry and high-technological production in the aerospace and defense industries. The changes in the modes of production are reflected in political-economic changes that include the rise of neo-conservatism and the rise of privatization ethos, the decline of social-welfare programs, and periods of economic recession and retrenchment.

Globalization

Globalization has impacted on Los Angeles through the use of tax dollars gained from international capital investment in the urban renewal downtown development of Bunker Hill. It also accounts for the reflux of low-wage manufacturing and the labor-intensive service industry as a consequence of Mexican and Central American immigration. Bank and real-estate capital has been overaccumulated in Southern California as a consequence of East Asian trade surpluses. The global/local dialectic is seen by Dear to "become an important leitmotif . . . of contemporary urban theory, most especially, via notions of 'world cities' and global 'city-regimes'" (2002:22)

Politics of Nature

The natural environment of Southern California is seen to be under attack by the onslaught of urbanization. The consequence has been a range of environmental problems including air pollution and the loss of animal habitats. The result is a politicalization of nature reflected in battles over environmental regulation policies and grassroot environmental movements.

   In a critical examination of the LA School and the ideas put forth by Michael Dear, Edward Soja, and as presented in a *Chronicle of Higher Education* essay by D.W. Miller (2000), the urban sociologist Mark Gottdiener takes issue with many of the underlying assumptions regarding the distinctiveness of Los Angeles. Gottdiener believes that proponents of the LA School place undue emphasis on Los Angeles as the exclusive geographical site for what the United States Census Bureau calls a consolidated metropolitan statistical area (CMSA). Gottdiener points out that in 1995 the Census Bureau recognized that there were 13 such areas, with the New York area being the most populous. He further argues that such features as edge cities, the city as theme park, deindustrialization, and globalization are not unique to LA. The proliferation of these emerging sprawling, developing, and urbanizing areas are seen by Gottdiener as calling for the "need for new concepts and theories of urban growth" (Gottdiener 2002: 161).

He strongly asserts that the study of sociospatial forms of land use and sociocultural patterns would benefit from an incorporation of the concepts and theoretical perspective of what has been called the "new urban sociology." This approach stresses the importance in understanding CMSAs of such key factors as governmental policies; real-estate development and speculation; wage differentials and union impacts; the growing importance of sign values and symbolic factors that affect growth, deindustrialization, and global economics; and the rising affluence of the general public (Gottdiener 2002). He sees the necessity of understanding the new social forces that are determining new land-use patterns. No city, not even Los Angeles, can be seen as both an existing city and an ideal type.

> Significantly more critical is the advancement by urbanists everywhere of our understanding of the processes that have worked and reworked settlement space by increasing its scale, fragmenting its communities and nodal points of interaction; by decentralizing its businesses and then recentralizing them in new, functionally specialized nodes; by perfecting a cultural array of themes that organizes business through franchising, centralized malls and decentralized strip zones; by fragmenting populations according to class, race, ethnicity, and even age; by producing uneven development and reproducing social inequalities across the generations; and finally by making it increasingly difficult for society to deal adequately with problems related to environmental quality, equality, governance, the quality of community life, the issue of social mobility, public transportation, and civic culture. (Gottdiener 2002: 178)

The New Urban Sociology: The Growth Machine and the Sociospatial Perspective

Many sociologists tend to see the urban environment in terms of its physical structure. Yet, the political, economic, and social components that make up that structure become the essence for understanding the environment. The social-psychological perspective focuses on the interactions of people who live in the city, viewing their activities, both ordered and disordered and planned and spontaneous, as the subject matter of urban analysis. For those who take this perspective the concern is with the analysis of the experience of the city with inclusion of emotions and feelings in the response to the built environment. This perspective goes beyond ecological and political economic analyses and seeks the inclusion of individuals' meanings and understandings and *actions* toward that built environment and not simply their *reactions* toward it. Two approaches that have sought to broaden the political economic perspective are *the growth machine* and the *sociospatial perspective (SSP)*.

John Logan and Harvey Molotch (1987) developed the conceptualization of the "urban growth machine." They are concerned with the growth of American cities and see this growth in a broad, political economy context. They argue that cities can be seen as machines for urban growth, machines that are developed and shaped by a select group of people representing institutions that can best profit from that growth. The key institutions that develop a consensus on stimulating investment and economic growth include realtors, local banks, influential politicians, corporate chairs, and chambers of commerce.

Logan and Molotch observe that while these key institutions may promote their own interests, debating, for example, whether a city should pursue a tourist, manufacturing, service, or residential real-estate emphasis, they do share a common pro-growth mentality. Together, they seek to operationally define the city as a growth machine. They pursue a pro-business agenda that often pits their city in economic competition with alternative investment opportunities and competing locales. Essentially, urban politics is dominated by the pursuit of business interests pursuing their own interests while limiting the redistributional function of the state. Further, while these key institutions are aware of, and are sensitive to, local community sentiments, they do not take these sentiments fully into consideration as a contributing factor in articulating how the growth machine operates. Logan and Molotch state, "As cities grow and government bureaucrats seek sites for devalued projects (for example, sewage plants, jails, and halfway houses), they look first—if they have any occupational competence at all—to poor people's neighborhoods" (Logan and Molotch 1987: 113).

While Logan and Molotch realize that growth may be problematic, they do not emphasize the importance of community representatives who may be against such growth if they feel that the growth may be in conflict with their community interests. The failure of Logan and Molotch to fully integrate a conflict orientation in their approach stems in part by their failure to give sufficient attention to the importance to the contestation of urban imagery and the conceptualization of space. The socio-spatial approach seeks to include a consideration of space as an important factor in the understanding of the political and economic actions of the real-estate developers and governmental agencies that comprise the growth machine.

Mark Gottdiener (1985, 1994, 1997), and with Ray Hutchinson (2000), has been one of the leading proponents of integrating urban political economy with a social-psychological perspective. He seeks to broaden the political economic perspective by integrating it with sensibility to the symbolic nature of environments with more traditional factors that comprise social behavior, such as class, race, gender, age, and social status. Space is seen as another compositional factor in human behavior. Gottdiener (1994) refers to the broader parameters of this perspective as the *new urban sociology,* and his own term for it is the *sociospatial perspective (SSP).*

He introduces the importance of symbolic processes within a political economic framework to analyze urban structures and the urban environment. Such an approach, he argues, overcomes the limitations of urban ecology. Urban ecology, while recognizing the importance of urban location, does so through a one-dimensional, technologically deterministic framework. It also overcomes the limitations of political economy. The sociospatial perspective expands the political economy analytical framework that emphasizes space as a container of political and economic activities but tends to ignore the importance of the symbolic meaning of spatial relations. The sociospatial perspective (SSP) emphasizes the social production and meaning of urban space.

> The SSP stresses the human dimension along with structural arrangements. It wants to know who the actors are and how they behave, not just the facts or figures about aggregate levels of growth and change. Activities involve people acting as part of social classes and class factions, or of gender, racial, and ethnic interests. How people come together to struggle over the patterns of development is an important question for the SSP; . . . but this is not viewed as a machine. (Gottdiener and Hutchinson 2000:141)

Sharon Zukin: "Whose Culture? Whose City?"

The sociologist Sharon Zukin has studied changes in New York City for most of her academic career. Based on her observations, she develops a point of view that ties a political economic perspective with what she sees as the emergence of a *symbolic economy.* This new "symbolic economy" is anchored on the economic importance of tourism, media, and entertainment for cities. She believes that with the disappearance of local manufacturing, culture is increasingly the business of cities. The cultural consumption of art, gourmet food, fashion, and music, as well as tourism, which often packages them all, is the driving force on which the city's symbolic economy rests. Zukin describes the symbolic economy created by cultural strategies of urban redevelopment and the privatization of public space. Zukin persuasively argues that the recent growth of the symbolic economy has tangible spatial repercussions: it "reshapes geography and ecology" (Zukin 1995:8). The symbolic economy creates new types of workplaces, commercial areas, and residences, and throws into turmoil conventional meanings of public versus private, local versus transnational, commodity versus culture.

> The growth of the symbolic economy in finance, media, and entertainment . . . has already forced the growth of towns and cities, created a vast new workforce, and changed the way consumers and employees think . . . The facilities where these employees work—hotels, restaurants, expanses of new construction and undeveloped land—are more than just workplaces. They reshape geography and ecology; they are places of creation and transformation. (Zukin 1995: 8)

The symbolic economy for Zukin is not a singular thing; rather, it involves a number of different ways in which the cultural symbols of a place are combined with capitalist activity: the "intertwining of cultural symbols and entrepreneurial capital" (Zukin 1995:3). She suggests that historically this economy takes three main forms and influences how a place is seen and used and the subsequent kinds of investment and economic development that can be used to regenerate a city. The first and most basic form of the symbolic economy implies profiting from its imagery—"the look and feel of a city" (Zukin 1995:7). The second form of symbolic economy refers to the concerns for profit through real-estate developments and jobs by "place entrepreneurs." She uses the concept developed by Harvey Molotch (1976), which refers to the development of the private sector through investments in retail and office developments or the housing market, as sought by real-estate developers, corporate organizations, and venture capitalists. The third form of symbolic economy involves traditional "place entrepreneurs," whose investments in the city are through such cultural forms such as museums, parks, and monuments. These businesses and municipal authorities operate for civic and philanthropic reasons to promote the public good, which indirectly reflects and promotes economic prosperity. What gives this third form its power is its increased importance since the beginning of the last quarter of the twentieth century, an importance brought on by the decline in the manufacturing and industrial sectors and the concomitant rise of the service-sector and consumer-culture industries, which are associated with the arts, music, film, theater, and sports, as well as entertainment complexes combined with food and drink establishments, retailing, and tourism.

Zukin's major concern is how the power of the symbolic economy in cities impacts on "social inclusion or exclusion, depending on your point of view" (Zukin 1995: vii). She argues that the cultural constructs of a city delegates "who belongs where" through its images and symbols, regulating the economy by producing goods and designing public space through planning backed by those in positions of power in the private sector. The control of images in the city is for the benefit of the middle class and the affluent as well as for tourists. Unsavory images are removed and concealed. "Controlling the various cultures of cities suggests the possibility of controlling all sorts of urban ills, from violence and hate crimes to economic decline" (Zukin 1995:2).

The symbolic economy becomes dependent on the creation of attractions, whether they be museums; entertainment zones, such as the new "family friendly" Times Square; sports stadia; parks; or festival marketplaces for the more affluent groups of the city. In Bryant Park in New York City for example, the establishment of an expensive sidewalk cafe was one means to establish the presence and control of these people over the park: "A sidewalk cafe takes back the street from causal workers and homeless people" (Zukin 1995:9)

Zukin's dominating concern is not only on issues of who occupies "real" space but on the utilization of "symbolic" space as well. In an allied work Zukin states: "To ask 'Whose City?' suggests more than a politics of occupation; it also asks who has a right to inhabit the dominant image of the city" (Zukin 1996: 43).

Zukin's analysis of the usage of Bryant Park will be discussed in greater detail in chapter 9.

In the next section of this chapter I would like to build on the importance of urban imagery and power to show how that leads us to define a given section of the city in a particular sort of way. It continues our examination of how physical space is redefined in terms of "place" by those in positions of power and economic control.

Urban Imagery, Power, and the Symbolic Meaning of Place

Power and economic factors combined with concerns for the symbolic meaning of space interact and have consequences on how people interpret their built environment. Earlier in this book we observed that in Park's concept of "the city as a state of mind" and Thomas's concept of "the definition of the situation," a basic premise of symbolic interaction thought is articulated on the importance of *urban imagery*, or on how cities are both conceptualized and acted upon. Anselm Strauss (1961)

The 2nd Ave Deli is one of the few food stores left that caters to its Lower East Side Jewish residents. It is currently being threatened with closure as its owners cannot afford the rapidly rising rent now being asked in the gentrifying East Village, New York City. Photo by author.

Cast iron buildings located in SOHO, New York City. Photo by author.

examined how the physical reality of cities is interpreted through the "images" that people have of them. The *feelings* that people have for cities impact on how they perceive and act toward them. Further, the spatial complexity and the social diversity of a city often becomes integrated by the use of "sentimental" history in selected landscapes, and an invariable characteristic of city life is that certain stylized and symbolic objects must be employed by people in order to "see" the city.

Strauss observed that people know best ("see") those parts of a city that they are intimately involved in; their perspectives "are constructed from spatial representations resulting from membership in particular social worlds" (1961: 67). For Strauss, then, the images that a person has of the city are based on relationships. Images can be seen as a spatial consequence of the different types of social relationships that people have with each other in different places. By extension, the meaning of the city, as well as its districts, neighborhoods, streets, and buildings, comes about through an interpretive process. With his colleague, R. Richard Wohl, Strauss observed that:

> The city, then, sets problems of meaning. The streets, the people, the buildings, the changing scenes do not come already labelled. They require explanation and interpretation. (Wohl and Strauss 1958:527)

However, Wohl and Strauss fail to make explicit how that "labeling" process is influenced by people in positions of power, who can influence and control the symbolic meaning given to a community. Proponents of the new urban sociology and the sociospatial approach are very much interested in the role played by real-estate developers and other power brokers, including bankers and big businesses through the consent and support of government agencies, in transforming urban space through the manipulation of images, symbols, and rhetoric. It would be useful to begin our discussion by starting with the contrast that cultural geographers have made between *space* and *place*.

Cultural geographers have given different meanings for the terms *place* and *location*. Location usually refers to a physical position within a specified space, often with objective specifications such as latitude and longitude. Place refers to a geographical location as well but also includes a subjective meaning that often alludes to a position on a social hierarchy: for example, "He knows his place," or "She was put in her place." Similarly, *sense of place,* often refers to subjective feelings designated to a given place. As the urban architectural historian Dolores Hayden (1995) states in her book, *The Power of Place*, "People make attachments to places that are critical to their well-being or distress. An individual's sense of place is both a biological response to the surrounding physical environment and a cultural creation . . ." (1995:16). Place, then, is simultaneously geographic and social. Place can also be seen in terms of power relations and the battle for control of urban imagery and the symbolic meaning of place. In this section, I want to illustrate this point by looking at the feminist approach of Melissa Gilbert (1999) and Mary Pardo (2004) and then the new urban sociology perspective of Christopher Mele (2000).

Melissa Gilbert (1999) takes Logan and Molotch's ideas of the "urban growth machine" to task for their failure to analyze power relations, their conceptualizations of agency, activism, and daily life, and their lack of attention to geographic scale, which has resulted in a romanticized notion of community and a failure to fully develop an analysis of the politics of place. Feminist theorists, on the other hand, she argues, are seen to understand the underlying politics of place and to realize that communities are often antidemocratic, patriarchal, and homogeneous. Local communities are often characterized by discriminatory political and social arrangements.

Gilbert sees the need for the development of an integrative politics of place and a politics of identity. There is a necessity to merge a feminist politics of place with a perspective that sees the importance of group interests based often on people's diversified identities. She observes that feminist urban geographers have been reconceptualizing space by moving beyond a spatially fixed entity to one that sees space both in geographical terms as well as in relational terms. By this she means that in terms of process, space is conceived, as nodes of networks of social relations. These feminist geographers have examined space in terms of how identity, difference, and place are mutually constituted. Gilbert observes that poor, racialized, minority urban women often develop a politics of place to challenge their marginality at the local level as well as to challenge the power relations that create and sustain their marginalization in the broader society. An illustrative example is how Latina and African American women have successfully organized to fight environmental racism in Los Angeles.

Mary Pardo (2004) discusses the community activities of a group of Mexican American women called the *Mothers of East Los Angeles (MELA)*. Pardo observed that the family structures of members of the MELA are composed of a developed social network comprised of extended kin and neighbors. This social support structure serves as an important mediating factor in a given family's involvement with the larger community. Women transformed traditional networks based on family, religion, and culture into political assets to improve the quality of their community life. They used their social network and family roles as a basis for political action that includes the building of new schools and safe work sites.

In 1984, the State of California decided to construct energy-producing waste incinerators in East Los Angeles, a low-income, predominantly Mexican American, community. This decision was made despite the fact that the air quality in East Los Angeles was already debilitating. In 1985, the California Department of Corrections selected a site in East Los Angeles for the first state prison in Los Angeles County. The prison was to be built in close proximity to 34 schools. The decisions to build the toxic waste incinerators and the prison in East Los Angeles were based on a belief that the residents of this community would be least likely to organize effective community opposition to these projects. This belief was based on the politicians' conceptions of Mexican Americans as having a low rate of participation in the voting process, their assigning Mexican Americans "to a set of cultural 'retardants' including primary kinship systems, fatalism, religious traditionalism, traditional cultural values, and mother country attachments" (Pardo 2004: 74). The politicians proved to be mistaken.

Pardo first discusses how women's gender-related "traditional" responsibilities, such as their active involvement in the education of their children, their concern for safety in the surrounding community, and their participation in church activities, led them to become involved with other mothers in fighting against the building of the prison in their community. Together, these women articulated similar complaints about past governmental injustices, including the building of freeway interchanges through their community that impacted on the quality of air. Pardo then discusses how their common concern's about such "traditional" issues as health, housing, sanitation, and the urban environment led them to take collective action as the MELA. The MELA proved effective in getting the State of California to reverse its decisions to build the incinerators and the prison in East Los Angeles.

The mobilization of the community through the actions of the MELA is seen by Pardo to disprove the belief that political involvement can be predicted by cultural characteristics. Indeed the MELA's defying of cultural stereotypes of apathy was based on their use of their ethnic, gender, and class identities as an impetus and a strength to foster political activism. Pardo concludes:

> The story of the MELA reveals, on the one hand, how individuals and groups can transform a seemingly "traditional" role such as "mother." On the other hand, it illustrates how such a role may also be a social agent drawing members of the community into the "political" arena. Studying women's contributions as well as men's will shed greater light on the network dynamic of grassroots movements. (Pardo 2004: 82)

The Politics of Power and Collective Memory

In a monograph on the construction of community imagery, Christopher Mele (2000) takes issue with Anselm Strauss's conceptualization of urban imagery as a result of a public consensus that is formed by shared symbols and understanding of the meaning of place. Mele draws on the new urban sociology and a sociospatial approach. He argues that the meaning of place is a result of "social power and contestation rather than as ad hoc by-products of consensual place image making." (2000: 14). Mele places the symbolic meaning of place in a perspective that is anchored in political, economic, and cultural stratification.

> Outstanding themes in place representations in any given historical period are reflective of wider political and social currents. These guideposts make sense of "different" places, people and social interactions in ways that cannot be considered neutral but rather are bound to political, economic, and cultural dimensions of inequality. (Mele 2000: 14–15)

Mele illustrates his view through both an historical and contemporary analysis of New York City's Lower East Side. While living there as a graduate student, he analyzed real-estate investors' manipulation of urban imagery and the symbolic meaning of place in a way that fundamentally changed that community's imagery and meaning to enhance their own economic interests at the expense of those who lived there. The New York's Lower East Side has a long history throughout the twentieth century as an area that has been the home for poor immigrants and working-class people. In the early twentieth century it was inhabited by poor Jewish immigrants from Eastern Europe and later, in the second half of the twentieth century, by poor Puerto Rican immigrants. It has also been the residential site for an assortment of bohemians—poets, painters, writers, musicians, and other artists as well as radicals—socialists and communists, union activists, and more recently youth of the counterculture.

Mele argues that real-estate developers and media personnel, with the compliance of local government, co-opted the area's reputation for social and cultural diversity and political radicalism and used that reputation as a marketing tool for residential and commercial development. Rather than ignoring the underlying poverty, reputed deviance, and problematic, nature of the community, these conditions were redefined as a marketable commodity for those upscale young professional members of the middle class who would find such a "rough" neighborhood an attractive place to pursue a faux-Bohemian lifestyle.

Mele observes that there has been resistance by the residents in this marginalized poor community to prevent its takeover. The battle has not only been over economic and political issues but also on symbolic ones as well. Latinos, many Puerto Ricans and Dominicans, as well as blacks refer to their community as *Loisaida*. Real-estate investors and brokers in their battle to economically restructure the area have appropriated the name *Alphabet City*, which was used in the late 1970s and early 1980s by those connected to the emerging art scene, and later the name *East Village*, a designation used earlier by hippies and later by members of the underground culture to distinguish the area from the adjacent West Village, which was perceived as stodgy and middle class.

> The somewhat playful name Alphabet City concealed the area's rampant physical and social decline and downplayed the area's Latino identity. The name East Village . . . was quickly appropriated by real estate brokers and developers. An "East Village" disassociated the identity . . . from its working-class past and the less developed streets and avenues . . . Since realtors, hippies, and other newcomers together referred to the northern part of the Lower East Side as the East Village, its use was picked up by the local, national, and international media . . . For many local activists, the name retains the distinct meaning of real estate developers and displacement. *That all these names continue to be used is strong testimony to the importance of cultural representation to neighborhood restructuring and resistance* (italics added). (Mele 2000: xi–xii)

Another example of the politics of place can be seen in the battles to restore to a geographical location its historical past. This historical past can sometimes become hidden from history as a consequence of economic, political and cultural factors. I want to illustrate this by first taking a brief look at the construction of a commemorative wall in Los Angeles to honor a previously forgotten American hero and then taking a more extended look at Independence Hall in Philadelphia and its forgotten history.

The historic preservation movement in the twentieth century has fought to keep structures and buildings that are defined as having historical importance. Often, however, the meaning of "historical importance" is seen to take on political and economic significance. By this I mean that "historical" and "important" tend to reflect the political and economic contemporary concerns of those who are in positions of power. In important books written by Christine Boyer (1994) and by Dolores Hayden (1995) they argue that the historical past that is reflected in structures and buildings reflects a subjective view of history that often minimizes the activities and involvements of women, people of color, and those who constituted the lower economic and less powerful social classes. Thus, only those structures and buildings that support the current view of the historical past are preserved and those that provide alternative evidence of a different historical past are destroyed.

Further, Boyer and Hayden in their respective works argue that history and collective memory of the past have significant instrumental value in influencing contemporary community consciousness and awareness of not only the past but of present urban and community politics as well.

In *The City of Collective Memory* (1994), Christine Boyer focuses on projects that would create meaningful and imaginative public spaces. These projects would illuminate a comprehensive and inclusive collective memory that would encompass those interpretations of the past held by marginal community groups. The projects envisioned by Boyer would go beyond the more traditional approach of city image building that merely reinforces an unblemished view of the historical past, an approach that attempts to preserve the "triumphant culture of consumption, designer skylines and packaged environments" that "enhance the prestige and desirability of place" (Boyer 1994: 5). Boyer decries, "The contemporary arts of city building (that) are derived from the perspective of white, middle-class architectural and planning professionals who worry in a depoliticized fashion about a city's competitive location in the global restructuring of capital, and thus myopically focus on improving a city's marketability by enhancing its imageability, livability, and cultural capital" (Boyer 1994: 4–5).

Christine Boyer is concerned with the relationship between history and memory and whether that relationship can foster the revitalization of the public realm in the urban landscape. She believes that this can occur when urban space more accurately reflects the historical past of all those who used it. She calls for the inclusion of the entire community into the design elements even when that historical past may prove bothersome to the official interpretation. "The public realm of the City of Collective Memory should entail a continuous urban topography, a spatial structure that covers both rich and poor places, honorific and humble monuments, permanent and ephemeral forms, and should include places for public assemblage and public debate, as well as private memory walks and personal retreats" (1994: 9). One such example of the type of project that Boyer favors has been the "Power of Place" project of Los Angeles's Community Redevelopment Agency.

The Power of Place Project: Los Angeles

Dolores Hayden is an urban historian who is concerned with the interpretation of historic places, people, movements, and events. She specifically writes about women's and ethnic histories in urban places in the context of the relatively new movement of historians and geographers who are reexamining the uses of space by society.

Hayden's book, *The Power of Place*, provides an account of the preservation of places of community memory in Los Angeles. *Power of Place* documents both a preservation project and the history that is to be preserved. Hayden argues that planners involved in historic preservation should understand that the historic preservation of the architecture and histories of multiple classes, ethnicities,

The wall commemorating the life of Grandma Biddy Mason, located in the park celebrating her life. This site was developed through the efforts of Dolores Hayden, the president of The Power of Place and project director, and others who sought to preserve the "public past in the downtown landscape." Photo by author.

and genders is important. Urban renewal and economic development is a powerful tool that can cleanse the landscape of any references to past inhabitants—their struggles, lives, and uses of place. Her work can be seen as part of a larger movement of historians, sociologists, and geographers who are reexamining the uses of space by society.

Hayden demonstrates how physical memory of a place can valorize a people's history—despite the onslaught of the urban growth machine. She defines the power of place as "the power of ordinary urban landscape to nurture citizens' public memory, to encompass shared time in the form of shared territory" (Hayden 1995: 9). She asserts that urban planners involved in historic preservation should understand that the historic preservation of the architecture and histories of multiple classes, ethnicities, and genders is important. Urban renewal and economic development is a powerful tool that can cleanse landscape of any references to past inhabitants—their struggles, lives, and uses of place.

The Politics of Power is a nonprofit program dedicated to celebrating the lives of people who have lived and worked in Los Angeles. Hayden focuses specifically on one project, the Biddy Mason wall and park in downtown Los Angeles. Biddy Mason Park includes a fountain, furniture, paving, lighting, signage, and permanent, public artworks that commemorate the life of Biddy Mason, a former slave who rose to prominence as a midwife, landowner, and church community leader in nineteenth-century Los Angeles. The Biddy Mason wall chronicles the story of Mason's life, along with aspects of Los Angeles history, on a black concrete wall with photographs on limestone, impressions of objects embedded into the concrete during construction, carved steel panels, and attached metal letters.

The commemorative park and wall honor the existence of an African American woman who once resided in the neighborhood, but who was largely forgotten. The Biddy Mason wall and park represent efforts to revitalize Los Angeles's downtown's historic center by the Community Redevelopment Agency. Hayden argues that the Biddy Mason wall reflects not only good design but it acknowledges the existence of previous uses even if no structure remains. She observes that there is a considerable amount of history yet to be acknowledged with appropriate monuments.

The events that surround the discovery of slave quarters in the historic Independence Hall area of Philadelphia also serve as prime examples of both Hayden's and Boyer's concerns about the hidden history of poor or disenfranchised people of color or gender.

Independence Hall, the National Park Service, and the Reinterpretation of History

In 2002 the National Park Service was excavating the ground near Independence Hall in Philadelphia, to build a $9 million pavilion for the Liberty Bell and for an interpretation and orientation center on the Revolutionary War and early nationhood period in Philadelphia. The planned entrance to the pavilion was discovered to be the site of slave quarters. It was here that George Washington housed some of his slaves when he lived in Philadelphia in the 1790s during his first term in office as the first president of the United States. Washington brought both "house as well as stable slaves with him from his Mount Vernon plantation to Philadelphia." This was despite the fact that slavery was illegal in Philadelphia (Washington, Jr., *The Philadelphia Tribune* 2002).

Initially, the government decided not to promote or even recognize the existence of slave buildings in Revolutionary-era Philadelphia. A spokesperson for the U.S. Park Service, Phil Sheridan, argued that the historical mission of the proposed Independence Mall and Liberty Bell Pavilion was to promote the Liberty Bell, not to focus on Washington's slaves. *The Philadelphia Tribune*, the major newspaper and voice of the African American community in Philadelphia, editorialized: "This not-the-right-time/right place posture of U.S. Park Service officials is fraught with irony beyond the fact the agency charged with preserving and interpreting American history is actively engaged in actions that ignore and annihilate a significant aspect of American history" (Washington, Jr., *The Philadelphia Tribune* 2002).

The National Constitution Center is located in the Independence Hall Historical area, the site of the Liberty Bell, Independence Hall, and the recently discovered slave quarters that existed in Philadelphia in the late eighteenth century. The National Park Service initially wanted to ignore the existence of the slave quarters but, bowing to public pressure, their history is now being told in the National Park Service Interpretive Center. Photo by author.

However, public outcry at the blatant attempt to hide history led to an accommodation that will have slavery and the Liberty Bell in spatial juxtaposition. The controversy has an added dimension. In the past, when National Park officials talked about the Liberty Bell, they observed that it gained symbolic importance after slavery abolitionists before the Civil War adopted it as their symbol. They named it the "Liberty Bell," and it became their icon for freedom. Later this symbol took on its contemporary "generic" quality. This historical fact has long been overlooked. The irony is that they initially wanted to ignore the historical circumstances of slavery in Philadelphia during and after the Revolutionary War. Bowing to political pressure this history has been incorporated in the commemoration of the site's link to slavery with the new Liberty Bell Pavilion.

Of further interest is the new realization that by including Philadelphia's historical past connection with slavery, the National Park Service's Independence Pavilion may attract a much sought-after diverse tourist population. Additional memorials, tours, and educational programs are being proposed that would explain in a much more comprehensive and inclusive manner a new emerging view of Philadelphia, its diverse early settlers, and the history of the new republic.

> What is at stake could have enormous consequences—for the city; which has been saddled with what many view as a stodgy, if not exclusionary, sense of its past; for the National Park Service, which is trying to engage an increasingly diverse America; for cultural tourism in a region that is aggressively seeking visitors of color; and for black and white Americans who seem more than ready to connect with the reality of the nation's origins and development. (Salisbury 2003:C1)

The list of potential projects include: a museum devoted to the African American experience and to Richard Allen, founder of the first African Methodist Episcopal (AME) church in America; the inauguration of an Underground Railroad walking tour by the Independence National Historical Park; the reconstitution of a Civil War Library and Museum; and further archaeological investigations that would include excavations of eighteenth-century free African homes. The initiatives for this and similar projects are based on grassroots interests (Salisbury 2003). Salisbury argues that "taken together, the museums, programs and other activities have the potential to alter the city's cultural and historical identity radically" (Salisbury 2003: C3).

Salisbury believes that, taken together, these projects will reframe Philadelphia's identity as not only the birthplace of the American polity but also as the birthplace of black American and contemporary American diversity. The economic benefits to the city are not being ignored. It is estimated that about a third of the visitors to Philadelphia are nonwhite. That translates into tourist dollars of about $1 billion in annual revenue. Tanya Hall, the head of the Multicultural Affairs Congress of the Philadelphia Convention and Visitors Bureau, observes that these projects, along with a more inclusive-oriented National Park Service, are essential in making Philadelphia a destination choice for *tourists of color* (cited in Salisbury 2003: C3, italics added). Of final note, Mary Bower, the new superintendent of Independence Park, realizes the potential for these new developments in the emerging new collective memory of Philadelphia: "There's going to be a cultural mind shift here, and a new vision for the park" (quoted in Salisbury 2003: C3).

However six months later, as of the July 4th holiday, 2004, the public outcry that led the Park Service to agree to revamp the Liberty Bell exhibits to include a commemoration mentioning the existence of slavery in colonial Philadelphia was still unrealized. Stephen Salisbury of the *Philadelphia Inquirer*, reports that, "there is still no mention, no marker, no sign acknowledging the fact that Washington's slaves were housed near the Liberty Bell Center entrance" (2004: B4). This has led to increased resentment within the African American community. Michael Coard, a representative of the Avenging the Ancestor Coalition, feels that a commemoration would reflect both "historical ammunition" as well as "cultural ammunition" and the lack of such a commemoration reflects on the "embarrassment" of the government: "It's the embarrassment of acknowledging that there was a hell of slavery right in the middle of their haven of liberty" (Coard quoted in Salisbury 2004: B4).

Nearly a year later, in June 2005, Stephen Salisbury (Salisbury 2005: B3), who has been following this unfolding story, reports that finally there has been a fundamental rethinking—"a seismic shift in the approach"—by the National Park Service. In collaboration with two other agencies, the National Park Service has opened the Independence Living History Center in a retooled part of the previously used Visitors Center. The center has implemented an innovative program that is a working archaeological laboratory open to the public. Professional archaeologists are involved in a detailed analysis of more than 30,000 artifacts found at various sites around Independence Park. Visitors can witness the archaeologists at work as they research the reclamation of old tools and everyday household items—housewares, fragments of clothing, weapons, and innumerable other artifacts.

The current focus of the archaeological research is the study of artifacts that were evacuated from the home of a former slave, James Oronoko Dexter. Dexter bought his freedom and became a confidant of some of Philadelphia's most wealthy families, devoting his life to the betterment of Africans living in Philadelphia and the United States. Salisbury reports that this man, a founder of Philadephia's first black church and a founding member of the nation's first black self-help organization, had been virtually forgotten by history and "his name had vanished from memory" (Salisbury 2005: B3)

The Independence Park area was one of the most significant neighborhoods of postcolonial Philadelphia. It was a community in which diverse groups of people lived and worked and is a prime example of what the historian Sam Bass Warner has called the "walking city." Salisbury (2005: B3) reports that the significance of the research is that a more complete profile on everyday city life can be made when the project is completed.

> When work on that is completed in several years, Independence Park will be able to paint a portrait of one of the most interesting neighborhoods in the early city, a place where free blacks lived next door to wealthy Quaker merchants, Irish laborers, German shopkeepers, and Welsh clerks . . . . The block shows how deeply rooted the nation's cultural diversity actually is. And the remaining artifacts will convey a detailed portrait of ordinary life as vivid as any such portrait anywhere, archaeologists hope. (Salisbury 2005: B3)

And to think that just three years earlier, when these artifacts were first unearthed, the National Park Service Planned to ignore them and keep them buried beneath a planned bus depot. The public outcry made those plans inoperable. As a consequence, the history of a community and its diversified people—a history that is older than the nation itself and that is located in the city which was the site where the nation declared its independence—has been reclaimed.

Part **III**

City Imagery and the Social Psychology of City Life

7

The City as a Work of Art

Paris and the Impressionists
New York City and the Ashcan School
Mural Art as Street and Community Art

Philadelphia's Mural Arts Program
The Murals of Los Angeles

People's impressions of a building, a street, a neighborhood, and, indeed, a whole city are more than visual awareness of their surroundings. Impressions and perceptions, experiences and memories are strongly influenced by a host of psychological and sociological factors. An individual confronts one's environment through social constructions based on mental pictures of that environment. Often we observe that one's mental map or image overlaps and complements another's. This is not surprising in that a person's mental map is a product of social interaction. The way we perceive space and the environment is socially learned and is based on experience.

The imagery of the city can be seen as a result of how people perceive the city. Urban imagery also has consequences in the shaping of city life itself. Urban images have a symbolic function. Images help provide strong associations with a place that help facilitate interaction between people who share a common environment. Shared images of places and communities are the facilitator in the development of strong bonds between people. The urban social geographer Kevin Lynch has pointed this out:

> The landscape plays a social role as well. The named environment, familiar to all, furnishes material for common memories and symbols which bind the group together and allow them to communicate with one another. The landscape serves as a vast mnemonic system for the retention of group history and ideals. (Lynch 1960: 126)

The urban historian R. Richard Wohl and the symbolic interactionist Anselm L. Strauss concurred with this observation. As pointed out in the introductory chapter of this book, Wohl and Strauss (1958) provide a number of examples of how people find a shorthand physical symbol for the city. This symbol helps to both organize impressions of the city and to facilitate daily activity.

What is not emphasized in the analyses of Lynch and Wohl and Strauss is the recognition that the image of the city is not based solely on the ease of perceptual readings of the city, but is influenced by underlying political, economic, and social factors. Probably the strongest proponents of this viewpoint are the followers of the urban political economy perspective. The ideas of Mark Gottdiener, who combines political economy within a sociospatial framework, are of particular relevance. Gottdiener is interested in the role of ideology in the structuring of urban space. In his essay "Culture, Ideology, and the Sign of the City" (1986), he takes issue with the socio-culturalist school of urban ecology represented by the work of Walter Firey, and the communications model of urban planners such as Kevin Lynch and his followers. Gottdiener argues that urban imagery is not simply a visibility cognitive matter as Lynch proclaims but rather is a result of ideological factors.

Urbanists such as the urban art historian Donald J. Olsen have long noted that great cities go beyond their economic dimension and should be appreciated as "deliberate artistic creations intended not merely to give pleasure but to contain ideas, inculcate values, and serve as tangible expressions of thought and morality" (Olsen 1986:4). In a wonderful and insightful book, Olsen (1986) examines three nineteenth-century European capitals, London, Paris, and Vienna, and suggests through the title of his importance of conceiving *"the city as a work of art."* In referring to these nineteenth-century cities as works of art, Olsen deliberately makes the contrast with contemporary historians and social scientists who have focused on the "pathological aspects of modernity" (1986: X). He argues for the necessity to approach the study of the city as "objects to be cherished and understood rather than as evils to be exposed, as works of art rather than instances of social pathology" (1986: X).

Olsen stresses the importance of understanding the importance of "history" as well as that of technology in "shaping the consciousness and determining the conduct of the ordinary European during the century preceding 1914." What he means by "history" is "not objective historical forces, in a Marxist or any other sense, but patterns of thought, systems of categorization, modes of perception associated with the study and interpretation of human history . . ." (Olsen 1986: 296–97).

In this Chapter I will be examining the city as a work of art that not only reflects an image of the city but that also is anchored by an underlying social, political, and economic agenda. I will provide two historical examples and two contemporary examples that convey different imagery of the city. The historical examples are nineteenth-century Paris seen through the eyes of the Impressionists, and early twentieth-century New York City as seen by the social realists, members of the Ashcan School. The two contemporary examples reflect current concerns: graffiti artists and street muralists whose work appears in Los Angeles, Philadelphia, and New York City.

Paris and the Impressionists

It is my business, to take foreigners 'round the city and show them all the beauties of the capital.

Operetta character, *La Vie Parisienne,* by Jacques Offenbach, libretto by
Henri Meilhac and Ludovic Halevy (1867) (Gache-Patin 1984:109)

The creation and development of the great industrial metropolitan cities of the nineteenth century, such as London, Paris, and Vienna, helped define that century. Social scientists and social reformers sought to understand the nature and character of the new urban life emerging in these metropolises. Initially, the sweeping changes affecting the newly migrated poorer working class groups caught the attention of social scientists, social commentators, and social reformers. Urban slums were characterized by social disorganization. The dramatic increase in such conditions as poverty, child labor, desertions, prostitution, illegitimacy,

Caillebotte's Paris: A Rainy Day *1877 has become one of the definitive images of the affluent Parisians strolling in Paris after Baron Haussmann's rebuilding of that city.*

and abuse of women and children shaped perceptions of city life. The vivid writings of such novelists as Charles Dickens in *Oliver Twist* and *Hard Times* provide startling portraits of a harsh new way of life.

Concomitantly, much attention was also given to the new way of life of the emerging bourgeois class. For example, the novels written by Jane Austen (for example, *Pride and Prejudice, Sense and Sensibility*, and my wife's favorite, *Emma*) examine the bourgeois character with its virtues and blemishes. In addition, the new industrial cities were being constructed and the narrow and twisted sections of the old city were being reconstructed and transformed to make the city a fit and *most proper* setting for the new bourgeois. Nowhere else but Paris do we see the transformation of cities to be *the* site for the upwardly mobile elite classes. And nowhere else do we see the city depicted so brilliantly visual. It was French Impressionism that bathed the city in dazzling sunlight.

As sociologists, we tend to think of the nineteenth-century European city in the Dickensian imagery of the gloom of industrial development and of dark and filthy streets and slums characterized by social disorganization—an image echoed in the conceptual frameworks of the early sociologists, including de Tocqueville, Marx and Engels, and Maine and Tönnies. Yet, when we think of nineteenth-century Paris, the imagery is of broad boulevards, of scenes of everyday street festivals, of happy people publicly congregating in its innumerable cafes and restaurants or promenading down these boulevards or spending leisurely time in parks. Our imagery is bathed in the luminescent light of French Impressionism paintings. The depiction of Paris by the Impressionists (Manet, Renoir, Monet, Caillebotte, Morisot, and Pissarro, among others) provides a luminous portrait of a city designed and conceived for the emerging bourgeois middle classes. In this discussion, I will examine the imagery of Paris and how it was created through the radical rebuilding of the city. I will also temper this portrait with an examination of the situation of the decidedly less affluent in that same city for whom the transformation of Paris meant something quite else.

In the nineteenth century, Paris, like its urban counterparts in England and Germany, witnessed tremendous growth. At the beginning of the century its population was a little more than a half million; by the end it had nearly three and one-half million people. In the early part of the nineteenth century, Paris became the central terminus of France's rapidly developing railway system. In the 1830s it experienced an industrial and financial boom. By 1848, it had become one of the leading manufacturing cities in the world. Over 400,000 people worked in small factories, very large textile mills, and heavy industry factories and chemical plants (Girouard 1985). Yet, Paris at mid-century still reflected its medieval past, with narrow, winding, and filthy streets, with little sanitation or outdoor lighting. It experienced daily traffic jams that severely handicapped the distribution of its working population and the conducting of economic activities. What the autocratic government believed was necessary was a radical transformation of Paris.

The new Paris was built in the aftermath of the revolutions of the mid-nineteenth century by the engineering prefect, Baron George-Eugene Haussmann, who worked under the authorization of the dictatorial Louis-Napoleon Bonaparte (Napoleon III). *Haussmannization* is the term used to refer to this radical restructuring of Paris. Baron Haussmann's plans were the obliteration of large swaths of land. Using modern technology, he bulldozed through poor and working-class communities. Entire neighborhoods were demolished; the evicted were forced to migrate to the outlining districts. The Paris before 1848 was characterized by narrow, twisting streets. Street design not only prohibited the speedy movement of traffic but it also served as a maze that prevented the deployment of troops to stop revolutionary activities and to apprehend and capture their perpetrators. The razing of much of the old Paris and its replacement by broad boulevards and new high-story apartment dwellings accomplished a number of objectives. It allowed for the deployment of brigades to march unobstructed and unimpeded, if need be, through the center of the city. The redeveloped districts allowed for the construction of restaurants and cafes, theaters and parks, where an affluent bourgeoisie could see and be seen by their peers.

The Paris of our contemporary imagination was constructed in the mid-nineteenth century. Impressionism must be seen in the context of the transformation of Paris and how it was integrated into the social and cultural bourgeois life of the times. Robert L. Herbert (1988) demonstrates how Impressionist painters were both participants and observers of the emerging modern life of consumption and display. The underlying themes of leisure and entertainment dominated Parisian life from 1865 until 1885. The streets, cafes, dance halls, opera houses, theaters, restaurants, and parks of Paris became the subject matter of the Impressionists.

Weinberg, Bolger, and Curry cite the belief of a contemporary commentator on the necessity to portray modern life in the "age of great cities" (1994:135). The portrayal of the urban scene became the quintessential aim of the French Impressionists. Edmond Duranty, a reviewer of the second Impressionist exhibition in 1876, proclaimed:

> It was necessary to make the painter leave his skylighted cell, his cloister . . . and to bring him out among men, into the world. The idea was to take away the partition separating the studio from everyday life. We need the particular note of the modern individual, in his clothing, in the midst of his social habits, at home or in the street. (quoted in Weinberg, Bolger, and Curry 1994:136)

Haussmann created broad tree-lined boulevards with adjacent areas of parks and squares. The boulevards were enormous thoroughfares, extremely wide and miles long. Lining the boulevards were shops, cafes, restaurants, theaters, and elegantly balconied apartments; these became the recreational and residential sites for the emerging bourgeois class. Picking up on the work of Walter Benjamin (1995), Sir Peter Hall proclaims "the boulevards are not everyday streets; they are theatrical spaces, designed for display" (1998:721). The ultimate goal was the creation of a city designed to impress and one that reflected civic and national pride. In Donald Olsen's words:

> The boulevard de Sebastopol, the boulevard Malesherbes, the future avenue de l'Opera, though dedicated to private residence and private business, were designed to elicit quite same surge of civic and national pride that the place de la Concorde, Notre Dame, and the Louvre called forth. Paris had its share of private retreats, hidden back courtyards, narrow passages, and unpretending sides streets in its older quarters, colonies of bourgeois villas in its outlying suburbs, where it put aside its

full-dress uniform. But no city anywhere has taken more seriously its duties to look and behave throughout as if the eyes of the world were on it and the honor of the nation at stake. (Olsen 1986: 291; also quoted in Hall 1998: 721).

It is Haussmann's Paris, which became the city as a work of art that was so vividly captured by the Impressionists, that is our concern. The public life of the bourgeoisie and their leisure pursuits was a central Impressionist theme. However, before I begin this examination, it is important that we also recognize and are fully aware of how Haussmannization can be seen as the precursor of the urban renewal and public works programs that occurred in the United States after World War II.

The eminent architectural historian, Spiro Kostof, reminds us that it is essential to understand the legal and political underpinnings of Haussmannization to understand twentieth-century policies of urban renewal. He observes that the redevelopment of Paris was one of the earliest manifestations of urban planning or "urban embellishment," in which the state had the right to designate parts of the cityscape as incompatible with urban change. This designation allowed the state to confiscate private property in favor of the "public good." Using the power of eminent domain, the power of condemnation, and compulsory purchase, Haussmann was able to expropriate land and develop it as the state chose without the consent of those who owned it. "Haussmannization is often synonymous with social engineering in that it relieves the cities of their populist ferment and isolates the possessing classes from the pressure of the poor and the unempowered" (Kostof 1992: 266).

The benefits of the reconstruction of Paris were for public health (the elimination of slums and opening areas to light and air), the creation of modern housing and business premises, and social order. It was the concern for "social order," through the ability to thwart the building of street barricades to allow armies to move easily down the broad boulevards, that many saw as a major purpose of the reconstruction. Walter Benjamin, the influential Marxist essayist of pre–World War II Europe, had commented that the true purpose for the design of the wide boulevards was to help secure the city in the case of civil war. Paris had witnessed horrible street battles during the French Revolution and the Revolutions of 1830 and 1848. Benjamin observed, however, that in the 1871 Commune uprisings, which occurred after the disastrous loss of the Franco-Prussian War, the barricades that were constructed were stronger and better secured than ever (Benjamin 1995).

The urbanization and transformation of Paris emphasized social stratification. The poor were forcibly removed from the cleared streets. By design, Haussmann failed to provide sufficient public housing for the poor in the redeveloped areas. When one of the older neighborhoods was "haussmannized" its economic residential makeup was inevitably altered. While the apartment houses along the boulevards were becoming occupied by the more affluent, some of the displaced people were able to find accommodations off the boulevards. But a much greater percentage of the people now living in the "haussmannized" areas were the bourgeoisie (Willms 1997).

Most of the poor were forced to move to the outskirts of Paris in what has been called the *ceinture rouge* ("red belt"), so named for the propensity of its residents to vote communist (Kasinitz 1995). A contemporary observer in 1863 remarked, "The transformation of Paris has evicted the working population from the center to the periphery, so that two circles have developed within the capital: one rich, the other poor; the one encircling the other. The needy class is like an enormous belt enclosing the wealthy class" (cited in Willms 1997: 271).

The streets were depicted as turbulent places and the sites for political upheaval. It was in the streets that the populace demonstrated their disenchantment and revolutionary fervor against the existing political structure. During the street fighting of the Revolutions of 1830 and 1848, the barricades in the street became a highly politicized imagery of the Parisian cityscape. "To represent the street was to represent a politically contested urban space, the principal arena where the 'people' periodically expressed their collective power and where the governing bodies of 'order' were forced to address or suppress such public displays" (Distel et al. 1995: 90). The depiction of liberty leading the people, by Eugene Delacroix, a leading romantic painter, is a symbolic presentation of the revolutionary meaning of the street.

The Haussmannization transformations of the city generated artistic and public interest in street imagery and photographs, prints, and literary expression. It was through the paintings of the group of avant-garde painters who would become known as the "Impressionists" that the new layout of Paris was depicted and glorified. "Haussmann's Paris, with its broad, elegant boulevards and vistas artfully focused on monuments, also became a model for something else—for urban life as a work of art, as esthetic experience, a public spectacle *san pereil*" (Kostof 1992: 266–67). The Impressionists painted the pageantry of the street and the movement of the pedestrians. Probably one of the most famous paintings of the ascendancy of the bourgeoisie in public space is Gustave Caillebotte's monumental painting *Paris Street: Rainy Day* (1877).

The nineteenth-century poet and social critic Charles Baudelaire wrote an influential essay, *La Peintre de la Vie Moderne* [The Painter of Modern Life] that served as the inspiration for many Impressionist painters to portray contemporary urban life. The painters were encouraged by Baudelaire to take the perspective of the *flaneur*—the personification of the modern spectator. "The perfect *flaneur* was the 'passionate spectator,' the modern man who was in his element wandering amid the ebb and flow of the urban crowd and whose most guarded possession was the anonymity made possible by life in the city" (Fer 1993: 30). In many paintings the *flaneur* is depicted as a man of leisure, a dandy, who observes life with cool detachment. The top hat is often his fashion symbol, reflecting Baudelaire's belief that fashion was an integral part of modernity and should be portrayed in art. Edouard Manet's painting *Music in the Tuileries Gardens* (1862) reflects the influence of Baudelaire's essay. In this painting of members of Parisian high society enjoying an outing in the Tuileries, Manet includes himself, Baudelaire, and the composer Jacques Offenbach, among others (Welton 1993).

The importance of transportation and industry to the new Paris was of special importance to the Impressionists. Caillebotte's *On the Europe Bridge (1876–1877)* and *The Pont de l'Europe (1876)* depicts pedestrians on the bridge. Monet used the train stations of Paris as a frequent subject matter for his paintings [*The Europe Bridge at Saint-Lazare Train Station (1877), Saint-Lazare Train Station (1877), Saint-Lazare Train Station, The Normandy Train (1877)*].

Another result of the Haussmannization of Paris was the reality of Paris as the site of tourism and consumerism. Rupert Christiansen in his historical account quotes a contemporary critic that Paris had become "an object of luxury, and curiosity more than of usefulness, a town of exhibition, placed under glass, hostelry to the world, the object of foreigners' admiration and envy, impractical for its inhabitants, but unique in the comforts and pleasures of all kinds it offers to the sons of Albion" (Fournel cited in Christiansen 1994: 106).

The *Paris of Commodity* was revealed in the grand, wide, and elegant boulevards of Paris, which were lined with the new "sidewalks." The parks and boulevards of the "new" Paris became the subject of many Impressionists, most notably Monet and Pissarro. It was here that the *flaneur* strolled among the gathering of strangers, watching and participating with them in the innumerable cafes, in theaters of drama, comedy, ballets, and opera, in dance halls, racetracks, and in gardens and parks. The themes of leisure and entertainment dominated the great years of Impressionist paintings. Auguste Renoir's paintings of life in the urban cafes continue to delight our imagination and lead to the desire to be a participant in its seemingly endless leisure time. It was here that Parisians enjoyed their leisure—the reward of industrialization and urbanization. Pierre Auguste Renoir's *Le Moulin de la Galette* (1876) is a celebration of the good life and the social glamour of the emerging urban life.

The brightness and gaiety of the sunlit day has its counterpart in the night scene. It was Henri Toulouse-Lautrec who portrayed the seamier side of urban life. His paintings of the urban underworld of prostitution and alcoholism, of risk and strangeness, run counter to the color of Renoir's brilliant daylight Paris. The life of the Paris night also captures our imagination by providing the opposite side of the coin of the reality of urban life. In *A Corner in the Moulin De La Galette* (1889), painted 13 years after Renoir's celebrative painting, Toulouse-Lautrec created a darker vision of cafe life. As Jude Welton (1993) points out, this composition of unsmiling girls and a sinister-looking man watching dancers is in stark contrast to the dance hall's sunny pleasures as seen by Renoir. Toulouse-Lautrec's paintings of life at the Moulin Rouge reveal a harsher, grimmer, and more depressing reality of Parisian life, one not reflecting the glorification of the bourgeoisie. It was the American Realist paintings, and particularly the members of the Ashcan School, that fully developed a depiction of urban life that could be seen as a reflection of the city's working classes and the lustiness of its urban life. For the Impressionists, the brightness of the new Paris served as their major theme.

> With its train stations, neighborhoods, and bridges, the Paris of the Impressionists was chiefly remarkable as an out-of-door city, a city of light, atmosphere, and space. Its life was what the French writer, Jean Schopfer called "life in the open air," a truly public and urban life. If the *real* city of Paris was filled with social tensions, class conflict, and urban alienation played out in small apartments and garrets and obsessively recorded by contemporary Realist writers, its inhabitants could escape from such pressures into the boulevards, parks, and quays of the "new Paris."

On the Steps. *George Luks (1867–1933), oil on wood panel. George Luks was one of the "Ashcan" painters whose social realism paintings evoked the aura of urban life in the early twentieth-century.*

The very grandeur and healthiness of this new city—that pictured by Monet, Pissarro, and the rest—is set into relief when compared to the patterned apartments of Pierre Bonnard and Edouard Vuillard and the claustrophobic brothels and dance halls of Theophile Steinlen and Henri Toulouse-Lautrec. (Gache-Patin 1984: 116)

New York City and the Ashcan School

"Come take a ride underground . . . In the city where nobody cares."
Edward Laska, Thomas W. Kelly, and Charles K. Harris

The lyrics cited above are from a popular, early-twentieth-century song that conveyed both the optimism and the despair of the urban future. Annie Cohen-Solal, a noted art historian, comments that this song, and others by Laska, Kelly, and Harris, "distilled the dynamism and abandon of the urban culture that was exploding in the world's new great metropolis" (New York City). At the same time that New York City and some other American cities were rapidly growing with new transportation systems, new train stations, and skyscraper buildings, they were also experiencing great housing shortages, inadequate water and sewage systems, and overcrowdedness and congestion.

In the late nineteenth and early-twentieth century, a reform movement developed in the industrial cities of the United States to combat the social disorganization problems that were so pervasive. This reform movement became the major underlying philosophy that influenced the proponents of the Chicago School and others in their analyses of city life. The muckraking novels of the early twentieth century, such as Frank Norris's *The Octopus* and Upton Sinclair's *The Jungle*, focused on the exploitation of immigrants. They took up the cause of the common man against organized corporate power and abuses of privilege. Sinclair and other writers took up the challenge of Theodore Roosevelt, who became president after the assassination of William McKinley in 1901 and who was elected president in his own right in 1904. Roosevelt bellowed the importance of studying the American urban site and admonished writers for being more interested in the picturesque marketplaces of Europe than in the Fulton Street Market in New York City (Hunter 1972). Roosevelt, the former police commissioner and mayor of New York City, observed in his essay "Dante in the Bowery" that "The Bowery is one of the great highways of humanity, a highway of seething life, of varied interest, of fun, of work, of sordid and terrible tragedy, and it is as haunted by demons as evil as any that stalk through the pages of *The Inferno*" (quoted in Hunter 1972: 39).

The art historian Sam Hunter (1972) has observed that novelists, essayists, and painters picked up on the challenge and, along with the social reformers, turned their attention to an examination of social injustice and the ills of social disorganization, including poverty, prostitution, drunkenness and acts of civil impropriety, which were running rampant in urban communities and skid rows.

Social realism was echoed in the works of writers such as Stephen Crane, *Maggie: A Girl of the Street* and Theodore Dreiser, *Sister Carrie*, whose books vividly depicted the deprivations that inevitably befell naive and relatively helpless young women as they encountered the harsh realities of urban life. These are stories of prostitution, of seduction, adultery, and bigamy that were a result of the overwhelming economic circumstances that were beyond their capabilities to control. These fictional accounts were written in a stark, nonjudgmental manner that heightened their impact and startled their middle-class and affluent audiences who had little awareness of the lives of the poor. The disruptive and dangerous nature of everyday street life was a theme that was conveyed in much of their work. Popular songs were also composed on the indifference and noncaring of the rising metropolis to the plight of the poor and the unfortunate.

Like London in the mid-nineteenth century, life in these American slums of poverty was almost unknown to the more prosperous residents of the city. Robert Hughes, the art critic, observes that these journalistic works had great appeal to the affluent. They encouraged them to see for themselves the reality of these urban conditions. "The 1900s were a time when the adventurous enjoyed a bit of class tourism: they went 'slumming' downtown, as their sons and daughters in the 1920s would go to Harlem, for a whiff of strangeness" (Hughes 1997: 332).

Rejecting the urban romanticism of the Impressionists, painters turned to social realism to convey their sensibilities to these concerns. The painters of the "Ashcan School," a name that did not come into common usage until the middle 1930s, were young realist painters who wished to portray the life around them, first in turn-of-the-century Philadelphia and then, more significantly, in New York City. Like Robert Park, the founder of the Chicago School of Sociology, they shared the journalistic conceptualization of urban reality.

The painters included George Luks, John Sloan, William J. Glackens, Everett Shinn, and George Bellows; their leader was Robert Henri. All but Henri and Bellows had experience serving as illustrators for the press. Their depiction of New York City gave graphic meaning to Park's concept of the city as a mosaic of social worlds populated by a world of strangers. "All six artists were newcomers to the city, and their work reveals experiences common to most New Yorkers at the time: the challenge of making sense out of encounters with strangers in a city of unprecedented scale and heterogeneity" (Zurier and Snyder 1995:14). Unlike the French Impressionists and their American followers, these painters sought to portray not only the vitality of city life but also the seamier side of that life.

Their subject matter was the emerging industrial city with particular focus on everyday street life and the nightlife of theaters, dance halls, bars, and fight clubs. They were interested in both the life of the slums and the bustling immigrant neighborhoods as well as of high society. All their work reflected their interest in the urban scene, and they painted it with a realism tinted with a positive affirmation of city life. Cohen-Solal describes their interests most descriptively:

> They reported the clash between the old and the new, the city by day and night, captured an urban civilization in evolution, with its construction sites, elevated trains, skyscrapers, slums, markets, excavation sites, accidents, and fires—elements of a chaotic world of intersecting realities. They painted crowds, boxing matches, and nightclubs. They described the masculine ideal, the changing role of women, and, above all, the immense flood of people that was fast becoming New York's most valuable resource. These were the themes they imported from periodical illustration, transforming them into art with formidable virtuosity in a variety of mediums—pencil pastel, watercolor, gouache, charcoal—and grounding the act of painting in a new spontaneity of execution. (Cohen-Solal 2001:170)

They were less inclined to study the skyscraper, the emerging symbol of corporate urban America, than the people who built it or lived in its shadow (Zurier and Snyder 1995). Yet, they were most aware of its symbolic importance. (I will have more to say on the meaning of the skyscraper as a symbol of corporate America in the next chapter.)

> "It is the fashion to say that skyscrapers are ugly. It is certain that any of the Eight will tell you: 'No, the skyscraper is beautiful. Its twenty stories swimming toward you are typical of all that America means, its every line indicative of our virile young lustiness.'" (Robert Henri, quoted in Cohen-Solal 2001:170)

John Sloan's painting of New York's Madison Park (later given the erroneous title, *Recruiting, Union Square*) is a park nestled among the newly built skyscrapers, including the colossal Metropolitan Life Insurance Company Building.

This skyscraper had made a profound symbolic import in the defining of New York City as a center of corporate capitalism. However, in Sloan's 1909 painting, the building has no such impact. It depicts a genre scene of an army recruiter talking to a potential enlistee on the virtues of military service while children in the foreground examine the recruitment poster, and young women in the background give a backward glance to the two men. Sloan, himself, commented, "I saw a mother explaining to her little son (about six years) the vastness of the Metropolitan Insurance Building tower. He was not apparently impressed!" (quoted in Zurier and Snyder 1995:16).

George Bellows's urban realist subject matter reflected the dynamism and energy of a changing New York—the teeming life in lower Manhattan, prizefighters,) and the excavation of ground for Pennsylvania Station. His paintings of the Lower East Side, especially that of the overcrowding of people captured in his masterful, *Cliff Dwellers* (1913, Los Angeles County Museum of Art) depicts the huddled masses in a way that matches Emma Lazarus's salutation to "the huddled masses yearning to be free . . ." located at the base of the Statue of Liberty. Bellows's preparatory drawing for *Cliff Dwellers* was published in *The Masses*, a socialist periodical. It has the satirical title, *Why Don't They Go to the Country for a Vacation?* The drawing is allegedly based on an uptown socialite's ignorance of poverty, the query implying that the poor people who overflow the streets, fire escapes, and roofs can so easily escape the stifling summer heat. Bellows's portrayals of children swimming along the docks of the Hudson River, *River Rats* (1906, private collection) and *Forty Two Kids* (1907, Corcorran Gallery) show the exuberance of childhood in the midst of a polluted river on a broken-down pier.

Prize fighting was illegal in New York City. To circumvent the law, private clubs like Sharkey's made both fighters temporary members of the club. Bellows's paintings, like his *Stag at Sharkey's* (1907, Cleveland Museum of Art) and *Both Members of This Club* (1909, National Gallery of Art), are graphic ringside level views of the fighters at the height of combat. The crowd is animated and women are noticeably absent, as these clubs denied admission to them.

Bellows was also fascinated by the dynamic changes occurring in New York's architectural structures. His paintings of the excavation of the Pennsylvania Railroad site and the building of Pennsylvania Station, the monumental train station (*Excavation at Night*, Berry Hill Galleries, New York; *Pennsylvania Station Excavation*, 1909, The Brooklyn Museum) evoke the image of a city in dramatic growth. The train station itself was demolished in 1962 to give way to the relatively bland Madison Square Garden. This caused great consternation and ushered in the era of historical preservation. Bellows's images of Pennsylvania Station attract the attention of the viewer to those who helped build it and the machinery that they used with the new skyline is in the background. "From a distance the symbol of the city was its new skyline, the product of the businessmen who directed city's forces of consolidation. But at street level, New York was defined not by buildings but by people, whose diversity gave the city its vital polyglot culture" (Snyder 1995:34).

However, a major theme present in the work of the Ashcan School was a depiction of the slum in a way that showed that the inhabitants, rather than being downtrodden by their situational circumstance, often arose above it. In Sloan's painting of the East Side, in Luks's study of Hester Street, and in Bellows's examination of urban cliff dwellers, we see a more optimistic view. Slum dwellers in these genre scenes are depicted with a vitality that transcends the downside of their environment and instead portrays an ability to redefine their situation in a way that makes even the most awful place a place for hope.

The locale of Luks's *Hester Street* is the vibrant market street where street vendors sell all the commodities necessary for daily life, including fruits and vegetables, meat and fish, pots and pans, towels and linens, and clothing. Similarly, in Michael Gold's classic novel, *Jews Without Money*, he provides a vivid dynamic description of the sights and sounds of the streets of the Lower East Side:

> I can never forget the East Side where I lived as a boy.
> It was a block from the notorious Bowery, a tenement canyon hung with fire escapes, bed-clothing and faces.
> Always these faces at the tenement windows. The street never failed them. It was an immense excitement. It never slept. It roared like a sea. It exploded like fireworks.
> People pushed and wrangled in the street. There were armies of howling pushcart peddlers. Women screamed, dogs barked and copulated. Babies cried.
> A parrot cursed. Ragged kids played under truck-horses. Fat housewives fought from stoop to stoop. A beggar sang.
> At the livery stable coach-drivers lounged on a bench. They hee-hawed with laughter, they guzzled cans of beer.
> Pimps, gamblers and red-nosed bums, peanut politicians, pugilists in sweaters, tinhorn sports and tall longshoreman in overalls. An endless pageant of East Side life passed through the wicker doors of Jake Wolf's saloon.
> The saloon goat lay on the sidewalk, and dreamily consumed a *Police Gazette*.
> East Side mothers with heroic bosoms pushed their baby carriages, gossiping. Horse cars jingled by. A tinker hammered at brass. Junkbells clanged.
> Whirlwinds of dust and newspaper. The prostitutes laughed shrilly. A prophet passed, an old-clothes Jew with a white beard. Kids were dancing around the hurdy-gurdy. Two bums slugged each other.
> Excitement, dirt, fighting, chaos! The sound of my street lifted like the blast of a great carnival or catastrophe. The noise was always in my ears. Even in sleep I could hear it; I can hear it now.
> (Michael Gold 1930/1996, *Jews Without Money*. New York)

In George Luks's 1996/1930:13–14 *Hester Street* the tumult of the street is being observed by the omnipresent *flaneur*, perhaps Luks's surrogate, who is in the scene but is not part of it. Ashcan painters often took on the role of flaneur—the nonparticipant observer of contemporary life who sees but does not partake. The art historians H. Barbara Weinberg, Doreen Bolger, and David Park Curry title a section of their catalog introduction to the exhibition, *American Impressionism and Realism, The Painting of Modern Life, 1885–1915*, which was organized by the Metropolitan Museum of Art and the Amon Carter Museum, Fort Worth in 1994–1995, "Passionate Spectators." *Passionate Spectators* refers to the mid-nineteenth century Parisian poet Charles Baudelaire's "exquisite insight(ful)" term for the *flaneur*"

(Weinberg, Bolger, Curry 1994:15). "For the perfect *flaneur*, for the passionate spectator, it is an immense joy to set up house in the heart of the multitude, amid the ebb and flow of movement, in the midst of the fugitive and the infinite." (Baudelaire cited in Weinberg, Bolger, Curry 1994:15).

Mural Art as Street and Community Art

From time immemorial, people have left their mark on both natural and manmade edifices, whether they be cave or building walls or floors, trees, or monuments. If one could leave one's message for posterity through writing or carving on almost any conceivable surface this has been done. Evidence of this goes back through the pleistocene age in ice-age caves; in ancient Rome in its catacombs and in the ruins of Pompeii; and in modern times to the infamous "Killroy was here." And this practice continues to the present era. *Graffiti* is the term used to describe the inscriptions made on a wall or any surface. The origin of the word is from the Italian word *graffio*, which means a scratching or scribbling.

Beginning in the 1950s and continuing in the 1960s, cities across the United States were confronting rampant graffiti. By the 1970s the graffiti took on "epidemic" proportions. The range of reactions ranged from bitter outrage to glorification of the perceived artistic creations. Some viewed graffiti as a celebration of the unbridled gift of untrained artists who used the public sphere to announce their presence, to use their voice. Some graffiti was perceived as quite artistic. Two of the most notable graffiti artists were Keith Haring and Jean-Michel Basquiat. Both individuals and their work took on almost mystic charismatic qualities, and both died at the height of their notoriety and fame. Basquiat died at the age of 27 of a heroin overdose in 1998; Haring died of AIDS in 1990, at the age of 31.

Some saw graffiti as reflecting the political activism of that time period. Influenced by the late 1960s Civil Rights movement, many local nontrained artists embraced the painting of public walls as a means of voicing the call for social change. Those who saw the positive in graffiti felt that it was a manifestation of the creative genius of heretofore unrecognized individuals, who were expressing their psychological needs or were making a social, economic, and/or political statement on their views of the society. Many young, local nonacademically trained artists depicted on neighborhood wall images that portrayed urban problems such as drugs and racial tensions. In poor neighborhoods the graffiti done by gang members often signified neighborhood gang turf markings. The writings were associated with aspects of city life and were seen as rebellious expressions. Other popular motifs include names, loves, sports, and gang identifications. The visual sociologist Camilo Jose Vergara (1997), through his own photographs, documents how neighborhood residents have brightly painted street-wall murals that depict local and cultural themes as well as street memorials usually of young gang members who perished in local turf battles. Pleading as well as frightening and menacing messages are also mural themes. Vergara observes how these murals provide a sense of presence and a response to the deprivations and realities of ghetto life.

The negative reaction to graffiti viewed it as manifestations of antisocial acts. As graffiti became more and more prevalent, in an effort to stop the graffiti that was defacing so much of public and private surfaces, a number of city governments' implemented anti-graffiti campaigns. The aim was to cover up graffiti as soon as it appeared. Graffiti was seen as a symbol of community neglect and abandonment. This was an echoing of what has been called the "broken windows" theory put forth by Wilson and Kelling. Nathan Glazer, in a 1979 article in *Public Interest*, makes this essential argument in his views on the consequences of graffiti in New York City subways: "While I do not find myself consciously making the connection between the graffiti-makers and the criminals who occasionally rob, assault, and murder passengers," Glazer admits, "the sense that all are a part of one world of uncontrollable predators seems inescapable" (cited in Chang 2002).

In July 2002, at the beginning of New York City's Mayor Michael Bloomberg's administration, Bloomberg grandstanded his opposition to graffiti by whitewashing its appearance on sections of walls in Williamsburg, New York City. Bloomberg announced his cleanup war on graffiti and the continued effort to police and punish offenders. He said: "Even with limited resources, we are not going to walk away from the needs of this city. Graffiti poses a direct threat to the quality of life of all New Yorkers . . . It's not just an eyesore. It is an invitation to criminals and a message to citizens that we don't care" (cited in Chang 2002). Bloomberg's actions follow a long-term battle by governmental officials not only in New York but also in other American cities to combat graffiti.

Philadelphia's Mural Arts Program

Philadelphia is one of those cities that have successfully implemented an anti-graffiti program. In addition to destroying graffiti as soon as it appeared, the idea was to hire graffiti artists under a street art mural program and have them involved in legal paintings that would essentially co-opt them. They would be working for trained artists employed by the municipality whose task was to go into communities and assess their desires for themes that would become manifested as murals on walls and which would replace the unwanted graffiti.

Philadelphia's mural program began in the 1970s as a reaction in part to the two decades of the 1950s and 1960s gang warfare and graffiti. The graffiti was often gang-related, reflecting memorials and turf battles. By the 1970s the gang warfare had mostly dissolved, but graffiti became rampant throughout the city. Jane Golden, the artistic director for Philadelphia's Mural Arts Program, speculates that former gang members "could travel through another gang's territory. They wanted to leave their mark wherever they went. It was a way to achieve an identity. They felt they didn't have one." In addition to "tagging" the term for name writing, scenes were drawn from comic books and original images were drawn on numerous walls.

The initial momentum for the Environmental Arts Program for the Philadelphia Museum of Art's Urban Outreach Program was not to combat graffiti but to beautify communities through street art. Its plan was to include community murals along with other activities. Later, during the administration of Mayor Wilson Goode in the 1980s, a Philadelphia Anti-Graffiti Network (PAGN) was established to combat graffiti wall writing. In 1984 the Philadelphia Department of Recreation Mural Arts Program (MAP) was instituted. In 1984 Jane Golden was hired by the PAGN and would eventually become the artistic director and head of PAGN. MAP would become a city-supported public program working with neighborhood residents, young people, arts, and a wide range of public and private organizations to create murals that reflect the aspirations and experiences of diverse communities (Tremblay 1999).

Golden was initially one of 10 field reps that met with graffiti artists. In exchange for amnesty from prosecution, teenage wall writers were asked to sign "The Pledge" to give up graffiti. In return they were to participate in PAGN's programs. Initially their jobs included cleaning walls but later it included other paid jobs with the city. Between 1986 and 1992 a summer program implemented by PAGN employed 300 to 3000 teenagers each year. In addition to providing summer work, teenagers were also taught art, provided with tutors for high school equivalency, and given apprenticeships with professional artists. The first murals were painted by a group of probationary graffiti artists; now the program includes art classes and internship possibilities for young artists. In 1996, with the death of the founder of the PAGN, Tim Spencer, the program was transformed to the Recreation Department and became MAP. MAP now works primarily with after-school programs and works less to provide community service opportunities to graffiti offenders (Tremblay 1999).

Since, 1984, MAP has sought to work with communities across the city to develop murals that reflect and restore the community. The program, which originally began as a citywide anti-graffiti initiative, redirecting graffiti writers to create arts, has since given birth to more than 2000 murals across the city—the work of local volunteer artists, community leaders, and children. It is one of the largest programs of its kind in the country and has allowed Philadelphia to claim the title of the "mural capital of the country." The argument is that not only do the murals serve to provide a beautified legacy in the neighborhoods in which they appear but they also play a role in changing the image of the city itself. Golden and her colleagues see the murals as giving members of the community an opportunity to express and define themselves; the murals serve as a mechanism to bring disparate elements in the community together. The program's success is seen to lie in the level of neighborhood involvement in each project, so that the resulting product is considered community art and not simply public art.

Murals are developed in consultation and partnership with the communities in which they are located. Neighborhood residents are canvassed, and their input is essential on the design and subject of the murals. Murals often reflect themes of community importance, such as "Safe Streets," "A Celebration of Community," "Compassion," and "Peace Wall." The "Peace Wall" was painted in the wake of a local racial incident in the Grey's Ferry area of Philadelphia. This community was the site of community tensions between the working-class whites and the working-class blacks living there. Through collective work in creating the mural, residents found commonality in the shared activity, which helped sooth tensions and broaden understanding between the two conflicting groups. It shows the hands of people of different ages and races holding hands in a celebration of community unity and contains the inscription "Blessed are the peacemakers: for they shall be called the children of God."

Initially, the murals were painted in North and West Philadelphia. These areas of the city were the site of great poverty, with many vacant lots and abandoned buildings of long-gone industrial and manufacturing businesses. Much of the housing was in a state of disrepair and neglect. The murals were designed to brighten the neighborhoods and to foster community togetherness and pride. "We started in the more impoverished neighborhood. Murals are signs of hope around which neighbors could rally. They're a catalyst for positive change. They change the way people see themselves, their lives, their future" (quoted in Clark 1998).

Ruth Birchett, one of the community leaders of a North Philadelphia neighborhood, describes one such community, one that is defined by what is missing:

> There used to be 50 houses on the street. There was an ice cream parlor and a bakery, a cleaners and a pharmacy. We have lost so very much. This is a government-forsaken neighborhood. (quoted in Halpern 2002)

The current neighborhood consists of no visible commerce. There are no stores. There is a homeless shelter at the end of the street, and around the corner there is a homemade memorial to three neighborhood youths who had been shot that year (Halpern 2002). The mural that was painted on the side wall of the last remaining house on that side of the street is described by Sue Halpern, the author of the *MotherJones* magazine article, as follows:

> Covering the entire side of the last house on the block, the mural shows an elderly black couple looking down on the younger generations—on an anguished woman bemoaning the senseless violence in the neighborhood and on an unwed teenage mother cradling a baby. Traditional African symbols decorate the center of the towering canvas, as do a rainbow and a pair of clasped hands, each meant to convey its own message of hope tempered by love and remembrance. Still, the eye is drawn to the outline of a crack pipe that hovers in the picture like a ghost—a symbol, surely, bust something more as well.
>
> "The main economy here is the drug economy, which is why the crack pipe is in the picture," Birchett explains. "The only people who had trouble with it were the "entrepreneurs." (Halpern 2002)

The success of the mural in fostering a sense of community pride was reflected in the disappearance of drug dealers in the immediate vicinity of the mural. Unfortunately, however, the drug dealers have moved to other streets in the neighborhood. Perhaps optimistically, Halpern sees the mural as becoming a catalyst for community action and neighborhood improvement ("neighborhoods are reclaimed, communities are reconstituted" [Halpern 2002]). She notes that a community garden has been planted and is being tended and people are once again using the streets.

In recent years, the Philadelphia Mural Project has taken on new assignments. Moving from depressed poverty communities, street murals have become symbols of hero worship, community self-pride, and a celebration of community life (Golden 2002). Among those so honored include the basketball star Dr. J (Julius Erving), and the late jazz musician Grover Washington, Jr. (The Dr. J mural is over 38 feet high and is located on the side of a house that overlooks a fenced-off lot.)

In the Italian-American ethnic enclave of South Philadelphia, probably the most famous murals are those that depict the legendary locally born opera singer Mario Lanza, the adopted native-son, Frank Sinatra, and the massive portrait of the former and late mayor, Frank Rizzo, with a backdrop of the 9th Street (Italian) food market. Rizzo was a most controversial figure. His white ethnic constituents viewed him as a staunch supporter of their political power in the face of the growing political strength of the African American community. A local artist who assisted in the creation of the Rizzo mural remarks: "It's the immigrant spirit, the triumph of turning what you have into something more. The murals show what this neighborhood is all about. They show what Philadelphia is all about" (Joe DiBella quoted in Golden et al. 2002: 100).

The mural served as the backdrop for a number of local community and political rallies. It also has been the target of politically motivated graffiti. In 1999,

The mural commemorating Frank Rizzo, a past mayor of Philadelphia, is located on 9th Street in the Italian market, South Philly, Philadelphia. Photo by author.

it was defaced by splattered gray paint and sprayed FREE MUMIA by supporters of convicted cop-killer Mumia Abu-Jamal soon after then–Pennsylvania Governor Tom Ridge signed Abu-Jamal's death warrant. The prime painter of the mural, Diane Keller, remarked after the defacement: "The people who don't like [Rizzo] see the mural as a symbol of his aggressive, larger-than-life imposing figure" (quoted in Golden et al. 2002:101).

The contemporary subject matter of the murals gives them an ephemeral quality reflecting the immediate concerns, secular, religious, and ethnic, of the current community residents. As the neighborhood undergoes change, the murals lose their salience to new residents. In a decade or two murals tend to fade and deteriorate unless there are attempts to preserve them. Golden et al. (2002) explains:

> The murals themes and symbols, even their aesthetic, reflect the concerns and character of the communities for which they are created. This grassroots genesis is both a strength and a vulnerability: Contemporary murals achieve an immediacy and relevance untouched by other forms of public art, but they are also more vulnerable to change. (Golden et al. 2002:21)

An "In Memory" mural located in the Puerto Rican community in Philadelphia. Photo by author.

However, as Golden emphasized on a World News Tonight feature of ABC News, while the murals are current they have great influence:

> "Murals can give visual representation to our past and our present," Golden says. "They're tools of education. Because they can last 20 years, kids, even people's grand kids, can walk by, look at that mural and see the history of this area." (quoted in Jennings 1999)

The Murals of Los Angeles

Two American cities, Philadelphia and Los Angeles, have a friendly competition for the title of "Mural Capital of America." In this section of the chapter I will examine the mural movement in Los Angeles.

Los Angeles is a city with a long history of street art that has promoted community themes. The contemporary murals of Los Angeles stem from a long tradition of public wall art. They were strongly influenced by Mexico's revolutionary governmental mural arts program implemented in the 1920s (Dunitz and Prigoff 1997). Utilizing the creative talents of such muralists as Diego Rivera, David Alfaro Siqueros, and Jose Clemente Orozco (Los Tres Grandes), panoramic murals conveying the spirit of the revolution covered public walls in Mexico City and elsewhere.

During the Great Depression of the 1930s, the United States Federal Government was inspired by the patriotic fervor that these murals generated in Mexico. Under the New Deal, the government implemented the Public Works of Art Projects

A homeless man sitting in a vest pocket park, Santa Monica, Los Angeles. Photo by author.

(PWAP) in 1933. It flourished until 1943 when World War II precipitated its end. Nationwide murals were commissioned, and, as elsewhere, in Los Angeles and other cities in California, murals were designed for the interiors and exteriors of public buildings. Critics have argued that this project often resulted in murals that reified a history of California from an Anglo American perspective to the neglect of the historical contributions of Mexican Americans and Asian Americans as well as other ethnic and racial groups (Westenberg 2001).

Cesar Chavez and the social ferment of the late 1960s and early 1970s also influenced the contemporary mural arts activities in Los Angeles. These murals have had a very strong Latino influence, reflecting the styles of the earlier Mexican muralists. Grassroots-arts organizations and collectives advocated social change, particularly for migrant farm laborers. This and similar advocacy calls for change resulted in the appearance of numerous murals in many urban centers including San Diego, San Francisco, and Los Angeles.

In 1974, the Los Angeles City Council funded the Citywide Mural Project (CMP) under the leadership of Judy Baca. However, CMP was confronted with opposition by the city council on the subject of many of the murals. In response, Baca, along with a number of associates founded the nonprofit, multicultural art center, Social and Public Art Resource Center (SPARC). Under the long-term directorship of Baca, SPARC has had a long history of street art that has promoted community themes.

SPARC was responsible for probably the most famous mural in Los Angeles, "The Great Wall of Los Angeles." This mural is more than 13 feet high and is almost a half-mile in length. The Great Wall is located in San Fernando Valley's Tijunga Wash, a flood-control channel built in the 1930s. A multiethnic history of LA is depicted. The time span goes from prehistoric times, with the major focus being on the post–World War II era. The project began in 1976 and was completed seven summers later. At the onset, 400 underprivileged teenagers executed the design with input from residents, social activists, and academics. Among the artists who contributed to the design were Judy Chicago, Christina Schlesinger, Gary Tokumoto, Yreina Carvantez, and Patricia Valdez (Tannenbaum 2002).

SPARC has become the leader in mural painting in Los Angeles with numerous murals in such Latin American neighborhoods as City Terrace, East LA, and Boyle Heights, and in African American neighborhoods, such as Watts and South Central. The subject matter of the murals reflects pride of community issues, portraits of prominent individuals as well as political figures, and political statements. Murals reflecting political statements can often run into censorship problems with city governmental agencies. *Revolution Evolution,* a mural depicting Emiliano Zapata, the early twentieth-century Mexican leader who advocated land reform and the redistribution of land from wealthy landowners to poor rural workers, aroused the indignation of the City of Los Angeles Cultural Affairs Department. So did the adjacent mural depicting Marcos, a current leader of the Zapatistas movement in Mexico, protesting the North American Free Trade Agreement (NAFTA) treaty. Both murals were seen by the Cultural Affairs Department as inflammatory. Not wishing to upset the Mexican Consulate located near the murals, and despite community support for them, they had them destroyed (Westenberg 2001).

Many of the murals in Los Angeles have a celebratory function (cf Dunitz (1993) for a comprehensive guide to Los Angeles Murals). Major events are depicted on the murals, such as the 1985 Olympics that were held in LA. However, the core of the mural art movement rests on themes that accentuate the positive aspects of community life. The importance of the LA mural movement, especially for its Latino community, is expressed by Raymond Paredes, a former vice chancellor at UCLA and the current director of arts and culture at the Rockefeller Foundation:

> I believe people are going to look back at Los Angeles in the period from the 1970's through the 1990's as having the equivalent importance for the Latino community as the Harlem Renaissance held for the African-American community. Those murals were one of the most significant creations of that historical phenomenon. Coming to terms with the murals will be a test of whether Los Angeles has come to terms with itself; whether it can become a world-class city with a great sense of pride in itself and its heritage. (quoted in Tannenbaum 2002)

Dunitz and Prigoff in their summary statement on the significance of mural arts programs conclude with a cautionary note. Murals should not be seen as solutions for the problems that continue to be manifest in impoverished communities.

> While it is true that mural art is achieving broader recognition and acceptance, those murals that include self-expression and self-definition by artists in impoverished neighborhoods, whose work seldom has been valued by the formal art community, are the heart of the mural movement. Murals are certainly no panacea for cities rife with decay or youth otherwise abandoned by government, schools, the job market and families. But community murals can be seen as an empowering force, giving visibility to community issues and serving as a means of communication between peoples and cultures. (Dunitz and Prigoff 1997:18)

8

The Skyscraper as Icon

Robert Park's description of the "city as a state of mind" proclaims a basic premise of symbolic interaction thought on the nature of urban imagery and urban identification: "The city is, rather, a state of mind, a body of customs and traditions, and of the organized attitudes and sentiments that inhere in these customs and are transmitted with this tradition" (Park 1925/1966:1). As you recall, R. Richard Wohl and Anselm L. Strauss (1958) pick up on that theme by informing us that given objects of the city become symbolically representative of the city as a whole. Thus the New York skyline, San Francisco's Golden Gate Bridge, and the French Quarter of New Orleans have all become the identification symbol of the given city and serve as a source of personal identification for the inhabitants. Wohl and Strauss point out how the spatial complexity and the social diversity of a city often become integrated by the use of "sentimental" history in selected landscapes such as the Water Tower in Chicago or Telegraph Hill in San Francisco. They build on this observation by arguing that an invariable characteristic of city life is that certain stylized and symbolic objects are employed by people in order to "see" the city. "The city, then, sets problems of meaning. The streets, the people the buildings, the changing scenes do not come already labeled. They require explanation and interpretation" (Wohl and Strauss 1958:527).

The complexity of the city calls for symbolic management. Yet few interactionists, aside from Anselm Strauss, have chosen to investigate, on the one hand, the interactional dynamics that lie at the center of urban imagery, and, on the other hand, the degree to which imagery acts as an independent variable in shaping urban life itself. Again as mentioned earlier, what Wohl and Strauss don't emphasize is how that "labeling" process is influenced by people in positions of power, who can redefine "space" in terms of "place."

In a significant essay, "Slums and Skyscrapers: Urban Images, Symbols, and Ideology", Sam Bass Warner, Jr. (1984), argued that photographic art transformed skyscrapers as symbols of corporate power into a "skyline." This skyline imagery revealed to urban dwellers a world of possibility and progress. For Warner, however, the transformation was illusionary in nature and in effect. Turning symbols of corporate power into objects of art deflected attention away from the source of urban problems in the slum and pacified those victimized by them.

Warner's analysis of the downside of urban imagery proposed to show how conflicts intrinsic to capitalist ideology became subterranean. Warner's work, in the least, demonstrates the potential for cross-disciplinary work and for bridging the micro-macro divide. In this chapter I want to look at the skyscraper as an icon of both the city and the society. I will first do a comparative historical analysis by examining the birth of the modern skyscraper in New York City (New York and Chicago are the two cities in the United States credited with "inventing" this cityscape.). The skyscraper symbolized the booming capitalist economy and political realities of this country's industrial power and also had symbolic meanings that helped define the modern urban experience. I then will analyze how, in mid-century, Stalinist Moscow sought to redefine its cityscape by destroying and demolishing most of its churches, cathedrals, and monasteries, seeking to transform its cityscape by substituting secular skyscrapers that would reflect the monumentality of Communism. Finally, I will turn my attention to the end of the twentieth century and the city of Hong Kong. Hong Kong epitomizes in many ways the booming emerging economy of unbridled capitalism as the city moved, perhaps unwittingly, to incorporation into the last great Communist power, China.

And, finally, I want to analyze the World Trade Center as a contemporary symbol of the United States. In this analysis, it will also be useful to understand, in part, the mentality of the terrorists who destroyed the World Trade Center. The symbolic meaning that the World Trade Center had for the terrorists was costly—it destroyed their own lives as well as that of thousands of people.

New York City

The skyscraper—the tall building with passenger elevators and steel-frame construction–was historically developed in New York City and Chicago. The skyscraper became the symbol of corporate America in the late and early twentieth century. The density and narrowness of Manhattan Island dictated the locational density of this innovative urban form and the emergence of New York's unique skyline. The *sight* of that New York City skyline from its harbor became the *site* for the symbol not only of corporate America but also of the United States itself. The story of a few such skyscrapers in New York City will highlight their symbolic and economic importance in the development of corporate America.

F. W. Woolworth holding a nickel and a bag of nickels and dimes is depicted in one of the grotesques supporting the lobby-arcade galleries. This caricatured sculpture is one of twelve depicting individuals involved in the construction of the Woolworth Building. Photo by author.

This section will focus on New York City's Singer, Municipal, Metropolitan Life, and Woolworth buildings and will follow the argument put forth by Fenske and Holdsworth (1991).

In the early years of the twentieth century, the emergence of giant national and soon-to-be international corporations required large amounts of centralized office space. These corporations sought to merge this need with the development of a memorable corporate image that would help advertise the company name nationally and internationally. In addition, smaller commercial and professional firms became interrelated through economic connections with the larger corporations, and they needed office space in close proximity to their larger partners. *Large* office buildings were needed, and *tall* office buildings were desired. The growing dominance in world trade and finance of New York City and its increasing concentration in lower Manhattan "influenced the shaping of the emerging skyscraper city" (Fenske and Holdsworth 1992: 129).

The Singer Building

When it was completed in 1908, the 47-story Singer Tower was the tallest skyscraper yet built—doubling the height of the tallest point on the lower Manhattan skyline. The Singer Tower was composed of two parts. There was a lower building

A view of the Singer Tower in New York, ca. 1908. This office building provided both image and office space for the Singer Sewing Machine Company. Until the destruction of the World Trade Center it was the largest skyscraper ever demolished.

that consisted of a base structure 14 stories high, containing 330,000 square feet of gross floor space. The 27-story tower that rose above it stood 612 feet tall but was very slender–only 70 feet square. The additional office space provided by the tower was only another 130,000 square feet of space.

The facade, the main entrance with a grand staircase, and the tower's two-storied galleried lobby with 16 Italian marble-sheathed columns supporting glazed saucer domes on heavily ornamented pendentives, was an architectural tour-de-force (Landau and Condit 1996). The tower was open to visitors who were willing to pay 50 cents (a considerable sum at that time) to go to its observation area, where they had unobstructed views of New York City, its harbor, and its environs.

From the outset the Singer Building was designed for two purposes—office space and image. The tower provided visibility and gave the Singer Corporation a landmark headquarters. The total office space went beyond the needs of the Singer Company. The president of the company occupied only one of the top floors in the tower; all the other offices was leased to tenants (Fenske and Holdsworth 1991). Nevertheless, the Singer Building became one of the first skyscrapers to become not a civic symbol of the city, like the Parliament buildings of London, but an advertising symbol of a corporation. The ornate beaux-arts style of the building designed by the architect, Ernest Flagg, has been described as of "exuberant elegance" (Landau and Condit 1996:359). Mardges Bacon, an Ernest Flagg scholar, observes that the building was "sumptuous, showy, and richly appointed . . . the kind of office building that corporate clients demanded. Above all else it was good business in an age of big business" (quoted in Landau and Condit 1996:359).

The Singer Building would hold its skyscraper world-height record for less than a year. The 43-story City Investing Building, a speculative office building whose office space was to be totally leased, was constructed directly north of the Singer Building and permanently blocked its northern view. However, the dramatic presence of the Singer Building transformed the New York skyline, and its setback design would set an example for future tower-skyscrapers. "The Singer Tower was an aesthetic triumph that enriched the city by demonstrating the sculptural possibilities of the steel-framed skyscraper . . ." (Landau and Condit 1996: 361). Unfortunately as architectural taste changed to modernism in the 1960s, the Singer Building achieved a second and final world record, albeit a most dubious one. In 1968, it became the tallest office building to ever be demolished. It gave way for the construction of the undistinguished United States Steel Building, which was never actually occupied by that company. It is now referred to as One Liberty Plaza. Paul Goldberger, the architectural critic observes: "The Singer Building may be gone, but what other building will be remembered by a 54-story tombstone? One Liberty Plaza, built on the site of Ernest Flagg's gentle, graceful, and utterly humane Singer Building is aggressively anti-urban" (Goldberger 1979:9).

The period from 1908 to 1915 was marked by a tremendous nationwide boom in office building construction, and New York City was in the forefront of that boom. The skyscraper radically transformed the New York skyline from one based on the prominence of the sacred church steeple to one based on commerce and civic government.

The Metropolitan Life Insurance Building

The increased acceptability of the skyscraper as the symbol of the modern city was no more—as evidenced by, first, the destruction of the Parkhurst Presbyterian Church and, later, by the destruction of one of the foremost churches in America, the Madison Avenue Presbyterian Church. This church was built by the architectural firm, of McKim, Mead & White and was among the finest and last buildings designed by Stanford White. This church stood for only 13 years before it was replaced by the continually expanding Metropolitan Life Building.

The Metropolitan Life Insurance Building and its campanile, built in 1909, symbolized both by its site location and by its architecture the replacement of buildings that had comprised the sacred skyline by ones that proclaimed the monumentality of a secular skyline. The 50-story Metropolitan Life Insurance Tower was the first building to exceed 700 feet in height. It was modeled after the campanile in St. Mark's Square in Venice. A light that Metropolitan Life linked to its advertising slogan topped the campanile: "The light that never fails" (Dupre 1996: 27).

The Metropolitan Life Insurance Company was incorporated in 1868 and by the end of the nineteenth century was one of the nation's largest insurance companies with its headquarters in New York City. Still, by 1906 its assets were still reported lower than its three other and older rivals, the Mutual, New York, and Equitable insurance companies. The tower was conceived to the space needs of Metropolitan Life and to enhance its image. Once built, excess office space was

The Metropolitan Life Insurance Building soon after its construction in 1909. The Madison Avenue Presbyterian Church (seen on the left of the Campanile) was among the finest and last buildings designed by Stanford White and stood for only thirteen years before being demolished by the continually expanding Metropolitan Life Building.

rented, and, as a company official observed, the tower served as "an advertisement that didn't stand the company a cent because the tenants footed the bill" (cited in Fenske and Holdsworth 1991: 140). Advertisements that incorporated the tower into letterheads and logos by tenants and by Metropolitan Life reciprocally benefitted both (Zunz 1990). During its construction Metropolitan Life proclaimed that it was writing more policies and that it "gained more insurance in force than all the other New York companies combined" (cited in Landau and Condit 1996: 361).

The Municipal Office Building

New York City long required a centralized location for its office needs. In 1907 a competition was announced for the design and construction of a municipal building in lower Manhattan adjacent to City Hall and near the Brooklyn Bridge. The architectural design had to incorporate the straddling of a street (Chamber Street) so that bridge traffic would be able to proceed below the building. (The street is now closed to through traffic under the building.) The competition was open to 13 prominent architectural firms. A three-person jury was selected and the ultimate decision was subject to the approval of the commissioner of bridges and the city's art commission. The architectural firms were given instruction to design a first-class office building for the city, one that reflected the monumentality of New York (Landau and Condit 1996). The architectural firm of McKim, Mead, & White submitted the winning design.

The Municipal Building was 559 feet tall and contained a massive 1,250,000 square feet of usable space. It was built in a beaux-arts style that was selected for its "civic character" (Landau and Condit 1996: 374). The various aspects of civic government, including "Guidance, Executive, Power, and Prudence," were represented by classic-style sculpture figures, as were sculpture cherubs representing "Civic Pride and Civic Duty," which adorned the building. The top of the building is a "wedding-cake sequence of colonnaded towers" (Goldberger 1979: 31). A statue of "Civic Fame" sculptured by Adolph Alexander Weinman tops it. Landau and Condit observe: "The Municipal Building attests to the increasing consolidation of expressive form and imagery in civic and commercial buildings, a quality that also characterizes the Singer and Metropolitan towers" (1996: 375).

The Woolworth Building

The Woolworth Building, constructed from 1911 to 1913, was one of the most famous skyscrapers in New York City and was the apex literally and figuratively of the skyscraper boom of the early twentieth century. F. W. Woolworth, the "five-and-ten-cent store" tycoon, commissioned this neo–Gothic-style structure. He instructed its architect, Cass Gilbert, to design the world's tallest building (the height had to be extended several times during the architectural design stage as taller buildings were completed elsewhere in Manhattan). At 792 feet it remained the tallest building in the world until it was surpassed in the 1930s by the Chrysler Building and the Empire State Building.

What both Woolworth and Gilbert had in mind for this head office was a building that would be an imposing urban monument and a tower that would be prominent in the New York skyline, and would be a constant advertisement for the Woolworth five-and-ten cent store. Yet, from its inception, the Woolworth Company planned to occupy just a small portion of the available office space. Indeed the company's headquarters occupied less than two stories of the available 50 floors. The Irving National Bank, which had been the financier from the beginning, occupied the first four stories. The rest of the building was comprised of speculative office use (Fenske and Holdsworth 1991).

The building's Gothic style was suggested by Woolworth and elaborated by Gilbert. He sought as his model the secular Gothic represented by North European town halls with towers. He felt that the Gothic style would give him the "possibility of expressing the greatest degree of aspiration . . . the ultimate note of the mass gradually gaining in spirituality the higher it mounts" (cited in Dupre 1996:29).

The lobby of the Woolworth Building repeated the Gothic-style motif. It also reflected the beaux-arts architectural theory. It has a cathedral-like cruciform layout that incorporates vaulted entrance and elevator halls. The lobby includes a stained-glass skylight, painted murals representing *Commerce* and *Labor* located on mezzanine galleries overlooking the center of the lobby, and walls and floors of various imported and native marbles. Neo-Gothic bronze doors and hardware are often embossed with a "W." The lobby grotesques that appear to support the ceilings of the north and south elevator halls are portraits of various people involved with the building's construction, including Woolworth (counting his nickels and dimes); Gilbert (with a model of the building);

The Woolworth Building, with the Singer Building visible in the background. Its neo-Gothic architectural style inspired its nick-name as the "Cathedral of Commerce."

Lewis Pierson, president of Irving Bank (with a safe deposit box); Louis Horowitz, the head of the building syndicate; and Gunwald Aus, the structural engineer, measuring a girder.

The Woolworth Building was quickly given a sacred name, "The Cathedral of Commerce." The name was coined by the Reverand S. Parkes Cadman at the building's grand opening and has been used ever since. In the opulent brochure that soon became available to its thousands of visitors, the Reverend Cadman alludes to how commerce has replaced religion in the public imagination. "Just as religion monopolized art and architecture during the Medieval epoch, so commerce has engrossed the United States since 1865" (Cadman 1916). In the following passage, he describes how he came to call it "The Cathedral of Commerce":

> Here, on the Island of Manhattan, and at its southerly extremity, stands a succession of buildings without precedent or peer. The vision of their grandiose effect from the Brooklyn Bridge at dusk, when the gathering darkness softens their bold outlines, and every one of the numberless windows coruscates with radiance, is beyond the brush of Turner to paint or the eloquence of Ruskin to describe. It outvies imagination in its most fertile moments. Of these buildings the Woolworth is Queen, acknowledged as premier by all lovers of the city and the commonwealth, by critics from near and far, by those who aspire toward perfection, and by those who use visible things to attain it. When seen at nightfall bathed in electric light as with a garment, or in the lucid air of a summer morning, piercing space like a battlement of the paradise of God which St. John beheld, it inspires feelings too deep

even for tears. The writer looked upon it and at once cried out, "The Cathedral of Commerce"—the chosen habitation of that spirit in man which, through means of change and barter, binds alien people into unity and peace, and reduces the hazards of war and bloodshed. (Cadman 1916: Forward n.p.)

To this day, the Woolworth Building and the Metropolitan Insurance Building remain in the ownership of their respective founding companies, and they, along with the now-demolished Singer Building and the Municipal Services Building, represent the supreme examples of the first skyscraper era, which became the symbol of corporate America.

Moscow

The aspect of Moscow, on approaching it, is extraordinary [Baron von Haxthausen wrote in 1856], and I know no city in Europe which can be compared with it: the finest view is from the heights called Sparrow Hills. (During Soviet period Lenin Hills). Those countless golden and green cupolas and towers (every church has at least three, most of them five, some even thirteen, and there are about four hundred churches) rising from a sea of red housetops, the Kremlin in the midst upon a hill, towering like a crown over all . . . . (quoted in Kostof 1991: 318, who cites E. A. Gutkind, *Urban Development in Eastern Europe, Bulgaria, Romania, and the USSR* [New York, 1972], 43)

It has been hard for outsiders to realize that Russian national feeling is a spiritual emotion largely detached from the mundane things of life, that for centuries past Russia has meant for her people much more than just a country to be loved and defended: "Russia" was more a state of mind, a secular ideal, a sacred idea, an object of almost religious belief—unfathomable by the mind, unmeasurable by the yardstick of rationality. (Tibor Szamuely, *The Russian Tradition,* quoted in Piers Paul Read, *The Patriot: A Novel,* 1995. New York, Random House)

The city of Moscow epitomizes this observation. Timothy J. Colton (1995), in his comprehensive examination of Moscow, observes that Socialist Moscow sought to redefine the cityscape of Moscow to reflect representations of the secular, the statist, and the collectivist over the religious, the commercial, and the individualist. The annihilation of cathedrals, abbeys, fortifications, and ceremonial gates and towers and their replacement by Soviet edifices is evidence of this belief. Similarly, in this post-Communist era changes in the Moscow cityscape provides continued support.

To illustrate this, I want to relate the story of the building, destruction, and the rebuilding of the great Cathedral of Christ our Savior. In the twentieth century the Moscow skyline underwent massive changes that reflected different ideological mentalities. In the early part of the twentieth century in the pre-Bolshevik period, Russian Orthodox churches and monasteries dominated. In 1933 there occurred the destruction of the highest building in Moscow, the Cathedral of Christ the Redeemer (Savior), also known as the Church of the Savior. After World

The new Cathedral of Christ Our Savior built in 1995 as a symbol of the reemergence of the Russian Orthodox Church and the downfall of the communist state. Photo courtesy of James M. Curtis.

War II on that site was built the great Moscow swimming pool. Beginning in the 1950s seven Stalinist skyscrapers were built along with massive apartment house complexes.

In 1947 there was a proposal to build a system of high-rise landmark buildings. The noted architect Spiro Kostof (1991) states that the intention was to re-establish the legibility of the skyline as a means of orientation, which was lost as a consequence of the destruction of many churches and cathedrals and their

A nineteenth century view of the Cathedral of Christ Our Savior. Destroyed in 1931.

replacement by uniform six- to eight-story housing developments in the 1930s. Eight skyscrapers were planned at different strategic visual sites. They were designed to celebrate the entry into the city, which was located at the intersection of major roadways and in close proximity to railroad stations. Two of the eight skyscrapers were hotels, one was the university, two were apartment buildings, and two were designed for governmental functions. Kostof notes that Soviet authorities felt that the placement of the buildings around the city rather than in a skyline cluster would give them a different symbolic meaning than that of the American skyline, which was seen as a symbol of capitalist greed whose disorderly cluster destroyed community values and urban quality.

The Soviet skyscrapers resembled the McKim, Mead & White's Municipal Building in New York City. They had rectangular bodies with recessed stages toward the top, culminating with a sort of thin spire. They were inevitably given the nickname "wedding cake" skyscrapers. Ringing Moscow, these buildings would dominate their respective surroundings.

In the summer of 1994, as a participant at a National Endowment of the Humanities (NEH) Summer Institute, I studied the architecture and art of Moscow. Our trip to Moscow began with a visit to the Sparrow (Lenin) Hill. Located on the southwestern outskirts of Moscow, this area provides an excellent view of the city. Quite evident is the Kremlin, which today has returned visually to its historic importance as the sacred site of churches, monasteries, and palaces, while also evoking memories of the former omnipresent Communist government. Competing for the domination of the skyline are the still innumerable churches and monasteries, (although there are far fewer the estimated 450 churches and 80 monasteries and nunneries that existed in Moscow before the Bolshevik Revolution) along with the post-Revolution government buildings, Stalinist skyscrapers, and the vast apartment housing complexes built during the Khrushchev and Brezhnev years. Looming behind the viewer is the massive Moscow State University.

Absent from the 1994 skyline was the huge Church of Christ the Savior, southwest of the city center. Built between 1839 and 1883, it covered an area of over 8,000 square yards, had five gilded domes, 48 exterior marble reliefs, and extensive interior decorations in gold and marble. The cathedral had a 7,000-person capacity that made it Moscow's largest. This massive church was dynamited under Stalin's orders in December 1931 along with many others during this time period. The Party's intention was to replace the cathedral with an even more grandiose Palace of Soviets.

The central part of Stalin's 1931 architectural scheme for Moscow under the first Five Year Plan was the placing of the Kremlin on the central axis between two huge buildings—the Palace of the Soviets, and the Commissariat of Heavy Industry. Ultimately neither was built. My attention will focus on the proposed Palace of the Soviets, for its history and the history of the site on which it would have been located tells us a lot about the history of Moscow and of Russia in the twentieth century. The Cathedral of Christ the Redeemer was a massive building that served as a monument to the victory of 1812 and to the glory of the Russian Orthodox

The Palace of the Soviets was a never-built structure that would have been twice the height of the Empire State Building with a statue of Lenin crowning the building. It was planned in the 1930s and its grandiose design was to serve as the secular icon of Russian Communism.

Church. It was built in the late nineteenth century and was demolished by the Soviets in 1933.

In 1933 Bris Iofan won the architectural competition for the Palace of the Soviets. He proposed a building that would have been 435 meters high. The palace was to be the largest building in the world—surpassing the Empire State Building and the Eiffel Tower. It was to be topped off by a 75-meter-high statue of Lenin. The building was to contain two large halls to seat 20,000 and 8,000 people. This would accommodate the meeting of the Supreme Soviet and Party Congresses. Offices, restaurants, and other amenities were also planned.

The 110,000-square meter site was excavated and work begun in 1937. However, construction problems caused complications (the site was on marshland with numerous underground streams that were offshoots of the Moscva River). International tensions that were building and which culminated in World War II (or The Great Patriotic War, as it is known in Russia) prevented its construction. During the War the building's unfinished steel framework was dismantled to provide materials for the war effort. After the war, the project was never subsequently revived, and the site was used for the world's largest open-air swimming pool. The great Moscow swimming pool accommodated more than 3,000 people. This pool fell into disrepair in the late 1980s. After the overthrow of the Communist regime, a new Cathedral of Christ the Redeemer began to be constructed

Moscow, Russia, the Stalinist Gothic skyscraper of the Moscow State University.

on this—with its strong encouragement and financial support of the city of Moscow; the cathedral was completed at the end of the millennium. The Russian Orthodox Church successfully argued for the rebuilding of a nearly exact replica of the Church of Christ the Savior on this very site. This desire raises one's awareness of the political and symbolic nature of these historic changes of the cityscape.

On September 26, 1995, the *New York Times* reported on the rebuilding of Cathedral of Christ the Savior on the original site ("Moscow Resurrecting Icon of its Past Glory: Evoking Image of Holy Russia, Moscow Rebuilds Cathedral Stalin Smashed; Steven Erlanger). Its account, which I will re-present here, provides a vivid portrayal of the importance of the symbolic meaning given to the built environment. The *Times* observed that the huge outdoor swimming pool itself is now only a memory. In its place more than 2,500 laborers are working 24 hours a day, 7 days a week, to create a new symbol that represents both state power in the post-Communist era and also the rising influence of the Russian Orthodox Church.

The *Times* reported that there are those who question the wisdom of the costs of such a massive undertaking, when the money spent could instead be used for the vital necessity of rebuilding the infrastructure of Moscow, as well as for satisfying the growing need for additional housing and new factories. Others, particularly the elderly who had not severed their religious ties to the Russian Orthodox Church, see the reconstruction of the cathedral as a symbolic event that reflects the repentance for past sins and the emergence of a new nationalistic Russia. Messages left in a visitors' book at a small museum adjacent to the work site reflect this view:

> "We must rebuild our churches! "We must redeem ours sins!" "Russia is freeing itself from evil. Good is triumphing."

The *Times* reported that the speed of the rebuilding is astonishing. The reconstructed Cathedral is already retaking a prominent place on the Moscow skyline along the river, just west of the Kremlin. When it is completed a huge cross will crown its tallest central dome. The structure itself will stretch 335 feet high, the equivalent of more than 30 stories. While in close proximity to the original structure on the outside (the original architectural plans were destroyed long ago), the interior will include a parking garage and electric elevators.

The mayor of Moscow, Yuri Luzhov, the driving governmental official behind this mega-construction project, is currently searching for the original 87-foot-high gold-encrusted iconstasis. (An iconstasis is a screen, decorated with icons, that separates the sanctuary from the rest of the church.) Rumor has it that it is either in the Vatican or was brought to and is secretly hidden somewhere in the United States. Eleanor Roosevelt is thought to have bought it before the Second World War as a means of preserving it from wartime destruction. There are some Russian officials who believe it lies in still-secret vaults of the Kremlin or in a museum, or that it was broken up and its icons sold separately.

The *Times* concludes by quoting a 33-year-old writer, Igor Yarkevich: "During Communism, the Soviet intellectuals used to say, 'There was a wonderful church here, and now there's a metro and swimming pool.' And after some time, the intellectuals will say, 'You know there used to be a wonderful swimming pool here, and now the new bosses have built a church.'"

Hong Kong

Toward the end of January 1996, the British government in Hong Kong announced that it would be replacing its postage stamps with newly designed stamps. Under British rule, the postage stamps traditionally featured images of the British monarchy from Victoria to Elizabeth II. The reigning monarchs profile was incorporated in a corner of the stamp. The new stamps would no longer carry that design; instead, the first set of new stamps would highlight the skyline of Hong Kong. This change in postage stamp design reflected the coming political reality in which the British government would turn over control of its former crown colony to China. It seemed fitting that the image of Hong Kong that the government wished to highlight was that of its skyline, which symbolizes its economic global power.

The treaty signed between Great Britain and China in 1984 essentially gave China political control of Hong Kong on July 1, 1997. The treaty of transfer commits China to guarantee Hong Kong at least 50 years of complete autonomy in terms of its internal economic, social, and political system. China gained control over Hong Kong's defense and foreign relations. Nothing better symbolically reflects the political duality of Hong Kong and its current economic dynamism than two buildings: the Hong Kong and Shanghai Bank (now called the Hong Kong Bank), and the Bank of China (Brunn and Williams 1993). The former, owned by the Hong Kong and Shanghai Business Corporation, represents the local financial stronghold of Great Britain and private capitalism; the latter represents the financial center for the People's Republic of China in Hong Kong.

The Bank of Hong Kong designed by Sir Norman Foster was built to demonstrate the economic importance of England. It dominated the Hong Kong skyline and dwarfed the adjacent Legislative Council Building. In turn it was dwarfed by the Bank of China designed by I. M. Pei.

Hong Kong Island, like the isle of Manhattan, is a confined space. Its economy is booming. As such, the decision to build high can be seen as a reflection of land prices. But even so, symbolic factors play a role in the design and execution of tall buildings in Hong Kong as well as in New York.

The Hong Kong Bank building, designed by the English architect Sir Norman Foster, was opened in 1987. Its costs (more than HK$5 billion) caused controversy, as it was the most expensive building in the history of Hong Kong, as was its design. The building is 52 stories high (586 feet [179m]) and is constructed of steel, aluminum, and glass. Architects have variously described the building as a "stainless steel ladder," a "Chinese lantern," "a megolith of super technology," "like an English cathedral," the "eighth wonder of the world," "of surpassing ugliness," and "somewhat in the style of a modern chemical works" (cited in Rafferty 1990:281). Raferty, in his account, quotes the *London Times* architectural critic Charles Knevitt, who puzzlingly referred to the building as "a meeting of technical sophistication of the west with the somewhat inscrutable mysticism and superstition one associates with the east" (Knevitt quoted in Rafferty 1990:281).

The skyline of the city center Hong Kong with the peak of the Bank of China building (designed by I. M. Pei).

There was another controversy regarding whether the building conformed to *feng-shui* principals. *Feng-shui*, which literally means wind and water, is based on a Chinese belief in the necessity of achieving balance and harmony with nature. The location, design, and placement of buildings, roads, and furniture must be placed in harmonious positions. If they are, they will bring good luck; if not, bad luck will prevail.

The exterior walls originally were designed to be finished in red or green with chevron-shaped crossbeams. These caused consternation both with the bankers and with the practitioners of *feng-shui*. The bankers did not like the colors but liked the chevrons; the Chinese practitioners did not like the chevrons but liked the colors. For the Chinese, the downward thrust of the chevrons could be interpreted as money and prestige dissipating. For the bankers, Foster's use of the colors was inappropriate even though they were traditionally used for important public buildings. Ultimately, the walls were painted in a more conservative silver finish with paint provided by the company that makes the paint for Porsche, and the chevrons were removed from the design.

The bank's *feng-shui* geomancer, Koo Pak Ing, was involved in deciding the best corner of entry to the new building and the most auspicious placement of the elevators, which were aligned with the tail of a dragon whose shadow fell from a nearby peak (Bennett 1992: 89). Similarly, in bowing to *feng-shui*, the two bronze guardian lions that stood watch in front of the old building were moved at the most propitious time and were lowered simultaneously into place by two cranes to avoid showing favor to either lion. Ultimately, the controversies surrounding the building and especially the cost in its construction could only be resolved on the continued financial success of the Hong Kong Bank when Hong Kong came under Chinese rule. The prevalent architectural view shared by many of its inhabitants: "We have a fine building. What does it cost?—A few years' profits, but its puts us on the world architectural map" (cited in Rafferty 1990:281–282).

The Bank of China was built by the Chinese government to serve as its main overseas headquarters. It is a concrete manifestation of its burgeoning economic interest in Hong Kong. Not only did the building reflect the increased dominance of China in Hong Kong's financial structure but it also dominated the Hong Kong skyline, dwarfing the adjacent Legislative Council Building and the Bank of Hong Kong.

I. M. Pei designed the Bank of China building. It is majestic, elegantly proportioned and engineered. Its external bracings are set off by a glass and aluminum curtain wall. The tower is 1,209 feet (369 meters) high and is considered by many to be the finest looking modern skyscraper.

At the time of its completion in 1988 it was the tallest building in Asia. But the Central Plaza Building (1,227 feet; 374 meters) soon topped it. This building, designed by Ng Chun Man and Associates, is located in Hong Kong's Wanchai area and stares out over the Kowloon hillside to mainland China (Bennett 1995: 80). It's a postmodern version of the Empire State Building and its gold and silver glass facade. At night, it is lit by colored neon lights that run in a series of vertical strips that has earned the nickname, "the catscratch." However, its distance from the skyline from the main Hong Kong skyline has diminished its impact on that skyline.

The Bank of China's topping-off ceremony was held on August 8, 1988— 8/8/88. This date was chosen because the number eight—baat—sounds like the word for prosperity—faat—in Cantonese.

Yet, *feng-shui* believers feel that the bank's shape, based on a series of interlocking traingles or pyramids, is unlucky. The Cantonese term for pyramid, *kam che tap,* is similar to *kam tap,* the term for the urns that contain remains of the dead (Rafferty 1989) Further, the bank has many sharp sides that gleam razor-like in the sun. It is seen as signs of danger and is avoided in traditional Chinese architecture. One *feng-shui* observer comments: "People are afraid the sharp points will cause danger to the surroundings. If an angle is pointing at you, it's like a knife pointing at you. It could cause bad health or economic damage" (cited in Jones 1988). Others observe that some of the points are directed at the Legislative Council Building, another is directed at Government House, while others seem to point inward to the Bank of China building itself (Rafferty 1989). Finally, the two electronic rods that top the building are seen to have dire meaning:

> There is also unhappiness about the two "chopsticks" on top of the building, giving it extra height. No good Chinese, says a local *fung shui* expert, would ever place chopsticks upright. The Chinese always lay them flat. To put them upright resembles placing incense sticks, a memorial for the dead. They hope it won't happen to the Bank of China building, still less to Hong Kong itself. (Rafferty 1989:345)

Hong Kong in the summer of 2004 was experiencing demonstrations for democracy. Over a quarter of a million people congregated in downtown Hong Kong, surrounded by its skyscrapers, demanding that the now ruling government of the People's Republic of China allow Hong Kong to exist as a democratic bastion of freedom within the larger country. Demonstrations periodically continue.

The Attack on the World Trade Center and the Media Response

On Tuesday morning September 11, 2001, without warning, four airplanes were hijacked. Two of them crashed into the World Trade Center killing nearly 3,000 people as well as all the occupants of the airplanes. A third plane was flown into the Pentagon in Washington, D.C., killing nearly 200 people there as well as all the occupants of the airplane. A fourth crashed in a farm field in rural Pennsylvania killing all on board.

Immediately after the destruction of the twin towers of the World Trade Center and the attack on the Pentagon, a number of newspapers and periodicals recognized the symbolic underpinnings of the attack. *The Wall Street Journal*, in the opening paragraph of the lead article by staff reporters David S. Cloud and Neil King (2001), states that: "By successfully attacking the most prominent symbols of American power—Wall Street and the Pentagon—terrorists have wiped out any remaining illusions that America is safe from mass organized violence." The subtitle of the article

The World Trade Center dominated the iconic New York City skyline before its destruction by terrorists on September 11, 2001.

as it appeared on the continuing page 12 was: "Attacks on Symbols of U.S. Power Alter Nation's View of World Role." *The Philadelphia Inquirer* proclaimed, "Symbols of U.S. capitalism crumble" (Saffron 2001), and "Terrorists strike symbols of U.S. culture, capitalism" (Bowden 2001). The World Trade Center, both in name and in its physical prominence, had become the most recognizable symbol of American capitalism. Similarly, the Pentagon is the symbol and site of the articulation of American's military prowess.

Immediately after the attacks, other symbols of America were quickly evacuated, including famous high-rise buildings like San Francisco's TransAmerica Pyramid; Detroit's Renaissance Center; Atlanta's Peachtree Center; and Chicago's Sears Tower (Firestone 2001). Also evacuated were some of America's leisure and consumer theme parks, including Disneyland in Anaheim, California, and Disney World in Orlando, Florida, along with Sea World, as well as the country's largest shopping complex, the Mall of America in Bloomington, Minnesota. Other landmarks with a clear American resonance were among those secured. In Philadelphia, the Liberty Bell Pavilion and Independence Hall were closed. Pedestrian access to the Golden Gate Bridge was denied, as was the highway above the Hoover Dam and its visitors' center. Other tall structures including the Stratosphere tower in Las Vegas, the Gateway Arch in Saint Louis, and the Space Needle in Seattle were similarly shut down. Major league and minor league baseball games were canceled, and the weekend was largely devoid of sporting events, including the postponing of Sunday's National Football League games.

Thomas L. Friedman (2001) relates that a day after the bombing of the World Trade Center an Egyptian television show called and asked him to give his assessment on the impact that it would have on Americans. Friedman gave the analogy that it would have a similar impact on Egyptians if the Pyramids were bombed and leveled *and* (my emphasis) if they had thousands of people inside them. Friedman states: "The World Trade towers were our Pyramids, built with glass and steel rather than stones, but Pyramids to American enterprise and free markets, and someone had destroyed them" (2001: A31).

Michael Lewis (2001), a contributing writer for the *New York Times Magazine*, shifts the focus of the symbol from the buildings to what the buildings represent and to the people who worked in them and to the people who destroyed them. In his essay, "Why You?" he makes the point that Wall Street and other financial centers are not merely places but ideas, and the dominant idea is that of liberty and capitalism. "The sort of people who worked in financial centers are not merely symbols but also practitioners of liberty" (Lewis 2001: 70). He observes that while the markets were closed temporarily, eventually they would reopen and continue their economic purposes. The economic system is seen to be impervious to terror. He contrasts the terrorists who destroyed the buildings, their inhabitants, and themselves as the spiritual antithesis of the bond traders and the other capitalists who worked in them. He sees the terrorists as religious fundamentalists "whose business depends on a denial of personal liberty in the name of some putatively higher power" (Lewis 2001:71). Rhetorically speaking to the World Trade Center, he asks:

> And so, Why you? The attack was designed by a keenly intelligent person who understood us better than we understand him. And so he must have also understood that the target he picked was fundamentally indestructible. The only answer I can come up with to my question is that you have become Exhibit A in the global display of modern capitalism, and modern capitalism is deeply disturbing to the sort of people who steer airplanes into buildings in the name of a higher power. Your friend in the north tower who was fixated on the prices on the computer screen when the first plane struck was as different from the young man with his eyes glued to the airplane's instrument panel as one ambitious young man can be from another. (Lewis 2001: 70)

Some years ago, Mark Abrahamson (1980) pointed out that many cities become so intimately identified with certain activities that the mere mention of their name becomes synonymous with that activity. So, for example, reference to Detroit implies reference to the automobile industry, Houston to the air and space industry, and Hollywood to the film industry. Similarly, New York City takes on a broader context, especially on the global level. The mention of its name, or its sites and buildings, e.g., Wall Street and the World Trade Center, had come to be a shorthand representation of not only American democratic capitalism but of American cultural values, including secularism and materialism.

The popular historian and novelist Caleb Carr (2001) has pointed out that American cultural predominance and global force had become personified in the buildings of lower Manhattan and particularly the World Trade Center. These buildings and the activities that occurred there were seen by some as a direct threat to their own values, to their own ways of life, and to their effective autonomy. To destroy the buildings was in essence a means of destroying the threat. Carr (2001: 92) states, "The terrorist obsession with the World Trade Center was not irrational. In fact it was, viewed in the context of a war of cultures, entirely understandable."

Terrorism picked its targets wisely. The columnist George F. Will (2001) points out that terrorism is not senseless. "Terrorism is a compound of the tangible and the intangible—of physical violence and political symbolism" (Will 2001: 57). Echoing Carr, he sees the terrorists' targets as symbols of American virtues as well as of American power.

> The twin towers of the World Trade Center are, like Manhattan itself, architectural expressions of the vigor of American civilization. The Pentagon is a symbol of America's ability and determination to project and defend democratic values. These targets have drawn, like gathered lightening, the anger of the enemies of civilization. These enemies are always out there. (Wills 2001: 57)

Wills further observed that terrorism is "cost-efficient" or, in the words of the stock exchange, terrorism is "highly leveraged." Similarly, the late Colombian

Mourners at the World Trade Center site. Photo courtesy of Michelle C. Dailey.

cocaine kingpin Pablo Escobar stated: "Terrorism is the atom bomb of the poor" (quoted in Bowden 2001: A4). The coordinated attacks on the World Trade Center and the Pentagon, while lacking the destructive power of an atomic bomb, had a similar psychological impact. "It's the monumentalism of this," said Elna Yadin, a psychologist at the University of Pennsylvania's Center for the Treatment and Study of Anxiety. "It's something that actually touches at the heart of people all over the United States. It was something that no one had ever thought possible" (quoted in Burling et al. 2001: A28). Wills (2001) quotes a Chinese theorist who said many years ago, "Kill one, frighten 10,000." A modern-day terrorist has updated the axiom, to "Kill one, frighten 10 million."

By attacking the most visible symbolic sites of the country's economic and political/military power, the terrorists were successful in causing many Americans to worry about the nation's security and the safety of their cities from coordinated attacks. The world "taken for granted" in the United States was shattered. *The New York Times* had a banner headline, "Physical and Psychological Paralysis of Nation" (Harden 2001). A headline in *USA Today* articulated this thought, "America's descent into madness: Attack destroyed lives, landmarks and nation's sense of security" (Willing and Drinkard 2001). And the *Philadelphia Inquirer* observed: "Peace of mind falls victim to mayhem" (Burling et al. 2001).

The newspaper accounts constructed this emerging attitude through selective quotes of observers of the day's events. A lawyer who was watching the ruins of the World Trade Center from a bluff in New Jersey said, "Things are never going to be the same in this country again. This is the worst day in the history of the country, with the exception of the Civil War" (cited in Hampson 2001). Cloud and King (2001) repeat this sentiment by quoting an office administrator in downtown Houston who was hurrying to leave her office building while carrying an armful of computer tapes and copies of account data for safekeeping, "This is the end of the world as we know it. The United States will never be the same" (Cloud and King 2001).

Echoing this sentiment other newspapers voiced these feelings in the titles and bodies of their reports. For example, *USA Today's* (September 12, 2001) front page subtitle of its cover story was: "Minute by minute, fear envelops the country: As jetliners strike U.S. landmarks, America's sense of security is shattered" (Hampson 2001). And, again, a *USA Today* article that had a graphic depiction of the attack included this headline: "Flights of terror strike symbols of U.S. strength" (Ahrens et al. 2001).

In its total destruction of the twin towers this attack was seen to have a massive psychological impact. Citing trauma experts, Burling et al. state, "Psychologically, yesterday's terrorist attacks were a watershed event likely to leave many Americans feeling afraid, unsure of their government and vengeful" (2001: A28). Its stunning impact can best be understood within the context of the symbolic importance of the buildings. Jim Hedtke, chairman of the history and political science department at Cabrini College in Philadelphia, observes that: "The World Trade Center is a symbol of American capitalism, and from the point of probable terrorists, a symbol of American decadence. The victims on the planes and the buildings were not the real targets of the attack. The intended victims were you and me" (quoted in Bowden 2001:A4).

From Civic Criticism to Sentimental Icon: A Brief History

The sentiment regarding the WTC has changed over the years. The story begins with the creation of the Port Authority of New York and New Jersey in 1921. The Port Authority was a semi-autonomous governmental organization that was responsible for the building of numerous bridges and tunnels between New York and New Jersey. In the late 1950s intertwined economic motives for a world trade center to serve as the central work site for the Port Authority were articulated. The Port Authority also was interested in moving the docks on the west side of Manhattan to ports in New Jersey. Both the State of New York and the State of New Jersey had additional motives for the building of the trade center. New York saw the construction of the towers as a way of transforming Lower Manhattan into an international financial center. Further, the landfill would cover the docks and create 28 acres of reclaimed land on the Hudson River where the World Financial Center and Battery Park City would eventually be built. For New Jersey, it would rid itself of an obsolete and money-losing rail connection between Manhattan and New Jersey. The Port Authority would take over the rail line and transform it into the Port Authority Trans-Hudson, or PATH, line, and New Jersey would gain the port business that New York would lose.

Construction on the World Trade Center began in 1966 amid protest and was officially dedicated on April 4, 1973. Minouri Yamasaki designed it in association with Emory Roth & Sons for the Port Authority of New York and New Jersey. (Minouri Yamasaki was also the designer of Pruitt-Igoe, the public-housing towers that were imploded in 1972 and which will be discussed later in this book.) At the time that the WTC was built, the towers exceeded in height the then-tallest building in the world, the Empire State Building. The twin towers of the World Trade Center rose 110 floors to over 1,350 feet. They were not identical twins. The north tower, 1 World Trade Center, was 1,367 feet tall; the south tower, 2 World Trade Center, was 1,362 feet. The excavated dirt was used as landfill to destroy the deteriorating west side docks, which became the site for the World Financial Center and Battery Park City.

The immensity of the World Trade Center can be measured quantitatively (Dunlap 2001). The workday population was around 50,000, with an additional 80,000 daily visitors. Each floor was more than 40,000 square feet, the equivalent of an area bigger than an acre. The towers had their own zip code (10048). While the bustling shopping streets that Le Corbusier so detested were gone, the interior concourse had more than 70 shops and restaurants and was considered as a functioning main street by its users.

The towers were designed to maximize office space. This was successfully accomplished. While the Sears Tower in Chicago and the Petronas Towers in Kuala Lumpur surpassed the twin towers in height, they were not surpassed in floor space. The office space in the twin towers was maximized by eliminating the interior support columns found in most skyscrapers. The towers relied on core columns and their exterior weight-bearing walls to hold them up. Because of this architectural reliance on the support of the outer shell, the hijacked commercial airplanes that struck the buildings, and the resultant jet-fuel fire, made the sides impossible to remain standing. Thus Yamasaki's two major architectural projects, the World Trade Center and Pruitt-Igoe, ultimately experienced implosions and were destroyed, albeit for quite different motives and means.

The twin monoliths were nick-named "David" and "Nelson" at the time of their construction in recognition of the Rockefeller brothers, who were instrumental in their coming into being (Stern et al. 1995; Dunlap 2001: A14). David Rockefeller was chairman of Chase Manhattan Bank and founder of the Downtown-Lower Manhattan Association. Nelson Rockefeller was the governor of New York. There was great controversy at the time of construction. The Le Corbusierian style was seen as antithetical to the city life of small-scale buildings and streets that dotted the area. The WTC replaced, and displaced, the electronics small businesses along "radio row."

The Trade Center's size and technological innovations did not transfer to either architectural or public acclaim. Its very size, as well as the large-scale temporary and permanent disruptions it would cause for the city's physical and human fabric, led to criticisms and opposition (Stern et al. 1995). The machinations of the Port Authority, David Rockefeller's financial empire, and the politicians of New York and New Jersey, including Governors Nelson Rockefeller and William Cahill, respectively, upset both the public and the press. Further, the architectural immensity of the towers disrupted the spatial arrangements and the coherence of the traditional low-scale buildings of the Hudson River's edge of Lower Manhattan.

After their construction and usage, they were, at best, tolerated, never loved. However, unanticipated and unusual events helped alter their image. The World Trade Towers were "humanized" on August 7, 1994, when a French high-wire acrobat, Philippe Petit, tightrope-walked and danced between the towers, and in 1997 when the self-titled "human fly," George Willig, illegally scaled the south tower. Willig was arrested when he reached the top floor and was fined $1.10, a penny a floor. Petit was sentenced to perform before children in Central Park. Reminiscing on *All Things Considered* on National Public Radio on September 28, 17 days after the destruction, Petit noted how he was able to handle potential wind and turbulence problems. He reports on how he felt the vibrations of the twin towers as he crossed between the towers. Petit concluded by noting how his feelings are now tainted with sorrow at the human tragedy. He waxed poetic, regarding the towers as his children and wished he could dance between them again.

The destruction of the World Trade Center on September 11, 2001, was the second attack on the World Trade Center. The first attack occurred eight years earlier in 1993. Terrorists bombed it. Six people died, many were injured, and the center suffered much damage. But the complex survived. Its survival altered people's perception of the World Trade Center. Their very visibility took on an emotional cast. Shortly after the 1993 attack, poet David Lehman expressed sentiments in his poem "World Trade Center"* that were shared by many:

> *I never liked the World Trade Center.*
> *When it went up I talked it down*
> *As did many other New Yorkers.*
> *The twin towers were ugly monoliths*
> *That lacked the details the ornament the character*
> *Of the Empire State Building and especially*
> *The Chrysler Building, everyone's favorite,*
> *With its scalloped top, so noble.*
> *The World Trade Center was an example*
> *   of what was wrong*
> *With American architecture,*
> *And it stayed that way for twenty-five years*
> *Until that Friday afternoon in February*
> *When the bomb went off and the buildings became*
> *A great symbol of America, like the Statue*
> *Of Liberty at the end of Hitchcock's* Saboteur.
> *My whole attitude toward the World Trade Center*
> *Changed overnight. I began to like the way*
> *It comes into view as you reach Sixth Avenue*
> *From any side street, the way the tops*
> *Of the towers dissolve into white skies*
> *In the east when you cross the Hudson*
> *Into the city across the George Washington Bridge.*
>
> (Lehman 1996)

Philippe Petit, a French high-wire acrobat, thrilled New Yorkers with his daring walk on a tight-rope that he illegally set up between the two towers of the World Trade Center on August 7, 1994.

After the destruction of the towers, Daniel Henninger (2001), a deputy editorial page editor for the *Wall Street Journal,* voiced a similar sentiment on the emotional impact related to their visibility. In his editorial of September 12, 2001, he remarked:

> In fact, you have no idea, unless you had ever seen it, just how extraordinarily beautiful this complex of buildings was on a dark, clear night looked at from the Hoboken ferry in the middle of the Hudson River; all the buildings would be lit up, and the fat, domed World Financial Center's buildings, designed by Cesar Pelli stood in perfect proportion to the two magnificent silver towers. I cannot believe I will not see it again.
>
> I loved the World Trade Center towers. I have worked in their shadow for almost 25 years. I came to see them the way I saw the Statue of Liberty. At night, in the fall, . . . when they and all the rest of Manhattan's buildings were alight against a dark sky, the World Trade Center's towers were just joyous. They shouted out on behalf of everyone in this city, where everyone seems to take pride in working long, hard hours. No matter what, those long, hard silver towers were always there. Way up there. (Henninger 2001)

As mentioned, the twin towers were never considered architecturally significant. Yet because of their sheer size they dominated the skyline of Lower Manhattan and indeed of the city and became an iconic feature of that skyline visible for miles. Their absence from that skyline will be a constant reminder of their terrorist destruction. The architectural historian of the *Philadelphia Inquirer*, Inga Saffron, observes, "Among the many shocking things about yesterday's coordinated attacks was the realization that two such immense, complex, human creations could be erased from our common landscape in the blink of an extremist's eye. Even in an age when building implosions have become routine, the gap in the New York skyline is likely to provoke shudders for a long time to come. Now the two immense towers have become a testament to the frailty of human endeavors and the vulnerability of a civilized society" (2001: A13).

The Future: How Do You Reconstruct an Icon?

The question has arisen on whether to rebuild or not, and if to rebuild what form should that take. *The New York Times Magazine* of September 23, 2001, asked a number of prominent architects for their thoughts. All their responses recognized the necessity of not simply replacing buildings and office space but of constructing a built environment that satisfies the practical, aesthetic, and symbolic needs. Themes that have been articulated in the media are reflected in the architects' assessments. Those of particular relevancy that speak to the historical importance of the skyscraper and the skyline as icons of American culture and society were voiced by Robert A. M. Stern, Elizabeth Diller and Ricardo Scofidio, and Peter Eisenman:

> We must rebuild the towers. They are a symbol of our achievement as New Yorkers and as Americans and to put them back says that we cannot be defeated. The skyscraper is our greatest achievement architecturally speaking, and we must have a new, skyscraping World Trade Center. (Stern cited in "To Rebuild or Not—Architects Respond," 2001: 81)
>
> What's most poignant now is that the identity of the skyline has been lost. We would say, Let's not build something that would mend the skyline, it is more powerful to leave it void. We believe it would be tragic to erase the erasure. (Diller and Scofido cited in "To Rebuild or Not—Architects Respond," 2001: 81)
>
> Whatever we do in the future has got to reflect the sense that the West, its culture and values have been attacked. I would hope that we would not be deterred from going as high as the old towers were. We should not move back from that point. We cannot retreat. (Eisenman, cited in "To Rebuild or Not—Architects Respond," 2001: 81)

Richard Meier gave the definitive summarization statement:

> It should be rebuilt. We need office space, though we don't want to build the same towers—they were designed in 1966 and now we live in 2001. What has to be there is an ensemble of buildings that are as powerful a symbol of New York as the World Trade towers were. The life of the city depends on people living and working in the city and loving it—we want people there. We want them in a place that can be magnificent. (Meier cited in "To Rebuild or Not—Architects Respond," 2001: 81)

What now remains is an icon of air.

Part **IV**

*The Social Psychology
of City Life*

9

Experiencing Strangers and the Quest for Public Order

The Private Realm, the Parochial Realm, and the Public Realm

Strangers and the "Goodness" of the Public Realm

Cheers: *"Where Everybody Knows Your Name"*

Anonymity and the Quest for Social Order

William H. Whyte: Public Spaces—Rediscovering the Center

Sharon Zukin: The Battle for Bryant Park

Elijah Anderson: On Being "Streetwise"

The dichotomies developed by Tönnies, Maine, Durkheim, Wirth, and others lead to the assumption that rural life is comprised of intimate and personalized primary relationships. Urban life, in contrast, is characterized by anonymous, segmented, fleeting, and secondary involvements of strangers with no biographical knowledge of each other. This false dichotomy has led many analysts to ignore the anonymity of rural life and the intimacy of urban life. Further, and most significantly in the study of the city, much of the attention had and has been directed to discover the nature of community. Left at the wayside is the failure to examine in more detail the world of strangers. But just as one can understand social interaction that exists in primary group relationships, one can also examine the social interaction patterns that exist in the world of strangers.

Sociologists have two major points of contention with the Wirthian definition of urbanism, which sees the city as alienating and anomic. The first point was to refute the "decline of community" argument. Sociologists sought to overturn the Wirthian perspective by emphasizing that there is vital community life in the city. Their aim was to broadcast the "rediscovery of community" based on community research, especially in working-class enclaves. Other sociologists take issue with Wirth's assumptions on the nature of urban life that prevails on the streets of the downtown central business districts. These sociologists seek to examine the public realm, what Simmel and Wirth saw as the world of the "lonely crowd," on its own grounds.

Their point of view is that this world is not the site of anonymous or anomic relationships. Rather, the very anonymity of these city dwellers is a social product governed by its own set of rules, regulations, and cultural patterns.

In vividly describing the importance of strangers in cities, sociologists sought to emphasize the importance of the social relationships that exist among strangers. Jane Jacobs (1961), in her masterful book, *The Death and Life of Great American Cities*, emphasizes the distinctive quality of city life: "Great cities are not like towns, only larger. They are not like suburbs, only denser. They differ from towns and suburbs in basic ways, and one of these is that cities are, by definition, full of strangers" (1961: 30). Lyn Lofland (1973), in her insightful book, *A World of Strangers*, emphasizes that to live in cities is to live with strangers. "The city . . . is the locus of a peculiar social situation; the people to be found within its boundaries at any given moment know nothing personally about the vast *majority* of others with whom they share this space" (Lofland 1973: 3). Erving Goffman, in a series of wonderful monographs, especially *The Presentation of Self in Everyday Life* (1959), *Behavior in Public Places* (1963), and *Relations in Public* (1971), studied the underlying and fundamental social order that exist among strangers. A fellow social psychologist, Richard Sennett, describes the contributions of Lofland and Goffman as follows:

> The works of Lyn Lofland and Erving Goffman have explored in great detail, for instance, the rituals by which strangers on crowded streets give each other little clues of reassurance which leave each person in isolation at the same time: you drop your eyes rather than stare at a stranger as a way of reassuring him you are safe; you engage in the pedestrian ballet of moving out of each other's way, so that each of you has a straight channel in which to walk; if you must talk to a stranger, you begin by excusing yourself; and so forth. (Sennett 1992: 299)

A certain type of etiquette governs behavior, an etiquette that requires a reserved and impersonal style interrupted as aloofness. The constriction on personal expression takes the form of a noninvolvement shield that, in turn, fosters a sense of tolerance for those acting in a nonacceptable manner. It allows strangers to deal with each other even without moral judgment or consensus.

In this chapter, we will investigate this world of strangers. We will study the underlying rules that govern the city as "a world of strangers," as Lyn Lofland has so dramatically described it, and the public realm—the city's "quintessential social territory"—that provides the setting for stranger interaction. To begin, it is first necessary to distinguish between three social realms—the private, the parochial, and the public.

The Private Realm, the Parochial Realm, and the Public Realm

In this discussion, I want to present another typology that examines urban life. Herbert Gans (1962b), in an important article, talks about urbanism and suburbanism as *ways* of life. He distinguishes the different types of urbanism and suburbanism—the cosmopolitan, the ethnic villagers, the poor, the trapped, the single and unmarried, and the suburbanite. The sociologist Albert Hunter (1995) and later Lyn Lofland (1998) examine urbanism as a way of life by focusing on three different urban realms that exist in the city. Each of these realms reflects a different set of interactional relationships among its inhabitants.

Albert Hunter (1995) distinguishes between three realms of city life—the private, the parochial, and the public. The private realm refers to the world of intimates—friends and family. He observes that while people in this group often live in close proximity to each other, this does not have to be. Friendships and family ties and relationships can transcend geographic boundaries. This is made possible by technological advances in transportation—the automobile, railroads, and airplanes—and through communication—the telephone and the internet/computer. The parochial realm refers to the residential community and its local institutions, which serve the needs of its populace. These institutions include local stores, schools, churches, and voluntary associations. The spatial domain of the public realm is found in those locations where the private and public realms intersect. These are the public places of the downtown, the street and the sidewalk, and parks and public transportation. The public refers to the broader city and society and to its formal, bureaucratic agencies. Hunter observes that the inherent social bond changes as one moves from the private to the parochial to the public realm. Further, there is a steady diminishing of affect and sentiment in the three social realms.

Hunter observes that in actuality there are three spheres, or social orders as he calls them, operating in the city. These three spheres may be arrayed on a continuum of decreasing sentiment from private, to parochial, to public (Hunter 1995: 211). The first, the private, is restricted to family and kinship relationships; the second, the parochial, is an expansion of the first and includes like-minded people, i.e., people who share at least one social class component. They may share ethnicity, race, stage of the life cycle, and economic backgrounds. A term frequently given to these type of communities are *urban enclaves* (cf. Abrahamson 2006). The public sphere is the faceless "center of the city" where social relationships are among "a world of strangers" (cf. Lofland 1973). It is in the public sphere that supposedly Wirth and earlier Georg Simmel postulate the anomic nature of city life.

Most importantly, Hunter observes that these three realms each have their own underlying basic social bond.

- Private realm: egalitarian mutual ties of socio-emotional support.
- Parochial realm: mutual aid and support and local community status and power local business people, religious leaders, directors and board members of local voluntary associations.
- Public realm: formal, bureaucratic agencies.

According to Hunter, three different types of statuses (and relationships) characterize these three different social orders.

The structural positions or statuses defined by these three bonds within the three social orders are, respectively, friend, neighbor, and fellow citizen. Each of these statuses implies its structural equivalent in dyadic interaction: friend to friend, neighbor to neighbor and citizen to citizen; and each also implies a larger collective unit of which it is part: a group of friends or kin, a local community, and the state. (Hunter 1995:211)

The focus of the following discussion is on the public realm.

Strangers and the "Goodness" of the Public Realm

The work of Lyn H. Lofland was introduced in the first chapter of this book. Here I want to focus on her (1973) view that the city is composed of a "world of strangers." Lofland sees the underlying dilemma of city life as interacting with and trusting people that you do not know—that is, how is it possible for social order to exist among strangers? By examining the "public realm"—the public space of parks, plazas, and streets—the dynamics of doubt and trust among strangers is fully articulated. Lofland (1998) claims that it is the diversity of the city played out in the public realm that gives it is essential quality; critics argue that this is exactly what makes the public realm and, in turn, the city such a dangerous place. Lofland spells out exactly what the public realm is good for, and why it should be valued, in a listing of six "uses" or functions performed in the public realm. Her intent is for us to understand the social values of the public realm in the same manner that we understand the social values of rural and suburban life.

The six functions of the public realm are:

1. an environment of learning
2. a place to enjoy respites and refreshments
3. a communication center
4. a place that allows the practice of politics
5. the enactment of social arrangements/social conflicts
6. the creation of cosmopolitans.

The first important function of the public realm is that it offers a learning environment. Lofland demonstrates this through an example of how city streets are intellectually stimulating for children and a place where people can learn to interact and accept others. Rather than see the public realm as a place that teaches social ills, Lofland points out that through experiencing life in the public realm one is able to quickly learn acceptable and essential social norms, such as the ability to relate to strangers, to move among crowds, and to feel comfortable with different types of people. These things can be taught in the private and parochial realms, but they are never actually learned until one experiences them firsthand.

The public realm as a place for rest and relaxation and a place that offers opportunities for entertainment is its second function. The public realm is the site for "hangouts," Oldenburg's third place, which in Lofland's terminology is the "locale for small, bounded pieces of the public realm" (Lofland 1998: 233). It offers cafes, restaurants, bars, and nightclubs, which give people a place to go, sit back, and take things in. These entertainments are not only in the form of things to do but in the development of relationships, fleeting perhaps, but friendships that can be forged in doing such things. Arenas such as the neighborhood store, the beauty parlor, and small cafes become settings of high social activity where the local inhabitants, many of whom are strangers, come together in a conducive, interactional atmosphere. This allows for the development of shared feelings among strangers, which is hard to duplicate elsewhere.

The third function of the public realm is a communication center, which has a high sociability level and which links other parts of the city together. Citing the work of Joseph Rykwert (1978), a British urban architectural historian, the public realm promotes and leads to daily human contact. On park benches, there are exchanges of ideas; people of different cultures share goods and endless services are performed. The public realm allows for the continual exchange of information in all its variant forms, be it political ideas or simply the exchange of goods. This allows for the quick exchange, growth, and acceptance of new radical ideas. It blends diverse individuals together by allowing a communal blending of ideas.

Lofland's fourth function is that of the practice of politics in the public realm. Using the ideas of Richard Sennett (1970, 1977), Lofland observes that the public realm teaches people to act together without the need to be the same. This, essentially, is the foundation of effective political action. In essence, the lessons learned when one interacts with strangers allows the learning of politics.

> Sennett developed a complex psychosocial argument that linked the city experience—especially the experience of the city's public domain (in my terms, realm)—with emotional, intellectual, and—of relevance here—*political* maturity. . . . Involvement in the public life of cities, in the nonmetaphoric "free spaces" that constitute the public realm, also provides citizenship schooling and allows people to practice . . . politics. (Lofland 1998: 235)

Lofland next describes the fifth function of the public realm. Given visual form, political realities are enacted through social arrangements and social conflict. Here the public realm performs various acts, public dramas, such as street parades, and demonstrations. Historically, these public displays were used for a variety of reasons including status order, power, loyalty, tradition, solidarity, and social/cultural change. The life and death pageants that occurred during the French Revolution provide a vivid example.

Last, the sixth function of the public realm is its creation of cosmopolitans. Lofland wonders why so many different types of people live together in the city. She makes a key point: "Cityphiles have implicitly answered this question with the claim that city living by itself generated tolerance and civility, that city living by itself created cosmopolitans" (Lofland 1998: 237). Compared to other places, cities are tolerant and for the most part allow human variety to be expressed. By living in the city, people must become tolerant of others; in smaller communities, residents are not introduced to as much variety of the human condition in their whole lives as city dwellers encounter in one day.

Lofland contrast two forms of tolerance, positive and negative. Negative tolerance is the ability to put up with differences in people who share a large area of space, but who are segregated within that space. This is also true for people who share smaller spaces but symbolically separate themselves from others in ways such as not "seeing" different people. Positive tolerance is the ability to put up with fully recognized difference even under circumstances in which people are not segregated into groups. They must learn to settle disputes. When these people know enough about the urban environment to feel safe in it, there is less cause for intolerance of others. When one is able to understand those different from themselves, they are able to tolerate them to a greater degree because there is less cause for fear.

For cosmopolitarianism—a positive tolerant atmosphere—to occur certain urban characteristics must be present. The city must be predominantly a walking city, where pedestrian behavior dominates or where mass transportation—buses, trains, trolleys, rather than the automobile—predominates. This allows for plenty of opportunities for strangers to interact as they move from place to place. If there is segregation it must be small scale so that people with diverse backgrounds can commingle and get to know each other. The diverse populations must have some significant differences, and there must be some "hard edge" to human interactions, in order to foster and teach tolerance of those who are seen as somewhat disagreeable. "Cleaned-up, tidy, purified, Disneyland cities (or sections of cities) where nothing shocks, nothing disgusts, nothing is even slightly feared may be pleasant sites for family outings or corporate gatherings, but their public places will not help to create cosmopolitans" (Lofland 1998: 243). Finally, mild fear must be integrated with the teaching of tolerance. This will allow citizens to feel safe enough to venture out, because if they never interact in the public realm they can never learn lessons of tolerance or become cosmopolitan.

Lofland's book ends on a cautionary and pessimistic note that fears the end of the public realm, as we now know it. She fears that the forces against the public realm may be greater than the forces for it. She gives prominence to three important aspects of the public realm: *technology, tourism, timidity.* Technology, which was so instrumental at removing the individual from the private world of the home, is now driving people back to it. Modern technology has given people choices; they are no longer forced to go out in public since the public realm can now be located in the home through the Internet and home entertainment centers. The popularity of tourism is turning the public realm into "theme parks" of sanitized and safe settings. Public realms are losing their hard edge in favor of "Disneyfication." Timidity refers to the fact that as that more and more people are removed from the hardness of the public realm, the less inclined people will be to venture out into an unknown, possibly dangerous place: "Less familiarity (less exposure), and, in the end, a preference for avoidance" (Lofland 1998: 249).

The examination of the decline of the public realm is a theme that has captured much attention (cf. Sorkin 1992). Why this has occurred, and how it has not only radically transformed the public realm but the private and parochial realms as well, are topics that are explored in this book. The study of small neighborhood institutions—the barber shop and beauty salon, the corner grocery, the local bar, coffee shops and candy stores—and their contribution to how urbanites experience cities is of particular interest in examining changes in the public realm. The work of Ray Oldenburg (1989), in what he calls the "great good place" or the "third" place, is of important significance.

Cheers: *"Where Everybody Knows Your Name"*

The Great Good Place by Ray Oldenburg identifies neighborhood spots ("hangouts) that serve as "the core settings of informal public life" (1989: 8). He focuses on the importance of what he calls "third" places—informal gathering places. His idea is that our "first" place is home; work is the "second"; and our "third" place, which has equal importance in everyday life after work and family. "Third places" provide a public balance between the increased privatization of the family and the home and the formal involvements in the work place. They have an important function in the health of communities.

Under "third" places we have places such as neighborhood taverns, restaurants, drugstores, hair salons, barber shops, and coffee shops. In a third place, people

A tourist exits the Bull & Finch bar in Boston, MA. The bar was the inspiration for the popular television sitcom "Cheers."

develop a sense of the community and their place in it. The third place is where members of a community interact with each other and come to know the ties that they share in common. In Durkheim's terminology, third places are sites that help establish mechanical solidarity. People interact with each other by virtue of their "name" not their title; in good third places, people are known through their social self, not through their work identity. Good places are characterized by informality where people are encouraged to "sit and set a spell." The casual gathering spot encourages talk, laughter, and a feeling of good camaraderie.

> The character of a third place is determined most of all by its regular clientele and is marked by a playful mood, which contrasts with people's more serious involvement in other spheres. Though a radically different kind of setting for a home, the third place is remarkably similar to a good home in the psychological comfort and support that it extends. (Oldenburg 1989: 42)

Oldenburg argues that the vitality of community life is dependent on the well-being of third places. "They are the heart of a community's social vitality, the grassroots of democracy, but sadly, they constitute a diminishing aspect of the American social landscape" (Oldenburg 1989: front-inside dust jacket). Without it, there is no escape from the endless home-to-work-to-home cycle. Social well-being and personal health are dependent on such places. Oldenburg sees the discussions on the demise of community as a reflection of the loss of the third place.

The loss of third places in cities was largely an outcome of post–World War II urban planning. Proponents of the city as highway, and tower proponents like Le Corbusier and Robert Moses in their urban renewal plans, ignored the necessity for the inclusion of informal gathering places. Third places—the corner store, the barber shop, the neighborhood parks, the tavern—had no place in the radiant city. The vehicle of choice was the automobile, not one's feet, and the thoroughfare was the highway, not the street. The resultant residential towers had no localized places for people to congregate, talk, chat, and gossip.

Third places also have no place in suburbia, and Oldenburg believes that the decline of third places is attributable, in part, to the sprawling suburbanization of cities. The suburbs, as defined by housing developments, are relatively isolated from shops and businesses, from a local pub or coffee shop, or from other community gathering places that bring people together. Oldenburg concurs with the feminist architectural historian Dolores Hayden, who says that "Americans have substituted the vision of the ideal home for that of the ideal city" (Hayden quoted in Oldenburg 1989: 7). Nor can the house substitute for the community. He takes to task the quest for larger and larger homes on bigger and bigger lots; they only result in a decline in community civilities and amenities. As a consequence, "We do not have that third realm of satisfaction and social cohesion beyond the portals of home and work that for others is an essential element of the good life" (Oldenburg 1989: 9). Oldenburg (1989) believes that the development of suburbia fostered the decline of community civic life.

Oldenburg concludes that social life requires these three places: home, work, and the "third place," the informal gathering spot. When the third place starts to disappear, the expectation is that home and work will fill in the social gap. Oldenburg believes, however, that home and work cannot fulfill all our needs for playful conversation, for surprise, for gaining new ideas and new stimulations. Home and work are limited to solving family matters or work concerns. Additional outlets for social discourse are required. Failure to provide such outlets leads to disenchantment with family and work. Oldenburg speculates that disappointment in marital relationships and subsequent divorce are a consequence of over-dependence on relationships and on the lack of alternative social outlets.

Finally, Oldenburg argues that the loss of third places ultimately contributes to the lessening of an individual's well-being, a decline in grassroots democracy and civic society. As the community has declined, the fear of public space has increased. Oldenburg's work can be seen in the broader thesis advanced by Harvard professor Robert Putnam (2000) in his *Bowling Alone: The Collapse and Revival of American Community.* Putnam uses statistics to document the decline of social ties and civic engagement in America. For now, let us make note of Putnam's major conclusion. He sees an overall plummeting in the levels of trust in government, reflected in low voter turnout; in a reduction in membership in labor unions, PTAs, and churches; and in many other voluntary associations. He asserts that in the past there was a strong association between the level of affluence and education and civic involvements. However, while the social and class levels are rising, there is a concomitant decline in participation in civic associations. The consequence of the decline in social engagement is civic apathy, which is ultimately a threat to both civic and personal health. Putnam's thesis will be examined later in this book. For now, I will illustrate in more detail the workings of the public realm and how social order is created and sustained among strangers.

Anonymity and the Quest for Social Order

Greta Garbo, the famous actress of the 1930s, effectively removed herself from the celebrity spotlight when she chose to retire from show business at the height of her career, ushering the plea, "I want to be alone." Through her subsequent actions, she was a daily participant in the passerby street life of Manhattan; she made the distinction of *being* alone and *left* alone. She wanted to be able to walk in the public realm undisturbed. She was fully cognizant that to be left alone on the streets of the city she would have to depend on the cooperation of strangers. They had to ignore her presence while at the same time they recognized it. To be anonymous requires rules of social engagement among nonparticipating participants in nonsocial action: people are involved in a form of social interaction that appears to be devoid of social interaction.

To understand this seemingly contradictory statement it is necessary to define what we mean by *interaction*. The discussion in this section is heavily dependent on the ideas put forth by the symbolic interactionists David Karp, Gregory P. Stone, and William Yoels. In their seminal work *Being Urban* (1997), they observe that interaction is more than simple *verbal* communication. "We advocate a view that

Greta Garbo, the famous movie star of the 1920s to the 1940s who preferred to be left alone when in the public sphere. This could only be accomplished by the kindness of strangers.

interaction is occurring in any social situation in which persons are acting in awareness of others and are continually adjusting their behaviors to the expectations and possible responses to others" (Karp, Stone, and Yoels 1977: 101). The key point here is "acting in awareness of others." By utilizing such a definition, avoidance behavior and noninvolvement can be seen as a form of social interaction even when no social interaction seems to be occurring. They illustrate their analysis through the utilization of such seemingly contradictory terms—*public anonymity, public privacy,* and *civil inattention.* In a later edition of their book, Karp, Stone, and Yoels observe:

> These descriptions of city interaction may seem strange, if not contradictory—intimate anonymity, public privacy, involved indifference—yet these subtle combinations of apparently opposite ideas do capture the quality of a good deal of city life. They suggest that while urban persons may spend relatively little time engaged in direct verbal interactions, with one another, they are deliberately acting in awareness of, and adjusting their own behaviors to, the possible response to others. (Karp, Stone, and Yoels 1991: 89)

A homeless man eating alone and being ignored by fellow customers at Pat's Steaks, South Philly, Philadelphia. Photo by author.

The necessity for strangers to interact while at the same time keeping their sense of anonymity and privacy is particularly interesting in understanding why people seem so indifferent to others even in situations where there seems to be a "natural" demand for intervention. What happens when an individual finds himself or herself in a desperate situation that requires the need for the help of strangers? Karp, Stone, and Yoels (1977) discuss this type of situation in their delineation of what they call the *mini-max hypothesis.* The situational case in point is the tragic circumstances that led to the death of a young woman whose cries for help went unheeded.

In 1964 a young women, Catherine (Kitty) Genovese, was killed late at night by a still-unknown assailant. She was returning home from a night job and was attacked near her home on the deserted streets in her neighborhood, Kew Gardens, located in Queens, New York City. She screamed for help as her murderer repeatedly stabbed her. Outside of a few neighbors who, disturbed by her cries for help, opened their windows and admonished the attacker to leave her alone, no one physically came to her rescue. Deterred momentarily, the attacker continued his assault until she cried no more and died.

Her tragic death and the nonresponsiveness of her neighbors led to much soul-searching by urbanites on why no one came to her rescue, why no one got involved. This shocking incident seemed to symbolize the image of a city that does not care, one where a sense of civic responsibility is absent. At first, sociologists and social psychologists put the "blame" on the city. They elaborated on the theoretical premises of Wirth (1995/1938) on "the superficiality, the anonymity, and the transitory character of urban social relations," and of Simmel (1995/1971/1903) that "the urban man reacts with his head not his heart." The conclusion reached was that the city was uncaring and callous, and that urbanites would not get involved in matters that did not directly affect them.

Stanley Milgram, a social psychologist, built on the work of Wirth and Simmel by postulating a theory of urban "overload." Simmel, as you may recall from our earlier discussion, believed that the urban dweller was constantly bombarded by a multitude of stimuli. This required an ability to "select-out" those stimuli that were of particular importance and ignore the others. The result was a rational response that favored the intellect over feelings and emotions. Milgram's concept of "stimulus overload" is relatively similar; it emphasizes the ability to adapt and cope with an overstimulated environment. The implications of stimulus overload are that the moral and social involvement of the city dweller becomes severely restricted. "The ultimate adaptation to an over-load social environment is to totally disregard the needs, interests, and demands of those whom one does not define as relevant to the satisfaction of personal needs, and to develop highly efficient perceptual means of determining whether an individual falls into the category of friend or stranger" (Milgram 1977a:26). Milgram goes on to observe that the Genovese murder appears at first glance to be a prime example of the "... most striking deficiencies in social responsibility in cities in crisis situations" (Milgram 1977a:26).

However, Milgram develops his thesis to explain that the lack of bystander intervention in crisis situations is *not* a reflection of urban indifference or callousness. Rather it is a reflection of what he calls *norm of noninvolvement.* The urban condition is one where people frequently find themselves in situations that demand involvement but often result in the opposite. It is impossible to attend to the needs of all people in all situations. If one did so, one could not keep up with one's affairs and concerns.

Milgram further believes that the urbanites' desire to grant others the rights of emotional and social privacy outweighs the norms of intervention. It is the belief that one should not meddle in the affairs of others, especially when one might not understand the underlying situational context that hinders involvement. Further, the heterogeneity of the urban populace encourages the desire of tolerance for the norms and behavior styles of other groups that one does not belong to and does not fully understand. "The heterogeneity of the city produces substantially greater tolerance about behavior, dress, and codes of ethics than is generally found in the small town, but this diversity also encourages people to withhold for fear of antagonizing the participants or crossing an inappropriate and difficult-to-define line" (Milgram 1977a:27).

This "live and let live" attitude serves as the cornerstone of a hypothesis developed by social psychologists David A. Karp, Gregory P. Stone, and William C. Yoels. The *mini-max hypothesis*—minimizing involvement in order to maximize social order—serves to underline the interactions among people, especially in cases where they are strangers to each other in the public realm. With a shared understanding of the definition of the situation, people often interact by not interacting overtly, by allowing the routine behavior among strangers that categorizes so much of life in the public realm. As mentioned earlier, Karp, Stone, and Yoels evoke the concept of "public privacy" to refer to the necessity for urbanites "to strike a balance between involvement, indifference, and cooperation with one another" (1991: 89).

A social-psychological study by Bibb Latané and John Darley, *The Unresponsive Bystander* (1970), came to the conclusion that the Genovese death can be situationally explained and does not reflect the indifference or callowness of urban dwellers. They argue that in a crowded situation, the individual assumes that someone else will intervene. Medical emergency workers, for example, are trained that in emergency situations they should point to a given individual and ask him or her to specifically do something, for example, to telephone for an ambulance. They are trained not to simply ask, "Would someone call an ambulance?"

Latané and Darley argue that the "indifference" of people in a crowd is actually a reflection of what they label as a "diffusion of responsibility." It is this social-psychological phenomenon of reacting with one's head rather than one's heart, rather than indifference or uncaring, that explains the behavior of people in crowds. Latané and Darley also stress that urban bystanders are less likely to know each other or to know the victim than nonurban bystanders, and they conclude that under these conditions the helping response is least likely to occur. Stanley Milgram concurs that it is the conditions of city life that ultimately account for the inattentiveness of city people to come to the aid of their fellow urban dwellers:

> There are, of course, practical limitations to the Samaritan impulse in a major city. If a citizen attended to every needed person, if he were sensitive to and acted on every altruistic impulse that was evoked in the city, he could scarcely keep his own affairs in order. A calculated and strategic indifference is an unavoidable part of life in our cities, and it must be faced without sentiment or rage. At most, each of us can resolve to extend the range of his responsibilities in some perceptible degree, to rise a little more adequately to moral obligations. City life is harsh; still we owe it to ourselves and our fellows to resolve that it be no more harsh than is inevitable. (Milgram 1977b: 46)

William H. Whyte: Public Spaces–Rediscovering the Center

William H. Whyte's study of the use of public plazas and parks vividly demonstrates the underlying rules that govern the behavior of strangers. People are attracted to public spaces provided that they are safe places to be in. For Whyte the safety of a place is not found in the absence of people but in their presence. Whyte's focus on urban life is the very heart of the public realm, the central business district (CBD)—center city, downtown, the loop. He takes issue with the perspective of Georg Simmel, Louis Wirth, and others who see the hustle and bustle of pedestrian patterns and street congestion as the antithesis of social order and the site of the "lonely crowd." Further, Whyte's research argues against the sterility of the radiant city and the planned absence of street life. Whyte instead finds that the streets and plazas of the CBD that are the most crowded are so by choice:

> What attracts people most is other people. Many urban spaces are being designed as though the opposite were true and what people like best are places they stay away from. (Whyte 1988:9)

City officials in many American cities including New York City developed zoning codes that required office towers to have setbacks, called plazas, in front of the buildings. However, the officials had a fundamental misunderstanding on how these plazas should be used. The plazas were designed to allow for more light and air but were seen to have no social purpose, and so the city planners deemed that such places would best serve the populace if they remained vacant. Indeed, some of these plazas' empty spaces became populated by derelicts and other undesirable people, and ultimately they were seen as dangerous places. In others, barriers were placed in the plaza to limit accessibility. It was Whyte's view that these plazas should be re-thought of as potential cites for social interactions. He also tested his theories in Bryant Park in New York City.

Whyte's findings were primarily responsible for the redefinition of urban parks. The case in point was Bryant Park, located behind the New York Public Library on 42nd Street. In the 1960s through the 1980s, this park was virtually unused by the people who worked in the surrounding office towers or by the patrons of the public library. The park was visually cut off from the walkways and streets by overgrown shrubbery. Its visual isolation made it a dangerous place for people to enter, and it became a haven for the homeless, drug dealers, and other miscreants.

Utilizing the public-use policies advocated by Whyte, city officials cut down on the shrubbery and opened the sight lines. Whyte proposed that moveable chairs be placed in these plazas and that pushcarts be allowed to sell food and drink. He advocated for public concerts and a center meadow that allowed for lounging on the grass (no "keep-off-the-grass-signs" permitted). All this came to be. By so doing, the space became redefined and became a much-frequented place for social interaction. People felt free to move about and move chairs as they so desired. The space became an attractive place for people to congregate in, and with its popularity more and more people used the plazas. The end result was a transformation of plaza space and a new Bryant Park that has become one of the most used public spaces in the city.

In a filmed series of marvelous street vignettes of pedestrian behavior and street conversations, Whyte documented the attraction of public spaces. Whyte and his students, over a period of more than a decade and a half, documented how people used public places, including plazas, parks, steets, cafes and stores, and train stations. People like being with other people; they like talking, eating, and "schmoozing" with other people in congested public spaces. In fact some of the actions of the participants of this street life are implicitly designed to accentuate that congestion: "To our surprise, the people who stopped to talk did not move out of the pedestrian flow; and if they had been out of it, they moved into it" (Whyte 1988: 8).

Whyte's filmed observations and his reports of them demonstrate the pervasiveness of social activity, revealing the underlying social order that characterizes these so-called "anonymous" social interactions. His findings echo that of Jane Jacobs, who describes the "ballet of the good city sidewalk" quoted earlier in this book:

> Under the seeming disorder of the old city, wherever the old city is working successfully, is a marvelous order for maintaining the safety of the streets and the freedom of the city. It is a complex order. Its essence is the intricacy of sidewalk use, bringing with it a constant succession of eyes. This order is all composed of movement and change . . . and we may . . . liken it to the dance—not as a simple-minded precision dance with everyone kicking up at the same time, twirling in unison . . . but to an intricate ballet in which the individual dancers and ensembles all have distinctive parts which miraculously reinforce each other and compose an orderly whole. The ballet of a good sidewalk never repeats itself from place to place, and in any one place is always replete with new improvisations. (Jacobs 1961:50)

Sharon Zukin: The Battle for Bryant Park

Whyte's (1980) *Social Life of Small Urban Spaces* became an important treatise on the use of urban plazas and provided a test case on his views of how people use public space. His ideas inspired the transformation of Bryant Park. Sharon Zukin (1995) adds a cultural, economic, and political dimension to Whyte's analysis of the usage of Bryant Park. Zukin observes that the management of the park was ceded to a private nonprofit corporation that reflected middle-class and corporate interests. She sees an implicit "battle" for Bryant Park between the homeless, poor, ethnic minorities, and drug dealers who came to colonize the park, and the more affluent middle class that worked in the surrounding areas or wished to use it for their own social and cultural purposes.

Zukin's account of Bryant Park is part of her broader analysis of the development of a new "symbolic economy" based on tourism, media, and entertainment, which we discussed earlier in Chapter 6. Zukin describes the symbolic economy created by cultural strategies of urban redevelopment and the privatization of public space. Zukin persuasively argues that the recent growth of the symbolic economy has tangible spatial repercussions: it "reshapes geography and ecology" and is a place of creation and transformation (Zukin 1995:8).

Bryant Park located in mid-Manhattan, New York City was for many years left abandoned by the local government. Now it has become a prime example of William H. Whyte's ideas on how to utilize public space. Unfortunately, many are now concerned that its very success has initiated a commercialization process that threatens its public accessibility. Photo by author.

Zukin's major concern is how the power of the symbolic economy in cities impacts on "social inclusion or exclusion, depending on your point of view" (Zukin 1995: vii). She argues that the cultural constructs of a city delegates "who belongs where" through its images and symbols; regulates the economy by producing goods; and designs public space through planning backed by those in positions of power in the private sector. The control of images in the city is for the benefit of the middle class and the affluent as well as for tourists. Unsavory images are removed and concealed. "Controlling the various cultures of cities suggests the possibility of controlling all sorts of urban ills, from violence and hate crimes to economic decline" (Zukin 1995:2).

The symbolic economy becomes dependent on the creation of attractions, whether they are museums, entertainment zones such as the new "family friendly" Times Square, sports stadiums, parks, or festival marketplaces for the more affluent groups of the city. For Bryant Park the establishment of an expensive sidewalk cafe was one means to establish the presence and control of these people over the park: "A sidewalk cafe takes back the street from casual workers and homeless people" (Zukin 1995:9).

Since the turnover of Bryant Park to Bryant Park Restoration Corporation, a private corporation, to its credit, the park has become an extremely popular gathering place and is heavily used. Bryant Park has become more accessible since the takeover, and the public is open to many of the events held in the park. However, the downside, predicted by Zukin in 1995, is that the park has to some degree ceased to be a public place, and has instead been transformed into a business that charges fees for holding events and allows corporate sponsorship (Williams 2005). In the last few months Timothy Williams (2005), a reporter for the *New York Times*, has observed that the park has hosted "Fashion Week" sponsored by the Olympics, as well as a summer movie festival sponsored by HBO; ABC has underwritten a summer movie series for the park; and the *New York Times* has supported a book fair. Currently, the park is being used for a privately operated holiday market and as an ice-skating rink that is sponsored by Citi (the rink is free but there is a charge to rent skates and lockers). The sponsors do pay a rental fee, but in return they are allowed to display their company logo throughout the park. The park is also closed at times for film and television crews; for private parties—you can rent the park's carousel for birthday parties or corporate events; for family celebrations; and for promotional events to spotlight new products, which have included Microsoft Windows Media Edition and Coffee-Mate.

Since many of the events are private, this has raised questions about not only the commercialization of the park but also about the function of a public park located in the middle of the city, an area supposedly always open to all but which is not. A further concern is that the private corporation that runs the public park is not publicly funded; instead, it raises operating funds through these commercialized activities. Richard N. Gootfried, a city elected official, believes that this has led to the commercialization of the park and has transformed it from a public park into a private "theme park."

> "Parks have never in this city's history been thought of as entities that would fund themselves, and I think that's a dangerous concept," Mr. Gottfried said. "This takes us way down the road of a public park becoming a theme park." (Williams 2005: B1)

Sharon Zukin's dominating concern is not only on issues of who occupies "real" space but on the utilization of "symbolic" space as well. In an allied work Zukin states: "To ask 'Whose City?' suggests more than a politics of occupation; it also asks who has a right to inhabit the dominant image of the city" (Zukin 1996: 43).

Elijah Anderson: On Being "Streetwise"

What would happen if the laws of civility that governed the behavior among strangers were not obeyed? That is, what would happen if the underlying social order of the world of strangers became a world of social "disorder"? In *The Fall of Public Man*, Richard Sennett is concerned that contemporary social life is suffering as a consequence of the collapse of public life, as people forget the forms of civility in settings marked without intimacy. Jane Jacobs (1961) emphasizes that for a city to be successful people must feel personally safe and secure among all these strangers. Sociologists have observed that poverty has had severe detrimental affects on people living in poor communities.

The study of the impact of poverty on African American communities and on street behavior reveals the impact of macrolevel economic and political factors on microlevel interactional dynamics. Loic J. D. Wacquant documents how the breakdown of the public sector has resulted in the development of a "hyper-ghetto." This "hyper-ghetto" is characterized by extreme segregation according to both class and race and has resulted in unprecedented levels of hardship and deprivation along with extreme social isolation and violence. The result is an accelerated destruction of the social fabric of the ghetto as its indigenous instititutional base collapses. Wacquant asserts that "the local businesses, churches, lodges, recreational facilities, and neighborhood associations that used to give structure to life in the inner city and a sense of collectivity to its residents have disappeared by the thousands, leaving behind an *organizational desert* filled largely by gangs, currency exchanges, liquor stores, and virulent relations with police and the courts, to institutions whose role is reduced to creating a protective buffer between the ghetto and the larger society" (Wacquant 1995: 440).

Elijah Anderson, a sociologist at the University of Pennsylvania, has spent his career studying race, poverty, and street culture. In *Code of the Street* (1999), he demonstrates how economic and social processes—joblessness, the stigma of race, rampant drug use—lead to psychological feelings of alienation and lack of hope, which, in turn, translates into an overzealous demand for respect in interactions, especially among the interactions of strangers. The result is a *code of the street*, an elaborate set of informal etiquette rules and rituals that govern people's behaviors as they negotiate problematic street life.

In an earlier work, *Streetwise* (1990), he studied two adjacent communities in Philadelphia over a 14-year period. The people in these two bordering communities are of divergent class and race and often find themselves in contact with each other on the streets. "Northtown" is the Mantua neighborhood that is home for many poor young blacks; "Village" is the Powelton neighborhood near the University of Pennsylvania and Drexel University that is undergoing gentrification by white professionals.

Anderson discusses the impact of national and international economic changes on these two communities. Northtown residents feel the full impact of reduced jobs and opportunities as a consequence of federal cutbacks in job training and social programs. Young blacks in particular feel the impact of economic depravation; a persistent drug culture prevails; and there is increasing violence and desperation. Anderson discusses the cultural breakdown in the community by examining the declining influence of older black men in the community ("old heads") on their younger counterparts. The "old heads" used to keep the young focused on family obligations and distilled a work ethic. The racial and class makeup of the residents of the Village is undergoing change and gentrification. This community is becoming increasingly white and middle- to upper-class, replacing poorer blacks.

What gives Anderson's work so much value is that he provides the macrolevel context for the microlevel interaction patterns of the street. He argues that the socioeconomic structure of society and debilitating public policies have resulted in a profound feeling that the street is unsafe. His macrolevel analysis sets the stage for his microlevel discussion of street etiquette at a time when the mere presence of young blacks on the streets evokes feelings of fear in the minds of the professionals. Anderson demonstrates how the street-interaction of blacks and whites who are strangers is influenced by the economic structure and linked to prevailing structures of racial stereotypes and prejudice. Based on a "definition of the situation" that perceives threat, to avoid any semblance of interaction, whites often cross the street when they see young blacks approaching or, if that is not possible, they speed up their gait and avoid all eye contact.

Anderson utilizes the dramaturgical framework of Erving Goffman (1959) in his analysis. Goffman described the techniques of "impression management," which guided individuals in their desire to make a good first impression. In assessing this first impression, individuals seek clues to confirm that the impressions put forth reflect the "true" character of the other. Goffman provides a now classic description on how social roles and statuses between strangers become articulated in given contexts or locations:

> When an individual enters the presence of others, they commonly seek to acquire information about him or to bring into play information already possessed. They will be interested in his general conception of self, his attitude toward them, his competence, his trustworthiness, etc. . . . . Information about the individual helps to define the situation, enabling others to know in advance what he will expect of them, and what they may expect of him. Informed in these ways, the others will know how best to act in order to call forth a desired response to him. (Goffman 1959: 1 quoted in Anderson 1990: 166)

Following Goffman and in a similar manner as Lofland (1973), Anderson discusses the importance of locational, temporal, behavioral, and appearance clues to help identify the stranger and determine in the event of an interactional encounter whether it would be a safe one or not. The time of day becomes important as does location. Of special interest to Anderson (1990: 166–67) is the importance of appearance: "Skin color, gender, age, companions, clothing, jewelry, and the objects people carry help identify them, so assumptions are formed and communication can occur." If any aspect of their appearance seems problematic, Anderson observes:

> If a stranger cannot pass inspection and be assessed as "safe" (either by identity or by purpose), the image of predator may arise, and fellow pedestrians may try to maintain a distance consistent with that image. In the more worrisome situations—for example, encountering a number of strangers on a dark street—the image may persist and trigger some form of defensive action. (Anderson 1990: 167)

Anderson delineates what Karp, Stone, and Yoels (1977) refer to as a "doubt-trust" continuum of age, race, and gender identities, often stereotyped, of those least likely to most likely to be considered dangerous: "In the street environment, it seems, children readily pass inspection, white women and white men more slowly, black women, black men, and black male teenagers most slowly of all" (Anderson 1990: 167). To be "streetwise" is to have the street wisdom to be aware of the underlying street etiquette that governs the interaction among strangers. The underlying strategy to assure safety is to avoid strange black men on the streets as much as possible.

> The public awareness is color-coded: white skin denotes civility, law-abidingness, and trustworthiness, while black skin is strongly associated with poverty, crime, incivility, and distrust. Thus an unknown young black male is readily deferred to. If he asks for anything, he must be handled quickly and summarily. If he is persistent, help must be summoned. (Anderson 1990: 208)

As trust gives way to doubt, the streets are seen as being more unsafe. The result is that the public realm of the streets is seen as the site of incivility and should be avoided as much as possible. Nighttime accentuates this belief.

> Increasingly, people see the streets as a jungle, especially at night, when all "cats are gray" and everyone may seem threatening. They are then on special alert, carefully monitoring everyone who passes and giving few people the benefit of the doubt. Strangers must pass inspection. Although there is a general need to view the Village as an island of civility . . . the underlying sense is that the local streets and public places are uncertain at best and hostile at worst. (Anderson 1990: 239)

In this chapter I discussed the nature of the public realm and how life is possible in a world of strangers. I noted that in recent years there has been fundamental change occurring in the public realm, which has served to undermine its underlying social order. This becomes the topic that will be discussed in greater detail in the next chapter.

10

"Seeing" Disorder and the Ecology of Fear

The concern for social order in a world of strangers has always been an underlying issue in the examination of city life. This is an underlying theme in the works of both Erving Goffman (1963, 1972), in his microsociological investigation of gatherings and behavior in public settings, and Lyn Lofland (1973, 1998), in her study on order and action in a "world of strangers" and of the "public realm." Albert Hunter (1995) in his analysis of the nature of social order in neighborhoods refers to three realms of social order (private, parochial, and public) and focuses his attention on problems of crime and *incivility*. Jane Jacobs's influential study, *The Death and Life of Great American Cities* (1961), redefined the way we look at everyday street life and public safety. She emphasizes that for a city to be successful people must feel personally safe and secure among all these strangers. A basic concern is the threat of disorder on neighborhood civility.

The Decline of Civility in the Public Realm

Jane Jacobs's (1961) work is an evocation of the importance of urban civility. It was on city sidewalks where people discerned differences in each other and developed a sense of public trust. Jacobs's views are based on her experiences living on

Hudson Street in Greenwich Village of New York in the 1950s and early 1960s. In her neighborhood there was a high rate of social interaction among neighbors and shopkeepers. A viable social network of interrelationships developed. Strangers, too, were a part of this interactive mix. While they may not have been personally known, over periods of time they became "familiar strangers." Through their everyday routine behavior and participation in sidewalk life they became to be trusted and became part of the urban mix. There were always people on the streets—literally 24 hours a day. Intensive street interaction patterns—children playing in the streets, neighbors gossiping and shopping, or people simply sitting in a front room observing street activity—assured that there were always "eyes on the street" (Jacobs 1961:35). "Eyes on the street" gives importance to the power of informal social control and serves as the basic defense against crime.

Jacobs believes that the successful street is self-policing. Further, this self-policing is not readily apparent; it is attained through the intensive use of and contacts among a wide diversity of people who are not aware that they are policing. "Public peace—the sidewalk and street peace—of cities is not kept primarily by the police, necessary as police are. It is kept primarily by an intricate almost unconscious network of voluntary controls and standards among the people themselves, and enforced by the people themselves" (Jacobs 1961:31–32).

Jacobs argued that "lowly, unpurposeful and random as they may appear, sidewalk contacts are the small change from which a city's wealth of public life may grow" (1961:71). She contends that "The tolerance, the room for great differences among neighbors . . . are possible and normal only when the streets of great cities have built-in equipment allowing strangers to dwell in peace together on civilized but essentially dignified and reserved terms" (Jacobs 1961:71).

But what would city life be like if strangers no longer dwelled in peace? What would happen if the behavior among strangers were no longer anchored in laws of civility? What impact would it have on the city and in turn on the entire society? What would happen if the underlying social order of the world of strangers became a world of social "disorder"? We began to answer these questions at the end of the last chapter in our discussion of the impact of poverty on poor African American communities in Philadelphia. Michael Walzer (1975) asks the "what if" question and builds on it. What if the street is not successful? What if it always seems dangerous and a place to avoid? What if it seems inadequately policed? What if the same holds true for parks, playgrounds, waiting rooms, lobbies, and other places in the public realm? What then? He believes that if this social disorder holds true, then these public places, without regular and confident users, will become the settings for social, sexual, and political deviance. The consequence will be the withdrawal of people into their private and controlled worlds and the abandonment of the public realm.

In the late 1960s and 1970s life in the city for many Americans became problematic. This chapter examines what happened to American cities when the public realm went into severe decline and the ramifications it had on the relationships among people not only in the public realm but in the private and parochial realms as well. Writing during this period, Richard Sennett (1977), in *The Fall of*

Public Man, is concerned that contemporary social life is suffering as a consequence of the collapse of public life as people forget the forms of civility in settings marked without intimacy. Many social commentators agreed with Sennett and saw the late 1960s and 1970s as a pivotal time period in the history of the American city. During these years much of American society was under scrutiny. In addition to the anti–Vietnam War movement, the feminist movement, and the civil rights movement, American cities were witnessing a period of decline in civility in the public realm. Erving Goffman (1971) commented that the social contract and the assumptions regarding the moral order were questioned and in some cases disregarded.

> In the last decade interesting things have happened to assumptions about the moral order within and around establishments. Ordinary policing, along with the mortification presumably consequent on public arrest, was thought to be all that was necessary in order to keep users of public and semi-public establishments effectively respectful of the property and persons within these places, and of the frame itself. But, of course, other factors were at work, such as actual respect and informal segregation by class, race, and age; and these factors seem to be much less effective in cities today. (Goffman 1971: 289)

In an insightful review of Goffman's (1971) *Relations in Public*, Marshall Berman (1972) follows him in cataloging what is now an all too familiar litany of examples of ways that establishments have sought to police what heretofore were not problematic areas. These include libraries instituting extensive checkout and search procedures; stores with elaborate antitheft devices or stores that simply give up and close; streetcars and buses employing exact change coin boxes and cashless drivers; taxicabs with protective glass dividers between front and back seats; and banks with remote control television tellers and the videotaping of all activities and transactions. Goffman observes the implementation of strict security measures and surveillance techniques at political conventions, public meetings, and governmental official appearances. To counter theft and vandalism, including the prevalent occurrence of the spray-paint defacement of buildings, there was a massive increase in crime preventive implements, the iron mesh and bars originally used for doors and windows in prisons and inner-city jewelry stores were extended to stores and homes in upscale commercial and residential areas. Doormen had taken on police-like guard functions in apartment houses, and building maintenance managers of urban public housing were confronted with an everyday terrifying atmosphere. Goffman observes the development of a new "garrison architecture" that includes orientation to an inner court and street sides that are nearly windowless. "And citizens at large have learned the sociological lesson that their easefulness had been dependent all along on the self-restraint sustained by potential offenders who have never had many reasons for being respectful" (Goffman 1971: 290 cited in Berman 1972:12).

Fred Siegel (1995, 1997), a sociologist who was very influential during Rudolph Giuliani's mayoral administration (1994–2002) in New York City, makes the argument that in the late 1960s and early 1970s the "built-in equipment" that allows people to trust and live together so eloquently extolled by Jacobs was being dismantled. He argues that it was those liberal policies concerned with the decriminalization of victimless crime, the deinstitutionalization of the mentally ill, and the decriminalization of minor civil offenses that ultimately led to the decline in urban civility and the abandonment of public space.

Siegel particularly takes issue with the municipal governments' handling of the riots and threats of riots by alienated African American city dwellers in the mid- to late 1960s. He vehemently opposes the liberal policies of big city mayors' abandonment of the stern principles of personal responsibility and their creating a vast social welfare system premised on the idea that dependence of government was healthy. Siegel sees these policies as being based on the mayors' beliefs that black anger was a legitimate response to poverty. Siegel blames this "riot ideology" on a crime explosion that he terms a "rolling riot" and the huge municipal government's expansion, which drove taxes so high that they chased out private industry and led to fiscal disaster.

Siegel also takes issue with the abandonment of the notions of civil responsibility under the guise that the decriminalization of vice and other minor offenses to civility would allow the police to concentrate on major crime. He argues that the movement to decriminalize "victimless" crimes (crimes in which none of the involved, consenting adults has either cause or desire to press for legal action) was part of a larger Vietnam era movement against the legislating of morality. The rights of the individual were pitted against the strictures of social conformity and the duty of the community to police "deviant" behavior. Further the battle for the decriminalization of vice was joined with the push for the deinstitutionalization of individuals who were incarcerated, often unjustly and unnecessarily, for violation of social norms. As a consequence the desire to protect the individual's rights was ultimately at the expense of the community and the concomitant decline in urban civility. The result was seen in the decline of public civility in New York City in the late 1960s, 1970s, and 1980s. In the following passage Siegel speaks specifically of the New York experience but he feels the discussion can be generalized to most American cities of that time period:

> New Yorkers understand that entering public places leaves them open to what have become the indignities of everyday interaction. Walking in the park outside city hall, the New Yorker faces an aesthetic assault in the form of mounds of swirling garbage. In the East Village and on Upper Broadway, "thieves' markets" set up by predatory peddlers block the sidewalks. On nearly every street, homeless men panhandle aggressively, often "rough tailing" passersby. Even those who drive must pay a toll to not-so-subtle shake-down artists, the "squeegee men." Writer Gil Schwartz tells of picking up his daughter from a play-date: "I told another parent we were moving out of the city. 'Why?' he asked. I quietly took my child, stepped over the wino sleeping in the vestibule, [and left]." (Siegel 1995:370)

In the next section, we want to take issue with the idea of the "decline" of the public realm. Our point-of-view is to emphasize the fact, that for many Americans, historically, the public realm should be seen in terms of "exclusion" rather than "decline" and that much of the battle in the public realm is over the policies of exclusion.

African Americans and the Exclusion from the Public Realm

Flora Dorsey Young was a colleague in the Department of Sociology at Rowan University. She was the daughter of prominent parents who were well established in the Philadelphia black community—members of its *Black Bourgeoisie*, to use E. Franklin Frazier's term. Her parents were highly educated, her father being a very successful dentist. Dr. Young vividly recalls that in pre–World War II Philadelphia, when African Americans went to Center City—the downtown shopping area—they knew to use the bathroom before they left home, as public toilet facilities were not available to them. If they shopped and wished to purchase clothes and hats they were not allowed to try them on for fit. The policy set for African Americans in downtown department stores was that anything purchased was not returnable. Street etiquette required them, both males and females, to give way to whites and to avoid eye contact and be as inconspicuous as possible. African Americans were required to sit in segregated sections of movie theaters. Philadelphia, a northern city, the city of Brotherly Love, was a Jim Crow city as were many others, both in the North and South, in early twentieth-century America. How can we reconcile the memories of Dr. Young, which are shared by so many African Americans who were systematically degraded, segregated, and often excluded from the public realm of the city until relatively recent years, with the perspective that views the public sphere of the past so fondly and laments on its "decline"?

Bryant Simon (2004: 13), an urban historian at Temple University in Philadelphia, reminds us that the perspective that laments the decline of the public sphere in America—"the lost city of sidewalks, and window shopping, corner stores and showy movie theaters"—is an idealized nostalgic image that ignores the exclusion of many from the public spheres. Simon argues that the public realm was never about democracy but rather of exclusion. He further observes that the failure to incorporate the experience of those who were excluded from the public sphere distorts its actuality in its reinterpretation of the past.

> This erasure of the meanness of the past and the walling off of public space is not that different from what goes on in current urban studies and urban planning. While there are innumerable books on the decline of American cities and the need for neotraditional designs to save them, they are frequently nostalgic, if only in subtle ways, for an urban past that we all too often forget was defined and shaped by exclusion. Keeping some people out because of how they looked or acted was not just an unfortunate aspect of these places; it was what made them public places to begin with. (Simon 2004: 18)

Simon uses as his case-in-point Atlantic City, New Jersey, to document his assertions. The use of this city is somewhat surprising given its popular past image

Couples and families strolling past storefronts and being conveyed in rolling chairs on Atlantic City Boardwalk, ca. 1915.

as one of America's great city playgrounds. James Kunstler (1993: 228), one of the prominent urbanists who polemically reports on the decline of the public realm and its replacement by a "geography of nowhere," refers to Atlantic City as "one of [the] nation's great public spaces." From 1900 until mid-century, Atlantic City was one of the premier tourists towns in America—an idyllic playground for the middle class. It is located within easy distance by rail and later by bus and automobile to Philadelphia, New York City, and Baltimore, as well as to smaller towns and industrial cities in the mid-Atlantic region. It was the home of a famed boardwalk, the Steel Pier's diving horse, and the Miss America Pageant, and its street names were immortalized in the board game *Monopoly*.

During this time period, Atlantic City became the city of fantasy, where white tourists could revel in their upward mobility and satisfy their leisure desires in an atmosphere of frivolity, fun, and safety without anxiety. Atlantic City as a tourist city was designed to provide a luxury experience city at middle-class prices. To be in Atlantic City, and to walk the Boardwalk, was an ideal setting for demonstrating that one had achieved respectability and the American dream of inclusion and social mobility. Yet, during that time period, the Boardwalk was completely segregated (Simon 2004).

At the height of its popularity, from the 1920s to the 1950s, African Americans were not allowed full access to the Boardwalk. Beach access was restricted to a specified area away from the tourist area. Just as Young reports for Philadelphia, African Americans faced similar patterns of discrimination in Atlantic City when entering establishments that implicitly catered to a white-only clientele. The African American presence in the tourist area and on the Boardwalk was limited to service occupations and pushing the rolling chairs—rickshaw-like, wicker baskets on wheels seating two people comfortably. Sitting in the rolling car and being pushed by African American men served as a moving symbol by middle-class whites that they had made it in America. "During the years before the resort slid into decline, the rolling chairs . . . represented the city's most accessible and visually arresting fantasy. This is where visitors let down their guards and acted out their dreams" (Simon 2004: 6).

By the 1960s Atlantic City was in its death throes, a symbol of urban decay and blight. Factoring into the city's decline were changing vacation fashions, inexpensive airplane flights, and a failure to modernize, as well as the closing of hotels, theaters, and middle-class shopping areas, which all led to the development of a honky-tonk atmosphere generated by cheap T-shirt and souvenir stores and fast-food stands. Simon reports that as theaters, stores, and shops closed along Atlantic Avenue, the main shopping district, there was less foot traffic on the streets and on the Boardwalk itself by the *right* people. This in turn accelerated the process of closure. Fewer and fewer shops meant less people on the streets and on the Boardwalk. Atlantic City was no longer the "fantasy" city for white middle-class tourists or for the white middle-class residents.

Simon believes that a significant factor in the decline of Atlantic City was the Civil Rights movement of the 1960s. It opened the tourist establishments as well as the Boardwalk to African Americans. With the democratizing of Atlantic City, the area was no longer a segregated fantasyland for the white middle class. Further, the riots of the late 1960s that occurred in Newark, in Detroit, and in Watts, Los Angeles, convinced the middle class that Atlantic City was unsafe and a place to be avoided. The perception of an increase in crime (actually crime rates were pretty consistent since the 1930s) began to frighten tourists away in the late 1950s. However, in the 1960s, crime did become more violent, more personalized, and more harrowing, and most importantly its occurrences were not restricted to the poorer areas of the city. The Boardwalk itself was not immune to crime, and each occurrence attracted much media attention (Simon 2004).

Simon believes that the end of segregation and the democratization of Atlantic City's public realm, including the Boardwalk and its neighborhoods as well, combined with the fear of crime, became the primary factors that led to the abandonment by the white middle class of the city as a whole. "Worried that public space was now unmanageable and out of control, [they] opted for self containment" (Simon 2004: 14). The white middle class found haven in the segregated suburbs and the controlled environments of the shopping mall and other *de facto* segregated leisure and amusement venues. While never explicitly proclaiming their desire for racial segregation, it "just happened" that where they lived, where they shopped, and where they played somehow was populated by people just like themselves.

> In their leisure time and in their neighborhoods, these families on the run didn't ask for explicit performances of racial deference and superiority any more; they didn't fantasize about being pushed down the Boardwalk by happy African American servants. They showed off their middle-class status in other ways, including by abandoning the city. When it came to organizing their new worlds away from the cities, they wanted to seal people of color off in their own spaces, as far away from them as possible. But they wanted to do this without calling attention to the new way of carving up public space. So they tolerated a handful of well-behaved Others on their streets and in their malls. That way, they could say to themselves and any-one who asked that the sorting of people along race and class lines was natural; it just happened that they lived in virtually all-white neighborhoods, sent their kids to virtually all-white schools, and vacationed in virtually all-white theme parks. (Simon 2004: 14)

In regard to the public realm, Simon observed that while being desegregated Atlantic City was also transformed into a more controlled environment with the restrictions based more on class and proper behavioral demeanor and shared rules of decorum. Indeed, in the mid-1970s gambling was seen as Atlantic City's salva-tion, with the first casino opening in 1978. Since then it has been restored as a desir-able tourist town for the middle class and the affluent, and while racial segregation is no longer blatant it takes more subtle forms in a highly regulated and policed environment.

Gambling *has* changed Atlantic City. The 12 casinos have invested $6 billion and have paid hundreds of millions of dollars in federal, state, and local taxes. More than 45,000 people work in the casinos. The number of people employed in the casinos outnumbers the number of people who live in Atlantic City. But higher paying jobs are mostly held by non-residents who live in the suburbs. The lowest-skilled, most poorly paid jobs are occupied by those who live in the city. The city itself has not revitalized—abandoned buildings are abundant and many blocks contain no built structures. The poor and their housing are still visible . . . but are some distance from the casinos. There is no large middle-class community. The land-use patterns reflect what Ernest Burgess called the zone of transition; nothing is done to maintain properties. The hope is that someday the casinos will expand and buy up whatever property they already do not own.

The fear of the city that was so prevalent in the 1960s and 1970s is still preva-lent. The irony is that this has worked to the favor of the casino. It provides a secured environment with the world outside perceived as being dangerous. The casino-owned parking garages are located within the casinos. The casinos are enclosed spaces detached from the surrounding environment. They could be any-where. Time is suspended—no clocks. The outside world is invisible—no win-dows. Sound is biased—the only sound that is heard is the sound of winning as coins clatter in the slot machine for the lucky few. There is no sound of losing. Space is distorted—bright lights and mirrors overstimulate the senses. It's easy to become disoriented. Doors to the Boardwalk and the ocean beach are hard to find. People who come to Atlantic City to gamble do so as their sole objective, with many not venturing out on the Boardwalk, with its still-tacky shops selling T-shirts, cheap souvenirs, and cheap food.

> Fear of the city keeps gamblers locked inside casino fortresses glued to the black-jack tables and slot machines, feeling safe under the watchful eyes of hundreds of surveillance cameras. And that's just where the casinos want them. They don't want them at the movies—so there aren't any in the city. They don't want guests sitting in the lobbies talking—so none of the hotels have lobbies; they just have high-speed computerized check-in desks. They don't want them eating at a local restaurant, and they don't want them watching the Surf, Atlantic City's minor league baseball team. (Simon 2004: 214–215)

Gambling has been a remarkably powerful economic engine. And the casinos have certainly brought the crowds back. More than 35 million visitors come to the city each year (Simon 2004). Yet, despite all the people on the Boardwalk and in the 12 casinos, Atlantic City, as a place to live and to play, is worse off than before the gamblers arrived in their cars and buses. Despite the hype, the casinos have not transformed the rest of the city. In the last quarter of a century, Atlantic City has lost a third of its housing stock, and its population has dropped by a third. Much of the retail businesses have closed; more than 200 restaurants have shut their doors since 1978. Relatively little everyday clothing and grocery shopping and entertainment venues such as movie theaters exist. While a pedestrian shopping mall has been constructed linking the convention center to the casino area, this mall is targeted for the tourist. Simon summarizes his view on what makes a city and its public realm viable and why casinos can be seen as the antithesis:

> "People make cities—people on the sidewalks, in cafes, in front of movie theaters and in stores," Simon said . . . This dance of people out in public is what brings life, vigor and energy to cities. Casinos spend a lot of time and money trying to create the opposite effect." (Baals 2004)

The historical experience of African Americans in Atlantic City in the twentieth century is similar, with some modification, to that experienced in many other American cities as well. In the next chapter I will elaborate on how the perception of disorder has resulted in a dramatic reconfiguration of American cities, particularly in how the built environment has been restructured and how the interactions among strangers has dramatically changed. The particular focus will be on ethnic enclaves and ghettos.

Wilson and Kelling: Broken Windows

As discussed, what Goffman and Siegel allude to was that in the late 1960s and into the 1970s and beyond there was a collective group of strangers, women, and minorities who refused to accept the underlying premises of the existing social order.

The denial of the rules of civility were in larger part a denial of the underlying legitimacy of the state, manifested in the order of everyday life in the city. George Kelling, who helped articulate the *broken windows* theory, elaborates on the consequences of this viewpoint in *Fixing Broken Windows*, coauthored with Catherine Coles (1996). They claim that the ethos of the 1960s resulted in "the expression of virtually all forms of non-violent deviance [that] came to be considered synonymous with the expression of individual, particularly First Amendment or speech-related rights" (quoted in Shapiro 2002:2). The consequences of nonviolent deviance and the necessity for control are the concerns of the broken windows theory.

The broken windows thesis of enforcement is a foundation stone in community policing. "Broken windows" was a term coined by James Q. Wilson and George Kelling (1982) to figuratively illustrate a theory that argues that untended and ignored petty crimes, such as breaking a window, send out the wrong signal that nobody cares. The perception that no one cares leads to further violations, some not as petty, and ultimately to an atmosphere of fear, serious crimes, and neighborhood decay. This theory asserts that to fight crime disorderly neighborhoods must appear more attractive, and disorderly individuals must be confronted. To combat the occurrence of social disorderliness aggressive enforcement of the law even against nuisance offenses was advocated.

New York City in the mid-1990s was one of the first to employ this "broken windows" thesis for law enforcement. The police commissioner of New York at the time, Bill Braxton, in the administration of Rudolph Giuliani, sought to change the attitudes of the police department and the entire community about crime. His mentor was George Kelling, who has been dubbed the father of "community policing." The development of what may be called the culture of community policing had as its goal making community life better by reducing crime through "order maintenance."

The old policy of the New York Police Department was based on the belief that they did not have the resources to counter "broken windows" crimes and needed to devote their energies solely to serious felonies. As a consequence many minor offensives were ignored. The new policy saw the necessity to move from a "reactive" policing response, such as the investigation of reported crime, to a "proactive" policing response that sought the prevention of crime. A police department publication and widely distributed articulates that new strategy:

> By working systematically and assertively to reduce the level of disorder in the city, the NYPD will act to undercut the ground on which more serious crimes seem possible and even permissible. (quoted in Norquist 1998: 61)

One particular target of the NYPD were subway-system fare beaters who would jump the turnstile. As a consequence of the police efforts, not only were such fare beaters apprehended, but as many as one out of ten turnstile jumpers were found to have outstanding felony warrants for previous crimes or were carrying drugs or weapons. One police officer commented: "We got this great new chief and this great new strategy: robbery, fare beating, and disorder, you deal with one, you deal with all" (quoted in Siegel 1997:193). Whether a coincidence or not, in the last five years of the 1990s tourism in New York City rose dramatically while fare beatings were down, public urination was down, windshield squeegee scamming was gone, and there was a dramatic fall in bigger and more serious crimes.

However, soon after the broken windows policy went into effect in New York City and elsewhere, numerous critics believed that there was a serious downside to how this policy was enforced. Broken windows policing often operates under a "zero tolerance" policy in law enforcement. Critics such as Bruce Shapiro (2002), a contributing editor at the magazine *Nation*, argue that this has resulted too often in excessive force and police brutality, which have violated basic human rights standards. A disproportionate number of people of color are the recipients of such violations. Complaints of excessive force have risen dramatically, resulting in a growing belief that questions police legitimacy.

In examining the broken windows thesis it is important to note the distinction made by Wilson and Kelling between what they call "untended property" and "untended behavior." "Untended property" focuses its impact on community life. "Untended behavior" focuses on the nature and character of street life. There is an interlinked relationship between untended *property* and untended *behavior*. The linkage is spelled out by Wilson and Kelling in their illustration of the processes that change a stable neighborhood into a neighborhood in decline:

> A stable neighborhood of families who care for their homes, mind each other's children, and confidently frown on unwanted intruders can change, in a few years or even a few months, to an inhospitable and frightening jungle. A piece of property is abandoned, weeds grow up, a window is smashed. Adults stop scolding rowdy children; the children, emboldened, become more rowdy. Families move out, unattached adults move in. Teenagers gather in front of the corner store. The merchant asks them to move; they refuse. Fights occur. Litter accumulates. People start drinking in front of the grocery; in time an inebriate slumps to the sidewalk and is allowed to sleep it off. Pedestrians are approached by panhandlers.
>
> At this point it is not inevitable that serious crime will flourish or violent attacks on strangers will occur. But many residents will think that crime, especially violent crime, is on the rise, and they will modify their behavior accordingly. They will use the streets less often, and when on the streets will stay apart from their fellows, moving with averted eyes, silent lips, and hurried steps. "Don't get involved." . . .
>
> Such an area is vulnerable to criminal invasion. Though it is not inevitable, it is more likely that here, rather than in places where people are confident they can regulate public behavior by informal controls, drugs will change hands, prostitutes will solicit, and cars will be stripped. That the drunks will be robbed by boys who do it as a lark, and the prostitutes' customers will be robbed by men who do it purposely and perhaps violently. That muggings will occur. (Wilson and Kelling 1982:31–32)

This breakdown, in turn, led to the development of crime as a way of life especially, for young men. Others have taken issue with Wilson and see the turning to crime as an adaptation to these men's perception that there was no economic future for them. Faced with a future of unemployment, crime was seen as an alternative, albeit illegal, activity.

In an earlier work, Wilson (1975/1983) made the broader point that the increase in crime is attributable to the breakdown in the social order in poorer neighborhoods and the "visible signs of [such] disorder." His fundamental argument is that people have a right to expect social order and proper behavior to operate in public places. When this does not occur people feel that the very foundation of community life is disintegrating. This breakdown in standards of behavior often results in a disregard for property. In what Wilson and Kelling (1982) later call "untended property" the interactive affects continue with the further development of other more serious forms of misconduct and ultimately to predatory criminal behavior.

Mitchell Duneier: Street People and Broken Windows

Mitchell Duneier, in a trenchant ethnographic monograph, *Sidewalk* (1999), examines the street lives of poor black men who make their livelihoods selling discarded magazines, or new and used books, or who panhandle. He believes that Wilson and Kelling (1982) and later Kelling and Coles's (1996) book, *Fixing Broken Windows*, fail to distinguish between *physical* disorder and *social* disorder. *Physical* disorder refers to the broken windows or other forms of property damage that

People browsing at one of the many street vendor book stands located in NYC. Photo by author.

provides symbolic evidence that no one cares in the community. As a consequence this leads to increased vandalism and ultimately to the breakdown of community social order. *Social* disorder refers to human beings who seem to evidence social behavior that is viewed as disorderly, threatening, and potentially criminal by the more affluent and powerful. "Unlike a broken window, social disorder consists of human beings such as the vendors, scavengers, and panhandlers on Sixth Avenue, who are capable of thinking and creating meanings that range from 'everyone cares', to 'someone cares' to 'no one cares'" (Duneier 1999:288). It would be instructive to see how Duneier reaches this conclusion based on his research.

The locale for Duneier's study is upper-middle-class Greenwich Village, New York City, the neighborhood made famous by Jane Jacobs in her influential work on urban life. He focuses his attention on the ongoing interaction of vendors, scavengers, and panhandlers with the more affluent passersby on the busy intersection of Sixth Avenue and W. Eighth Street in Greenwich Village. What often seems from afar to be the problematic nature of these relationships is examined within the context of the influential "broken windows" theory and the quality of life issues that have been a cornerstone of Rudolph Giuliani's administration and have been supported by other municipal governments as well.

Duneier examines the everyday street life that occurs. He analyzes the rules and regulations set up by the street people to self-regulate their spatial distribution of who sells and who does what and where. The rules of decorum that are worked out between the street people and the passersby and between the street people and the police indicate an underlying sense of social order. In his examination of the street life of these poor black men, many of whom are homeless, Duneier demonstrates how social order develops and is sustained among them and with many of the passersby and residents of the community.

One of the vendors characterizes his role in the neighborhood as that of a "public character." The vendor cites Jane Jacobs on his perception that he fulfills many of the characteristics that she attributes to this type of individual:

> The social structure of sidewalk life hangs partly on what can be called self-appointed public characters. A public character is anyone who is in frequent contact with a wide circle of people and who is sufficiently interested to make himself a public character. (Jacobs 1961 cited in Duneier 1999)

Duneier argues that such public characters serve a useful function in making the street life safe even though they seem to be exhibiting "social disorder" in their behavior. He believes that their behavior is not the equivalent of vandalized public telephones and that they should not be seen as "social" broken windows.

> The men working on Sixth Avenue may be viewed as broken windows, but this research shows that most of them have actually become public characters who create a set of expectations, for one another and strangers (including those of the criminal element—as indeed, many of them once were), that "someone cares" and that they should strive to live better lives. (Duneier 1999: 289)

The Criminalization of Poverty

One of the most vocal and influential critics of the broken windows theory was Mike Davis. Davis, a social activist and academician, was living in Los Angeles, where a similar law enforcement policy had been undertaken. The policy was called "take-back-the-streets." Davis argued that the police department had developed strategies of social control that in essence has sought to criminalize much of the behavior of the poor and of the "undesirables" such as vagrants and panhandlers. I will discuss Davis's ideas in more detail later in this chapter.

Another critic of the broken windows theory was Bernard E. Harcourt (2001), a political scientist at the University of Arizona, who makes the point that broken windows policing is basically a detrimental conservative philosophy that is portrayed as an enlightened pragmatic public policy, Harcourt believes that the underlying causes of much of the physical and social "disorder" of communities stems from underlying "root causes" of crime—such as poverty, discrimination, poor education, and lack of jobs and economic opportunities in the inner city. To support this viewpoint, others have observed that the decline in crime after the implementation of broken windows policing is more likely the result in underlying changes in other factors, such as demographic shifts from teenage and young adults to less crime-prone age populations, the return of many teenagers to school, a decline in the crack cocaine market, and increased employment opportunities even for those with little occupational skills.

Underlying issues of doubt and trust permeate the interaction of strangers. Where strangers meet (the location) and the individualistic characteristics (appearance) of the stranger become important cues. The depiction of the stranger as a lone individual who, for whatever motives, personal or psychotic, disrupts the underlying social order adds to the fear and distrust. The homeless are often depicted as symbols of the decline in public civility. Special attention is given to those who break the civil norms of public propriety by sleeping in the streets, colonizing public parks, and aggressively panhandling. The call for the implementation of "quality-of-life issues" has led to the call for legislation against those who defy the rules of civility. Critics see this call as an example of the desire to "criminalize poverty." Let's examine some of this legislation.

The question of whether the homeless should be allowed to sleep in parks and other public areas has become a flashpoint in the debate over the rights of individuals and the rights of the collective (Kendall 2001). In a number of cities, including San Francisco, Portland, Baltimore, Santa Monica, and Philadelphia, the local government has sought to improve the downtown areas and public spaces. One of the tactics that they have employed is to enforce city ordinances that control loitering (which includes standing around or sleeping in public spaces) and disorderly conduct.

The enforcement of these ordinances has been seen by advocates of the homeless and civil liberties groups as direct attacks on the rights of individuals whose presence, for whatever reasons, is deemed undesirable. In the case of the homeless, their advocates assert that they have a right to use and sleep in parks, as there is no affordable housing available for them. The argument is also made that panhandling or begging is a legitimate activity to make a living and should be seen as a form of speech protection guaranteed by the First Amendment.

Local governments have controlled the homeless through various means, including the redesigning public benches to include separation arm rests that prevent people from spreading out over the length of the bench, systematically harassing and imprisoning the homeless, and providing them with one-way transportation tickets to other destinations.

An example of what has been referred to as the criminalization of poverty was the debate over a "sidewalk" bill in the Philadelphia City Council in June 1998 to regulate and control sidewalk behavior. The ordinance would ban sitting or lying on city sidewalks and aggressive panhandling (begging). Opponents of the bill, many of them advocates of the homeless, see it as an attempt to criminalize homelessness. In response, the proponents of the bill argued that violators would not be assessed criminal penalties. Instead, they would be fined and assessed community service penalties.

The underlying issue is the council's attempt to balance the economic needs of the business community and the rights of the homeless. Businesses believe that potential customers are scared away by the presence of homeless people and panhandlers. A mentioned case-in-point is the presence and panhandling that occurs near automatic teller machines and bank entrances. Opponents of the bill are concerned that the rights of the homeless would be violated. They are particularly concerned that hardcore homeless people would be forcibly placed in shelters or treatment centers for substance abuse or mental illness.

The City Council President John F. Street (quoted in Burton 1998) argues in favor of the bill: "We can't have them (hardcore homeless people) in the street. It's unfair to them and it's unfair to the general public. The commitment is to make the services available (and to) take them off the street in a fair, humane, safe, decent way."

Mike Davis: The Ecology of Fear and the Fortressing of America

As previously mentioned, Mike Davis has a much different perspective on the "broken window" thesis of policing. The "ecology of fear" and the "militarization of public space" are phrases coined by Mike Davis (1992a, 1992b, 1992c). He refers to an "ecology of fear" that has impacted on the ecological zones of contemporary Los Angeles. Davis applies Burgess's concentric zonal model but with a twist. Rather than seeing land patterns based on economic factors, "fear" is the underlying new factor, and is based on an "obsession with security" (Davis's term; Davis 1992a:155; Sorkin 1992:xiii). Mike Davis writes that a "second civil war," which began in the summers of the late 1960s, has been institutionalized into public space. He observes that "the old liberal attempts at social control, which at least tried to balance repression with reform, have been superseded by open social warfare that pits the interests of the middle class against the welfare of the urban poor" (Davis 1992a:155). He observes architecture, urban planning, and a militarized police force set out to control public space and to criminalize much of the behavior of the poor.

> To reduce contact with untouchables, urban redevelopment has converted once vital pedestrian streets into traffic sewers and transformed public parks into temporary receptacles for the homeless and wretched. The American city . . . is being systematically turned inside out—or rather, outside in. The valorized spaces of the new megastructures, and super-malls are concentrated in the center, street frontage is denuded, public activity is sorted intor strictly functional compartments, and circulation is internalized in corridors under the gaze of private police. (Davis 1990: 226)

Davis's viewpoint is echoed in the works of Neil Smith, who sees a new form of urban policy that he calls *revanchism* taking shape in American cities. *Revanche* means the act of retaliating or revenge, and Smith coins the term the *revanchist city* as a label for those cities that use the "broken windows" form of policing to counter the behavior of those who are seen to breach the code of civility.

In his analysis of the revanchist city, Smith (1997) makes an interesting point. He distinguishes between the concepts of identity and individualism. The concept of social justice is seen to have traditionally centered on *individual* rights regardless of the individual's identity—male or female, rich or poor, white or black. He gives the example of a homeless person asserting: "Why do we as homeless individuals have no right to housing?" Here the individual's identity, in this case a homeless person, is used to assert one's right to "equal justice" and the importance of identity over individualism. Siegel's example cited earlier of the man who feels that he has a right not to be interactively molested is restated by Smith as "Don't I have a right to live without homeless people messing up the neighborhood; don't men also have rights?" Identity here becomes a vehicle for a reasserted individualism that is the hallmark of the revanchist city. By so doing, the rights of individuals assert themselves to only those whose identities have political clout, such as the rich over the poor, whites over blacks, and men over women.

Surveillance of the Street

As part of the enforcement policies many cities for public safety reasons have instituted the use of closed-circuit television cameras (CCTV) to monitor activity over public space. Citing a small survey by the Security Industry Association, Allan Reeder (1998), in a July 1998 issue of the *Atlantic Monthly*, reports that more than 60 American cities have employed video technology for public safety. These surveillance monitors are not limited to just monitoring the streets but increasingly are also being utilized for surveillance purposes in housing projects, parks, and subways. In San Francisco, closed-circuit cameras are found in every subway car; in Baltimore, cameras monitor traffic as cars proceed through traffic lights. The use of surveillance cameras is not limited to the city. Gated communities more often than

Chicago Mayor Richard Daley announced in 2004 that more than 2,000 surveillance cameras in public places, similar to this one in downtown Chicago, would be tied to a network armed with software to alert authorities to suspicious behavior or emergency situations. Daley said the cameras are the equivalent of hundreds of sets of eyes and are the next best thing to having police officers stationed at every potential trouble spot.

not employ CCTV cameras to monitor gate activity as well as thoroughfares within the community.

In addition to their utilization by various levels of governmental agencies, the private sector has also employed CCTV cameras in offices, apartment buildings, garages, stores, banks, and restaurants. *USA Today* estimates that in the year 2000 more than a million closed-circuit cameras, most with videotape recording capability, were being employed in the United States (Zuckerman 2001 cited in Gumpert and Drucker 2001).

The United Kingdom is reported to be the country that has employed such devises more systematically than any other country (Reeder 1998; Bulos & Chaker 1998 cited in Gumpert and Druker 2001). A criminologist observes that in London, "A million cameras could be a conservative estimate. On an average day in London, or any other big city in the United States, more than 300 cameras from 30 different CCTV networks can film a given individual. The filming goes on throughout the day, and in some areas, such as the London Underground, it is constant" (citied in Gumpert and Drucker 2001).

New York City is one of the most surveilled cities in the United States. It is reported that over 200 cameras monitor every community in the borough of

Manhattan (Gumpert and Drucker 2001). The New York Civil Liberties Union (NYCLU) has undertaken the Surveillance Camera Project to record the number of visible surveillance cameras in Manhattan. Over two thousand cameras have been located, and many more are expected to exist. The NYCLU report estimates that only 11 percent of the watching is by governmental agencies; the rest is by private companies, employers, landlords, and coworkers (NYC Surveillance Camera Project Information 1999 cited in Gumpert and Drucker 2001).

The NYCLU found that on the West Side of Manhattan, over a three block area between West 32nd Street and 35th Street, over 70 cameras were observed. Similarly, Reeder (1998) surveyed a three-block area of midtown Manhattan and found the use of CCTV cameras so prevalent that virtually the entire area was under surveillance. His map of the locations of 72 easily visible CCTV cameras leads him to conclude that virtually all street-level activities were being monitored. The implications of this ubiquitous monitoring policy is that "Surveillance cameras portend consequences for freedom of association and the less clearly articulated right of anonymity associated with public places as well as the right to move freely" (Gumpert and Drucker 2001:4).

Sampson and Raudenbush: "Seeing" Disorder and the Social Construction of "Broken Windows"

A major research study conducted in Chicago neighborhoods fundamentally questions the basic assumptions of the broken windows theory. The study, by a research team under the direction of Robert J. Sampson and Stephen W. Raudenbush at the University of Chicago, is reported in two articles that we will cite here (Sampson and Raudenbush 1999 and Sampson and Raudenbush 2004). They report in their 1999 paper that social disorder and crime were the consequence of concentrated poverty and low "collective efficacy," the capacity of neighbors to work together to strengthen their community (Sampson and Raudenbush 1999). The extent of neighborhood orderliness was not a crucial factor. They found little empirical evidence for the connection between disorder and crime. Further, they report in their later article (Sampson and Raudenbush 2004) that the perception of disorder is more important than actual objective signs of physical and social disorder in orienting people's feelings about their community. And the perception of disorder is influenced by the racial, ethnic, and class composition of that community. Let's examine their research in more detail.

Sampson and his research team studied Chicago in the mid-1990s. They surveyed thousands of families with children and, very creatively, they rated over 23,000 street segments in 196 neighborhoods for physical and social disorder. They did this by videotaping these blocks from a sports utility vehicle. Trained observers systematically coded and audiotaped everything in public view. Signs of physical disorder included the prevalence of garbage/litter and empty beer bottles on the streets and sidewalks, graffiti, needles and syringes, condoms on the sidewalks, abandoned cars, the prevalence of bars, and broken windows and vacant houses.

The signs of social disorder included loitering, people drinking alcohol and/or people who appeared intoxicated, the presence of prostitutes, adults fighting or arguing, and people selling drugs on the sidewalks and streets.

Their ratings of neighborhoods for physical and social disorder were correlated with different types of predatory crimes, including homicide, robbery, and burglary. They found that once they accounted for other neighborhood characteristics, such as poverty and instability, the connection with disorder disappeared in all but the category of robbery. They speculate that robbery may constrain social interaction and reduce social control; robbery offenders may be enticed by social and physical disorder in neighborhoods. However, after careful analysis of all their data, Sampson and Raudenbush conclude overall that "disorder is a moderate correlate to predatory crime" (1999:637). They put forth the argument that "collective efficacy" and structural constraints that are "defined as cohesion among residents combined with shared expectations for the social control of public space" are important factors in lowering crime rates and observed disorder (Sampson and Raudenbush 1999: 603). In communities where there is underlying trust and where there is a collective action to improve and protect the neighborhood, lower crime rates are achieved.

Sampson and Raudenbush (1999) further argue that the emphasis placed on the enforcement of ordinances to curb "broken window" offenses through tough police actions may be misplaced. They favor more attention to policies to encourage the development of collective efforts among residents to combat disorder and to work toward enhancing collective efficacy that may, in turn, lower the rate of crime. They conclude:

> The current fascination in policy circles on cleaning up disorder through law enforcement techniques appears simplistic and largely misplaced, at least in terms of directly fighting crime. . . . Put differently, the active ingredients in crime seem to be structural disadvantage and attenuated collective efficacy more so than disorder. Attacking public disorder through tough police tactics may thus be a politically popular but perhaps analytically weak strategy to reduce crime, mainly because such a strategy leaves the common origins of both, but especially the last untouched. A more subtle approach . . . would look to how informal but collective efforts among residents to stem disorder may provide unanticipated benefits for increasing collective efficacy . . . , in the long run lowering crime. (Sampson and Raudenbush 1999:638)

In their 2004 article, Sampson and Raudenbush pose fundamental questions. Granted that disorder may serve as evidence that there is a more fundamental problem in neighborhoods, they ask: "what triggers our perception of order?" (2004:319). Do people react solely to the objective cues found in their neighborhoods, or do they "see" disorder through such social psychological filters as the presence or absence of certain racial, ethnic, or class groups found in those neighborhoods? Sampson and Raudenbush (2004) found that people's perception of disorder does not always match the actual disorder found in their neighborhoods. The researchers discovered that the objective signs of physical disorder, such as "broken windows," and social disorder, such as vagrancy, did not shape people's perceptions of neighborhood disorder. Much more influential was the racial, ethnic, and class composition of that neighborhood. Social structure more than observed disorder was the more powerful predicator of perceived disorder.

Further, and surprisingly, they found that neighborhood residents of all races perceived heightened disorder in their neighborhoods when African Americans lived in that neighborhood or when that neighborhood was poor. The fact that blacks as well as whites and Latinos associate the presence of blacks with neighborhood disorder leads Sampson and Raudenbush to conclude that this viewpoint is not simply a case of racial prejudice. Rather, it is a reflection of the long-standing empirical association between ethnicity, poverty, and disorder by *all* ethnic, racial, and class groups in our society, and also, citing Wacquant (1993), by "prior beliefs informed by the racial stigmatization of modern urban ghettos" (Sampson and Raudenbush 2004:336).

Sampson and Raudenbush (2004) believe that their findings have implications not only for the salience of the broken windows theory but, even more importantly, for the understanding of the continued prevalence of racial segregation in this country. In regard to the broken windows theory, these researchers argue that it is more than "seeing" disorder that is relevant in changing neighborhoods. They reason that if the "meaning" of disorder is socially constructed, then the underlying causes of the perceptions of disorder must be addressed; simply fixing "broken windows" or policing residents who have various forms of social deficiencies is an insufficient policy to combat crime and disorder. To change neighborhoods it is mandatory that underlying social-psychological processes of implicit bias and discriminatory policies must be ended.

> Attempts to improve urban neighborhoods by reducing disorder—cleaning streets and sidewalks, painting over graffiti, removing abandoned cars, reducing public drinking and the associated litter, and eliminating sources of blights such as prostitution, gang gatherings, and drug sales—are admirable and may produce many positive effects . . . Our results suggest that these steps may have only limited payoffs in neighborhoods inhabited by large numbers of ethnic minority and poor people. The limitations on effectiveness in no way derive from deficiencies in the residents of such neighborhoods. Rather, it is due to social psychological processes of implicit bias and statistical discrimination as played out in the current (and historically durable) racialized context of cities in the United States. In other words, simply removing (or adding) graffiti may lead to nothing, depending on the social context. (Sampson and Raudenbush 2004:337)

In regard to the spatial segregation of people by race and class, Sampson and Raudenbush believe that it is necessary to not only investigate the importance of structural factors but also the relevance of social-psychological processes for the understanding of urban inequality. They assert "neighborhoods with high percentages of minority and poor residents are stigmatized by historically correlated and structurally induced problems of crime and disorder" (Sampson and Raudenbush 2004:337). Over time, the image of the disorderly slum has led to negative racial stereotypes. This, in turn, has led people to not only move out of such neighbor-hoods but ultimately to social policies that have augmented and fostered racial segregation. A self-fulfilling prophecy is seen to operate whereby people are likely to divest and move away from black or other minority neighborhoods that are viewed as high in risk for crime and disorder. The researchers speculate that the continued racial segregation that exists in this country may be in part accounted for by the correlation of racial stereotypes with the perception of disorder (Sampson and Raudenbush 2004).

In the discussion of the development of the suburbs and the simultaneous development of segregated housing projects in cities, we will see how both of these developments were a consequence of both private practices and governmen-tal policies to foster racial and class segregation in American communities, cities, and suburbs.

Part *V*

City People

11

Urban Enclaves and Ghettos: Social Policies

Ghetto and Enclave

White Ethnic Enclaves

African American Ghettos

Assimilation versus **Hypersegregation**

Urban Renewal and Urban Removal

Project Living in Public Housing

Stuyvesant Town

Gentrification

Hollow City: The Gentrification of San Francisco

Homelessness

In this chapter I will look at people residing in different types of urban communities. I begin the chapter by first distinguishing the concepts of *ghetto* and *enclave*. This will allow the examination of the historical development of ethnic enclaves in American cities. A discussion of the emergence and consequences of African American ghettos in early twentieth-century cities follows. Of particular relevance to us here is the experience of African Americans in the high-rise apartment projects of post–World War II—the quintessential *hyperghetto*. The chapter will also discuss gentrification processes and the transformation of American cities. I conclude with a study of urban homelessness.

Ghetto and Enclave

The study of immigrant groups and southern black migrants and how their communities established, emerged, and transformed American cities has been of great interest to urban planners, officials, and academicians. Indeed, the dramatic changes that occurred in cities because of this massive urban migration were the very impetus for the development of the Chicago School—which virtually defined American sociology in the early part of the twentieth century. The analytical viewpoint developed by the Chicago School was a reflection of predominant public views of these new arrivals and a distillation of previous sociological perspectives. In subsequent years, as social, cultural, as well as economic and political changes have occurred in American cities, so has the viewpoint of urban sociology. It would be instructive to begin the discussion by looking at these new urban dwellers and their communities—ghettos and enclaves.

The *ghetto* as defined by sociologists Douglas S. Massey and Nancy A. Denton in their important book, *American Apartheid,* as "a set of neighborhoods that are *exclusively* inhabited by members of one group, within which virtually all members of that group live" (italics added)(1993: 18–19). Implicit in their definition is that the residents of the ghetto are involuntarily segregated.

Enclaves, on the other hand, are defined as communities where a high percentage of members of the same group, often of the same cultural and ethnic background, voluntarily reside. The neighborhoods are *not* segregated and often are composed of a number of different ethnic groups. The members of a given group live in a given neighborhood in part because of their desire to live in close proximity with people "like themselves." They frequent the same commercial establishments and institutions, such as neighborhood groceries and restaurants that provide the food that they eat, bars and theaters that cater to their leisure tastes, and parochial churches and schools. Each distinctive group along with their stores and institutions occupies part of a geographic area shared with members of another group. Over time, these stores and institutions become associated with specialized meanings for the particular group (Abrahamson 2006).

In the opening chapter of this book, I described my experiences in growing up in Bensonhurst, a community inhabited by two ethnic groups—Italians and Jews. Bensonhurst was spatially integrated and symbolically segregated. The Italians and Jews residing side-by-side had their own ethnic groceries, candy stores, and fruit and vegetable and butcher shops, and each group attended either Catholic churches or synagogues. Indeed, if you would ask members of the two different groups to draw their mental map of the neighborhood, their own establishments and institutions would be on the map and the establishments and institutions of the other group would often be missing.

The concept *ghetto* traditionally applied to segregated Jewish communities of central and northern Europe during the preindustrial period. The origin of the term, *ghetto,* is Italian and referred to the Jewish neighborhoods that were segregated by both custom and law. Louis Wirth [1927 (1964), 1938(1956)] wrote the classic account of the ghetto and its application to the Jewish community in Chicago. In Wirth's account, he observes that while the medieval ghetto is thought to have developed by government decree, in fact, it was often voluntarily developed because of the desire of members of a group to be amongst themselves.

> The factors that operated toward the founding of locally separated communities by the Jews are to be sought in the character of Jewish traditions, in the habits and customs, not only of the Jews themselves, but of the medieval town-dweller in general. To the Jews the spatially separated and socially isolated community seemed to offer the best opportunity for following their religious precepts, their established ritual

and diet, and the numerous functions which tied the individual to familial and communal institutions. . . . In addition, there were the numerous ties of kinship and acquaintanceship which developed an *esprit de corps* as a significant factor in community life. (Wirth 1927/1964:86)

In Wirth's (1938/1956) account he observes the fact that the population in Chicago's Jewish ghetto were not forcibly segregated nor was the neighborhood exclusively Jewish. (The term "enclave" would convey a more exact description of the community described by Wirth than his use of the term "ghetto"). Yet, through symbolic segregation a Jewish cultural community existed whether it either shared a neighborhood with another ethnic group or was geographically dispersed. Echoing his mentor, Robert Park, Wirth stated, "the ghetto. . . was a state of mind." He further generalized to the fact that all ghettos, regardless of ethnic or racial composition, should be thought in social psychological rather than in geographical (physical) terms.

> What makes the Jewish community—composed as it is of heterogeneous cultural elements and distributed in separate areas of our cities—a community is its capacity to act corporately. It is a cultural community and constitutes as near an approach to communal life as the modern city has to offer. The ghetto, be it Chinese, Negro, Sicilian, or Jewish, can be completely understood only if it is viewed as a sociopsychological, as well as an ecological, phenomenon; for it is not merely a physical fact, but also a state of mind. (Wirth 1927/1964:98)

Wirth predicted that the ghetto would eventually disappear as the Jewish residents would experience assimilation over a few generations, as cultural isolation would decrease and intermarriage would increase. Earlier, Robert Park (1925) described Chicago as composed of *mosaics of social worlds* and described the same processes of assimilation.

> The Chinatowns, the Little Sicilies, and the other so-called ghettos with which students of urban life are familiar are special types of a more general species of natural area, which the conditions and tendencies of city life inevitably produce.
>
> The keener, the more energetic and the more ambitious very soon emerge from their ghettos and immigrant colonies and move into an area of second immigrant settlement, or perhaps into a cosmopolitan area in which the members of several immigrant and racial groups live side by side. (Park 1925:9 quoted in Peach 2005:37)

As the English geographer Ceri Peach (2005:47) pointed out, the ghetto came to be seen as a *stage* in the assimilation process that *all immigrant groups* would go through. Peach argues that the Chicago School and Wirth's conceptualization saw the *ghetto* then the *enclave* and finally the fully integrated and assimilated *suburb* as the communities that all immigrant groups would pass through. While proving to be true for white immigrant groups, this assimilation process was not the experience of African Americans. That failure stems from an inability to distinguish between assimilation and cultural plurality. Assimilation refers to the situation in which the majority and minority become socially and residentially intermixed. Cultural pluralism, or "multiculturalism" (the contemporary term) occurs when a high degree of segregation remains distinguished by social encapsulation and residential separation.

The Chicago School did understand that the ghetto model can be a result of two different causes—voluntary action or coercive actions, as I noted earlier in Wirth's discussion of the Jewish ghetto. Peach makes a similar observation: "Ethnic segregation may be either voluntarily adopted as a strategy for group survival or else it may be negatively imposed upon a weaker group" (2005:36). However, the Chicago School downplayed the significance of coercion in forcing African Americans into segregated neighborhoods and keeping them there. Finally, the fundamental problem with the Chicago School was its failure to realize that the movement of population from highly centralized inner-city neighborhoods to dispersed suburban communities was not inevitable. This failure stems from the Chicago School's inability to distinguish between the melting pot and assimilation with the mosaics of social worlds and pluralistic models, and between the ghetto and the enclave. Peach (2005) concludes that this failure led proponents of the Chicago School to not see or predict the continuation of processes of forced segregation in inner-city ghettoes, which many African Americans have experienced to the present time.

> Worse still, not only did the Chicago School fail to distinguish between the ghetto and the enclave, it believed that the ghetto was a stage within the melting pot model. It saw the ghetto as the first stage of three-generational progression of (1) ghetto, (2) enclave, and (3) suburb. In this fundamental misunderstanding, the Chicago School falsified the ethnic history of long settled groups, misunderstood the processes affecting blacks and mistakenly forecast their future in American cities. (Peach 2005:37)

In the following section, I want to expand on a discussion of the experiences of immigrant groups in the United States. A discussion of the experience of African Americans as they moved from the rural south to the urban north then follows.

White Ethnic Enclaves

The last quarter of the nineteenth century and the first quarter of the twentieth century were periods of massive industrial growth in the United States. New industries like oil refining and iron and steel, new processes of economic organization like trusts, and new overseas markets all led to greater labor needs. Manufacturing and industrial-based cities were rapidly growing. The nonagricultural workforce rapidly accelerated. In 1890 there were over 8 million employed in factories, mines, construction, and transportation. Twenty years later, in 1910, 15 million were employed in these same industries, almost double the earlier figure. The birthrate and the movement from farms to cities simply could not provide the labor demanded by this economic explosion. Further, an underutilized black labor force because of persistence racism and discrimination accelerated the labor short-age in cities (Dinnerstein, Nichols, and Reimers 2003).

Fortunately, the United States had another source of labor: between 1880 and 1930, due to a combination of immigration laws and the onset of a worldwide depression, over 25 million immigrants came to the United States. From 1880 to 1924, when immigration laws placed severe limitation on movement into the United States, there was a massive exodus of people from southern and eastern Europe. This "new" immigration was from countries like Austria-Hungary, Greece, Italy, Poland, Rumania, Russia, and Serbia. Others joined these immigrants, espe-cially individuals from China and Japan, Mexico, French Canada, and the West Indies. In contrast, the people of the "old" immigration, those who arrived between 1820 (when federal statistics of origin were first recorded) and 1880, were made up almost entirely of northwestern Europeans, who came from countries such as England, Ireland, Scotland, France, Germany, Norway, and Sweden.

Immigration in the three decades before the Civil War totaled 5 million. Between 1860 and 1890 that number doubled, and between 1890 and the begin-ning of World War I in 1914 it tripled. The peak years of immigration were in the early twentieth century, with over a million people entering annually in 1905, 1906, 1907, 1910, 1913, and 1914. The main explanation for this massive movement of people to the United States was that the countries of origin of the "new" immi-grants were experiencing population explosions and dislocations. By the latter part of the nineteenth century, the pressures of overpopulation, combined with the prospects of economic opportunity in the United States and the availability of rapid transportation systems that included railroads and steamships, set the wheels of world migration moving. Maldwyn Allen Jones, whose study of American immigration (1960) has been a standard work on the subject, comments on the shared motives of the culturally diversified immigrants for coming to America.

> The motives for immigration . . . have been always a mixture of yearning—for riches, for land, for change, for tranquility, for freedom, and for something not definable in words . . . . The experiences of different immigrant groups . . . reveal a fundamental uniformity. Whenever they came, the fact that they had been uprooted from their old surroundings meant that they faced the necessity of coming to terms with an unfamiliar environment and a new status. The story of American immigration is one of millions of enterprising, courageous folk, most of them humble, nearly all of them unknown by name to history. Coming from a great variety of backgrounds, they nonetheless resembled one another in their willingness to look beyond the horizon and in their readiness to pull up stakes in order to seek a new life. (Jones 1960:4–5)

Prior to the 50-year dramatic growth period (1876–1925) of the industrial centers of the United States, the "old" immigration had a geographically dispersed residential pattern. The "new" immigrants bunched together because of concen-trated large-scale urban employment and the need for low-cost housing near the place of employment. Immigrants arrived, were drawn to the urban areas of eco-nomic expansion, and the migration chain—the subsequent arrival of relatives and friends—continued the concentrated settlement pattern. Immigrants from southern and eastern Europe concentrated in the industrial cities of the Northeast and the Midwest because it was in these urban areas where job opportunities were plentiful and chances of success were greatest. By 1920, almost 60 percent of the population of cities of more than 100,000 inhabitants was made up of first- or second-generation ethnic Americans (Seller 1977).

The immigrants settled in ethnic enclaves that people referred to as "Little Italys," "Polonias," "Little Syrias," and "Jewtowns." Each enclave reflected its distinctive ethnic flavor with its own church, stores, newspapers, clothing, and gestural and language conventions. The Chicago newspaper journalist Mike Royko, reminiscing on his own Slavic community background, recalls that you could always tell where you were "by the odors of the food stores and the open kitchen windows, the sound of the foreign or familiar language, and by whether a stranger hit you in the head with a rock" (cited in Seller 1977:112).

Yancey, Ericksen, and Juliani (1976) explain that the establishment of immigrant "ghettos" reflects a stage in the development of American cities because there was a great need for occupational concentration due to the expansion of the industrial economy. Low-paid industrial immigrant workers were forced by economic pressures to live close to their places of work. The presence of friends and relatives strongly influenced the particular choice of residence and occupation. *Chain migration* refers to the connections made between individuals in countries of origin and destination in the process of international migration and to the influence of friends and relatives in the choice of residence and occupation.

Networks of friends and relatives established in America maintained their European kinship and friendship ties and transmitted assistance across the Atlantic. Relatives acted as recruitment, migration, and housing resources, helping each other to shift from the often-rural European work background to urban industrial work. A number of social historians (Anderson 1971; Hareven 1975; Yans-McLaughlin 1971) have observed that nineteenth-century, as well as twentieth-century, migrants chose their residential and occupational destinations in large part because of the presence of kin-group members in the new area.

Chain migration facilitated transition and settlement. It assured continuity in kin contacts, and made mutual assistance in cases of personal and family crises an important factor in the adjustment to the new American environment. Workers often migrated into the new industrial urban centers, keeping intact or reforming much of their kinship ties and family traditions. As previously mentioned, a prevalent practice was for unmarried sons and daughters of working age, or young childless married couples, to migrate first. After establishing themselves by finding jobs and housing, they would send for other family members. Through their contacts at work or in the community, they would assist their newly arrived relatives or friends with obtaining jobs and housing. In a classic work, *Old World Traits Transplanted (1925)*, Park and Miller present a map of the borough of Manhattan in New York City in the mid-1920s. The map depicts the distinct ethnic villages created in this city by *paesani* (countrymen) from different parts of Italy.

The family was an important intermediary in the recruitment of workers to the new industrial society. Family patterns and values often carried over to the urban setting and provided the individual with a feeling of continuity between the rural background and the new industrial city. Immigrants tended to migrate in groups; often entire rural communities reconstituted themselves in ethnic enclaves. They helped recruit other family members and countrymen into the industrial workforce. Migration to industrial communities, then, did not break up traditional kinship ties; rather, the family used these ties to facilitate its own transition into industrial life. Tamara Hareven (1983), after examining the historical evidence,

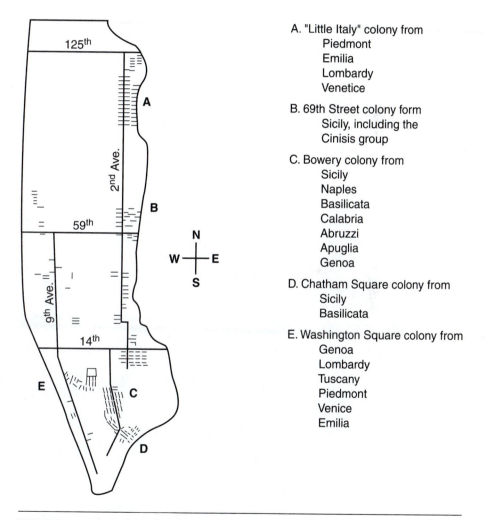

A. "Little Italy" colony from
    Piedmont
    Emilia
    Lombardy
    Venetice

B. 69th Street colony form
    Sicily, including the
    Cinisis group

C. Bowery colony from
    Sicily
    Naples
    Basilicata
    Calabria
    Abruzzi
    Apuglia
    Genoa

D. Chatham Square colony from
    Sicily
    Basilicata

E. Washington Square colony from
    Genoa
    Lombardy
    Tuscany
    Piedmont
    Venice
    Emilia

FIGURE 11.1 *Location of Italian Ethnic Villages in New York City, with Sources of Emigration from Italy.*

Source: *Old World Traits Transplanted* by Robert E. Park and Herbert A. Miller, 1925. New York: Harper.

concludes that it is grossly incorrect to assume that industrialization broke up traditional kinship ties and destroyed the interdependence of the family and the community. What is of particular interest is that these findings on the viability of
kinship involvements of urban immigrants in the early twentieth century goes
counter to the beliefs of the proponents of the Chicago School. Park, Burgess, and
McKenzie (1925) and later Wirth (1938b) postulated that extended family ties as
well as the immigrant communities are not only of little importance but rather
than providing help for individuals, they promoted social disorganization. This is
a subject that I will turn to shortly.

African American Ghettos

As mentioned earlier, the period of the large eastern and southern European
migration was from 1880 to 1924. In 1921, bowing to anti-immigrant sentiments,
the United States government passed a quota law that placed severe limits on
immigration from southern, central, and eastern Europe. Another quota law
passed in 1924, which virtually restricted immigration, followed this. Nonetheless, city migration continued to rise through the Great Depression of the 1930s,
as well as before, during, and after World War II. However, this city migration

African American boys on Easter morning, Southside, Chicago, Illinois. 1941.

was a domestic one of African Americans from rural southern states to the industrial urban centers of the Northeast and Midwest states. The migration that began right before World War I was so large, in fact, that the ratio of black to white population rose from 17 percent in 1910 to 48 percent in 1950 in these cities (Glabb and Brown 1976). In 1910, nearly nine out of ten African Americans lived in the south, and nearly three quarters of them lived in rural areas. By 1930, Chicago's South Side and New York City's Harlem comprised the densest concentration of African Americans in the world with a higher population than found in southern states.

Push-pull factors explain this migration. Changes in southern agriculture, particularly in cotton production, first decimated by the boll weevil and then dramatically altered by mechanization, combined with the lure of industrial jobs in northern cities, led to "The Great Migration." Initially, the labor shortage brought on by the number of young men entering the military provided some opportunities for black men. Unfortunately, discriminatory hiring practices and later the drastic decline of entry-level manufacturing jobs severely curtailed job opportunities. Equally important was the lack of availability of low-rental housing because of racism and an overall housing scarcity. Consequently, poverty became a way of life for many African Americans without jobs, and housing became restricted to overcrowded and dilapidated segregated ghettos.

The experience of African Americans in cities during the period of the Great Migration from 1910 through World War II was worse than that of their poor white counterparts. The prevalence of racism increasingly found African Americans and other racial minorities housed in growing segregated ghettos. The continuing arrival of more and more rural southern blacks displaced by agricultural technology resulted in even more crowded conditions. The ghettos expanded into adjacent white working-class neighborhoods that increasingly became vacant as socially mobile whites moved to suburban areas.

After World War II, the expanding slums, the lack of well paying work, the constantly increasing costs of social services, the movement of industrial and manufacturing jobs, and the beginning of a mass movement of white middle-class city residents to the suburbs caused many cities to go into steep decline. Federal policies that channeled federal funds away from cities to help finance suburban development exacerbated the plight of American cities. The millions of returning servicemen were in dire need of housing for themselves and their families. The war and the previous ten years of the Great Depression left much of urban housing in dreadful condition. The federal government's response was to earmark vast sums of money to the development of an interstate highway system that would aid in the development of the suburbs. In addition, federal housing policies made it economically viable for young families to buy homes in the suburbs. Easy mortgage credits and tax incentives that included the deduction of mortgage interest and local and state taxes from federal taxes made it more attractive to buy a single-family detached home in the suburb than rent a much smaller apartment in the city. Further, "redlining," a government sponsored real-estate policy, made mortgage monies unavailable to many urban communities, which the government viewed as being "problematic" and a poor investment. Such communities were instrumentally defined as those containing minority populations.

The decline of the cities was becoming so acute that the federal government turned to urban renewal policies to halt the decline and provide housing for the urban poor that increasingly were minority peoples of color. The resultant Urban Renewal Program proved to make the situation even worse for the working class and the poor. During the 1950s, 1960s, and into the 1970s, the federal government destroyed hundreds of working-class and poor neighborhoods—characterized as "slums"—and tore down low-income housing in large sections of central cities. Millions of people and small businesses were evicted. In their place, the government built, using New York City as the prime example, entertainment centers such as Lincoln Center, corporate office complexes such as the World Trade Center, and middle-class housing such as Stuyvesant Town. Relatively little acreage was devoted to meeting the housing needs of those displaced. When housing for the poor was built it took the shape of massive high-rise apartment projects that became communities in themselves.

Assimilation versus Hypersegregation

In 1945, *Black Metropolis*, a monograph on the South Side of Chicago, also known as *Bronzeville*, written by St. Clair Drake and Horace R. Cayton, gave an account of the experiences of blacks in this black community. The book focused on the interracial tensions that existed between blacks and whites and the role of the government, which affected the black community (Peretz 2004). Drake and Cayton (1945) research shows the limitation of the Chicago School's urban ecology concept of "natural area." Rather than natural areas emerging as a consequence of processes of invasion and succession operating in the creation and development of the black community, racism and discriminatory patterns are seen as the major contributing factors. Other studies by E. Franklin Frazier (1964) and Alan Spear (1967) reached similar conclusions.

The Chicago School developed a cycle that consisted of stages from initial contact through competition, conflict, accommodation, and assimilation. The held belief was that ethnic groups would eventually go through these stages and become assimilated into American society. Initial contact was through both primary and secondary interaction processes. Competition and conflict naturally occurred as different groups confronted each other over jobs, housing, and community control. However, through the elaboration of a moral and political order, accommodation and assimilation would take place (Persons 1987).

The adjustments that groups made to each other is defined as accommodation. Assimilation, in turn, was the end result, in which the given group adopted and shared the culture and tradition of the larger society. Park and Burgess, as was described, saw assimilation as the eventual outcome for immigrant ethnic groups. E. Franklin Frazier was probably the most prominent African American to come out of the Chicago School in the 1930s. His work on the Negro family led him to question the saliency of the cycle. He found conflict in various forms throughout the cycle and did not see that assimilation was occurring in the black community. Rather, race relations prevented the full assimilation predicted by the Chicago School. Frazier concluded that it was necessary to distinguish between ethnic relations and race relations (Persons 1987). The intellectual historian Stow Persons (1987), in his analysis of the Chicago School and its treatment of ethnic studies, summarizes Frazier's view as expressed in his "Theoretical Structure of Sociology and Sociological Research," which appears in Edwards (1968):

> Assimilation was defined as a larger process incorporating acculturation but signifying complete identification with the group. . . . An assimilated population might contain any number of racial or ethnic groups so long as the racial or ethnic identification constituted no barrier to involvement in the full range of primary or secondary institutions, including intermarriage. An assimilated people would identify themselves with the traditions of the dominant group, whereas American blacks still thought of themselves as blacks first and Americans second. They were acculturated but not assimilated. (Persons 1987: 141)

As mentioned earlier, Ceri Peach (2005), summarizing the work of the Chicago School on the issue of ethnicity and race, asserts that there was a failure to fully predict the future of urban segregation patterns experienced by African Americans but not that of their European immigrant counterparts. Massey and Denton (1993) provide a contrasting summarization of the differences between the immigration experience of Europeans and the migration of southern African Americans into Chicago, which also held true for other northern cities. Massey and Denton focus on three essential differences. First, European immigrant groups did not live in segregated communities. Neighborhoods were composed of a number of different ethnic groups. Except for one enclave of Poles, who comprised 54 percent of the population, no ethnic group had a majority of residents. In contrast, African Americans resided in neighborhoods that were as high as three-quarters black. Second, European ethnic groups were dispersed throughout the city; they did not all live in an ethnic enclave. They thus did not experience the same degree of isolation as did African Americans. Third, and most importantly, the ethnic enclaves eventually conformed to the assimilation patterns predicted by the Chicago School. African Americans lived and continue to live in black ghettos that have become a permanent feature of their residential urban experiences.

> For European immigration, enclaves were places of absorption, adaptation, and adjustment to American society. They served as springboards for broader mobility and adjustment to American society, whereas blacks were trapped behind an increasingly impermeable color line. (Massey and Denton 1993:33)

Massey and Denton (1993) argue that the black ghetto, the specific urban form of racial segregation, has been the major contributory factor for the prevalence of black poverty and has had the most detrimental effect on racial relationships. The black ghetto was a result of a deliberate governmental policy supported by the institutional discrimination practices of private real-estate investors, bankers, and businesses to segregate the African American urban population. Even those successful African Americans found it very difficult to find housing outside of the ghetto, and even when located they would experience threatening and unwelcoming behavior from their white neighbors. Massey and Denton further find that city neighborhoods continue to be highly segregated. They refer to the contemporary black ghetto as characterized by *hypersegregation*—segregation patterns so complete that people have virtually no contact with people in the larger society.

Geographic variations associated with segregation are identified by five distinct dimensions: *unevenness, isolation, clustered, concentrated,* and *centralized.*

> Blacks may be distributed so that they are overrepresented in some areas and underrepresented in others, leading to different degrees of *unevenness;* they may also be distributed so that their racial *isolation* is ensured by virtue of rarely sharing a neighborhood with whites. In addition, however, black neighborhoods may be tightly *clustered* to form one large contiguous enclave or scattered about in checkerboard fashion; they may be *concentrated* within a very small area or settled sparsely throughout the urban environment. Finally, they may be spatially *centralized* around the urban core or spread out along the periphery. (Massey and Denton 1993: 74)

Hypersegregation is when a given area ranks "high" on each dimension of segregation. Hypersegregation can characterize a given ghetto and even an entire metropolitan area. Massey and Denton (1993:75–77) developed indexes to measure hypersegregation. Using 1980 census data, they report that 16 metropolitan areas were hypersegregated: Atlanta, Baltimore, Buffalo, Chicago, Cleveland, Dallas, Detroit, Gary, Indianapolis, Kansas City, Los Angeles, Milwaukee, New York, Newark, Philadelphia, and St. Louis. They further point out that no other group, including Hispanics, has anywhere near the level of hypersegregation as that experienced by African Americans. While many Hispanic Americans are also poor and disadvantaged, they were highly segregated typically on only one dimension of segregation, and that is centralization. Massey and Denton (1993) conclude that a consequence of hypersegregation is the perpetuation of urban poverty. To overcome perpetuating urban poverty and racial inequality and injustice, the various forms of institutional discrimination that have resulted in hypersegregation must be ended. Unless this occurs, dire consequences are predicted, and the very future of the nation is in peril.

> As racial inequality sharpens, white fears will grow, racial prejudices will be reinforced, and hostility toward blacks will increase, making the problems of racial justice and equal opportunity even more insoluble. Until we face up to the difficult task of dismantling the ghetto, the disastrous consequences of residential segregation will radiate outward to poison American society. Until we decide to end the long rein of American apartheid, we cannot move forward as a people and nation. (Massey and Denton 1993:236)

In the next section, I will discuss how governmental policies regarding the housing of African Americans were reinforced by racism and discrimination. The building of high-rise, low-income segregated housing projects had major ramifications on the experience of African Americans in many major American cities, including Chicago, New York, and St. Louis. The discussion will be framed within the context of urban planning and urban politics.

Urban Renewal and Urban Removal

> The projects in Harlen are hated. They are hated almost as much as policemen, and this is saying a great deal. And they are hated for the same reason: both reveal, unbearably, the real attitude of the white world, no matter how many liberal speeches are made, no matter how many lofty editorials are written, no matter how many civil-rights commissions are set up.
>
> The projects are hideous, of course, there being a law, apparently respected throughout the world, that popular housing shall be as cheerless as a prison. They are lumped all over Harlem, colorless, bleak, high, and revolting. (James Baldwin 1961)

In the United States after World War II, proponents of urban renewal and slum clearance projects saw the Le Corbusier advocacy of high-rise dwellings and spacious park areas linked by high-speed motorways as the economically feasible solution to urban ills. At first, the federal program of slum clearance and rebuilding was viewed very favorably. Lewis Mumford was highly critical of the Le Corbuserian radiant city model. Yet, in 1950, he had positive things to say about the New York Housing Authority's accomplishments. They did more "to improve the living quarters of the lowest-income housing groups than all the earlier housing reformers did in a hundred years. Acres of dark, musty, verminous, overcrowded tenements have been replaced by clean, well-lighted sanitary quarters—also overcrowded" (Mumford quoted in Vergara 1995:42).

However, many areas were ruthlessly cleared without consultation and often with the opposition of their residents. Such high-rise projects as Pruitt-Igoe in St. Louis, Cabrini-Green in Chicago, and numerous high-rise projects in the New York City's boroughs of Manhattan and Brooklyn were built in their place. Most of these projects were built without social amenities like meeting places or localized small shopping areas that would enable the informal congregation of residents. Also not built were childcare centers, shops, or recreational areas. All poor and low-income people were housed cheaply. Under the Urban Renewal Act of 1949, government-subsidized housing replaced demolished old slums. This housing took the form of high-rise apartment house complexes. Designed for the poor, most proved absolute failures.

In the 1950s, public housing was known as "black housing." Urban renewal programs involved with slum clearance were referred to as "Negro removal." Thousands of low-income, inner-city housing units were replaced with middle-income apartment projects, probably the most famous being Stuyvesant Town in New York City, or with entertainment centers, such as New York City's Lincoln Center, which had auditoriums that included those for the Metropolitan Opera Company and the New York Philharmonic Orchestra. (Soon thereafter, the neighborhood site for the shooting of the film *West Side Story* was leveled for the building of Lincoln Center.) The displaced poor were not able to afford living in the more middle-class housing developments. Instead, they were forced to move into subsidized housing. Initially designed for "poor deserving families," these housing projects quickly became segregated housing of African Americans.

The most infamous was the Pruitt-Igoe housing project constructed in 1956 in St. Louis, Missouri; this project was inspired by Le Corbusier and was the winner of numerous architectural awards. The architect was Minouu Yumasaki, the designer of the World Trade Center in New York City. Pruitt-Igoe consisted of 43 eleven-story buildings containing 2,762 apartments housing twelve thousand people on a sparsely landscaped 60-acre site. A high proportion of the tenants were on public assistance.

Five years after completion, occupancy rates began a steady decline. In 1970, vacancy rates reached nearly 50 percent with 27 of the 43 buildings completely empty. Two years later, the decision was reached that Pruitt-Igoe was an uninhabitable environment and demolition began. The entire project was demolished by 1976. Charles Jencks, the architectural critic, dates the beginning of the destruction of Pruitt-Igoe at 3:22 p.m. on July 15, 1973, as representing the end of modernism, in which the dominant belief was that architecture could solve social problems, and the beginning of post-modernism, where no longer would there be an assertion that architecture could inspire social progress (Harvey 1989).

What accounts for the failure of Pruitt-Igoe? Part of the responsibility lies in the very nature of its architectural design, and part is a combination of political, social, and economic factors. Under the Roosevelt Administration's New Deal Policy, the Public Works Administration Program (PWA) in the 1930s initially built public housing that was of substantial quality. Fearful that federal "tenement" housing would prove to be too attractive and so would discourage homeownership, the building and real-estate interests lobbied successfully for the government to stop building structures that would compete with private builders. The result was that by the end of World War II, the government housing that was being built was made up of cheap, austere buildings whose construction costs were closely watched by congressional regulations (Wright 1981).

William L. Yancey (1973), a student of Lee Rainwater, and his colleagues studied Pruitt-Igoe for three years in the 1960s. Yancey argues that the architectural design had an "atomizing" effect on the informal social networks that characterize lower-income and working-class neighborhoods. The massiveness of Pruitt-Igoe separated its residents from the surrounding communities. Further, the architects and builders were more concerned with providing housing for people than with having knowledge of what is required to develop a community and neighborhood.

Yancey ironically points out that *Architectural Forum* in 1951 praised the housing project for not having "wasted space" between dwelling units. However, the lack of such "wasted space" proved to be a fundamental problem. While residents praised the "private" space within apartments, they had highly negative opinions on the "public" space inside buildings. There were long narrow hallways and corridors leading to stairwells and a single elevator. This design pattern discouraged informal interaction and prevented people from gathering. Thugs would linger in the hallways, stairwells, and in the elevator. Muggings, beatings, and rapes were all too frequent occurrences.

Similarly, the "public" space between buildings was not integrated with the private space of the apartment. These areas were too open with no common areas for people to congregate. Owing to the height of the building, apartments were vertically segregated from the outside areas. The large expanses of open space made it difficult for the recognition of strangers. Parents, in particular, felt that once children were out of their sight they were out of their control and were likely to get into trouble. The exterior walkways between buildings were dimly lit and became sites for crime. The interior construction of the buildings proved conducive to vandalism and crime: corridor systems that provided good hiding places for muggers and the lack of ground-level public toilets led people to urinate in the elevators. Thin walls made privacy virtually impossible. Fear of crime led mothers to keep their children inside their apartments. The lack of childcare and transportation further confined people and exacerbated the feeling of being overcrowded (Rainwater 1970).

Yancey concludes that "wasted space" should be seen as "defensible space" and is essential for the formation of informal networks of friends and relatives and for the development of social support, protection, and informal social control required in lower-income and working-class neighborhoods. He observes that the trash-filled alleys, streets, and backyards of perceived "slums" are, in fact, the semi-public settings in which such informal networks develop. Without them, "atomization" of the community can occur and families will withdraw into the sanctity and privacy of their own homes as the last defense from the intrusion of a hostile neighborhood.

Architectural Forum was lavish in its praise of Pruitt-Igoe at its inception. It saw in Pruitt-Igoe the development of "vertical neighborhoods" anchored by galleries that contained laundry facilities, play spaces, and communal porches, and the winding spaces between buildings were seen as the potential site for a "river of trees" that would develop into a park area. Ten years later, the foremost journal on architectural design, reported that Pruitt-Igoe was an architectural disaster. *Architectural Forum* observed that the spaces between Pruitt-Igoe's buildings now consisted of scrubby grass, broken glass, and litter, and the galleries were "anything but cheerful social enclaves" (Teaford 1986: 125). Crime was rampant, with the elevators proving to be convenient sites for rapes and muggings.

Architectural housing design must take into consideration the needs of its residents. Public space designed for no one should be replaced by semi-public space that maximizes social interaction and informal controls and allows for neighboring, visiting, and mutual aid. Yancey asserts that "if housing must be designed for the ghetto—if we must reconcile ourselves to not being able to change the social forces which produce the world of danger for lower-class families—the architect can make some small contribution by facilitating the constructive adaptations that have emerged as a means of defense against the world of the lower class" (Yancey 1973: 120).

To redress the disastrous outcomes of high-rise "radiant city" public housing, Chicago is pursuing an ambitious new plan—replacing the two public housing projects that were built from 1937 to 1970: the Cabrini-Green development on Chicago's North Side, and the more massive Robert Taylor Homes in the South Side. Robert Taylor Homes was the largest public housing project in the world. It consisted of 4,415 units in 28 identical 16-story high-rises over a 4-mile corridor. The project originally contained 27,000 poor, black residents (Teaford 1986). In their place will be mixed-income townhouse-style developments. Housing will be spatially integrated with schools, parks, stores, and social-support services. The plans call for a cost outlay of over $1 billion to be spread out over a period of 15 to 20 years (Siegel 1998). Current public housing residents will be eligible to occupy the new mixed-income communities as they are built. Alternatively, residents will have the option of accepting Federal government Section 8 vouchers, which could subsidize their rent in privately owned apartment buildings located elsewhere.

Cabrini-Green is located in a rapidly gentrifying area of Chicago. In the first phase of the development, residents of now demolished high-rises are moving into townhouses, paying 30 percent of their incomes. Their more affluent neighbors will be paying $250,000 for their homes. The goal is for the establishment of a new racially and economically integrated community. One of the higher-income owners expressed optimism rather than trepidation for the future of the community: "There was definitely some hesitation, because they [the public housing residents] come from a different environment. But that doesn't mean they're bad people" (cited in Siegel 1998).

Project Living in Public Housing

Sudhir Alladi Venkatesh is a sociologist who, while a graduate student, spent nearly a decade in the Robert Taylor Homes. Built and managed by the Chicago Housing Authority, the Robert Taylor Homes were designed with the best of intentions to serve the city's poor and needy. In his ethnographic study of Robert Taylor, Venkatesh (2000) attacks the notion that the demolition of high-rise public housing is the solution to the problems. Rather, he moves away from a "blaming the victim" model based on architectural determination. He wishes to avoid perspectives that

Low-income garden housing has replaced two high-rise housing projects. The remaining high-rise building is now set aside for senior citizens. Philadelphia, Photo by author.

focus on the pathology of residents or the view that high-rise projects are pathologically built environments. Venkatesh focuses instead on the daily struggles of the people who reside in this public housing project to make it a habitable community in which they can live peacefully. He emphasizes the strengths of the residents, their utilization of resources, their sharing of goods and services, and the networks they established to cope with the challenges of their everyday lives.

He asserts that a shift in governmental policy from a liberal agenda never fully realized, due to the disastrous cut in federal funding to the nation's public housing project from the mid-1960s, combined with the disappearance of manufacturing and industrial job opportunities for low-skilled workers are major contributing factors for failures in public housing. The problem rests not within the built environment of high-rise public housing or with the occupants of it but rather with the failure of the governmental agency to provide the necessary supports that would have helped residents combat the difficulties of living in this environment. Venkatesh believes that the true culprits were poor law enforcement, diminished federal funding, socioeconomic hardships, and increased gang violence. These impediments had staggering consequences for life in the projects. The culmination of daily struggles for survival in the face of crime, vandalism, and lack of economic opportunities led eventually to feelings of general despair that went beyond the capacity of the residents to overcome. Venkatesh documents how residents sought to utilize various resources, including the sharing of goods and services and the development of social networks, but that their efforts ultimately proved inadequate when the residents were faced with the challenges of the harsh circumstances they encountered in their everyday lives.

Venkatesh observes how the efforts of tenants to band together to fight for better living conditions—including working elevators, a safe and accessible playground, and needed health and employment services—must be evaluated within the larger economic and political context of federal government policies, Chicago's municipal political machine, the Chicago Housing Authority, and the surrounding communities. Ultimately, these often-debilitating external forces could not overcome the disintegration of the communities in the Robert Taylor Homes, despite the best efforts of residents to mobilize all available resources. Venkatesh states that: "The example of Chicago suggests that government, civic, and private-sector support plays a key role in the viability of any community, not just that of public housing—the inability to perceive this connection being perhaps the most glaring error of the consensus view" (Venkatesh 2000:272).

Venkatesh concludes that the tenants "impressive efforts to cope and make life meaningful amid a dearth of resources" was doomed to failure (2000:274). "If these innovative survival strategies had been buttressed with government resources and adequate economic development in public housing neighborhoods, perhaps tenants' networks and associations could have been strengthened and the capacity of the overall community to meet its needs could have been restored" (Venkatesh 2000:275). But they were not. The Robert Taylor Homes are in the process of being demolished and, unfortunately, much of the blame for their destruction has been put on the residents and not on the policies and forces that are the true sources.

Stuyvesant Town

Before we leave this discussion of urban public housing, a brief look at a middle-income apartment-housing complex would be instructive. After World War II, in New York City, a large section of the lower east side of Manhattan, dominated by congested tenement houses, was to be replaced by a "town" for 24,000 residents. The Metropolitan Life Insurance Company with the generous financial support of Robert Moses's agencies built Stuyvesant Town. However, unlike many of the other urban renewal projects, this complex was designed for the middle class rather than for the poor. While replacing a poor neighborhood with ramshackle houses, the residents who would move into Stuyvesant Town were middle class residents who did not come from the demolished neighborhood. No provisions were made for the poor who were evicted from their homes to make way for Stuyvesant Town. Everyone who applied to live there was screened for acceptability, and often inspectors visited their current dwellings to see how well they maintained their homes (Demas 2000). Everyone who moved in was white—Irish and Italian Catholics and Eastern European Jews. The chairman of Metropolitan Life, Frederick H. Ecker, justified the exclusion of African Americans: "Negroes and whites don't mix. Perhaps they will in a hundred years, but they don't now" (quoted in Retica 2005). It wasn't until 1950 that African Americans were allowed

Begun in 1944, Stuyvesant Town replaced tenements, commercial buildings and gas tanks under the redevelopment plans developed by Robert Moses, New York City Park Commissioner, with financial backing from the Metropolitan Life Insurance Company (now called MetLife). In Stuyvesant Town and the adjacent slightly more upscale Peter Cooper Village, there are 110 buildings from 13 to 15 stories each, housing more than 25,000 people. Photo by author.

to become residents. In more recent years, Stuyvesant Town has contained a diversified population of Hispanics and South and East Asians.

It's instructive to look at this successful housing complex to see why it succeeded while others, such as Pruitt-Igoe, failed. The story that is told reflects, in part, how people rather than architecture may determine one's adaptation to the environment. And, more significantly, the story reflects what proper funding can accomplish in building a housing complex for people to live in rather than a housing complex designed primarily to separate and segregate people, as was done in low-income government housing projects such as Pruitt-Igoe.

Stuyvesant Town is a Le Corbusier radiant city located in a more concentrated area. However, the buildings are linked by walkways and park-like green areas, not by highways. The landscape of curved walkways passing playgrounds, lawns, and park benches prevents the building from dominating the environment. The apartments contained within them have nice layouts and are well maintained. The tenants are primarily from the middle class. Corrine Demas is a professor of English at Mount Holyoke College. She grew up in Stuyvesant Town and has written a memoir of her childhood there. She describes its physical layout:

> Stuyvesant Town. If this were a novel you would think I made it up. Imagine some giant hand leveling eighteen square blocks of Manhattan tenements, and in their place constructing a utopia of brick apartment buildings laid out around a large central green called the Oval. The only streets, four semicircular drives, one on each side of the perimeter, and a maze of paved walking paths and twelve fenced playgrounds, some with swings and slides, some with basketball hoops, some simply square open spaces.

Demas further observes that there was strict control over the activities of children:

> Everything in Stuyvesant Town was regulated and manicured. Order always prevailed. The playgrounds, all surrounded by metal fences too high to climb over, were locked up at night, although it was never clear what was being kept out. During the day the children inside the playgrounds looked like zoo animals, caged in. (Demas 2000: 8)

Yet her memoirs reflect warm memories of the vitality of child-play and her continued association with many of her childhood friends. Aaron Retica (2005), the chief of research for the *New York Times Magazine*, who also grew up in Stuyvesant Town, observes as does Demas that there were no stores located within the housing complex. The absence of stores usually means relatively little street activity. Retica quotes Jane Jacobs (1961) in her *The Death and Life of Great American Cities* that the absence of stores usually means the absence of community life: "middle-income housing projects which are truly marvels of dullness and regimentation, sealed against the buoyancy of city life" (Jacobs quoted in Retica 2005:last page). But Retica observes that even with regulations and even with the absence of stores, features of the housing complex not examined in Jacobs's assessment led to the development of a viable community life. He notes that there are 15 playgrounds within the confines of Stuyvesant Town. Further, the Oval described earlier by Demas has served as a form of town square, which provides a common area for public interaction by all residents. He compares the design of Stuyvesant Town to that of a Spanish hacienda—both face inward. The result is a city neighborhood unlike that predicted by Lewis Mumford or Jane Jacobs. He concludes:

> The tower-in-a-park model has failed in most of the places it has been tried. And it remains to be seen whether it can continue to work in Stuyvesant Town, now that Met Life has taken every newly vacated apartment out of the rent-regulation system. But, five generations on, it seems to me that this particular experiment, conducted day by day, for almost 60 years, proves that the richest kind of civic life can be found in unlikely places. (Retica 2005; last page)

Taken together, Paul Goldberger, for many years the influential architectural critic for the *New York Times* asserts: "Maybe these factors counted for more, in fact, than the architecture—perhaps Stuyvesant Town's most important lesson is that architecture is not always crucial" (1979: 104).

Gentrification

Gentrification is the process by which higher-income people move, in sufficient numbers to lower income communities, renovate existing housing, and transform the neighborhood to fit their style of living patterns. This results in the displacement of the lower-income groups and results in a change in neighborhood identity. The origin of the term stems from the early 1960s when affluent people moved to rundown areas of London. The press depicted them as members of the *landed gentry*, people of good family and high social position in the class just below that of the nobility. Ruth Glass, a British sociologist, in 1964 was one of the first to use the term: "one by one, many of the working class quarters of London have been invaded by the middle classes—upper and lower . . . Once this process of 'gentrification' starts in a district, it goes on rapidly until all or most of the original working-class occupiers are displaced and the whole social character of the district is changed" (quoted in Solnit 2000:59–60).

Soon thereafter, this phenomenon occurred in many cities in the United States and Canada. Transformed areas include the fan area of Richmond; Georgetown in Washington, D.C.; Society Hill in Philadelphia; Yorkville in Toronto; and the Lower East Side and SoHo in New York City. As the housing becomes more expensive and the taxes increase, lower-income residents find themselves squeezed out of their homes and neighborhoods.

Neil Smith (1996), in *The New Urban Frontier*, speaks of the process of gentrification in political-economic terms. He speaks of the importance of an influx of private capital by middle-class homeowners and renters and business owners in inner cities, in poor working-class neighborhoods that had experienced disinvestment and an exodus of a previous generation of more affluent residents. In this book, and earlier in his (1992) essay, "New City, New Frontier: The Lower East Side as Wild, Wild West," Smith uses the notion of the frontier to depict this transformation. Smith shows how the ideology of the frontier becomes associated with

Stores catering to the needs of a working class community are rapidly being replaced by stores that reflect the needs and wants of an affluent populace moving into a gentrified neighborhood in Washington D.C. Photos by author.

the economic belief in the necessity to develop previously devalued urban land. In turn, these ideologies are linked with investment flows into and out of the city as part of global economic restructuring processes.

> The gentrification frontier is also an imperial frontier . . . Not only does international capital flood the real estate markets of New York, but international migration provides a workforce for the new service jobs associated with the new urban economy. In New York, the greengrocers are now mainly Korean; the plumbers fitting gentrified buildings are often Italian and the carpenters Polish, while the domestics and nannies looking after the houses and offspring of gentrifiers come from El Salvador or the Bahamas. (Smith 1992:92)

Demand-side arguments and supply-oriented arguments provide explanations of why gentrification occurs. The demand-side argument emphasizes cultural and quality-of-life arguments. A number of factors explain the move to inner city sites. At the outset, economic restructuring has occurred in many cities. There are an increasing number of high-income professional, research, and administrative jobs in service industries in the central business district. The workers who fill these jobs are often highly educated young singles—men and women—or cohabiting or married couples without children. These *yuppies* (young urban professionals) and *dinks* (dual income, no kids) prefer an "urban lifestyle." They chose to live close to work and near shops, restaurants, theaters, clubs, and museums. Without the concern to raise children new patterns of consumption develop, also reflected in their housing preferences. In many older cities, large existing housing and industrial sites are available that can be converted into housing at an affordable rental or condominium rate. This housing can vary from older Victorian brownstones, to apartments in formerly luxury buildings, to reconverted industrial and storage lofts.

A supply-side argument that focuses on economic factors can explain the availability of such affordable housing. Political economists like Neil Smith (1992, 1996) point out that it is not so much the movement of people back to the city that is the primary factor for gentrification but the movement of capital back to the city. He observes that in suburban locations so much capital has been invested that there occurred a disinvestment from many inner-city neighborhoods. To maintain and repair inner-city buildings, smaller and smaller amounts of capital were used. Ultimately, there is a decline in the value of land in the inner city. A "rent gap" results in which the difference between the land value and the potential land value creates conditions for new forms of investment, with prospects of greater profit capital returned to the inner city. "At the most basic level, it is the movement of capital into the construction of new suburban landscapes and the consequent creation of a rent gap that create the economic *opportunity* for restructuring the central and inner cities" (Smith 1996:347).

Elijah Anderson's (1990) *Streetwise: Race, Class, and Change in an Urban Community* was discussed in Chapter 9. Gentrification provides the macrolevel context for his study of the relationships among residents of the two communities. The housing renovations and the increased presence of upscale neighborhood shopping because of the movement into that section of the city resulted in increased real-estate values. But the price paid was the removable of the low-income residents who could no longer afford to live there as a result in the rise of property taxes and rents. These residents also felt that yuppies had a view of communities that favored class homogeneity rather than cultural diversity.

> The yuppies are seen by most others within the community as having very little interest in getting along with their black and lower income neighbors. People are inclined to view the young professionals as bent on profiting from their investments over the short run. From this perspective, hastening the exodus of undesirables would improve the values of their homes as well as their own comfort on the streets. Further, instead of welcoming color differences as old residents did, the newcomers are believed to feel fear, hostility, or at least indifference toward blacks. Their agenda is not cultural diversity but class homogeneity. (Anderson 1990:144–45)

The relationship between demographic and lifestyle patterns and changing economic conditions can be illustrated by the development of "loft living" in the SoHo district of the lower Manhattan area of New York City. SoHo [*South of Houston* (pronounced House-ton) Street] is a section of lower Manhattan characterized by cast-iron buildings that were manufacturing sites (Wolfe 2003). Cast iron is a building material composed of pig iron, cast into sand molds of the desired shapes and sizes. Used as fronts for many commercial buildings during the period from 1860 to 1890, many of these buildings first housed textile manufacturing. Later SoHo became a millinery-manufacturing center. By the late 1960s, diverse light manufacturing and warehousing dominated the area, but these commercial endeavors were in economic decline. It was at that time that many young artists and craftsman were attracted to the area by the spaciousness and high ceilings of the many lofts found there and the low rents required to occupy them.

Soon thereafter, attracted by the low rents, numerous art galleries opened, followed in turn by chic bars and restaurants, clothing boutiques, and home decorating and antique shops. The resulting gentrification has gradually transformed SoHo and has posed a threat to the future of the artist community and the remaining commercial industry. Indeed, movement to another area of "rent gap" Manhattan, the Chelsea pier area, has begun in earnest.

Sharon Zukin (1989) in a very interesting monograph, *Loft Living*, examined the development of the SoHo district. In the 1960s, a government-sponsored plan was to demolish this cast-iron area and replace it with high-rise buildings suitable for corporate redevelopment. By this time, the artist community was developing and ultimately was influential in the designation in 1971 of the area as an "artist district" for the "historic preservation and the arts." Zukin, however, makes the important point that this designation did not necessarily mean the triumph of culture over capitalism; rather it meant using preservation rather than new construction as an alternative strategy for the revalorization of SoHo. Zukin (1989: 352) explains, "In Lower Manhattan the struggle to legalize loft living for artists merely anticipated. . . . (that) the widening of the loft market after 1973 provided a basis for capital accumulation among new, though small-scale developers."

Neil Smith has observed that soon thereafter large-scale developers replaced the small-scale developers. Where groups of prospective residents banded together

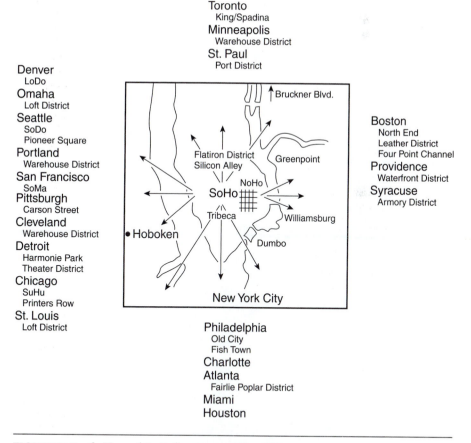

FIGURE 11.2 *SoHo and its Influence on Other Cities.*

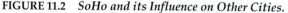

Source: Roberta Brandes Gratz with Norman Mintz, 1998. *Cities Back From the Edge: New Life for Downtown.* New York: Wiley. Page 301.

to buy and develop loft co-ops, today real-estate developers who purchase buildings do the necessary renovations and sell lofts out of the income range of most artists. Smith (1996: 354) concludes: "The point here is that even SoHo, one of the most vivid symbols of artistic expression in the landscape of gentrification, owes its existence to more basic economic forces . . ."

Hollow City: *The Gentrification of San Francisco*

The beat poet and long-time owner of City Lights Books, observes that "A place for artists, activists, and working folks. That's what made San Francisco the great city it is, or was. The city we love is disappearing almost overnight and turning into just another sector of corporate monoculture. (Lawrence Ferlinghetti and Nancy J. Peters, clb) http://www.semcoop.com/detail/1859843638 Seminary Co-op bookstore (Ferlinghetti 2005)

San Francisco's cable cars have become a symbol of this gentrified city whose symbolic economy is anchored by tourism. Photo by author.

In an interesting photo-essay monograph (Solnit 2000), Rebecca Solnit (text), an environmental activist, and Susan Schwartzenberg (photographs), an urban archaeologist and photographer, examine how gentrification processes can extend beyond given neighborhoods to incorporate an entire city as well. Solnit's thesis is that in the case of San Francisco, gentrification does not simply refer to location transformation processes in selected areas of a city but to the whole city. She follows the lead of Neil Smith and Peter Williams, who as early as 1986 reported on a major transformation of cities.

> The direction of change is toward a new central city dominated by middle-class residential areas, a concentration of professional, administrative, and managerial employment, the upmarket recreation and entertainment facilities that cater to this population (as well as to tourists) . . . The moment of the present restructuring is toward a more peripheralized working class, in geographical terms. (quoted in Solnit (2000: 20)

Solnit (2000) provides a visual sociological study of San Francisco. San Francisco has the nation's most expensive housing market. Writing at the height of the dot.com economy in the late 1990s, Solnit believed that gentrification would undermine the city's economic and cultural diversity through its real-estate boom and an accelerated crisis of housing displacement. The dramatic growth of the Internet economy and inflated incomes generated by venture capitalism had led to soaring rents and housing prices. Old neighborhoods lost their sense of community as artists, bohemians, and many of the lower and working classes were forced to move out of their neighborhoods, and many were finding the city as a whole unaffordable and uncongenial. Solnit contrasts the activities of those who work in the dot.com economy with those who live a barely adequate economic life as bohemians, artists, and activists. She sees a movement from a blue-collar port city of manual labor and material goods to a white-collar center of finance administration, tourism, and knowledge industries. Although the dot.com economy went into decline, the economic forces that were a by-product still impact on the San Francisco economy.

Solnit (2000) outlines a two-step gentrification process that first transforms neighborhoods and ultimately can transform a city. The first step in the process is the displacement of the poorer people by artists who begin the transformation of the community and neighborhood. The artists lay the groundwork that often ultimately results in their displacement by more affluent individuals and groups who benefit by the economic changes in the community. In the second step in the process, the artists who themselves can't economically compete with those who have more money are forced out of the community.

Solnit elaborates on the consequences of this two-step gentrification process. First, bohemians and artists moved into different affordable sections of the city and transformed neighborhoods as a by-product of their effort to find the space to do their work. This process of urban gentrification leads to the creation of a highly viable creative civic culture. Solnit is concerned with the consequences of the second step of the gentrification process when artists are forced to relocate from the creative communities that they established. More affluent but much less creative individuals transform these communities into mundane and suburban-like environments. Solnit takes the perspective of those hit hardest by gentrification, the creative and nonprofitable people, such as artists, musicians, and the working poor. She believes that the consequences of these new economic developments means the death knell for those who wish to spend their time in artistic and other less economically productive pursuits in the city.

Solnit argued that the Internet boom transformed San Francisco into a suburb of Silicon Valley. She argued that the Internet economy is leading to a cultural die-off because of the resulting housing squeeze and accelerated gentrification. There has been a displacement of artists, activists, and members of diverse racial and class groups from the low-income neighborhoods in which they no longer could afford to live. The new technology results in a spatial privatization that goes counter to the public sphere that has been a hallmark of San Francisco's city life. The new arrivals driven by the dot.com revolution treat city streets not as places to be in, but rather as conduits to go through. Solnit decries the abandonment of civic life and cultural life by people whose primary involvement is in economic pursuits. "An increasing urgency governs everyday public acts—and the public sphere itself is more and more merely the space people pass through on errands and commutes" (Solnit 2000: 122). The acceleration of work involvements means less time spent in public involvements.

> Urban life, like cultural life, requires a certain leisure, a certain relaxation, a certain willingness to engage with the unknown and unpredictable. For those who feel impelled to accelerate, the unknown and the unpredictable are interference as the city's public space becomes not a place to *be* but a place to traverse as rapidly as possible. (Solnit 2000: 123)

Solnit advocates the importance of the artistic class for giving the city its cultural vitality and making it such an attractive place to work and live in. She argues that artists help create the city's culture. The creative forces that are unleashed generate the city's economy. Ultimately, if artists are economically displaced by the more affluent there would be consequent negative ramifications for the city's culture and economy. Dire consequences are predicted both for the decline in public sphere activities and ultimately to the city itself. The ultimate results will be cities that take on more of a tourist and unauthentic reality than the creative city. She concludes that cities like San Francisco were sanctuaries for those who were different—the queer, the eccentric, the creative, the radical. As they are forced out, cities like San Francisco will become a "Hollow city," with the distinct urban culture eroding under an onslaught of new-economy money.

For the irony is that the city and its public realm are being destroyed not by poverty and urban decay, but by wealth.

> Cities are the infrastructure of shared experience. Thirty years ago we worried that cities were being abandoned to desperate poverty and decay. Even five years ago the threat seemed to be redesign and new development that eliminated public

space and public life, a suburbanization by design. *No one foresaw that cities could be abandoned to the ravages of wealth,* or that public life and public space could be undermined by acceleration and privatization of every day life, by spatial practice rather than the alteration of actual space. (emphasis added, Solnit 2000: 166)

Very soon after the publication of *Hollow City,* the dot.com economy burst; the housing crisis in San Francisco was somewhat alleviated, and the "siege of San Francisco and the crisis of American urbanism" was substantially lifted. Initially, higher-priced apartments became vacant and real-estate prices started to drop. However, economic forces and the transformation of such new economy and tourist cities like San Francisco have seen a stabilization in the high cost of living, especially in terms of housing stock. While the pace of change in urban centers like San Francisco, New York, Austin, Portland, and Seattle, to name just a few, may be slowing down along with the national economy, the long-range prospects continue to be the withering away of the old city. Yet the inextricable thing about the city is that it is in a constant state of change.

Solnit focuses on the artists, who she sees as the "indicator species of this ecosystem," similar to the canaries that coal miners took into the mine shafts—when they stopped singing it was an indication that there was a major foul-up in the air quality and that it was time to leave. Solnit was severely castigated for her seeming sympathy to the economic plight on this group rather than on the poor who were displaced by them. She was also criticized for ignoring how other groups have also been transforming the population demographics of San Francisco. Of particular importance are the large numbers of Asians, Pacific Islanders, and Chinese who have moved into San Francisco, followed by the large numbers of Latinos who have moved into adjacent communities and suburbs and whose movement to those communities may reflect the economic realities of living in high-cost-of-living San Francisco and their preference for the suburban lifestyle. I will have more to say about how immigrants are changing American cities in a later chapter of this book.

Homelessness

In the 1980s increasing numbers of homeless besieged America's urban centers. The estimates on the number of homeless ranged from the the United States Department of Housing and Urban Development's figure of 350,000 to the U.S. Department of Health and Human Services' figure at 2 million. Advocates of the homeless put the figure much higher—10 to 20 million. The variations in these estimates are attributable to the difficulty in getting accurate assessments of counting people who are transient. Censuses and sample surveys are inadequate in that the data they collect are based on tabulating people who have relatively permanent residences (Rossi 1994).

Who are these homeless people? The evidence collected indicates that they vary greatly. The "old" homeless who populated the nation's skid rows of the 1950s and 1960s, were almost all white males with an average age of around 50 years old. The new homeless are much younger—around 30 years of age—25 percent are women,

The homeless have colonized a large segment of the park adjacent to the famous Santa Monica Pier, Los Angeles. Photo by author.

and proportionately blacks and Hispanics constitute an increasing number of them (Rossi 1994). Worsnop (1996) as reported in Lindsey and Beach (2004), found that 36.5 percent were families; almost all of whom were female headed. Forty-six percent were single men; 14 percent single women; and the remaining 3.5 percent were runaway and throwaway children. In 1996 the U.S. Conference of Mayors reported that 56 percent of the homeless are African American and 10 percent are Hispanic. Thirty percent of them are white (U.S. Conference of Mayors 1996). Macionis (2005) in his summary of a HUD (Housing and Urban Development) study of 4,000 homeless interviewed throughout the United States that around 9 out of 10 live in urban areas. Of this number 71 percent reside in central cities and 21 percent live in suburbs. Only 9 percent live in rural areas (HUD 1999).

What accounts for the vast number of Americans who are homeless? Frequently cited factors include individuals who are mentally ill but never diagnosed and the deinstitutionalization of those classified as mentally ill; unemployment; cutbacks in public assistance and the consequent falling through the alleged "safety net"; and the decline in affordable housing, especially in urban areas. The growing shortage of affordable housing occurs as rents increase above what the increasing number of poor people can afford to pay. The decline in affordable housing also results from redevelopment in which poorer housing stock is converted either through extensive renovation to much more expensive apartments or condominiums or demolished to give way to luxury housing or to other uses such as office build-ings or shopping malls. This process of "gentrification," while beneficial to the "revitalization" of cities, often leaves the dispossessed without housing.

Talmadge Wright (1997) examined the relationship between urban redevel-opment and the resistant homeless mobilizations. He examines how inner-city redevelopment programs are manifestations of dominant social constructions of marginalized populations. Wright discusses the theoretical connections among social constructions of space, redevelopment visions, and homeless identities, demonstrating how the social constructions of space play a crucial role in the socially constructed nature of marginalized identities. He argues that urban rede-velopment policies exclude certain groups from urban spaces. Using the South Loop of Chicago and downtown San Jose as illustrative cases, Wright demon-strates how exclusionary and authoritative land-use policies are grounded within a pervasive context of socioeconomic polarization.

What distinguishes Wright's theoretical analysis is his examination of how the homeless combat the restructurings of their everyday life and how they seek to establish a "place" through various resistance tactics that include civil protests, squatting, and legal advocacy. He analyzes the positive agency of these marginalized populations of homeless in Chicago and San Jose. In Chicago, Tranquility City, a homeless squatter camp, is the center of resistance and squat-ting activities. In San Jose, the homeless worked together with the Student-Homeless Alliance, which directly challenged the city's affordable housing policies. In sum, Wright makes the argument that homelessness is not merely an issue for social welfare. Rather, in the broader context, it is an issue of land use that is directly connected to issues of gentrification displacement and the cul-tural imaginings of what a city should look like by those who are in positions of power to shape its development.

David Snow and Leon Anderson (1993) provide overwhelming evidence that to understand the plight of the homeless in contemporary America it would be misguided to employ a pathological and medicalized view of them. In their field research of homeless people in Austin, Texas, they found that the vast majority of homeless men and women were highly adaptive, resourceful, and pragmatic as they cope with their situation. They argue that to focus on disabilities is a distorted characterization of the homeless. Their differences are a result of consequence of the dismal situation in which they find themselves, not from character frailties. "Confronted with minimal resources, often stigmatized by the broader society, fre-quently harassed by community members and by law enforcement officials, and repeatedly frustrated in their attempts to claim the most modest part of the Ameri-can dream, they nonetheless continue to struggle to survive materially, to develop friendships, however tenuous, with their street peers, and to carve out a sense of meaning and personal identity" (Snow and Anderson 1993:316).

In an earlier study, Snow and his associates (1986) make the point that the emphasis on the personal sources of homelessness is another example of blaming the victim. It also deflects attention away from the economic sources of homelessness, leads to faulty generalizations, and channels social policies that are doomed to fail.

It is demeaning and unfair to the majority of the homeless to focus so much attention on the presumed relationship between mental illness, deinstitutionalization, and homelessness. To do so not only wrongfully identifies the major problems confronting the bulk of the homeless, it also deflects attention from the more pervasive structural causes of homelessness, such as unemployment, inadequate income for unskilled and semi-skilled workers, and the decline in the availability of low-cost housing. (Snow et al. 1986:422)

Similarly, in the aforementioned work of Talmadge Wright (1997), he argues that it would be wrong to assume that the homeless are on the streets because they "choose" to live in their own "subculture." This "volunteerist" perspective along with the previous mentioned "individualistic" perspective both follow "blame the victim" rhetoric. He sees both perspectives reflecting earlier twentieth-century research based on skid row residents and transients that were predominantly white, middle-aged, older men who were often labeled as "hobos," "bums," and "tramps." Wright concludes that "Thinking of homeless as primarily an individual problem, to be solved by clinically based therapies, displaces the concern over structural social inequalities onto concerns over 'proper' components and individual responsibility" (Wright 1997: 12).

Peter Rossi (1994) observes that the primary reason for the upsurge in homelessness is related to the structural changes occurring in the economy as it moves from a manufacturing base with large numbers of low-skill manual jobs to a service base requiring higher educational attainment and greater occupational skills. The deteriorating value of Aid for Dependent Children payments and the crisis in affordable housing are contributing factors. The most significant change in the demographic composition of the new homeless was the appearance of homeless families (Rossi 1994). These families are identified as being single-parent, mostly young mothers in their twenties with very young children. Rossi (1994) attributes the rise in homeless families to the country's economic restructuring, which eliminated most low-level manufacturing jobs. He observes that while the low-level job prospects of both men and women were adversely affected directly by this economic restructuring, women were also affected indirectly by the decline in the supply of economically stable men who earned enough to provide for a family. How these economic changes have impacted on families is given a human dimension in the following passages. The first is from an underemployed African American who saw his job designing and building conveyer belts end when the company he worked for went out of business. Faced with the job loss and a medical emergency, his family was forced out of their home in an affluent city east of Seattle, and they moved to temporary housing in a large public housing project in Seattle.

"But minimum wage—that's insulting. I don't knock if for high school students. They're getting training, learning about working, making their pocket money. That's fine. But you take a person . . . I got six kids. $3.35, $4 an hour, I spend more than that wage in a day's time on a grocery bill. I mean you can accept some setbacks, but you can't tell a person, 'I don't care if you've been making $15 something an hour, the minimum is what you've got to make now.' If I hand you this letter, give you my resume, my military record, show you the kind of worker, I am, talk about my family, how can you degrade me by offering me the minimum wage?" (cited in Vanderstaay 1992:173)

A minister in a depressed industrial town in Pennsylvania echoes the under-employed man's sentiments. This Lutheran church leader witnessed the loss of hundreds of truck and auto manufacturing jobs when companies left the area. Families saw their savings dwindle, their unemployment benefits and pensions disappear at the same time food and rent costs rose while their federal benefits declined.

"Yes, there are new jobs. There's a new McDonald's and a Burger King. You can take home $450 in a month from jobs like that. That might barely pay the rent. What do you do if somebody gets sick? What do you do for food and clothes? These may be good jobs for a teenager. Can you ask a thirty-year-old man who's worked for G.M. since he was eighteen to keep his wife and kids alive on jobs like that? There are jobs cleaning rooms in the hotel . . . Can you expect a single mother with three kids to hold her life together with that kind of work? All you hear about these days are so-called service jobs—it makes me wonder where America is going. If we aren't producing anything of value, will we keep our nation going on hamburger stands? Who is all this 'service' for, if no one's got a real job making something of real worth?" (quoted in Kozol 1988:6)

Rossi (1994) also observes that the processes that produce family homelessness operate selectively along ethnic lines. He explains that extreme poverty is more prevalent among minority families, and single-parent families are more prevalent among minority families. Shelter and welfare systems, in turn, are geared to these single-parent families and particularly toward African American and Puerto Rican families located in urban areas. Finally, minorities are also the ones disproportionately affected by difficult housing situations at the local level. A final key factor is the failure of the social network of friends and relatives to provide the support needed to keep these families from experiencing homelessness. Rossi states: "They [homeless families] may not be complete isolates, but there are certainly few among their friends and kin on whom they can count for support" (1994:364). The population at risk at becoming homeless, the "precariously housed," is forced to rely on the benefice of a fragile support network of relatives or acquaintances for their shelter, individuals who are also vulnerable to economic uncertainties and downturns.

Shinn and Weitzman (1994), based on their earlier study (Shinn, Knickman, & Weitzman (1991) of homeless families in New York City, found that those who requested shelter were not isolates. Rather they had mothers and grandmothers living, had other close relatives, and had a close friend they saw on a regular basis. The homeless families were unable to stay with relatives and friends—in large part because they had already "worn out their welcome" by staying with them previously. The researchers, agreeing with Rossi, believe "that the kin of homeless families may themselves be too poor to offer much assistance . . . Also, the parents of homeless families were more likely than the parents of housed public assistance families to have been on public assistance themselves" (Shinn and Weitzman 1994:441).

Let us zero in on this last point, the relationship of kinship (including quasi-kin) networks and homeless families. It will be instructive to do this by comparing Latino poor families and African American poor families. Susan Gonzales Baker (1994) in examining the research literature finds that Latinos (predominantly Mexican Americans), in light of their high poverty rate, are underrepresented among the homeless. She attributes this underrepresentation to variations in patterns of familial support and network ties.

Baker (1994), observes that close-knit, family-based social networks are important to both Latinos and African Americans. Both are sources for not only emotional support but also for the exchange of guidance, useful information, personal services, and material assistance. However, these groups functioned in different ways when dealing with social services under different conditions. Latino family networks do not provide enabling information assistance on social services regarding shelters for families who are faced with homelessness. However, they do provide alternative residential arrangements, including living with parents, nonrelated adults sharing living quarters, multiple families doubling up, and, in the case of older immigrants, living with their adult children. The data sources are Mexican Americans living in the Southwest and West. Puerto Ricans living in New York City do not as readily avail these family-residential assistance options. Instead, they use social services and shelters and are found to be demographically represented among the homeless.

For African Americans, social service usage was encouraged by family networks, which also provided enabling information and assistance. Baker (1994) believes that a primary motive in doing so was the inability of the network to provide the necessary support and constrained housing and economic opportunities. The southwestern and western Latinos, on the other hand, may find such social services not as geographically readily available and may not face the same racial discrimination in housing as African Americans.

Baker concludes that the explanation for the "Latino paradox"—their underrepresentation among the homeless—may be explained by an interaction between culture and economic necessity.

> Latino social support seems to be more likely to include diverse housing arrangements within the interpersonal network as a strategy for avoiding life on the streets in the face of persistent poverty. Thus it appears likely that the Latino paradox can be explained in large measure by the particular way in which Latino populations have adapted to their constrained opportunity structure by sharing housing as a material resource more frequently and in more varied ways than may be true of other ethnic groups. (Baker 1994:498)

In summary, our investigation of homelessness in America indicates that poverty is the central causal factor. More fundamentally, governmental redevelopment policies exacerbate this poverty by excluding the poor from social space previously available to them. Land-use policies, in effect, redefine the city landscape in a manner that excludes, represses, and displaces the poor through punitive police actions, city zoning practices, and negative identity conceptualizations of the poor. Further, the inability of social networks to provide the necessary resources to help those in need exacerbates homelessness. These social networks, themselves, are overburdened, and cannot subsidize homeless families. They can barely make it on their own.

12

Gender Roles in the City

Any discussion on the nature of the social realm would be remiss unless attention is paid to how social exclusion operates in that realm. In an earlier chapter, the focus was on how race is a factor in understanding the dynamics of exclusion and how that exclusion has affected African Americans in particular. Further, the fear of the stranger was legitimized by spatial-segregation policies that extended beyond the public sphere to the entire city as well. This chapter will investigate the articulation of ideologies of social exclusion based on gender and sexual preferences in the city.

In this chapter, we will also discuss what Richard Florida (2002) has called the people of the "creative class," and the reasons on why creative people, many of whom are young and single, are attracted to living in the downtown areas of cities. Florida observes that these people are not attracted to downtowns that have large sports stadiums, tourist sites, or "theme park" shopping. Rather they are attracted to areas where they can live in communities that respect social and cultural diversity; where there are sites where one can establish a sense of identity and develop relationships with others who are similarly "creative"; and where one can find high-quality personal experiences. He further observes that businesses are often attracted to cities where there are large numbers of creative people. Florida, in essence, believes that businesses follow people, rather than people going where the jobs are. The implications of these ideas have ramifications for the redevelopment of the downtowns of many American cities and are of interest to us in this chapter.

Gender and Public Space

The urbanist John Rennie Short (1996: 231) cites the term *manmade city* as indicative of the social construction of urban space, and of male domination of the design and planning professions and in the very designs that reinforce gender bias. A common theme articulated by feminist geographers is that patterns of urban structure reflect the construction of space into masculine centers of production and feminine structures of reproduction. In thinking of gender and space, definitions of masculinity and femininity are constructed in particular places—the home as the site for women, work and the public sphere as sites for men. Yet even the private sphere, while seemingly defined as feminine space, was still controlled by men. "A man's home is his castle," is a popular folk saying that conveys this view. The private sphere was organized for the convenience of men. It was their site for rest, recreation, and relaxation: "Wife, get me my slippers." As feminists have observed, the private sphere was the *workplace* for women, and the public sphere was controlled or excluded spaces.

Ann Oakley (1974) investigated contemporary Victorian documents to find the rationale for the confinement of women to the household and their restriction or prevention from seeking outside employment. Four main reasons are delineated: "female employment was condemned on moral grounds, on grounds of damage to physical health, on grounds of neglect of home and family, and lastly, simply on the grounds that it contravened the 'natural' division of labour between the sexes" (Oakley 1974:45).

The middle and upper classes originated the ideology of women's confinement to the home. A woman's idleness was a mark of prosperity. The leisured lady-at-home was the ideal. The development and elaboration of society and rules of etiquette became the epitome of the later Victorian era. For the working classes, the doctrine of female domesticity began to crystallize in the last quarter of the nineteenth century. It ran counter to the economic needs of the family, yet became prevalent. For the working classes, too, "the idea that work outside the home for married women was a 'misfortune and a disgrace' became acceptable" (Oakley 1974:50). A closer look at Victorian society and its accompanying etiquette rules can be enlightening, for it was these rules established by the emerging bourgeois upper class that proved to be influential in affecting gender-role relationships not only for that class but also for the entire society.

During the nineteenth century, England saw a radical transformation of its ruling classes. As newly rich families began to gain eminence, these families, through individual achievement in industry and commerce, were supplanting the traditional rich, whose positions were based on heredity and family connections. To govern the social mobility of these new personnel, an elaborate formalized society developed. The rules of etiquette set down in housekeeping books, etiquette manuals, and advice columns in magazines were most relevant for highly structured social gatherings. Presentations at court, country, and city house parties, and the round of afternoon calls, regulated the behavior of all participants.

The rules of "society" were created to control entrance and involvement within social classes. This was necessary since Victorian "society" was undergoing unprecedented social change; rigid rules of social acceptance provided a haven of stability. The elaborate code of etiquette created barriers to social entry. Ceremonial behavior included rites of passage, especially during certain important events as births, marriages, and deaths. The introduction of new individuals and families into group membership and activities was also a sensitive area and marked by etiquette rules. Introductions, visits, and dining patterns became formalized and vastly elaborate.

The home became increasingly an important area for social gatherings. It served to control and regulate the contacts that the "ins" wished to have with their equals and the new people seeking entrance into their group. The private clubs served a similar function. The "society" controlled access to and involvement with those of the upper classes. For the newcomer it necessitated the abandonment of old allegiances, family and nonfamily, for this new prestigious social group.

The role of women was paradoxical. Influenced by the male-dominant patriarchal ideology, Victorian "society" was elaborated by its women. Women were exhorted to act as guardians of the home; men were exhorted to leave the home for the struggles of the business world, the army, the church, or politics. Women's duties were to regulate and control social gatherings and thus keep order in the ever-changing social scene. However, their sequestration in the home, and the confinement of their activities to domestic and "society" matters, occurred at the same time that men were expanding their influence and involvement in the new industrial world. This, ultimately, proved disastrous for women's independence and autonomy.

Socialization practices reinforced this dichotomy. Men were being socialized to operate in the ever-changing and complex world of industry, finance, and commerce. Women were socialized into the complexities of etiquette and the running of the home with its hierarchy of servants. Dress was a sign of social position and achievement.

> Every cap, bow, streamer, ruffle, fringe, bustle, glove and other elaboration symbolised some status category for the female wearer; mourning dress being the quintessence of this demarcation. A footman, with long experience in upper-class households, said "jewelry was a badge that women wore like a sergeant major's stripes or field-marshall's baton; it showed achievement, rank, position." It is not surprising, then, that girls and women of all classes were preoccupied with dress. (Davidoff 1975:95)

The rules governing sexual behavior for women were also paradoxical. The emphasis was on respectability through control of sexual behavior and desire. Victorian women gained status by denying their own sexuality and treating the Victorian masculine sex drive as sinful. Purity beliefs and the elaborate etiquette norms, which stressed modesty, prudishness, and cleanliness—as well as the rules governing demeanor and appearance, served to provide a sense of order, stability, and status in the everyday world. However, they also served to be psychologically stultifying. Further, the placing of women on a virginal pedestal, limiting their involvement to the home, and excluding them from the economic sphere served to reinforce the patriarchal ideology. Through idolatry, subservience emerged (Bartelt and Hutter 1977).

Feminist scholars have often pointed out that the dichotomization of space into public and private spheres has ramification for the articulation of gender roles. Public space has often become the province of men and is defined as masculine space. It is here that material manifestations of masculine ideas of order and authority are articulated. A "feminine" presence on the street, in public space, is viewed as threatening (Wilson 1991).

In a broad historical sweep, the social historian Elizabeth Wilson (1991) argues that what is wrong in the design of cities is the masculine desire to control disorder and especially men's need to control the "place" of women. Men define the public sphere as their spatial territory and by virtue of that belief women are "fair game" when they venture into this masculine sphere. Affluent women are virtuous and given some amount of protection from unwanted contacts. Poor and working class women, on the other hand, are often viewed as prostitutes, lesbians, or "loose" women who do not warrant protection. A paradoxical situation confronts women.

Wilson felt that the anonymity combined with the excitement of the late-nineteenth and early-twentieth-century city provided an opportunity for women to free themselves from the patriarchal control of either their fathers or husbands. Rural and suburban settings, as well as the home, are seen to be controlling environments. The city has the possibility of being the site for freedom and autonomy, but often, instead, it becomes the site of danger. It provides the anonymity to allow women to gather with other women of different backgrounds and to develop their sense of independence, but the potential for work opportunities and sexual freedom is offset by the presence of danger. The way to "protect" women in the city is not by the offering of police protection, but rather changing in a fundamental way the perception of women as sexual objects because of the impersonality and anonymity of city life.

Etiquette: Governing Gender Roles in the Public Sphere

A long-held justification for the relative absence of women from the private realm is the belief that women need to be protected from the uncertainties of social interaction with strangers in that realm. The ideological construction of women as a fragile being in need of protection has important implications for women politically, economically, and socially and, of particular concern here, it severely limits her rights to and freedom in the public realm. To understand the nature of women in the public realm it is necessary to understand the broader context of gender stratification in both private and public spheres.

Gentleman Meeting a Lady. "One should always recognize lady acquaintances in the street, either by bowing or uttering words of greeting." Woodcut from old-time etiquette book, ca. 1880.

Nancy Henley and Jo Freeman (1975) have observed that everyday interaction patterns reflect the subordination of women to men and are a fundamental source of social control employed by men against women. A study of the historical role of etiquette books and the part they played to control and regulate the behavior of men and women in both the private and public spheres is illuminating (Bartelt et al. 1986). Etiquette books played an important role in the socialization process of the nineteenth-century Victorian lady. They emphasized the importance of proper modes of acting to socially conscious Americans whether they were a part of the upper class or not in the areas of deference, demeanor, and manners. Stemming from the sexist pedestal model of their English counterparts, American etiquette books continue a patriarchal viewpoint from the Victorian era to the present. An unbroken tradition continues of female subservience most symbolically represented in the restriction of women to the home and limited access to the public sphere.

Contributing to the lowly position of women during the Victorian industrial period was the development of an ideology whose explicit goal was to assure the safety and well-being of women. This *ideology of domestic confinement* implicitly added to her political and social demise. A central tenet of this philosophy was the belief in women's natural domesticity. This belief prevented and restricted the employment of women outside the home. It advocated the economic dependence of married women on their husbands and their sole involvement with household tasks and childcare. This ideology was in direct contrast to the practices of the preindustrial era when women were a part of domestic industry. It was the Victorian answer to the harshness and severity of early industrial labor practices. Numerous laws were passed that restricted or prevented female and child labor in mining, factories, and the textile industries. This protective legislation led to the creation of the modern housewife role, which has become the prime source of feminine subservience. It is ironic that this legislation passed by "chivalrous" Victorian gentlemen to alter the brutality of industrial work had as its ultimate effect the substitution of a different form of subjugation.

David Reisman (Reisman et al. 1950) has observed that in societies which are relatively stable, people's conformity reflects their membership in particular age groupings, and in clan and caste groups. Behavior patterns are well established and have endured through a considerable period of time. However, in societies undergoing rapid social change such normative guidelines are inoperative. Etiquette rules are then established to control and regulate the important relationships of life.

In everyday life situations—walking, taking a streetcar, dining in public restaurants, attending theater and other cultural events, traveling—there arises the necessity to develop rules governing one's behavior in order to provide predictability in such relatively anonymous situations. This was particularly true in the United States during the turn of the twentieth century. America was undergoing major social and industrial changes. Cities were expanding at a phenomenal rate. People were moving to urban areas from the rural areas of the South and Midwest. There was an unprecedented wave of immigration from eastern and southern Europe. To control this disparate population in these emerging communities, etiquette manuals were developed as one attempt to teach these norms of conduct and to do so explicitly. This was an attempt to maintain the status quo.

An examination of etiquette books in nineteenth-century England and the United States at a time of rapid social change and urbanization provided few rules in governing the relationships among strangers. The problem was seen to be particularly acute when the strangers were male and female. Male advisements often took the form of etiquette guidelines on the proper ways that women should comport themselves in the public realm. Through rigorously controlled patterns of noninvolvement, or very limited involvement, women would be able to shelter themselves from uninvited male overtures. The preferred way to avoid public difficulties was to avoid public places and sequester them in the private place, the home. Nonetheless as Lyn Lofland notes, "Given what we know about nineteenth- and early twentieth-century trends in female employment, leisure activity, and political participation, it seems unlikely that such efforts kept any significant numbers of women cowering in their domestic 'havens'" (1973).

Lofland (1973) found in a review of etiquette books from 1881 to 1962 that there was a concentration on explicit instructions for public behavior during the earlier period and a gradual decreasing concern with these matters during the later one. This reflects the instability and unpredictability which people felt in the emerging industrial cities in the United States and the growing regularities felt in the cities of the mid-twentieth century. These concerns of the early etiquette books are demonstrated in such topics as:

> Street Etiquette: Recognizing friends on the street—Omitting to recognize acquaintances—Shaking hands with a lady—Young ladies conduct on the street—Accompanying visitors . . . —Conduct while shopping . . . —Carriage of a lady in public . . . — Meeting a lady acquaintance . . . —Riding and Driving . . . —Travelers and Traveling.

These early guidebooks provide the reader with explicit instructions on how to behave in these public places. The general pattern of admonitions revolves around the areas of controlling the relationship of males and females who are strangers to each other. [The following examples are from Bartelt et al. 1986, who examine gender deference and formal etiquette.] The following excerpt from Lillian Eichler's etiquette book in 1922 is illustrative:

> If a woman drops her bag or gloves and they are retrieved by a passing man, it is necessary only to smile and say "Thank you." No further conversation is permissible. (1922:194)
>   When a gentleman sees that a woman passenger is having difficulty in raising a window he need feel no hesitancy in offering to assist her. However, the courtesy ends when the window has been raised. (1922:224)

Writing in 1967, Amy Vanderbilt continues to argue for the control of interaction among strangers in public places:

> A man touches his hat but does not look more than briefly at a woman to whom he gives up his seat (in a streetcar). He then stands as far away from her as possible and does not look in her direction. (1967:211)

Shifting attention to other areas of public life—pedestrian behavior, shaking hands, opening doors, smoking in public, restaurant behavior, women's dress—a pattern continues to be enunciated in contemporary etiquette books. The underlying rationale for this pattern is giving deference to women—opening doors, walking on the outside of sidewalks (to prevent women from being littered by splashes from the street or by garbage), asking women for permission to smoke. Underlying these deferential patterns is imputation of women's helplessness and fraility. This is, of course, accompanied by the more subtle but direct premise of women's subservience. This is the price exacted. The following guidelines illustrate this:

> A man accompanying a woman "opens the door for her and holds it for her to go through. At a revolving door, he starts it off with a push and waits for her to go through." Also he "allows a woman to precede him, if single file formation is necessary, unless there is some service he can do for her by going first." (Fenwick 1948:29)
>   A man kissing a lady on the street—in greeting or farewell (only)—should always remove his hat, no matter what the weather. He should be careful concerning this courtesy even—or perhaps I should say especially with his wife or daughter. (Vanderbil 1974:20)
>   Well-bred women do not smoke when it will make them conspicuous, or when it will embarrass or offend anyone who is with them. (Hathaway 1928:43)

In their analysis of the "politics and politesse" inherent in etiquette, Bartelt et al. (1986) conclude that underlying etiquette admonitions are the basis for the philosophy of female helplessness. The authors argue that this type of thinking still pervades contemporary etiquette books. Deferential patterns are in reality forms of social control that perpetuate and continue the power and superior status enjoyed by men.

> While it is true that "wiser" people know that women are not weak and helpless and continuation of these patterns for whatever motive—femininity, courtesy, or whatever—when it is solely based on sexual differentiation criteria continues to serve as a common means of social control employed against women. The fixing of these patterns into codified vocabularies defining propriety in inherently iniquitous terms, in day-to-day situations, links these definitional processes to the overarching structure of sexual politics—the persistent power differential between the sexes. (Bartelt et al. 1986:213)

In essence, etiquette guidelines controlled interactional involvements through a dictation of norms of silence and decorum between the sexes. Yet, by so doing, they had a liberating effect in that they minimized the risk for women in the public sphere. As Clare Olivia Parsons (1997: 60) puts it, "Paradoxically, the institution of these mechanisms for regulating the actions of the urban bourgeoisie succeeded in reducing the anxiety of women on the street." She goes on to observe that in the case of Paris after the modernization of that city by Baron Haussmann (1850s and 1860s) the constructed broad boulevards promoted commerce and circulation. These designed boulevards proved conducive for the emergence of the female shoppers in the department stores created for that purpose. This is a topic for a later chapter. Returning to the function of rules of etiquette, when they did not govern the interactions of strangers, problems did occur. The case of gender harassment in the public sphere is the prime case-in-point.

Gender Harassment in the Public Sphere

In her (1975, 1998) analyses of women in the city, Lofland observes that urban sociology was derelict in its study of women in public places. In her opinion, this was largely because women were relegated to the home and neighborhood and had not been significantly visible in the public sphere. She argues that given the problematic orientation of the field of urban research, even in the study of women in the public sphere, the focus is more on the impact of male troublemakers than on the nature of women's involvement of the public sphere. She believes that the overemphasis by some feminist scholars and intellectuals on the ubiquity of sexual "harassment" as an integral feature of life in the public realm is misplaced. She does not deny that it "happens" but she feels that the "magnitude of its occurrence has been widely exaggerated" (1998: 161). The consequence is that women's involvement in the public realm has not been given the attention it deserves. Further, the

Young males harassing, whistling, catcalling, flirting and intimidating a young women as she walks by on a city street.

generated fear and loathing of the public realm often leads to the further withdrawal of women from it.

The feminist geographers Mona Domosh and Joni Seager (2001) observe that women fear the city, especially urban public spaces such as streets, parks, and public transportation, because they see it as the place where their own physical safety is most at risk. This is despite the fact that violence against women is most frequent in the private spaces of home. "There are real risks to women who venture into the wrong street at the wrong time, but our culture also tends to exaggerate those risks, thereby keeping women in their 'place' (at home)" (Domosh and Seager 2001:101). The geographer Gill Valentine speaks of a "spatial expression of patriarchy" referring to the self-imposed "curfews" that women utilize to minimize their perceived risk factors in venturing into public space (cited in Domosh and Seager 2001:101). This takes the form of not entering certain areas alone or only during certain hours during the day.

In *Passing By: Gender and Public Harassment*, Carol Brooks Gardner contends that an important characteristic of the public realm has been neglected: "the highly gendered nature of public place" (1995:44). She argues that there are significant differences in the way women and men experience the city. Fearing male violence, women's use of urban space is more constrained than men's. Women are more sensitive to the fear of sexual violence, and this structures their behavior in many cities.

Her ethnographic monograph examines the issue of gender-related public harassment. Going beyond the benign notion of harmless "standing by the corner watching the girls walk by," Gardner sees that various forms of unwanted public attention, including wolf whistles, verbal slurs, pinches, and stalking, are in reality manifestations of males controlling women's presence in public places. Public spaces become not neutral territory but one in which men exert control of women's sense of comfort.

Mitchell Duneier (1999), in his study of panhandlers on the streets of Greenwich Village, observes that some homeless ("unhoused" in his terms) black men use unreciprocated conversation to white women passersby as an articulation of gender power. "A few poor and unhoused men behave like some workingmen—black and white—who engage in sexually suggestive banter" (Duneier 1999:213). He believes that this unwanted verbal interaction is a form of norm violation on the social etiquette that should govern the behavior of strangers on a street.

> Much more is going on than the breaking of conventional rules of etiquette or even the expression of outright vulgarity. Through the pacing and timing of their utterances, the men offer evidence that they do not respond to cues that orderly interaction requires. The men deprive the women of something crucial, not just to them but to anyone—the ability to assume in others the practices behind the social bond. (Duneier 1999:213)

Duneier goes on to explain the behavioral motivation of these men, which arises because of their belief that these women would not normally engage them in conversation. Therefore, these women are treated "as objects upon whom interaction tricks can casually be put into play" (Duneier 1999:216). The men's behavior only reinforces the women's view that the street is unsafe and that these men need to be avoided and ignored—treated as "nonpersons" to use Goffman's term. A behavioral cycle comes into play that justifies the stereotypes they have of each other.

> In avoiding the street men's gaze, walking past them as they were not there, they further reinforce the men's view of them as beyond human empathy and, in their coldness and lack of respect, appropriate as interactional toys. For the women, the men's behavior and the predicaments to which it leads further reinforce their view of these men—and others who appear to be like them—as dangerous. Anxiety transforms to innocent panhandlers, book vendors, and to some degree, perhaps, black men in general. Stereotypes are given their life. (Duneier 1999:216)

Elizabeth Wilson (1991) and Lyn Lofland (1998) do not deny the existence of such forms of gender harassment. Nevertheless, they see that representatives of a body of feminist literature give excessive attention and express hostility toward urban public place. Concerns over safety, welfare, and protection dominate that analysis and view the city in a social problem context. Elizabeth Wilson believes that such a perspective only serves to perpetuate paternalistic thought and keep women within their place in the domestic realm. She advocates a more balanced view that sees both the positive benefits and pleasures of women being visible and viable in city public places while recognizing the potential dangers that too often lurk there as well. She argues for a recognition that while city life poses risks and dangers, it also provides women with freedom and opportunities. "Surely it is possible to be both pro-cities and pro-women, to hold in balance an awareness of both the pleasures and dangers that the city offers women, and to judge that in the end, urban life, however fraught with difficulty, has emancipated women more than rural life or suburban domesticity" (Wilson 1991: 10).

Lyn Lofland (1998) in her examination of the role of women in the public realm of the city makes a similar argument. Lofland goes on to observe that late-twentieth-century "feminist intellectuals and movement activists are evoking that same specter of the fearsome *male* and there is at least some suggestion. . . that *their* warnings are falling on more receptive ears" (Lofland 1998).

In essence I agree with the position of Wilson and Lofland, although I would not underestimate the extent of sexual harassment behavioral patterns. However, the heightened attention to these patterns may have reached such epidemic proportion that a *culture of fear* has developed in regard to the public sphere. The negative reaction to the public sphere has a threat of being counterproductive. Unfortunately, often the effect of the heightened attention is not to stop the problem of sexual harassment but rather to remove women from the public sphere of which they are an integral part. This feminist anti-urban view, therefore, plays into the hands of those who prefer, for whatever reason, to see the removal of women from the public realm. The solution, however, is not to deny the legitimacy of those who express concern over public sexual harassment, but to institute enforcement policies both by the police and by the passersby to make those who perpetuate harassment feel extremely uncomfortable if they do so.

Gays and Lesbians in the City

The attitudes of social scientists toward the opportunities that cities provide for the gathering and intermingling of strangers have varied widely. Simmel and his later twentieth-century counterpart Stanley Milgram emphasized the negative effects of the "multitude of stimuli" (Simmel) or "stimulus overload" (Milgram) that could affect urbanites. The analysis focused on the "lonely crowd" and the resultant feelings of alienation and anomie that were a result of asocial stranger interactions. Countering this image was the more positive assessments of sociologists like Lofland, who saw the world of strangers as an opportunity for like-minded people who shared similar lifestyles that may be radically different and diverse from the cultural mainstream to meet and interact.

Fischer's subcultural theory points out that the city, because of its size, density, and heterogeneity, allows for the development of a critical mass of people to gather and develop their own enclave. Cities offer the opportunity to those whose lifestyles may be considered deviant to find people of a similar fashion, interact, and develop their own enclaves. Karp, Stone, and Yoels (1977), citing

These statues of gay and lesbian couples are found in the vest pocket park situated across from the Stonewall Inn on Christopher Street, Greenwich Village, New York City. Photo by author.

Charles Horton Cooley, an early twentieth-century social psychologist and pioneer observer of the human condition, emphasize that through one's social relationships with others one's individuality can be realized. Further, self-expression premises intimate social association.

No better example of Fischer's subcultural theory and Cooley's observation of the linkage of identity and community is the investigation of the development and vitality of gay enclaves. For gays, social and spatial identities are interwoven, and gay enclaves are mutually constructed. Today, the Castro area in San Francisco and Greenwich Village in New York are visible examples of recognized gay areas that have been established in numerous other cities throughout the United States and worldwide. Gay enclaves emerged more than 100 years ago, at the same time that industrialization fostered the growth of American cities. Before we discuss this development, it would be instructive to frame the account in a broader social-psychological analysis of the development of "homosexual" identity.

Attitudes and behavior toward homosexuality have historically changed. Today, we are experiencing great debate on the nature and significance of homosexuality. The debate centers on whether homosexuality is a lifestyle determined by various cultural factors, a reflection of some sort of biological or genetic "imbalance," or a manifestation of psychological deviance. Of particular interest to us is the scholarship that examines the cultural conceptualization of sexuality, heterosexuality, and homosexuality. A very influential study has been Michel Foucault's (1978) *The History of Sexuality, Volume I: An Introduction*. Foucault sees the modern conceptualization of sexuality as developing because of the decline in the importance of kinship and extended family ties in controlling individuals. He observes that, beginning in the eighteenth century, there was a shift in emphasis away from marriages constructed to control individuals through the continuation and development of kinship and lineage ties. This movement accelerated during the Industrial Revolution and continued into the Victorian era, and a new control system developed that placed emphasis on marriage and conjugality within a broader context of the control of sexuality and its modes of expression. Foucault writes,

> "The deployment of alliances (kinship ties) has as one of its chief objectives to reproduce the interplay of relations and maintain the law that governs them; the deployment of sexuality, on the other hand, engenders a continual extension of areas and forms of control. For the first, what is pertinent is the link between partners and definite statutes; the second is concerned with the sensations of the body, the quality of pleasures, and the nature of impressions. . . ." (1978:106)

Foucault argues that Victorian society was not, as popularly depicted, a society that denied and suppressed sexual discussion; rather, it was a society that sexualized all social relations and was consumed with the study of sexuality and its control as part of its obligation to assume total responsibility for its citizens' lives and welfare. The study of sexuality becomes incorporated into the world of therapists, psychologists, social scientists, and educators as part of an all-encompassing attempt to shape and influence people, not only in terms of their acting in socially, economically, and politically appropriate ways, but also in terms of their views of their bodies, their sex, and their human potentials. Foucault's analysis of sexuality shares a similar orientation to that of his French associate, Jacques Donzelot (1979), and of Christopher Lasch (1977a), all of whom call attention to the perceived intrusion of the state and subsidiary medical and social agencies (the "helping" profession) on the family beginning in the nineteenth century and continuing today. Let us see its applicability in regard to the conceptualization and policies regarding homosexuality.

In a book with the seemingly curious title, *The Invention of Heterosexuality*, Jonathan Ned Katz (1995), examines the development of the conceptualization of *heterosexuality* in the nineteenth century. Katz is not arguing, of course, that the sexual relationship between men and women was invented but rather he refers to the way that this concept became distinct from the emerging concept of *homosexuality*. The concept of heterosexuality is seen to have changed over time; the current conceptualization is our particular historical arrangement of perceiving, categorizing, and imagining the relationship between the sexes.

Katz (1995) traces heterosexuality's conceptual development as a term meaning "perverted desire" to one of "normal sexuality." The term heterosexuality was invented in Germany in the 1860s, and the concept appears in an American medical journal in 1892. It originally referred to a perverse desire for both sexes. In the ensuing decades, the term changed and by the 1930s it came to mean normal sexuality manifested in sexual passion for one of the "opposite sex."

Katz picks up on the construct "opposite sex" to investigate this construct in broader terms, terms that dichotomize things—such as black and white, good and bad, us and them. By referring to men and women as opposite sexes and homosexuality and heterosexuality as opposite sexual orientations, the tendency is to focus on differences rather than similarities. This is at a time when we have seen that men and women are more alike than different in terms of nurturance, aggressiveness, and emotionality. The differences are more attributable to historical periods and cultural differences than any innate biological differences. Katz further argues that while the media focuses on biological differences between homosexuals and heterosexuals, the evidence shows a convergence in lifestyles, diverse family arrangements, and a sexual pleasure ethic. He believes that the desire for dichotomous labels of homosexual and heterosexual is fostered by the conservative elements of our society in a misguided determination to reinforce the "naturalness" and "superiority" of heterosexuality and masculinity as currently conceptualized.

While Katz sees the concept of heterosexuality as a recent social invention, other scholars [see Berube (1981), D'Emilio (1983a, 1983b), Walkowitz (1980), and Weeks (1981)] on gay history have assembled evidence that homosexuality as it is currently conceptualized is also of relatively recent origin. John D'Emilio (1983b), in his excellent historical study of the formation of the gay community, reminds us that in colonial America there was no concept of "homosexuality." Erotic behavior between individuals of the same sex was viewed as a sporadic and exceptional activity that did not differ essentially from other sexual transgressions such as adultery, bestiality, and fornication. Heterosexuality was assumed to be the natural way of sexuality. Colonial society placed such a great emphasis on the family and on reproduction (the average pregnancy rate for white New England women was eight) to populate the vast American wilderness that "homosexuality" was inconceivable.

It was not until the second half of the nineteenth century, with the advent of full-blown industrial capitalism and the modern city, that gay and lesbian conceptualizations and identities emerged. These conceptualizations linked the formation of gay enclaves at this time. This fact may surprise many. The popular but erroneous belief is that the development of the gay community began with the Stonewall Rebellion in New York City in 1969 when gays publicly protested police harassment of gay bars as the beginning of the gay liberation movement. (The Stonewall Inn, in June 1999, was officially placed on the National Register of Historic Places. It was the first gay site in the country to be so honored.) According to this view, it was thought that prior to this period gay life existed privately, "in the closet." Gay men were depicted as being isolated with profound negative feelings of self. However, an extensive literature has developed that has disproved this historical misconception.

John D'Emilio (1983b) traces the movement of large populations from kinship-dominated, closely knit rural communities into the more impersonal urban centers. The family, in turn, shifted from a public community institution into a private insular one. For individuals, industrialization and urbanization created the social context for the development of a more autonomous personal life. Affection, intimacy, and sexuality became more a matter of personal choice than a determination by family members. Homosexually-inclined men and women, who would have been visible and vulnerable in small rural communities, began moving into the city. In this setting, men and women who wished to pursue active and public sexual involvements with others of their own sex felt free to do so and began to fashion from this desire a new sexual identity and way of life (D'Emilio 1983b).

George Chauncey (1994), in his book, *Gay New York*, investigated the emergence of a gay world in the early 1890s and studied its development through the next 50 years. Chauncey also takes issue with the assertion that public gay life first came into existence in the 1960s. Using multiple resources, including newspapers, diaries, legal records, books, and letters, Chauncey discovers a multilayered public life of rooming houses; community centers, including the YMCA; restaurants and cafeterias; bathhouses; drag balls; and streetlife. Further, this gay world was diverse, composed of different class and racial groups who lived in different neighborhood enclaves, including Greenwich Village, Times Square, and Harlem.

The motive, then, for the movement of large numbers of gay people to the city, in addition to employment opportunities, was for the opportunities to pursue a gay lifestyle, a lifestyle curtailed to the extreme in the small town and rural areas. Chauncey emphasizes the importance of the creation of a gay male world both for the individuals who participated in it and for the culture they created. "The men who participated in that world forged a distinctive culture with its own language and customs, its own traditions and folk histories, its own heroes and heroines" (Chauncey 1995:1).

John D'Emilio also traced the development in urban settings of male homosexual bars, cruising areas, public bathhouses, and parks, settings that enabled men to meet each other at the beginning of the twentieth century. Lesbians, more constrained in terms of both economic dependence on husbands and patriarchal ideologies, developed more private meetingplaces, which included literary societies, social clubs, faculties of women's colleges, and settlement-house involvements. By the 1920s and 1930s, public institutions such as lesbian bars made an appearance, although they never assumed the size of their male equivalents.

World War II had a similar effect in developing gay male and lesbian community and identity. The war geographically mobilized young people—at the time that their sexual identities were just forming—from the heterosexual settings of their families, communities, and hometowns. D'Emilio asserts, "Because the war removed large numbers of men and women from familial—and familiar—environments, it freed homosexual eroticism from some of the structural restraints that made it appear marginal and isolated" (1983b:38). This was the case for men and women in the sex-segregated armed forces. It also held true for nonmilitary females who entered the work force to fill America's labor needs. D'Emilio reminds us that this analysis should not let us think that heterosexuality did not continue as the predominant form of sexual expression, but the war did temporarily weaken the patterns of daily life that fostered heterosexuality and inhibited homosexuality. The war provided a new situation in which those who were sexually attracted to their own sex but were previously constrained by their circumstances from acting on this attitude could do so. Further, the war reinforced the identities of gays and lesbians and strengthened their ties to homosexuality as a way of life.

By the 1950s, gay urban territories—such as Greenwich Village in New York City and similar enclaves in Chicago, Los Angeles, and San Francisco—were established. Gay and lesbian subcultures also came into existence in smaller cities such as Worcester, Massachusetts; Buffalo, New York; and Des Moines, Iowa. Activist groups such as the Mattachine Society and the Daughters of Bilitis formed to provide a vehicle for self-expression and protection against hostile actions and discrimination in government and the work world.

As mentioned earlier, the "Stonewall Riots" of late June 1969 was one of the pivotal events that helped spark the Gay Rights movement. The Stonewall Inn in New York's Greenwich Village was a gay bar that served the gay community. One patron interviewed by a newspaper reporter shortly after the incident expressed the importance of the bar for gays:

> You felt safe among your own. You could come down around here without fear of being busted or of being beaten up by some punk or to prove his masculinity to himself. Around here, we outnumber the punks. (quoted in McGarry and Wasserman 1998:5)

As part of the continuous policy of harassment employed by the city's police force and extenuated by an upcoming mayoral election, police raided the bar. Rather than submitting to the raid, the bar's clientele reacted with fury. Subsequently, Stonewall has taken on mythic importance. It was the catalyst for the gay liberation movement and for the organization of lesbian and gay men. As pointed out by others (cf. McGarry and Wasserman 1998; and Murray 1996), the activism triggered by Stonewall strengthened and organized an extensive gay and lesbian organizational structure that was already present in most large American cities, especially in New York, Chicago, and San Francisco. The Stonewall Riots politicized the movement especially in New York City.

> Stonewall has been an extraordinarily appealing—and useful creation myth for lesbians and gay men trying to define themselves as a community. The riot has become the symbol of a community shared heritage that has deep meaning for gay people. . . . A generation has passed since the Stonewall Riots of 1969, but Stonewall retains enormous power as a symbol of collective resistance and beacon of hope for lesbians and gay men around the world. (McGarry and Wasserman 1998:20)

Coinciding with and reinforced by the gay rights movement, gay communities continued to organize and develop in the late 1970s and early 1980s; in that short time period they made a significant impact on urban politics in the United States, with San Francisco being the most notable example (cf. Castells 1983, Murray 1996). In San Francisco and elsewhere, gays have moved into centrally located, but rundown, areas and have successfully sought to transform these areas into hospitable neighborhoods. The most successful attempts have been marginal sections of New York's Greenwich Village and San Francisco's Castro Street area. However, gays have often faced the competition and hostility of other groups for control of the limited supply of cheap and moderate housing. Low-income gays have been the victims of street violence exacerbated by economic conditions and homophobia. In addition, in cities such as San Francisco that are undergoing massive downtown business development and high-cost condominium construction, gays are either being forced out or are depicted as the cause of the evaporation of affordable housing. Rubin notes that in San Francisco, "The specter of 'the homosexual invasion' is a convenient scapegoat which deflects attention from the banks, the planning commission, the political establishment, and the big developers" (1984:296).

Manuel Castells (1983) has observed that the gay community has transformed the city of San Francisco. The artistic talent of many gay men, which has become a major element in the gay culture, is reflected in the enhancement of urban aesthetics that has made a significant architectural improvement in the San Francisco cityscape. Gays have been responsible for a significant proportion of renovations of the "Painted Ladies" (Victorian era houses) and other old buildings, and in neighborhood improvement that has played an instrumental role in the upgrading of the real-estate market in San Francisco.

The liveliness of street life, popular celebrations, and festivals first initiated in the Castro area has become a vital component of the urban culture of San Francisco and has contributed to the rise of San Francisco as one of the most popular tourist destinations of any American city. The importance of a viable public realm has been one of the quintessential elements of city life (Lofland 1998). The significance of the contribution of the gay community to the vitality of San Francisco cannot be underestimated. As Castells (1983) states:

> Although the appreciation could be somewhat subjective, most urbanists seem to value public life, street activity, and intense social interaction as one of the most distinctive positive dimensions of city life. Cities all through history, have been spaces of diversity and communication. When communication ends, or when diversity is swallowed by social segregation, as in the uniform backyards of American suburbs, the urban culture is endangered,—the sign perhaps, of a sick civilization. (Castells: 167)

John D'Emilio (1983b), in his analysis of the emergence of gay and lesbian identity and the creation of their respective communities, observes that structural changes in industrial urban society made possible the emergence of gay and lesbian identity and the creation of their respective communities. Yet, at the same time, society is unable to accept homosexuality. He asks what accounts for societal heterosexism and homophobia and finds the answer in the contradictory relationship that exists between this form of society and the family. His analysis is provocative.

D'Emilio notices the theme shared by many sociologists that industrial capitalism shifted the family away from a productive economic unit into one that emphasized the affective function of the family in terms of the nurturance of children and the emotional happiness of its members. Consequently, sexuality ceased to be defined primarily in terms of reproduction and instead became defined largely in terms of emotional expressiveness. Indeed, affection, intimacy, and sexuality became more and more a matter of individual choice and no longer solely defined in terms of the family. This attitudinal and behavioral shift provided the setting and opportunity for people who wished to fashion their notions of sexuality with people of their own sex.

The increased reaction against the development of gay and lesbian identities and their communities stems from recent developments in heterosexual marriage that point to its failure to satisfy the emotional demands and needs of its members. D'Emilio points out that since the mid-1960s there have been a plummet in birthrates, a continuing decline in average household size, a rise in divorce rates, and an increase in the variety of living arrangements that people are choosing. The reason for these developments lies in the inherent contradictions of capitalism, which allows individuals to live outside the family in relative economic independence while at the same time dictating, ideologically, that men and women marry and have children to assure the perpetuation of society. As D'Emilio has indicated elsewhere (1983a), "Thus while capitalism has knocked the material foundation away from family life, lesbians, gay men, and heterosexual feminists have become the scapegoats for the social instability of the system. . . . The elevation of the family to ideological preeminence guarantees that capitalist society will reproduce not just children, but heterosexism and homophobia" (1983a:109, 110).

At the beginning of the Clinton administration in 1992 and 1993, the issue of gays in the military crystallized opinion about gay people and gay rights. Homophobia, like racism, anti-Semitism, and sexism, reflects a fear and intolerance toward others. An executive for a gay rights group observes that, "Homophobia . . . serves a purpose in society. It preserves privilege for some people, maintains an uneven playing field and limits who has access to the job market" (cited in Angier 1993). Homosexuality, because of its linkage to feelings about sex and procreation, also provides a reason for homophobia. In Judaism and Christianity, especially Catholicism and Protestant fundamentalism, there is a clear separation between sex for procreation and sex for pleasure. The former is encouraged, the later rejected. Historians have observed that the religious injunction against homosexuality can be understood in the context in which the Bible was written. Lillian Federman, a historian on gay issues, states: "Fundamentalists refuse to see that whoever wrote the Old Testament was part of an endangered tribe. They had to emphasize procreation, and therefore homosexuality for men was taboo" (cited in Angier 1993). Finally, AIDS, with its linkage of sexuality with pleasure and punishment, has exacerbated uneasiness about homosexuality (Angier 1993).

The AIDS epidemic impacted on the gay community at the same time that a severe sexual counterrevolution was gaining fervor among conservatives. This counterrevolution advocated a return to "family values" and the restriction of sexual practices to the heterosexual marital relationship.

Urban Tribes, Gays, and the Creative Class

"Urban tribes," a concept formulated by Ethan Watters, refers to what he sees as a new phenomenon among young people in their late 20s and early 30s. Those people, who remain single, form friendship groups—*urban tribes*—characterized by caring and commitment. These tribes can vary from being intricate, tightly knit, mixed-set groups of singles, who develop emotional support systems, exchange favors, and often vacation together, to more loosely knit groupings. They can be composed of both straight and gay members, and they can vary in size from six members to more than two dozen. What makes them different than other friendship groups are their long-term character and the fact that so many young urban professionals are involved.

The television sit-com *Friends* immediately comes to mind as an example of an urban tribe. Peterson (2003), in a *USA Today* article on urban tribes, writes that a member of one tribe in the Washington D.C. area observed that the characters in the television show are too attached to each other, while another in New York City observed that in the group she belongs to, the members are much more culturally and racially diverse.

The family historian Stephanie Coontz, who has written widely on historical changes in the American family, comments on the concept of urban tribes: "This idea is a creative adaptation to the fact people are marrying later in order to establish careers. Like it or not, we are having to seek a number of alternative ways to make and sustain commitments rather than just relying on marriage" (quoted in Peterson 2003: 5D).

The major factor for the development of such groups is the desire of young people to delay marriage until their careers have been established. Another factor in their decision to delay marriage is a desire to spare themselves from the fate of their cohorts who married young and who subsequently have divorced. Watters delineates the characteristics *not* present among this group.

> We were a curious new breed, those of us treading water in the cities—outside of our families of origin and seemingly unwilling to begin families for ourselves. We were interested in (often devoted to) our careers and avocations, but we stayed strangely off the social map in other ways. Devotion to blood ties didn't seem to interest us enough to stay in our hometowns, and the idea of finding community among our neighbors was a quaint anachronism. While we worried about the "breakdown of community" and bemoan the current level of selfishness in the country, we didn't seem to be taking much action. Although we were part of the fastest-growing demographic group in America, our Census Bureau designation, the "never-marrieds," implied a type of stasis—we were a population by what we weren't doing. (Watters 2003: 19–20)

Watters takes issue with those who have argued that people, especially young people, are disconnected in a city. From the work of Robert Putnam's (2000) "bowling alone" thesis to the earlier social disorganization approach of the Chicago School, social analysts have defined the city in terms of disconnections. Putnam's thesis argued that there has been a diminishing amount of community spirit as well as a substantial reduction of community participation that has resulted in the loss of "social capital." Robert Park, the founder of the Chicago School, wrote in 1925 that "A very large part of these populations of great cities . . . live much as people do in some great hotel, meeting but not knowing one another. . . .

The effect of this is to substitute fortuitous and casual relationships for the more intimate and permanent association of the smaller community" (Park quoted in Watters 2003: 115).

Watters believes that the prevalence of urban tribes composed of young people belies the argument that the young experience a loss of community in the city. He supports the beliefs of the sociologist Claude Fischer who observes, "Even if . . . Americans have withdrawn from public activities such as politics and civic clubs, the question arises as to whether they have withdrawn all the way into their isolated lonely selves, or have withdrawn into a more private world of family, work and friends" (Fischer quoted in Watters 2003:116).

Watters argues that the social network formed by members of urban tribes works in many beneficial ways to solidify feelings of community through involvements and supports among each other. These involvements and supports cover both emotional and practical needs, e.g., networking to help obtain jobs. Watters believes that the bonds that exist among members of urban tribes provide a form of "social capital" that goes beyond Putnam's defining the term synonymously with joining civic groups. In a nice touch, Watters quotes from a school supervisor from 1916 who sees social capital as composed of:

> Those tangible substances [that] count for most in the daily lives of people: namely good will, fellowship, sympathy, and social intercourse among the individuals and families who make up a social unit. If [an individual] comes into contact with his neighbor, and they with other neighbors, there will be an accumulation of social capital, which may immediately satisfy his social needs and which may mean a social potentiality sufficient to the substantial improvement of living conditions in the whole community. (quoted in Watters 2003: 137)

Richard Florida, the author of *The Rise of the Creative Class* (2002), sees support for his ideas in Watters's discussion of urban tribes. Florida believes that urban tribes provide evidence on "the rise of new kinds of cities and support structures for the growing class of creative, single people inhabiting leading urban centers in the United States and around the world" (Florida cited on back cover jacket of Watters 2003). Let us turn to Florida's work to build on this point.

Florida (2002) has put forth a provocative theory of metropolitan economic redevelopment driven by members of a creative class cluster. He asserts that people do not move to where the jobs are, but rather jobs move to where talented, highly creative people choose to live based largely on quality-of-life considerations. "My conclusion was that rather than being driven exclusively by companies, economic growth was occurring in places that were tolerant, diverse and open to creativity—because they were places where creative people of *all* types wanted to live" (Florida 2002: x).

Florida defines the "creative class" as being composed of artists, musicians, writers, inventors, architects, and entrepreneurs, as well as professors. These are people who are seen to be in the forefront of the next wave of economic prosperity in this country. Their common linkage is that all are part of a creative group that produces new forms or products in knowledge-based industries, such as the high-tech sector, financial and legal services, business management, educational institutions, and healthcare. The unifying element in their work is that they have to utilize their minds and think on their own. Florida developed a creativity index with a mix of four equally weighted factors that rank all metro areas. The index includes a creative class share of the workforce; percentage of high-tech industry; innovation, as measured by patents per capita; and diversity measured by a gay index—the percentage of gays in a given locale. The creativity index that is employed by Florida to determine a city's potential for economic vitality is a composite of many smaller indexes, *High-Tech, Bohemian, Working Class, Melting Pot, Gay*, and others.

Among those metropolitan areas with a population of 1 million or more the top ranked is the San Francisco Bay Area, followed by Austin, San Diego, Boston, and Seattle. The bottom five of the 49 listed are Louisville, Buffalo, Las Vegas, Norfolk–Virginia Beach–Newport News, and Memphis. For those with populations between 500,000 and 1 million Albuquerque ranked first, while Youngstown ranked last. Among medium-size cities of populations between 250,000 and 500,000, Madison is number one; the last is Shreveport. Finally, the list of small metropolitan areas (50,000 to 100,000) is headed by Santa Fe, while Enid, Oklahoma, ranks last in the creativity index rankings.

His book has stirred controversy because Florida's central thesis is that a city that attracts diversity—and namely, large numbers of gays and bohemians, will do better economically than a city that does not. The places that are poised for economic growth are those that are most open to diversity. This discussion also focuses on those individuals who have the most mobility and freedom from the constraints of family and old community ties. These include gays, single Yuppies (young urban professionals), DINKS (double income, no kids), and single men and women. Interestingly, Florida finds an inverse relationship between those regions that score high on his creativity index and Robert Putnam's (2000) surveys of social capital. Putnam argues that social mobility is associated with involvement with community and social ties within community. Florida argues the reverse. He feels that when an individual is enmeshed in a tight social network of family and friends this inhibits social advancement. He argues instead that social mobility occurs when people are free of the constraints of the community and are free to move into communities that are high in the "3ts"—technology, talent, and tolerance. It is these type of communities that attract businesses. *Technology* refers to regions that have a strong technology base, often found in communities with research universities and with strong investment in technological enterprises. *Talent* refers to creative people who embody excitement and energy and have stimulating minds. *Tolerance* refers to communities that are tolerant of diversity and thus can attract all sorts of people—including foreign-born immigrants, women as well as men, gays as well as singles, and people who have different appearances from the mainstream.

Of the 3ts, "tolerance" has gotten the most media attention. Florida's development and usage of indexes labeled as the "gay" index and the "bohemian" index reflect the combination of creativity and diversity. Florida emphasizes the importance that diversity and openness play in attracting creative people to metropolitan regions. He demonstrates that there is a correlation between creative places and openness to alternative lifestyles. Tolerance and diversity are the wellspring of creativity in our regions. The people who make up the creative class are seen to welcome places that are composed of different kinds of people. Citing his colleague Gary Gates, gays are the canaries of the creative economy. Gays often locate themselves in communities notable for their tolerance of alternative lifestyles.

Florida believes that many of his ideas support the prescriptions of Jane Jacobs in her seminal study, *The Death and Life of Great American Cities* (1961). Jacobs focused on the importance of walkable neighborhoods, compact rather than sprawling environments, and civic spaces. Similarly, Florida sees a linkage with the ideas of Ray Oldenburg on the importance of "third places" as crucial sites for the fostering of community among mobile creative individuals. Like Oldenburg, he recognizes the importance of "authentic" places rather then the ersatz chain stores or the shops that too often comprise the core of gentrified downtowns or suburban malls.

Members of the creative class are not attracted by gentrification and homogeneity. Nor are they involved in the traditional forms of entertainment such as the symphonies, operas, or ballet. Nor do they advocate center-city sports stadiums. Their focus is on street-level cafes and local music scenes. Florida sees the development of new communities of individuals with high degrees of social mobility. They use the third places in these communities exclusively with less linkage to the surrounding community or with their families and kin. Finally, members of the "creative class" have little self-recognition of their own existence or identification as a specific class. Their importance lies in how they are part of, and the generators of, the development of a creative economy that fosters metropolitan economic redevelopment.

Jobs Move to Where People Are: Meet Me in St. Louis

> Meet me in St. Louis, Louis
> Meet me at the Fair,
> Don't tell me the lights are shining
> Anyplace but there.
> We will dance the Hoochee Koochee,
> I will be your tootsie wootsie,
> If you will meet me in St. Louis, Louis
> Meet me at the Fair.
>
> Andrew Sterling, lyricist, and
> F. A. Mills, composer, 1904

As previously noted, Richard Florida's (2002) theory of metropolitan economic redevelopment asserts that people do not move to where the jobs are, but rather

A large mall and hotels utilize the former train shed of Union Station, St. Louis, Missouri. This site serves as a major attraction for both tourists and residents in this city's design for the revitalization of its downtown. Photo by author.

jobs move to where talented, highly creative people chose to live based largely on quality-of-life considerations. Recently, a number of cities, including Philadelphia, Vancouver, British Columbia, and St. Louis, have witnessed a boom in downtown residential development. Many people who share the creative class cluster discussed by Florida are moving to the downtowns of these cities to live; they spend their leisure time there but do not work there. A discussion of St. Louis will serve to illustrate this urban redevelopment phenomenon.

St. Louis has a very interesting demographic history. In 1900, a few years before its World's Fair (the 1904 Louisiana Purchase Exposition), it had a population of 575,238 people and was the fourth largest city in the United States. For the first half of the twentieth century it was a very viable city. It was known for its "booze and shoes"—a leading beer manufacturer (Budweiser) and shoe manufacturer. However, in the late twenties and into the thirties, signs of decline were becoming evident. And plans for the redevelopment of deteriorating communities were forced to be put on hold because of the Depression and World War II. By 1950, its population reached its maximum of 856,796. The population rise in mid-century was attributable to an influx of poor, unskilled workers. After World War II there were large areas of deteriorated housing because of the earlier neglect. Following urban renewal practices occurring in other cities as well, many old areas were bulldozed and replaced by smaller-scale housing projects and large high-rise, low-income housing projects, most notably Pruitt-Igoe. The smaller-scale housing projects were relatively successful. Pruitt-Igoe, as was discussed earlier in this book, was an abject failure and was eventually demolished.

Like other cities, St. Louis experienced a massive movement out of the city. First, the businesses left, followed by the city's largely white, middle-class, inhabitants, to the suburbs. By 1980 St. Louis had less than half a million people (453,083). Its tax based eroded; crime increased; and the quality of its education system appreciably declined. Many neighborhoods continued to decline and some with the oldest housing in the Midwest were virtually abandoned (Greer 1989). The Brookings Institute in the early 1980s saw it as one of the worst of the "rust belt" cities based on demographics, mobility data, and economic indicators (Greer 1989). In 2003 its population shrunk by more than 100,000 people to 332,223, ranking it 53rd in the country. Based on 2002 U.S. Census bureau estimates, St. Louis is the fastest-shrinking big city in the United States (*The World Almanac and Book of Facts* 2005). Since 1950, the greater St. Louis metropolitan area remains about the same, 2,500,000. Thus, the metropolitan growth has been in the suburbs.

In November 2005, the National Collegiate Honors Council had their annual meeting in St. Louis. At a plenary session, Easley Hamilton, a prominent urban architectural historian who is the Preservation Historian for the St. Louis County Department of Parks and Recreation and is also an Affiliate Assistant Professor at Washington University's Department of Agriculture, reported that there has been a major residential explosion in downtown St. Louis and that many of those residents reverse-commute to work in the adjacent suburbs. Where there were few downtown residents just a few years ago, more than 10,000 residents now live there. James A. Cloar, the president and CEO of the Downtown St. Louis Partnership, a private, not-for-profit organization representing the downtown business community, estimates that by the end of 2008 the expectation is that 15,000 will live downtown (Cloar 2005). Just north of the central business district and the Renaissance Grand Hotel (see discussion below), is an emerging Warehouse District containing loft apartment units in buildings that were formerly used by the shoe, hat, and garment industries. The buildings are now becoming condominiums with apartments above and boutique and restaurants on ground level. The buildings are handsome, early-twentieth-century, brick and stone buildings that provide the requisite "urban-feel" reminiscent of SoHo in Manhattan.

Cloar reports that since 2000, over $3 billion dollars have been invested in downtown St. Louis. This money has been spent on the building of thousands of new residences, new hotels, and the restoration of office buildings and renewed public spaces. Restaurants, shops, and galleries have opened and The Robert's Orpheum Theater has reopened. There are plans to restore the historic Kiel Opera House. A new baseball park has been built alongside the waterfront near the Gateway Arch.

In its initial efforts to rebuild and redevelop its downtown, St. Louis built a downtown baseball stadium, Busch Stadium. Partially funded ($5 million) by the Anheuser-Busch Brewery Company, which owned the St. Louis Cardinals, and by the city ($15 million), the stadium was opened on May 12, 1966. The stadium was surrounded by acres of vacant land converted into parking lots. Baseball fans, who were primarily from the suburbs, went to the ballpark, ate at the ballpark, got back into their cars, and returned to the suburbs. The stadium was demolished after the end of the baseball season in 2005 and was replaced, as mentioned earlier, by a new stadium in 2006 in the same downtown location. The stadium, while an attractive draw for those in attendance, in the long run did not prove to be the needed catalyst for the rebuilding of the downtown. A more multivaried strategy was needed.

In the later part of the 1980s, St. Louis began its long road to recovery. Various strategies include neighborhood preservation and renewal. In the quest for increased tourist business, Union Station, at one time the largest and busiest passenger rail terminal in the world, ceased operation in 1978 and was transformed and reopened as an upscale market place in 1985. It was the largest adaptive re-use project in the United States. Union Station includes over 90 shops and restaurants and adjacent hotels, including a 539-room Hyatt Regency Hotel. The Hyatt transformed the magnificent former passenger train waiting area into a hotel lounge that has preserved much of the old grandeur. Tax incentives are designed to encourage businesses to return to the downtown, and the city's universities and hospital systems are growing in economic importance. The building of a light-rail transit system, Metrolink, ties the region together, linking the airport; Clayton, the suburb where many businesses are now located; downtown St. Louis; and the area across the river in East St. Louis, Illinois.

To develop its tourist and convention business, the former Statler Hotel, which had won design awards when it opened in 1917 and was later vacant for 13 years after being damaged by a fire, was restored to its former elegance and opulence by Historic Restoration Inc., in partnership with Kimberly-Clark Corporation. This hotel has been renamed the Renaissance Grand Hotel and is part of the Marriott hotel chain. This hotel and others that have opened since 2000 have added 2,000 new rooms to the existing base of 3,000 rooms, an increase of 67 percent. Almost all the new rooms are in historic landmarks (Downs 2003).

Rebecca Gratz and Norman Mintz (1998), in their evaluation of St. Louis's urban redevelopment, are somewhat pessimistic about its potential for success. They point out that much of the urban fabric of the downtown was destroyed. Too many businesses left the city; too many buildings were destroyed in the name of urban renewal. The former manufacturing district was replaced by the Gateway Arch, baseball and football stadiums, an indoor arena used for hockey and other activities, and open park areas that are under utilized. At the time that they wrote their assessment, only 1 percent of the city's population lived downtown. As reported here, that figure is rapidly rising. But, still, the downtown area is still relatively bereft of business and commerce activities; the central business district is still underutilized; and the suburbs are where businesses are located. Today, the streets are virtually deserted after 5:00 p.m. Retail stores are few and far between; theaters and movie houses are not located downtown. Whether, as Richard Florida predicts, businesses will follow the new residents of the downtown into the downtown remains to be seen. Until that occurs, even with the development of new residential areas in former commercial districts, the rebirth of downtown urbanism remains problematic, given the previous dismantling of St. Louis's downtown. Gratz and Mintz's concluding assessment of St. Louis and cities that share a similar history is as follows:

> In most places, loft or commercial building conversions are occurring in fragmented areas of cities. Decades of "renewal" projects have severed most of the close-grained connections of a functioning urban fabric, leaving cleared, empty areas between urban fragments. Reweaving those fragments is a challenge. Understanding of and sensitivity to the fundamental characteristics of urbanism are imperative. (Gratz and Mintz 1998:320)

13

City Families and Kinship Patterns

The Public World of the Preindustrial Family

The Industrial City and the Rise of the Private Family

The Rise of the Suburbs, the Cult of Domesticity, and the Private Family

The City and the Rediscovery of the Family and Urban Kinship Patterns

Urban Kinship Networks and the African American Family

Mexican Americans in Urban **Barrios**

The Suburban Working-Class and Middle-Class Family

The Dispersal of Kin and Kin-Work

In this book we have seen that the emergence of the industrial city led to the development of three forms of spatial segregation. The first form of spatial segregation was the separation of work and the home. Mixed land-use for work and home characterized the preindustrial city. In the industrial city people no longer worked where they lived. Segregated land-use patterns were based on function; factories, commercial, business, and shopping areas were separated from residential areas. The second form was the segregation of neighborhoods by class, race, and ethnicity. In the preindustrial city people of different classes intermingled. Lyn H. Lofland (1973) observed that you could not tell who the strangers were by their locale but rather by their appearance. In the industrial city, Robert Park and his colleagues at the University of Chicago, in the first part of the twentieth century, refer to the "mosaic of social worlds"—the Little Italys, Chinatowns, Greek Towns, and Skid Rows. The previous chapter was concerned with the third form of segregation, the segregation of people by gender-based activities. In this chapter we want to extend that discussion by examining the nature of family and kinship relationships and involvements and how they were affected by urbanization.

Sociology has long maintained that the fundamental characteristic of modern life has been the creation of an area of social activity referred to as *private life* or the *private sphere*. The private sphere is an area of social life that is removed from and segregated from the public institutions of the community, the economy, and the state. The family—the most important institution that comprises the private sphere—is given primary responsibility for the socialization of children. The mother, in Western industrial societies, is often seen as the primary socialization agent. The argument is made that historically the larger kinship group, the clan, and the community had more direct control over individuals. In the premodern, preindustrial historical period, the family was more of a public institution integrated within an elaborated kinship system that was part of the larger community. This integration of the family with the larger community is absent from modern society, and the segregation of the family from the community is the primary characteristic of the family concerning the contemporary society.

In this chapter I would like to examine the underlying premises of the above depiction and to examine their implications for both the family and the community. This investigation falls within the prevalent sociological perspectives on how family life and city life are experienced by families and by women and men both within and outside of the family.

The Public World of the Preindustrial Family

Philippe Ariès, a French social historian, has written a seminal work on the analysis of the historical evolution of the Western family. This analysis lies within the context of the changing relationships of the family with larger kinship, friendship, neighborhood, religious, and community ties. Ariès's *Centuries of Childhood: A Social History of Family Life* (1962) traces the developments in the conceptualization of the family from the Middle Ages to the present. His data sources include paintings and diaries, the history of games and pastimes, and the development of schools and their curricula. Ariès's basic thesis is that the contemporary conceptualization of family life and the modern image of the nature of children are recent phenomena. He argues that the concept of the family did not emerge until the seventeenth century. He does not deny the existence of the family prior to that time but makes a critical distinction between the family as a *reality* and the *idea* of the family, which is sensitive to change. Ariès states that the physical existence of the family is not in question: Fathers and mothers and children exist in all societies. But the point is that the ideas entertained about family relations can be radically dissimilar over lengthy periods of time.

> ... it would be vain to deny the existence of a family life in the Middle Ages. But the family existed in silence: it did not awaken feelings strong enough to inspire poet or artist. We must recognize the importance of this silence: not much value was placed on the family. (Ariès 1962:364)

The low valuation placed on the family in preindustrial Europe occurred because of the individual's almost total involvement with the community.

People lived in their communities; they worked, played, and prayed in them. The communities monopolized all their time and their minds. They had very little time for their families. The gathering point for the community was the "big house," which contained up to 25 people, including families, children, and servants. The big house fulfilled a public function by serving as a place for business and sociability. Here friends, clients, and relatives met and talked. The rooms of the house were multifunctional: they were used for domestic activities as well as for professional purposes. People ate, slept, danced, worked, and received visitors in them.

> They ate in them, but not at special tables: the "dining table" did not exist, and at mealtimes people set up folding trestle-tables, covering them with a cloth. . . . It is easy to imagine the promiscuity which reigned in these rooms where nobody could be alone, which one had to cross to reach any of the communicating rooms, where several couples and several groups of boys or girls slept together (not to speak of the servants, of whom at least some must have slept beside their masters, setting up beds, which were still collapsible in the room or just outside the door), in which people forgathered to have their meals, to receive their friends or clients, and sometimes to give alms to beggars. (Ariès 1962:394–95)

The general situation was one in which most activities were public and one where people were never left alone. The density of social life made isolation virtually impossible. Families were part and parcel of the society and were intertwined with relatives, friends, clients, protégés, debtors, and so on. Aries argues that the lack of privacy attributed to this overwhelming community sociability and hindered the formation of the concept of the family. The concept of the family developed as other specialized institutions relieved the home of its multifaceted functions. The growth of the taverns, cafes, and clubs provided alternative outlets for sociability. The establishment of geographically distinct business and occupational places freed the family from its business functions. The strengthening of the family was to be seen in the increased privacy for family life and a growing intimacy among family members. Gradually, the family cut itself off from the outside world, and a separate and distinct family life emerged. As we see, this isolation has had critical implications for women and children.

Edward Shorter—in a provocative book, *The Making of the Modern Family* (1975)—continues the general theme of Philippe Ariès. He sees the family tied integrally with the community. Shorter states that ordinary families in western and central Europe from 1500 to the end of the eighteenth century were "held firmly in the matrix of the larger social order" (Shorter 1975:3). The family was secured to the community by two ties: one was the intricate web of extended kin, including uncles, aunts, and cousins; the other was to the wider community. The family had no sense of privacy or separation from the community. The marital roles were not viewed as independently important. Marriage was frequently arranged on the basis of advancing the extended family's economic interests.

Shorter's central argument is that the history of the family can be seen in the shift in the relationship between the nuclear family and the surrounding community. During the preindustrial period, the physical matrix discouraged privacy and intimacy within the traditional family. However, unlike Ariès—who presents a rather rosy, idealized depiction of preindustrial life, where all peoples of different ages, sexes, and classes intermingled in a Bruegelesque scene—Shorter stresses the negative characteristics of marital and family life. Emotional coldness between husband and wife and an emotional isolation through a strict division of work assignments and gender roles characterized family life.

In summary, a much greater involvement of the family with the surrounding community characterized traditional life in preindustrial Europe. The relationship between husband and wife was not as intimate or private, as it is in today's contemporary industrial societies. In addition, the status and treatment of women varied with their involvement in economically productive work. When a woman contributed, she had more power and control over her own life. When she did not, her life was that of a domestically confined slave, servile and subservient to her master—her husband.

Although the majority of households studied historically were composed of nuclear families, they did not conform to the characteristics of the modern private family. Historically, the family was not intimate and did not encourage domesticity or privacy. It was neither detached from the community nor highly mobile, either socially or geographically. The modern private family, in contrast, is mobile both socially and geographically with relatively few extended kinship ties and with relatively little involvement with the community.

Why did this transformation take place? Why did the personal life in the eighteenth and nineteenth centuries move toward privatization and domesticity? Why is the significance in the change of the historical family seen not so much in terms of size and composition of the household but in the detachment of the nuclear family from the outside world? Why did the family develop an ideology that saw it as the center for emotional support and gratification? What were the implications of these changes for the family, for the husband, for the wife, and for the children? How successful has the family been in becoming a private institution? What are the implications of this change for the community and for the city? I have only briefly sketched out some of the answers so far.

The Industrial City and the Rise of the Private Family

To help answer some of the questions just posed let me return to a theme that I introduced earlier in this chapter. Family and urban sociologists have emphasized that changes in Western society resulted in the gradual separation of the public institution of work and community from the private sphere of the family. Since the nineteenth century, the removal from the community setting distinguished middle class family life in America.

The Chicago School has long influenced the study of families and kinship patterns in the city. The Chicago School developed a distinct contrast between urban and rural life. Proponents saw traditional patterns of life being broken down by debilitating urban forces, resulting in social disorganization within the family. Louis Wirth (1938), in his seminal work on "urbanism as a way of life," set down the definitive statement on the impact of the city on the family. His words, quoted in Chapter 4, are worth repeating: "The distinctive features of the urban mode of life have often been described sociologically as consisting of the substitution of secondary for primary contacts, the weakening of the bonds of kinship, and the declining social significance of the family, the disappearance of the neighborhood, and the undermining of the traditional basis of social solidarity" (Wirth 1938: 21–22). The Chicago School essentially saw the consequence of urban life on the family and kinship in terms of family disorganization. Its litany on the crisis and decay of the family continues to be echoed in contemporary views of family breakdown.

Beginning in the late 1930s and accelerating after World War II, many of the views of the Chicago School of Sociology either merged with or influenced newer perspectives. By the 1950s, the dominant school of American sociology was structural-functionalism, under the intellectual leadership of Talcott Parsons (1902–1980). Parsons was one of the most predominant and influential sociologists of the twentieth century. He noticed the Chicago School's view on cities weakening the bonds of kinship, but rejects the view that the social significance of the family is in decline. Parsons persuasively developed a more positive, or functional, view of the contemporary American family. According to Parsons, the isolation of the nuclear family "is the most distinctive feature of the American kinship and underlies most of its peculiar functional and dynamic problems" (1943:28). The typical American household consists of a husband, wife, and children economically independent of their extended family and frequently located at considerable geographical distance from it.

Parsons believes that industrialization and urbanization are greatly changing American society. In particular, he believes that society has become highly "differentiated," with the family system's previous educational, religious, political, and economic functions being taken over by other institutions in the society. By "differentiation," Parsons means that functions performed earlier by one institution in the society are now distributed among several institutions. Thus, schools, churches, peer groups, political parties, voluntary associations, and occupational groups have assumed functions once reserved for the family. Rather than view industrialization and urbanization negatively, Parsons sees the family as becoming a more specialized group, concentrating its functions on the socialization of children and providing emotional support and affection for family members.

Parsons further suggests that the isolated nuclear family may be ideally suited to meet the demands of the occupational and geographical mobility that is inherent in industrial urban society. Unencumbered by obligatory extended kinship bonds, the nuclear family is best able to move where the jobs are and better able to take advantage of occupational opportunities. In contrast, the traditional extended-family system bond of extensive and obligatory economic and residential rights and duties is seen to be dysfunctional for industrial society.

Arguing against the social disorganization thesis on the breakdown of the contemporary family, Parsons (1955) finds support for the importance of the nuclear family in the high rates of marriage and remarriage after divorce, the increase in the birthrate after World War II, and the increase in the building of single-family homes (particularly in suburbia) during this time period. All these trends provide evidence of the continuing visibility, *not* the social disorganization, of the family and *increased* vitality of the nuclear family bond. Thus, a specialized family system functionally meets the affectional and personality needs of its members. Further, a family system that is a relatively isolated and self-sustaining economic unit of mother, father, and children, living without other relatives in the home and without close obligations and ties to relatives who live nearby, may be admirably fitted to this form of society.

In summary, Parsons emphasizes the importance of the nuclear family—in the absence of extended kinship ties—in that it meets two major societal needs: the socialization of children and the satisfaction of the affectional and emotional demands of husbands, wives, and their children. Further, the isolated nuclear family not handicapped by conflicting obligations to extended relatives can best take advantage of occupational opportunities even when geographical mobility is required and is best able to cope with the demands of modern industrial urban life.

The Rise of the Suburbs, the Cult of Domesticity, and the Private Family

An analysis on the rise of the suburbs in the nineteenth century in conjunction with the emerging ideology—the cult of domesticity—are seen as the forerunners of the "isolated nuclear family" described by Parsons. The development of the American suburbs can be seen, in part, as a reaction against the perceived deterioration of family life in the city. In my discussion I follow the model developed by Kenneth T. Jackson (1985) in his important work, *Crabgrass Frontier: The Suburbanization of the United States.*

Between 1820 and 1920, a major social and cultural revolution was transforming life in America. The small-town agrarian society was rapidly giving way to the emergence of a vast industrial urban society. Further, this new society was being populated by two major waves of immigrants that differed remarkably from the predominant England-derived population and from each other. The first wave of immigrants began arriving in the 1830s; for the next 50 years, in addition to those who came from England, many came from Ireland, Germany, and the Scandinavian countries. A second wave of equal duration coming from Eastern and Southern Europe and comprised in main part of Poles, Italians, Greeks, Slavs, and Jews, soon followed.

Many of these immigrants, especially the Irish from the first wave and almost all the others from the second wave, moved to the job-rich urban centers, and by so doing dramatically transformed not only these cities but the country itself. For the descendants of the original English immigrants, especially those in the emerging American middle class and those even more affluent, the city became the symbol of the new America. And that symbol often was fraught with danger of the unknown paths that the future of city life would take.

As these changes began in the second-third of the nineteenth century, the growing industrial cities of the United States, began to be perceived by many as a place to be feared. The city was depicted as the site of sinfulness and greed. The antidote was seen in the family and in the virtues of domestic life. This was a reaction to the new roles taken by men and women in adapting to industrial life.

The growth of manufacturing meant that men left the home for outside worksites. For the more affluent families, wives did not work in the paid labor force. The residence soon became their sole responsibility. As a consequence, the husband and wife relationship assumed the "traditional" division of labor that we for so long took as a given. The men's sphere was tied to paid work, and the women's sphere was tied to the home and children. Furthermore, this sphere came to be regarded as morally superior. It was during this period that the "cult of domesticity" developed, anchored by what Barbara Welter (1966) has called the "Cult of True Womanhood." Four cardinal virtues—piety, purity, submissiveness, and domesticity—were tied to the idealization of feminine roles of mother, daughter, sister, and wife.

During this period, women's magazines and religious pronouncements began extolling the virtues of domesticity, privacy, and isolation. Ministers, such as the Reverend William G. Eliot, preached to a female audience in 1853: "The foundation of our free institutions is in our love, as a people, for our homes. The strength of our country is found in the declaration that all men are free and equal, but in the quiet influence of the fireside, the bonds which unite together in the family circle. The corner-stone of our republic is the hearth-stone" (quoted in Jackson 1985:48).

The song "Home, Sweet Home" came to be the most widely sung lyric of the period (Jackson 1985). This song, written in 1823, gives an account of the wistfulness of a wanderer yearning for his childhood home—a theme quite appropriate to a society undergoing major changes. Christopher Lasch (1977a) refers to the home as a sought "Haven in a Heartless World." It is here that the privatization of the family could occur and it is here that the home could serve as a refuge and a private retreat. The home would serve as the center for the development of a new form of emotional intensity between husband and wife, and parents and children. The home was also seen as the ideal site for women to pursue their god-given destiny as wives, mothers, and homemakers.

Further the ideal site for the private home was seen as being the suburb, not the city. Kenneth T. Jackson provides an historical overview of the development of the private family ideology and the suburbanization of the United States. He documents how "the suburban ideal of a detached dwelling in a semirural setting was related to an emerging distinction between 'Gemeinschaft,' the primary face-to-face relationships of home and family, and 'Gesellschaft,' the impersonal and sometimes hostile outside society" (Jackson 1985: 46).

The nineteenth-century ideology of female domesticity was wedded to the ideology that glorified the sanctity of the home. The ideal setting for both was the middle-class suburb. The city was reviled as the setting for infamy and anonymity; the suburb, with its green spaces and clean air, was the setting in which women could provide the proper wholesome and moral atmosphere to raise children (Palen 1995).

In an era when activities were divided between men's and women's spheres, the city was Gomorrah—a world of men, factories, crowding, and vice. The suburban home, by contrast, was sacred space in which, under the wife's tutelage, men would be encouraged to become more civilized and children would be raised in health and virtue. (Palen 1995:153)

I will be devoting considerably more attention to the development of the suburbs and "suburbia as ways of life" in a later chapter of this book. For now, however, let us make note of the fact that the privatized home located in the privatized middle-class suburb became the American ideal. But what of those who remained in the city? Let us turn our attention now to the nature of family and kinship relationships in the city.

The City and the Rediscovery of the Family and Urban Kinship Patterns

Was city life as destructive to family life as those who chose to leave the city for the suburbs think? How had urban industrial society altered kinship solidarity? The contention put forward by sociologists such as Talcott Parsons (1943) and his

An urban playground used by young professional families.

"isolated nuclear family" hypothesis was that the family had to change to meet the needs of the industrial system, which required a mobile labor force that was detached from rigid rules and the economically irrational demands of extended kin. The isolated nuclear family was viewed as the functionally ideal institution to meet the labor demands of modern industry.

Studies of long-distance overseas migration during the mass-immigration period in America that extended from 1880 to 1920 revealed that relatives on both sides of the Atlantic maintained ties and transmitted aid and assistance. We examined these immigrant family groups in the previous chapter. Let us now turn our attention to the post–World War II research that has documented the persistence of kinship interaction and mutual support in contemporary American society outside the confines of the nuclear family. This research cast serious doubts on the assumption that the city is antithetical to family life.

Since 1950, a mass of empirical data has accumulated that questions the basic assumptions of theorists such as Louis Wirth and Talcott Parsons on the isolation of the nuclear family in the city. These studies have shown that viable relationships exist among relatives and that they constitute a family's most important social contacts; they also demonstrate that relationships with kin are a major source of recreational and leisure activities and that there is a considerable interchange of mutual aid among related families. The studies directly contradict the prevalent notions about the social isolation of the urban nuclear family and the underlying theme of social disorganization as a characteristic of urban life that leads to the disintegration of families and the alienation and anomie of individual city dwellers.

The following studies of urban family relations in New Haven (Sussman 1953); East Lansing (Stone 1954; Smith, Form, and Stone 1954); Detroit (Axelrod 1956); Los Angeles (Greer 1956); San Francisco (Bell and Boat 1957); Philadelphia (Blumberg and Bell 1959); Cleveland (Sussman 1959); and Buffalo (Litwak 1959–1960, 1960a, 1960b) all provide evidence of the significant role played by extended kin in contemporary American families. Sussman and Burchinal (1962) summarized this relevant research and concluded that the urban nuclear family must be seen within the context of an interrelated kinship structure that provides services and aid in a reciprocal-exchange system.

They find that the major forms of help and service include the following: help during illness, financial aid, childcare, personal and business advice, and valuable gifts. Social activities were found to be the principal functions of the interrelated family network. The major forms include interfamily visits; joint participation activities; and participation in ceremonial activities, such as weddings and funerals, which are significant demonstrations of family unity. These findings led Sussman to answer the question of whether "the isolated nuclear family . . . is fact or fiction?" as "mostly fiction" (1959:340).

Sussman (1953, 1959), Litwak (1960a, 1960b), and Sussman and Burchinal (1962) provide a theoretical explanation that accounts for the existence of viable kinship relations in urban centers when the early theorists hypothesized that they did not exist. Whereas Parsons (1943) suggests that the isolated nuclear family is ideally suited to the demands of occupational and geographical mobility, which are an inherent part of urban industrial society, these researchers suggest that it may not be the most functional family type. They hypothesize that the *modified extended family* (a term coined by Litwak) may be more functional than the isolated nuclear one.

Litwak (1959–1960, 1960a, 1960b) found that an extended family kinship structure existed in a modern urban center–Buffalo, New York. This extended-family structure differed from the classical extended family in that there was no authoritarian leader and it was not dependent on geographic mobility or occupational similarity to assure its viability. This modified extended family structure consisted of a series of nuclear families joined together on an egalitarian basis for mutual aid. It differed from the isolated nuclear family in that considerable mutual aid is assumed to exist among these family members, and thus the family does not face the world as an isolated unit.

A common shared characteristic of all the families that were investigated by the above researchers was that they were from the working class, and the communities that they lived in took on the characteristics of what Herbert Gans's (1962b) has described as "urban villagers." As discussed in a previous chapter, Herbert Gans described urban villagers as being highly integrated into an ethnic working-class community. These communities tended to resemble homogenous small towns more than they resembled depersonalized, isolated, and social disorganized urban communities. Far from being depersonalized, isolated, and socially disorganized, as predicted by Louis Wirth, Gan's observes that these communities put an emphasis "on kinship and the primary group, the lack of anonymity and secondary-group contacts, the weakness of formal organization, and the suspicion of anything and anyone outside their neighborhood" (Gans 1962b:630).

John Mogey (1964), in his essay "Family and Community in Urban-Industrial Societies," draws on the descriptive writings about urban villages in England, France, and the United States and develops a theoretical dichotomy between *open communities* and *closed communities*. The closed community is the urban village, characterized as one in which scenes of intense interfamilial cooperation exist, and that is cohesive, homogeneous in cultural values, and closed against outsiders. The open community, on the other hand, is similar to Gans's depiction of the urban way of life of the cosmopolites, the unmarried, and the married without children. In these communities, people have voluntary attachments to a variety of associations and secondary groups. Families who live in these communities interact with individuals from other areas as well as from their own.

An open community has an in-and-out migration of population, whereas the closed community is characterized by relatively little mobility. The closed community or urban village has families who are acquainted with each other and have extensive ties with neighbors; in the open community, each family lives in relative anonymity and few personal relationships exist among members of the community.

Mogey states that the conjugal family is not prevalent in the closed community. No isolated nuclear family structure exists since it requires an open community structure, with secondary group relationships predominating over primary ones. Family mobility is also seen as leading to the abandonment of segregated family-role patterns.

Elizabeth Bott (1957), in what has become a classic study, presented an influential typology that focused on the husbands' and wives' involvement with social networks comprised of kin, friends, and neighbors in the community as well as their relationship and involvement with others. The settings were communities in England. Bott found that if either family member maintained ties with a network of friends, neighbors, and relatives who knew one another and interacted, husband-wife ties would be minimal. Husbands and wives who are members of such close-knit networks when they marry and continue to maintain such relationships during their marriage have a marital-role organization based on a clear differentiation of tasks with few shared interests or activities. If either needs assistance, whether economic or emotional, he or she does not ask the spouse but rather seeks help from network members. The result is that the husband-wife relationship is not close. The couple lives in relatively separate worlds with different involvements and activities.

Young and Willmott (1957/1963), in their classic study of the working-class community of Bethnel Green in east London, report that the extensive family ties, far from having disappeared, were still very much prevalent. Young and Willmott provide an interesting illustration of the extensiveness of family relations in Bethnel Green—the report by one of their children who was attending a local school. The child came back from school one day and reported the following.

> The teacher asked us to draw pictures of our family. I did one of you and Mummy and Mickey and me, but isn't it funny, the others were putting in their Nannas and aunties, and uncles and all such sorts of people like that. (Young and Willmott 1957/1962:14)

Gans (1962a) made a similar observation. He reports that the Italian Americans residing in the working-class community on the West End of Boston have a family system that shares some of the characteristics of the modified extended family and the classical extended family. Although each of the households is nuclear—composed of husband, wife, and children—there are extended family ties.

> But although households are nuclear or expanded, the family itself is still closer to the extended type. It is not an economic unity, however, for there are few opportunities for people to work together in commercial or manufacturing activities. The extended family actually functions best as a social circle, in which relatives who share the same interests and who are otherwise compatible enjoy each other's company. Members of the family circle also offer advice and other help on everyday problems. There are some limits to this aid, however, especially if the individual being helped does not reciprocate. (Gans 1962a:46)

Mogey describes the impact of the closed community on marital roles as one characterized by husbands and wives each performing a separate set of tasks. The wife is in charge of household tasks and child raising; the husband is primarily responsible for being the breadwinner. Leisure-time activities are similarly segregated. In times of emergency, aid for either the husband or wife is provided by same-sex relatives. Within families with segregation-role patterns, mother-daughter relations tend to be stronger than father-son relations. This is particularly true when the husband has moved his residence at the time of marriage to the street of the wife's mother. Both Gans (1962a) as well as Young and Willmott (1957/1962) report that a particularly strong relationship exists between married daughter and mother:

> Marriage divides the sexes into their distinctive roles, and so strengthens the relationship between the daughter and the mother who has been through it before. The old proverb applies:
>
> *My son's a man till he gets him a wife, My daughter's a daughter all her life.*
>
> The daughter continues to live near her mother. She is a member of her extended family. She receives advice and support from her in the great personal crisis and on the small domestic occasions. They share so much and give such help to each other because, in their women's world, they have the same functions of caring for home and bringing up children. (Young and Willmott 1957/1962:61)

Let's return to Gans's study of working-class Italian Americans in Boston to see how family relationships were articulated in the urban village of West End Boston. Gans emphasizes the particular importance given to the peer group relations with friends and kin of the same generation. Social gatherings of married adults do not revolve around occupational roles as they do among the middle class, but rather among the same-age kin and longstanding friends. Social gatherings tend to occur regularly—for example, once a week to play cards—and usually with the same people. These activities as well as major family events, such as christenings, graduations, and weddings, are all sex segregated—men staying in one group, the women in another.

The working-class families are an adult-oriented family system. Children do not have center stage as they do among families of the middle class and upper-middle class. Gans reports that in the West End of Boston, the child is expected to develop and behave in ways satisfying to adults. Little girls are expected to assist their mother with household tasks by the age of 7 or 8; little boys are treated in a similar way as their fathers are, free to go and come as they please but staying out of trouble. Thus, the children tend to develop a world for themselves that is relatively separate from their parents and in which the parents take little part:

> . . . parent child relationships are segregated almost as much as male female ones. The child will report on his peer group activities at home, but they are of relatively little interest to parents in an adult centered family. If the child performs well at school or at play, parents will praise him for it. But they are unlikely to attend his performance in a school program or a baseball game in person. This is his life, not theirs. (Gans 1962a:56 57)

The question naturally arises as to how these later findings on the viability of extended kinship relationships can be reconciled with the earlier sociological accounts reporting the existence of isolated nuclear families and the absence of a viable kinship network (cf. Hutter 1970). William Key (1961) suggested that the hypothesis on the disintegration of the extended family was focused on the experiences of immigrant groups coming to the city during the period of urbanization in Western society before these immigrants had the opportunity to establish families. In addition, this period of industrialization was characterized by rapid change and great geographical mobility from rural areas to newly urbanized ones. The events that occurred in many American cities, such as Chicago, during the first 30 years of the twentieth century dramatically illustrate this point.

It is my contention that the earlier theorists, particularly Wirth and Parsons, did not look at the effects of the Americanization experience on generational relationships in the extended family when they examined the relationship between industrialization and kinship solidarity. That is, when they looked at that relationship, they did not control for the "transformation of identity" of family members as a result of their different socialization experiences—the older generation's European experiences with the younger generation's American experiences (Hutter 1970).

This belief is shared by Peter L. Berger (1963). Berger believes that kinship ties are weakened by social mobility when social mobility has consequences in terms of the reinterpretation of our lives. Berger argues that individuals reinterpret their relationship to the people and events that used to be closest to them because their self-image changes as they move up the occupational and ethnic assimilation ladder. "Even Mama, who used to be the orb around which the universe revolved, has become a silly old Italian woman one must pacify occasionally with the fraudulent display of an old self that no longer exists" (Berger 1963:60).

During the first half of the twentieth-century stage of industrialization and urbanization, then, social mobility was accompanied by differential socialization experiences that accounted for the "transformation of identity" of the younger family members and the resultant weakening of kinship ties. This period of rapid social change—great geographical mobility from rural areas to newly urbanized ones and, in the United States, a great influx of Europeans emigrating from their homelands—caused great social and cultural mobility and separation among intergenerational families. Once the descendants of these immigrants went through the Americanization process and emerged as ethnic Americans, their social-class differences based on cultural diversity became moderate and shrank.

Litwak (1960b) maintains that among white Americanized groups, especially those of the middle class, upward mobility does not involve radical shifts in socialization and, therefore, does not constitute a real barrier to extended family communication. Here, then, is one key intervening variable between social mobility and kinship solidarity—transformation of identity caused by differential socialization experiences. The fact that the differential socialization experiences shrank among these studied groups helps to account for the appearance of the modified extended family.

A further limiting aspect of the isolated family ideal type was its failure to take into consideration differences in class and ethnicity. The working-class extended family still served as a basic economic unit. It had a strong influence on the work and occupational careers of its individual members. Working-class and ethnic families banded together in their attempt to overcome their poor economic circumstances. The middle-class family with its values of privacy and individualism best approximates the ideal type of the isolated urban family, but the working class developed their own "modern" and urban family value system to allow them to cope with the vicissitudes of urban industrial life. As we shall see next, the African American family also developed an urban adaptation form that took shape from historical experiences as well as from city involvements. It, too, differed radically from the isolated nuclear family model. Thus, within the same historical period there was a myriad of urban adaptation processes.

Urban Kinship Networks and the African American Family

The first part of the twentieth century witnessed a "great migration" of African Americans from rural areas of the south to the industrial cities of the north. Beginning during the First World War, when Eastern and Southern European white immigration was halted, approximately 500,000 rural southern African Americans moved to northern cities, in the years 1916 to 1919. Nearly one million more followed

From generation to generation and across racial and ethnic group lines, people enjoy the simple pleasure of gathering on the stoop in front of their homes.

in the 1920s. The Depression of the 1930s temporarily put a halt to the migration. However, with the mechanization of the cotton picker in the early 1940s and another labor shortage precipitated by World War II, the great black migration resumed in even greater numbers. In a 20-year period, more than 5 million African Americans joined their compatriots to the big cities of the north. Nicholas Lemann in his gripping account of this migration observes that this was "one of the largest and most rapid mass internal movements of people in history—perhaps *the* great-est not caused by the immediate threat of execution or starvation" (1991:6). These migrants not only transformed their way of life, but in the process transformed American society (cf. Grossman 1989; Lemann 1991).

Like their white immigrant counterparts, African Americans found them-selves in urban ghettos. However, to a larger extent than for the southern and east-ern Europeans, societally imposed patterns of segregation and discriminatory employment practices defined the residential patterns and economic experiences of African Americans. Forced to live in segregated housing, they were gouged for higher rents. Often they were barred from jobs by employers and denied admission into unions that controlled access to other jobs. When they got jobs, they were paid lower wages than whites. Yet, a majority of these migrants helped establish the black middle class, the working class, and the lower working classes in northern cities. For them and for those who found themselves ravaged by poverty, it was the strengths of the African American family and its strong kinship support structures that helped them prevail. In this discussion, we will look at the African American family in these urban centers with particular focus on their kinship networks.

The strength of the African American kinship system stems from its western African origins as well as from the extraordinary historical experience it has had in the United States. Niara Sudarkasa (1988) in a much-cited article provides an overview of African family and African American family structure as it developed in the political and economic context of American history. The cultural and histori-cal importance placed on the extended consanguine kinship relationship over the importance of the marital or conjugal relationship is seen to distinguish the African American family from the American family of European origin.

Sudarkasa observes that the most important properties in African societies— land, titles, and entitlement—were transmitted through lineages. Spouses did not inherit through each other. Women played a distinctive role in the articulation of family dynamics. Western African women were important economically; they were farmers, traders, and craft makers. Decision making was centered in the con-sanguine extended family group. Polygyny also played a role distinguishing this nuclear unit from the monogamous Western model. The stability of the African family system was rooted in the extended family, not in the nuclear family. The socialization of the young was seen as an involvement shared by the entire extended family and not by separated nuclear units. Overall, the emphasis was on the col-lectivity and not on the nuclear family.

Sudarkasa then sees how the African family dynamic was transposed under slavery. Citing Herbert Gutman's (1976) major analysis, *The Black Family in Slavery and Freedom*, Sudarkasa observes that in addition to a fairly stable nuclear family pattern there is evidence that a strong extended-kinship structure existed. This system was integrated with a strong sense of community and interdependence. Sudarkasa argues that the extended family networks that were formed during this period and were carried to future generations have their source in the institutional heritage of African culture. But "the specific forms they took reflected the influence of European-derived institutions as well as the political and economic circumstances in which the enslaved population found itself" (Sudarkasa 1988:35).

In reviews of the evidence, scholars have observed that historically—from slavery, reconstruction, the Great Depression, and the Great Migration from the 1940s through the 1960s—a major source of strength in African American families has been the extended kin networks composed of grandparents, uncles, aunts, cousins, and adult siblings. Extended living arrangements in all socioeconomic statuses were found to be twice as common in African American families as in white families (Farley and Allen 1987). These kin provided economic as well as emotional supports. They have been pivotal, despite a history of racial oppression and material deprivation, in the remarkable resilience and adaptive capacity of the African American family to survive relatively intact despite severe urban conditions (Billingsley 1968).

Robert Staples (1971) argues that, regardless of the role of African American women in the family, it is necessary to stress that the female role evolved out of the struggle for African American survival. His position is similar to that of Rodman (1965, 1971), who views the behavioral adaptations of people living in poverty as solutions to the problems of economic deprivation. Andrew Billingsley (1969) has shown that many families in the black inner-city ghettos have demonstrated an impressive capacity to adapt to the social, cultural, and economic deprivations fostered on them by the larger society and have developed strong family relationships. Finally, Rainwater (1966) contradicts the notion that female-centered households are dysfunctional; in research of families living in poverty, Rainwater finds an *adaptive* urban matricentric family form (among others) that successfully copes with the problems of poverty. Carol B. Stack (1974), an urban anthropologist, offers additional support for this position.

Stack's *All Our Kin* (1974) is an anthropological study of a poor black community, which she called The Flats, located in a midwestern city called Jackson Harbor. She examines how families cope with poverty by adapting domestic networks to link people who are not necessarily related. Stack emphasizes that a census-defined, female-headed, single-parent household does not indicate separatedness or isolation. A cooperative-support network exists that is composed of both relatives and fictive kin, who are treated as kin by family members and are given such kinship terms as sister, aunt, and uncle. These people unite for mutual aid and to meet daily needs.

> Black families living in The Flats need a steady source of cooperative support to survive. They share with one another because of the urgency of their needs. Alliances between individuals are created around the clock as kin and friends exchange and give and obligate one another. They trade food stamps, rent money, a TV, hats, dice, a car, a nickel here, a cigarette there, food, milk, grits, and children.

> . . . Without the help of kin, fluctuations in the meager flow of available goods could easily destroy a family's ability to survive. . . . Kin and close friends who fall into similar economic crises know that they may share the food, dwelling, and even the few scarce luxuries of those individuals in their kin network. Despite the relatively high cost of rent and food in urban black communities, the collective power within kin-based exchange networks keeps people from going hungry. (Stack 1974:32–33)

Stack stresses that social scientists who employ such culture of poverty terms as *pathology* and *social disorganization* fail to understand the adaptive forms of familial and quasi-familial relationships and structures that have developed in these economically deprived communities. Further, these social scientists are not aware of how resilient urban black families are to the socioeconomic conditions of poverty, to the inexorable unemployment, and to the limited access to scarce economic opportunities of single-parent mothers and their children who receive welfare under such programs as Aid to Families with Dependent Children (AFDC) and later by the Temporary Assistance for Needy Families Program (TANF). Stack points out that these structural adaptations do not lock people into a cycle of poverty or prevent them from marrying or removing themselves from the networks. But her study does indicate that the very success of these cooperative networks forces women to think twice about marriage:

> Forms of social control both within the kin network and in the larger society work against successful marriages in The Flats. In fact, couples rarely chance marriage unless a man has a job; often the job is temporary, low paying, insecure, and the worker gets laid off whenever he is not needed. Women come to realize that welfare benefits and ties within kin networks provide greater security for social mobility. A woman may be immediately cut off the welfare roles when a husband returns home from prison, the army, or if she gets married. Thus, the society's welfare system collaborates in weakening the position of the black male. (Stack 1974:113)

In summary, Stack's work graphically reveals how viable family structures develop to handle chronic poverty and governmental programs that reinforce welfare dependency and unemployment. Unfortunately, in the years since Stack's research, poverty has significantly increased among African Americans. As we shall see later in this chapter, this poverty has undermined these extended family network support systems and has had a particularly negative impact on female-headed households. However, without them the plight of the African American poor would be in even worse condition.

In a later work, *Climbing Jacob's Ladder: The Enduring Legacy of African-American Families*, Billingsley (1992) reviews the literature and finds that the values of kinship and mutual assistance are characteristic features of family relations that encompass all family income levels as well as both single-parent and two-parent types in both city and suburb. A fundamental characteristic of the African American family is love of children and emphasis on family cooperation. However, Billingsley points out that beyond such family values is the need for a caring society to provide opportunity structures. "The family, church, school, and workplace in dynamic interaction can become an ecosystem which surrounds, protects, and enhances the emotional, intellectual, physical, social and economic well-being of all our children" (Billingsley 1992:333).

Unfortunately, for many Americans, including African Americans, the larger "caring society" has been absent with devastating consequences in the last three decades. Despite its strengths, the support networks of African Americans have not been able to overcome significant changes in the structure and stability of families living under poverty conditions. These changes include declining rates of marriage, higher rates of divorce, a reduction in fertility rates, and an increase in female-headed families, higher percentages of births to unmarried mothers, higher percentages of children living in single-parent households, and a larger percentage of children living in poverty (Farley and Allen 1987). These demographic trends have affected all Americans. However, they have particularly affected African American families.

In coping with poverty, I would remind the reader of the existence of extended kinship networks for both black and white ethnic groups, including those who experienced economic uncertainties. In the next section I turn attention to the Mexican American urban experience.

Mexican Americans in Urban Barrios

Mexican Americans have a unique place in American immigration history. They can be considered to be both a native American group as well as an immigrant group. Their historical immigration patterns have shown great variation. Within the last

A shopping street in a Mexican-American barrio *in Los Angeles. Photo by author.*

65 years there has been a major change in the living conditions of Mexican Americans, as they have gone from being a major ethnic group with the largest rural population to being strongly urbanized, with 88 percent living in the city (Baca Zinn 1994). The crowded urban *barrios* attract most of the newly arriving immigrants. According to the 2000 census, of the 35.3 million Hispanics in the United, States, nearly 20 million are of Mexican origin or descent. This figure, which represents 65 percent of the total Hispanic population, is about five times the estimated number of Puerto Ricans in the United States, the second-largest Hispanic minority. About 87 percent of Mexican Americans live in the southwestern states, with the vast majority in California and Texas.

An increasing number have migrated to urban areas throughout the United States, and especially in the southwest and in California. Chicago has more than 700,000 Mexican Americans, representing the largest Hispanic group in that city. They, combined with other Hispanic groups, comprise more than 25 percent of that city's population. Los Angeles has more than 3 million Latinos, most of whom are Mexican Americans, a figure that is larger than the African American population in this city. More than 25 years ago, Carlos E. Cortes (1980:697) observed, "The shifts from regional to national minority, from farm to city, and from field to factory have set in motion a series of other changes whose consequences are still unfolding." What was true then is even truer today. Here I focus attention on the impact of these changes on family life in American cities.

Initially, conquest and annexation, rather than immigration, was responsible for the creation of Mexican Americans. The Mexicans were here when what is now Texas, New Mexico, Arizona, California, and parts of Colorado, Nevada, Utah, and Wyoming were acquired by the United States through the war of separation of Texas from Mexico, the United States–Mexican War, and the Gadsden Purchase during the period between 1845 and 1854. This annexed regional minority experienced a diminishing influence in the economy of the southwestern states throughout the nineteenth century. Queen and his associates (Queen, Habenstein, and Quadagno 1985) make the point that as slavery is a key element in understanding the black American experience, so too is the labor utilization of Mexican Americans and Mexicans in understanding the Mexican American experience. This historical experience has influenced their contemporary social position and, to a lesser extent, their family patterns.

In Texas, first cattle ranching, then land ownership, and then cotton farming determined economic superiority, and the Mexican Americans became a subjugated, exploitable minority group. What land they owned was obtained both legally and illegally during this time. Anglo-dominated agricultural production became large scale and labor intensive. Relegated to serve as cheap labor, Mexican Americans had to compete economically with job-starved Mexican nationals who were willing to work for even lower wages. The immigration policy allowed for the crossing back and forth over the border of Mexican migrants, and this further undermined the economic position of Mexican Americans.

In New Mexico, the situation was somewhat better. When Mexican Americans were in the demographic majority through the 1860s, they dominated the economy and controlled the territorial legislature. However, with the expansion of the railroads, the depletion of grazing lands, the development of industrial mining, and the consequent movement into New Mexico of Anglos or Anglo-Americans (white persons of non-Hispanic descent), the balance of power gradually shifted. Still, by the turn of the century, Mexican Americans retained some economic and political power. However, many were forced to become part of the unskilled labor force.

In southern and central California, powerful rancheros dominated the economy at the time of annexation. However, the Gold Rush of 1849 brought more and more Anglos into both the northern and the southern parts of the state. Prejudice, reinforced by legislative actions biased against Mexican Americans, resulted in the loss of most of the old Mexican land grants. By 1900, their political and economic power plummeted throughout the Southwest, with only New Mexico being the notable exception.

The dominant Anglos gained economic and political control of the Southwest, and ethnic stereotypes prevailed. Characterized as an inferior people, the religion, language, and culture of Mexican Americans were seen as antithetical to the "American" way of life. Being relegated to manual labor, poverty, and subjugation only reinforced the stereotype of Mexican Americans as ignorant, shiftless people.

The United States shares a 2,000-mile boundary with Mexico. Two rivers, most notably the Rio Grande, and open land separate the two countries. Mexican immigration into the United States during the second half of the nineteenth century was relatively modest compared to what it is in the twentieth century. The total estimated number of native-born and foreign-born Mexican people in the United States was between 381,000 and 562,000 in 1900 (Cortes 1980).

Social, political, and economic factors in both countries led to a substantial rise in the number of immigrants from Mexico to the United States in the first three decades of the twentieth century. Political upheavals, social unrest, and poverty in Mexico, combined with the growth of the American Southwest, accounted for the movement of more than 500,000 legal immigrants in the 1920s alone. Dinnerstein and Reamers (1975) observe that Mexican laborers provided more than 60 percent of the common-labor force in the railroad-track gangs, the mines of Arizona and New Mexico, the fruit and truck crops of Texas and California, and the packing plants on the West Coast. They also dominated the sugar-beet farming industry, which extended from Colorado to Montana, Michigan, and Ohio. The use of these laborers coincided with the rapid growth of the Southwest and with changes in the immigration laws that severely restricted the immigration of Chinese and Japanese laborers at the beginning of the century and European immigration in the mid-1920s.

Mexican immigration began to decline in 1928 and remained low through the Depression and the coming of World War II. Indeed, during the 1930s, many Mexicans either returned home voluntarily or were pressured to do so because of the high rates of unemployment in their communities. During the war, labor shortages encouraged American industry to welcome Mexican workers. The number of Mexicans with permanent visas continued to grow in the 1940s expanded rapidly in the 1950s and exceeded 30,000 in every year from 1960 to the end of the 1970s.

In addition, countless numbers of Mexicans entered the United States illegally throughout the twentieth century and into the twenty-first century.

The Center for Immigration Studies, an independent, non-partisan, non-profit research organization founded in 1985, based on Census Bureau and other government data, reports (Camarota 2005) that the foreign-born population of the United States is currently 35.2 million (legal and illegal), equal to 11.5 percent of the U.S. population. This is the highest number ever recorded—two and a half times the 13.5 million during the peak of the last great immigration wave in 1910. Of this total, the Census Bureau estimates 8–9 million are illegal immigrants. Between January 2000 and March 2005, 7.9 million new immigrants (legal and illegal) settled in the country, making it the highest five-year period of immigration in American history. Nearly half of post-2000 arrivals (3.7 million) are estimated to be illegal aliens. Other estimates indicate a considerably higher number of illegal immigrants. The Pew Hispanic Center, another private research group in Washington, based on Census Bureau and similar government data, that the estimated total of undocumented immigrants is 10.3 million as of March 2004. This is 23 percent increase from the 2000 estimate. Of that number more than 50 percent of that growth is attributable to Mexican nationals living illegally in the United States. The total number of illegal migrants from Mexican is estimated to be 5.9 million (Moreno 2005).

The proportion of Mexican Americans born in the United States and those born in Mexico has radically changed in the last 45 years. For example, in 1960, Mexican-born immigrants were a rarity in California; nearly 9 out of 10 Mexicans Americans were born in the United States. By 1990 the ratios were reversed because of the massive immigration to California (Baca Zinn 1994). Commenting in 1994, Baca Zinn stated that "The concentration of immigrants was so high that it formed a virtually new population with family characteristics that differ from those of the native-born Mexican or 'Chicano' brethren" (1994:65). Since 1990 more than 6.7 million Mexicans have migrated to the United States further dramatically increasing the size ratio differential of the Mexican to the native-born Mexican.

Especially in light of the recent new wave of immigration, we recognize that there is no such thing as *the* Mexican American family, and that there are social-class variations and historical-experience variations in relation to when these people settled in the United States. Yet a distinct set of values centering on the family and not on the individual has been an overriding cultural feature. The *familia* is the center of Mexican American culture and is seen as the single most important social unit (Queen et al. 1985). Traditionally, it has been an extended family containing not only parents and children but also grandparents, uncles, aunts, and cousins. Migration patterns usually require the relocation of both the nuclear family and the consanguine one.

Familism, incorporated in a theme of family honor and unity, is seen to persist in today's ethnic enclaves, or *barrios*. *Barrios* are the equivalent of the urban villages that characterized the urbanization patterns of such "new" immigration groups as the Italians, Poles, and eastern European Jews in the Northeast and Midwest. Baca Zinn (1994), in reviewing research reports, concludes that the familism of Mexican Americans can also be seen as having important roots that developed as a response to socioeconomic depravation conditions of United States society. An example of the persistence and adaptation of traditional cultural family values can be seen in the changes that have affected *compadrazqo* (godparentage), a special form of ritual kinship that promotes continuing close relationships among extended families.

The compadrazqo is designed to generate social and interpersonal cohesion and, at the same time, to reduce the potential extrafamilial conflict that might arise in a highly family-centered society. Mutual patterns of obligations between *compadres* (people or groups) are expected to develop. In the event of trouble or difficulty, compadres are expected to offer help and advice. Cortes (1980) has observed that the practices of the traditional family and the compadrazqo have been declining in the face of the pressures of the more militant young Mexican Americans (Chicanos). Similarly, these practices are in decline throughout Latin America and in many Mediterranean nations; however, they still maintain a viable force in the barrios, even where the dynamics of urban life strain traditional practices. Cortes explains: "Although these traditional structures and practices have eroded among all immigrant groups, it is likely that they have survived more widely among Mexican Americans because of their historical isolation, residential segregation, continuing immigration, geographical proximity to Mexico, and deep commitment to these social institutions" (1980:714).

Ruth Horowitz's (1983) monograph, *Honor and the American Dream*, is an excellent study of an inner-city Chicano community in Chicago. (She refers to all people of Mexican ancestry in the United States as Chicanos, and therefore her use of this term differs from the political implications noted previously.) She finds support for Cortes's belief that compadres serve, in part, to maintain cultural continuity. In addition, the naming of friends as compadres not only strengthens the relationships with each other, but also "the mutual obligations further strengthen the relationship of the entire expanded family unit both as a symbol of their cohesiveness and because they need each other" (Horowitz 1983:56). Horowitz observes that the exchange of economic and personal services is frequently needed since these families rarely turn to outside agencies such as public welfare or public employment. This help is regarded as a failure of a family's solidarity and social worth. In addition, compadres and relatives provide emotional and social support.

> Having a large, close family that can be augmented by *compadres* who can and will readily help in time of need is very highly valued. Being seen as a cohesive family transcends economic success. In such a family on 32nd Street and in other Chicano communities, members lend each other money, locate a car mechanic, and help out in innumerable other situations. "We can hardly keep track of all the money that goes around between us anymore. We just assume it's about equal," a young couple declared while discussing the state of their finances and their family's aid. (Horowitz 1983:57)

Horowitz goes on to observe that the strong network of intergenerational ties among the families fosters the continuation of traditional gender-role relationships in the family. Horowitz sees the articulation of gender-family role relationships in terms of male domination, virginity, motherhood, and respect. Independence, personal strength, situational control, and dominance over wives and daughters defines manhood. Great importance is given to a daughter's identity as a virgin. Tension is seen in the more-assimilated young woman's attempt for autonomy over parental control regarding dating and freedom to do things unsupervised, and the parents' desire to assure that such activities are not perceived as the activities of nonvirgins. Motherhood is the culturally acceptable identity; the role of independent career-woman is not. Women's identities are anchored in their familial roles as wives, sisters, and mothers. Respect, another symbol of family life, refers to systems of chivalry and etiquette that formalize social inter-action both in the family and in the community. Formal rules delineate ways of acting; for example, swearing in front of females is strictly forbidden, older people must be greeted with courtesy, and insolence or rudeness is not tolerated within the home.

Horowitz believes that these symbols of family life, taken together, provide order and stability for everyday social interactions in the context of an urban community that is highly industrialized and educated. Yet the changing nature of urban life results in many circumstances that prove problematic for the traditional culture. Horowitz focuses on the ambiguity and conflict that are found in the expectations concerning gender-role behavior and child-parent relationships particularly faced by youths. "Youths are caught between the traditional model of social relationships and the urban Chicago reality: the streets, the school, the media, and the job scene. With the freedom they take or are given, the youths are faced with many dilemmas as they venture beyond the confines of the communal and familial order" (Horowitz 1983:76).

Similarly, Lea Ybarra (1982) has investigated changes in Mexican American family life in Fresno, California. Her study of 100 married couples found that marital role relations ranged from a patriarchal pattern to a completely egalitarian one. However, the most prevalent pattern was one in which the husband and wife shared in decisions. The factor that appeared to have the strongest impact on whether household chores and childcare would be shared between spouses was whether or not the wife was employed outside the home. Families in which the wife worked outside the home demonstrated a more egalitarian family pattern relative to decision making, sharing of household tasks, and caring of children. Further, in her investigation of other studies of Mexican American families in different regions of the United States, Ybarra found that egalitarianism was the predominant conjugal-role relationship. Similarly, Staples and Mirande (1980) found that "virtually every systematic study of conjugal roles in the Chicano family has found egalitarianism to be the predominant pattern across socioeconomic groups, educational levels, urban rural residence, and region of the country." Such findings led Ybarra to question previously accepted assumptions on the nature of Mexican American family life that more often than not viewed it negatively, especially compared to "mainstream" American family life.

Ybarra touches on an important critique that has been made of the biases inherent in many of these studies. Staples and Mirande (1980) have observed that much of the research has a pejorative view of the Mexican American family. This research, based on psychoanalytical assumptions, examines *machismo* (masculine patriarchal authority) as the key variable in explaining the dynamics of both family life and culture, seeing machismo as a compensation for powerlessness resulting from feelings of inadequacy, inferiority, and rejection of authority. However, beginning with the influential studies by Miguel Montiel (1970, 1973), "the social science myth of the Mexican American family" has been exposed.

This myth developed a pathological view of Mexican American culture in terms of three characteristics: fatalism, patriarchy, and familism (or strong orientation to kin). Machismo was not equated with honor, respect, and dignity; it was defined in terms of power, control, and violence (Staples and Mirande 1980). Murillo (1971) has redefined machismo in positive terms: "An important part of the [father's] concept of machismo . . . is that [of] using his authority within the family in a just and fair manner." Similarly, the family is depicted in terms of its warmth and nurturance and providing emotional security and a sense of belonging to family members. This pattern continues through generations and "the mother continues to be close and warm, serving and nurturing even when her children are grown, married, and having children of their own" (Murillo 1971:104).

In discussing the Mexican American family it is imperative to understand the impact of poverty, especially as it is experienced in the barrio. In an important anthology, *In the Barrios: Latinos and the Underclass Debate*, Joan Moore and Raquel Pinderhughes (1993) bring together a collection of articles about the nature of poverty among Latinos in different communities. Of particular interest to us here are the studies that examine the Mexican American poverty experience.

One common theme addressed by many of the authors in this collection of essays is the impact of economic "restructuring" on these families. Economic restructuring refers to the changes in the global economy that has resulted in a shift from a manufacturing to a service economy in the United States. This shift, which has led to deindustrialization, loss and relocation of jobs, and a decline in the number of middle-level jobs, has had a devastating impact on the economy of so-called "rustbelt" cities in the northern and midwestern sections of the United States. But it also has had an impact on many regions, both urban and rural, in the "sunbelt" as well. A second concern addressed by Moore and Pinderhughes is that of immigration, which has had major significance for poor Latino communities. For Mexican Americans, the large numbers of Mexicans migrating to the United States have impacted on their community, on economic conditions, and on family life.

Moore and Vigil examine four separate barrios in Los Angeles, the Chicano "capital" of the United States" (1993:27). They report three major changes within the past decade. The first change is the economic restructuring combined with immigration that has changed, for the worse, the economic opportunities for Mexican Americans. The second change is that these communiites are increasingly becoming

"Mexicanized." The third major dimension of change is the reconfiguration of community-based organizations in the light of governmental policies that have contracted the welfare state in the 1980s.

What this means in regard to the family is that the recent Mexican immigrants bring with them many traditional family extended networks. In addition, Mexican American families are moving toward more egalitarian, dual leadership arrangements, while some are becoming single-parent households. The overall result is that the addition of new immigrants has helped enliven and regenerate Mexican culture within a broad configuration of family styles and patterns (Moore and Vigel 1993).

In addition, despite the era of welfare state contraction, the community has developed its political voice and has become more adapt in airing its grievances. While street problems exist and youth male gangs are quite visible, the process of "choloziation" (social, familial, and economic marginalization) has been resisted by the traditions of family solidarity exhibited both by Mexican American and newly arived Mexican families. Together they seek to regenerate community social controls (Moore and Vigel 1993).

Velez-Ibanez (1993) studied Mexican Americans living in poverty in a number of southwestern borderland communities, with a focus on Tucson, Arizona. He emphasizes the need to examine the individual who is poor within the context of localized kin groups made up of a number of related households involved in extended social and economic exchange relations. He argues that poor persons "should be understood as *individually poor* but not part of a cluster that is necessarily impoverished" (Velez-Ibanez 1993:209).

Phillip B. Gonzales (1993) provides an historical examination of poverty, restructuring effects, and integrative ties in Mexican American neighborhoods located in Albuquerque, New Mexico. Here again we see the emphasis that is placed on the structures of integrative ties and the impact of economic restructuring on them. The historical importance of residential stability and the importance of strong ties of ethnic culture and family relations in combating economic and social problems are delineated. He observes how economic changes can erode the structures of these legacies. "Assaulting traditional neighborhoods are increasing poverty among families, drug and alcohol problems, crime, gentrification, changing development patterns resulting in the loss of primary jobs to fringe areas, and other threats to a historic stablity" (Gonzales 1993: 170). Yet, these families are better able to resist these threats than other communities where residents lack a strong sense of neighborhood identity, familiarity, and belonging.

Earlier in this book, I reported on the activities of the *Mothers of East Los Angeles* (MELA) and their successful efforts to mobilize and prevent the building of polluting incinerators and a prison that potentially threatened the safety of the community. Both Pardo and Moore and Pachon [(1976) cited in Myers 2003] report that in the recent past the barrios of Los Angeles lacked political power. Writing 30 years ago, Moore and Pachon commented on the impact that urban renewal policies had on the destruction of a number of barrios in the Southwest and in Los Angeles, including the one in Chavez Ravine that became the site, in the early 1960s, of the then-recently-moved Brooklyn Dodgers' baseball stadium.

Often, as in the near downtown area of Los Angeles, Mexican American *barrios* have been destroyed by the march of civic progress. A railroad station, a baseball stadium, and a cluster of government buildings each cost the existence of a separate Los Angeles neighborhood. Mexican neighborhoods have been destroyed by the march of freeways across many southwestern cities. This easy eradication of Mexican American communities reflects both their political impotence and the fact that these neighborhoods never enjoyed the great rise in land values so characteristic of the urban Southwest. (Moore and Pachon (1976) quoted in Myers 2003: 473)

Pardo's (2004) study emphasized how traditional networks based on the family, religion, and culture emerged and proved to be political assets in improving the quality of community life in the East Los Angeles barrio. Myers (2003) comments that the barrio provides the geographical base for the maturation and development of various culturally based centers of political power. The election of the first Mexican American mayor of Los Angeles in 2005 is testimony of the barrio's political clout. The barrio has been the site for the articulation of cultural as well as political cohesion for Mexican Americans, much as ethnic enclaves have proven to be for other minority groups, a fact noted by Myers:

> Like the urban enclaves of other minority groups, the *barrios* promoted the formation of ethnic unity for Mexican Americans. The *barrio* gave a geographic identity—a feeling of being at home—to the bereft and the poor. It was a traditional place that offered security in the midst of social and economic change and turmoil. Life in segregated *barrios* allowed Mexican Americans to continue to function within a closed Mexican society and culture. The *barrio* enabled and ensured the continuity of Mexican society and culture. (Myers 2003: 473)

In summary, both social and intellectual biases distort the understanding of this ethnic group. Ruth Horowitz has observed that in the context of community involvement one gains the understanding of Mexican American family structure and dynamics. The economic hardships often faced by Mexican Americans, whether in the urban barrios or in agricultural regions where they make up a large percentage of the migrant labor force, play a crucial role in the articulation of patterns of adaptation and survival of the family. In recent years, the Chicano movement has resulted in an attempt to overcome economic discrimination and subordination while maintaining familial cultural values. As Ruth Horowitz observes of the Mexican American family system (which, in principle, also holds true for the other groups that make up America's ethnic heritage):

> Some aspects of culture, such as the expanded family network, will survive, even if their content alters slightly by ecological or class changes. Not only do Mexican Americans have a low divorce rate compared with other ethnic groups, regardless of the length of United States residency and location, but the expanded family network remains the valued and predominant family form. Some traditions may persist much longer than any class-based theory would hypothesize, while other symbols, values, and norms may change as community members achieve greater economic stability and begin to spread through the city and into the suburbs. The United States as a melting pot may not only be unachievable but undesirable. Why should everyone be the same? (Horowitz 1983:235)

The Suburban Working-Class
and Middle-Class Family

Earlier in the chapter I examined the experience of the family in working-class ethnic enclaves. Of considerable interest were the studies that report the effects of social and geographical mobility—from the inner-city's ethnic villages to the outer city and the suburbs—on the family's way of life. Now, I would like to turn my attention to a more detailed look at the family life of working class and middle-class residents in this geographical area.

Young and Willmott (1957/1963) contrasted the working-class urban village of Bethnel Green in east London with the upwardly aspiring working-class suburban community of Greenleigh, located outside London. They found that the migrants from Bethnel Green did not leave because of weaker kinship attachments. Rather, they left for two main reasons: the first was the attraction of a house with modern conveniences, as opposed to the antiquated, crowded flats that pervade Bethnel Green; second was that Greenleigh was generally thought to be "better for the kiddies." These migrants left their extended kin in Bethnel Green with regret. However, these people were not deserting their family so much as acting for it, on behalf of their children rather than the older generation.

The effect of moving to Greenleigh was a significant drop in the frequency of visiting relatives in Bethnel Green, despite the close proximity of the two areas. Life in Greenleigh became much different than life in east London. In day-to-day affairs, the neighbors rarely took the place of kin. Even when neighbors were willing to assist, people were apparently reluctant to depend on or confide in them. For the transplanted Bethnel Greeners, their neighbors were no longer relatives with whom they could share the intimacies of daily life. This had a particularly strong impact on wives, who were no longer in daily contact with their mothers and sisters; their new neighbors were strangers and were treated with reserve. The neighbors did not make up for kin. The effect on the family was that the home and the family of marriage became the focus of a couple's life far more completely than in Bethnel Green.

Young and Willmott (1957/1962) conjecture that, since Greenleigh was a newly developed community populated by upwardly aspiring working-class couples, the couples neither shared longtime residence with their neighbors nor had kin ties to serve as bridges between themselves and the community. Young and Willmott believed that it would not have mattered quite so much in their neighborhood relationships if the migrant couples from Bethnel Green had moved into an established community. Such a community would have already been crisscrossed with ties of kinship and friendship; thus, one friend made would have been an introduction to several more.

A parallel study of working-class suburban life in Los Angeles by Bennett Berger (1960) reached a similar conclusion to that of Young and Willmott. In Berger's *Working Class Suburb*, male workers and their families were forced to move to an outlying suburb when their automobile factory relocated. Separated from extended kin and their extensive involvement with them, these families had great difficulty in readjustment. They found that their new neighbors, even though they were much like themselves, did not provide the same support and social relationships as did their now-distant kin.

The working-class wives, who were relegated to spend all their daytime hours in their new "bedroom" suburbs, had a particularly rough time in adjusting. The effect of the move on working-class couples from inner-city communities in Minneapolis–St. Paul to a suburban community outside the Twin Cities is a case in point (Tallman 1969; Tallman and Morgner 1970). Researchers were concerned with what effect social and geographical mobility had on couples who had lived in urban villages and who were intimately tied to networks of social relationships composed of childhood friends and relatives. The researchers found that, despite the considerable amount of neighborhood contacts established by these couples after they moved to the suburban community, the wives experienced a considerable amount of dissatisfaction and personal unhappiness and feelings of anomie and personal disintegration.

The wives believed that their feelings resulted from the loss of contact with their relatives and their longstanding childhood friends in the city, as well as the failure of the couple to reorganize their conjugal relationship. The emotional and psychological supports that the wife received from her relationships with her relatives and friends were severed by the move to the suburbs, and this required fundamental changes in the husband-wife relationship to make up for this loss. The working-class wife, who was very dependent on her extra-nuclear family and on primary-group relations, was not able to make adequate adaptations to the suburban move.

> The disruption of friendship and kinship ties may not only be personally disintegrating for the wife but may also demand fundamental changes in role allocations within the family. Suburban wives may be more dependent upon their husbands for a variety of services previously provided by members of tightknit networks. In addition, the ecology of the suburbs makes it necessary for the women to interact with strangers and to represent the family in community relations. Such a reorganization can increase the strain within the nuclear family and take on the social psychological dimensions of a crisis in which new and untried roles and role expectations are required to meet the changing situation. (Tallman 1969:67)

Tallman's work suggests, then, that the movement from working class urban villages of the inner city to outer city and suburban open communities necessitates fundamental reorganization of conjugal and community roles of working-class couples to the middle-class type, which emphasizes the importance of the conjugal-role relationship. To support this contention, research indicates that the anomie and alienation characteristic of working-class couples does not exist to the same extent with middle-class families in suburban communities.

The study of middle-class families who voluntarily moved to the suburbs is a different story. Earlier in this chapter I examined how suburbia was developed as the antidote to the perceived deterioration of urban life, as the haven in a heartless world for the privatized family. Studies of the middle-class suburbs of the post-war era report, first, on the motives for movement to them and, second, the family life experienced there.

The study by Wendell Bell (1958) of 100 middle-class couples residing in two adjacent Chicago suburbs provides a vivid contrast to the experiences of working-class couples. Bell tested the hypothesis that the move to the suburbs expressed an attempt to find a location in which to conduct family life that was more suitable than that offered by inner cities; that is, familism—spending the time, money, and energy of the nuclear conjugal family—was chosen as an important element of the couples' way of life.

Bell devoted his concern to probing the reasons why the couples moved to the suburbs. He found three themes shared by the overwhelming majority of new suburbanites. The first theme had to do with better conditions for their children, a finding similar to Young and Willmott's (1957/1962) study of the Greenleigh couples. The second theme had to do with "enjoying life more." This classification was composed of such responses as being able to have friendlier neighbors, greater participation in the community, and easier living at a slower pace than in the city. A third major theme was classified as "the people like-ourselves" motive. These couples wanted to live in a neighborhood where people were the same age and had the same marital, financial, educational, occupational, and ethnic status as themselves.

It is important to note that the latter two themes, "enjoying life more" and "the people like ourselves," were not given by the working-class couples of Young and Willmott's study of Greenleigh. The different social-class compositions of these two suburban populations account for these differences; only one-third of Bell's couples were identified as blue collar, whereas all of Young and Willmott's couples fell into that category. It is particularly relevant in Bell's finding that only 14 percent gave as the reason for their moving to the suburbs more space inside the home; this was the major factor for the Greenleighers. Finally, the fact that the Greenleighers all had moved from the closed community of Bethnel Green, as opposed to Bell's couples who moved from transitional inner-city neighborhoods or from the outer city, may account for the differences in their attitudes toward the suburban community and their neighbors.

A most important variation in these two groups of people is the overwhelming familistic orientation of the Chicago suburban couples. This familism, as it enters into the suburban move, largely emphasizes the conjugal family system. This is indicated by the fact that only a small percentage of the respondents moved to be closer to relatives. In fact, in vivid contrast to the working class couples described by Young and Willmott (1957/1963), several of the middle-class couples moved to get away from their relatives, a condition they considered desirable. In conclusion, Bell's (1958) findings support his hypothesis that the suburbanite couples have chosen familism as an important element in their lifestyles and, in addition, have a desire for community participation and involvement in neighborhood affairs. Both factors are absent as motivators for the blue-collar families of Greenleigh and the Twin Cities and may be the crucial reasons for the instability and unhappiness of the transplanted urban villagers.

In contrast to the adult-centered life of the urban villagers and the transplanted couples in the outer city and suburbs is the child-centered orientation of their middle-class counterparts. Wendell Bell has indicated the importance of familism and the involvement of parents with their children, as opposed to their extended family. John Seeley and his collaborators (1956) reached a similar conclusion in their study of an upper-middle-class, outer-city suburban community in Toronto. Seeley reports that the focus in these families is on the children; close, continuous attention is given to them. Tied with this is the extensive involvement of the couple with each other, a condition that is not present to the same degree in working-class couples of the city and suburbs. The Crestwood Heights suburban couple of Toronto is characterized by intense interaction and exchange by all family members. The family is viewed as a refuge from the trials and tribulations of the outside world. The dominant theme is home-centeredness; family members are expected to ask for and achieve psychic gratifications from each other.

Willmott and Young (1960) report a similar pattern in a predominantly middle-class suburban community (Woodford) in England. The young middle-class couples see little of their relatives and do not depend to any great extent on the extended family for regular help or companionship. Instead, they create social networks with people of their own age in the community. However, Willmott and Young believe that, although they have a larger circle of friends outside the family than do the urban villagers of Bethnel Green, their social relationships are not as closely knit nor are their loyalties as strong. The "friendliness" does not have the same characteristics in the two districts. In Bethnel Green, people are seen to take each other for granted based on long-term friendship ties; in Woodford, relations are not so easygoing. This results in sociability becoming a sort of how-to-win-friends-and-influence-people contest, with a great amount of superficiality and noncommitment—and with people leaving out some part of their inner self in the process. This corroborates Gans's (1962b) observation that the common element in the ways of life of the outer city and suburban family is quasi-primary relationships that are more intense and occur with greater frequency than secondary contacts, but that are more guarded and less intimate than primary relationships.

Gans's own work, *The Levittowners* (1967) provides us with the classic study of suburban family life. Levittown, now Willingboro, New Jersey, located about 25 miles from Philadelphia, was one of three vast postwar suburban developments built through the application of mass-production techniques for the white lower-middle class by Levitt and Sons. Restrictive covenants against selling to African Americans were based on the notion that community harmony could best be achieved if racial, although not religious, homogeneity could be achieved by people who shared similar regional, class, and white ethnic backgrounds.

The majority of Levittown wives developed social ties with neighbors and did not feel the sense of aloneness and isolation as reported by their working-class counterparts. These people shared similar attitudes toward family togetherness—particularly on the attention given to raising and involvement with their children.

While some reported missing relatives left in the city, most compensated through the use of the phone and through regularly scheduled family gatherings.

Gist and Fava (1974) have concluded that the vast literature on suburban family relationships makes similar observations. Finally, as with the research on suburban couples in America, Willmott and Young find that the area for intense emotional relationships for their English suburbanites lies not in contacts with friends, neighbors, or relatives, but within the nuclear family. The conjugal-role organization of these families is home-centered; couples share in many household tasks, including the raising of the children.

The Dispersal of Kin and Kin-Work

A parallel theme, regarding the relationship of family and community, centers on the changing nature of kinship relationships among extended family members. I have been observing that the privatization of the family was the result of the gradual separation of the public institutions of work and community from the private sphere of the family. Middle-class family life since the nineteenth century has been distinguished by this removal from the community setting. The American suburb fostered this privatization process.

Many sociologists see the privatization of the middle-class family as antithetical to women's independence. More specifically, the spatial segregation of residence from home and the development of the single-family house led to the increased dependence of women on income-earning husbands. In addition, and most significantly, the house became the setting that required the full involvement of women. As Ruth Schwartz Cowan (1983) and Susan Strasser (1982) have demonstrated, women's domestic labor paradoxically increased with the development of mechanized techniques, e.g., vacuum cleaners and sewing, washing, and dishwashing machines that were designed supposedly for efficiency's sake but in fact have set new housekeeping standards.

In addition, suburbia, with its low-density housing community and minimal public transportation services, further increased women's household and domestic involvements. The automobile fostered the end of home delivery services for all kinds of goods and services, thus requiring that families own an automobile to perform these services. These new tasks include driving spouses to commuter stations, picking up and delivering children to after-school activities, and taking sick family members to doctors, who no longer make house calls. The automobile became "mom's taxi."

All of these factors impacted on the nature of community involvements and also led to the relative separation of the nuclear family from extended kinship ties. However, kinship ties, rather than being permanently broken and destroyed, have emerged in a new form. In this section I will first examine how the middle class has responded to the dispersal of kin and then on how the working classes have utilized a women's "kin-work" to maintain such relationships.

Claude Fischer, a sociologist at the University of California–Berkeley, has conducted an important research study (1982a, 1982b) that provides information regarding kinship involvements in today's automobile society. Fischer investigated kinship patterns of almost 1,000 adults living in northern California. He was concerned with the following: the geographical distribution of relatives deemed active and important in those individuals' lives; the respondents' social characteristics associated with their various patterns of spatial distribution; the nature of the interaction patterns that they had with kin who lived outside the household; and the role played by distance in shaping the interaction patterns.

Fischer described the social networks of "modern" California kinship as being geographically dispersed. Individuals were not necessarily isolated from kin, but dispersed kin were infrequently used as helpers. The type of specified aid included borrowing money, considering opinions for decisions, talking about personal matters, and joining in social activities. Those relations that were most viable with ongoing exchanges were most likely to be with parents, siblings, and children. Extended-kinship ties were not actively utilized. This dispersal of kin was greater for educated and urban individuals than for their less educated and rural opposites, and these educated individuals were least dependent on kin.

Fischer reasons that educated people lived further away from relatives as a consequence of a number of interrelated processes. These people may be participating in a continental job market that demands that they be highly mobile. (For example, college and university teachers often find that jobs in their areas of specialization are not regionally located but may be found throughout the country.) The likelihood of their living near kin is further diminished by the fact that these kin may also be well educated, so that even if they remain geographically stable, their kin may be mobile. A third possibility is that the value system of the educated may place relatively little value on maintaining kinship ties (a "modernity" ideology). Finally, educated people may be better able to keep in touch with and call on their kin than the less educated. In such circumstances, there may also be greater reliance on the telephone and mail to keep in contact with kin.

Urban residents were also likely to have less kin living in close geographical proximity. Fischer believes that migrants to large cities, particularly in the West, may be transplanted easterners who have moved large distances. Another explanation is that people who reside in metropolitan areas are likely to have alternative opportunities for social affiliations—business associates, activities, and social worlds that would permit them to disregard nearby kin. Finally, urban residents, like their well-educated counterparts, may exhibit a "modernity" ideology that places less emphasis on kinship.

Overall, Fischer believes that modern American patterns of kinship may be limited to involvements and commitments with parents and siblings (family of orientation) and with children (family of procreation), rather than with other relatives. The ties with parents, siblings, and children may thus survive distance and competing social involvements with nonkin, whereas other kin ties may not survive. The result is a family form that is neither the isolated nuclear family nor the extended family. Fischer states that "Modern extended kin networks are distinctive in being spatially elongated, in losing out to nonkin relations in certain regards, and perhaps in being more functionally specialized" (1982a:366).

Fischer concludes his work by asking how his findings might be explained. He outlines three fruitful areas for speculation: industrialization, culture, and technology. He does not feel that contemporary geographical dispersion patterns are a result of industrial or factory work; rather, they may have been generated more by office work and white-collar occupations. He reasons that, during the rise and establishment of the industrial order, work and extended kinship may have been intertwined as scholars such as Michael Anderson (1971, 1980) and Tamara Hareven (1978) have argued. But during the period of growth in white-collar and professional work, there may have been little necessity to connect work and extended kinship. "Such jobs—in law, medicine, corporate management, academia, specialized accounting, etc.—have national job markets, tend to be insulated from nepotism and cronyism more than is factory work (although not as much as we think), tend to be filled through 'weak tie' networks . . . and have as entry requirements educational credentials which can often be most advantageously gotten by leaving home" (Fischer 1982a:362).

The second area of speculation centers around ideological changes regarding kinship structures and involvements. The emerging view may be toward tolerance, or even preference, for spatial dispersion of kin. The well-educated and the urban respondents conform to this belief in their opinion that living close to relatives or seeing them frequently is not very important to them. But Fischer believes that this cultural value alone is insufficient explanation and, rather, it is more likely that the spatial dispersion of kin was stimulated by structural changes in the society.

Some of these structural changes that Fischer deems to have facilitated the geographical dispersal of kin may be the advent of rapid mass communication and transportation: the telegraph, telephones, trains, planes, and automobiles may be as important to dispersion as is industrialization, since these means of communication/transportation make possible dispersion without isolation.

Fischer cites an interesting study of rural France by Eugen Weber (1976), entitled *Peasants into Frenchmen*, to indicate how transportation changes can impact on kinship ties. In his chapter "Roads, Roads, and Still More Roads," Weber discusses how previously isolated back-country regions were opened up by roads, rail lines, bicycle paths, and the like. These conduits to the outside world removed the necessity for the rural French people to remain in the village for either a day or a lifetime. It, of course, also removed the mandatory requirement for the individual to participate in extended-kinship networks.

Fischer concludes by bemoaning the lack of attention given to this topic by historians and sociologists and the potential significance that mass communication and transportation may have to understanding contemporary family-kinship patterns.

It may be that, in our effort to understand the nature of "modern" as opposed to "traditional" social and personal life, of which spatially dispersed kinship networks are but one element, we have been too mesmerized by the dramatic sight of the "satanic mills," gargantuan dynamos, and seemingly endless assembly lines to give due notice also to the car keys in our pockets and the telephones on our nightstands. These mundane symbols represent dramatic changes in the material "givens" of social life, changes that alter the context within which people negotiate and manage their personal relations, including their kin ties. (Fischer 1982a:369)

The historical changing role of the telephone in our lives serves as a lead-in to my next point. And that is that technology, while permitting the geographical dispersal of kin, can also serve to help maintain kinship ties. One technological advance that ran counter to the prevailing "more work for mother" pattern described earlier was the residential telephone. Fischer (1992), in a fascinating account, examines the telephone and its use by women to foster gender-linked social relationships and involvements. At the turn of the twentieth century the telephone was seen by the industry to be of great aid in the business world. By extension, telephone companies saw it as a tool that would help manage the housewife's household activities by ordering goods and services. It was not viewed in the way that it began to be used and continues to be used—for purposes of sociability, especially by women.

Fischer locates three sources that account for the fact that most people see the domestic phone as being in the women's domain. The first source was women's "structural position," i.e., her increasing isolation from daily adult contacts as a consequence of her extensive involvement within the house. The second was "normative gender rules" where the expectation was that women would serve as the social managers. "Both men and women commonly expect the latter to issue and respond to social invitations; to organize the preparations for group dinners, outings, church affairs, and so forth, and more generally, to manage the family's social networks—keeping in touch with relatives (including the husbands' kin), exchanging courtesies and token gifts with neighbors and the like" (Fischer 1992:138). The third source is "personality differences." Fischer contends that in our society women's greater comfort with the phone than men's is a reflection of their greater sociability. In summary, by the mid-1990s the use of the telephone for social contacts was not only taken for granted but was also used as the basis for calculating long-distance telephone rates, "calling circles of family and friends," by at least one major telephone company. "Circles" in particular are used by women to aid in "kin-work."

Micaela Di Leonardo (1992) develops the concept of *kin-work* to refer to all forms of work that include the "conception, maintenance, and ritual celebration of cross-household kin ties, the organization of holiday gatherings; the creation and maintenance of quasi-kin relations; decisions to neglect or to intensify particular ties; the mental work of reflection about all these activities; and the creation and communication of altering images of family and kin. . . . " (Di Leonardo 1992: 248). She distinguished kin-work from two other types of women's work so familiar to us all that we rarely think about them. The first is housework and childcare; the second is work in the labor market. Essentially, Di Leonardo develops this third category to distinguish between those forms of work that are tied to the paid labor market and those forms of work that are geared to the nurturance of children and the maintenance of family life. Kin-work is seen to fuse both the labor perspective and the domestic network categories of female work. The concern is with the interrelationships between women's kinship and economic lives.

Kin-work, like housework and childcare, is largely an exclusive female work activity. Often women are more knowledgeable not only about their own family relations but of their husbands' as well. Citing cross-cultural evidence as well as research from the United States, di Leonardo asserts that kin-work should be seen as gendered-based rather than class-based. She attributes this to the ideology of separate spheres, which often resulted in men being responsible for work activities with non-kin and women being responsible for the maintenance of kinship ties, in addition to childcare and housework.

The role of the telephone in the early twentieth century and the role of the Internet in the late years of that century have provided a technological tool that has enhanced kin-work activity. I will turn to a discussion of these technologies in Chapter 17.

Part VI

City Places

14

Downtown Stores: Shopping as Community Activity

In this chapter and the next, I wish to investigate the role of shopping, with particular focus on the downtown department store, and the role of spectator sports, with particular focus on baseball, as sources of both community activity and community identification. Their respective roles as an integral component of urban culture and their contribution to the urban economy will also be studied. I use two orienting perspectives. The first ties into a social-psychological definition of community. This definition notes the importance of geographical or spatial characteristics of a community and shared characteristics and attributes, such as social class, race, ethnicity, gender, stage of life cycle, and attitudes and values. It places its emphasis on the nature and form of the social interaction patterns shared by participants in that community. The second is W. I. Thomas's dictum that "what persons define as real is real in its consequences." Erving Goffman (1959), in his *Presentation of Self in Everyday Life*, fully recognized that the "definition of the situation" is not simply a mentalistic activity but a staging activity, situations defined through the manipulation of settings and props. Similarly, one's appearance is staged through appropriate dress and behavior. The second theme focuses on macrolevel factors that have transformed neighborhood and downtown institutions. Utilized will be the perspective of new urban sociology that combines an urban political economy model with the symbolic meaning of place and collective memory.

Previous chapters discussed how the industrial city divided space into two broad land-use patterns. The public space of the city was the manufacturing, commercial, and financial district—the central business district. The residential district was the location of communities containing homes, schools, churches, and other local institutions, including neighborhood shopping districts. A closer look at the central business district reveals that it was divided into an office district and a commercial district. By the late nineteenth century this commercial district became a consumer district of department stores, smaller specialized boutiques, theaters, and restaurants and bars.

"Working" women were found in textile factories. The infamous Triangle Shirt Waist Factory, which experienced a calamitous fire that claimed the lives of over 100 women, revealed the extent of women's employment in downtown factories and the horrible working conditions that they endured. In addition to factory production work, working women were employed in retail selling positions. Indeed, Frances Donovan (1929) authored one of the earliest Chicago School studies, *The Saleslady*. Susan Porter Benson (1986) studied the ambivalent roles that these saleswomen occupied. They were expected to personify the middle-class lifestyles that were symbolized in the merchandise that they sold. At the same time, they were poorly paid and most came from the lower economic strata of the society. The historians Gunther Barth (1980) and Kathy Peiss (1986) have explored the presence of women in places of leisure, including museums, theaters, restaurants, and amusement parks. This chapter's focus is on the role of shopping as an urban activity and examines shopping within the context of gender role relationships.

The Downtown Department Store

In the early years of the twentieth-first century, we still see the downtown department store as one of the key institutions that helped define the central business district of the twentieth-century American city. For many department stores in

Macy's, Herald Square, New York early twentieth century.

many cities—including Hudson's in Detroit and Wanamaker's in Philadelphia—the glory days are gone and so are the department stores. In other cities, they continue in various forms. For many citizens these massive downtown stores epitomized the prosperity and urbanity of their cities. The following discussion, based on the author's earlier work (Hutter 1987), explores the downtown department store as a symbol and as a social force.

Lyn Lofland (1975, 1983) and Gerda R. Wekerle (1980), among others, note that urban sociology has neglected women's involvement in the city. Lofland (1983), in her examination of the legacy of the Chicago School, sees this as part of the wider omission of urban sociology to public-sphere analysis. She argues that the Chicago School was primarily concerned with the relative existence or nonexistence of primary relationships in the city and was oriented to general problems, reform, and policy. Consequently it "left largely unexplored the possibility of relational meaningfulness residing in the public realm" (Lofland 1983:501).

In an earlier paper, Lofland (1975) observed the lack of scholarly attention to the study of women's involvements in public space and services. Lofland observes that in the public areas that women do frequent and "colonize," such as beauty parlors or, as in the case with their children, urban playgrounds, no studies exist. Similar neglect also holds for the study of shopping, a largely female-involved activity.

Gerda Wekerle (1980) focuses on the lack of attention to the nature of the public environment, especially on how the public places of the city inhabit or encourage women's participation in the urban public world. She argues that the exclusion of women from urban public places and facilities is due to nineteenth-century industrialization that led to the privatization of family life and women's isolation to the family sphere, and men's dominance in the public sphere.

One area of urban public life that women have been involved in is the downtown department store. The rise of the modern department store was concomitant with the rise of the industrial city in the nineteenth century. The most famous, the *Bon Marche* in Paris, which opened in 1852, has long been regarded as the first modern department store. Similar stores also came into existence around mid-century in England and the United States. American cities were characterized by job and resident concentrations with mass transportation systems giving easy access to the central business district. The department store provided a convenient one-stop, one-price shopping establishment.

The growth of these department stores was first aided by such new inventions as pneumatic tube systems, the elevator, and improvements in gas lighting. Later inventions included the telephone, the escalator, and electric lighting. However, the social phenomenon of consumption and consumerism provided much of the impetus for its growth. The giant department store, the "grand emporium," embodied a new ethic that glorified consumption not only in terms of particular goods but in terms of a "world" of goods symbolically manipulated by the store into objects of desire and ways of life. Ewing and Ewing (1982:68) observe that "the department store was more than a site for consumption, it was a 'sight' of consumption; goods were graced in monumental splendor." Architecturally, department stores were designed as "palaces of consumption," with monumental neoclassical fronts, elaborate carriage entrances, ornamental doorways, and large picture windows. The interiors were equally impressive with central courtyards and rotundas containing leaded glass ceiling domes that dramatically lit plush carpets, sweeping staircases of marble and wood, lavish display counters, and opulent chandeliers.

John Wanamaker, for example, saw the desirability of monumental architecture. In his instructions to the architect of the Philadelphia store, which would contain a huge auditorium with almost 2,000 seats, a pipe organ of nearly 3,000 pipes, a Grand Court with towering marble columns and a massive sculpture of an eagle, and a Greek Hall with 600 more seats, he demands:

> What you must do for me is to strive to say in stone what this business has said to the world in deed. You must make a building that is solid and true. It shall be granite and steel throughout . . . simple, unpretentious, noble classic—a work of art, and humanly speaking, a monument for all time. (quoted in Rothman 1978:19)

It is no wonder that Lewis Mumford observed: "If the vitality of an institution may be gauged by its architecture, the department store was one of the most vital institutions of the era 1880–1914" (quoted in Hendrickson 1979:40).

Socially, shoppers were advised on the use, purpose, and necessity of the purchase of myriad goods. Alan Trachtenberg points out that "in department stores, buyers of goods learned new roles for themselves, apprehended themselves as 'consumers,' something different from mere users of goods" (1982:130). In addition, the store organized the world as consumable objects, each in its own department. As a whole, "the store 'represented' the world . . . in a form of an ideal home inhabited by role-playing characters" (Trachtenberg 1982:132).

The role of the department store for urban women in the public spheres of the city countered the nineteenth-century movement toward the privatization of middle- and upper-class women and their relegation to the home. Concurrently, women were forced to withdraw from the emerging occupational opportunities of the city. As Gunther Barth (1980) astutely states, the department store provided access for women to downtown city life. It did this in two ways. For the more affluent middle- and upper-class women, it served as the site for consumption. For the less-affluent women, it became one of the few urban occupational sites available. The department store was the major downtown institution that provided women with a safe haven in the city and an alternative, albeit a brief interlude, from the home. Gordon Slefridge, a turn-of-the-century department store executive from Chicago's Marshall Field's, saw the department store as a community center for women: "You know why they come here? It's so much brighter than their homes. This is not a shop—it's a community center" (quoted in Barth 1980:180; see also Hower 1943; Duncan 1965).

The mottos of Marshall Field's, "Give the Lady What She Wants" [Chicago] and of Thalhimer's, "Free Showers for the Ladies" [Richmond, Virginia], testify to the importance of women as their primary customers. Reciprocally the department store provided women with access to the city and taught them new social roles.

The downtown department store provided a number of services for women to foster the image of a "community center." Macy's opened the first ladies' lunchroom in 1878. In 1892 its ladies' waiting room is self-proclaimed in the following terms:

> It is the most luxurious and beautiful department devoted to the comfort of ladies to be found in a mercantile establishment in the city. The style of decoration is Louis XV, and no expense has been spared in the adornment and furnishing of this room. On the way to it you will pass our new art room containing a most complete and carefully selected line of onyx, bronze. (quoted in Hower 1943:284)

Additional amenities found in Macy's and other early department stores included reading and sitting rooms, stools for customers, wheelchairs for old or infirm customers, "dark rooms" lit to simulate dim ballroom gaslights so women could see how their evening gowns would look in that setting, tables and chairs where customers could sample foods, and even "silence rooms" to soothe the tired and worn customer. There were special writing rooms supplied with paper and pens, art galleries filled with oil paintings, and newspaper reading rooms. Many department stores had nurseries and beauty parlors. Hudson's amenities in Detroit included a room where mothers could nurse their babies and change their diapers and a fully staffed medical clinic where up to 200 customers a day could be treated for everything from scrapes and cuts to heart attacks (Green 1982). An ultimate convenience was free bath showers for women customers to make their shopping more comfortable in Thalhimer's during the hot summers in Richmond, Virginia (Hendrickson 1979). Through advertising, women were depicted as the family member exclusively involved in the purchase of family apparel and household furnishings and allied products. The display, presentation, and clear pricing of department store goods provided the customer not only ease but the justification for the purchase. The shopper was informed on the social desirability of the merchandise and was provided a new standard of the "good life" for herself and for her family. Hugh Dalziel Duncan describes the "feminization of spending" as an additional component of her domestic way of life:

> The feminization of spending . . . depended on the transformation of traditional woman's role as mother, mistress, wife, and lady. As mothers . . . women must be taught to spend properly for their families, as mistresses, they must translate erotic appeal into money; as wives, they must learn the nuances of the "pecuniary cannons of taste" required in public and private appearance. All must learn how to translate traditional forms of gentility into pecuniary form of gentility. It was not simply a matter of giving the lady what she wanted, but of seeing to it that she wanted things and sevices that money alone could buy. (Duncan 1965:127)

The department store used the fashion cycle. Through newspaper advertising and window displays, department stores informed women consumers when, where, and why to buy new goods and informed them of the obsolescence of what they had. Stuart and Elizabeth Ewing (1982) see the commercialized activities of the downtown department store as reinforcing and reflecting the atmosphere of this new cityscape and what they term "the commercialization of the self." Elizabeth Hurlock, in her 1929 treatise, *The Psychology of Dress: An Analysis of Fashion and Motive,* describes the importance of fashionable dress in a manner reminiscent of Charles Horton Cooley and his concept of the "looking glass self":

> No one likes to be considered mediocre, or to be so like every one else that he is passed over unnoticed. From the cradle to the grave, no one is totally free from regard for the opinions of others . . . One of the chief values of clothing is that it enables people to advertise themselves in a way that will win the attention and admiration of others. Many who lack any ability and could not hope to rise above the "average" on their merit alone, find a satisfactory outlet for this desire for recognition through the medium of dress. (Hurlock 1929:28–29)

Thus, shopping in the downtown department store became an integral feature of a woman's life. Through her shopping a woman found a place in the downtown. Barth persuasively argues that downtown shopping was not simply a fashionable activity but also an urban activity that helped form a woman's identity as an urbanite:

> [Women] . . . went window shopping, strolled through the stores, gazed at the displays and each other, chatted with friends, listened to clerk's explanations, assessed the articles and other shoppers, bought something they considered a bargain, and under fortunate circumstances went home with the feeling that they had not only done something women were supposed to do, but had actually enjoyed doing it. This experience, repeated almost daily, intensified their identity as modern urban women . . . (Barth 1980:44)

Barth also points out how the department store provided one of the few urban occupational opportunities for women, and this also provided an avenue for urban identification:

> Moreover, though the women who worked as sales clerk may have earned low salaries and worked long hours, this form of employment opened up a major avenue into the male-dominated urban job market. The total effect was to introduce women as a new social force in city life. (Barth 1980:44–45)

In summary, the department store reintegrated women into downtown, albeit in the form of a consumer and within its domain as a member of the urban workforce. It helped change the character of the downtown from an exclusive business district to a shopping one as well. By opening up the downtown area to women, it assured the development of a more socially ordered urban life. It also provided additional justification for the continued development of urban mass transportation. It did this by providing transit services for women during off-peak rush hour travel when the railroads, subways, and trolleys would otherwise be unoccupied.

The examination of the downtown department store provides additional counterarguments toward the erroneous prevalent notion that life in the public realm is devoid of meaningful interactions. Shopping is revealed not as an alienating, impersonal activity but one meshed within a complex matrix of social relationships among strangers. Further, the department store user identified with the broader values of urbanism as reflected in the downtown department store as an urban institution. Processes of urban identification differ significantly from neighborhood identification. Neighborhood identification emerges through involvement with local community institutions, an area we will discuss next.

Neighborhood Stores and Community Identification

Local stores are often the social and economic hub in their communities. They serve as community centers and are the sites for repeat and continuous encounters not only between customers and clerks but between customers themselves. Going shopping serves a number of different functions. The purchase of goods is not the only reason to visit a local store. It's also a means of getting out of the house and entering a different social milieu. It is a social occasion, a chance to interact with neighbors and friends. In the case of neighborhood food stores, this interaction often occurs on a daily basis. Jacqueline Wiseman (1979), in her study of women's thrift stores, categorize the interactions that occur as "quasi-primary." Women not only comment on how a particular garment looks on a fellow customer but that conversation is often extended to other facets of life . . . if one is married, has children or grandchildren, if one is employed, etc.

The role of neighborhood stores as a source of community identification has been recognized in Gregory P. Stone's seminal paper, "City Shoppers and Urban Identification" (1954). Stone focused on female shoppers and salesperson relationships in terms of the potential for quasi-primary characteristics to develop in local urban communities. Among the four types of shoppers identified by Stone (economic, personalizing, ethical, and apathetic), it was the "personalizing" shopper who defined shopping as fundamentally interpersonal. These women expressed a tendency to personalize and individualize the customer role in the neighborhood store in terms of closeness of relationship between the customer and sales personnel.

Stone links this type of shopper with local, independently owned stores in contrast to the larger department store. His striking finding is that these women, who sought to personalize relationships through their shopping, were the most recently arrived residents who had the least amount of community institutional and personal attachments. These newcomers sought to develop their relationship with sales personnel in the local independent store. Stone concludes (as does Charles Horton Cooley) that relationships may become primary in nature in any area of life where communication is frequent and regular. The "secondary" institution of the store integrates the "personalized" shopper into the larger community in which he or she lives.

Ray Oldenburg's *The Great Good Place* (1989) notices this theme. The subtitle of his book *Cafes, Coffee Shops, Community Centers, Beauty Parlors, General Stores, Bars, Hangouts, and How They Get You Through the Day*. He refers to the "Great Good Place" as a *third place*, "a generic designation for a great variety of public places that host the regular, voluntary, informal, and happily anticipated gatherings of individuals beyond the realms of home and work" (Oldenburg 1989:16). These "third places" are characterized by the participants' feelings that they are not faceless consumers solely defined by their economic value, but rather they are "regulars" at places where socializing and lingering are not considered economic liabilities. Here, conversation, sociability, and camaraderie are welcome. The place a home away from home. Think here of the television show *Cheers*.

Oldenburg observes that *third places* have been disappearing quite rapidly as the proliferation of chain stores and the onslaught of suburban malls continue unabated. He bemoans the loss of such places. We observe that *third places* have characterized much of small-town, downtown business districts, and as third places decline, so does Main Street. In post–World War II America, significant changes altered the character of shopping as an urban institution. This decline was felt in both the neighborhood as well as in the central downtown. The downtown department stores were severely affected economically by the development of suburbia. At first, the movement of the middle-class residential base to the suburbs meant just a further commute to the downtown to do shopping. However, with the building of first strip malls and later enclosed malls, the downtown department shopping district meant a drastic change in shopping patterns. In neighborhoods, the insidious effects of urban renewal proved particularly detrimental for local stores. Later, gentrification and immigration were responsible for the transformation of neighborhood shopping patterns and community identification processes.

Suburbia, the Mall, and the Decline of Downtown Shopping

Let's turn our attention here to an investigation of the suburban mall, which has proven to be a poor substitute for the community identification processes provided by neighborhood shopping areas that are integrated into the residential community. Malls have become pseudo-town centers for many suburban communities. They have taken on such importance that often they become the focal point for the community and a source of community identification. Indeed, a suburban South Jersey township changed its name to Cherry Hill to gain the cachet of its regionally prominent shopping center, Cherry Hill Mall. Teenagers have often colonized the malls in the evenings, especially on Friday nights, while their elderly counterparts and housewives with children use the malls during weekdays. The popularity of malls stems from default, ("there's no other place to go") and a feeling that the mall is a safe environment. Malls seem to have taken on the appearances of a public realm but legally they are not. From a legal standpoint, malls are private spaces owned by the malls' proprietors whose primary objective is to make economic profit through the shopping activities of its consumers. Mall owners have the right to remove the "unwanted," whether they be unruly teenagers, the homeless, charity workers, or political protesters. Private security guards whose uniforms give the appearance of real police officers often do this.

The loss of economic vitality of the downtown has been attributed to the development of suburban strip malls and later to the development of the enclosed megamalls. Giant stores, called "category busters," like Wal-Mart, also moved to the outskirts of small towns and further accelerated the decline of the downtown. Through an economic policy of first focusing on small profits, these giant stores drove the small downtown stores into economic ruin and eventual collapse. This led to disastrous consequences. Main Street was dying. In many communities, downtown stores closed, were boarded up, and left to decay. The downtown was beset by various types of vandalism. First windows were broken, and graffiti on buildings proliferated. Then, vagrants, criminals, and "no-goods" colonized downtown areas. And finally, residents of the community deserted their downtowns and Main Streets.

Erving Goffman, in his *Relations in Public*, talks of "fixed territories" where an "individual's sense of privacy, control, and self respect is tied to the dominion he exerts over his fixed territories" (1971:288). Similarly, Moe and Wilkie (1997:102) point out that to overcome crime and decay in a community, it is necessary to foster a shared sense of turf or "territoriality" among its residents. In this context, we can analyze how businesses in the downtown areas, in their desire to revitalize shopping patterns for economic gain, also provide a most beneficial, highly significant latent function: they help to develop a sense of local community identification.

In the later part of the twentieth century, just as small-town stable neighborhoods were being threatened and were in decline, so were the downtown business districts. A major concern facing the downtown business proprietors was a growing public perception that shopping downtown was not safe. The belief developed that the downtown needed to change its image in order to change shopping patterns and to get people to return. This could be accomplished through physical changes as well as by bringing in new stores to replace those that went out of business. To help accomplish this and to redevelop a sense of community, people in a number of small towns saw a need to restore their downtowns. A major player in that restoration was the group of businesses already located there. If successful, both businesses and the local community would benefit. However, initial attempts at such restoration often resulted in failure. The strategy was to emulate strip malls and change building facades to echo those of the uniformly designed strip malls. Downtown streets were converted into pedestrian malls. These strategies proved wanting.

Gratz and Mintz (1998) talk of the importance of "character and history" as an essential need of downtowns. "If nothing distinguishes downtown from the strip, the mall, the nearest megastore, or the formula-design chain store, why would someone bother to come downtown? Character is what old buildings contribute best. History disappears from view when they do" (Gratz and Mintz 1998:262–63). Moe and Wilkie provide some examples of the successful attempts by local businesspeople to accomplish downtown revitalization. Moe and Wilkie found that this revitalization occurred through the enhancement of the individualistic character of the existing buildings, which reflected historical patterns of architectural design. By so doing, "(T)hese places seek to steer new investment into downtown historic buildings to preserve the local pride of place from being overwhelmed by sprawl" (Moe and Wilkie 1997:151).

Pedestrian malls were reconverted back into streets. Since the inherent nature of the street as a conduit for traffic and parking accessibility did not detract from pedestrian activity, "cruising" and "window shopping" once again became indications of active streets. Businesses began to realize that to change their downtown image they, in effect, had to redefine the overall "situation" or "look". In addition to reemphasizing the character and historical sense of the downtown it was necessary to restage the downtown look through the re-design of signage, storefronts, picture windows, sidewalks, benches, bike racks, etc.

The concern for safety also takes on paramount importance for both the shopper and mall-shop proprietors and for the mall owners. A magazine for shopping mall executives, *Chain Store Age,* informs its readers, "In a business that is as dependent as film or theater on appearances, the illusion of safety is as vital or more so, than its reality" (cited in Baxandall and Ewen 2000: 230). Contemporary malls use up-to-date surveillance systems that include highly illuminated parking lots and visible video cameras that contain closeup lenses that can see any activities occurring in those lots. In Denver, a manufacturing company has gone so far as to construct a female mannequin facetiously named "Anne Droid" that has a camera in her eye and a microphone in her nose as a deceptive decoy to augment store surveillance (Friedberg 2002: 446). Surveillance cameras as well as security police who wear specialized uniforms patrol parking lots and the malls.

The conflict between public responsibility versus private property has been resolved in favor of malls being defined as private space. In a 1972 landmark Supreme Court decision, *Lloyd Corp. v. Tanner,* and in a followup 1976 decision regarding union picketers at another mall, the majority opinion ruled that malls were private property and did not have any public responsibility to serve as a setting for civic activity. In a dissenting opinion, Supreme Court Justice Thurgood Marshall observed that shopping center owners have assumed the role of a traditional town square and that the majority court ruling allows them to escape the assumption of public responsibilities. (cf. Kowinski 1985; Crawford 1992).

Malls have not restricted themselves to suburbia. In many cities, urban malls have appeared and have taken on the same character as their suburban counterparts. Often these upscale malls have taken the place of the traditional department stores located on public streets in the more public-transportation accessible section of cities. In Chicago, to provide one example, Water Town Place and a nearby mall anchored by Nieman Marcus, on posh Michigan Avenue, have provided privately controlled shopping centers catering to the well-to-do. The department stores still located on State Street in the older "loop" are now frequented primarily by less affluent black and Hispanic customers. The result then is class segregated shopping areas with one store, Marshall Fields, having stores in both areas.

Whose Stores? Whose Neighborhood?

Just as urban renewal destroyed housing in "slum" communities, it also destroyed its stores. Shopping was an integral part of the public and civic life of the community. Shopping was the venue where people in the community met and socialized. It was in the public realm of the street with its neighborhood stores that one saw one's friends and the familiar strangers that were so important to maintaining the sense of community continuity and well-being.

Both Herbert Gans in his account of the West End of Boston and Jane Jacobs in her account of Greenwich Village point out the significance of neighborhood stores. Gans reports on how the stores, restaurants, and taverns "served as the ganglia in the area's extensive communication network" (1962a/1982: 117). Gans is referring to how these social establishments provided a "message service"—taking and passing on messages and serving as centers for the exchange of news and gossip. Lunch counters, "variety stores," taverns, and barbershops often provided hangouts for unemployed men. Neighborhood grocery stores combined both shopping and socializing for women. Those small neighborhood stores that were able to compete with modernized larger stores treated their customers more as peers than as customers. Similarly, Jane Jacobs (1962) saw the neighborhood store as essential to the life of community. Store proprietors were often "public characters" that had as an unofficial duty to serve as the eye on the street, to be aware of the everyday activity of street life. They were the "designated street watchers."

Jacobs uses the vehicle of neighborhood stores to talk about two models that came to identify urban planning. The first model, employed by professional urban planners, focused on the importance of order, rationality, uniformity, and the necessity for urban "renewal." The second, identified by neighborhood advocates, focused on the neighborhood itself, which was often ugly, messy, and complex, with mixed-use housing, recreation, and commercial activities. Jacobs comments on a friend, a professional planner steeped in orthodox planning, who on the personal level recognized the "goodness" and vitality of multifaceted neighborhoods for both people and the city, yet, professionally, felt that such neighborhoods had to be destroyed in order to save them:

> "I know how you feel," he said. "I often go down there myself just to walk around the streets and feel that wonderful, cheerful street life . . . But of course we have to rebuild it eventually. We've got to get those people off the streets." (Jacobs 1961: 20)

Urban renewal was dominant for more than a quarter of a century after World War II. During that time, mixed-use neighborhoods of homes and stores were destroyed and replaced by segregated high-rise projects and separately located shopping areas. In the suburbs, residential developments were exclusively devoted to housing, and shopping was relegated to highway strip malls and ultimately to large enclosed shopping malls. The decline and near-death of many "mom and pop" stores selling all sorts of merchandise raises the question of what affect this decline had on neighborhood shopping patterns and community identification patterns. Karp, Stone, and Yoels (1991) point out that it is necessary to understand the policy implications of neighborhood stores, which acquire a symbolic meaning that transcends their economic importance and becomes key in maintaining the social fabric of the community:

> Small stores, taverns, cafes, and the like are not just places to purchase goods; they also constitute meeting places for neighborhood residents and crucial communication centers for informal news about the community. The demolition of such stores does not just eliminate a few more buildings from the community; it may also rupture the fabric of social life in that neighborhood. (Karp, Stone, and Yoels 1991:61)

The title of this section, "Whose Stores, Whose Neighborhood?" paraphrases Sharon Zukin's "Whose Culture, Whose City." Zukin emphasized how the battle that exists in contemporary cities for control of the culture of the city as the symbolic economy transformed neighborhoods on the local level and the city on the metropolitan level. In earlier chapters the impact of gentrification on communities was examined. Now, I want to revisit an earlier discussion on the relationship of place to memory with specific emphasis on the impact of gentrification on this relationship.

As you may recall Rebecca Solnit (text) and Susan Schwartzenberg (photographs) 2000, in their case study of San Francisco, *Hollow City* (2000), are of the opinion that gentrification need not simply refer to locational transformation processes in selected areas of a city but to the whole city. Solnit is especially concerned with the destruction of the memory of place as the places resided by artists, bohemians, activists, organizations, and small businesses are pushed out of neighborhoods being displaced by the gentrification; Solnit believes that the movement of the affluent participants of the dot.com economy into the community neighborhoods completely transforms the community. Schwartzenberg illustrates the point by photographing 60 Starbucks coffee shops that dot San Francisco's commercial streets; Schwartzenberg juxtaposes each photo with text on what used to be on each site: a hardware store, a restaurant, an auto shop, a grocery, etc. The captions emphasize the loss of "third places," which are so important to giving character and life to a community. The 60 Starbucks have replaced 60 history-laden small businesses. This brings to mind a scene from the movie *You've Got Mail*, which depicts the economic demise of a neighborhood bookshop when a megastore moves in. In an unintended ironic scene, the owner of the local bookstore, played by Meg Ryan, is seen to frequent a Starbucks instead of a local neighborhood coffee shop that is also competing with a national chain store at the same time she is bemoaning the fate of her own store.

New Immigrants, the Revitalization of Inner-City Stores, and the Rise of the Consumer City

In the last 15 years, there has been a resurgence of inner-city neighborhoods in many American cities. There are myriad reasons for this resurgence. Grogan and Proscio (2000) in their analysis of contemporary "comeback cities" identify the constantly increasing number of neighborhood-based nonprofit organizations as leading to a grassroots revitalization movement. This movement has energized residents and has led to the renovation of individual houses, apartments and commercial areas, and the development of civic institutions, educational programs, and block watches. Four positive trends are seen to constitute a "surprising convergence of positives" that account for a broad inner-city recovery (Grogan and Proscio 2000: 3). They include community development, the rebirth of retail markets, a decrease in crime through policing practices, and the "unshackling of inner city life" from giant bureaucracies, especially the welfare system, public housing authorities and public schools (Grogan and Proscio 2000: 6).

Given centerstage in their analysis, Grogan and Proscio highlight the importance of Community Development Corporations (CDCs). CDCs are an outgrowth of the "riot ideology" of the late 1960s, when inner-city residents sought to take control over their neighborhoods. From their confrontational, ideological beginnings, CDCs developed a more politically sophisticated operation, working in partnerships with governments, businesses, and nonprofit agencies. The federal government also played a key role with the passage of the Community Reinvestment Act (CRA), passed during the Carter Administration. The CRA obligated banks to make credit available to the communities where they did business. Banks were to direct loans to people and areas that were formerly redlined and denied such loans by these lending institutions. Banks feared federal regulations that would look unfavorably on them. Banks would not be allowed to merge unless

The ethnic diversity of immigrant groups is reflected in these three adjacent stores in Washington, D.C. Such stores have taken a vital role in the revitalization of local shopping areas in many American cities. Photo by author.

they could show a good CRA rating. To obtain this credit rating banks opened credit to inner-city neighborhoods. CDCs initially focused on the building of affordable housing, and by 1994 they were responsible for the building of over 40,000 units a year, a rate that surpassed the federal government's pace during the public housing construction period of the late 1950s and 1960s. Between 1994 and 1998, bankers pledged to invest more than $355 billion to inner cities.

With money and work beginning to flow into these communities, crime began to decline. Together, these factors led to the slow but steady growth in the economic revitalization of inner-city neighborhoods. With the increase in improved housing, there has been a concomitant growth in neighborhood shopping centers. Precipitating this growth is the realization by retailers that profits are to be made in the servicing of the shopping needs of neighborhood residents.

> The social magnet of that development—and of its solid affirmation that life in this community is sustainable and improving—amounts to an explosive economic force as well as a social one. The message is: This is once again a neighborhood with large-scale pedestrian traffic to feed other businesses, with community assets that benefit residents and call forth their vigilant protection, and most of all, where owning real estate starts to look like a promising investment as well as a route to better housing. Those are the essential messages for attracting further investment to the area. Without them, the neighborhood remains a charity case. With them, it becomes a market and an enterprise. (Grogan and Proscio 2000: 136)

Sharon Zukin (2005), in her analysis of the significance of shopping in shaping American culture, reports on the importance of recent immigrant entrepreneurs and merchants in the revitalization of neighborhood shopping districts. She confines her discussion to the localized shopping experience in New York City neighborhoods. She reports that in the Brooklyn neighborhoods of Brighton Beach and Bensonhurst, which have witnessed a large migration of Russian Jews, stores have opened to meet the needs of its new populace. Delicatessens and grocery stores selling Russian ethnic food items, such as caviar and smoked sturgeon, as well as clothing stores stocking merchandise that reflects both the style and specialized larger sizes of larger Russian shoppers, have proliferated. Similarly, the emerging three new Chinatowns in New York City now have stores that sell herbalist and food items that appeal to the new Chinese immigrants. The West Indian Caribbean community in Brooklyn has music stores that sell reggae as well as rap tapes and CDs, and groceries stock mangoes and other types of melons found in the Caribbean.

Zukin also describes the activities of immigrant store merchants who have moved into abandoned neighborhood stores and who not only fill market niches but have also served to revitalize their respective neighborhoods. These include Koreans, who have opened up fruit and vegetable stores and have also created a new market for manicures in "nail salons"; Dominicans, who followed Puerto Ricans and in turn are being followed by Mexicans in opening neighborhood bodegas (grocery stores); and Syrians, who are working in newsstands and small stores selling a variety of goods as well as magazines. Long-time shopping districts noted for bargain stores have been revitalized in lower Manhattan's Broadway and Canal Street areas, on Fourteenth Street, and in downtown Brooklyn's Fulton Mall—all of these areas are now vibrant with a multitude of stores that appeal to recent immigrant groups. Reinforcing the shopping venues are numerous, albeit illegal, street vendors, dispensing various types of inexpensive merchandise and knockoff counterfeit merchandise ranging from sweatshirts to sunglasses to handbags and watches.

Zukin (2005) sees the revitalization of neighborhood shopping by newly arriving immigrants as just one segment in a much broader pattern in which shopping and consumerism are becoming the linchpins of an urban redevelopment strategy anchored in the transformation of public spaces into commercialized consumption spaces. She describes the reinvigoration of shopping streets by new luxury trade and mass-market stores as well as design boutiques and trendy restaurants. A prime example is the gentrification of the revitalized SoHo cast-iron buildings first by artist lofts, then by artist galleries, and eventually by upscale stores selling merchandise to attract the shopping needs of well-to-do new residents and tourists. This now-commercialized area has expanded into the adjacent NoLIta, which was previously an Italian-American working-class neighborhood; NoLIta has also experienced this changeover, as have other lower Manhattan downtown areas. It should be pointed out that other well-known areas of New York City, such as Fifth Avenue, Madison Avenue, and Times Square, have also undergone a consumer-oriented reemphasis powered by such national and international corporations as Ralph Lauren, Nike, and the Walt Disney Corporation. Zukin believes that the revitalization of neighborhood shopping and downtown shopping that has happened in New York City is not unique to that city but is shared by other large American cities, although it has particular importance to New York City, especially since 9-11.

> Much of the street-level revitalization in all big cities since the 1980s is due to these kind of changes. Both products and stores have become more individualized by name and more standardized by type, and shopping districts are widely recognized as both a force and a symbol of economic development. The wealth and variety of new shops in New York enable the media to present shopping as one of the city's cultural attractions—an alternative to the suburbanization and standardization that have engulfed the rest of the country, if not the rest of the world. After September 11, 2001, these distinctions were even more important to maintaining the city's image and economy. (Zukin 2005:27)

Indeed, Zukin sharing the viewpoint of others, most notably Lizabeth Cohen (2003), believes that since the Great Depression of the 1930s and accelerating with the rise of post–World War II suburbia, the United States has increasingly become "a consumers' republic." It has only been in recent years, however, that there has been such a widespread transformation of public space into consumer space. It has become a commonplace occurrence in many cities and has resulted in an economic development that has broad economic impact extending beyond the neighbor-hood to the entire restructuring of the city, if not the entire country, into a con-sumer society.

> America has become, more than ever, a nation of shoppers. In 1987, the country had more shopping malls than high schools. More Americans shopped while they traveled—and took trips in order to shop—than relaxed in outdoor recreation or visited historical sites, museums, and beaches. Airlines offered special excursion rates for one-day trips to the Mall of America in Bloomington, Minnesota, and the Potomac Mills outlet mall near Washington, D.C. (Zukin: 2005:16)

Money Has No Smell: *African Street Vendors and International Trade*

Paul Stoller is an anthropologist who teaches at West Chester University, Pennsylvania. From July 1992 to December 1998 he studied West African street vendors in New York City. These vendors—from Mali, Niger, Senegal, and Ghana—sold wooden masks and statues as well as baseball caps, "knockoff" brand-name watches, and various forms of clothing and jewelry. The title of his book, *Money Has No Smell,* refers to the inherent ethical dilemmas and religious contradictions of selling idolatrous statues and epithet-explicit baseball caps when their Islamic faith does not permit such activity.

> Seeing no dissonance between his views on Islamic morality and his business prac-tices, he said: "We are here in America, trying to make a living. We have to do this to look after our families. Money has no smell." (Stoller 2002:xi)

The population of West African street vendors is predominantly male; their fami-lies are usually back in Africa. Stoller states that many of these men are devout Muslims who are in New York City and other northeastern cities, most notably Washington, D.C. They also form caravans of vendors who travel through what they call the "bush"—Indianapolis, Kansas City, Detroit—as part of African American trade shows and conventions. He notes that their cultural backgrounds and per-sonal backgrounds, as well as their hopes and values, are virtually unknown to the thousands of passersby who encounter them on the streets of the city:

> Although he worked daily on the streets of New York City, he remained like Ralph Ellison's *Invisible Man,* an unseen person. Like his brother traders, he walked among the shadows, earning money but maintaining a judicious distance from a society whose values he found both fascinating and disturbing. (Stoller 2002:6)

The focus of Stoller's account is on the "new immigration" experience, the changing character of communities in cities, and also on the impact of globalization on local shopping patterns. These men form culturally distinct international West African communities within larger culturally diverse communities. Stoller observes that since their prime focus is to make money and eventually return to Africa, these men have little involvement with the larger community. Their separation is further reinforced because many of them are here illegally. Further, their separation from the larger community is a reflection of their belief that America is a "violent, insensitive, and rushed society where morally depleted people (non-Muslims) haven't enough time to take care of one another" (Stoller 2002:23). As a consequence, they have created mutual protection societies as well as informal associations to dispense immediate credit. These separatist activities along with their aloof attitude have engendered hostile feelings among their African American shoppers and neighbors who are attracted to the Afrocentric merchandise.

Their street presence as vendors has had an impact on the business of stores in commercial districts. This was notable in Harlem, where an accommodation among vendors, local businesses, and political leaders had to be made to legitimize their previously illegal street activities into a market area that could become part of the larger commercial thoroughfare. Stoller discusses the international network of trade that exists in the city. Merchandise, legal and illegal, from Africa and Asia, particularly Taiwan, Korea, and China, is bought by these street vendors and sold by them to many shoppers, including foreign tourists from Japan and elsewhere as well as to African Americans. In addition, there is a diversity of West African nations involved including Niger, Nigeria, Cote d'Ivoire (Ivory Coast), as well as individuals from India, Pakistan, Afghanistan, and Indonesia. A complex transnational and transcultural interaction exists. Stoller documents how the lucrative market in selling Afrocentric textiles, caps, T-shirts, jewelry, and art is supplied by Koreans who operate "sweatshops" in the lower Manhattan Chinatown area. Stoller further reports that the international contacts maintained among West Africans fosters their business activities. "West African merchants in New York City use their familial traditions to construct long-distance trade networks to facilitate the marketing of Afrocentricity" (Stoller 2002: 87).

Strategies for Main Street Redevelopment

The renewal of the downtown area in St. Louis, discussed in Chapter 12, is but one example of attempts being made in many American cities to revitalize downtowns. In the 1990s, many cities employed a strategy to revitalize downtowns based on the assumption that the economic success of those downtowns was essential for future urban growth. The activities of "can-do" mayors in Milwaukee, Fort Worth, Denver, Portland, and Seattle, captured the attention of the media. Books with such titles as *Comeback Cities* (Grogan and Proscio 2000), *Changing Places: Rebuilding Community in the Age of Sprawl* (Moe and Wilkie 1997), and *Cities Back From the Edge: New Life for Downtown* (Gratz and Mintz 1998) highlighted those efforts.

Gratz and Mintz (1998) discuss such efforts as spreading the "SoHo syndrome" of gentrification and cultural investment from its origins in New York City to other cities that have either abandoned and underutilized centrally located former industrial districts or that have never fully developed their downtowns. SoHo was a former industrial area in New York City that contained numerous nineteenth-century cast-iron buildings that were converted to residences, art studios, and art galleries. This transformation was done without the use of government funds. Rather, local people were instrumental in the change. Gratz and Mintz refer to this strategy of urban revitalization as *urban husbandry*. *Urban husbandry* refers to the encouragement of local businesses and people in the community by supporting small businesses, reinvigorate existing downtowns, and supporting new residents moving into old buildings and neighborhoods. Gratz and Mintz argue that SoHo's emergence has transformed the ways that cities are seen and has provided a blueprint for revitalization in many other cities. Other cities, including San Francisco and St. Louis, as mentioned earlier, have seen private enterprise investing heavily in residential redevelopment as a spur to economic revitalization.

Even cities that historically have not had viable downtowns are seeing the necessity to develop downtowns to spur city growth. For example, Fort Worth, Texas, created a pedestrian-friendly city center with buildings representing different historical periods. Houston, Texas, has created a downtown cultural center with theaters and restaurants and a light-rail transit system. Phoenix, Arizona, another quintessential Sunbelt sprawling city, is pursuing a similar strategy with the development of a theater-cultural complex and an adjacent new downtown campus for Arizona State University. Phoenix is also building a light-rail transit system that will provide convenient public transportation from the near-downtown Heard Museum of Native American Art and the Phoenix Art Museum, to the downtown, and further to Tempe, with its Mill Avenue shopping area and the main campus of Arizona State University, nearly 20 miles away.

The building of light-rail transit systems in downtowns that are linked to outlying areas have also been built in recent years in other cities, including Portland, Denver, San Jose, San Diego, and Baltimore, in addition to the aforementioned St. Louis, Houston, and Phoenix. Gratz and Mintz (1998), in observing this development, caution that such light-rail transit systems are often built at the expense of struggling public bus systems that tend to cater more to the poor and working class. They believe that both forms of public transit are critical to the redevelopment of cities.

Many small towns are employing similar strategies to revitalize their "Main Streets" through gentrification, cultural investment, and encouragement of retail shop redevelopment. In the face of suburban retail development personified by strip malls, local enclosed malls, regional malls, and megastores like Wal-Mart and Home Depot, downtown shopping districts in big cities as well as in small towns, have employed economic survival strategies. The downtown department store has both downsized and has set up branch stores in the suburbs. "Main Streets" have been employing a number of different strategies to revitalize their downtowns. Four small towns in southern New Jersey provide a microcosm that is worth examining to shed light on how the nation's small towns are economically coping with various forms of economic competition.

If you find yourself in a suburban mall or a megastore in a different part of the country in which you live, you may momentarily forget what mall or store you are in. Indeed, the sameness of these shopping institutions, with their nationwide chain stores, provides no visual place reminder of what region of the country you are in. The detachment to a sense of place is an underlying characteristic of contemporary retail suburban shopping. Joel Kotkin (2001), in his analysis of the essential identical nature of malls and chain stores, speaks of the "retail homogenization of America," brought forth by the power of mass marketing in such specialty stores as The Gap, Banana Republic, Benetton, Pottery Barn, and Williams-Sonoma (2001:142). He goes on to observe that the technological efficiency of these specialty stores has resulted in a "place-destroying process" (Kotkin 2001).

In New Jersey in recent years, downtown business districts in small towns are revitalizing. Many South Jersey communities are utilizing an "urban husbandry" revitalization approach. What Main Streets are attempting is to define themselves in unique ways that break the "place-destroying process"; revitalizing local stores not found elsewhere recaptures the interest in shopping and identifies Main Street as an integral part of the community. These revitalization efforts seek to set Main Street apart from the ubiquitous suburban mall and the megastores. The hope is that not only will neighborhood shopping patterns be revitalized but that such revitalization will also have consequences for the restoration of community interaction and identification patterns. However, in the attempt for revitalization, what is happening is not the restoring of older communities but the creation of new ones. The next section investigates four different revitalization strategies in four different small communities in South Jersey. To start, let's look at one of the most successful BIDs (Business Improvement Districts) in New Jersey—Collingswood. (A business improvement district is comprised of local stores that self-tax each other to provide needed funds for the physical improvement of that built environment.)

Collingswood

Collingswood was originally composed of a largely white, working-class population of about 15,300 people. Located about eight miles from downtown Philadelphia, Collingswood in recent years has undergone gentrification. The Benjamin Franklin Bridge links provide relatively convenient access from Collingswood to Philadelphia. A high-speed rapid train system, PATCO, gets you into Philadelphia in less than 15 minutes. Collingswood borders similar working-class towns; Camden City is about four miles away, and the more affluent suburban communities of Haddonfield/Cherry Hill/Vorhees are located toward the east.

The residential area of Collingswood has both smaller houses and stately Victorian houses. The Victorians have wraparound porches, ornate moldings, and fireplaces and are located on large lots. Since the mid-1950s, the wealthier residents have moved out of Collingswood to the more affluent adjacent town of

The downtown shopping area in Collingswood, New Jersey. In the last five years major changes have occurred that are transforming what was once a working-class shopping area into one with more up-scale stores. Photo by author.

Haddonfield and into newly created suburbs such as Cherry Hill. In the 1970s, Collingswood, like older small towns, was undergoing rapid economic decline. Downtown stores were closing and were being replaced by thrift stores or becoming vacant. The Victorian houses were being transformed into as many as four apartments, providing affordable housing for Collingswood's working-class population. Associated with this housing transformation were more cars on the street, increases in garbage and liter, and more petty crime. The town mayor has described the situation as one in which out-of-town landlords rented apartments to unruly tenants: "Everybody used to be able to point out the problem duplex on the block. It was the big pimple on the end of the nose" (Mayor Jim Maley quoted in Ruderman 2005: A21). What occurred was a two-pronged attack to change both the downtown and the housing situation.

A major concern facing the downtown business proprietors was the perception that shopping downtown was not safe. To rectify the situation, the perceived need was not only to restage the downtown through changing signage, store fronts, picture windows, sidewalks, benches, and bike racks, but to also change the downtown image through the development of a new mix of retail stores that would cater more to an affluent population than a poorer one. Collingswood Partners Inc., a private nonprofit organization, was formed and funded by borough merchants in May 2000. Collingswood Partners is working with New Jersey State's Business Improvement District program to help revitalize its downtown shopping strip and two other business districts. Merchants in Business Improvement Districts assess themselves a special tax to finance improvements ranging from street repavement, to new store facades and signage, to advertising campaigns. In Collingswood, business owners pay $250 per $100,000 of their property assessment annually to belong to the district.

Collingswood and the people involved in its BID seek to take advantage of the town's location near the affluent suburbs of Haddonfield, Cherry Hill, and Vorhees, and the fact that it is only a short train ride to Philadelphia, to attract upscale shoppers. Initially, Collingswood sought to satisfy the everyday shopping needs of its local populace. At the onset, the battle waged among its storeowners on how to make this vision materialize. Numerous skeptics contended that Collingswood's working class would not shop in these stores and that competition from downtown Haddonfield, surrounding regional shopping malls, and nearby center-city Philadelphia would be economically overwhelming and would ultimately lead to failure for these revitalization plans. The immediate concern, then, was to strike a balance of local versus regional retail stores and the types of clientele and services that would be attracted to these groups. In addition, issues were raised regarding the autonomy of existing storeowners within the BID.

In the last four years, Collingswood has undergone a restaurant renaissance with more than six restaurants opening. Restaurant owners are taking advantage of Collingswood's convenient location. The town does not permit restaurants to have liquor licenses; however, customers can bring in their own alcohol and save an appreciable amount of money by doing so. Many restaurants, predominantly upscale, have opened and prospered. Their success has not transferred over to nonrestaurant stores, however. In the 10-block central business district, upscale home furnishing, gift, and craft shops have opened and closed. In addition, the lower-income service shops, small groceries, and hardware stores previously there are also closing. Stores on both ends of the economic scale find that they cannot generate enough business profits to pay for the increasingly higher rents. Many storeowners report that restaurant sales do not translate into retail sales: "I love the town, and the people, but it's impossible to make a living here. There are a lot of princesses walking around here in fur coats after dinner, but there are no bags. For the business owner, all this means is more hours to stay open, but no sales" (a store owner quoted in Stilwell 2005: 1B).

The result is that, now, Collingswood has an improper balance of many restaurants but few retail stores. The upscale stores are opening and closing; the low-end stores are closing. Neither can afford the rents. The major problem for renters is the skyrocketing price of real-estate. New owners are forced to pass rising prices onto renters; older owners do the same as their taxes rise. As the downtown goes through its revitalization process, it is finding that a balance is missing between the type of stores it wants and the type of customer it wants to attract. As of now, only the restaurants prosper. People go there to eat but then leave immediately thereafter. It is a downtown still searching for its identity and its shoppers.

Collingswood saw a decrease in its population of 6.3 percent between 1900 and 2000, and a significant decline in seniors ages 60 to 84. During this period and continuing to the present the cost of housing is dramatically rising in South Jersey. Young professionals—mostly young couples with school-age children as well as straight and gay singles—saw an affordable housing opportunity and started to move into Collingswood. The Collingswood municipal government, seeing the opportunity to attract this younger population, has embarked on a program to convert the towns many duplexes back into single-family homes. This program would also help it rid itself of its more "problematic" poorer residents and increase the town's property rateables. This program began four years ago and provided financial incentives to buyers who pledge to reconfigure the dwellings back into single-unit homes. Owners who convert a duplex can obtain a guaranteed, low-interest loan and pay no interest for a year.

For the government, the aim is to take advantage of the real-estate market by "promoting their historic charm, and attract the kinds of families who once served as a neighborhood's social and economic backbone" (Ruderman 2005: A1, A21). The hoped-for result would be more spacious houses that would continue to attract younger families. It would also result in a Collingswood with reduced density, higher property values with increasing tax revenue, and an upgrade of declining properties. At the same time, the poorer people who are renting apartments in these houses would be forced to move out. This duplex-conversion strategy has not been totally welcomed. Some duplex owners complain that local officials are zealously enforcing building codes and zoning regulations to force them to sell their converted Victorian houses. At present, about 150 Victorians have been reconverted into single-family dwellings, although only 60 have participated in the conversion program. Ruderman reports on one family that participated in the program:

> "We wanted a big Victorian that we could work on," Molly Phillips said. "The location was perfect, and you could see the potential."
>
> She said she would not have been able to buy her Stokes Avenue home without Collingswood's program. The home, built in 1881 by William Reed, a sea captain from England, had been converted into a triplex about four decades ago.
>
> Phillips and her husband, Greg, both 34, bought the house for $144,000 in 2001. The 14-room home, with five bedrooms and three full baths, is now worth about $500,000, she said.
>
> "It was a no-brainer," she said. (Ruderman 2005: A21)

The newspaper accounts do not report on what has happened to the displaced tenants of this and the other houses, nor do they comment on where the lower-income residents who remain in Collingswood shop.

The situation for the poorer residents and lower-profit retail stores will only get worse. Announced in November 2004 was a proposed condominium and retail complex using the space previously occupied by a lumberyard, "The Lumber Yard" will include between 100 and 125 condominiums (selling from $175,000 to $400,000), 20 retail spaces, and 400 parking spaces. The complex will both enlarge the downtown commercial district and connect the main shopping area with a smaller commercial district. This project seeks to take advantage of the propensity of more affluent suburban dwellers who want to partake in condo life without living in the center city of Philadelphia. The Lumber Yard is located within a very short walk to the high-speed rail connection to downtown Philadelphia. This project, plus another redevelopment plan to allow for additional residential development, has already had financial ramifications. The borough commissioners approved a $12 million spending plan that comes with a 10-cent municipal tax hike per $100 of assessed property value.

The borough also developed a plan to lease a large 1,500 capacity facility, the Scottish Rite Temple, which was previously used for Masonic ceremonies and had been underutilized in more recent years. Working with a Philadelphia-based concert promoter, the borough has begun to present pop concerts, with music ranging from David Crosby and Joan Baez to a local symphony. The borough has created the Collingswood Foundation for the Arts and has signed a 50-year lease with the Masons, which has transformed a structure that was destined to be destroyed into a viable theater. A further strategy to utilize the arts to foster community revitalization is a "2nd Saturday Avenue of the Arts" event that brings artists, crafters, and musicians to the downtown area from 5 to 9 p.m. on the second Saturday of each month.

Sharon Zukin's important article, "Whose Culture, Whose City," discussed earlier in this chapter, emphasized the battle that exists in contemporary cities for control of the culture of the city, as the symbolic economy transforms both neighborhoods (on a local level) and the city, (on the metropolitan level). The problems discussed by Zukin mirror the major underlying issues facing Collingswood in its quest for downtown revitalization.

Haddonfield

Haddonfield is a small municipality founded in the seventeenth century. It is located about 2 miles east of Collingswood and 10 miles east of Philadelphia. It also has a PATCO high-speed line station and the train ride to downtown Philadelphia takes about 20 minutes. The town has 11,659 residents and a median income of $86,872, making it one of the most affluent communities not only in South Jersey but in the entire Philadelphia metropolitan area as well (Mathis 2005). Its public school system is highly regarded. It prides itself as being a family oriented community—the July 4th parade and evening fireworks show, and the "First Night" celebration, are designed for children and their parents. Throughout the year, weekend classic car shows and arts and crafts show (the most recent drawing over 125,000 visitors) occur along its main street. Its population is largely composed of professional families who can afford both the high cost of housing as well as the highest real-estate taxes in South Jersey. It's largely a residential community with very few large businesses and no industrial properties. Many of its streets are tree-lined with historic architecture reflecting its colonial and Victorian past; the neighborhoods are located within easy walking distance of the downtown business district, which contains more than 200 shops, restaurants, and cafes, as well as its most prominent architectural structures—churches, a Masonic Hall, and a bank. Kings Highway, its main street, also contains historic buildings from the eighteenth and nineteenth century; many are two-story with a shop on ground level and

The downtown affluent shopping area in Haddonfield, New Jersey. Photo by author.

housing above. The downtown has served as the shopping center for clothes, groceries, and banking.

In the 1960s and 1970s, faced with the competition of the first regional mall,
the Cherry Hill Mall, and the strip malls of the growing adjacent suburb of Cherry
Hill, the downtown retail stores suffered. As stores closed some were converted
into professional offices. The municipality had an image that a downtown composed primarily of professional offices would be the wave of its future. To counter
this development, the borough sought to market itself as an historic business district with specialty shops. Implemented was an historic district ordinance. The
goal was to maintain an image that would reflect its historical past. The Indian
Head Tavern, a colonial-era tavern turned museum, was designated a New Jersey
historical site. No radical changes were permitted to storefronts and an historic
facade was to be maintained on all downtown stores. Strict rules were adopted to
assure signage conformity. The economic situation of the downtown retail store
stabilized and a viable core of gift and jewelry shops, and women and children's
clothing stores catering to its affluent population, prospered. The cafes and restaurants located there were geared to serving daytime shoppers and office workers,
and most closed when the stores closed, in the early evening.

However, in the late 1990s, at the same time that Collingswood was undergoing its redevelopment, Haddonfield's downtown was faltering. In response the
municipality, working with local businesses and groups, hired consultants who specialized in retail and economic development. The aim was to encourage downtown
business and residential development. To do this, the consultants worked to cut

the red tape for incoming businesses, encouraged the local government to pay interest on business loans, built more parking facilities, and undertook a recruitment drive to bring in specialty retailers to move into vacant stores. The underlying philosophy was to foster an image of Haddonfield as an attractive community with a small-town, more personalized environment than that offered by suburbia and its malls and their chain stores (Van Allen 2004).

> "There was an emerging demand for an urban-type environment, an 'urbanesque' environment. People were looking for a downtown—a kind of 'urban light,'" said Louis S. Bezich, president of Haddonfield-based *Public Solutions*, which helped develop the strategy. "Many people moved to the suburbs to cocoon. But often when people find that, they also find there's something missing, a social element, the energy of human connectedness." (Van Allen 2004)

To revitalize King's Court, a small pedestrian-walkway with retail stores that was built in the 1970s, the borough approved the construction of townhouse apartments over the existing stores. On vacant land, near the train station and off Kings Highway, a small townhouse development was built. Its location is convenient, both to get to Philadelphia and to walk into town. These condo developments and the aforementioned one in Collingswood are reflections of plans by officials in Camden County, where both towns are located, and officials in Lower Merion Township outside of Philadelphia to build small town-centers near their rail-transit systems. These centers are also envisioned on land now designated for car parking at a total of 45 train stations in the Delaware Valley regional area near Philadelphia in both Pennsylvania and New Jersey. These centers are referred to as "transit-oriented developments"—TODs, for short (Saffron 2005). These TODs meet the needs of people who want to live within easy commuting distance to downtown Philadelphia but prefer to live in a small-town environment rather than in a suburban housing development. In both Collingswood and Haddonfield, many of the early condo buyers were empty-nest suburbanites or young couples without children who worked in Philadelphia's Center City. The location of these TODs is of value for the small towns, as they provide additional shoppers and help maintain viable town centers.

The Partnership for Haddonfield, a management corporation for the business improvement district, was formed in 2004. Its aim was to foster self-financing programs and to enhance the commercial viability and attractiveness of the downtown in order to promote growth and employment. A consultant was hired who saw that the best strategy for competing with the upscale shopping centers that were recently built in nearby Marlton and Mount Laurel was to focus on attracting apparel stores, bakeries, restaurants and cafes (Mathis 2005). The inclusion of restaurants and cafes was designed to counter the "restaurant renaissance" in nearby downtown Collingswood. Haddonfield, while having more established affluent retail-store establishments than Collingswood, has relatively few upscale restaurants. Most of the restaurants serve the day shoppers and local businesspeople. But they close in the evening at the same time the stores close. The one restaurant establishment that caters to the more affluent has undergone different owners every few years.

Now, changes are becoming apparent. New restaurants are opening and transforming the daytime only eateries to serving evening dinner meals as well. Starbucks has opened a store on the busiest corner of the downtown that has proved to be highly popular both during the day and into the late evening, staying open even after most retail stores close by 6:00 p.m. Two upscale retail shops, one catering to high-end women's shoes, the other selling bath and body products, are examples of the kind of retail establishments that Haddonfield is seeking. To solidify its image as a family-oriented downtown, Haddonfield commissioned a nine-foot construction of a dinosaur and placed it in the center of town. During the day, it attracts the attention of young children—many in strollers—and their parents. The ultimate goal is to attract not only the affluent Haddonfield residents but the affluent shoppers in the surrounding suburban areas as well. Guy Elzey III, a member of the partnership's board of trustees, has lived in Haddonfield his entire life. He comments that when he was a student in the local high school in the 1970s, a math teacher referred to students as "young Athenians," a reference to the historical center of Western civilization and culture. "We lived in the Athens of South Jersey. Back then, it was more understated and quiet. It was maybe a better-kept secret" (quoted in Mathis 2005). Today, Elzey observes that Haddonfield has a different view of itself:

> It's a different vision, a different approach . . . What we need is great businesses. If you bring the right shops and restaurants, people will come, and we're recruiting great businesses. (quoted in Mathis 2005)

Glassboro

Glassboro New Jersey is located in Gloucester County in south Jersey approximately twenty-miles southeast of Philadelphia. It has a population of a little over 19,000 people. It's a predominantly working class town with nearly 75 percent of its population being white non-Hispanic. The remaining population is composed of nearly 20 percent blacks and 4 percent Hispanic. Esther DeEugenio, the President of the Glassboro Historic Preservation Commission, reports that the town was founded in the late eighteenth century and grew during the nineteenth century, with the glasswork industry serving as the center for its economy. By the end of that century its glass factory operations were one of the largest and most prosperous in the state (DeEugenio, 2006). In 1918 the Owens-Illinois Glass Company opened in 1918 and built one of the most advanced glass-making factories on the east coast. However, faced by stiff economic competition, glass manufacturing soon became a less viable economic activity and declined in importance. In 1923 Glassboro, became the site of the New Jersey Normal School, a college designed to prepare students to become teachers in South Jersey classrooms. It later became known as Glassboro State College. In 1967 it was the site for a summit meeting between President Lyndon Baines Johnson and Premier Aleksei Kosygin of the Union of Soviet Socialist Republics.

With a $100 million endowment gift from a wealthy industrialist, it began an extensive expansion program in the mid-1990s and became Rowan University. Currently, the university is divided into a Graduate School and six academic colleges: Business, Communication, Education, Engineering, Fine & Performing Arts, and Liberal Arts & Sciences. Rowan's nearly 10,000 students can select from among 36 undergraduate majors, seven teacher certification programs, 26 master's degree programs and a doctoral program in educational leadership. The growth plan calls for more than doubling the size of its campus within the next ten years. It has acquired more than 250 acres of farmland on which it will build a technological center and sports center anchored by a major-league professional soccer league stadium and athletic facilities. It is very actively transforming itself from its history as a state college into a major regional comprehensive university in South Jersey and the Delaware Valley.

Today, Glassboro's main street is barely economically viable. Some of its business owners have a vision that seeks the transformation of Glassboro's downtown into a middle-class shopping district anchored by stores catering to the needs of its more affluent citizens and to the university's faculty, staff, and students. This vision is shared by the university's administration that seeks not only the transformation of its institution but the transformation of the town of Glassboro.

For the university, Glassboro will become a "college town" aimed to enhance the involvement of members of the university community with the town as well as to draw people from surrounding areas. Rowan University's president, Donald Farish, advocates the development of a "'campus village' in which students and staff would leave the college grounds to spend their money in town" (cited in Bitman 2005: B4). He observes, "Campuses can no longer wall themselves off from the community in which they are located" (quoted in Bitman 2005: B4).

The university has announced its desire to build a street corridor, "Rowan Boulevard," that would link the campus to the downtown area. This corridor would include stores designed to appeal to students and faculty. The plans call for a hotel, a conference center, and residential apartments above the stores. Some funding will come from the Casino Reinvestment Development Authority and the university; the majority will come through private investment.

Other projects to build relationships between the university and the state include the creation of a fiber-optic loop throughout the town that businesses will be able to use. In 2004, the university bought a vacant public school, transformed it into offices for various Rowan University centers, and leased out much of the space to a private company that has 150 employees. Three scholarships for township high school seniors have been created. Implemented is a $15,000 financial incentive paid over 10 years to Rowan University employees who move to Glassboro. So far, 50 employees have moved into Glassboro. In April 2005, Rowan University committed $1 million to help with the economic redevelopment of Glassboro. These monies are allocated at the rate of $100,000 annually over a 10-year period. The mayor of Glassboro has indicated that the monies are targeted for a number of downtown revitalization projects, including landscaping and new building facades.

Millville

Millville, a town of nearly 27,000 residents, is located on the banks of the Maurice River in Cumberland County in southern New Jersey, about 40 miles from Philadelphia. Its name derives from the numerous mills and factories that operated there. Of great importance was the glass producing factories that processed the abundance of silica sand located in South Jersey. The city was also the site for the nation's first defense airport built in the 1940s and is known as "The Holly City of America" for its holly growing production. Wheaton Village, a major glass museum that attracts 80,000 visitors a year, is located in Millville, as is the Millville Airport Museum. An annual air show draws large numbers of people. Like most small towns in South Jersey, Millville went into economic decline in the 1950s and has had a stagnant economy through most of the later part of the twentieth century.

The building of a four-lane highway, Route 55, in the late 1990s has allowed for a relatively easy and convenient commute to Philadelphia and other South Jersey communities and has been a key factor in the city's revitalization. In very recent years Millville is in the process of reinventing itself through the development of a downtown arts district. It builds on its heritage as a center for the glass industry and as the site of the Wheaton Village museum. The city initiated a comprehensive center-city redevelopment strategy that includes physical improvements, neighborhood revitalization, and the establishment of the Millville Development Corporation.

In 1998, the Millville Development Corporation—a nonprofit organization designed to direct revitalization through a public, private partnership—acquired a downtown department store and an adjacent building. A local developer converted these structures into a gallery and community center known as the Riverfront Renaissance Center for the Arts (Rolland 2004). The city enlisted the local county college to open a ceramic studio, and the county's improvement authority renovated a vacant bank building to use for offices for further revitalization. Since then, 48 new businesses—primarily galleries and retail stores—have located in the arts district, a two-block-by-six block area that is mostly dedicated to the visual arts. A brick paving system, ornamental lighting, and site amenities upgraded numerous parking areas. Millville is planning to put up banners downtown that will provide visual clues to let visitors know they are in the Arts District. The banners are just one feature of an effort to set apart and popularize the arts district (Makos 2005).

These revitalization efforts worked in conjunction with earlier and continuous city actions to improve the area's infrastructure and maximize the beauty of its riverfront location. The city used state funds from a designated urban enterprise zone program to add new sidewalks, streetlights, parking, and landscaping, and to help owners repair business facades. In 2004 the city was inducted into the Main Street New Jersey Program (Monaghan 2004). This program, established in 1989, is a comprehensive revitalization program that provides economic redevelopment of traditional business districts in New Jersey (Monaghan 2004). Every two years the state's Department of Community Affairs selects communities to join the program.

These communities receive technical support and training to restore their Main Streets as centers of community and economic activity. Chosen towns had to demonstrate public and private support for improving its downtown areas. The Main Street Program builds on the town's accomplishments and jump-starts a new beginning for the community.

The focus of Millville's strategy for the revitalization of its deteriorating downtown area was the creation of an "arts overlay zone" (Ficcaglia n.d.). Activities central to or supportive of the arts would be encouraged. The Riverfront Renaissance Center for the Arts provides educational programs to the community in an effort to promote an understanding and appreciation of the arts. It offers working, teaching, and exhibition space for artists. Every third Friday, the Center is open until 9 p.m. The public is invited to meet the artists and to enjoy an evening in celebration of the arts. Other shops and restaurants remain open for this event and live entertainment is often included. The goal was that the arts district would attract new businesses to the downtown area. As noted above, 48 new businesses have located in the arts district since 1998.

The real-estate market has been profitable. Since the development of the arts district, the city has witnessed an increase in property values. The smaller buildings on the main street have tripled in value over the last five years, the larger buildings have doubled in value, and private investors are showing a strong interest. A housing boom has developed. Construction will soon begin on 25 upscale single-family homes that will cost over $250,000 (Makos 2005).

A challenge is downtown property speculation. Those particularly affected are the very artists who were so instrumental in the downtown's revitalization. They viewed Millville's old buildings, some a century old, as irreplaceable pieces of history, not as old and dilapidated structures (Rolland 2004). They moved in, and both lived and worked in those buildings. With real-estate speculation and rental prices rising rapidly, many artists find themselves being priced out of the very buildings that they rehabilitated. To counter this, the city is exploring the feasibility of developing affordable artists' housing. This has taken the form of a "Pioneer Artist" program. Fourteen Pioneer Artists have located in the arts district (Miller n.d). Dozens of building owners have applied for and received grants and loans to facilitate capital improvements. The maximum loan available to a Pioneer Artist is $5,000 (Ayres n.d.). The loan may be used for relocation expenses and/or establishing the artist in a rented or purchased property located in the arts district. The artist must make a two-year commitment as a resident in the arts district. In a community development offshoot of the arts district, the city is requiring artists who receive pioneer artist grants to paint murals and engage in beautification activities in the city's neighborhoods. An artists' guild is also being formed to improve communication among city leaders, residents, and business owners. The city and the neighborhood associations are considering additional ways in which public art can become a significant part of the center-city neighborhoods.

Many residents were initially skeptical of Millville's plans for the revitalization of the downtown. They changed their minds when they saw how their children benefited from the arts district. Early on, the city created an annual summer arts program for young people, as well as arts and crafts programs linked to the schools. Some students are now pursuing arts-related education, partly with the help of federally funded job training programs.

In summary, the arts have played a key role in the revitalization of this town. Millville used public and private partnerships to support economic diversification, city beautification, special events, and recreational opportunities. The strategy utilized the city's riverfront, its industrial arts heritage, and its historic downtown to create and develop a new town image based in large part on an arts district that captured and enhanced its cultural and structural past. Recently, Millville was named the fourth best urban center in the state of New Jersey.

Conclusion

All four towns, then, have different definitions of a redesigned main street. One is in a gentrification transformation process (Collingswood); one wants to maintain its upscale reputation (Haddonfield); one is interested in transforming itself into a college town (Glassboro); and the fourth is developing its downtown as an arts-district to redefine itself (Millville). Each town's vision of the future is broad in scope. Collingswood sees itself as a downtown retail site for selected businesses and commercial enterprises that cater to the larger surrounding affluent populations. In the process it is undergoing gentrification that may fundamentally change the character of the town. The affluent borough of Haddonfield seeks to maintain its high status and its image as a family-oriented town whose downtown will appeal to both residents and upscale out-of-town-shoppers. In partnership with Rowan University, Glassboro seeks to transform its main street into a viable economic entity, one that will also service the expanding and growing university community. Glassboro ultimately wants to transform itself into a college town that will appeal both to the college community and to its residents. Millville seeks to transform itself both as a tourist destination for those oriented toward the arts, and for middle-class workers by building a speedway. The revitalization plans of all four, therefore, do not seek the return of nostalgic small-town main streets. The plans are for more complex downtown centers that can serve their respective regions and that can provide competitive goods and services that can economically compete against regional malls. Moreover, in the cases of Collingswood and Haddonfield, the plans are to provide an attractive alternative experience to revitalized areas in Philadelphia and to the innumerable shopping malls in South Jersey.

15

Baseball as Urban Drama

An Urban Game

Boosterism and Civic Pride

Spectators and Fan(atic)s

Image Building Through Technology and Newspapers

The National Pastime

A Spectacular Public Drama

This chapter will focus on a social historical analysis of professional baseball as a shared social world and as a source of urban imagery and identification. A basic premise of symbolic interaction thought on the nature of urban imagery and urban identification follows Robert Park's notion that the "city is a state of mind." Building on that premise, given objects in the city can become symbolically representative of the city and can serve as a source of personal identification for the inhabitants. R. Richard Wohl and Anselm Strauss (1958) inform us that given objects of the city become symbolically representative of the city as a whole. Thus the New York skyline, San Francisco's Golden Gate Bridge, and the French Quarter of New Orleans are all identification symbols of these cities and each serves as a source of personal identification for the inhabitants.

Further, the shared social world of urban dwellers is linked to shared symbolization and networks of communication that transcend local contacts and involvements and allow people to belong to this shared world. For as Tamotsu Shibutani has said: "Each social world . . . is a culture area, the boundaries of which are set neither by territory nor by formal group membership but by the limits of effective communication" (1955:566). Strauss states the general importance of symbols in the city as follows:

> When the city has been symbolized in some way, personal action in the urban milieu becomes organized and relatively routinized. To be comfortable in the city—in the widest sense of these words—requires the formulation of one's relations with it, however unsystematically and crudely. (Strauss 1961: 17)

Partisan baseball fans attending a New York Giants baseball game at the long-gone Polo Grounds in New York City. The stadium was demolished after the Giants moved to San Francisco and the New York Mets moved to Shea Stadium in Queens, New York City in the mid-1960s.

This discussion seeks to integrate two types of historical analysis: social history, with an emphasis on the structure and institutions of baseball; and cultural history, with an emphasis on the emotional component of baseball. Elliot J. Gorn (1990) has observed that sports history's great emphasis has been placed on the "supply side"—how sports have developed within modern urban structures—and less on the "demand side"—on audience response and on the interplay between producers and consumers of sport. "Supply side" refers to the examination of "the structures of sports ownership and control, the structure of city politics, the structure of sport utilization, and the relationships between these structures" (Gorn 1990: 27).What is often missing is an examination of the "guts" of the baseball experience: what it is like to attend a baseball game, how baseball becomes part of a fan's emotional life, and the nature of the occupational culture of baseball (Gorn 1990). In addition, it is important to also study how baseball becomes part of urban imagery and identification and becomes a community representation. Gorn concludes that to be successful sports history must integrate these two forms of analyses: "Only when we begin to reconcile structure with tone, ethos, values, context— social institutions with cultural details and nuances—will we begin to have fully fleshed out the history of American sports" (Gorn 1990: 32).

By extension, I seek to broaden the understanding of organized baseball not only as a spectator entertainment in the same category as vaudeville, variety shows, and movie theaters but also as a form of entertainment in which the audience is active in defining its activity and importance. John Kasson (1978), in his important work on Coney Island, relegates baseball involvement to a passive spectator activity. By studying baseball fans we hope to demonstrate how baseball too can be seen as another form of amusement in which the participants are also actively involved in the development of American mass culture.

Kasson (1978) observes that the new mass culture that was to emerge in the early twentieth century had its origins in commercial amusements "which were creating symbols of the new cultural order, helping to knit a heterogeneous audience into a cohesive whole" (1978: 4). Commercial amusements are seen to have developed and fought for their specific form of mass culture through the active activity of participants, often of the working and lower-middle classes. These participants sought to overcome the "moral" constraints of a "genteel" elite primarily composed of middle-class Protestant critics, ministers, educators, and reformers who sought to define not only their work activities but their recreational and leisure activities as well.

Proponents of the genteel culture were most active in the creation and development of organized baseball and sought to foster their definition of the sport. As we shall see, the spectators and fans were not solely reactive to these imposed definitions but were active participants in the fashioning of baseball into the "national game" and were active in utilizing it as a tool for community representation and urban identification.

An Urban Game

The rise of professional baseball in the last quarter of the nineteenth century coincided with America's transformation from a predominantly rural agricultural society to an increasingly industrial one. Baseball is one form of urban landmark that

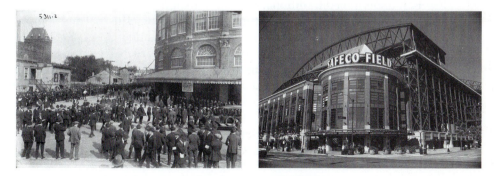

Crowd at Ebbets Field (left), October, 1920 waiting to buy tickets to a World Series Game between the Brooklyn Dodgers and Cleveland Indians. Ebbets Field as was true of most baseball stadiums of that time was located in urban neighborhoods. The Dodgers were so-named as a reference to the many trolley lines located near an earlier ball field that fans had to cross to get to the ball field. Safeco Field (right) in Seattle is a postmodern stadium that seeks to replicate the emotional context for experiencing baseball games.

drew people together, became a source of subjective identification with the larger community, and also contributed to the rapid industrialization of the city. This is especially important for urban dwellers. In the city setting, faced with potentially alienating and impersonal situational circumstances, individuals can reassign meanings to objects, make different usages of existing institutions, and thus create new sources of meaning, sentiment, and identification. Gregory P. Stone (1968, 1973) viewed involvement in spectator sports as a source of subjective identification with the larger community, and sports teams can be considered as a kind of collective representation of the community.

Baseball originated in the city, not in the country. Prior to 1845, baseball was a relatively simple child's game with informal rules. The sports historian Melvin L. Adelman chronicles where, how, and when (between the years 1845 and 1860) baseball became an organized sport with standardized rules. The sport developed in the cities of New York and Brooklyn, where the Knickerbocker Club was created in 1842 and where a dozen additional clubs emerged between 1845 and 1855. Adelman's analysis leads him to conclude that "Baseball propagandists have long sought to give the sport a pastoral image, but from the outset organized baseball was an urban product" (1986:121).

The rise of professional baseball in the post–Civil War period of the nineteenth century and into the first 20 years of the twentieth coincided with America's transformation from a predominantly rural agrarian society to an increasingly urban industrial one. The Civil War is popularly viewed as giving baseball the opportunity to expand the scope of its popularity from northeastern cities to the midwest and to the south. This came about, in part, through the interactions of Union and Confederate soldiers in prisoner-of-war camps.

The popularity of baseball spread with rapid urban expansion. The rise of professional baseball was part of the emergence of spectatorship as a recreational component of the new urban way of life that emerged in the 1860s. A "substitution theory" advanced by such historians as Foster Rhea Dulles argues that urbanization undermined traditional recreation patterns. The theory's underlying premise is that the increase in momentum and intensity of industrial and commercial activities led spectatorship to become a form of recreation. Spectatorship began to take shape with admissions being charged to watch baseball games. City playgrounds, municipal recreation programs, and park systems were not developed as they would be later toward the end of the century. Further, underdeveloped transportation systems prevented the convenient movement of people to more open areas where they could spend hours in their former rural environment. For the vast majority of the working classes there was little practical opportunities for sports and outdoor leisure activities. As a necessity, entertainment and recreation became passive, commercialized, and cheap (Dulles 1965).

Adelman (1986) observes that baseball, more than any other sport, has come to symbolize spectatorship. Yet, baseball does not fit the substitution theory. Based on his research, Adelman observes that in its pre–Civil War period, baseball, like other antebellum spectator sports, including horse racing, did not attract fans from all social ranks. He argues that the inadequate transportation system also prohibited the lower economic class dweller from attending sporting events. He takes issue with the "substitution theory," believing that it has an anti-urban bias that falsely dichotomizes participants and spectators in the same way that it falsely dichotomizes rural and urban and leads to the erroneous conclusion that "the artificial city produced artificial sport" (Adelman 1986:149).

Recognizing that commercialized spectator sports were an urban phenomenon, Adelman asserts that "The rise of spectator sports did not derive from the urban masses seeking a vicarious substitute for the 'real thing' but was rooted in the urban and economic expansion of the period" (1986:150). Spectator sports emerged in cities in the second half of the nineteenth century because there were sufficient numbers of people with sufficient incomes to sustain organized sports on a permanent basis. The individual and communal functions of spectator sports and other forms of organized and commercial entertainment and amusements were not, in Adelman's view, "a manifestation of, or response to, the antinatural urban environment" (1986:150).

Similarly, Dale A. Somers asserted that "Commercial pastimes and organized activities such as the theater, the circus, burlesque, vaudeville, and sports, arose to fill this recreational void" (1972:vii). Somers believes that while people from rural areas supplied their own leisure pastimes, many features of urban life, including the six- and even seven-day work weeks, the remoteness of the countryside, and the temporary loss of any sense of community, made the informal, unorganized, and often spontaneous leisure diversions of rural America unsuitable or inaccessible for many urban dwellers. Another sports historian, George B. Kirsch, echoes this view. The nature of the urban social milieu led to the formation of more organized and structured forms of involvements. "As cities became more diverse in race, religion, and ethnicity, their inhabitants sought community in voluntary associations for political, religious, cultural, or sporting purposes" (Kirsch 1987:54).

Somers (1972) points out that industrialization and urbanization caused dramatic shifts in the basic structure of the society, and sports and other forms of formal, organized and commercial recreation reflected that transformation. Organized recreation and entertainment were created as a source of amusement. Professional baseball provides a prime example of what happened to commercial entertainment during this period. In the late 1840s and early 1850s, baseball was predominantly a team sport for urban gentlemen who wiled away their leisure hours on this activity. The early baseball teams and informal leagues that developed within the northeastern cities of Boston, Philadelphia, Brooklyn, and New York had a decidedly amateur and upper-class character, with social exclusiveness as well as athletic exclusiveness predominating. But it was the emerging urban centers with their new urban populations that fundamentally changed the character of the game. Beginning around 1855 baseball players represented the middle and lower-middle classes, reflecting the occupational structure of such cities as Brooklyn and New York (Adelman 1986).

Improvements in transportation affected baseball as a spectator sport both on the intracity and intercity levels. The increased importance of the railroad as a basic form of transportation allowed professional baseball teams to conveniently travel from city to city. For example, intercity competition among southern cities like New Orleans, Mobile, St. Louis, Memphis, and Vicksburg was immeasurably aided by railroads (Somers 1972). In turn, the largely amateur teams were forced to standardize their rules and regulations, and the competition fostered improvement in the quality of play.

The first all-professional baseball team, the Cincinnati Red Stockings, made its historical eastern tour in 1869 and then went to the West Coast, playing before an estimated 200,000 people altogether. Somers (1972) reports on the significance of the Red Stockings tour for the rise of professional baseball in New Orleans. The visit of the Cincinnati team in August 1869 and the inevitable defeat of the more amateurish New Orleans team spurred the desire for a local professional team. A New Orleans newspaper commented: "Their defeat by the Red Stockings was to have been expected, as the latter club have been severely trained, and are what are known as 'professionals'—that is to say, they make a business of pleasure" (*New Orleans Daily Picayune*, August 8 and 29, 1869, cited in Somers 1972:126). Subsequently, professional baseball teams were formed in southern cities and their intercity travel was financed through private contributions, fundraising festivals, and gate receipts (Somers 1972).

The success and popularity of the Cincinnati Red Stockings and other touring professional teams soon led to the formation of a professional baseball league in 1871, with nine teams. Baseball rules became standardized; gambling was practically eliminated; equipment was improved; and team uniforms were designed. However, continued problems with gambling and scandals relating to the bribery of ballplayers led to that league's demise. But in 1876, the National League was founded, ushering in a period of stability. Its chartered member teams were located in Chicago, St. Louis, Cincinnati, Louisville, Philadelphia, New York, Hartford, and Boston.

Boosterism and Civic Pride

Boosterism and intercity rivalry were important elements in later nineteenth-century American cities (see Boorstin 1973; Callow 1973; Strauss 1961). As Stephen Hardy (1981) has observed, intercity baseball rivalries served to stimulate and exaggerate feelings of civic pride. In Stone's words, "Inter-urban rivalry destroyed the exclusiveness of baseball, was extended by the proliferation of rail transportation, stimulated professionalization, and established true collective representations of the urban masses as teams bearing city names—Chicago, Louisville, Buffalo, Cincinnati, St. Louis, Philadelphia, and New York, to name only a few" (1981:222). Rivalries are seen to heighten urban solidarity by involving the populace in the outcomes of baseball games and the competition among teams representing different cities.

As a case in point, for Cincinnati, the meaning that these victories might have for the city's image was not lost on its politicians. Upon the team's return, a tumultuous crowd met them at the railroad station and paraded them through the city streets, where they were received by the mayor at city hall. He presented them with a 27-foot-long bat (Durant and Bettman 1965). The local newspaper quoted two citizens who indicated the symbolic importance of the team's victories. The first citizen admitted he knew little "about baseball, or town ball, now-a-days, but it does me good to see those fellows. They've done something to add to the glory of our city." His companion chimed in, "Glory, they've advertised the city— advertised us, sir, and helped our business, sir" (cited in Voigt 1976:36). It was in Brooklyn the following year that the Cincinnati team lost their first game, ending their unbeaten winning streak at 92 games before a standing-room crowd estimated at between 10,000 and 20,000 people.

Similarly, Chicago's amateur baseball teams were losing to the more skillful and experienced professional touring teams. Chicago's newspapers argued that the losses incurred by its baseball teams were discrediting the city's image, dynamism, and enterprise (Freedman 1978).

> Chicago has heretofore succeeded only in great things. The city was never famous for its small undertakings. Our citizens . . . make of a low and unhealthy swamp, a bright and beautiful and happy city. . . . It is true that we have other achievements to fall back on as a community . . . (b)ut that only makes the record glaringly patent . . . when it comes to baseball . . . Chicago ain't there. These things have always been left to such cities as Milwaukee, Saint Louis, and Cincinnati . . . There was a time when Chicago thought otherwise. Our people went to work organizing a baseball club with the same energy as they would build a tunnel or construct a railroad. This was some years ago. (*Chicago Tribune*, July 10 and 31, September 1, 1869, cited in Freedman 1978:60)

Boosterism and civic pride were integral parts of the sport's newspaper coverage. Gregg Lee Carter (1975) examined newspaper accounts of victorious baseball games of St. Louis over Chicago teams from 1867 to 1875. He found that the descriptions and hyperbole of the newspaper accounts demonstrated how baseball became one of the symbols that reflected a mythic self-image and bolstered St. Louis's claim to civic greatness. Such baseball victories were seen as symbolic evidence of the economic and cultural supremacy of St. Louis over Chicago in the Midwest in the post-bellum period: "In the continuing drive to maintain her mythic self conception, St. Louis began to manipulate every possible symbol that would proclaim her to be 'The Future Great City of the World' . . . Baseball became one of these symbols" (Carter 1975: 263). The following editorial in the *St. Louis Republican* reflected on the meaning of the victories of the St. Louis Brown Stockings over its intercity rival, the Chicago White Stockings:

> St. Louis is happy. Chicago has not only been beaten at baseball, but outrageously beaten. With all the bragging of that boastful city . . . the result only illustrates once more the old truth that bluster does not always win. In this, as other things, St. Louis proves stronger . . . Chicago came, saw, and was conquered. (May 7, 1875, cited in Carter 1975: 256)

Not to be outdone, the *St. Louis Democrat* provided the following poem to convey the symbolic importance of those baseball victories:

A Tale of Two Cities—A.D. 2000

By Jack Frost

A village, once of low degree,
A city's rival tried to be.
The city now in triumph stands.
The village—leveled to the sands.

This mournful tale's designed to tell
How, like the frog who tried to swell
Until he'd be an ox in size,
Soon burst this town of many lies.

From out her miasmatic smells
One morn came nine athletic swells,
Who would their humbler rivals meet,
And crush them with a sore defeat.

They met these rivals on the green;
They ne'er were more surprised, I ween,
For though they hard and harder fought,
Their puny efforts counted naught.

Again they met—but, while, you know,
Brains fed on lake fish larger grow,
And while to man great use they've been,
A game of ball they cannot win.

As lions, came this buffer crew,
Intending mighty deeds to do;
Like badly beaten fowls they went,
With feathers drooping, crushed and bent.

This little village seemed accursed;
Soon all her gaudy bubbles burst.
She proved what me thought her before,
A wind-bag burgh—and nothing more.

Where this wretched village stood
Now stands a sign of painted wood,
On its these words; "Upon this spot
Chicago stood, but now stands not;
Her time soon came, she had to go;
A victim, she, of too much blow."

(May 15, 1875 reprinted in Carter
1975: 254–55)

Similarly, Brooklyn newspapers saw symbolic meanings in the victories of their teams. In the opening lines to his history, *The City of Brooklyn 1865–1898,*

Harold Coffin Syrett (1944:11) states that, "The city of Brooklyn, like the borough of today, suffered from an inferiority complex which could have been overcome only by widening the East River to the proportions of an ocean or by the destruction of its elephantine neighbor." The city's newspaper, *Brooklyn Eagle,* grabbed onto the early successes of baseball teams in Brooklyn to boost the city's morale. Commenting on the victory of a Brooklyn all-star team that defeated its New York counterpart during the 1862 season, the paper declared, "Nowhere has the National game of baseball taken a firmer hold than in Brooklyn and nowhere are there better ballplayers" (*Brooklyn Eagle*, March 12, 1862, cited in Adelman 1986:132). A few months later the newspaper, reflecting on Brooklyn's inferiority complex, comments on the victories of a team from Brooklyn over a New York City rival: "If we are ahead of the big city in nothing else, we can beat her in baseball" (May 10, 1862, cited in Adelman 1986:132).

Spectators and Fan(atic)s

However, baseball as a community representation was handicapped by its perceived lower-class popularity. Through the last quarter of the nineteenth century baseball was caught in a dilemma. While its attendance was increasing, it continued to be plagued by unruly crowds. Spectators at National League games comprised a different demographic profile than those who watched amateur games during the pre–Civil War period. As its attendance increased, it attracted a large working and lower-class audience. The more prosperous members of the middle class were reluctant to attend these professional games. Allen Guttmann (1986) observes that photographs in the lavishly illustrated *Book of Sports*, published in 1901, contains numerous photographs of members of the leisure class on the tennis courts and golf links of their private country clubs. No photographs of their attendance at baseball games are shown.

The photohistorian Peter Bacon Hales comments that the lack of "grand-style" photographs of baseball that would add to the glorification of the city can be attributed to the fact that baseball was viewed by many as a "lower-class" spectator sport. He observes that organized middle-class recreational activities in urban parks became a fitting subject for grand-style urban photography. But "the 'lower class' status of spectator sports may . . . have been responsible for 'grand-style photographers' neglect of those sports" (Hales 1984:111).

Further detracting from the image of baseball as the representation of a city was the fact that baseball spectators were not particularly noted for their sportsmanship and fairplay. Rather, rowdyism, gambling, and drinking were more typical of the everyday activities at the baseball park. The behavior of spectators at baseball games is truly reflected in the term "fan," which is a shortened form of the word "fanatic." Robert Smith (1961), who has written one of the more informative as well as entertaining popular histories of baseball, tells us that spectators were particularly nasty in Detroit. It was in Detroit where distracting rhythmic clapping, stomping, and organized noises of every sort originated. Baltimore fans also had a notorious reputation.

Umpires were berated and cursed at routinely. In one graphic incident, a gang of fans holding a length of rope with a noose at the end of it waited for an umpire to leave the sanctity of the dressing room after a game in which the local team lost due to the umpire's "bad" calls. These fans also developed the technique of using small mirrors to reflect the sun into the eyes of opposing team's players.

George B. Kirsch (1987), in his analysis of baseball spectators during the period 1855–1877, observes that proper fan behavior, courtesy, and civility concerned promoters and clubs. During the early years of team sports, amateur clubs did not restrict attendance, and admission fees were charged only for all-star baseball games. Rules of etiquette such as the "Manual of Cricket," also adopted by baseball officials, stated: "It is always a proper courtesy, and tends to the popularity of this noble exercise, to allow any respectable and quiet strangers to come on the ground to witness either play or practice; but it is always good policy, likewise to have it understood by the visitors that it is a privilege, not a right" (quoted in *Porter's Spirit of the Times* III:228, December 12, 1857, cited in Kirsch 1987:5).

The majority of spectators tended to be from the middle and upper classes since they could afford to pay for the transportation to the different baseball parks. However, for the more important games, attendance included members of the lower classes as well. It was only after the Civil War that admission fees began to be routinely charged. Kirsch speculates that the promoters and clubs were motivated, in part, to charge admission fees because of their desire to exclude lower-class fans. A particular concern was the appearance at baseball games of assorted troublemakers, including "roughs," con men, thieves, and pickpockets. However, Kirsch observes, such troublemakers still became an integral part of the baseball audience.

To counter the negative image of baseball spectators, promoters sought to encourage the attendance of females to games, hoping that they would "enhance the respectability of their pastimes while restraining the behavior of males in the crowd" (Kirsch 1987:12). To illustrate, Frank Queen, editor of a prominent sports newspaper of the 1860s, sought the attendance of females at sporting events so that they could exert their positive influence on spectator behavior:

> Let our American ladies visit the cricket grounds, the regattas, the baseball matches, and the most rough or rude among the spectators would acknowledge their magic sway, thus conferring a double favor upon the sports they countenance, because the members of our sporting organizations are usually gentlemen and always lovers of order, but they can no more control the bystanders than they can any other passengers along a public highway. When ladies are present . . . no class of our population can be found so debased as not to change their external behavior immediately, and that change is always for the better. (*The New York Clipper*, VII:29, May 14, 1859, cited in Kirsch 1987:6)

Gambling continued to be a pervasive feature of nineteenth-century baseball. "Hippodroming" was the popular name for gambling, and betting scandals were common in baseball and other spectator sports. Drinking and drunkenness also characterized spectator behavior and were so extensive that they threatened the very popularity of the game. Other recreational activities, including bicycling, golf, and football, became serious contenders as the preferred middle-class recreational activity. An 1877 newspaper article accounts the problems of attracting a middle-class audience to baseball:

> It would be difficult to name any recreation which can be conducted in public, from horse-racing to base-ball, that has not been debased by the infusion of the gambling element. Base-ball indeed, has steadily declined in popular interest during five years past . . . If the promoters of these games cannot cure the evil nobody can. And if dishonest managers persist in their schemes, they will soon find nobody simple enough to attend their humbug shows. (*New York Times*, July 6, 1877, cited in Betts 1974:221)

Image Building Through Technology and Newspapers

Despite the difficulties with fans, however, interest in baseball continued. A steady increase in paid attendance figures through the 1870s led to a wave of new stadium construction in the 1880s, which continued through to the end of the century. The earlier stadiums were wooden constructions surrounded by wooden fences with spaces for up to 10,000 spectators. Stadiums increased in size to 15,000 seats when double-decked stands replaced the single-storied pavilions in the 1880s. But the continued increase in baseball crowds soon exhausted the technical capacities of wooden stands. Innovative technological improvements culminated in the early twentieth century with the building of concrete-, brick-, and steel-constructed stadiums, such as Shibe Park in Philadelphia, Forbes Field in Pittsburgh, Brush Stadium (later the Polo Grounds) in New York, Comiskey Park in Chicago, and Ebbets Field in Brooklyn—all with seating capacities of over 30,000. And in 1923, Yankee Stadium in New York was built, with seating for over 72,000 people.

To make the spectator sport more attractive to a middle-class audience, baseball tried to change its image. It did this by building sections of new stadiums designed for the affluent, sections segregated from the cheaper seats. It scheduled games to make it easier and more convenient for its prospective middle class clientele to attend. And, it worked in collusion with newspapers to promote a positive image of the game. Let's turn our attention to how this was done.

Leading the drive for middle-class respectability was one of the founders of the National League, A.G. Spalding, who later became a major sporting-goods entrepreneur (Levine 1985). He saw an immediate demand for more comfortable facilities that would attract the middle class to baseball games. Spalding's first stadium for his Chicago White Stockings was built in 1883 and was designed not only to provide the average spectator with unobstructed views, free scorecards, and the opportunity to rent seat cushions but also included 18 private boxes for the more affluent. As one Chicago newspaper reported, these private boxes were replete with "cozily draped curtains . . . and luxurious arm chairs for the accommodation of reporters, club officials, and parties of ladies and gentlemen" (*American Sports*, April 28, 1883, cited in Levine 1985:46).

The above newspaper quote also reflects baseball's desire to attract not only middle-class men but also middle-class women. To achieve that end, new stadiums constructed such amenities as ladies' toilets. "A necessity in all well ordered grounds," declared Chris von der Ahe, the president of the 1880s St. Louis Browns, when he built his stadium in the 1880s.

Stadiums from the 1870s and onward were built by the baseball owners with the travel convenience of fans in mind. The stadiums were constructed with easy access to the technologically improving forms of public transportation, such as the electric streetcar and subway lines. As electric streetcars and trolleys replaced horse-drawn omnibuses, it became possible to move thousands of people many miles quickly and cheaply. Baseball entrepreneurs like A. G. Spalding were always cognizant of the need to arrange for convenient transportation schedules so their middle-class business clientele could leave work and arrive at the ballpark in time for afternoon games. Communications to rail officials encouraged them on ways to increase business: "For their 'mutual interest' he (Spalding) told Lake (superintendent of the West Division Rail Company), it was important to improve service on the Van Buren Street and State Street lines by providing extra cars and better scheduling on game days, so that patrons could get from the business district to the club's Lake Front Park in time to enjoy the afternoon's entertainment" (Levine 1985:45–46).

Owners of transportation facilities were among the earliest entertainment and sports promoters. To increase passenger traffic and to increase financial profit, streetcar lines went into the amusement business and established amusement or "trolley" parks at the end of the line. Many early baseball magnates also were involved in the transportation business, owning both the team and the streetcar lines. For example, when the aforementioned Chris von der Ahe built Sportsmen's Park in St. Louis, he gave his railway company adjacent land for a trolley loop with a resultant financial gain both for the baseball team and the railway company (Seymour 1960).

Brooklyn baseball teams reflected this pattern. The owners of the Brooklyn National League team was owned from 1891 to 1898 by trolley line operators. These owners moved the team from Washington Park in South Brooklyn to Eastern Park in Brownsville, which was serviced by their trolley lines. Indeed, the team gained its nickname, the "Trolley Dodgers," which was subsequently shortened to "Dodgers," as a consequence of fans who had to dodge trolleys as they crossed the tracks of the New York & Manhattan Beach Railroad to get to the ballpark (Reiss 1980; Cohen 1990).

Baseball owners saw the necessity of getting public attention through the use of the city newspaper, and some of them also owned newspapers. For example, the owner of the *Chicago Herald* was a principal investor of the Chicago White Stockings. Indeed, there was an immediate affinity between the rise of professional baseball leagues and the metropolitan newspapers. By promoting baseball and treating baseball games as newsworthy events, newspapers not only increased their daily circulation but added to baseball's growth and popularity. Newspapers were instrumental in transforming baseball from a recreational activity to a spectator sport. The cities that had the most profitable and stable franchises were located in

Boston, Philadelphia, New York, Washington, and Chicago—where press coverage was most available and plentiful.

Newspapers, sports weeklies, and other printed materials played a pivotal role in developing the image of baseball and seeing it as a source of community representation. Space allotted to daily sports events and activities began to increase in the 1870s; made appreciable gains in the 1880s when Joseph Pulitzer's *New York World* organized the first separate sports department; and became an integral and vital circulation builder when William Randolph Hearst's *New York Journal* introduced the separate sports section in the 1890s (Barth 1980).

Newspapers not only reported the game but determined its image. Fully aware that sports coverage, and particularly baseball coverage, sold newspapers, the sportswriters, whenever possible, underreported the rowdyism and roughhousing that occurred on the field and the gambling, drinking, and fighting that occurred in the stands. They did this because they knew that ultimately such activities would mean the end of baseball's popularity. Robert Smith reports that, outside of a few muckraking journalists, a sort of gentleman's agreement developed where the disreputable side of the game was virtually ignored. In turn, baseball teams treated the writers in rather high style, with free access to lavish food buffets after the game and various perks such as complementary tickets. Smith observes that the journalists' reporting practices are in keeping with the American pattern of playing down unpleasantries:

> This was right in the literary tradition of that day—and even of this, to some extent—when focusing attention on the less cheerful aspects of American life was deemed unchristian, immoral and unpatriotic. Many a juicy story of petty mayhem was suppressed and thousands of Boy Scout legends invented on the ground that to do otherwise would "hurt baseball." (Smith 1961:95)

Sociologists have long noted the influence of the newspaper on city life. Robert Park in his writings [most notably *The Immigrant Press and Its Control* (1922) and "The Natural History of the Newspaper" (1923/1967)] points out that for the immigrant both the foreign-language newspaper and the native American newspaper provides essential functions. In particular, the later serves as a "window looking out into the larger world outside the narrow circle of the immigrant community in which he has been compelled to live" (Park 1923/1967:98).

Shibutani (1961) picks up on this theme when he observes that the individual has as many reference groups as the number of communication channels that he or she participates in, and that an individual's viewpoint is both shaped and limited by this involvement:

> Each time a man enters a new communication channel—subscribes to a new periodical, joins a new circle of friends, purchases a television set, or begins to listen regularly to some radio program—he is introduced into a new social world. People who communicate develop an appreciation of one another's tastes, interests, and outlook upon life; and as one acquires new standards of conduct, he adds more people to his audience. (1961:258)

In his examination of the immigrant press, Reiss (1980) notes that sports stories were reported differently depending on whether the story was in a foreign-language newspaper or in the English-language section of that newspaper. In the foreign-language newspaper, the appearance of a sports item usually referred to a matter of ethnic pride (typically the exploits of a fellow ethnic player). (A notable exception was a 1907 article, "The Fundamentals of Baseball Explained to Non-Sports," accompanied by a diagram of the Polo Grounds, that appeared in Abraham Cahan's *Jewish Daily Forward*.) By the 1930s when the immigrant press developed English-language sections, sports items appeared on a regular basis and were oriented toward the second-generation reader (Reiss 1980).

In this light, the newspaper can be seen as providing a social world for the reader by serving as a communication channel with collective symbols that give substance to another world and an additional urban perspective. Daniel Boorstin shares this view regarding the newspaper and baseball: "People who could not watch the games, much less play them, could follow sporting 'news,' enjoying a suspense and elaborating a cultic lore missing elsewhere in their lives" (1973:404). We can now also understand the social and symbolic significance of the press use of baseball coverage not only in terms of circulation building but in terms of the Americanization process.

Sports jargon, and most notably baseball slang, was a prominent feature of this sporting news (Gipe 1978). Sports jargon, too, has symbolic significance. Much of it was ephemeral, quickly passing out of usage by contemporary writers and fans. Another type became limited only to baseball and still has some currency ("Baltimore chop," for example). The third type consists of words or phrases that have become incorporated into the larger language and can be used by those with no knowledge of the game whatsoever. For example, the phrase "pinch hit" has become part of everyday speech. It refers to a substitute who carries on a job for an unavailable person in an emergency situation. In the same manner "in there pitching" describes a determined person. The ubiquitous phrase "game plan," used ad nauseam, is another example.

The significance of baseball terminology for us is that it became, in symbolic interaction parlance, "significant symbols" for many fans who shared a "universe of discourse" and who otherwise lived in different social worlds. Or as Seymour puts it in more standard sociological terms:

> The argot of baseball supplied a common means of communication and strengthened the bond which the game helped to establish among those sorely in need of it—the mass of urban dwellers and immigrants living in the anonymity and impersonal vortex of large industrial cities. Like the public school, the settlement house, the YMCA, and other agencies, baseball was a cohesive factor for a diverse, polyglot population. With the loss of the traditional ties known in a rural society, baseball gave to many the feeling of belonging. (1960:350–351)

The National Pastime

I have observed that boosterism and civic pride also served to enhance baseball's popularity. In addition, organized baseball itself, from its founding in the 1870s to the present, has wrapped itself around a "baseball creed" in its quest to become the "national game." This creed is expressively stated in the fanciful alliteration of Albert G. Spalding, the foremost baseball entrepreneur:

> I claim that Base Ball owes its prestige as our National Game to the fact that as no other form of sport it is the exponent of American Courage, Confidence, Combativeness; American Dash, Discipline, Determination; American Energy, Eagerness, Enthusiasm; American Pluck, Persistency, Performance; American Spirit, Sagacity, Success; American Vim, Vigor, Virility. (1911/1992: 42)

The baseball creed can be seen to have three component myths (Reiss 1980). The first was the pervasive myth that the game had a rural origin. The second, myth was that baseball was a locus for social integration. The third, integrally related to the second, was the myth of social democracy. Further, all three creeds, in actuality, may be more fanciful than factual (Reiss 1980; Hardy 1981).

In regard to the pastoral origins of the sport, Peter Levine (1985) demonstrates in his biography of A.G. Spalding, the baseball entrepreneur, how baseball developed the myth of the American pastoral origins of the sport. Disregarding the historical evidence that baseball developed from the English game of "rounders," Spalding, in 1907, on his own initiative appointed a national board of baseball commissioners to discover the origins of baseball. He then put forth the myth of baseball's creation by Abner Doubleday, later to be a Civil War general, of Cooperstown, New York, in 1839. The evidence was a letter received from a mining engineer in Denver, Colorado, who recalled that in his childhood he saw Doubleday interrupt a game of marbles and diagram a baseball diamond, explain the rules, and give the sport its name. Spalding used this story to legitimate his claim and justified it by adding that ". . . it certainly appeals to an American's pride to have the great national game of Baseball created and named by a Major-General in the United States Army" (cited in Levine 1985: 114). Levine comments:

> Spalding's plea for baseball as America's immaculate conception only served to underline his personal feelings about baseball's important contribution to American development. Some thirty years later, in 1939, as testimony to the persuasiveness of his beliefs, the Baseball Hall of Fame opened at Cooperstown and celebrated baseball's mythological centennial by posthumously admitting A.G. as one its charter members. Anyone familiar with baseball lore who attended that event should have known that if it had not been for Spalding there would have been no festivities at all to commemorate the one hundredth anniversary of the "invention" of America's national game. (Levine 1985: 115)

The function of the myth of baseball's pastoral origins and its linkage to rural and small-town America gives emphasis to the superiority of such settings over the urban environment. As we have noted, club owners as well as sportswriters used this myth to promote the idea that, through such rural and small-town ideals as self reliance, hard work, honesty, and individualism, city dwellers, often immigrants, would become good Americans by either playing baseball or participating in the rituals of spectatorship (Reiss 1980: 228).

The second myth, that of social integration, sees baseball, and by extension other sports as well as other recreational activities, as developing health and character, civic pride, and a crime-free environment. According to this myth, baseball was also seen to provide a recreational diversion for the emerging nineteenth-century, urban working-class populace. Baseball, it was argued, was a spectator sport that gave the working class the opportunity to rub shoulders with each other irrespective of their ethnic or social class backgrounds, thereby aiding in the Americanization process of the foreign born. Morgan Bulkeley, the first president of the newly formed National League in 1876 who would later serve as a governor of Connecticut, was the ideal image of the solid citizen and civic leader. He expressed this view and even extended it in his recommendation that baseball could serve as an antidote to revolution:

> There is nothing which will help quicker and better to amalgamate the foreign born, and those born of foreign parents in this country, than to give them a little good bringing up in the good old-fashioned game of Base Ball. They don't have things of that kind on the other side of the ocean, and many spend their hours fussing around in conspiring and hatching up plots when they should be out in the open improving their lungs. (cited in Seymour 1971:4)

Reiss (1980) sees this myth of social integration fitting in with the prevailing sentiments of Progressive America. This myth is tied to the belief that it is through baseball that traditional American values would be taught, that Americanization would occur, that civic loyalty and boosterism would be enhanced and urban identification would occur, and that social control of the city dweller would be established. The function of this myth can be seen in terms of what many contemporary social historians propose as a "social control" thesis (cf. Hardy 1981; Boyer 1978). In essence, this view argues that the primary motives of middle- and upper-class social reformers in promoting sport spectatorship and recreational activity was not for purposes of social and moral uplifting but rather for control and containment goals.

Social democracy, the third myth making up baseball's creed, is integrated with the myth of social integration. Essentially, this myth stated that anyone who wished to could attend baseball games, and/or if one had sufficient talent one could participate in the professional game as well. This myth was expressed by a 1909 writer who saw fans of all races, classes, and religions going to baseball games and enjoying "a glow of fellow-feeling, so strong and so genuine as in some sort to bespeak a realization of that noble American ideal, the brotherhood of man" (R. L. Hartt, *The People at Play*, [Boston: Houghton-Mifflin], cited in Hardy 1981: 202).

Reiss (1980), however, observes that the quest for social integration at the ballpark was hampered by game-scheduling factors. The scheduling of baseball games usually coincided with the convenience of the more independent worker, who could forgo work or leave work early to attend a baseball game. For many working-class people this was not possible. Further, on Sundays, when most workers would have the opportunity to attend baseball games, no baseball games were scheduled. Sunday blue laws put forth by rural Anglo-Saxon Protestant members of the Sabbatarian movement, whose goals were a strict observance of the Sabbath, worked against the goals of social integration and social democracy. It was not until the early twentieth century that Sunday baseball began to become a reality.

Baseball functioning as an urban institution that facilitated the acculturation and assimilation of immigrant children continued to be a common theme in both popular literature and in the press. In Abraham Cahan's novel *Yekl* (1896), baseball serves as a symbol of Americanization. The novel, which became the basis of the film *Hester Street*, opens with the title character Yekl, who Americanized his name to "Jake," espousing on the importance of sports to fellow immigrants. Meeting criticism that boxing was a brutal sport not worthy of an educated and civilized person, Jake exclaims the importance of baseball: " . . . But what will you say to *baseball*? All *college boys* and *tony peoplesh* play it" (Cahan cited in Guttmann 1988: 58). (Cahan italicized the interspersed English words to indicate that Yekl spoke primarily in Yiddish.)

Hugh Fullerton, a prominent contemporary sportswriter, citing correspondence from Chicago settlement workers who believed baseball to be ". . . one of the best means of teaching our boys American ideas and ideals," wrote in the *Atlanta Constitution* in 1919 that:

> Baseball . . . is the greatest single force working for Americanization. No other game appeals so much to the foreign-born youngsters and nothing, not even the schools, teaches the American spirits so quickly, or inculcates the idea of sportsmanship or fair play as thoroughly. (cited in Reiss 1980: 25)

A Spectacular Public Drama

On another point, much has been written (cf. McKelvey 1963; Barth 1980; Smith 1961; Voigt 1976) on how attendance at a baseball game is linked with the Americanization process and the egalitarian premises of American society and of American sportsmanship and fairplay. For example, the urban historian Blake McKelvey (1963) argues that baseball provided a powerful antidote to the impersonality of the congested crowds in American cities. It gave the spectator the opportunity to be out in the relatively spacious baseball park sharing in the pleasures and excitement of the emerging national sport and sharing in a community camaraderie:

> Participants learned a new sense of discipline, called sportsmanship, as well as a team spirit, and the great host on the sidelines enjoyed the excitement generated by the contest. Many acquired a team loyalty, which often helped to breach social barriers and create a new sense of group or community solidarity. Intercity contests abetted this trend and enabled regional rivals to work off their hostilities in a harmless fashion. (McKelvey 1963:192)

McKelvey, however, in an earlier passage, attributes the integrative function of baseball game attendance to have occurred at a much earlier date than that reported by Reiss. McKelvey claimed that the middle classes "often rubbed shoulders with factory workers too, at the ballpark on a Sunday or holiday, and developed a keener sense of community solidarity than any other experience afforded, as Baltimore, during the heyday of the Orioles in the nineties, and many other cities demonstrated" (1963: 187). As Hardy points out, "McKelvey has confused the *perception* of reality with reality itself" (1981: 202). Hardy emphasizes that it was true that the keen sense of community was developing among a wide range of urban inhabitants. "But, the crucible for this reactions was not the ballpark; it was the *symbolic* status that baseball had attained" (Hardy 1981: 202).

Given the above caveat, we nevertheless can attribute some of the power of baseball as a symbol of urban identification to attendance at ballgames, albeit for some at a later date than first thought. For those who did attend baseball games the ballpark served as, in Lewis Mumford's terms, "a spectacular public drama" (1934/1963). Durkheim (1915/1965), in his discussion of religion, refers to the "collective effervescence" that is experienced in the sociability of commonly shared ritualistic or exhilarating activities. Durkheim defines religion as "a unified system of beliefs and practices relative to sacred things, that is to say, things set apart and forbidden—beliefs and practices which unites into one single moral community called a Church, all those who adhere to them" (1915/1965: 62). In this sense religion is seen as primarily a social phenomenon and should not be construed as a theological or psychological phenomenon. The content of the symbolic system is insignificant compared to the fact that the ritual process itself serves to join the individual to a community of moral order. The symbol is a "collective representation" because it is a concrete manifestation of the values of the community to which all members of the community must subscribe and through which they maintain their community identity.

Sports, and baseball in particular, can be seen in this light as having an "encompassing power . . . to join together the individual and the community for the benefit of both" (Birrell 1981: 354). This point is explicitly delineated by the philosopher Morris Raphael Cohen, who grew up in the Brownsville section of Brooklyn in the 1890s and who lived in close proximity to Eastern Park, the predecessor to Ebbets Field. He compares the ritual of attending a baseball game and being a baseball devotee or fanatic to that of a religious experience. Further, he anchors that religious experience in the identification of baseball with the city.

> Is there any other experience in modern life in which multitudes of men so completely and intensely lose their individual selves in the larger life which they call their city? . . . In baseball the identification has . . . (a) religious quality, since we are absorbed not only in the action of the visible actors but more deeply in the fate of the mystic unities which we call the contending cities. (1919:57)

According to this view, the experience of belonging and the resultant group "spirit" can take place at a baseball game. By extension, this is also Gregory Stone's view, as stated previously that involvement in spectator sports may serve as a source of subjective identification with the larger community.

> Sports teams should be thought of as collective representations of the larger urban world. Teams represent the world. Significant then are the names of the teams. Such names have in the past designated urban areas . . . Identification with such representations may be transferred to identification with the larger communities or areas they represent. (Stone cited in Karp, Stone, and Yoels 1977:80–81)

Stone's view is shared by many social historians. Bruce Kucklick (1991) makes a similar point in his analysis of Philadelphia's Shibe Park, the first concrete and steel baseball facility, which was built in 1909 and was demolished in 1976. Shibe Park, later renamed Connie Mack Stadium, was the major league home of first the Philadelphia Athletics and then the Philadelphia Phillies, who played their last game there in 1970. Kucklick gives the above position a slightly different interpretation. He anchors collective memory in the physical site, and in this case, Shibe Park. "Group remembrance made the location part of the silent infrastructure of a shared life" (Kucklick 1991: 192). It is at the ballpark, that, collectively, memory is reinforced as the drama of the baseball game is played out within the broader context of city identification:

> During much of the period that Shibe Park stood the city was the principal entity through which multitudes of people escaped solitude, and Philadelphia was the unifying force at the stadium. The link to the city's accomplishment and status enlarged the compass of people's lives. Glory became imperishable because it was civic. This enlarged meaning was usually exaggerated, idealized—it certainly is in sports—because individuals needed to put so much weight on the collective expression of conquest. . . . The competition between cities—with Detroit, Chicago, but especially with New York—nurtured a taste for combat but also an array of community emotions, the feelings of pride, triumph, and perhaps most of all in Philadelphia, resignation. (Kucklick 1991:192)

Kucklick goes on to speculate on the implications when a site, such as Shibe Park, is abandoned, neglected, and destroyed. He argues that memories and meanings are fragile and need to be connected to specific objects, and thus he makes the case for historic preservation. "The destruction of artifacts can thus sever the present from the past and the accumulated significance the past embodies" (Kucklick 1991:193). The impoverishment of the individual and the city is seen as the outcome when the things that are the carriers of the collectively shared past are no longer there. Kucklick states that "We do not create the legacy of the city but find it in our memories, because in cooperation with others we locate this legacy in the world around us and make it salient in our lives" (1991: 193). Kucklick argues this point by observing how the movement of the Athletics to first Kansas City and then to Oakland is tied to the fact that many Philadelphians are not aware of this historical connection. This lack of awareness demonstrates the fragility of memory and keeping faith with the past.

While we share Kucklick's view on the importance of the site as a locus for community identification, we must reiterate our earlier point that urban identification need not be rooted in space but in the more salient shared symbolization and shared networks of communication. Kucklick, himself, demonstrates this point in his discussion of how the renaming of Shibe Park to Connie Mack Stadium resulted in the disruption of shared memory. Indeed, the continued presence of the Phillies in Philadelphia makes them a continued locus and source of community identification and history, even though they no longer play in Shibe Park (Connie Mack Stadium), while the Philadelphia Athletics, who left Philadelphia after 1954, are now only a distant memory.

One can speculate on the truly devastating effects on community identification when there is both the abandonment of a historic site and the abandonment of a team to another city. Further, this can have especially traumatic importance when that team was the only one in town. This, of course, was true of the Brooklyn Dodgers, who moved to Los Angeles after the 1957 baseball season.

In this context, the baseball spectacle can be seen to serve as the common meeting ground, a place where the crowd experienced the importance of how rules regulated not only the action on the field, but served also as a metaphor for how rules governed American city life.

In this light, it is interesting to note how George Herbert Mead's discussion of "the game" in terms of the genesis of the self may tie in here. It may not be incidental that Mead uses baseball and its rules as a metaphor to examine how the generalized other comes into being. Mead states that, "Any thing—any object or set of objects, whether animate or inanimate, human or animal, or merely physical— toward which he acts, or to which he responds, socially, is an element in what for him is the generalized other; by taking the attitudes of which toward himself he becomes conscious of himself as an object or individual and thus develops a self or personality (Mead 1934). In Meadian terms, then, interactions at baseball games or interactions with the rules of baseball itself can be seen as influencing the socialization process in American urban society.

If this is true, we can speculate that shared feelings must have developed among strangers representing diverse ethnic groups and social class backgrounds as they collectively shared the "thrill of victory and the agony of defeat" of a ball game or as they shared a knowledge of the game, through reading stories in the printed media. And, we can also understand why there were tears in Mudville when "mighty Casey had struck out."

In conclusion, baseball may be seen as one form of urban landmark that drew people together and became a symbolic representative of the city as a whole. Baseball also contributed to the rapid urbanization of the country. For as Mark Twain had so astutely observed, "Baseball is the very symbol, the outward and visible expression of the drive and push and rush and struggle of the raging, tearing, booming nineteenth century" (cited in Dulles 1965:191).

Part **VII**

The Urban World

16

The Suburbanization of America

> *"Little Boxes on the hillside, Little Boxes made of ticky tacky . . . Little Boxes all the same."*
>
> —Malvina Jones, 1963

Students of the suburb have long pointed out that the suburb is defined both in terms of its spatial location and its symbolic meaning. Following Robert Park's dictum that the "city is a state of mind," Kenneth T. Jackson, who has written the definitive history of American suburbia, states, "Suburbia is both a planning type and a state of mind based on imagery and symbolism." And, building on that point, the urban architect and critic Robert A. M. Stern observes that the suburb is not defined solely in terms of location and legalities. "The suburb is . . . a state of mind based on imagery and symbolism. Suburbia's curving roads and tended lawns, its houses with pitched roofs, shuttered windows, and colonial or otherwise elaborated doorways all speak of communities which value the tradition of the family, pride of ownership and rural life" (Stern cited in Rybczynski 1995: 179).

Writing before World War II and the post-war suburban development period, Lewis Mumford observes some of the key elements of the suburb. He sees it as "a collective attempt to live a private life" (Mumford 1938: 215). Mumford observes that suburbia represented a new type of community, one that was segregated both in terms of space and by economic class. And suburbia was a residential suburb that separated consumption from production: "There was no visible connecting link, except the iron rails that led to the city, between the barbarous industries that manufactured the goods and the romantic suburban homes, remote from the grime and the sweat, where these things were consumed" (Mumford 1938: 215).

Mumford continued his criticism of the emerging residential suburbs by pointing out a characteristic "loss of community" that has framed much of the debate on the quality of suburban life. Mumford sees the failure of the suburb to develop a more adequate social environment as leading to its being a specialized urban fragment both geographically separated from the city and segregated from its heterogeneous class structure:

> Hence it lacked the necessary elements for extensive social co-operation, for creative intercourse, for an expansion of the social heritage as a whole. Consuming much, it produced little, created less. The stimulus of variety, the shock and jostle and challenge of different groups, were largely absent from its life. For the inhabitants of the suburb lived divided lives. Their purses were in the central city; their domestic affections were concentrated one or two hours away, in the villa. Neither side of their lives could be wholly active, wholly efficient. The necessary routine, with its daily shuttling between home and workplace, between nest and market, undermined life at both extremes. Spatial concentration has an essential part to play in psychological focus—and that above all was lacking in this new regime. (Mumford 1938: 217)

It was after World War II, with the advent of the full blossoming of the automobile age with its network of interconnecting highways, that the residential suburb as described by Mumford realized its full fruition in the United States. The historian Robert Fishman provides us with the most clearcut definition of the residential suburb:

> I shall use the words "suburb" and "suburbia" to refer only to a residential community beyond the core of a large city. Though physically separate from the urban core, the suburb nevertheless depends on it economically for the jobs that support its residents. It is also culturally dependent on the core for the major institutions of urban life; professional offices, department stores, and other specialized shops, hospitals, theaters and the like. (Fishman 1987: 5)

This chapter will begin with a look at the garden-cemeteries and parks that came into being in American cities in the first half of nineteenth century and which served as precursors to the suburban movement.

Nineteenth-Century Garden-Cemeteries and Parks: Precursors of Suburbia

Lucia and Morton White (1977), in their influential book, *The Intellectual versus the City*, delineate a series of anti-urban sentiments by American intellectuals to argue the point that the United States has a long history of hostility toward the American city.

They observe that "fear has been the most common reaction" to the city and our intellectual history has "expressed different degrees of ambivalence and animosity toward the city" (White 1977:1). Leo Marx (1964), in his book, *The Machine in the Garden*, adds to this thesis by looking at the other side of the landscape coin—the pastoral ideal, which he sees as defining the meaning of America. Marx believes that in the United States the goal was to create a natural landscape environment that would encompass technological innovations while at the same time obscuring the impact of the machine. A number of historians have severely criticized this anti-urbanism, pro-agrarian dichotomy as being overly simplistic (cf. Sussman 1984; Bender 1982). Even so, the fact remains that the incorporation of the pastoral and rural ideal into the city—first through the construction of the garden-cemetery and later by extensive park systems—did manifest itself in nineteenth-century American cities. Ultimately, the desire to construct communities in a natural landscape environment became incorporated in the building of American suburbs.

As Thomas Bender (1982) has shown, a mid-nineteenth century urban vision developed out of the interplay between the agrarian ideals and the modernizing forces that were becoming prevalent within the industrial city. This perspective sought to combine the values of city and country life into a modern urban vision. It was in the thoughts and works of Frederick Law Olmsted that this vision was articulated. Its physical manifestation was Olmsted's work in the development of elaborate urban park systems, the City Beautiful movement, and the development of the late nineteenth-century suburbs. Frederick Law Olmsted was the key figure in these developments.

Olmsted's work encompassed the broader public-parks movement of the nineteenth century. This movement had its origins in the 1840s as an outgrowth of the rural-cemetery (also known as the garden-cemetery) vogue (Dal Co 1980). Prior to the 1840s, the absence of leisure and open spaces characterized American cities. Cities were designed in a grid pattern that made it easy for the economic development of businesses and houses but that paid little if any attention to public parks. Prior to Olmsted, the major type of open space found in the nineteenth-century city, dramatically speaking, was designed not for the living but for the dead—the garden-cemetery.

In truth, the garden-cemetery was designed not only for the dead but for the living as well. The garden-cemetery was located in close proximity to the city. The garden-cemetery was magnificently landscaped, and often provided a vista of the city. The first garden-cemetery was Mount Auburn outside of Boston; it was swiftly followed by Philadelphia's Laurel Hill Cemetery in 1836, Brooklyn's Greenwood cemetery in 1838, and similar cemeteries in other cities. Cemeteries were the precursors of municipal parks, visited by thousands of people during the spring and fall seasons, and were the sites for "country" picnics and excursions (Rosenzweig and Blackmar 1992). Bender (1982) sees the cemetery as providing access to nature, which was increasingly seen as an essential condition of urban life. "The city of the dead would purify the city of the living" (Bender 1982: 82).

These garden-cemeteries, which helped to develop an urban appreciation for pastoral and picturesque landscapes, would have great influence on the future development of American urban and suburban planning. This appreciation of nature reached its full fruition in American cities with the building of various municipal parks beginning in the late 1850s, with New York City's Central Park being the first. As Paul Boyer (1978) has observed, municipal parks are so much a part of the contemporary urban landscapes that it is difficult to imagine American cities without them. Yet that was the historical case. The park movement was comprised of a broad-based coalition of social moralists and reformers, businesspeople, civic boosters, labor leaders, physicians, and other health-service workers, politicians, and landscape designers. Advocates saw the parks as an antidote to moral anarchy, vice, and corruption in urban life, especially as it affected the lives of the lower classes. Advocates believed that parks would mollify class antagonisms by promoting inter-class mingling in a pastoral setting communing with nature. Through observation of their upper-class fellow citizens, the belief was that the lower classes would learn from their betters. Park activities would be beneficial to both the physical and mental health of their users. There were economic benefits of parks also; they increased adjacent land values and would increase a city's image.

Olmsted was a leading player in the public-parks movement. He was an urbanist as well as an urban planner who saw the future of American democracy dependent upon the conditions of life in its cities.

> Our country has entered upon a stage of progress in which its welfare is to depend on the convenience, safety, order and economy of life in its great cities. It cannot prosper independently of them; cannot gain in virtue, wisdom, comfort, except as they also advance. (Olmsted cited in Dal Co 1980: 164)

The great lawn in Central Park. Photo by author.

Cities were identified with progress and civilization; they were the centers for learning, culture, and the arts. However, Olmsted felt that city living was characterized by the loss of small-town values, by a loss of sociability, neighborliness, and community. Further, the diversity of a city's population led to the emergence of social tensions and antagonisms. In writing reminiscent of George Simmel in his *Metropolis and Mental Life*, Olmsted saw this evident in everyday interactions on the crowded city streets: "to merely avoid collision with those we meet and pass upon the sidewalks we have constantly to watch, to foresee, and to guard against their movements" (cited in Bender 1982: 176). And, again, Simmel's view on how city life ultimately leads to calculating rational thought is reflected in Olmsted's words: "Our minds are thus brought into close dealings with other minds without any friendly flowing toward them, but rather a drawing away from them" (quoted in Bender 1976: 176).

To counter this destructive trend, Olmsted urged the development of large urban parks and, as would be discussed later, suburban communities. He proposed that natural parks containing picturesque landscapes and tree-lined parkways would not only bring a sense of rural beauty to the city but would help inculcate a feeling of community. Recreational pursuits in the form of ball fields and playgrounds was not Olmsted's vision. Rather, he envisioned pastoral setting of open spaces and wooded areas that would provide a world of contemplation, a setting that would be psychologically uplifting and a valued escape from the tumult and hustle and bustle of city life. Further, visiting these settings would serve as an alternative activity to frequenting saloons and other destructive activities.

> Civilized men, while they are gaining ground against certain acute forms of disease, are growing more and more subject to other and more insidious enemies to their health and happiness, and against these the remedy and preventive cannot be found in medicine or in athletic recreations but only in sunlight and such forms of gentle exercise as are calculated to equalize the circulation and relieve the brain. (Olmsted cited in Beveridge and Rocheleau 1998: 35)

Olmsted believed that all classes would benefit through their common usage of parks and that the parks could serve as a meeting ground for people of different backgrounds (Beveridge and Rocheleau 1998). However, he was particularly concerned with the benefits that the park would hold for the poor and for women. He felt that the workers who did not have the time or finances to go to the country could partake of the natural environment that the parks provided. Further, following the lead of the social moralists, Olmsted thought that the parks and their surrounding private villas "would exert an elevating influence upon the masses who visited the park" (Bender 1976: 179).

Women who incessantly toiled with petty household chores would benefit from the relaxation and broadening experiences that parks could provide. He had a vision of women who would spend summer days in the park with their younger children joined by their working husbands and working children for evening picnics. The effect that such frequent use of a park had on the largest class of a city's inhabitants was, according to Olmsted, "incalculable" (Beveridge and Rocheleau 1998: 46).

Olmsted's vision saw fruition in the construction of Central Park in New York City in 1857–58, which he designed along with his associate, Calvert Vaux. The park, located in the center of Manhattan Island, extends from 59th Street to 110th Street and from Fifth Avenue to Central Park West (about Eighth Avenue). It incorporates both pastoral and picturesque elements. Central Park was followed by park systems in Boston, Brooklyn, Buffalo, Rochester, Detroit, Louisville, Milwaukee, Hartford, Bridgeport, and Wilmington, as well as in Montreal, Quebec. His followers were responsible for many other urban park systems, including those built in Minneapolis, Omaha, and Kansas City, as well as small park systems in Cincinnati and Indianapolis (Mohl 1985).

For Olmsted, the park was an integral part of the city fabric. He extended this idea in his development of the suburban community. He observed that the spatial nature of the industrial city led to the separation of the workplace from one's residence, which, left unchecked, could result in congestion and the division between city and country. To counter this undesirable trend, Olmsted saw the importance of the development of suburban communities. He believed that urban problems could be alleviated through the efficient planning of urban services, a functional use of technology, and the creation of suburban neighborhoods that would be integrated with the city and which would be provided with all the necessary services (Dal Co 1980). The building of Riverside, a suburb of Chicago, in 1868–69 would be the primary example of how to accomplish this desired end. Other suburbs, Llewellyn Park in New Jersey and Tuxedo Park in New York, are other examples of affluent suburbs designed to put housing communities in park-like settings.

Suburbs: The Bourgeois Utopia

The social historian Robert Fishman (1987), in his important book, *Bourgeois Utopia*, traces the development of the suburbs in the nineteenth century to the emergence of a new ideology based on the primacy of the family and domestic life. Prior to that time, in the period before the Industrial Revolution, the residence choice of place was the center of the city, its core. In preindustrial England and the United States, the peripheries, the suburbs, were disreputable areas that were resided in and frequented by prostitutes, thieves, and the lower classes; the peripheries were defined as a "place of inferior, debased, and especially licentious habits of life" (*Oxford University Dictionary* as cited in Fishman 1987: 6).

The "bourgeois utopias" that developed with the Industrial Revolution were a reflection of not only a desire to escape threatening elements in the city, but also a desire for a utopian community based on the sanctity of the private family and a world of leisure embedded in a natural setting. "Suburbia embodies a new ideal of family life, an ideal so emotionally charged that it made the home more sacred to the bourgeoisie than any place of worship" (Fishman 1987: 4). Fishman defines bourgeoisie as meaning "that part of the middle class which through its capital or its professional standing has attained an income level equal to the landed gentry, but whose daily work in urban offices ties it to a middle-class style of life" (1987: 12). The bourgeois utopias originated in early nineteenth-century England and were soon transplanted to the United States.

Fishman goes on to say that the growth of suburbia meant a transformation of urban values, with the periphery becoming the place of choice, rather than the core center of the city, with the mixed-land use of that core being replaced by a separation of work and family life, and with suburbia becoming both class-segregated and exclusively residential.

The implications of this new form of suburban life were many. For the family, it meant the segregation of gender roles; men were assigned the role of commuting to the world of work in the core city while women were contained in the world of the domestic household, where they were primarily responsible for domestic work and the rearing of children. For the larger metropolitan area, it meant the spatial segregation of classes and, in turn, of ethnic groups. The middle-class bourgeoisie came to reside in the residential suburbs, while the working and immigrant ethnic classes were relegated to the areas surrounding the central business district.

Fishman's thesis is quite similar to that developed by Kenneth T. Jackson (1985) in his book *Crabgrass Frontier*. In summary, Fishman stresses the importance of the "suburban ideal" in the development of suburbia. He calls suburbia the "bourgeois utopia," and defines it in terms of a vision of community that emphasizes the importance of private property and the individual family. Jackson sees as the key factor manifested in the suburban ideal the development of new cultural values centering on the sanctity of the home and the private family. I introduced Jackson's thesis in Chapter 11 and will elaborate on it here.

Jackson traces the development of the suburban household—where the emerging values of domesticity, privacy, and isolation reached full expression—as the American middle-class ideal. He further explains that a number of key factors led to the growth of the American suburb in the nineteenth century. These factors include the ready availability of cheap land, the importance of land developers, transportation innovations such as the railroad and the street car, inexpensive construction methods, the abundance of energy, and the affordability of houses. Of particular importance were governmental subsidy policies and racial-stress factors.

Jackson further observes that the suburbanization of the United States must be seen in the context of the detrimental effects it has had on American cities. He asks, "Why have we neglected our cities and concentrated so much of our energy, our creativity, and our vitality in the suburbs? Clearly, no single answer can be held accountable for such an important phenomenon, but I will argue that there were two necessary conditions for American residential deconcentration—the suburban ideal and population growth—and two fundamental causes—racial prejudice and cheap housing" (Jackson 1985: 287).

Technological advances in transportation from the streetcar to the commuter railroad to the automobile helped usher in a new pattern of urban and suburban growth. However, although changes in the modes of transportation allowed for the development of new residential patterns, these changes were not the fundamental cause of the growth of the suburbs. The fundamental cause was a combination of economic factors and the emergence of suburbia as the American ideal.

The suburban ideal, by itself, cannot fully explain the massive suburbanization movement in the United States. What also must be taken into account are the economic and political forces and the people who stood to gain the most, both economically and politically, from suburban development. These include real-estate developers, the railroad industry, streetcar companies, the automobile industry, and the highway lobby—who all often worked hand-in-hand with the local, regional, and federal government. The government, both at the federal and state levels, instituted policies that encouraged economic investment in the suburbs and tax subsidies for residential homes in the form of income-tax mortgage deductions. Together, these components of the "suburban growth machine" are the major contributing factors for the development of suburbia.

As discussed earlier, the *new urban sociology* is made up of social scientists who have studied the development of the built environment of cities and suburbs with an emphasis on political and economic factors. Their focus is on the forces that drive urban and suburban growth. They have examined the political economy of places and have focused on how the built environment has been financed, planned, designed, constructed, and marketed. Harvey Molotch's (1976) essay, "The City as a Growth Machine," is a prime example of how land development can be seen in terms of a market commodity that provides wealth and power. Dolores Hayden (2003) picks up on this and sees the importance of studying the relationships between real-estate developers, government agencies, and the wide range of suburban residents and workers in the historical development of suburbia.

Race, Suburbs, and City

Race issues have long been an underlining and explanatory variable in understanding residential patterns in both cities and suburbs. Kenneth T. Jackson (1985), in his treatise on the suburbanization of America, observes that there was a concentration of energy, creativity, and vitality in the suburbs at the same time as there was a neglect of American cities. "This was a consequence of two necessary conditions—the suburban ideal and population growth—and two fundamental causes—racial prejudice and cheap housing" (Jackson 1985: 287). Reinforcing these factors was the development of government policies that encouraged the movement of the middle class out of cities.

Bruce Katz of the Brookings Institute shares Jackson's viewpoint and has made the following observation:

> Race has fundamentally influenced the policies of exclusion that are practiced in suburbs throughout the country. These policies have exacerbated the concentration of racial poverty in the central cities and helped construct the metropolitan dividing lines that separate areas of wealth and opportunity from areas of poverty and distress . . . In many respects, sprawl is the inevitable flip side of racial segregation

Three generations of an African American family eating outdoors on the deck in suburbia. The movement of African Americans to the suburbs has been a late-twentieth century occurence. Prior to that time various forms of racial restriction policies prevented that from happening.

and social exclusion. Race shapes growth patterns and drives business and residential decision in ways that no single other factor can match. (Katz quoted in Breen and Rigby 2004: 19)

The overall effect of American urban policy was the dispersal and division of people in metropolitan areas, which has consequentially resulted in a segregated society and has drastically diminished the number of places that people of different classes and racial groups can encounter each other. The political scientist Gerald Frug (1999) asserts that through zoning and redevelopment, we have created a segregated society of "two nations," to use Andrew Hacker's phrase, of rich and poor, white and black, and expanding and contracting. The cumulative results of these urban and suburban policies led to what has been facetiously called "chocolate" cities and "vanilla" suburbs.

The federal government has generated numerous government policies that have fostered suburban growth often at the expense of cities. The federal highway programs created a whole new transportation system that served the outlying suburbs far better than meeting the needs of the city. The Federal Aid Highway Act of 1956 made possible the movement to the suburbs by linking suburbs with central cities. This allowed the middle class, predominantly white people, to reside in the suburbs while still gaining the economic benefits of city employment, while not being burdened by the city tax structure. At the same time, federal government policies were reluctant to support urban-centered rail and mass public transportation that would have benefited local urban populations. Federally insured mortgage programs, which were created in the 1930s but which blossomed after World War II, had at their core a pro-suburb, pro-white, and anti-city and anti-black social policy. The Federal Housing Authority (FHA) sponsored long-term, low-interest mortgages and other incentives for new suburban housing. Through "redlining," entire older urban neighborhoods were defined as ineligible for federal mortgage funding. Mortgages for suburban housing, secured with government backing, and federal income-tax policies allowed for the deduction of local property taxes from federal income-tax obligations.

The segregation of classes and racial groups was not limited to the movement of whites to the suburbs and to blacks remaining in the city—the city itself became more segregated. Federal government policies of urban redevelopment and urban renewal were given the somewhat accurate name "Negro removal" by the black community. The Housing Acts of 1937, 1949, and 1954 led to the creation of black ghettos comprised of existing older housing and high-rise housing projects.

As we discussed earlier, governmental housing policies in effect resulted in what the historian Arnold R. Hirsch (1983) has called the "making of the second ghetto." Using post–World War II Chicago as the case in point, Hirsch documents how idealistic urban planners first argued for the development of "scatter-site" integrated housing projects in all-white neighborhoods. However, faced with overwhelmingly negative reaction by white constituents, the city government changed its policies to not only support de facto segregation but to actually reinforce it.

Herbert Gans's *The Levittowners* (1967, revised 1982) provides us with the classic study of suburban life. Levittown, now Willingboro, New Jersey, is located about 25 miles from Philadelphia. Levitt and Sons built immense post–World War II suburban developments through the application of mass-production techniques. Levittown, New Jersey was one such development. Gans lived in Levittown during the formative years of this community. He observes that restrictive covenants against selling to blacks were present; only Caucasians were allowed to live there. The covenants were based on the notion that community harmony could best be achieved if racial, although not religious, homogeneity could be achieved by people who shared similar regional, class, and white-ethnic backgrounds.

Gans, in his reexamination of his landmark analysis of suburbia, presents both the downside and upside of homogenous communities and puts forth an interesting, albeit debatable, point of view. He is a strong advocate of the importance of community heterogeneity, as it should reflect the pluralism of American society. Most importantly, since most of the funding for community services is derived from local taxes, community homogeneity would result in severe disparities and inequalities. Rich communities would be able to more than adequately fund high-quality facilities, including modern schools. Low-income communities without a sufficient tax base would result in neglectful public services and a restriction in the democratic process necessitated by the need to keep taxes minimal (Gans 1982).

Gans argues, however, that people do not live in cities or suburbs as a whole, but rather they live in specific neighborhoods. He advocates, especially in communities with small children, for *"selective homogeneity at the block level and hetero-geneity at the community level"* [italicized by Gans (Gans 1982: 172)]. Gans believes that socio-economic class rather than race should be the criteria for block homogeneity. He believes that the major barrier to integration is the fear of status deprivation that is a result of a loss in people's property's value. He feels that when whites and Blacks have similar socioeconomic class backgrounds then block integration becomes a more viable option. Unless this occurs, block integration is very problematic.

> Whereas a mixture of population types, and especially of rich and poor, is desir-able in the community as a whole, heterogeneity on the block level will not pro-duce the intended tolerance, but will lead to conflict that is undesirable because it is essentially insoluble and thus becomes chronic. Selective homogeneity on the block will improve the tenor of neighborhood relations, and will thus make it easier—although not easy—to realize heterogeneity at the community level. (Gans 1982: 172)

Gans is seeking to find a balance between homogeneity and heterogeneity. He argues that if like-minded people with similar interests and skills can gather on behalf of the interests of the entire community, even if these people do not live on the same block, all will ultimately benefit.

Broadening the discussion beyond the strategies needed to achieve commu-nity heterogeneity, let's look at the benefits of community heterogeneity. Gerald E. Frug (1999) has written a powerful book on what he calls "community build-ing," which is linked to the role of the stranger for individuals who live in com-munities. Frug "seek[s] to avoid the romantic sense of togetherness often associated with the term 'community' by offering a much more modest goal: the purpose of community building is to increase the capacity of metropolitan resi-dents to live in a world composed of people different from themselves," (1999: 115). "In a world composed of people different from themselves," Frug is referring to communities that are composed of strangers that differ from each other in fundamental ways. They have different class, racial, and ethnic backgrounds. By "community building," he is referring to the ability of these diversified strangers to live together not necessarily in a spirit of togetherness but rather in a spirit of negotiation and tolerance.

Frug builds on this viewpoint by contrasting the difference between suburbs, especially large suburbs where many people don't know each other but share sim-ilar homogeneous backgrounds, and the city, where many people don't know each other but have heterogeneous backgrounds. These different worlds of strangers have different consequences for their inhabitants. Frug examines property law as applied to walled enclaves such as gated residential communities, shopping malls, and office parks. He observes that the fortressing of such enclaves deals with vio-lent crime spatially. By this, he means that the creation of protected, often walled spaces does not confront crime directly but ensures that it takes place elsewhere. Further, walled enclaves have a psychological impact on insiders. It provides them with a sense of assurance that the physical separation reinforced by surveillance video cameras, security guards, and alarm systems are a primary defense against crime. "Keep Out" symbolizes the legal essence of one's property rights.

Frug (1999) believes that the key legal policy issue that accompanies the spread of walled enclaves is, "What is the proper nature and extent of one's property rights?" The point raised is: should walled areas be understood in terms of one's own home or rather of the city as a whole? While he notes, as did Weber, that walled cities did exist in the past, it seems unacceptable today to wall off a whole city. Frug believes that walled enclaves should be treated more in terms of public space than as private space. He observes that in the past, railroad stations and businesses that were open to the public, such as inns and later hotels, theaters, and restaurants, were required to serve the public without discrimination. He argues that similar laws of openness should govern shopping malls and office parks. He believes that this ruling should be extended to gated communities as well, even though they themselves are not open to the public. The idea of "one's home is one's castle" should be restricted to the house and not be extended to the streets of residential communities. These gated communities should be open communities. Frug justifies this belief in "terms of the public values that free expression represents. Simply admitting these outsider would demonstrate to insiders and outsiders alike that walled communities cannot wall their residents off from the rest of society at will" (Frug 1999:2).

The sociologist Nancy Kleniewski sees enclosed enclaves as a consequence of the "suburbanization of everything," which has led to a decline of public space and an increase in privatization. Kleniewski elaborates: "The public street has given way to the privately owned (and security guard controlled) mall, the public park has been superseded by backyard pools and commercial theme parks, and the public cafeteria has been replaced by drive-up, fast food establishments" (2002: 108). The desire of wealthy people to move into walled and secured gated communities is associated with their desire to further isolate themselves from civil responsibility.

Gated Communities

In his brilliant comparative analysis of historical cities, Max Weber (1962) asserted that one of the defining features of these cities was the fact that they were walled. The wall served as a fortification that protected the inhabitants of the city from potential outside intruders. Indeed, fears of outsiders have often been cited as one of the fundamental motives for the creation of cities in the first place.

> To constitute a full urban community a settlement must display a relative predominance of trade-commercial relations with the settlement as a whole displaying the following features: 1. *a fortification*; 2. a market; 3. a court of its own and at least partially autonomous law; 4. a related form of association; 5. at least partial autonomy and autocephaly, thus also an administration by authorities in the election of which the burghers participated (italics added). (Weber [1905] 1962: 88)

Weber does observe that the walled fortification is no longer a prominent feature of the city, as it was in many cities in medieval Europe. Indeed, the city as fortress was not universal even in the past. However, Weber does observe that there has been an important relationship between the city as a political fortress and the civil economic population. Many sociologists observe that the wall as a defining feature of the city gradually declined in importance with the creation of the state. However, in recent years, in the United States we have seen the wall re-emerge in various new forms. In thinking of contemporary walled enclaves, whether they be residential communities, shopping malls, or office parks, the desire for protection is closely associated with economic assets.

In an examination of urban sprawl, Duany, Zyberg-Plater, and Speck (2000) examine the state of contemporary American housing. They note that the continued emphasis on the private realm versus the public realm has ultimately reached its zenith in two form of housing—the *McMansion* and the *gated community*. The McMansion is a huge single-family dwelling, with two, three, or four times the square footage of the ubiquitous four-bedroom colonial. It is often located in large developments consuming much acreage that separates one McMansion from the other. Duany et al. see it as the prime example of "suburban nimbyism": "'I like living here, but I don't want any others like me living here'" (2000:42). Residents of the McMansion epitomize the desire for the separation of themselves from the larger community and are not all that concerned about the ecological impact that this form of housing generates. The irony pointed out by the authors is that these residents don't gain a satisfying private

Gate man checking approaching car at a gated community.

realm and further distance themselves from a gratifying public realm that they may yearn for.

An alternative form of housing that also emphasizes the segregation of the private realm from the public realm is the rapid ascent of *gated communities.* Gated communities have become one of the defining characteristics of edge cities (the sprawling automobile-dependent suburbs of housing developments, shopping malls, and commercial centers located at the intersection of major highways). They are becoming a standard new form of development that increasingly has domi-nated the real-estate market. In 1997, in the United States, there were more than 20,000 gated communities consisting of more than 3 million housing units (Blakely and Snyder 1997). Gated communities are particularly prevalent in California and in the West, the Southwest, and the South and have become a standardized feature of many affluent retirement communities and in many suburban developments. The *South Florida Sun-Sentinel* reports that a national homebuilders association estimates that eight out of ten new communities are gated, and surveys report that as many as eight million people are now living in secured neighborhoods (Allman et al. 2001).

Ed Soja (1996) documents the development of the "edge city" through his discussion of Mission Viejo and other gated communities located in the Orange County–south Los Angeles area. Soja coins the term *exopolis* [the city without] to describe the "non-city-ness" of what others have called "edge cities," "technopoles," "technoburbs," "postsuburbia," "silicon landscapes," and "metroplex." Among the towns that comprise Orange County are Irvine, Anaheim, and Fullerton. Among the theme parks located here are Knott's Berry Farm and Disneyland. Both of these theme parks try to evoke a sense of a traditional idealized America, and both reflect the conservative leanings of their founders. Mission Viejo, built by the Philip Morris conglomerate, is a prototypic community that reflects a specialized residential niche market with a tightly packaged local environment and lifestyle. This includes community proscriptions on the color of one's home, assuring that the exterior landscape reflects the residential theme of the housing "Greek Island, Capri Villa, Uniquely America" (Soja 1992: 115).

The authors of *Fortress America: Gated Communities in the United States,* Edward J. Blakely and Mary Gail Snyder (1997), point out that the gates are denoted as protective barriers of status to residents of prestige communities. Blakely and Snyder have developed a typology of gated communities, which includes "lifestyle communities," "prestige communities," and "security zones." Lifestyle communities are often found in the Sunbelt: California, Arizona, Texas, and Florida. There are three types of lifestyle communities: the retirement commu-nity, the golf and leisure community, and suburban new towns.

Retirement communities are the predominant form of lifestyle communities. These communities are designed for middle- and upper-middle class retirees who seek an all-encompassing environment to meet their recreational and social needs. Sun City and Leisure World are nationwide chains of retirement communities. Another type of retirement community, the golf and leisure community, is designed for the more affluent retirees, and includes the Blackhawk Country Club near

An over-55 gated community built by Toll Brothers located in East Windsor, New Jersey near Princeton University. Toll Brothers is one of the largest real estate developers in the country. Photo by author.

San Francisco and Hilton Head in South Carolina. Suburban new towns, a third type of lifestyle community, are very large, comprising several thousand housing units, and they often incorporate with commercial/industrial activities. A prime example is Irvine Ranch in Irvine, California, which contains both gated and nongated areas. There are an extensive number of gated communities in these new town residential areas. These new towns are not to be confused with the urban village development designed by the new urbanists like Andres Duany, Peter Calthorpe, and others.

The second type, the prestige community, is the fastest growing form of gated community. The gates symbolize prestige and distinction. "The gates are motivated by a desire to project an image, protect current investments, and control housing values" (Blakely and Snyder 1997: 41). These are the enclaves of the "rich and famous," those in the top fifth of the income bracket, and corporate executives.

The third category, the gated security-zone community, is a new type of community developing because of fear of crime and outsiders. There are three classes of security communities—the city perch, the suburban perch, and the barricade perch—called "perches" because it is the residents themselves, not developers, who build the security gates. Neighborhoods have been retrofitted with gates and barriers to limit traffic access and outside threats. The goal effectively creates a barricaded community isolated from its surroundings.

All three broad classifications of gated communities are seen by Blakely and Snyder (1997: 1) as manifestations of a new "fortress mentality" developing in the

United States. The setting of boundaries is a political act. Gated communities determine membership, separating those on the inside from those on the outside. They create and delineate space to facilitate activities that sustain political, economic, and social life. Further, "Using physical space to create social place is a long and deep American tradition" (Blakely and Snyder 1997: 1).

An underlying theme in Blakely and Snyder's analysis of gated communities is that the residents "want control over their homes, their streets, their neighborhoods" (1997: 125). Personal safety and protection of property values are high priorities for choosing a secured gated community. The creation of physical barriers restricting access defines gated communities. The underlying assumption is that crime can be excluded and safety secured if an elaborate security system is developed. Gated communities are designed to fulfill the promise of a crime-free residential area. Critics have argued that they are designed as "high security residential environments in which the predominantly white upper middle-class residents can turn their backs on the growing social and economic problems of the ethnically diverse central cities and retreat behind the walls, protected by security staff, electronic surveillance and 'rapid response' units" (Hannett 1999:247).

Let's first look at whether these gated communities are truly safe. Then, I will address the more important question about their implications for civil society. But, first, are they safe? In a comprehensive survey of more than two-dozen communities in South Florida, the *South Florida Sun-Sentinel* reported that the sense of security of gated communities is often illusionary (Allman 2001). The newspaper compared 14 sets of communities. Each pair consisted of a gated and a non-gated community that were roughly equivalent in terms of size, price range, and location access to major roads. Reporters examined three years of crime statistics, focusing on auto theft, home burglary, vandalism, and reports of suspicious vehicles or persons. They observe that gated entrances, by themselves, while designed to be intimidating, imposing, and impenetrable, do not deter crime. In combination with roving security patrols, visitor sign-ins, and single-access roads, there were significant safety differences. But, there is a price to pay for this security . . . and it's not only financial.

The cost of security can run as high as or higher than $4,000 a year, as is the case in Fort Lauderdale's upscale Bay Colony. Bay Colony consists of 103 homes and is located on the Intracoastal Waterway. Its security includes a gated entrance, at least two guards on duty at all times, a security system that requires all visitors to sign in, and movement restrictions including those for construction vehicles and real-estate agents. In comparison with its counterpart, Riviera Isles, a similar affluent community, there was not a substantial difference in reported crimes. The newspaper notes that despite Bay Colony's security system, a reporter was able to jog past the security gate without being stopped.

Indeed, no matter how elaborate security systems are, they are not foolproof. Reporters were able to breach the security systems of 51 out of 83 gated communities through various forms of subterfuge, including simply walking, jogging, or driving through open gates, or by showing relatively easily attainable newspaper identification badges. A police official observes that one of the best crime deterrents is to have neighbors watch out for each other and call the police when they see something unusual happening. But the privacy character of gated communities often results in many residents not knowing their neighbors or the people employed by them. In contrast, a case in point is a non-gated community in the small town of Lighthouse Point, just north of Pompano Beach. The residents of Lighthouse Point, which is comprised of very expensive single-family houses and less expensive townhouses, keep the crime rate low by relying on their neighbors and the police. A resident conveys the prevalent attitude: "I think we feel more secure because we have our own police and there's a real sense of community. If this were a gated community, we wouldn't have the same character we have" (Allman 2001).

In addition to the financial cost of gated communities, there are social and community costs as well. Gated communities privatize community space as well as individual and family space. Also privatized are many of the larger community's civic responsibilities, including police protection, as well as education, recreation, and entertainment communal services. The goal is the creation of a private sphere that shares little with either the outside community or inside with its own inhabitants.

Duany et al. (2000) observe a prevalent historical pattern of housing developments based on segregation—whether by race, immigration status, or class. Historically, zoning and city planning laws tried to preserve the geographical space of the select. However, the gated community is taking this segregation even further through the invention of "market segment" segregated housing that sells the "concept of exclusivity": *If you live within these gates, you can consider yourself a success* (Duany et al. 2000: 43). Gated communities are socially as well as economically selective.

Gated communities are one manifestation, albeit a most visible and symbolic one, of the increasing division of America by race and economic opportunity. Blakely and Snyder argue that "Gated communities create yet another barrier to interaction among people of different races, cultures, and classes and may add to the problem of building the social networks that form the base for economic and social opportunity" (1997: 153).

The urban critic Mike Davis has reported on the rise of gated communities as part of a larger pattern of systematic withdrawal of the affluent behind defensive barriers and the erosion of public space. As you may recall from our earlier discussion of Davis, the "ecology of fear" and the "militarization of public space" are phrases coined to what he sees as the development of "Fortress Los Angeles" (1992a, 1992b, 1992c). Davis refers to an "ecology of fear" that has determined the ecological zones of contemporary Los Angeles. Davis applies Burgess's concentric zonal model but with a twist. Rather than seeing land patterns based on economic factors, "fear" and an "obsession with security" are the new underlying factors (Davis 1992c). He writes that a "second civil war," which began in the summers of the late 1960s, has been institutionalized into public space. Davis observes,

"The old liberal attempts at social control, which at least tried to balance repression with reform, have been superseded by open social warfare that pits the interests of the middle class against the welfare of the urban poor" (Davis 1992a:155). Architecture, urban planning, and a militarized police force have set out to control public space and criminalize much of the behavior of the poor. The gated community is a prime example of the "fortressing of America."

Suburbs and Morality

The above discussion of race, gated communities, and the spatial race and class segregation of suburbia raises morality concerns on the nature of our society. In 1831, a young French magistrate named Alexis de Tocqueville toured the United States. He contrasted the European approach to civic responsibility with that of the United States. In Europe, to sacrifice on behalf of the multitude was justified in terms of patriotism and honor. In the United States, sacrifices were justified as being in the enlightened self-interest of those who incurred them. "The Americans are fond of explaining almost all the actions of their lives by the principle of self-interest rightly understood; they show with complacency how an enlightened regard for themselves constantly prompts them to assist one another and inclines them willingly to sacrifice a position of their time and property to the welfare of the state" (de Tocqueville cited in Reich 1991: 23–24). That is, an American's sacrifices for the good of the nation and the community were seen as being in the person's own best interests.

The former secretary of labor in the Clinton administration, Robert B. Reich (1991: 24), wonders whether that attitude still prevails: "What if Americans have grown far less dependent on one another, so that sacrifices no longer benefit them personally?" He finds that the evidence seems to indicate that civic virtue is not surviving. Reich (1991) linked the development of a wealthy class to the increased economic disparity between rich and poor. Furthermore, he believes that the wealthy more and more have secluded themselves spatially. This has led to the spatial segregation along class lines of much of the country. This spatial segregation has extended to more use of private facilities, including shopping in exclusive shopping malls, withdrawing children from public education institutions, finding recreation in private clubs, new executive seating areas in professional sports arenas, and living in gated communities with their own security systems. The consequence is the increased segregation of geographical space both in the suburb and in the city and the development of a spatially segregated society based on wealth and class.

Reich observes that in cities, those who are making much more have always effectively separated themselves from those making much less through occupational spatial segregation. Yet in the past, albeit in a very limited and constrained manner, those making more often found themselves interacting in the public sphere. They used the same public parks and streets, and their children interacted in the same geographical areas. Recently, however, there has been a significant trend, associated and concomitant with the increased decrease in governmental support of the public sector, for the "secession of the successful":

> In many cities and towns, the wealthy have in effect withdrawn their dollars from the support of public places and institutions shared by all and dedicated the savings to their own private services . . . Condominiums and the omnipresent residential communities dun their members to undertake work that financially strapped local governments can no longer afford to do well—maintaining roads, mending sidewalks, pruning trees, repairing street lights, cleaning swimming pools, paying for lifeguards and notably, hiring security guards to protect life and property. (Reich cited in McKenzie 1994: 229)

Alan Wolfe (1998), a knowledgeable observer of suburban life, has examined the broader morality of the middle class. He argues that the study of the suburb is an "indispensable symbol" of the changing political and moral outlook of the middle class. The suburb is seen as the site for the withdrawal of middle-class morality from the concerns of the nation. He contrasts the conservative and liberal positions: "When social critics and social scientists write about the battle over middle-class morality America is presumed to be experiencing, their focus unconsciously shifts directly to the suburbs: conservatives find in suburbanization support for the importance they attach to beliefs about property, physical safety, and economic independence, while for liberals, suburbs represent a retreat from the problems of the inner city" (Wolfe 1998: 19).

The push-pull factors of why people live in the suburbs center on the desire to escape the problems of the city and the desire for a better suburban life is seen. Wolfe sees these push-pull factors as being central in the moral debate about the quality of suburban life. "The particular shape and location of the suburb, its relationship to the city, its ethnic and racial composition, its density, the physical design of its houses—all these are held to be pregnant with symbolic significance" (Wolfe 1998: 181–182).

M. P. Baumgartner (1988) has written an interesting study on the impact of the withdrawal of middle-class morality from the concerns of the nation on life in the suburbs. She observes that suburbs have long been analyzed as the site for a lack of neighborliness and involvement with one's neighbors. Baumgartner studied a suburb of New York City noted for its tranquility and social order. She was concerned with how people handled the interpersonal tensions of everyday life as they occurred in their families, neighborhoods, and in public places. Extrapolating from her findings, she discovered that the "moral order of the suburbs" was part of a subculture of avoidance of contact and involvement with strangers, even though these "strangers" were neighbors. Also operating was a strategy of withdrawal from confrontations and conflict. She describes the suburbs as a place of "weak cultural ties" and "moral minimalism." The alleged harmony of the suburbs is a reflection of this non-involvement rather than a result of intensive interactions and involvements. The moral order of the suburbs was a reflection of an emerging and distinctive social environment that was becoming increasingly prevalent.

> People in the suburbs live in a world characterized by nonviolence and nonconfrontation in which civility prevails and disturbances of the peace are uncommon. In this sense, suburbia is a model of social order. The order is not born, however, of conditions widely perceived to generate social harmony. It does not arise from intimacy and connectedness, but rather from some of the very things more often presumed to bring about conflict and violence—transiency, fragmentation, isolation, atomization, and indifference among people. The suburbs lack social cohesion but they are free of strife. (Baumgartner 1988: 134)

Moral minimalism is Baumgartner's term for this phenomenon. The "indifference among people" extends not only to a desire to withdraw from potential social conflict but an indifference and lack of concern to the fate and well-being of others. Weak social ties not only generate weak social control but they also undermine the potential for meaningful patterns of mutual support as well.

> If people in such places cannot be bothered to take action against those who offend them or to engage in conflicts, neither can they be bothered to help those in need. Positive obligations to assist others are thus also minimal where moral minimalism flourishes. (Baumgartner 1988: 131)

"Moral minimalism" operates on both the suburban community level and the national level as well. Baumgartner's findings are an interesting twist on the viewpoint that contemporary society is in a state of collapse of civility with a declining sense of community.

Edge Cities and Urban Sprawl

Accompanying the development of the post-war residential suburb was the development of shopping centers—first strip malls and then enclosed malls. Moving shopping to the suburbs decreased the necessity of going into the downtown areas with their department stores to satisfy shopping needs. The next step was the movement of work from the central cities to the periphery, a movement made possible because the nature of work changed. The industrial and manufacturing centers located in cities were first moved to fringe areas, often in rural communities, away from labor unions, and then outside of the United States entirely into third-world countries with the development of a worldwide globalization economic structure. It was this last development that led a number of social scientists to speculate that the era of the residential suburb was over, replaced by a decentralized metropolitan development that combined, work, residential, and consuming locales. The new names that came into vogue included "post-suburbs," "exopolis," and two terms that became more popular—"technoburbs," coined by Robert Fishman, and "edge cities," so-named by Joel Garreau.

Fishman coined the term *technoburbs* to refer to a peripheral area, which may be as large as a county, that serves as a viable economic unit that is no longer dependent upon the adjacent city. Highway corridors of shopping malls, industrial parks, campus-like office complexes, schools, hospitals, and a wide range of housing types characterize the technoburb. "Technoburbs" were so named because they could function independently from a centralized city due to advances in communication technology. Fishman asserted that this independence was the most significant feature of contemporary suburbia.

> In my view, the most important feature of postwar American postwar development has been the almost simultaneous decentralization of housing, industry, specialized services, and office jobs; the consequent breakaway of the urban periphery from a central city it no longer needs; and the creation of a decentralized environment that nevertheless possesses all the economic and technological dynamism we associate with the city. This phenomenon, as remarkable as it is unique, is not suburbanization but a *new city.* (Fishman 1987: 184)

Joel Garreau (1991) describes this same phenomenon but uses a different term for it—*edge city.* Edge cities are defined as "urban" centers containing corporate headquarters, industrial parks, shopping malls, and the ubiquitous private home. Garreau argued that the factories and the skyscrapers of the city were being replaced by low-rise, glass-enclosed buildings in park-like settings surrounded by parking lots, all within easy distance to highways located in suburban areas. These office complexes reflect the change from a manufacturing economy to a post-industrial, information- and service-oriented economy. Edge cities are geographical areas where people work and live with little or no necessity to travel to cities. Replacing the train and the subway are the automobile and the ribbon of highways that tie the edge city together. Edge cities are seen as becoming new cities, socially, culturally, economically, and politically independent from the central cities in their region.

We can look at post–World War II Los Angeles as a distinctive new prototype. Los Angeles developed a different ecological pattern that in some regards has more of the characteristics of the *technoburb* and edge cities than the metropolitan cities of the Northeast and Midwest. Los Angeles was one of the first cities to develop suburbs that were not simply residential bedroom communities. Both Fishman and Garreau stress the importance of Los Angeles as being the prototype for this new form of suburban development. It was in Los Angeles that office complexes, shopping centers, and industrial parks were intermixed with residential housing to form a new type of suburbia.

Garreau asserts, "Every single American city that is growing is growing in the fashion of Los Angeles" (1991: 3). He sees 16 similar cities within a five-county area in Southern California, with eight more emerging. Garreau classifies edge cities into three major types:

- *uptowns,* are peripheral pre-automobile communities that have subsequently taken on the characteristics of an edge city (Pasadena, California, and Stamford, Connecticut are prime examples);
- *boomers,* the classic edge city that is located at highway intersections and centered by a shopping mall; and
- *greenfields,* the current phenomenon representing urban sprawl that occurs at the intersection of several thousand acres of farmland and is a result of some developer's grand scheme (Irvine, California, and the "Disneyed" world around Orlando, Florida are examples here).

In all, Garreau identifies more than 200 edge cities across the country; not all are confined to the Sunbelt and Western parts of the country. They are also prevalent at the periphery of older metropolitan areas like Washington, D.C., New York City, and Philadelphia. Examples of edge cities are Tyson's Corner, Virginia, outside of Washington D.C.; in the Philadelphia region, there are three edge cities identified by Garreau—King of Prussia and Willow Grove/Warminster, Pennsylvania, and Cherry Hill, New Jersey. In northern New Jersey, outside of New York City, one edge city is identified not by name but by the intersection of two highways, Interstate 287 and Interstate 78 in Bridgewater Township. Classic edge cities in the Sunbelt region include Buckhead, outside of Atlanta, and the Galleria area outside of Houston.

Advances in both technology and telecommunications made the *technoburb* or *edge city* possible. These advances permit urban dispersal since there is less dependence on close urban proximity and face-to-face interactions. In the last 20 years, further advances in communication technology, including mobile phones, fax machines, and the Internet, have made edge cities even more viable. Garreau points out that in edge cities "community" is scarce; when it occurs it's not through propinquity but rather through the use of the telephone, fax, and private mail service—and we can now add through e-mail and the Internet.

An integral factor in the growth of edge cities is the active involvement of local, regional, and national governments in subsidizing them through tax incentives for both residences and businesses and the building of highways. Edge cities are not "natural" developments resulting from ecological or location considerations (Abrahamson 2004). Tyson's Corner, a major edge city located some distance from Washington D.C. in Virginia, become financially viable because of the decision of the federal government to build a beltway bypassing that city. Local roads were also constructed using state funds. The county government in turn passed the necessary rezoning legislation to allow the land formerly occupied by apple orchards to be used for commercial and retail use (Abrahamson 2004). Further, no master plan characterizes edge cities; rather residential developments and office complexes provide recognizable boundaries rather than broad community organizers.

The mixed-land use combining both residence and work sites has proved beneficial to women. Garreau observes that the "empowerment of women" through their increased involvement in the work force has led them away from their entrapment in suburban domesticity:

> Edge cities doubtless would not exist the way they do were it not for one of the truly great employment and demographic shifts in American history: the empowerment of women . . . It is no coincidence that Edge Cities began to flourish nationwide in the 1970s, simultaneous with the rise of women's liberation . . . they were located near the best-educated, most conscientious, most stable workers—underemployed females living in middle-class communities on the fringes of the old urban areas. (Garreau 1991: 111–112)

A recent phenomenon that has captured attention in the early twenty-first century has been the development of *boomburgs*. "Boomburgs" (a play on words following Fishman's term "technoburbs') is the term coined by demographers Robert Lang and Patrick Simmons (2001) to refer to what they see as a new urban form. Boomburgs have populations of 100,000 people or more, but essentially they are massive subdivisions of residential communities that have no central business district. Their unique character is that they are *not* the largest metropolitan area in their region but rather they are massive suburban residential communities whose subdivisions are governed by homeowners associations. Lang and Simmons report that the 2000 census identifies 53 boomburgs, with 43 being located in Arizona, California, Florida, and Texas. Mesa, Arizona, adjacent to Phoenix, is the largest with a population that exceeds 400,000 people. Additional boomburgs that have received national attention include Irving, Texas, outside of Dallas; Henderson, Nevada; outside of Las Vegas; and Westminster, Colorado, outside of Denver. The growth of boomburgs has been spectacular, with most having less than 10,000 people 50 years ago.

Ann Breen and Dick Rigby (2004), in their discussion of boomburgs, report that race is an underlying motivation for their rapid growth. They cite the demographer William Frey, who found that in the 40 fastest-growing rural areas, the population is almost exclusively white. Calvin Beale of the United States Department of Agriculture also observes:

> It's fairly clear to me that a certain amount of the movement into rural areas can fairly be described as white flight. I have rarely heard anyone mention race in the context of talking about this. They talk about getting away from urban crime, drugs, congestion and school problems. But it also means getting away from areas that have significant percentages of blacks, Hispanics and Asians. (quoted in Breen and Rigby 2004:18)

The real-estate activities of mega-developers shed light on the economic factors that propel the housing market. Jan Gertner (2005), in a major cover story in *The New York Times Magazine*, examines what he calls the "house-building industrial complex." He focuses on the activities and viewpoint of one of the major mega-developers, Toll Brothers. Toll Brothers, an upscale housing developer, was one of the first to build what it calls "estate-houses" but what its detractors call "McMansions." This developer, located in the Philadelphia area, has expanded its real-estate activities throughout the northeast and the rest of the country. Toll Brothers has been very active in housing trends in suburban developments including the accelerated development of condominium communities and retirement communities earmarked for those over the age of 55. In addition, Toll Brothers has taken the initiative in building residential communities in urban areas. Toll Brothers plans to build very large condominium complexes on former industrial sites occupied by Maxwell House Coffee on the Hoboken, New Jersey, waterfront across the Hudson River from midtown Manhattan and at other locations in Jersey City and in Manhattan.

Toll Brothers and other mega-developers keep their pulse on the American real-estate market, and their long-range development plans anticipate future housing needs. They monitor demographic trends on which segments of the population will require housing, what type of housing they prefer, and the costs that they are willing to pay. To assure that they can economically benefit, these developers continually purchase land for future housing developments. Toll Brothers controls enough land to build nearly 80,000 houses. And, they are not the biggest developer: K. Hovanian has accumulated enough land to build more than 100,000 houses, and Pulte Homes can build more than 350,000 houses on its sites (Gertner 2005).

For the most part, the land purchased is located further and further from cities—resulting in suburban sprawl—as well as along traffic corridors. In addition, in their quest for land, developers, including Toll Brothers, have purchased properties located in abandoned industrial sites or vacated urban land. In post–World War II suburbia, developers like William Levitt were able to obtain and build housing of 17,000 units on thousand-acre tracts of land. Today, developers are forced to buy smaller parcels of land. This is especially the case in New Jersey, where even 200-acre lots are rarely available. New Jersey is viewed as the first fully "built-out" state in the nation.

The type of housing built on the available land will be a reflection of the wants and desires of the customers. Toll Brothers is known for its high-end, single-family, detached estate houses on large amounts of land. Yet, Toll Brothers has also built high-density condominium complexes, most notably in San Francisco. In responding to critics who feel that "McMansions" are not desirable, as they are impediments to community development, Zvi Barzilay, the president of Toll Brothers, states:

> "There are some buyers who love to live in this kind of environment, because of the dream of socialization and the next-door neighbor," Barzilay said. "But, I think it is only suited for a certain type of buyer and not for others." Most people, he added, would say, "Give me my one acre and I want to have my privacy." (Gertner 2005:81)

Barzilay adds that an additional impediment in building high-density mixed-use development is often the involvement of local government officials. These officials are often reluctant to overturn existing zoning regulations. Barzilay would rather build more housing units on less land, as that would increase his company's profitability as well as for social practicality, but he does not think that building denser developments will become feasible. Jon Gertner (2005) speculates on the future of housing in America. He wonders what happens when "build-out" is achieved: when a state like New Jersey becomes closed to new business or when a city like Los Angeles reaches the San Gabriel Mountains and there are no longer any parcels available to be built on, when even the "boomburgs" are someday built out, what then? Gertner believes that there may be some positive consequences and that the future may not be so dismal. Better usage can be made of remaining acreage or developers may begin the process "to use open lots, transform defunct shopping malls, convert old industrial space . . . ." (Gertner 2005:81).

One of the major problems facing the country is that in the next 50 years the population will grow by 140 million people, and this population has to be housed. The Northeast, itself, may have more than 18 million more people. Such growth demands regional planning. Unfortunately, as Gertner points out, such regional planning is unlikely to happen given the strength of local municipalities and the culture of *NIMBY* (not in my backyard) politics. Local townships, especially in the Northeast, often have more power than counties or states. Bob Toll, of Toll Brothers, pessimistically predicts:

> "That is the answer," Toll says, "but it can't be done, unfortunately. In order for you to take power for zoning and planning and put it in a regional council, you would have to take the power from the township. It'd be the last move you ever made in politics. The larger and more powerful the regional council, Toll says, the better it would be. "You would get something that makes a lot more sense" than the development we're getting today. The $4 million house in an older suburb, in other words. Or the newer (and cheaper) one-acre house in the most remote exurbs. (Gertner 2005:81)

New Urbanism

A contemporary movement in urban planning is to build new towns with neotraditional designs that recapture and preserve positive features of historic small towns. Because these architects draw inspiration and seek architectural ideas from historic towns and villages, they are referred to as neotraditionalists and their work as "the new urbanism." Note, however, that "new urbanism" is a misnomer in that its ideal is the small town or village and not the high-density urban villages described by Herbert Gans (1962a) and others. New urbanism can be seen as a response to the effects of both suburban sprawl and the development of quasi-autonomous "technoburbs" or "edge cities" or "boomburgs."

Technoburbs, edge cities, and boomburgs are post-suburban areas. Characterized by the decentralization of industrial, service, and residential areas, these new areas are relatively autonomous from the metropolitan area. They are highly dependent on the automobile and extensive highway systems and are criticized for isolating people in their homes and in their cars. Advocates of the new urbanism see suburban sprawl as responsible for the loss of community and neighborhoods; they see suburban sprawl as destroying cities, replacing them with what James Howard Kunstler describes as "the geography of nowhere" (Kunstler 1993). New urbanists, like Kunstler, feel that the post–World War II suburbs are "placeless" environments. They find fault with the gasoline and automobile industry, the greediness of developers, and the shortsightedness of civic officials.

A major concern of the new urbanists is the disappearance of public space and the increased development of the privatization of that space. Shopping malls, businesses, and commercial parks have essentially transformed the public space of streets and downtowns into privatization havens controlled by their owners. Only the "right" sorts of people are allowed to use this space. The poor and the homeless are not welcome nor do they have any right to be there. As Palen (1995) has observed, what such sites have gained is safety at the expense of democracy. "In many ways, the edge cities' privatization of public space and activities represents a shift back to the medieval and Renaissance concept of a city as a collection of essentially privately managed places controlled by an oligarchy" (Palen 1995).

The end result was the devastation of the built environment. Peter Katz (1994), a leading proponent of the new urbanism, observes that this underlying philosophy seeks to incorporate the traditional "new town" city planning concepts of 1900–1920 first articulated by Ebenezer Howard's garden-city movement in England, concepts later transferred to the United States in the designs for Radburn, New Jersey, and the Greenbelt cities during the Great Depression. Yet, proponents of new urbanism also recognize that many of the realities of modern life, including the automobile and "big-box" mega-stores, must also be addressed.

New urbanism seeks to channel suburban growth through the creation of small towns and communities in both suburban and urban areas. These communities are designed for residences, shopping, schools, and parks within walking distance of each other. They use pedestrian-friendly architecture and design principles to create vibrant communities. The automobile does not reign supreme. An anchoring idea is to get people out of their cars and to use the sidewalk. Pedestrians become a defining element of the new urbanism.

The physical layout of the community is also designed to heighten social interaction and civic action. New urbanism goes beyond a simple nostalgic return to small-town main streets as a substitute for the strip malls and enclosed malls of suburbia. Rather, it has as its ultimate goal the addressing and correcting of the perceived evils of suburban sprawl, environmental damage, and the loss of community. Highly visible examples of new urbanism communities include Kentlands, Maryland; Seaside, Florida, which was the setting in *The Truman Show*; and Celebration, Florida, the Disney-designed community adjacent to Disneyworld.

The architect Peter Calthorpe is associated with this movement. His ideas seek to incorporate the work of Ebenezer Howard's garden city as a response to suburban sprawl. Calthorpe's solution is the development of "Pedestrian Pockets"— relatively dense residential communities that allow easy walking access to commercial and workplace sites. Greenbelts of permanent agricultural space surround them. The density and integration of pedestrian pockets allow for less dependency on the automobile and the utilization of light-rail transit. Pedestrian Pockets are designed not to be entirely self-sufficient. Rather, each Pocket in a greater region has a specialized emphasis, such as manufacturing, culture, office work, etc., and they are all linked in their totality.

Laguna West, designed by Calthorpe, is a planned community of 800 acres in Sacramento County, California. It is based on Calthorpe's assumption that walking is the preferred means to travel short distances. Laguna West is a community is so designed with a light-rail transportation system as a supplement. Calthorpe himself coins the term "TODS," or transit-oriented developments, to refer to this type of community.

Laguna West is also designed to overcome the over-privatization of suburban developments. Front lawns are kept to a minimum; houses are pushed forward to the front lot lines and are designed with front porches as a "public face" to the street. Cars may be parked on the tree-lined streets but garages are located in back alleys. The overall plan for Laguna West includes five park-centered neighborhoods around a 65-acre artificial lake. Three central causeways run across the lake and converge in a town center with a tree-lined plaza comprised of stores, schools, office buildings, apartments, and townhouses. Calthorpe, in thinking of Laguna West, echoes the sentiments of many who advocate the new urbanism by making a distinction between tradition and nostalgia: "Tradition evolves with time and place while holding strongly to certain formal, cultural, and personal principles. Nostalgia seeks the security of past forms without the inherent principles" (Calthorpe cited in Kunstler 1993: 262).

Calthorpe's Laguna West accepts suburban housing design in its urban plan. Seaside, located in the panhandle area of Florida, is another "new urbanism" community that follows a housing format from "traditional towns." Designed by Andres Duany and Elizabeth Plater-Zyberg, Seaside is compact, covering only 80 acres. The design of the streets—narrow with sharp corners—discourages auto travel and fosters pedestrian and bicycling traffic. Whereas the garden cities of Letchworth and Hampstead Garden in early twentieth-century England used hedges as defining private and public space, Seaside uses white picket fences. Front porches are part of the architectural design of the houses to encourage passersby to interact with porch-sitters.

The new urbanism, however, does not simply want to return to a nostalgic way of life, but rather to a new way of life that would advocate a movement to a diverse new community comprised of people of different racial and class groups who share a common emphasis on the importance of community life. A basic tenet of the new urbanism is a call for affordable housing in an open, pedestrian-oriented neighborhood in which public space is an integral component of neighborhood life. If there is nostalgia to new urbanism it is not a suburban nostalgia characterized by a withdrawal into privacy and seclusion but to urban nostalgia of highly dense mixed land-use, public life, and vitality.

However, the actuality of most new urbanism communities goes counter to the wished-for diversity. Predominantly affluent white residents populate the vast majority of these communities. Douglas Frantz and Catherine Collins (1999) report on their experiences in living with their two children in Disney-built, Celebration, Florida. Celebration is a new urbanism style community built close to Disneyworld near Orlando. Celebration, like the 40 fastest-growing rural communities reported by Frey, is also predominantly white. Frantz and Collins attribute the lack of racial diversity to economic and location factors. Further, they do not have sufficient affordable housing. Frantz and Collins believe that the Disney Corporation abrogated its responsibility by its failure to provide for affordable housing "and ignored the need for a more inclusive vision of new towns in America" (Frantz and Collins 1999:219).

In developing Celebration, the Disney company had created a town that appealed predominantly to white, middle-class Americans, the same segment of the population that grew up with its animated films and made its theme parks such enormous successes. Disney's planners talked about their desire to build a community that could be replicated elsewhere . . . But the company was willing to go only so far, and it was not far enough. Imagine the impact if Disney's Celebration, the subject of intense public and scholarly scrutiny, had provided a showcase for innovative affordable housing as an integral part of its blueprint for a new utopia. As in Levittown fifty years before, it was an opportunity tragically lost. (Frantz and Collins 1999:225)

From Front Porch to Backyard to Front Porch: An Assessment

The new urbanism strives to recognize the insights of Jane Jacobs (1961) on the necessity to ensure that a safe community means face-to-face contact and interaction. In contrast to gated communities, street patterns are designed to enhance the gathering of people, not their isolation.

The architectural historian and critic Vincent Scully, in his investigation of vernacular architecture, which is the architecture of everyday life, observed how architecture often embedded and conserved cultural memory. Scully expressed his views in both his writings (see especially 1969) and his lectures at Yale University. Scully (1988), in his major work, *American Architecture and Urbanism,* is highly critical of suburban sprawl and of the "super-blocks" of Le Corbuserian inspired high-rise towers. Scully was scornful of single-income residential developments, of high-rise business complexes, and large-scale shopping malls surrounded by vast parking lots. He felt that these developments destroyed the diversity of pedestrian-centered neighborhoods. He called for the examination of neighborhoods using those in New Haven as prime examples to see how people used the streets and front porches of their homes to foster a sense of community involvement and neighborhood identification. His ideas had strong impact on two of his students, Elizabeth Plater-Zyberg, and Andres Duany. Based on long interviews with Scully, Plater-Zyberg, and Duany, Michael Dolan (2002) reports how Plater-Zyberg and Duany sought to replicate the positive attributes of community life in their architectural plans for many of their new urbanism projects. "On the streets of New Haven, as they followed Scully's instructions to look at the sidewalks, trees, and porches. Plater-Zyberg and Duany saw what their teacher had intended, and more: a harmonious arrangement of elements, yes, but also a way of living that Americans had forsworn" (Dolan 2002: 273).

The "front porch" became the architectural symbol of the old way of life. Picture in your mind a house on a tree-lined street in a small town on a summer evening in the early years of the twentieth century. On the front porch sits a family, drinking lemonade, watching as people promenade, often stopping to say hello, share conversations . . . James Agee's prose poem, *Knoxville: Summer of 1915*, set to music by Samuel Barber, the bittersweet remembrance of a time gone by, of parents, now long-dead, rocking, seemingly forever, on the front porch, conveys the tone. Now picture the suburban house of the late twentieth century. No front porch, no one on the streets, and the only activity seems to be the occasional car driving by or turning into a driveway with the garage door opening and the car disappearing into the garage.

In his historical study of the American porch, Michael Dolan observes that the front porch was the linkage site for family life, for neighborhood socializing, and for community connection at a time when life had a slower pace. The "walking" community prevailed, and from the front porch one greeted, relaxed, and entertained one's neighbor (Dolan 2002):

> Especially entertainment. With automobiles still few in number, walking was the main means of locomotion, whether to the corner store or the streetcar stop. In the evening, people amused themselves by going out for a stroll or sitting on their porches and watching other people stroll. In bungalow neighborhoods, where economics dictated small lots and shallow setbacks, front porches served as a line of box seats for the passing human show. Anyone who has spent time in the company of Americans of a certain age knows the litany of recollection: the summer nights on the front porch, the conversations of the adults at their end and the uproar of the children at theirs, the rasp and chitter of the bugs, the call-and-response chorus of greeting and counter-greeting exchanged with passersby, the young gentleman caller appraised, the kiss stolen, the last long look into the black sky before turning off the porch light and going to bed. (Dolan 2002: 197–98)

While this account has a nostalgic air, there are some sound elements of truth contained. Houses were built with front porches to foster community involvement as an inherent quality of life. Yet, by the end of World War I and the beginning of the 1920s, and continuing through most of the century, the front porch disappeared as an architectural feature of the house only to make a return by advocates of the new urbanism.

Carter Wiseman (1998) observes that the new urbanism propounds a neotraditional planning view. Front porches were a staple of the early twentieth-century neighborhood where people were less geographically mobile and where relationships among neighbors had the opportunity to flourish. However, with the advent of television and air conditioning and a more fluid population, the front porch lost favor. Wiseman questions whether the architectural return of the front porch would generate that same sense of traditional neighborhood camaraderie. Likewise, the restoration of the alleyway as an architectural feature of these new towns to encourage pedestrian flows may have sentimental appeal. Still it carries the baggage associated in more recent years with trash and muggings (Wiseman 1998).

Reflecting Wiseman's point of view was the experience that builders had with a new suburban development outside of Philadelphia. In a three-part series for *The Philadelphia Inquirer*, Diane Mastrull examined why a "traditional neighborhood development," or TND, has encountered stiff resistance in an upper-class Philadelphia suburb. The idea was for the development of a self-contained community comprising 107 homes, to be called "Woodmont." The designers and builders of Woodmont articulated a "smart growth" concept of suburban design that would create a village with small homes on tiny lots to allow for more open spaces and to create a community. The builders found great resistance from would-be buyers who were trying to escape what they perceived as the intrusive and overly public life of the high-density row-home neighborhoods of Philadelphia.

Wiseman goes on to raise a basic question on the neotraditionalist trend: " . . . why, if the principles on which its advocates were operating were valid, so many of the small towns from which they had derived their design guidelines were suffering" (1998: 380). He finds the explanation in a complex array of social and economic forces. These forces range from societal-wide economic changes that include the decline of industrial and manufacturing jobs, to changes in retail business patterns—from the small mom-and-pop neighborhood stores to the giant merchandise outlets, to the decline of the traditional two-parent single wage earner family, to the emergence of the single-parent household and the two-parent, dual-income family.

Robert Putnam (2000) makes a similar assessment on the factors that have resulted in the decline of civic society. Putnam is a professor of government at Harvard University who has written a provocative book that argues that there has been fundamental changes that have transformed how people relate to one another in American communities. His argument can be summed up by both the figurative as well as the literal title of his book, *Bowling Alone*. Bowling alone evokes an image where social isolationism has replaced group togetherness not only in the failure of people to join bowling leagues but also in people's wariness of social involvements of any sort with neighbors. The usual suspect, television, is joined by the debilitating effects of computers, which together work to separate people from one another and limit interpersonal ties. The fears of personal safety combined with the beliefs of the importance of non-involvement and the ideology of privatism has led to the reduction of neighborhood life and the decline of civic engagement.

All these factors transcend architectural preferences for either front porches or enclosed backyards. Wiseman contends that such towns as Seaside and Celebration, designed by the neotraditionalists, were a "facsimile—not just of a bygone architecture, but of a way of life that had largely vanished by the time their projects began construction" (1998: 381).

17

Social Capital and Healthy Places

Robert Putnam: **Bowling Alone**

The Internet and Virtual Communities

Chicago's 1995 Heat Wave

The Paris Heat Wave

Low Ground, High Ground: New Orleans and Hurricane Katrina 2005

Social capital refers to the social "glue" that holds a community together and provides the structural and interaction resources that enable people to benefit from their association with each other. It refers to the norms and networks that make social cohesion possible and that enable collective action. The term is often used in the context of organizational involvement. It is often seen that involvement in organizations or in social networks has social benefits. Such involvement ("social networking") allows individuals to foster mutual obligations, promote cooperation, and expand social connections for the benefit of all. Social capital promotes social networks, trust, and civil society.

Robert Putnam's (2000) provocative book, *Bowling Alone,* elaborates on the meaning of social capital for American society. He defines social capital in the following way:

> Whereas physical capital refers to physical objects and human capital refers to the properties of individuals, social capital refers to connections among individuals—social networks and the norms of reciprocity and trustworthiness that arises from them. In that sense social capital is closely related to what some have called "civic virtue." The difference is that "social capital" calls attention to the fact that civic virtue is most powerful when embedded in a sense network of reciprocal social relations. A society of many virtuous but isolated individuals is not necessarily rich in social capital. (Putnam 2000: 19)

In recent years sociologists have explored the connection between social capital and the physical and social well-being of residents of communities. This chapter begins with a discussion of the work of Robert Putnam, who is concerned with the nature of social capital, the decline of civic involvement and responsibility, and the implications for communities. It is followed by a discussion of the nature of the Internet and the development of virtual communities. In this chapter I also want to investigate a type of community in which social capital is minimal, with the result that many of its poor and aged residents live in virtual isolation. Our particular focus will be on the impact of two heat waves that occurred first in Chicago in 1995 and then in Paris in 2003 and the devastating effects they had on poor elderly residents in their respective communities. I then turn attention to the impact of Hurricane Katrina on New Orleans and particularly how it had a differential affect on the poor and the rich in that city. This chapter begins with an elaboration on Putnam's ideas on social capital.

Robert Putnam: **Bowling Alone**

Robert Putnam (2000) sees a predominant characteristic of contemporary life as the decline of community involvements, figuratively referred to as *bowling alone,* and the resulting decline of civic society. As discussed in the last chapter, *bowling alone* evokes an image in which social isolationism has replaced group togetherness not only in the failure of people to join bowling leagues but also in people's wariness of social involvements of any sort with neighbors.

Putnam reports that nearly every kind of political, cultural, or recreational activity that involves personal contact—church-going, card playing, dinner parties, neighborhood get-togethers, and even family members having dinner together—has declined in the last 50 years. Activities that have increased involve minimal social interaction, and many are solitary. They include watching television, going to the movies, and playing video games. In recent years, playing home computer games and "surfing the Net" have become increasingly popular.

Putnam believes that the consequence of the increase of solitary activities at the expense of more social undertakings is the shrinking access of "social capital"—the trust and reciprocity with others—that is the reward of communal activity and community sharing. Social capital can be thought of as the social networks and reciprocal norms of social trust that contribute to the functioning of a strong community. The consequence of the decline in social engagement is civic apathy that is ultimately a threat to both civic and personal health.

Putnam places part of the blame on financial pressures, which has resulted in two-income families who have less time available for civic engagement. For example, women's employment often results in less involvement with family, friends, neighbors, and with community organizations like school-parent associations. Suburbanization is partly responsible in that it demands considerable time spent commuting; people live in one suburb, work in another, and shop at malls in a third location. Electronic home entertainment, and particularly television-watching, consume large amounts of time and offer little socially redeeming value.

The American Bowling Congress, Bowling Tournament, Milwaukee, Wisconsin, c. 1905. Through most of the twentieth century, local bowling leagues served as a community activity. Today there are fewer bowling leagues and, as Robert Putnam argues, more people "bowling alone."

The implications of Putnam's analysis has been investigated in a landmark study developed by Putnam and fellow social scientists through a program at Harvard University's John F. Kennedy's School of Government, *The Saguaro Seminar: Civic Engagement in America.* The "Social Capital Community Benchmark" survey was developed to test the underlying supposition of Putnam's work that without adequate supplies of "social capital"—that is, without healthy networks of civic engagement, shared responsibility, and trust within a community—social institutions falter and lose effectiveness. The consequence is that the shortage of civic involvement has critical implications to our social well-being.

The survey was conducted in 40 American communities, large and small, located throughout the United States. Nearly 30,000 individuals were surveyed to assess the level of social capital in the United States. They were interviewed about 11 aspects of social capital, including trust, political engagement, informal socializing, giving and volunteering, faith-based engagement, involvement in association, civic leadership, diversity of friendships, and equality of civic participation. The survey results revealed differences in civic engagement around the country. It provides a baseline that can measure future progress and changes in the relative strengths and areas for improvements in a community's civic behavior.

In Philadelphia, in a followup study, investigators sought to find out the relationship between feelings of community connectedness and neighborliness to the physical and mental well-being of residents. The study was conducted by the Philadelphia Health Management Corporation. As reported in *The Philadelphia Inquirer* (Uhlman 2004), adults who had strong community ties were twice as likely to report good health as compared to their neighbors who reported poor or fair health. Those who had weak community ties were nearly twice as likely to experience extreme stress and be diagnosed with a mental disorder. Allen Glicksman, the research and evaluation director at the Philadelphia Corporation for Aging, who used the data, explains, "It has become crystal clear that health is not just in the individual. You can't separate it from the physical and social environment" (quoted in Uhlman 2004).

These findings support the argument made by Robert Putnam that social connectedness is one of the key determinants of well-being.

> "The more integrated we are with our community, the less likely we are to experience colds, heart attacks, strokes, cancer, depression, and premature death of all sorts. Such protective effects have been confirmed for close family ties, for friendship networks, for participation on social events, and even for simple affiliation with religious and other civic associations. In other words, both *machers* and *schmoozers* enjoy these remarkable health benefits. (Putnam 2000: 326)

The article in *The Philadephia Inquirer* focuses on two poor communities in north Philadelphia. While both communities are near the poverty level, one of them reports a much higher level of civic participation and willingness to help neighbors. It is in this community that, while there are still a lot of health problems, their severity is not as great as in the community that has a lower level of social capital. The community that ranks higher on the level of social capital is also reported to have a larger proportion of pockets of small, clean homes that are in a better state of repair, even though they are surrounded by blocks of deteriorated houses. One of the residents of this community believes that the positive differences lie in the close-connectedness of the residents, that they look after each other. This includes looking out for elderly neighbors who reciprocate by providing soup when others are ill. Neighbors exchange house keys and watch each other's children.

> "It is a close-knit community of people that are still trying to keep the area together . . . And there are more of them than people who don't care. That's why we are surviving." (Grace Garnet quoted in Uhlman 2004)

The Internet and Virtual Communities

The role of the computer and use of the Internet have raised questions about whether these new forms of technology and communication are an enhancement of social capital or a deterrent. Putnam rejects the belief that the Internet holds the promise of developing a viable "virtual" community. Putnam concedes that while

Internet cafés, many located in city downtown centers, provide dual functions. They allow users access to the Internet while at the same time provide a "third" place setting for social interaction within the café.

the Internet makes it possible to be in touch with more people, it has not fostered social and political awareness. It has not led to greater organizational involvement, nor has it stimulated personal action and interaction. Putnam would argue that social capital is primarily generated by face-to-face communal interactions.

Putnam's position discounts the importance of technological advances in communication that have permitted people to interact in ways that overcome long geographic distances. The telephone is a prime example of a technology that has enabled people to converse without face-face physical proximity. Claude S. Fischer (1991) examined how women used the telephone to foster gender-linked social relationships and involvements. He looked at the development of the residential telephone in its first 50 years (1890–1940) to emphasize how the linkage between gender and technology resulted in the usage of the telephone as a "technology of sociability"(Fishcer 1991:137). He observes that women who were housewives were relatively more isolated in their homes than men, who had more opportunities for daily adult contact. The telephone served to keep women in touch with friends and family and to help manage their everyday lives. Women thus developed an "affinity" for the telephone more than men because it provided them with a technology that permitted them to pursue their social activities without necessitating physical presence with others. "Women developed a greater affinity for the residential telephone than men did, because it was more useful to them in overcoming isolation, in performing their network tasks, and in pursuing an activity that they typically both enjoyed more and were better at than men—social interaction" (Fischer 1991:139).

Barry Wellman is a much-cited sociologist who studies social networks. He and his colleagues at the University of Toronto are particularly interested in the investigation of the social uses and developments of the computer and social "networking" over the Internet. Over the years, in studies of the prevalence of virtual communities, Wellman and his associates observed the relative decline in community life on the streets and public places in the Toronto, Ontario, metropolitan area. The absence of visible community life did not, however, mean that community life itself was absence. The residents were involved in community networks enhanced through interaction over the Internet. Wellman's research led to a broader redefinition of the way we conceptualize community life by conceiving it in terms of social networks not bound by geographic space.

Wellman argues that social relations are complex and involve more than physical proximity. He emphasizes the importance of technological innovations that have helped create new ways for people to find social relationships. With Milena Gulia (Wellman and Gulia 1999), Wellman pointed out that a social network can exist among people who do not live in the same neighborhood. The Internet is seen as a communications technology that offers specialized interactions—virtual communities. Wellman and Gulia go beyond the space-bound gemeinschaft community, which can provide support and be a source for companionship, emotional aid, information, services, goods, and money, to point out that one's "gemeinschaft" or "village" could be global. People can develop "villages" and create their own social networks that transcend a given locality (Wellman 1999).

With colleague Keith N. Hampton, Wellman (2004) examined the experiences of the residents of "Netville," a suburban neighborhood with access to some of the most advanced new communications technologies available. Wellman and Hampton are concerned with how this technology affects the amount of contact and support the residents have with members of their distant social networks. They look at relatives and friends who live outside of Netville. "Community" is defined by them as relations that provide a sense of belonging, rather than as a group of people living near each other. Wellman and Hampton (2004) find that through "networking," ties that were "just out of reach" geographically are increased and supported as a result of access to computer-mediated communication. Hampton and Wellman's research suggests that the Internet can provide new opportunities for family and social relationships and engagements with the community. Their research leads to speculation that as the emerging electronic technology becomes more and more part of our everyday life, it may influence the nature of family as well as community relationships in ways that may lead once again to "bowling together."

Paul DiMaggio and his colleagues (2001) provide a summarization of the relationship of the Internet and community. Unlike Putnam, they see no intrinsic effect of the Internet on social interaction and civic participation. They argue that the Internet can intensify already-existing inclinations toward sociability and community involvement. The need still exists to know more about the qualitative character of relationships that develop over the Internet. The long-range effectiveness of virtual communities still needs to be ascertained. Finally, there remains a need to investigate how utilizing the technology provided by the Internet can enhance civic associations, voluntary associations, and social movements.

Chicago's 1995 Heat Wave

Now I would like to elaborate on the connections between community involvement and the well-being of a community's residents by looking at the catastrophic effects of two heat waves—the first occurring in Chicago in 1995 and the other in Paris in 2003. Each provides a vivid illustration of the selective and devastating impact that living in isolation has on local populations.

Chicago's summer heat wave from July 14 to 20 of 1995 killed an excess of more than 700 people than was typical during a hot summer week. High humidity and high ozone levels compounded the heat wave. This heat wave was the worst (deadly) disaster in Chicago's history. By comparison, the Chicago fire of 1871 killed half as many, when it virtually destroyed the downtown of Chicago. Most of the victims of the heat wave were elderly African Americans who lived in the poorest sections of Chicago.

Eric Klinenberg (2002), then a graduate student at the University of Chicago, in a brilliant investigation examined underlying social factors to explain the devastating impact the heat wave had on elderly Chicagoans. Klinenberg looked at housing conditions, city services, government response, racial factors, news coverage, and numerous other aspects of the heat wave and tied them into a broader picture of the decay of urban life. He studied the social impact of living and dying alone and why certain neighborhoods lost more people than others. He explained why an ill-prepared city was unable to handle the mounting number of deaths. Klinenberg continued with an assault on the politics of Chicago, the response of the mayor and those around him, and finished with an insightful look at the media's role and response to the deaths of 739 people.

Klinenberg's "social autopsy" examined the underlying conditions that had such deadly consequences for people virtually living alone in a highly populated area of Chicago. Of particular interest is Klinenberg's comparison of two adjoining neighborhoods, North Lawndale and Little Village. Both neighborhoods had heavy concentrations of poor and elderly people living alone. The basic premise would suggest that they would have similar fates as they confronted the heat wave. But North Lawndale, an African-American neighborhood characterized by a wasteland of abandoned industries, businesses and stores, and dilapidated houses, had ten times the fatality rates of Little Village. Little Village, in contrast, was a Latino community thriving with a very busy commercial thoroughfare crowded with restaurants, stores, and street vendors.

Klinenberg attributes the difference in the fatality rate to the vibrant street life and commercial activities that contribute to a feeling of safety and security in this bustling close-knit Hispanic neighborhood. Further, most of the elderly, even those who lived alone, had ties with family and friends who lived nearby who could look after them. The Catholic church in the community was another source of community involvement and provided additional sources of protection. The sense of community in Little Village gave the elderly residents the incentive (initiative) to venture out of their hot apartments onto the cooler streets and into the air-conditioned establishments found there.

By contrast, North Lawndale had empty lots, abandoned buildings, and streets with few stores. Crime and violence was rampant, and the neighborhood was drug-infested. This menacing neighborhood had few places for seniors to go to escape the suffocating heat of their apartments. The elderly were fearful to go outside, and few had friends or relatives to visit them. The neighborhood churches could not overcome these social problems. Ironically, their apartments, which they saw as their only refuge from the neighborhood, in effect became their prison, and in too many cases they died there.

Klinenberg's place-based analysis is strongly influenced by the ideas of Jane Jacobs (1961). It was Jacobs, as has been noted elsewhere, who argues that it is in communities where there is viable street life with "eyes on the street" that crime is low and people have a feeling of safety. By contrast, the abandoned neighborhood with little street activity is the place where there is a high crime and violence rate. It is in such neighborhoods that a "culture of fear" permeates the community.

Broadening his analysis, Klinenberg explains that North Lawndale did not develop the same type of viable community as Little Village because of the consequences of discriminatory racism. He sees that the ghettoization of blacks in Chicago prevented them from reaping the economic benefits of the urban revitalization that was occurring during this time period. They had no alleviation from the effects of extreme poverty, failed schools, inferior housing, and massive unemployment.

Four underlying conditions are identified that contribute to the vulnerability often experienced by the old and poor and their consequent withdrawal from public life and activities (Klinenberg 2002). The first is the *demographic shift* in which more and more people, and especially older people, are living alone. More people are not marrying and more are separated from their families as a consequence of geographical mobility.

The second is a *cultural condition* described by Barry Glassner's (1999) concept of the "culture of fear," which is a byproduct of the increased violence found in everyday life combined with the culture's emphasis on the value of individual autonomy, privacy, and independence. (Glassner argued that the perception of the poor in a host of different circumstances has influenced a wide range of cultural and behavioral practices.) This culture of fear often results in people becoming housebound, as was the case during the height of Chicago's heat wave when it would have been in people's best interest to leave their hot and poorly ventilated living quarters.

The third factor is the *spatial transformation* of communities with particular emphasis on the degradation, fortification, and elimination of public spaces and the deterioration of public senior housing and housing projects as well as single room occupancy (SRO) dwellings.

And the fourth factor is a *gendered condition,* the tendency for older men, especially those living alone or those with substance abuse problems, to have dissolved or fragmented social and support networks.

Klinenberg places his sociological analysis within the context of the Chicago School paradigm. He observes that the Chicago School focused on the characteristics of distinct communities. The Chicago School's depiction of the city as a "mosaic of social worlds" emphasizes the separation of each area. Park's assertion was that communities "touch but do not interpenetrate" (Park cited in Klinenberg 2002: 12). Klinenberg's emphasis is that the city itself should be analyzed as a "complex social system of integrated institutions that touch and interpenetrate in a variety of ways" (Klinenberg 2002: 22). The Chicago School's ecological and biotic framework focuses on the segmentation of communities and does not emphasize the sources of contact and connections. By so doing, the Chicago School fails to see the consequences of the heat wave and its impact on individuals who were in literal isolation as a consequence of contemporary urban conditions.

> Assessing the social processes and spatial patterns that foster such isolation requires exchanging the Chicago School's biotic vocabulary for describing urban social processes with concepts and categories that recognize the significance of socially engineered inequality and difference. Moreover, it demands a method of investigation capable of comprehending the city as a complex system, where nature, culture, and politics conspire to determine the fate of its inhabitants. (Klinenberg 2002: 22–23)

Klinenberg makes a particularly interesting point that American sociology has been long concerned with the predominance of the characteristics of 'loneliness" and the decline of community. Indeed, Herbert Gans (1997) has reported that five of the six best-selling sociology books in the United States (*The Lonely Crowd, Tally's Corner, Pursuit of Loneliness, Fall of Public Man,* and *Habits of the Heart*) all deal with themes of loneliness and alienation (cited in Klinenberg 2002). [The sixth, *Blaming the Victim,* is not explicitly concerned with issues of the collapse of community, loneliness, or being alone.]

Klinenberg further observes that stemming from beliefs of the Chicago School and Wirth's "urbanism as a way of life," sociologists have been interested in the issue of alienation, loneliness, and isolation as a condition of living in the city. Sociologists have also discovered, as we have observed in this book, that in actuality, for most urban dwellers community life is in fact quite viable either through the persistence of ethnic enclaves (Gans book, *Urban Villagers,* is a prime example) or through the development of new subcultural groups (cf. Fischer 1975: 19).

But Klinenberg makes the key point that sociology's interest in this topic really focuses on a conceptual interest in isolation rather than in "literal" isolation and disconnection. "Instead, sociologists have used the concept of isolation to describe the relationships among rather than within communities, a metaphor that draws upon images of literally isolated individuals and extends it to the neighborhood or group level" (Klinenberg 2002: 251). The study of literal social isolation is seen to be the subject of interest of more specialized researchers in the field of epidemiology, social gerontology, and community psychology. And these researchers often fail to place their analysis in the historical and sociological context that is required.

The Paris Heat Wave

In the summer of 2003, eight years after the almost forgotten heat wave that claimed over 700 deaths in Chicago, a more devastating heat wave was experienced in Europe. This heat wave killed more than 19,000 people, with France hardest hit with nearly 15,000 deaths. Portugal (1,300), the Netherlands (between 1,000 and 1,400), and Italy (at least 1,176) all had more than 1,000 deaths; Great Britain had nearly a thousand; and Belgium (150), Spain (141), and Germany (40) had much lower death figures (Sampson/Associated Press 2003). In France, which experienced the highest death rates, the heat was relentless for nearly a two-week period, from August 5 to 13, reaching suffocating temperatures of up to 104 degrees Fahrenheit. Temperatures were never below 73 degrees Fahrenheit (this low temperature occurred briefly at night in Paris). In France, the majority of the victims were elderly, dying alone at home or in inadequately staffed and overwhelmed hospitals and nursing homes, from heat stroke and dehydration.

In the Chicago heat wave, government officials as well as the media focused on the disaster as a natural consequence of a heat wave. Social factors and city governmental policies were not deemed to be a contributing factor. In France, however, it was a different story. Newspaper stories put the blame either on the abandonment of the elderly by their vacationing children or on inadequate governmental health-service programs. As we shall see in this account, it was a combination of these two major factors that contributed to the death of so many.

Initially, governmental officials in France attributed the high death rate of elderly people to the "natural disaster" of a heat wave and to the "decline in family values" (Hart 2003). Government officials, upon their return from their holidays, took no responsibility for the high death rates and instead put the blame on the victims themselves rather than on their own inactions (Dubois 2003). Hart reports that politicians and the media blamed "families for abandoning their old folks as they took off to beaches and campgrounds" (2003). Hart quotes both the mayor of the city of Amboise, who blamed "young generations that don't want to take care of the elders," and the health minister, who argued that the deaths were a "brutal revelation of a social fracture, of the solitude and isolation of the aged" (Hart 2003).

Soon after the heat wave broke, a 37-page report appeared following an inquiry by France's lower house of Parliament. The report squarely put the blame on the nation's healthcare system (Hauser 2003). A combination of factors was identified. The French lifestyle, which traditionally has defined August as the time for lengthy vacations when families leave their elderly parents to go on holiday, was mentioned. However, of greater importance was a breakdown in communication by France's healthcare system and the absence of a large number of doctors, hospital staff, and many supporting medical personnel, who were also away on the traditional August vacation break. Governmental officials were away at their vacation retreats and did not react to the emerging health emergency quickly enough. In addition, the severe cutbacks in healthcare and other services, such as retirement homes, that France experienced under both the conservative government and the previous Socialist Party government had devastating consequences. Faced with a vast public protest over the inadequacies of the health system, one senior French health official resigned (Associated Press 2003b).

Compounding the social devastation and miserable situation was that morgues and cemeteries were overwhelmed. Those who staffed these facilities, from gravediggers to funeral undertakers, were also on summer holiday. In addition, many priests were similarly on vacation. Bodies were stored in the vast storerooms of a farmers market in Paris or kept in refrigerated tents until burials were once again performed (Doland 2003). The absence of relatives was reflected in the fact that, at one point, several hundred bodies laid unclaimed in Paris morgues. Three weeks after the heat wave subsided, there were still 57 bodies unclaimed (Associated Press 2003b). The health minister, making political capital of this and trying to deflect criticisms, said that this was evidence of "poor family values," and at the funeral of the 57 unclaimed bodies, an aide to French president Jacques Chirac proclaimed that the president wanted to "show the solidarity of the entire nation with the isolated people" (Hart 2003).

An underlying factor that seemed to many to be a major contributor to the high death rate of the Parisian elderly was the nature of city life as experienced by the elderly. The managing directory of the parent company of the largest undertaker funeral services commented: "Among the elderly, there's a lot of anonymity. Paris is a city with a lot of anonymity" (quoted in Tagliabue 2003). The Associated Press picked up on this theme by observing: "Now France is trying to answer painful questions about why so many of its most vulnerable citizens were abandoned" (Associated Press 2003a):

> One tearful young Parisian, Celine Rocquain, said the deaths were testaments to the loneliness of big-city life. In Paris, she said, people often keep to themselves and don't know their neighbors. "Paris is the capital of individualism," said Rocquain, who carried a bouquet of pink lilies. She was distraught that so many elderly people had no one checking in on them. "I think a small gesture could have saved some of them," she said. (Associated Press 2003a)

Low Ground, High Ground: New Orleans and Hurricane Katrina 2005

> "In New Orleans, income and elevation can be correlated on a literary sliding scale; the Garden District on the highest level, Stanley Kowalski in the swamp." (McPhee 2005: 58)

Nowhere is the elevation in New Orleans higher than along the river's natural bank. Underprivileged people live in the lower elevations, and always have.

Hurricane Katrina destroyed much of the poorer areas of New Orleans. Photo courtesy of DeMond Shondell Miller.

The rich—who live by the river—occupy the highest ground. There are two New Orleans: one for the tourists and the affluent, and one for the poor. One New Orleans is the French Quarter and Bourbon Street—the home of the Mardi Gras, of fine food and drink, of music—jazz and zydeco—of Brennans for breakfast—of Café Du Monde and late night/early morning beignets and chicory coffee—of po' boys and crawfish—of the stately mansions of the Garden District—of Audubon Park—of Jackson Square and buggy rides and steamboat river cruises—of the aquarium and of professional football at the Superdome. The other New Orleans—the invisible New Orleans—is for the poor. It is composed primarily of blacks, who account for nearly three-quarters of the total population and who reside in cheap, below-sea-level housing. More than a quarter of the population (28 percent) in New Orleans live in poverty, and nearly all (84 percent) of that poverty population is black.

The spatial segregation was a consequence of long-time decisions by government to straighten the Mississippi channel and to drain marshland to increase the capacities of the Port of New Orleans and to aid oil production. The resulting low-lying areas were increasingly vulnerable to flooding, but here again political and economic factors shaped the decision not to provide the needed improvements to the levee system to counter potential disaster. When Hurricane Katrina struck New Orleans right before Labor Day weekend 2005, the city that survived is the city of the rich and the tourist; the city that was destroyed was the city below sea level—the city of the poor. Also severely impacted were the low-lying coasts of Mississippi and Alabama.

The Associate Press (2005) examined census records of the disaster areas in the three states of Louisiana, Mississippi, and Alabama and found that nearly 25 percent of those living in the hardest-hit areas were below the poverty line, about double the national average. More telling, about 60 percent of the 700,000 people in the three dozen neighborhoods hardest hit were from an ethnic minority. Nationwide, one in three Americans are from a racial minority. This discussion

Tourism was a vital component of the symbolic economy of pre-Katrina New Orleans. The French Quarter largely escaped that city's devastation. Photo by author.

will focus on the impact of the storm on New Orleans, reflecting both media attention and national interest. But although our focus will be on New Orleans, the reality of the destruction of the coastal cities of Mississippi does warrant mention. According to the *New York Times:*

> If the levees had held in New Orleans, the destruction wrought on the Mississippi Gulf Coast by Hurricane Katrina would have been the most astonishing storm story of a generation. Whole towns have been laid flat, thousands of houses washed away, and, statewide, the storm has been blamed for the deaths of 211 people, a toll far higher than those from Hurricanes Andrew, Hugo and Ivan. (Robertson 2005:1)

The sociological concept of *environmental injustice* (*or environmental racism*) aids in the understanding of why Hurricane Katrina was so devastating. Rose Weitz (2005), a professor of sociology at Arizona State University and the chair of the medical sociology section of the American Sociological Association states: "*Environmental injustice* (or *environmental racism*) refers to the disproportionate burden of environmental pollution experienced by disadvantaged groups, including racial/ethnic minorities." She further lists the underlying factors that make environmental injustice possible:

- Political weakness of disadvantaged communities, so they cannot fight against the location of toxic industries or dumps in their neighborhoods.
- Lack of representatives from disadvantaged communities on decision-making bodies (city councils, government regulatory agencies, etc.).
- Regulatory agencies that only weakly enforce existing environmental regulations in disadvantaged communities.
- Extreme poverty and lack of job options, which makes disadvantaged communities welcome even polluting industries that promise to bring jobs.
- Lack of awareness or concern among majority groups regarding the living conditions of disadvantaged groups. (Weitz 2005)

The psychological and sociological traumatic consequences of environmental injustice and racism have been of concern to social scientists. Kai Erikson (1976, 1994, 1998) has been a leading authority on the study of the emotional impact that disasters have on the people in affected communities. He reports on the sociological as well as the psychological damage that the loss of communities has on disaster victims. His classic study *Everything in Its Path* chronicles the events that unfolded after a flood in Buffalo Creek in West Virginia in 1972. The six close-knit poor communities suffered both from the consequences of the flood and from the inefficiency of government experts. Policies designed to help these communities often impeded recovery and did not accommodate the expressed solutions proposed by community residents.

In his later works, Erikson (1994, 1998) focuses on a new source of disasters—"a new species of trouble"—that is an outcome of environmental injustice. His concern is on the policies of large industrial corporations, which pollute, contaminate, and wreck environmental havoc as a byproduct of their quest to maximize profits. The victims are usually the poor and minorities who reside in these communities. In one notable exception, Erikson studied the impact of a gasoline spill in a middle-class community of private homes whose residents were middle-aged or elderly. He observes that the psychological anxieties felt by residents because of the environmental damage included sleeplessness, anger, and other forms of emotional distress and were linked to a sociological malaise caused by the disruptions in their affiliations with their neighbors. Similar to the earlier findings of Marc Fried (1963), who related the "grieving for a lost home" after the destruction of a West End Boston community by urban renewal, Erikson observes that one's physical house, one's "home," is more than the sum of its contents and often becomes an extension of one's sense of self. The pioneer social psychologist Charles H. Cooley captures this in his vivid phrase, the "self as sentiment." Erikson (1976, 1994) finds that a pervasive trauma often goes beyond the physical importance of what has been lost and can haunt people's memories for years to come. Erikson has a pessimistic outlook that the restoration of communities impacted by disasters may often be to the disadvantage of its poor residents as housing often is not provided for them.

Prior to and in the immediate aftermath of Hurricane Katrina, at the local, state, and federal levels government agencies failed to fully anticipate the devastation that could occur. All were fully aware that New Orleans's system of levees was inadequate to protect against anything above a Category 3 hurricane. Yet collectively, there was no pre-hurricane action. More significant was that even *after* the devastation, all three levels of government either failed to act or responded with actions that were clearly inadequate. The flooded areas were home to more than 346,000 people—71 percent of the city's population—and contained more than two-thirds of the city's homes. The reason many give for the high number of people affected is that these were the people with the smallest political capital. The people who lived in the areas most impacted by flooding were more likely to be black, to have more children, to earn less money, and to be less educated than the rest of the city. They were the poor, the weak, the sick, the old, and the very young. The areas of the city with the least amount of flooding included the Uptown/Garden District, Audubon, and Lakeshore—residential areas of the city where the wealthiest lived and where the major universities were located—and the French quarter, which is the main tourist attraction (Constantine, Ericson, and Tse 2005: A15).

The early calls for the evacuation of New Orleans were aimed at those folks who had cars, and those people left the city. Those who remained, the estimated 57,000 households without cars, were poor and soon were the ones who suffered the most. More than a third of the poor population is without cars, and many of them are too poor to use buses even in the wake of a catastrophe. In one of the devastated neighborhoods, the median income is less that $7,500 and only about one in three people had a car (Freedland 2005). In "blaming the victim" remarks, Rick Santorum, the junior senator from Pennsylvania, told a Pittsburgh television station that people who failed to leave should be punished for putting others at risk (cited in Moore 2005: D7). Santorum failed to realize that these poor people—both black and white—did not have the resources to leave. Hundreds of school buses that could have been utilized to aid in the evacuation were left unused and were submerged by flood waters—illustrating not only the lack of systematic evacuation plans but the realization that whatever plans there were never included the utilization of such buses.

The invisibility of the poor in New Orleans was inadvertently expressed by the frequent characterization of them as "refugees" rather than "evacuees." The term *refugees* usually refers to people from a *foreign* country who flee to escape political turmoil. The term *evacuees* refers to people that are removed from a place of danger. *What was the media thinking?* Was the media's misuse of this term a reflection of the view that these poor people are not part of "our" America? Similarly, the media's usage of "looting" as a descriptive caption of images of poor blacks taking food from flooded stores while at the same time writing of whites "finding" food while exhibiting the same behavior speaks to an underlying ideology that has both racial and class-bias overtones.

The image of the United States has without doubt suffered. The question raised globally is, "How could this have happened in the world's richest and most powerful country?" Trudy Rubin (2005: A17), a political analyst for *The Philadelphia Inquirer*, speculates that "If people abroad see our leaders failing to help poor blacks or unable to cope with domestic crises, our model of government becomes less appealing. It no longer stands as a global example for emulation." For Americans, no longer can they think of their country as a country of "haves" without recognition of the ubiquitous presence of "have-nots." This reality was reinforced by the various forms of foreign aid given to this country by past recipients of such aid. No longer can a city like New Orleans project an image of a fantasyland without at the same time conveying a nightmare image.

There is no question that New Orleans will be rebuilt. The question remains, however, *whose* New Orleans will be rebuilt? Lawrence J. Vale and Thomas J. Campanella (2005), in their edited volume on what they call the "resilient" city— modern cities that recover from disasters—observe that the process of post-disaster recovery is a strong indication of the underlying power structure of the society. They go beyond the problem of "disaster management" to focus on what they see as "value-laden questions about equity" (Vale and Campanella 2005a: 12). These include:

- Who sets the priorities for the recovering communities?
- How are the needs of low-income residents valued in relation to the pressing claims of disrupted businesses?
- Who decides what will be rebuilt where, and which voices carry forth the dominant narratives that interpret what transpires?
- Who gets displaced when new facilities are constructed in the name of recovery?
- What roles do nonlocal agencies, national disaster-assistant policies, and inter-national relief organizations have in setting guidelines for reconstruction?
- How can urban leaders overcome the lingering stigma inflicted by their city's victimization?
- What place is there for visionary architecture and long-range planning? (Vale and Campanella 2005: 12–13)

In any discussion on the rebuilding of a city it is essential to also realize that the rebuilding effort transcends the built environment. It must also include rebuilding the lives of the people caught up in the disaster. Not only must these people be psychologically restored but their social networks of family, friends, neighbors, and their communities must once again become viable to their lives.

> Rebuilding cities fundamentally entails reconnecting several familial, social, and religious networks of survivors. Repairing, improving, and reusing the predisaster physical infrastructure are means to reestablishing the human connectivity that such networks fostered. Urban recovery occurs network by network, district by district, not just building by building; it is about reconstructing the myriad social relations embedded in schools, workplaces, childcare arrangements, shops, places of worship, and places of play and recreation. (Vale and Campanella 2005b: 347)

Vale and Campanella conclude that the "*resilient* city is a constructed phenome-non" (2005b: 353). By this they mean that cities that recover from disasters do so in both the literal, physically-built sense, and in the figurative, social, and psychological sense as well. "Urban resiliency is an interpretive framework proposed by local and national leaders and shaped and accepted by citizens in the wake of disaster. However, equitable or unjust, efficient or untenable, that framework serves as the foundation upon which the society builds anew (Vale and Campanella 2005b:353).

The future of New Orleans is now in the hands of the government. Soon it will be in the hands of the "growth machine"—land speculators and investors, real-estate developers, commercial banks, corporate property owners, and politicians. Decisions will be made on how to "rebuild" the city. The poor have been scattered outside New Orleans to nearby cities, including Baton Rouge, Houston, and San Antonio, as well as throughout the south, the southwest, and into the Midwest, and as far away as Pennsylvania and Michigan. No one is sure how many of them will ever return.

> "The people of New Orleans will not go quietly into the night, scattering across this country to become homeless in countless other cities while federal relief funds are funneled into rebuilding casinos, hotels, chemical plants. We will not stand idly by while this disaster is used as an opportunity to replace our homes with newly built mansions and condos in a gentrified New Orleans." (Community Labor United quoted in Klein 2005)

Fearful that the poor would be excluded in future decision-making processes the Community Land United, a coalition of low-income groups in New Orleans, put out the above statement. It sought recognition as a committee made up of evacuees that would provide a voice to FEMA, the Red Cross, and other organizations that may become involved in the rebuilding of the city. Naomi Klein (2005) reports that this coalition fears that the $10.6 billion earmarked for the poor who suffered the most for the rebuilding of their communities may be diverted to other uses. Klein quotes the chairperson of the New Orleans Business Council, Jimmy Reiss, who told *Newsweek* that the council wants "to use this catastrophe as a once-in-an-eon opportunity to change the dynamic" of the city. She notes that the council has long been advocates of low wages, low taxes, and luxury condominiums and hotels. Klein observes that in past years thousands of poor blacks were being displaced at the same time that their music and culture was an integral part of the French Quarter.

Sharon Zukin has noted similar processes in her analyses of contemporary *symbolic economies* where culture has become an important urban economic commodification. New Orleans is dependent on both domestic and international tourism, ranking with New York, San Francisco, and Los Angeles as a popular tourist site. Daniel Libeskind, the architectural planner of the World Trade Center site in New York, sees a similar opportunity to rebuild New Orleans, as occurred in Berlin after World War II. He believes that the cultural heritage of New Orleans provides a great foundation for the rebirth of the city:

> "To work with history doesn't mean to imitate it or make it kitsch, or simply simulate it, but really take the roots of great culture and build upon it. And what could be more creative than jazz? It's the right theme. You can build in a rich way with a variety of voices, yet create an overall structure of harmony." (Quoted in Campbell 2005)

Klein quotes Jordan Flaherty, a New Orleans–based labor organizer, who expresses his concern about the future of New Orleans.

> "For white tourists and businesspeople, New Orleans's reputation means a great place to have a vacation, but don't leave the French Quarter or you'll get shot. Now the developers have their big chance to disperse the obstacle to gentrification— poor people." (Flaherty quoted in Klein 2005)

For sure, the French Quarter and other major tourists areas will be rebuilt, as will the downtown buildings. The port of New Orleans will be rebuilt as well as the oil and natural gas facilities. Housing for the people to serve these industries will be rebuilt. The fear is that if the class, ethnic, and racial diversity of the city's population does not return, then the unique culture of the city will be lost and in its place will be just another theme park. Shirley Laska, director of the Center of Hazards Assessment, Response and Technology at the University of New Orleans, expresses these sentiments:

> The reason the world loves New Orleans is because of its culture, created by the diversity of its people. If you don't find a way to build a New Orleans that sustains that culture, then all you've done is to just build a Disney World. (Laska quoted in Maykuth 2005:A15)

Voicing optimism, Bill Taylor, the owner of Tipitina's, the legendary music club, feels that the art and music and the mystique of New Orleans will be reestablished:

> New Orleans is a frame of mind. There is a tie to that region and that place that is unbreakable. Eventually, when the time is right, New Orleans will be born again. (Taylor quoted in Gray 2005: A7)

John Logan is a sociologist at Brown University. Earlier in his career he, along with Harvey Molotch (Logan and Molotch 1988), developed the concept of the "growth machine." Soon after Hurricane Katrina, Logan was given funds by the National Science Foundation to provide the first in-depth demographic analysis of the impact of Hurricane Katrina. His (2006) study was based on a comparison of maps from the Federal Emergency Management Agency that documented detailed flood and wind damage, with data from the 2000 U.S. census to determine which people and areas were most affected, (Logan 2006).

Logan observes that about 650,000 people, more than a third of the region's population, lived in areas that sustained moderate to catastrophic damage. Logan's study found dramatic social demographic disparity between those who lived in undamaged areas and the people hardest hit. Logan notes that suffering from the storm cut across racial and class lines. However, he reports that "the odds of living in a damaged area were clearly much greater for blacks, renters, and poor people. In these respects the most vulnerable residents turned out also to be at greatest risk" (Logan 2006:7). Logan found that nearly half of the population (48.5 percent) in the damaged areas was African American compared with less than a third (30.9 percent) in undamaged areas. Similar figures applied to those living in rental properties.

Logan argues that decisions not to rebuild in heavily flooded areas would therefore disproportionately affect African American residents. Logan believes that New Orleans is at risk of losing as much as 80 percent of its African American population, who might not return because their neighborhoods would not be rebuilt, because they could not afford the costs of relocation, or because they may have put down roots elsewhere.

Logan's assessment can be seen in the context of the statement of New Orleans's mayor, C. Ray Nagin, who urged that New Orleans remain a "chocolate city" and that "this city will be a majority African American city; it's the way God wants it to be" (Dao 2006). Mayor Nagin's remarks, which he soon thereafter apologized for, were meant to urge African Americans to return to New Orleans and to allay fears that they would not. Logan, addressing Mayor Nagin's comments, is quoted in *The New York Times* as saying: "Certainly Mayor Nagin's comments reflected a concern on the ground about the future of the city. My report shows that there is a basis for that concern." Logan (2006:16) concludes:

> The analysis in this report suggests that if the future city were limited to the population previously living in zones undamaged by Katrina it would risk losing about 50 percent of its white residents but more than 80% of its black population. This is why the continuing question about the hurricane is this: whose city will be rebuilt?

William H. Frey, a demographer at the Brookings Institute, cautions that Logan's projection is "a worst-case scenario that will come about only if these evacuees see that they have no voice in what is going on" (quoted in Dao 2006).

DeMond Shondell Miller and Jason David Rivera (2006), in their analysis of public policy in the aftermath of Hurricane Katrina, see the demographic future of New Orleans in terms of the necessity to rebuild trust in government. They argue that the development of trust in government is essential and that trust can only occur when there is "an inclusive government that gives voice to racially and economically diverse groups that were once politically alienated and marginalized" (Miller and Rivera 2006: 45).

The persisting problems of infrastructure, disinvestment, poverty, and racial inequality are all part of the existing landscape that serves to deepen the ongoing tragedy caused by geographic displacement after the hurricane. Improving the discrepancy in social conditions, which were brought about by the natural disaster, has to be on the agenda in the same way as securing the levees and rebuilding the business infrastructure. Continuing to fail to address the social conditions in the Gulf Coast region will set the stage for another human tragedy, as well as a socially corrosive community (Miller and Rivera 2006: 39).

18

Experiencing World Cities

World Urbanization

Modernization Theory and Global Urbanization

Development Theory: An Alternative Perspective

Cities, the Global Economy, and Inequality

World Cities, World Systems Theory, and the Informational Revolution

Squatter Settlements

Paris: Riots in Suburban Housing Projects

This last chapter of the book deals with modernization processes and the world-wide urban explosion of the last 50 years. My thrust will be on the effect of world urbanization on people as they migrate into the city and on their consequent city lives and experiences. Modernization theory—its strengths and limitations—will be analyzed. Of particular importance will be the development of world systems theory and dependency theory. We will examine the rise of this perspective through an examination of the works of Wallerstein, Harvey, Castells, Walton, Feagin, and Logan and Molotch.

World Urbanization

The last half of the twentieth century saw an urban explosion never seen before in the history of the world. The first urban revolution, which began about 10,000 years ago, saw the origin and development of cities. It was followed nearly 11,800 years later (1800 AD) by the second urban revolution, which was brought about by the Industrial Revolution led by England, France, Germany, and later the United States. Spurred by Western capitalism and by European colonization, the entire world began to feel the impact of industrialization and urbanization. From our current perspective, the beginning of the twenty-first century, we can see the globalization of urbanization patterns that began in earnest after World War II. Indeed, a third urbanization revolution is occurring, one characterized by massive urban growth in non-Western cities, resulting in the urbanization of the entire world.

As was stated in the first chapter of this book, five years after World War II, the list of the 15 largest cities in the world was made up predominately of Western cities, with New York City the largest metropolitan area in the world. Also on that list were London, United Kingdom; Paris, France; Moscow, Russian Federation; Essen, Germany; Chicago, United States of America; Los Angeles, United States of America; Milan, Italy; and Berlin, Germany. Yet by the year 2000, only two United States cities, New York City and Los Angeles, remained on that list, and they ranked third and tenth respectively (United Nations 2004). *No* European city remained on the list. In 1950 only seven cities in the world had populations over 5 million people; in 2000, the number dramatically rose to 48, and nearly three-quarters of them (32) were in less developed nations (Brockerhoff 2000, *Time Almanac 2001).* By the year 2015, the United Nations predicts that 112 cities will have populations over 5 million; the less developed regions will account for 45 of them. In 1950 there were only two cities, New York and Tokyo that had populations over 10 million. In 2003 that number swelled to 20 cities, and the United Nations predicts that by the year 2015, 22 cities will have attained populations of 10 million or more. Of this number, 19 cities will be located in Asia, Africa, and Central and South America (United Nations 2004).

What are the key factors for such urban population growth? Growth is associated with economic, political, social, and environmental global interconnections. Sociologists have begun using the term *postindustrial city* to describe cities anchored in a new economic reality based on global finance and the electronic information superhighway. Multinational corporations that operate globally in, what Saskia Sassen calls, *global cities* control economic production. These new cities, themselves, are not based on production this occurs elsewhere in decentralized areas locally, nationally, and increasingly globally. Sassen defines *global cities* as "cities that are strategic sites in the global economy because of their concentration of command functions and high-level producer-service firms oriented to world markets; more generally, cities with high levels of internationalization in their economy and in their broader social structure" (Sassen 1994: 154). These global cities are the centers of the global economy and are the pushers in the development of international urban centers that are in constant flux. Not only is the global economy fluid but also so is space that is constantly being reutilized for the economic benefit of these corporations.

What are the consequences of this third urban revolution for the post-industrial city? Often, the consequence is that the urban poor suffer greatly. In nineteenth-century European and American cities, industrialization and urbanization often led to inadequate housing, deplorable sanitation systems, unbelievable crowding, and social problems, including high crime rates, juvenile delinquency, and high rates of marital divorce and separation. In addition, the urban infrastructures—sewage, water, transportation, fire, safety protection facilities, and medical care facilities—were inadequate to meets the demands of an exploding urban population. The consequences of rapid urbanization in underdeveloped third world countries are even more severe.

TABLE 18.1 *The 15 Largest Urban Agglomerations Ranked by Population Size*

	1950			1975			2000			2015	
Rank	Agglomeration and Country	Population (millions)	Rank	Agglomeration and Country	Population (millions)	Rank	Agglomeration and Country	Population (millions)	Rank	Agglomeration and Country	Population (millions)
1	New York-Newark, USA	12.338	1	Tokyo, Japan	26.615	1	Tokyo, Japan	34.450	1	Tokyo, Japan	36.214
2	Tokyo, Japan	11.275	2	New York-Newark, USA	15.880	2	Mexico City, Mexico	18.066	2	Mumbai (Bombay), India	22.645
3	London, United Kingdom	8.361	3	Shanghai, China	11.443	3	New York-Newark, USA	17.846	3	Delhi, India	20.946
4	Paris, France	5.424	4	Mexico City, Mexico	10.690	4	São Paulo, Brazil	17.099	4	Mexico City, Mexico	20.647
5	Moscow, Russian Federation	5.356	5	Osaka-Kobe, Japan	9.844	5	Mumbai (Bombay), India	16.086	5	São Paulo, Brazil	19.963
6	Shanghai, China	5.333	6	São Paulo, Brazil	9.614	6	Calcutta, India	13.058	6	New York-Newark, USA	19.717
7	Rhein-Ruhr North, Germany (1)	5.295	7	Buenos Aires, Argentina	9.143	7	Shanghai, China	12.887	7	Dhaka, Bangladesh	17.907
8	Buenos Aires, Argentina	5.041	8	Los Angeles-Long Beach-Santa Ana, USA	8.926	8	Buenos Aires, Argentina	12.583	8	Jakarta, Indonesia	17.498
9	Chicago, USA	4.999	9	Paris, France	8.630	9	Delhi, India	12.441	9	Lagos, Nigeria	17.036
10	Calcutta, India	4.446	10	Beijing, China	8.545	10	Los Angeles-Long Beach-Santa Ana, USA	11.814	10	Calcutta, India	16.798
11	Osaka-Kobe, Japan	4.147	11	Calcutta, India	7.888	11	Osaka-Kobe, Japan	11.165	11	Karachi, Pakistan	16.155
12	Los Angeles-Long Beach-Santa Ana, USA	4.046	12	Moscow, Russian Federation	7.623	12	Jakarta, Indonesia	11.018	12	Buenos Aires, Argentina	14.563
13	Beijing, China	3.913	13	Rio de Janeiro, Brazil	7.557	13	Beijing, China	10.839	13	Cairo, Egypt	13.123
14	Milan, Italy	3.633	14	London, United Kingdom	7.546	14	Rio de Janeiro, Brazil	10.803	14	Los Angeles-Long Beach-Santa Ana, USA	12.904
15	Berlin, Germany	3.337	15	Mumbai (Bombay), India	7.347	15	Cairo, Egypt	10.398	15	Shanghai, China	12.666

Source: United Nations Department of Economic and Social Affairs/Population Division *World Urbanization Prospects: The 2003 Revision.*

The chapter concludes with a look at the urban riots in France in the fall of 2005. These riots in suburban housing projects by poor Arab-French and West African–French descendants of 1960s immigrants is revealing in illustrating the impact of urbanization on, third-world populations in first-world cities. It also provides a very interesting comparison of the impact of Le Corbuserian urban planning ideals in French housing projects, projects that closely resemble those found in the United States.

Modernization Theory and Global Urbanization

Modernization theory was an outgrowth of much of the writings in the late nineteenth century. We have seen how sociologists such as Maine, Tönnies, Durkheim, Marx, and Weber had as their underlying basis the belief in stages and phases of urbanization. The Chicago School of urban ecology in the first half of the twentieth century adhered to these underlying assumptions as well. In the post-war period of the 1950s and 1960s, sociologists broadened their understanding of urbanization through worldwide comparative analysis. The post–World War II period witnessed the rapid dissolution of the colonial empires of the Western industrial societies and the concomitant transformation of what Westerners called "underdeveloped and backward" societies.

In addition, Western societies were also undergoing processes of social change during this time period. Structural functionalism, and particularly its offshoot, modernization theory, became involved in the endeavor to develop cross-cultural and historical analyses of social change. Structural functionalism views every society as a system made up of subsystems, called "institutions"; the major ones are the family, religion, economy, politics, and education. These institutions are intertwined so that a change in one institution, such as the economy, invariably affects other institutions, such as the family and education. Structural functionalism is concerned with the changing functions of institutions such as the family, religion, and education, in light of industrialization and urbanization. Change results as society seeks to restore its equilibrium in the light of institutional changes. Structural functionalism has an implicit evolutionary theme integrated into its concern with functional changes.

Modernization theory combines the conceptual orientation of nineteenth-century evolutionary thought and structural functionalism to elaborate the theoretical relationship between political, economic, and societal development and urbanization. Modernization theories developed from a combination of conceptualizations derived from evolutionary theory and structural functionalism. Modernization theory is concerned with the changes that societies and individuals experience because of industrialization, urbanization, and the development of the nation-state. Modernization theories have been widely used in sociology since World War II. However, the basic conceptual problems of both evolutionary theory and structural functionalism in their handling of social change have also led to similar problems in the development of adequate conceptual tools by the proponents of modernization theory.

The concept of modernization and the theories stemming from it have been the dominating perspective in the analysis of global social change. *Modernization* is a term that refers to processes of change in societies characterized by advanced industrial technology. Science and technology guide societies from traditional, preindustrial social institutions to complex, internally differentiated ones. Modernization is linked with wide ranges of changes in the political, economic, social, and individual spheres—changes such as the movement from tribal or village authority to political parties and civil-service bureaucracies; from illiteracy to educational literacy, which increases economically productive skills; from traditionalistic religions to secularized belief systems; and from ascriptive hierarchical systems to greater social and geographical mobility, resulting in a more achievement-based stratification system. Likewise, the extended family kinship ties lose their pervasiveness, and nuclear families gain in importance (Smelser 1973).

Modernization theorists have attempted to make the development of the Western European and American technological society the model for the comparative analysis of developing countries. Daniel Lerner, in his influential study, *The Passing of Traditional Society: Modernizing the Middle East*, argued, "The same model reappears in virtually all modernizing societies on all continents of the world, regardless of variations in race, color, creed" (1958:46). *Diffusion theory* is the belief that most nations would eventually imitate Western societies by industrializing and urbanizing. In examining urbanization processes in less-developed countries, proponents of modernization theory presumed that urbanization would evolve in a series of stages similar to the phases of growth of nineteenth-century industrial Western cities. They believed that urbanization was tied to industrial and economic growth.

In the 1970s, widespread dissatisfaction with many of the underlying assumptions of modernization theory and its relationship to urbanization patterns manifested itself. Here I will group these criticisms into three major categories. The first questions modernization theory's reliance on an evolutionary model grounded in the notion of progress. Critics believe that it erroneously supports the idea that progress is a more-valued phenomenon than traditional stability and that modern societies—that is, Western industrial societies—are superior to traditional nonindustrial societies. The second questions the belief that modern social systems are without problems. Critics argue that modernization theory fails to see the negative affects of modernization on such institutions as the church, education, and the family. The third questions the "liberating" effects of modernization and the perceived benevolent impact of modernization on less-developed societies and the people within these societies. I will focus on how these criticisms will heighten our understanding of changes in the city in relationship to modernization.

Development Theory: An Alternative Perspective

Proponents of modernization theory assumed that economic development was a path that all nations would follow. Further, they believed that the cultures of the less-developed nations could increasingly come to resemble those of the modernized world.

Modernization theory, while it recognized to some extent that cultural values of non-Western societies might affect the pace of industrialization, argued that it would not affect its inevitability. Modernization theory made the basic assumption that *the* model for development is that which occurred in Western Europe and the United States after the Industrial Revolution. Diffusion theory and the convergence hypothesis, offshoots of modernization theory, predicted that cultural differences would diminish as less-developed countries industrialized. As societies modernized, they would come to resemble one another more and more over time (individual characteristics would converge) and their cultural uniqueness would give way as they began to act and think more like one another and more like the more-developed societies. This prediction by diffusion theory is called the *convergence hypothesis.* The hypothesis is that unique cultural traditions would diminish when less-developed countries achieve a certain level of industrial production, education, and urbanization. Then, these countries' economies would experience a similar sustained economic growth to the industrialized West. This would allow these countries to compete in world markets with the advanced industrial economies. This change would first occur in urban areas and then proceed to the more economically backward rural areas. Accompanying that economic development would be a shift to "modern" attitudes and beliefs and a change in such institutions as family and kinship system.

Dependency theory takes strong exception to these predictions articulated by modernization theory's hypotheses. Further, and more importantly, proponents of dependency theory have changed the focus of the analysis of the impact of industrialization and globalization of the economy. Rather than focus on whether or not there is a convergence to Western models of modernity and family structure, they have focused on the impact of the globalization of the economy on the poor, not only in third-world societies but in industrial ones as well.

In opposition to modernization theory are the more radical "dependency/underdevelopment" approaches, also known as development theory or world system theory. Scholars studying Latin America, including Andre Gunder Frank (1966/ 1995), first put these viewpoints forth. Immanuel Wallerstein (1974) extended the analysis historically and internationally, and his perspective has been called *world system theory.* Frank argued that Western nations modernized by exploiting other nations and that continued exploitation prevents less-developed nations from becoming fully modernized. Economic underdevelopment, according to this view, is not so much an original condition shared by all societies but rather it is created from the outside by more advanced societies. Frank observes, "The now developed countries were never *under*developed, though they may have been *un*developed" (Frank 1966/1995). It was through colonization of other countries that Western nations became developed and non-Western countries became underdeveloped. Using the title of Franks seminal article, Sandeson observes, "Development for some is underdevelopment for others—it is 'the development of underdevelopment'" (1995:135).

Essentially, dependency theory saw that more developed societies have put third-world countries in a state of economic dependency. These less-developed

A parade in New York City protests the impact of globalization on third world nations. Photo by author.

countries are handicapped in their economic development because multinational corporations control their economies, as does the international banking community, which is located in and controlled by the more economically developed societies. Thus, while less-developed countries provide the raw resources and the cheap labor required by economically developed countries, they remain economically weak and exploitable. In essence, dependency theory argues that the development of modern industrial countries is enhanced by and in turn impedes the development of the less-developed countries. Dependency theory would argue that the major barrier to economic development is not the tradition or traditionalism of less-developed countries but their economic domination by others. For broad-based industrialization and urbanization to occur, economic profits must stay in the countries where the profits are earned, so they can be invested and consumed there. As things now stand, the societies that export raw materials remain poor. This is so because the demands for such materials have remained virtually stable because industrial societies have had negligible population growth. In addition, the dependency of the less-developed countries usually prevents them from forming economic coalitions to enhance the economic worth of their products. Therefore, rather than being in economic cooperation with each other, they are often in direct competition.

A final point, and one that is crucial for my analysis, is that dependency theory observes that a dual economic system develops in less-developed countries that make up the third world. In this dual system, one economy is modern and profitable, the one that involves the export of raw materials. However, the export economy does not provide either incentives or resources for modernizing the rest of the society. Unfortunately, the other economy is the one in which most of the population finds itself. Moreover, it is in this economy that poverty is so prevalent.

Cities, the Global Economy, and Inequality

Financial services, marketing, and high technology characterize the modern city's global economy. David A. Smith (1996) has pointed out that urbanization is an integral part of broader patterns of national, social, and economic development. In this context, the case in point is often cities in the core countries such as the United States, Western Europe, Australia, and Japan. All of these countries contain highly educated people who are employable in this type of global economy. In less-developed countries, while there is a similarly educated population, those who do not have the education suffer the economic consequences. In many countries, the disparity between the highly educated and rich, and the poorly educated and poor, are very visible. The *New York Times* columnist Thomas Friedman describes his experience in riding on a train taking him from Cairo to Alexandria, Egypt. On the train were educated Egyptians constantly communicating on their cell phones as they passed fields of barefoot farmers tilling their fields with water buffalo, as their ancient forebears did. Mark Abrahamson, who provides this illustration, remarks, "Inside the train, Friedman concluded, it was AD 2000, but outside the train, it was 2000 BC" (2004:9).

Dependency theory is of particular relevance in its analysis of global inequality on those who are most economically vulnerable—women, children, the elderly, and families living in poverty, especially those in third-world cities. Modernization theory attributes third-world poverty to environmental deficiencies and overpopulation, detrimental traditional customs and values, political unrest, and inadequate technology. Dependency theory, on the other hand, argues that poverty occurs in less-developed countries because of their subservient economic position.

Poverty in the less-developed economic societies tends to be more severe and extensive than in the more advanced economic societies. Lack of adequate food, shelter, and healthcare characterizes much of the everyday life situation of much of the world's poor. The estimate is that about 20 percent of the population—at least 800 million people—in the less-developed countries feels the brunt of the devastating effects of poverty, while some 15 million people, many of them children, die of starvation every year (Macionis 1995). Women are particularly impacted by global poverty. Lynne Brydon and Silvia Chant (1989) in their analysis of women in the third world are critical of modernization theory, and to a lesser extent of dependency theory, for taking essentially "top-down" views of development (1989). In particular, they fault both theories for their failure to examine the place for women as societies undergo change. The failure stems from a lack of realization that women should be analyzed as a social group in their own right. Brydon and Chant state, "Those who suggest that women's status improves with economic development, frequently fail to take into account the widespread structures of patriarchy which keeps women in subordinate positions" (1989: 7).

Patriarchy is the ideology of masculine supremacy, which emphasizes the dominance of males over females in virtually all spheres of life, including politics, economics, education, religion, and the family. Its worldwide pervasiveness is particularly acute in the third world. In third-world countries, women have relatively little political power. Economically, when women's work is not solely relegated to the household, women are still often found in lower echelon jobs, where they work longer hours for less pay than men. Men continue to control land, the principal source of wealth in most third-world countries. Education is a male prerogative, and lacking education, women have fewer economic options. Women's role in religion often is of secondary or little religious importance. In addition, modernization, rather than significantly increasing women's independence, often results in and perpetuates their dependency and subordination. Even the movement to urban centers does not impact on the power of patriarchy.

World Cities, World Systems Theory, and the Informational Revolution

Immanuel Wallerstein has been one of the most influential American sociologists in the development of *world system theory*. In his (1974) *The Modern World System,* and amplified in subsequent publications, Wallerstein (1979, 1984) put forth the idea that stratification exists among nations. Taking both an historical as well as a cross-cultural perspective, he argues that in the nineteenth century, Western Europe established an international economy as nations began their rapid industrial development through the economic exploitation of other nations. Within a short time an international worldwide economic system developed. Wallerstein sees the contemporary world divided into a three-tier system comprising nations differentially placed according to the state of their incorporation into the global capitalist economy. This hierarchy of three major types of nations—core, semiperiphery, and periphery—allows for upward or downward mobility based on the resources and obstacles that characterize their placement in the international system.

Those societies that gained a dominant position developed a diversified economy, modernized, industrialized, and urbanized. Wallerstein referred to them as *core nations*. They include the most industrialized and urbanized nations—United States, Great Britain, Germany, and Japan. Their control over world trade, which is reinforced by international economic agreements, results in a position of dominance. Politically, they exhibit marked governmental stability and have minimal internal class conflict. The high standard of living of their workers assures stability as these workers, in effect, are co-opted by the economic system. Considerable political freedom and individual liberty is extended to the large middle class. The major cities of some of these core nations have been given the status, *global cities* (Sassen 1991), reflecting their importance as international centers for economic, political, and cultural matters. They include New York, Tokyo, and London; all are home to the headquarters of large, transnational corporations and provide extensive financial, technological, and consulting services.

Semiperipheral nations have some development of industry and financial institutions, and can provide raw resources or finished products. Nevertheless, they remain dependent upon the capital and technological resources provided by the core nations. Falling into this category are nations such as Spain and Portugal in Southern Europe; some of the oil-producing nations, such as Brazil and Mexico; some of the Middle Eastern countries, including Saudi Arabia and Kuwait; South Korea and India in Asia; and the sub-Saharan African nations of Nigeria and South Africa. The cities of particular importance in these nations are Madrid (Spain), Lisbon (Portugal), Sao Paolo (Brazil), Riyadh (Saudi Arabia), Seoul (South Korea), Calcutta (India) and Bombay or Mumbai (India). Two Asian cities, Singapore and Hong Kong, are of particular importance to the international economy. China is very rapidly joining this group of nations, although it still has an economy highly dependent upon raw materials.

The third tier of nations, *peripheral nations,* have highly specialized economies usually dominated by a particular raw material such as timber, fiber, or food. Their economy is highly dependent on either semiperipheral nations or core nations. Unlike the core nations, the nations that fall into the peripheral grouping have a low standard of living, class conflict, and political instability. The result is often a repressive government. Most of sub-Saharan Africa, Latin America, and the Caribbean contain peripheral nations. These nations have uneven urbanization and fall under the domination of *primate cities.*

Primate cities are in nations where one city has economic, political, social, and cultural prominence. They are centers of tremendous population growth because they are the centers for industrial and economic activities and political governance. Whatever potential the society has for economic, political, and cultural advancement is located in urban institutions in primate cities. Primate cities tend to attract vast numbers of migrants from rural areas and much smaller urbanized areas. They overwhelm other cities in the country in terms of their size and their importance.

The population found in primate cities accounts, in some cases, for a substantial percentage of the total population of the country. For example, in South America in 1940, prior to the rapid urbanization that occurred in the later half of the twentieth century, two-thirds of the population lived in the rural countryside. By 1990, two-thirds of the population lived in cities, and especially in the primate cities (Short 1996). To cite some examples, Montevideo in Uruguay has a population of 1,341,000 out of 3,399,237, and Buenos Aires in Argentina has a population of 13,047,000 out of 39,144,753. The numerical tale of domination also holds true for Mexico City in Mexico (18,660,000 out of 104,959,594) and Sao Paolo and Rio de Janeiro in Brazil (17,099,000 and 10,803,000, respectively, out of 184,101,109) (World Almanac 2005). In Asia and sub-Saharan Africa, a similar pattern prevails.

Manuel Castells (1989, 1996) has suggested modifications of Wallerstein's schema of stable core, periphery, and semiperiphery countries. Castells argues that because of an informational revolution, the traditional sources of wealth tied to land—agriculture and mining, to trade, and to industrial manufacturing are giving way to wealth accumulated through the creation and manipulation of information.

To illustrate, in the past the richest and most economic influential Americans source of wealth was in resources such as fur—John Jacob Astor—and steel—Andrew Carnegie—or industrial products such as automobiles—Henry Ford. Today, the richest man in America—Bill Gates—has knowledge as his source of wealth. Within a generation, a communications revolution, ushered in with innovative technologies—the mobile phone, the fax, and the Internet—has spurred the creation of new mass-market products in virtually everything that people buy, including automobiles, electronic equipment, clothing, and food.

Castells also observes that *megacities*—cities characterized not only by size but also as centralizing points between extremely high population agglomerates and the global economy. These cities concentrate political, economic, media, and communications activities. Megacities are demographic magnets for the cities and world regions in which they are located. Further, Castells believes that cities in the world that have a population with the skills needed to work with this new information revolution will prosper. These cities are in Southeast Asia, in parts of India and China, and in South America, particularly in Mexico and Argentina (Kleniewski 2006).

Nancy Kleniewski (2006), in her assessment of Castells, believes that he makes three important modifications to world systems theory. His first modification differs most: "The new international division of labor is increasingly organized not along the lines of nations but rather in networks and flows of information" (Kleniewski 2006: 165). Second, from a global perspective, Castells argues that "informational labor" will have greater salience than populations with lower-cost labor, and both forms of labor are superior to labor based on the production of raw resources. "Thus, it follows that education and technology are increasingly important because the type of labor valued by the informational economy is intellectual labor rather than manual labor" (Kleniewski 2006: 165). Third, and finally, some regions of the world where labor is irrelevant to the world economy will themselves become irrelevant and excluded from economic participation in that world economy. Castells sees the sub-Saharan areas as having the potential to become a "fourth world" isolated from the global flow of capital. Kleniewski concludes that Castells "argues that being structurally irrelevant to the world economy is a more threatening position than being dependent upon it" (2006:165).

Squatter Settlements

More than 30 years ago, the geographer Brian J.L. Berry (1973) pointed out that it was in the third-world societies of Latin America, Africa, and Asia where the major thrust of urban growth was occurring. In the previous 50 years, the industrializing societies of the world had increased in urban population from 198 million to approximately 546 million. The urban population of third-world societies had an even higher growth rate, increasing from 69 million to 464 million. Although the third world accounted for only 25 percent of the world's urban population in 1920, it accounted for 51 percent in 1980.

The urban sociologist J. John Palen (2005) points out that Europe and North America saw the process of large-scale urbanization occurring over a hundred year period. In contrast, the process of urban growth in the less-developed countries (LDCs) of the third world is occurring more rapidly and in even greater population numbers in a much smaller span of time. In 1950 there were only two cities in the third world with populations of over 5 million; today there are 26 cities in LDCs with as large, or larger, population, and by the end of the century 46 of the 60 cities in the world with populations over 5 million will be found in LDCs.

Palen further observes that as the world's population increases by 90 million persons each year, 90 percent of this population growth is accountable in the less-developed countries. For example, Mexico City reached a population of 1 million in 1930 and became one of the most populated city in the world with a population of nearly 18 million by the year 2000. Similarly, other third-world cities such as Sao Paolo (24 million), Bombay and Calcutta (16–17 million), and Seoul and Jakarta (14 million) have experienced startling increases in population. In essence, "the so-called population explosion is in actuality an urban population explosion" (Palen 2005:277). Moreover, that urban population explosion is in the third world.

It is important that I emphasize a major variation in the urban growth patterns of third-world societies and industrial societies. The rapid urbanization of the industrial societies of Western Europe and North America occurred at the time when these societies had the highest level of economic development. In contrast, the contemporary accelerated growth occurring in the third world is taking place in the countries with the lowest level of economic development. This urban growth is also occurring in countries with the lowest life expectancy at birth, and with low levels of nutrition, energy consumption, and education. In addition, although third-world urbanization involves greater numbers of people than urbanization did in the industrial societies, the third-world countries have less industrialization. One consequence of this is that many of the population are unemployed or are finding only marginal employment in the cities.

A further striking variation in the third-world urbanization patterns is the development of peripheral settlements, or squatter settlements, around a city, which serve to transform rural societies into urban societies and which account for a substantial percentage of the urban population. Unbridled urbanization in most of the peripheral and semiperipheral nations is occurring without industrialization. The limited technology makes it difficult to provide for and support the mushrooming urban population. Consequently, while these cities have become the center for the economic activities and political governance and the home for much of the affluent populations, there are also vast undeveloped urban poverty areas. For the poor, adequate housing is most often non-existent. The vast majority winds up living in *squatter settlements*.

Squatter settlements are unplanned structures that contain housing often constructed of scrap and corrugated metals and cardboard. No city facilities are provided—no roads, electricity, water or sewage lines, or transportation lines. People illegally settle on land located on the periphery of primate cities that are growing rapidly. It is estimated that nearly 4 million people live in such settlements around Mexico City. The squatter settlements are shantytowns that have sprung up around large cites, largely because of the inability of the governments in those cities to provide adequate housing for the overwhelming influx of migrants. The residents are migrants from rural areas who have banded together and have established squatter settlements by constructing their own houses on land, both publicly and privately owned, usually against the armed opposition of the government. Often these settlements, as in Latin America, disregard urban planning and building regulations; nevertheless, they provide "uniquely satisfactory opportunities for low-income settlers" in that they are built according to the needs of the inhabitants in terms of social and economic urban changes (Turner 1970: 10).

A less pejorative term, *autonomous settlements*, reflects the fact that often these squatter settlements contain so many people, in some cases nearly half the total population of a given city, that the government politically ignores their existence and lets the populace police themselves. The people have to fend for themselves: securing stable water supplies, developing makeshift sanitation systems, constructing roads, and providing fire protection. Often an informal economy develops, with small home-based businesses that include grocery and clothing stores. Other signs of social organization include the presence of neighborhood churches and men's and women's clubs; at times quasi-governmental groups form to petition the city government for municipal services (Castells 1983; World Bank 2003).

Overview of slum neighborhood, Buenos Aires, Argentina. Squatter settlements are a commonplace phenomenon in cities worldwide.

While they do try to meet the needs of their inhabitants, squatter settlements throughout the world—whether they are known as *barriadas* (Mexico), *favellas* (Brazil), *bustees* (India), *kampongs* (Southeast Asia), *bidonvilles*, "tin-can towns" (Africa), *poblaciones* (Chile), or, the most appropriately named, *villas miseria* (Argentina) are cites of crushing poverty and public health crises. Yet as Palen (1992) points out, squatter settlements everywhere function to provide housing and community to those who have the least resources and who have no alternatives.

It has long been observed (Turner 1969, 1970) that squatter settlements vary greatly in terms of permanency and security of tenure settlement and in the financial and social resources of their inhabitants. A correlation exists between the conditions of the settlement and the wealth and income levels of a given society's population. The *bustee* settlements of Old Delhi, India, are among the poorest; whereas the *cuevas barriada* of Lima, Peru, has residents whose income approaches that of the average working-class level. Twenty-five years ago, it was believed that settlements such as those in Peru were transitory phenomena that would eventually evolve into working-class suburban areas. Their state at that time was merely at, or a little above, the poverty level. William Mangin (1960) presented a vivid picture of the *barriardas* around Lima and noted that "Construction activity usually involving family, neighbors, and friends is a constant feature of 'barriada' life and, although water and sewage usually remain critical problems, a livable situation is reached with respect to them" (1960:911–17). The people who inhabit the barriada are portrayed in the following manner:

> The early stereotype held by most middle- and upper-class Peruvians of the barriada dwellers; is illiterate, nonproductive, lawless, recent communistic Indian migrants is still held by many—but is giving way among young architects, politicians, academics, and anthropologists to an equally false picture. Perhaps as an antidote to the first, it paints them as happy, contented, literate, productive, adjusted, politically conservative-forever patriotic citizens. They are, in fact, about like the vast majority of Peruvians, moderately to desperately poor, cynical and trusting of politicians, bishops, outside agitators, and their own local leaders. They are alternately hopeful and despairing about the future of their children and themselves. They love and resent their children and their parents. They are, in short, human beings. (Mangin 1968:56)

By 1986, of Lima, Peru's, four million residents, an estimated one-third lived in these shantytowns, now called *pueblos jovenes*, or young towns (Bissinger 1986). Villa El Salvador, one of the largest of these shantytowns with a population of 300,000, had become a separate political district with its own mayor, 15 years after its illegal founding. While massive poverty still prevails, improvements were everywhere. While streets remain unpaved, there are sandy strips between rows of brick houses in various states of completion, and electricity and drinkable water have become available. The community established medical centers, schools, nurseries, and a sports complex; communal kitchens feed the needy. The progress was so great that Villa El Salvador was nominated for the Nobel Peace Prize in 1986.

Two predominant conceptualizations portray life in the squatter settlements. The first, and more prevalent, emphasizes the chaotic and socially disorganized aspects of the settlement—marital breakdowns, anomie, alienation, poverty, and misery are the lot of the migrant population. The second position takes an opposite stance; it argues that the settlement is able to maintain community organization and family continuity and that the residents have the general ability to adjust to the somewhat overwhelming demands of the potentially debilitating consequences of urban poverty.

As discussed, the social-disorganization approach stems from the intellectual tradition in the social sciences that has developed an ideal-type dichotomization of rural and urban life. The ideal typification of rural life stresses group solidarity and the primacy of personal relationships anchored by familial and kinship bonds. The typification of urban life, on the other hand, sees the development of secondary relationships based on a pragmatic philosophy of looking out for oneself; the absence of viable family and neighborhood relationships, which ultimately leads to social and personal disorganization; the breakdown of personal integration; and crime, delinquency, and individual isolation. A third approach may be most appropriate. Such an approach recognizes the strength of families and individuals to adapt to social misfortunes and economic poverty. This often takes innovative and creative forms. However, the life of quiet desperation, a life without rest or relaxation, is often the everyday reality of people living under poverty.

The account of the experience of Nancy Scheper-Hughes in Brazil provides us with a realistic picture of the plight of the third-world poor. She was a Peace Corps volunteer who came to Alto do Cruziero, a hillside shantytown adjacent to the factiously named town of Bom Jesus de Mata in northeast Brazil in the 1960s, and returned as an anthropologist on and off for the next 25 years. Scheper-Hughes reports that the inhabitants of this shantytown are rural people and are descendants of African slaves. Their diet is at the subsistence level. The central focus of her research is on the everyday violence experienced by the women and children and more specifically on "mother love and child death" (Scheper-Hughes 1992:15).

The high infant mortality rate is an everyday reality; 25 percent of babies succumbed to inadequate diets. What strikes one is the reaction of mothers to apathetic and dying infants. Rather than mourn, the mothers have adopted behavioral patterns that hasten the death of children identified by their mothers as unlikely to survive. *Mortal neglect* is Scheper-Hughes's term for a fatalistic withholding of not only emotional commitments but also of a systematic withholding of nourishment and maternal care.

In essence, the behavior of these mothers can be seen as just as natural as those of mothers who under different political circumstances and situations nurture and protect their children. Politically based distress caused mothers to emotionally protect themselves by refraining from forming attachments to their infants until they are assured that these infants will survive. Emotional detachment takes many forms including not registering children's deaths at the civil registry office and not attending their children's funerals.

The underlying point of Scheper-Hughes account is that the political and social environment creates a situation in which part of learning how to be mothers includes knowing when to let go of a child who shows that he or she wants to die. To not learn this would cause emotional turmoil and grieving that would be devastating. The resulting cultural climate enables the women of the Alto to minimize the individuality of each infant and to become stoic in the face of such high rates of infant mortality. Yet, women know the horrors of their lives. Scheper-Hughes provides one account that summarizes the plight of these women. Black Irene's husband was murdered and then an assassination death squad murdered her oldest son, Nego De.

> "I am three times cursed. My husband was murdered before my own eyes. And I cannot protect my son. The police made me pick over the mutilated bodies in the morgue to find my De. And now I am forced to go on living. I only wish I had the luxury to hang myself. My husband could die. My son could die. But I *cannot die* . . . Don't pity the young men and the infants who have died here on the Alto do Cruziero. Don't waste any tears on them. Pity us . . . Weep for the mothers who are condemned to live." (quoted in Scheper-Hughes 1992:408)

The geographer David Clark (1996), in his assessment of squatter settlements, makes a number of important observations. He notes that they can emerge as vibrant communities with strong forms of social organizations. They provide an important transition destination for many rural migrates into cities, serving as the initial site for assimilation and acculturation. They also provide a source of cheap and accessible labor for urban industries. Many governments realize this and have adopted a more accommodative approach instead of opposing and even demolishing squatter settlements. This accommodative approach includes providing essential services and helping to upgrade housing. Clark states that the granting of legal rights to the land is a crucial component in maximizing the legitimacy of squatter settlements, as that would give residents voting rights and full participation in the economic and political life of the city. This process, when it does occur, has been the principal means of urban growth in many developing countries. Clark concludes, "Whether it can accommodate the expected increases in urban populations in the future and so produce sustainable cities" remains to be seen (1996: 97).

Paris: Riots in Suburban Housing Projects

Unlike the pattern in the United States, in France and most notably in Paris, low-income, high-rise projects dominate the suburban landscape. The projects, built in the mid-1960s, follow Le Corbuserian urban-planning principles: high-rise buildings containing small apartments clustered around lawns and playgrounds, social centers, and stores. Initially, these projects attracted people from surrounding cramped and old tenements around the city or from cramped old housing in the provinces. Later, immigrants from former French colonies in North and West Africa arrived as guest laborers and moved into the projects as well. The initial response was positive; older residents describe feelings of pervasive optimism and hope (Smith 2005d). Soon thereafter, however, in the 1980s, most of the middle-class native French residents moved out, attracted by government sponsored home-buying programs. A more uneducated and destitute immigrant population replaced them. Today these suburban poor are the children and grandchildren of those North African Muslim Arabs and West Africans.

Like American projects, the Parisian housing projects today are the residences of an unemployed, poorly educated population. Many residents live on public assistance, the equivalent of $600 per family with half of that amount paying for subsidized monthly rent of $300. What makes their economic situation more acute is the heavily regulated economy: Those who have jobs are well paid and have high job security, and it is very difficult to fire workers. This regulated economy has made it very difficult for the Arab minority and for West African blacks to break into the labor force, especially in low-skilled jobs. Unemployment in these neighborhoods is double and sometimes triple the national average of 10 percent; income is 40 percent lower (Smith 2005c). "The suburbs have become the French equivalent of America's inner cities" (Smith 2005a: A8).

The French housing projects do not have the same degree of physical disintegration that characterizes many American projects. Smith (2005b) reports that well-maintained green lawns and flowerbeds provide vivid contrasts to the gray concrete. Crime is not as manifest as in the United States; strict gun-control laws make gun-related crimes rare. The family structure remains strong, with generational ties still functioning. However, the younger generations are becoming more and more alienated from the larger society. Like their American counterparts, teenagers exhibit similar cultural manifestations of specialized jargon and distinctive clothing, similar to the baggy-jeans look found in American inner cities. These teenagers, even more marginalized than their parents and grandparents, do not share their cultural values nor are they culturally integrated into the French mainstream culture (Dilanian 2005). Smith makes a similar observation:

> But that tight social fabric is fraying as the second and now third generations of French-born immigrant come of age. On two levels, many young immigrants find themselves questioning where they really belong. They have weaker ties than their parents did to their ancestral countries, but they are also discovering that, contrary to what they have been taught in school, they are not fully French. (Smith 2005b:WK3)

On October 27, 2005, two teenage boys, one of Mauritian origin and the other of Tunisian origin, were electrocuted while attempting to elude the police. Their deaths touched off unrest that reflected long simmering anger against joblessness, inadequate housing, and other forms of discrimination. Riots ensued, first in the Parisian suburbs, then spread to nearly all the other low-income communities of France's 25 main urban areas. Ultimately, 300 cities and towns experienced some form of rioting and violence, the most serious riots and violence in the last 40 years in France. In two weeks, more than 6,000 automobiles were destroyed along with dozens of public and private buildings, and ten police officers were shot and many

A resident of a high-immigration suburban neighborhood in France looks at his car. Gangs of youths torched thousands of cars in the weeks of street violence. The rioting began after the accidental deaths of two youths who hid in an electrical substation to escape a police identity check. The rioting reflected the anger and hostility felt by many residents of these neighborhoods as a consequence of the discrimination and low job opportunities available to them.

more were injured (Landler 2005b). Most of the youths involved in the mayhem were Muslim, although there was little ideological or religious overtones or political agendas. Yet there is a concern that Islamic political radicalism may take hold if alienation and resentment deepen (Smith 2005a, 2005c). There was also fear throughout Western Europe in countries with sizeable Muslim populations that the violence would spread (Landler 2005b; Bernstein 2005).

Craig S. Smith (2005b) notes the similarities between the rioting in France and the rioting that occured in various cities of the United States in the 1960s and in Los Angeles in 1992. All are responses to very high degrees of isolation, especially as experienced by the young. In response to these social protests and urban upheavals, the United States has implemented policies designed to overcome discrimination patterns by providing political and economic opportunities within a context of recognition of cultural diversity, France, however, does not recognize such diversity. France has what some call a "myth of national homogeneity"—a policy of officially ignoring ethnic differences and promoting French identity. There is no formal recognition of ethnic heterogeneity. The consequence of this policy is that there are no policies of affirmative action, leading to what the French and other Europeans call "positive discrimination." Yet, the reality and the dilemma is that these Muslim-Arab-French citizens do face discrimination. A French sociologist highlighted their situation in a study conducted in 2004. Two thousand fictitious resumes with identical qualifications and photos were sent out in response to 258 help-wanted ads. White males with French names received nearly six times as many invitations for job interviews as did males with Arab names (30 percent compared to 6 percent) (cited in Dilanian 2005).

Prior to the riots, the French government chose to deal with this discrimination through providing relatively expensive measures to feed, house, and educate its poor Islamic Arabs and West Africans. However, it did not address the underlying problems of social and political isolation that many felt because of joblessness, discrimination, and geographical isolation in the suburban housing projects. The mayor of a suburb south of Paris that experienced the rioting and violence observes, "We've combined the failure of our integration model with the worst effects of ghettoization, without a social ladder for people to climb" (Manuel Valls quoted in Smith 2005b:WK3).

The government's immediate response was to promise money for community associations and housing renovations and to provide more help for job-seekers. In the face of these riots, French premier Dominique de Villepin has promised to confront discrimination, calling this a "moment of truth" for France:

> "The struggle against all discriminations must become a priority for our national community," he said in a speech to parliament. "They are a reality today for all the inhabitants of troubled neighborhoods when they look for housing, a job or even . . . leisure activities." (Dilanian 2005:A16)

Alain Touraine is an expert of integration in France. He sees the fundamental problem as not of poverty but of underlying deeper problems of segregation. "What we are living through is a general process of rapid reverse integration that is the problem on both sides" (quoted in Smith 2005c:A12). Craig S. Smith concludes that people who live in these neighborhoods have a simpler solution: "pull back the police and help idle people find jobs" (2005d: A12).

References

Abbott, Andrew. 1999. *Department & Discipline: Chicago Sociology at One Hundred.* Chicago: University of Chicago Press.

Abrahamson, Mark. 1980. *Urban Sociology Second Edition.* Englewood Cliffs, New Jersey: Prentice-Hall.

Abrahamson, Mark. 2004. *Global Cities.* New York: Oxford University Press.

Abrahamson, Mark. 2006. *Urban Enclaves: Identity and Place in the World.* 2nd ed. New York: Worth Publishers.

Adams, Robert McC. 1960. "The Origins of Cities." *Scientific American* 203 (September): 143–68.

Adams, Robert McC. 1966. *The Evolution of Urban Society: Early Mesopotamia and Prehispanic Mexico.* Chicago: Aldine.

Adelman, Melvin L. 1986. *A Sporting Time: New York City and the Rise of Modern Athletics, 1820–70.* Urbana and Chicago, IL.: University of Illinois Press.

Ahrens, Robert, Web Bryant, and Bob Laird. 2001. "Flights of Terror Strike Symbols of U.S. Strength." *USA Today* (September 12): 3A.

Allman, John W., Robin Benedick, and Nancy L. Othon. 2001. Special Report: Gated Communities How Safe are They? *South Florida Sun-Sentinel.* February 25, 26, 27.

Anderson, Elijah. 1990. *Streetwise: Race, Class, and Change in an Urban Community.* New Brunswick, NJ: Rutgers University Press.

Anderson, Elijah. 1999. *Code of the Street: Decency, Violence, and the Moral Life of the Inner City.* New York: W. W. Norton.

Anderson, Michael. 1971. *Family Structure in Nineteenth-Century Lancashire.* Cambridge, England: Cambridge University Press.

Anderson, Michael. 1980. *Approaches to the History of the Western Family 1500–1914.* London and Basingstoke: The Macmillan Press Ltd.

Angier, Natalie. 1993. "Bias Against Gay People: Hatred of a Special Kind." *The New York Times* (December 26).

Appleton, Lynn. M. 1995. "The gender regimes in American cities." Pp. 44–59 in Judith A. Garber and Robyne S. Turner (eds.), *Gender in Urban Research.* Thousand Oaks, CA: Sage.

Ariès, Philippe. 1962. *Centuries of Childhood: A Social History of Family Life.* Robert Baldick (trans.). New York: Knopf.

Associated Press. 2003a. "France Buries Forgotten Victims of Heat Wave." *St. Petersburg Times OnLine Tampa Bay* (September 4). wysiwyg:// 48http://www.sptimes.com200...Idandnation/ Franceburies_forgott.sh.

Associated Press. 2003b. "French Official Resigns After Heat Deaths." *abcNews* (August 18). http://abcnews.go.com/wire/World/ap20030818_591.html

Associated Press. 2005. "Money and Motorcars—The Difference Between Safety and Despair." *The Guardian* (September 6). http://www.guardian.co.uk/katrina/story/0,16441,1563533,00.html

Axelrod, Morris. 1956. "Urban Structure and Social Participation." *American Sociological Review* 21:13–18.

Ayres, D. (N.d). *Industrial and Economic Development.* Retrieved April 20, 2005, on the World Wide Web: http://www.millville.nj.com.

Baals, Barbara. 2004. "The Death and Life of Atlantic City." *Temple Times Online Edition* September 16. http://www.temple.edu/temple_times/9-16-04/ simon.html.

Baca Zinn, Maxine. 1994. "Adaptation and Continuity in Mexican-Origin Families." Pp. 64–81 in Ronald L. Taylor (ed.), *Minority Families in the United States: A Multicultural Perspective.* Englewood Cliffs, NJ: Prentice.

Baker, Susan Gonzalez. 1994. "Gender, ethnicity, and homelessness: Accounting for demographic diversity on the streets." *American Behavioral Scientist* 37, 4 (February):476–504.

Baldwin, James. 1961. *Nobody Knows My Name: More Notes of a Native Son.* New York: The Dial Press.

Bartelt, Pearl W., and Mark Hutter. 1977. "Symbolic Interaction Perspective on the Sexual Politics of Etiquette Books." Paper presented at the American Sociological Association Annual Meetings, Chicago, IL (September).

Bartelt, Pearl W., Mark Hutter, and David W. Bartelt. 1986. "Politics and Politesse: Gender Deference and Formal Etiquette." *Studies in Symbolic Interaction* 7, Part A:199–228.

Barth, Gunther Paul. 1980. *City People: The Rise of Modern City Culture in Nineteenth-Century American.* New York: Oxford University Press.

Baumgartner, M.P. 1988. *The Moral Order of a Suburb.* New York: Oxford University Press.

Baxandall, Rosayln Fraad and Elizabeth Ewen. 2000. *Picture Windows: How the Suburbs Happened.* New York: Basic Books.

Bell, Wendell, and Marion D. Boat. 1957. "Urban Neighborhood and Informal Social Behavior." *American Journal of Sociology* 62:391–98.

Bell, Wendell. 1958. "Social Choice, Life Styles and Suburban Residence." Pp. 225–47 in William Dobriner (ed.), *The Suburban Community.* New York: G.P. Putnam's Sons.

Bender, Thomas. 1978. *Community and Social Change in America.* New Brunswick, NJ: Rutgers University Press.

Bender, Thomas. 1982. *Toward an Urban Vision: Ideas and Institutions in Nineteenth Century America.* Baltimore: Johns Hopkins University Press.

Bender, Thomas. 1982. *Toward an Urban Vision: Ideas and Institutions in Nineteenth Century America.* Baltimore, MD: The Johns Hopkins University Press.

Benjamin, Walter. 1995. "Paris: Capital of the Nineteenth Century." Pp. 46–57 in Philip Kasinitz (ed.), *Metropolis: Center and Symbol of our Times.* New York: New York University Press.

Bennett, Martin F. 1992. *Update Hong Kong.* Yarmouth, ME: Intercultural Press.

Benson, Susan Porter. 1986. *Counter Cultures: Saleswomen, Managers, and Customers in American Department Stores, 1890–1940.* Urbana, IL: University of Illinois Press.

Berger, Bennett. 1960. *Working Class Suburb: A Study of Auto Workers in Suburbia.* Berkeley, CA: University of California Press.

Berger, Peter L., 1963. *Invitation to Sociology: A Humanistic Perspective.* Garden City, N.Y.: Doubleday (Anchor Books).

Berger, Peter L. and Thomas Luckmann. 1966. *The Social Construction of Reality.* New York: Doubleday.

Berman, Marshall. 1988. *All That Is Solid Melts into Air: The Experience of Modernity.* New York: Penguin Books.

Berman, Marshall. 1972. "Weird But Brilliant Light on the Way We Live Now." A book review of Erving Goffman's *Relations in Public: Microstudies in Public Order. The New York Times Book Review,* Section 7. (February 27):1,2,10,12,14,16,18.

Berman, Marshall. 1999. "The Lonely Crowd: New York After the War." Pp. 536–41 in Ric Burns and James Sanders, with Lisa Ades (eds.), *New York: An Ilustrated History.* New York: Knopf.

Bernstein, Richard. 2005. "Despite Minor Incidents, Chance of Large-Scale Riots Elsewhere in Europe is Seen as Small." *The New York Times* (November 8):A7.

Berry, Brian J.L. 1973. *The Human Consequences of Urbanization: Divergent Paths in the Urban Experience of the Twentieth Century.* New York: St. Martin's Press.

Berube, Allan. 1981. "Marching to a Different Drummer." *The Advocate* (Oct. 15).

Betts, John Rickards. 1974. *America's Sporting Heritage: 1850–1950.* Reading, MA: Addison-Wesley.

Beveridge, Charles E. and Paul Rocheleau. 1998. *Frederick Law Olmsted: Designing the American Landscape.* Edited and designed by David Larkin. New York: Universe Publishing Company.

Billingsley, Andrew. 1968. *Black Families in White America.* Englewood Cliffs, NJ: Printice-Hall.

Billingsley, Andrew. 1969. "Family Functioning in the Low Income Black Community." *Social Casework* 50:563–72.

Billingsley, Andrew. 1992. *Climbing Jacob's Ladder: The Enduring Legacy of African-American Families.* New York: A Touchstone Book.

Birrell, Susan. 1981. "Sport as Ritual: Interpretations from Durkheim to Goffman." *Social Forces* vol. 60, no.2, 60: 354–76.

Bissinger, H.G. 1986. "Residents of a Lima shantytown improve their lot." *The Philadelphia Inquirer* (August 9).

Bitman, Terry. 2005. "Rowan Pledges $1 Million to Borough." *The Philadelphia Inquirer* (April 28): B1, B4.

Blakely, Edward J. and Mary Gail Snyder. 1997. *Fortress America: Gated Communities in the United States.* Washington, DC: Brookings Institution Press.

Blumberg, Leonard, and Robert R. Bell. 1959. "Urban Migration and Kinship Ties. *Social Problems* 6: 328–33.

Blumer, Herbert. 1969, *Symbolic Interactionism.* Englewood-Cliffs, N.J.: Prentice-Hall.

Boorstin, Daniel J. 1973. *The Americans: The Democratic Experience.* New York: Random House.

Bott, Elizabeth. 1957. *Family and Social Network.* London: Tavistock Publications.

Bowden, Mark. 2001. "Terrorists Strike Symbols of U.S. Culture, Capitalism." *The Philadelphia Inquirer.* (September 12): A4.

Boyer, M. Christine. 1994. *The City of Collective Memory: Its Historical Imagery and Architectural Entertainments.* Cambridge, MA: MIT Press.

Boyer, Paul. 1978. *Urban Masses and Moral Order in America 1820–1920.* Cambridge, MA: Harvard University Press.

Breen, Ann, and Dick Rigby. 2004. *Intown Living: A Different American Dream.* Westport, CT: Praeger.

Briggs, Asa. 1970. *Victorian Cities.* New York: Harper Colophone Books.

Briggs, Asa. 1976. "The Human Aggregate." Pp. 83–104 in H.J. Dyos and Michael Wolff (eds.), *The Victorian City: Images and Realities. Volume 1 Past and Present/Numbers of People.* Boston, MA: Routledge & Kegan Paul.

Brinkhoff, Thomas. 2004. *City Population.* World Wide Web. http://www.citypopulation.de/Accessed June 16, 2004.

Brockerhoff, Martin P. 2000. "An Urbanizing World." *Population Bulletin* (September):55, 3.

Brunn, Stanley D. and Jack F. Williams (eds.). 1993. *Cities of the World: Regional Urban Development.* New York: HarperCollins College Publishers.

Bryden, Lynne and Sylvia Chant. 1989. *Women in the Third World: Gender Issues in Rural and Urban Areas.* New Brunswick, NJ: Rutgers University Press.

Bulmer, Martin. 1984. *The Chicago School of Sociology: Institutionalization, Diversity, and the Rise of Sociological Research.* Chicago, IL: University of Chicago Press.

Bulos, M., and W. Chaker. 1998. "Changing the Home Environment: The Case of Closed Circuit Televison (CCTV) Surveillance," paper delivered at the International Association of People Environment Studies conference, Eindhoven, The Netherlands, July, 1998, cited in Gary Gumpert and Susan J. Drucker. 2001. "Public Boundaries: Privacy and Surveillance in a Technological World." *Communication-Quarterly* vol. 49, no. 2 (Spring):115–29, retrieved on 10/30/2003 from http:/web5.silverplatter.com/webspirs/ showFullRecordContent.

Burgess, Ernest W. 1966. "The growth of the city: An introduction to a research project." Pp. 47–62 in Robert E. Park, Ernest W. Burgess, and Roderick D. McKenzie, *The City.* Chicago: University of Chicago Press. (Originally published, 1925.)

Burling, Stacey, Marie McCullough, and Marian Uhlman. 2001. "Peace of Mind Falls Victim to Mayhem." *The Philadelphia Inquirer* (September 12): A28.

Burns, Ric, and James Sanders, with Lisa Ades. 1999. *New York An Illustrated History.* New York: Alfred A. Knopf.

Burton, Cynthia. 1998. "Sidewalk Bill on Agenda Again." *Philadelphia Inquirer* (June 11) p. R1.

Cadman, S. Parkes. 1916. "Foreward." *The Cathedral of Commerce.* New York: Broadway Park Place Co.

Cahill, Spencer E., and Lyn H. Lofland (eds.). 1994. *Research in Community Sociology: The Community of the Streets,* Supplement 1. Greenwich, CT: JAI Press.

Callow, A. (ed.). 1973. *Urban American History: An Interpretive Reader with Commentaries,* 2nd ed. New York: Oxford University Press.

Calthorpe, Peter. 1994. "The Region." Pp. xi–xvi in Peter Katz (ed.), *The New Urbanism: Toward an Architecture of Community.* New York: McGraw-Hill, Inc.

Camarota, Steven A. 2005. Immigrants at mid-decade: A snapshot of America's foreign-born population in 2005. Center for Immigration Studies *Backgrounder,* December 2005. Retrieved from the Internet June 23, 2006. http://www.cis.org/articles/2005/back1405.html

Cambell, Scott and Susan Fainstein (eds.). 1996. *Readings in Planning Theory.* Cambridge, MA: Blackwell Purblishers.

Campbell, Duncan. 2005. "From the Ruins, An Opportunity for Rebirth: Planners Face Huge Challenge to Rebuild City—But it could Take Years." *The Guardian* (September 2).

Carr, Caleb. 2001. "Americans Don't Understand That Their Heritage is Itself a Threat." *The New York Times Magazine* (September 23): 91–92.

Carter, Gregg Lee. 1975. "Baseball in Saint Louis, 1867–1875: An Historical Case Study in Civic Pride." *Missouri Historical Society Bulletin* 31:253–63.

Castells, Manuel. 1979. *The Urban Question: A Marxist Approach.* Cambridge, MA.: MIT Press.

Castells, Manuel. 1983. *The City and the Grassroots: A Cross Cultural Theory of Urban Social Movements.* Berkeley, CA: University of California Press.

Castells, Manuel. 1989. *The Informational City: Information Technology, Economic Restructuring, and the Urban-Regional Process.* Oxford, UK; Cambridge, MA: Blackwell.

Castells, Manuel. 1996. *The Rise of the Network Society.* Oxford: Blackwell.

Chandler, Terius, and Gerald Fox. 1974. *3000 Years of Urban History.* New York: Academic Press.

Chang, Jeff. 2002. "American Graffiti." *Village Voice,* wysiwyg://79/:http://www.villagevoice.com/issues/0237/chang.

Chang, Te-K'un. 1960. *Archaeology in China*. Toronto: University of Toronto Press.

Chauncey, George. 1994. *Gay New York: Gender, Urban Culture, and the Making of the Gay Male World, 1890–1940*. New York: Basic Books.

Childe, V. Gordon. 1950. "The Urban Revolution." *Town Planning Review*. 21:3–17.

Childe, V. Gordon. 1951. *Man Makes Himself*. New York: American Library, A Mentor Book. Originally published in 1936.

Childe, V. Gordon.1964. *What Happened in History?* Baltimore: Penguin. Originally published in 1942.

Christiansen, Rupert. 1994. *Paris Babylon: The Story of the Paris Commune*. New York: Viking.

Chudacoff, Howard. 1975. *The Evolution of American Urban Society*. Englewood Cliffs, NJ: Prentice-Hall.

Chudacoff, Howard, and Judith E. Smith 2000. *The Evolution of American Urban Society,* Fifth Edition. Englewood Cliffs, NJ: Prentice-Hall.

Chudacoff, Howard P. and Judith E. Smith. 2005. *The Evolution of American Urban Society,* Sixth Edition. Upper Saddle River, NJ: Prentice-Hall.

Clapp, James A. 1984. *The City: A Dictionary of Quotable Thought on Cities and Urban Life*. New Brunswick, NJ: Center for Urban Policy Research, Rutgers University.

Clark, David. 1996. *Urban World/Global City*. London and New York: Routledge.

Clark, Joe. 1998. *Philadelphia Daily News*. "Philly: A Place for Good Wall Hunting: Artists Making Bold Strokes with City's Mural Masterpieces." http://www.nograffiti.com/temp/Wall%20Hunting.html

Cloar, James A. 2005. "Real Life in the New Downtown." *The Downtown Living Tour, September 17–18, 2005*. St. Louis, MO: Downtown St. Louis Partnership.

Cloud, David S., and Neil King. 2001. "Terrorists Destroy World Trade Center, Hit Pentagon in Raid with Hijacked Jets." *The Wall Street Journal.* (September 12): A1, A12.

Cohen, Lizabeth. 2003. *A Consumers' Republic: The Politics of Postwar Consumption in Postwar America*. New York: Knopf.

Cohen, Morris R. 1919. "Baseball." *The Dial*. 47 (July 26): 57–58.

Cohen, Stanley. 1990. *Dodgers! The First 100 Years*. New York: Carol Publishing Group, A Birch Lane Press Book.

Cohen-Solal, Annie. 2001. *Painting American: The Rise of American Artists Paris 1867—New York 1948*.

Colton, Timothy J. 1995. *Moscow: Governing the Socialist Metropolis*. Cambridge, Mass.: Belknap Press of Harvard University Press.

Constantine, David, Matthew Ericson, and Archie Tse. 2005. "The Neighborhoods That Were Hit the Hardest and Those that Weren't." *The New York Times* (September 12):A15.

Coon, Carleton S. 1962. *The History of Man from the First Human to Primitive Culture and Beyond,* 2nd ed. London: Cape.

Cortes, Carlos E. 1980. "Mexicans." Pp. 697–719 in Stephen Thernstrom (ed.), *Harvard Encyclopedia of American Ethnic Groups*. Cambridge, MA: The Belknap Press of Harvard University Press.

Coser, Lewis A. 1977. *Masters of Sociological Thought: Ideas in Historical and Social Context*. Second edition. New York: Harcourt, Brace and Jovanovich.

Crawford, Margaret. 1992. "The World in a Shopping Mall." Pp. 3–30 in Michael Sorkin (ed.), *Variations on a Theme Park: The New American City and the End of Public Space*. New York: Hill and Wang, The Noonday Press.

Curtis, William J. R. 1996. *Modern Architecture Since 190,* 3rd ed. London: Phaidon.

Cowan, Ruth Schwartz. 1983. *More Work for Mother: The Ironies of Household Technology from the Open Hearth to the Microwave*. New York: Basic Books.

Dal Co, Francesco. 1980. "From Parks to the Region: Progressive Ideology and the Reform of the American City." Pp. 143–291 in Girio Ciucci, Francesco Dal Co, Mario Manieri-Elia, and Manfredo Tafuri (eds.), *The American City From the Civil War to the New Deal*. London: Granada.

Daniel, Glyn. 1968. *The First Civilizations: The Archaeology of Their Origins*. New York: Thomas Y. Crowell.

Dao, James. 2006. "Study Says 80% of New Orleans Blacks May Not Return." *The New York Times.* (January 27).

Davidoff, Lenore, 1975. *The Best Circles: Women and Society in Victorian England*. Totowa, NJ: Rowman & Littlefield.

Davis, Kingsley. 1955. "The Origin and Growth of Urbanization in the World." *American Journal of Sociology* 60(March):429–37.

Davis, Mike. 1990. *City of Quartz: Excavating the Future in Los Angeles*. New York: Verso. Reprinted 1992, Random House, Vintage Books.

Davis, Mike. 1992a. "Fortress Los Angeles: The Militarization of Urban Space." Pg. 154–80 in Michael Sorkin (ed.), *Variations on a Theme Park: The New American City and the End of Public Space*. New York: Hill and Wang, The Noonday Press.

Davis, Mike. 1992b. "Beyond Blade Runner: Urban Control the Ecology of Fear." *Open Magazine Pamphlet, No. 23*. Westfield, NJ: Open Media.

Davis, Mike. 1998. *Ecology of Fear: Los Angeles and the Imagination of Disaster.* New York: Metropolitan Books.

Dear, Michael, and Steven Flusty. 1998. "Postmodern Urbanism." *Annals, Association of American Geographers,* 88 (1): 50–72.

Dear, Michael. 2002. "Los Angeles and the Chicago School: Invitation to a Debate." *City and Community,* vol. 1, no. 1 (March):5–32.

de Coulanges, Fustel. 1956/1864. *The Ancient City: A Study on the Religion, Laws, and Institutions of Greece and Rome.* Garden City, NY: Doubleday.

Demas, Corinne. 2000. *Eleven Stories High: Growing Up in Stuyvesant Town, 1948–1968.* Albany, NY: State University of New York Press.

D'Emilio, John. 1983a. "Capitalism and Gay Identity." Pp. 100–113 in Ann Snitow, Christine Stansell, and Sharon Thompson (eds.), *Powers of Desire: The Politics of Sexuality.* New York: Monthly Review Press.

D'Emilio, J. 1983b. *Sexual Politics, Sexual Communities.* Chicago: University of Chicago Press.

d'Eramo, Marco. 2003. *The Pig and the Skyscraper: Chicago: A History of Our Future.* London, New York: Verso.

DeEugenio, Esther. 2006. "The history of Glassboro, New Jersey." Retrieved from the Internet June 23, 2006. from the Rowan University website. http://www.rowan.edu/subpages/about/area/glassboro_history/

Dilanian, Ken. 2005. "Riots Strike Deep at a French Ideal: "The Myth of National Homogeneity." *The Philadelphia Inquirer* (November 9):A1, A16.

di Leonardo, Micaela. 1992. "The Female World of Cards and Holidays: Women, Families, and the Work of Kinship." Pp. 246–61 in Barrie Thorne (ed.) with Marilyn Yalom, *Rethinking the Family: Some Feminist Questions.* Revised edition. Boston, MA: Northeastern University Press. First published in *Signs: Journal of Women in Culture and Society.* 1987:12(3).

Di Maggio, Paul, P. Hargittai, E. Neuman, W.R., & J.P. Robinson. 2001. "Social Implications of the Internet. *Annual Review of Sociology* 27:307–36.

Dinnerstein, Leonard, and David M. Reamers. 1975. *Ethnic Americans: A History of Immigration and Assimilation.* New York: Dodd, Mead.

Dinnerstein, Leonard, Roger L. Nichols, and David M. Reimers. 2003. *Natives and Strangers: A Multicultural History of Americans.* 4th ed. New York: Oxford University Press.

Distel, Anne, et al. 1995. *Gustave Caillebotte: Urban Impressionist.* New York: Abbeville Press Publishers.

Dolan, Michael. 2002. *The American Porch: An Informal History of an Informal Place.* Guilford, CT: The Lyons Press.

Doland, Angela. 2003. "French Heat Wave Overloads Cemeteries." *net127: a scrapbook of words and images* (August 15): Associated Press. http://www.net127.com/archives/000873.html

Domosh, Mona, and Joni Seager. 2001. *Putting Women in Place: Feminist Geographers Make Sense of the World.* New York: The Guilford Press.

Donovan. Frances. 1929. *The Saleslady.* Chicago, IL: University of Chicago Press.

Donzelet, Jacques. 1979. *The Policing of Families.* New York: Pantheon.

Dubois, Francis. 2003. "France: Heat Wave Catastrophe Exposes Health Care Crisis." *World Socialist Web Site* (September 9). http://wsws.org/articles/2003/sep2003/fran-s09_prn.shtml.

Downs, Peter. 2003. "A catalyst for downtown redevelopment." *St. Louis Commerce Magazine* (March). http://www.stlcommercemagazine.com/archives/March2003/hospitality.html

Drake, St. Clair and Horace R. Cayton. 1945. *Black Metropolis, A Study of Negro Life in a Northern City.* New York: Harcourt, Brace and Company.

Duany, Andres, Elizabeth Plater-Zyberk and Jeff Speck. 2000. *Suburban Nation: The rise of Sprawl and the Decline of the American Dream.* New York: North Point Press.

Dulles, Foster Rhea. 1965. *A History of Recreation: America Learns to Play, Second Edition.* New York: Appleton-Century-Crofts.

Duncan, Hugh Dalziel. 1965. *Culture and Desire.* Totowa, NJ: Bedminster Press.

Duncan, Otis Dudley. 1982. "From Social System to Ecosystem." Pp. 123–28 in George Theodorson (ed.), *Urban Patterns: Studies in Human Ecology.* University Park, Pa.: Pennsylvania State University Press. Originally printed in *Sociological Inquiry,* 31 (1961):40–49.

Duneier, Mitchell. 1999. *Sidewalk.* New York: Farrar, Straus and Giroux.

Dunitz, Robin J. 1993. *Street Gallery: Guide to 1000 Los Angeles Murals.* Los Angeles, CA: RJD Enterprises.

Dunitz, Robin J., and James Prigoff. 1997. *Painting the Town: Murals of California.* Los Angeles, CA: RJD Enterprises.

Dunlap, David W. 2001. "A Birth of Great Praise, A Death Beyond Words For a Symbol of Strength." *The New York Times* (September 13, 2001): A14.

Dupre, Judith. 1996. *Skyscrapers.* New York: Black Dog & Leventhal Publishers.

Durant, John, and Otto Bettman. 1965. *Pictorial History of American Sports: From Colonial Times to the Present, Revised Edition*. New York: A.S. Barnes.

Durkheim, Emile. 1915/1965. *The Elementary Forms of the Religious Life*. New York: Free Press.

Durkheim, Emile. 1951. *Suicide: A Study in Sociology*. John A. Spalding and George Simpson (trans.). New York: The Free Press of Glencoe. (Originally published, 1897).

Durkheim, Emile. 1964. *The Division of Labor in Society*. George Simpson (trans.). New York: The Free Press. (Originally published, 1893).

Economist. 1996. "Will Crime Wave Goodbye?" January 6, 19–20.

Edwards, G. Franklin (ed.) 1968. *E. Franklin Frazier on Race Relations: Selected Writings*. Chicago, IL: University of Chicago Press.

Eichler, Lillian. 1922. *Book of Etiquette, Vol. 2*. Garden City, NY: Doubleday.

Elliot, David. 1986. *New Worlds: Russian Art and Society 1900–1937*. New York: Rizzoli.

Engels, Friedrich. 1999. *The Conditions of the Working Class in England*. Translated by Florence Kelley-Wischnewetsky. Oxford, England: Oxford University Press. Originally published in1887.

Erikson, Kai T. 1976. *Everything in its Path: Destruction of Community in the Buffalo Creek Flood*. New York: Simon and Schuster.

Erikson, Kai T. 1994. *A New Species of Trouble: Explorations in Disaster, Trauma, and Community*. New York: Norton.

Erikson, Kai. T. 1998. "Trauma at Buffalo Creek." *Society* 35:153–62.

Ewing, Stuart and Elizabeth Ewing. 1982. *Channels of Desire*. New York: McGraw-Hill.

Farberman, Harvey. 1979. "The Chicago School: Continuities in Urban Research." In *Studies in Symbolic Interaction: A Research Annual*, edited by Norman Denzin. 2:3-20. Greenwich, Connecticut: JAI Press.

Farley, Reynolds, and Walter Allen. 1987. *The Color Line and the Quality of Life in America*. New York: Oxford University Press.

Feagin, Joe R. 1999. *The New Urban Paradigm: Critical Perspectives of the City*. New York: Rowman and Littlefield.

Feagin, Joe R., and Robert Parker. 1990. *Building American Cities: The Urban Real Estate Game*, 2nd ed. Englewood Cliffs, NJ: Prentice-Hall.

Fenske, Gail, and Deryck Holdsmith. 1992. "Corporate Identity and the New York Office Building: 1895–1915." Pp. 129–59 in David Ward and Olivier Zunz (eds.), *Landscape of Modernity*: Essays on New York City, 1900–1940. New York: Russell Sage Foundation.

Fenwick, Millicent. 1948. *Vogue's Book of Etiquette*. New York: Simon & Schuster.

Fer, Briony. 1993. "Introduction." Pp. 2–49 in Francis Frascina, et al., *Modernity and Modernism French Painting in the Nineteenth Century*. New Haven: Yale University Press.

Ferlinghetti, Lawrence. 2005. quote retrieved from the Seminary Co-op bookstore internet site. http//www.semcoop.com

Feuer, Alan. 2002 "Hell on Wheels, and Nerves: If Ever There Was a Mean Street, It's the Cross Bronx." *The New York Times* (September 20):B1 and B10.

Ficcaglia. L.M. (N.d.). *The Birth of the Gallery*. Retrieved March 7, 2005 on the World Wide Web: http://www.riverfrontcenter.org.

Firestone, David. 2001. "Security Alerts Go Into Effect Across Nation." *The New York Times*. (September 12): A17.

Firey, Walter. 1945. "Sentiment and Symbolism as Ecological Variables." *American Sociological Review* 10:140–48.

Firey, Walter. 1947. *Land Use in Central Boston*. Cambridge: Harvard University Press.

Fischer, Claude. 1975. "Toward a Subcultural Theory of Urbanism." *American Journal of Sociology* 80:1319–41.

Fischer, Claude. 1976. *The Urban Experience*. New York: Harcourt Brace.

Fischer, Claude S. 1982a. "The Dispersion of Kinship Ties in Modern Society: Contemporary Data and Historical Speculation." *Journal of Family History* (Winter)7:353–75.

Fischer, Claude. 1982b. *To Dwell Among Friends: Personal Networks in Townand City*. Chicago: University of Chicago Press.

Fischer, Claude. 1991. "Gender and the Residential Telephone: 1890–1940." Pp. 128–47 in Mark Hutter (ed.), *The Family Experience: A Reader in Cultural Diversity*. New York, NY: Macmillan Publishing Company. First published in *Sociological Forum* 1988. 3(2):211–33.

Fishman, Robert. 1982. *Urban Utopias in the Twentieth Century: Ebenezer Howard, Frank Lloyd Wright and Le Corbusier*. Cambridge, MA: MIT Press.

Fishman, Robert. 1987. *Bourgeois Utopias: The Rise and Fall of Suburbia*. New York: Basic Books.

Florida, Richard. 2004. *Rise of the Creative Class: and How It's Transforming Work, Leisure, Community and Everyday Life*. New York: Basic Books.

Flusty, Steven. 1994. *Building Paranoia: The Proliferation of Interdictory Space and the Erosion of Spatial Justice*. West Hollywood, CA: Los Angeles Forum for Architecture and Urban Design.

Fogelson, Robert. 2001. *Downtown: Its Rise and Fall, 1880–1950*. New Haven: Yale University Press.

Foucalt, Michel. 1978. *The History of Sexuality. Volume 1, An Introduction.* New York: Random House.

Frank, Andre Gunder. 1966/1995. "The development of underdevelopment." Pp. 135–41 in Stephen K. Sanderson (ed.), *Sociological Worlds: Comparative and Historical Readings on Society.* Los Angeles: Roxbury Publishing Company.

Frankfort, Henri. 1954. *The Birth of Civilization in the Near East.* Bloomington, Indiana: University of Indiana Press.

Frantz, Douglas, and Catherine Collins. 1999. *Celebration, U.S.A.: Living in Disney's New Town.* New York: Henry Holt and Company Owl.

Frazier, E. Franklin. 1964. "The Negro Family in Chicago." Pp. 404–18 in Ernest W. Burgess and Donald J. Bogue (eds.), *Contributions to Urban Sociology.* Chicago, IL: University of Chicago Press.

Freedland, Jonathan. 2005. "Receding Floodwaters Expose the Dark Side of America—But Will Anything Change?" *The Guardian* (September 5).

Freedman, Stephen. 1978. "The Baseball Fad in Chicago, 1865–1870: An Exploration of the Role of Sports in the Nineteenth-Century City." *Journal of Sport History*, vol. 5, no. 2 (Summer): 42–64.

Friedberg, Anne. 2002. "Window Shopping: Cinema and the Postmodern." Pp. 442–54 in Michael J. Dear and Steven Flusty (eds.), *The Spaces of Postmodernity: Readings in Human Geography.* Malden, MA: Blackwell Publishers.

Friedman, Thomas L. 2000. "One Country, Two Worlds." *The New York Times* (January 28): A23.

Friedman, Thomas L. 2001. "Talk Later." *The New York Times* (September 28): A31.

Fromm, Erich. 1941. *Escape From Freedom.* New York: Holt, Rineheart and Winston,.

Frug, Gerald E. 1999. *City Making: Building Communities without Building Walls.* Princeton, NJ: Princeton University Press.

Fustel de Coulanges, Numa Denis. 1955. *The Ancient City.* Garden City, New York: Doubleday Anchor. Originally published in 1864.

Gache-Patin, Sylvie 1984: "The Urban Landscape." Pp. 109–35 in Richard R. Brettell, Schott Schaefer, Sylvie Gache-Patin, and Francoise Heilbrun (eds.), *A Day in the Country: Impressionism and the French Landscape.* New York: Abradale Press, Harry N. Abrams, Inc., Publishers.

Gans, Herbert. 1962a/1982. *The Urban Villagers: Groups and Class in the Life of Italian Americans.* Updated and Expanded Edition. New York: The Free Press.

Gans, Herbert. 1962b. "Urbanism and Suburbanism as Ways of Life: A Reevaluation of Definitions." Pp. 624–48 in Arnold Rose (ed.), *Human Behavior and Social Process.* Boston: Houghton-Mifflin.

Gans, Herbert. 1967. *The Levittowners.* New York, NY: Vintage Books.

Gans, Herbert. 1997. "Best-Sellers by Sociologists: An Exploratory Study." *Contemporary Sociology* 26:131–35.

Garber, Judith A., and Robyne S. Turner (eds.). 1995. Introduction pp. x–xxvi in *Gender in Urban Research.* Thousand Oaks, CA: Sage.

Gardner, Carol Brooks. 1995. *Passing By: Gender and Public Harassment.* Berkeley, CA: University of California Press.

Garreau, Joel. 1991. *Edge City: Life on the New Frontier.* New York: Doubleday.

Gately, Gary. 2005. "Two Views of Baltimore Compete for Public Money." *The New York Times* (July 6: A12).

Gelernter, David. 1995. *1939: The Lost World of the Fair.* New York: The Free Press.

General Motors. 1939. *The General Motors Exhibit Building: Highways and Horizons, 1939 New York's World Fair.* U.S.A.: General Motors Corporation.

General Motors. 1940. *Futurama.* U.S.A.: General Motors Corporation.

Gertner, Jon. 2005. "Chasing Ground." *The New York Times Magazine* (October 16):46–53,68,81–82.

Gibson, Campbell. 1998. *Population of the 100 Largest Cities and Other Urban Places in the United States: 1790 to 1990.* Population Division Working Paper No. 27. Washington, D.C.: Population Division, U.S. Bureau of the Census.

Gilbert, Melissa R. 1999. "Place, Politics, and the Production of Urban Space: A Feminist Critique of the Growth Machine Thesis." Pp. 95–108 in Andrew E.G. Jonas and David Wilson (eds.), *The Urban Growth Machine: Critical Perspectives Two Decades Later.* Albany, NY: State University of New York Press.

Gipe, George. 1978. *The Great American Sports Book: A Casual but Voluminous Look at American Spectator Sports from the Civil War to the Present Time.* Garden City, NY: A Dolphin Book, Doubleday.

Girouard, Mark. 1985. *Cities & People: A Social and Architectural History.* New Haven, CT: Yale University Press.

Gist, Noel P., and Sylvia Fava. 1974. *Urban Society. Sixth Edition.* New York: Thomas Y. Crowell.

Glaab, Charles N., and A. Theodore Brown. 1976. *A History of Urban America, Second Edition.* New York: Macmillan Publishing Company, Inc.

Glassner, Barry. 1999. *The Culture of Fear: Why Americans are Afraid of the Wrong Things: Crime, Drugs, Minorities, Teen Moms, Killer Kids, Mutant Microbes, Plane Crashes, Road Rage, and so Much More.* New York: Basic Books.

Goffman, Erving. 1959. *The Presentation of Self in Everyday Life.* New York: Doubleday Anchor.

Goffman, Erving. 1963. *Behavior in Public Places: Notes on the Social Organization of Gatherings.* New York: Free Press.

Goffman, Erving. 1971. *Relations in Public Order: Microstudies of the Public Order.* New York: Basic Books.

Gold, John R. 1998. "The Death of the Boulevard." Pp. 44–57 in Nicholas R. Frye (ed.), *Images of the Street: Planning, Identity and Control in Public Space.* London and New York: Routledge.

Gold, Michael. 1996. *Jews Without Money.* 2nd ed. New York: Carroll & Graf Publishers. Originally published in 1930.

Goldberger, Paul. 1979. *The City Observed: New York A Guide to the Architecture of Manhattan.* New York: Vintage Press. A Division of Random House.

Golden, Jane, Robin Rice, and Monica Yant Kinney. 2002. *Philadelphia Murals and the Stories They Tell.* Philadelphia, PA: Temple University Press.

Gonzales, Phillip B. 1993. "Historical Poverty, Restructuring Effects, and Integrative Ties: Mexican American Neighborhoods in a Peripheral Sunbelt Economy." Pp. 149–71 in Joan Moore and Raquel Pinderhughes (eds.), *In the Barrios: Latinos and the Underclass Debate.* New York: Russell Sage Foundation.

Gorn, Elliot J. 1990. "Doing Sports History." *Reviews in American History,* vol. 18, no. 1 (March): 27–32.

Gottdiener, Mark. 1985. *The Social Production of Urban Space.* Austin: University of Texas Press.

Gottdiener, Mark. 1986. "Culture, ideology, and the sign of the city." In. M. Gottdienter and N. Komninos (eds.), *Capitalist Development and Crisis Theory: Accumulation, Regulation and Spatial Restructuring.* London and NY: Macmillan.

Gottdiener, Mark. 1994. *The New Urban Sociology.* New York: McGraw-Hill.

Gottdiener, Mark. 1997. *The Theming of America: Dreams, Visions, and Commercial Spaces.* Boulder, CO: Westview Press.

Gottdiener, Mark. 2002. "Urban Analysis as Merchandising: The 'L.A. School' and the Understanding of Metropolitan Development." Pp. 159–80 in John Eade and Christopher Mele (eds.), *Understanding the City: Contemporary and Future Perspectives.* Oxford, UK and Madden, MA: Blackwell Publishers.

Gottdiener, Mark, and Joe R. Feagin. 1988. "The Paradigm Shift in Urban Sociology." *Urban Affairs Quarterly* 24 (December): 163–87.

Gottdiener, Mark, and Ray Hutchinson. 2000. *The New Urban Sociology,* 2nd ed. New York: McGraw-Hill.

Gratz, Roberta Brandes, with Norman Mintz. 1998. *Cities Back from the Edge: New Life for Downtown.* New York: Preservation Press, John Wiley & Sons.

Gray, Chris. 2005. "Saving Cultural Treasures: Restaurants, Musicians Struggling after Storm." *The Philadelphia Inquirer* (September 12): A1, A7.

Green, L. 1982. "As Hudson's Doors Lock, a Piece of Detroit Will Die." *The Philadelphia Inquirer* December 5.

Greer, Norma Richter. 1989. "St. Louis, Comeback City." *Architecture* April: 62–73.

Greer, Scott. 1957. "Urbanism Reconsidered: A Comparative Study of Local Areas in a Metropolis." *American Sociological Review* 21:19–25.

Grogan, Paul S., and Tony Proscio. 2000. *Comeback Cities: A Blueprint for Urban Neighborhood Revival.* Boulder, CO: A Westview Book.

Grossman, James R. 1989. *Land of Hope: Chicago, Black Southerners, and the Great Migration.* Chicago: University of Chicago Press.

Gumpert, Gary, and Susan J. Drucker. 2001. "Public Boundaries: Privacy and Surveillance in a Technological World." *Communication Quarterly,* vol. 49, no. 2 (Spring):115–129. Retrieved on 10/30/2003 from http:/web5.silverplatter.com/webspirs/showFullRecordContent.

Gutman, Herbert. 1976. *The Black Family in Slavery and Freedom: 1750–1925.* New York: Random House.

Guttmann, Allen. 1986. *Sports Spectators.* New York: Columbia University Press.

Guttmann, Allen. 1988. *A Whole New Ball Game: An Interpretation of American Sports.* Chapel Hill, NC: University of North Carolina Press.

Hales, Peter Bacon. 1984. *Silver Cities: The Photography of American Urbanization, 1839–1915.* Philadelphia: Temple University Press.

Hall, Peter. 1996. *Cities of Tomorrow: An Intellectual History of Urban Planning and Design in the Twentieth Century.* Updated ed. Oxford, UK; Cambridge, MA: Blackwell.

Hall, Peter. 1998. *Cities in Civilization.* New York: Pantheon Books.

Hall, Peter. 2002. *Cities of Tomorrow,* 3rd ed. Madden, MA: Blackwell Publishing.

Hall, Peter, and Colin Ward. 1998. *Sociable Cities: The Legacy of Ebenezer Howard.* New York: John Wiley & Sons.

Halpern, Sue. 2002. "The Art of Change." *Mother Jones.* (July/August). Retrieved from the Internet. http://www.motherjones.com/cgibin/print_

article.pl?url=http://www.motherjones.com/ commentary/commons/2002/07/art_of_change .html

Hamblin, Dora Jane. 1973. *The First Cities..* New York: Time Inc.

Hampson, Rick. 2001. "'Act of War' Terrorists Strike; Death Toll 'Horrendous'". *USA Today* (September 12) 1A, 2A.

Hareven, Tamara K. 1971. "The History of the Family as an Interdisciplinary Field." Pp. 211–26 in Theodore K. Rabb and Robert L. Rotberg (eds.), *The Family in History: Interdisciplinary Essays.* New York: Harper (Torchbooks).

Hareven, Tamara K.1975. "Family Time and Industrial Time: Family and Work in a Planned Corporation Town, 1900–1924." *Journal of Urban History* 1:365–89.

Hareven, Tamara K. 1976. "The Last Stage: Historical Adulthood and Old Age." *Daedalus* 105:13–27. (Fall issue titled, "American Civilization: New Perspectives.")

Hareven, Tamara K. 1978. "The Dynamics of Kin in an Industrial Community." Pp. 151–82 in J. Demos and S.S. Boocock (eds.), *Turning Points: Historical Points: Historical and Sociological Essays on the Family.* Chicago: University of Chicago Press.

Harcourt, Bernard E. 2001. *Illusion of Order: The False Promise of Broken Windows Policing.* Cambridge, MA: Harvard University Press.

Harden, Blaine. 2001. "Physical and Psychological Paralysis of Nation." *The New York Times* (September 12): A18.

Hardy, Stephen. 1981. "The City and the Rise of American Sport: 1820–1920." *Exercise and Sport Sciences Reviews*, vol. 9:183–219.

Harris, Chauncey O., and Edward L. Ullman. 1945. "The Nature of Cities." *The Annals of the Academy of Political and Social Sciences* 242 (November): 7–17. Boston, MA: Harvard University Press.

Hart, Lauren. 2003. "French Capitalism Kills 12,000 During Heat Wave, Paris Blames 'Mother Nature'." *The Militant*, vol. 67, no.32 (September 22). http://www.themilitant.com/2003/6732/ 673202.htm

Harvey, David. 1973. *Social Justice and the City.* Baltimore, MD: The Johns Hopkins University Press.

Harvey, David. 1985. *Consciousness and the Urban Experience.* Oxford: Basil Blackwell.

Harvey, David. 1989. *The Conditions of Postmodernity.* Cambridge, MA: Basil Blackwell.

Harvey, David. 2000. *Spaces of Hope.* Berkeley, CA: University of California Press.

Hathaway, Helen. 1928. *Manners.* New York: Dutton.

Hauser, Philip, and Leo Schnore (eds.). 1965. *The Study of Urbanization.* New York: Wiley.

Hauser, Jim. 2003. "French Blame Heat Wave Deaths on Health Care System." *GOPUSA* (September 29): Talon News. http://www. gopusa.com/news/ 2003/september/0929_french_heat_wave.shtml

Hawkes, Jacquetta and Sir Leonard Woolley. 1963. *Prehistory and the Beginnings of Civilization.* New York and Evanston: Harper & Row.

Hawley, Amos. 1981. *Urban Society: An Ecological Approach.* Second edition. New York: John Wiley & Sons.

Hayden, Dolores. 1984. *Redesigning the American Dream: The Future of Housing, Work, and Family Life.* New York: W.W. Norton.

Hayden, Dolores. 1995. *The Power of Place: Urban Landscapes as Public History.* Cambridge, MA: MIT Press.

Hayden, Dolores. 2003. *Building Suburbia: Green Fields and Urban Growth 1820–2000.* New York: Pantheon.

Hendrickson, R. 1970. *The Grand Emporium.* New York: Stein and Day.

Hendrickson, Robert. 1979. *The Grand Emporium: The Illustrated History of America's Great Department Store.* New York: Stein and Day.

Henley, Nancy, and Jo Freeman. 1975. "The Sexual Politics of Interpersonal Behavior." Pp. 391–401 in Jo Freeman (ed.), *Women: A Feminist Perspective.* Palo Alto, CA: Mayfield.

Henninger, Daniel. 2001. "I Saw It All, Then I Saw Nothing." *The Wall Street Journal* (September 12): A18.

Herbert, Robert L. 1988. *Impressionism: Art, Leisure, & Parisian Society.* New Haven, Connecticut: Yale University Press.

Hine, Thomas S. 1979. *Burnham of Chicago: Architect and Planner.* Chicago: University of Chicago Press.

Hine, Thomas, 1989. "Savoring the Cities' Vitality." *The Philadelphia Inquirer* (February 29): 1H,16H.

Hine, Thomas. 1999. "Just How Good was Ed Bacon, Really?" *Philadelphia Magazine* (March);84–90; 92–93.

Hirsch, Arnold R. 1983. *Making the Second Ghetto: Race and Housing in Chicago, 1940–1960.* Chicago, IL: University of Chicago Press.

Horowitz, Ruth. 1983. *Honor and the American Dream: Culture and Identity in a Chicano Community.* New Brunswick, NJ: Rutgers University Press. http://www.phil.frb.org

Hosken, F.P. 1985. *Academic American Encyclopedia,* vol. 5. Danbury, CT: Grolier. Cited in George J. Bryjak and Michael P. Soroka, 2001. *Sociology*

Changing Societies in a Diverse World. Boston: Allyn & Bacon.

Howard, Ebenezer. 1898. *To-morrow! A Peaceful Path to Real Reform.* London: Swan Sonnenschein.

Howard, Ebenezer. 1902/1965. *Garden Cities of Tomorrow.* Cambridge, MA: MIT Press.

Howard, Ebenezer. 1996. "Author's Introduction" and "The Town-Country Magnet" (from *Garden Cities of To-Morrow* 1898). Pp. 346–53 in Richard T. LeGates and Frederic Stout (eds.), *The City Reader.* London and New York: Routledge.

Howells, William. 1963. *Back of History: The Story of Our Own Origins*, rev. ed. Garden City, New York: Doubleday Anchor.

Hower, R.M. 1943. *History of Macy's of New York 1858–1919.* Cambridge, MA: Harvard University Press.

Hoyt, Homer. 1939. *The Structure and Growth of Residential Neighborhoods in American Cities.* Washington DC: Federal Housing Administration.

HUD. 1999, "The Forgotten Americans: Homelessness—Programs and People They Served." (December). [Online] Available October 21, 2002, at http://www.huduser.org/publications/homeless/homelessness/contents.html

Hughes, Robert. 1997. *American Visions: The Epic History of Art in America.* New York: Alfred A. Knopf.

Hunter, Albert. 1995. "Private, Parochial and Public Social Orders: The Problem of Crime and Incivility in Urban Communities." Pp. 204–25 in Philip Kasinitz (ed.), *Metropolis: Center and Symbol of Our Time.* New York: New York University Press. First published in Gerald Suttles and Mayer Zald (eds.), *The Challenge of Social Control.* Norwood, NJ: Ablex Publishers. 1985.

Hunter, Sam. 1972. *American Art of the 20th Century.* New York: Harry N. Abrams, Inc., Publishers.

Hurlock, Elizabeth. 1929. *The Psychology of Dress: An Analysis of Fashion and its Motive.* New York: Ronald.

Hutter, Mark. 1970. "Transformation of Identity, Social Mobility and Kinship solidarity." *Journal of Marriage and the Family* 32:133–37.

Hutter, Mark. 1987. "The Downtown Department Store as a Social Force." *The Social Science Journal.* Vol. 24, No. 3, 1987, Pp. 239–246.

Hutter, Mark. 1991. "Immigrant families in the city." Pp. 170–177 in Mark Hutter (ed.), *The Family Experience: A Reader in Cultural Diversity.* New York: Macmillan. Originally appeared in *The Gallatin Review* 1986/1987 6(Winter):60–69.

Hutter, Mark. 1998. *The Changing Family 3/e* 1998 Allyn & Bacon.

Hutter, Mark. 2003. "The World Trade Center: The Icon and Terrorism," Pp. 67–73 in Will Wright and Steven Kaplan (eds.), *The Image of the City: Selected Papers—2003.* Conference, "The Image of the City," Society for the Interdisciplinary Study of Social Imagery. Colorado Springs, Colorado, March 2003.

Hutter, Mark. 2005. "'Bensenhoist': A Jewish American Ethnic-Autoethnography," Pp. 265–280 in John P. Myers (ed.), *Minority Voices: Linking Personal Ethnic History and the Sociological Imagination.* Boston: Allyn & Bacon).

Huxtable, Ada Louise. 2004. *Frank Lloyd Wright.* New York: A Lipper/Viking Book.

Jackson, Kenneth T. 1985. *Crabgrass Frontier: The Suburbanization of the United States.* New York: Oxford University Press.

Jackson, Peter. 1998. "Domesticating the Street: The Contested Spaces of the High Street and the Mall." Pp. 176–91 in Nicholas R. Fyfe (ed.), *Images of the Street: Planning, Identity and Control in Public Space.* New York: Routledge.

Jacobs, Jane. 1961. *The Death and Life of Great American Cities.* New York: Random House, Vintage Books.

Jacobs, Jane. 1969. *The Economy of Cities.* New York: Random House, Vintage Press.

Jencks, Charles. 1993. *Heteropolis: Los Angeles, the riots and the strange beauty of hetero-architecture.* London: Academy Editions: Ernst & Sohn.

Jennings, Peter. 2000. "21st Century Lives: Jane Golden: Making Beautiful Murals Out of City Walls. *World News Tonight.* http://abcnews.go.com/onairWorldNewsTonight/Wrt000728_21st_golden_feature.html

Jones, Maldwyn Allen. 1960. *American Immigration.* Chicago: University of Chicago.

Karp, David A., Gregory P. Stone, and William C. Yoels. 1977. *Being Urban: A Social Psychological View of City Life.* Lexington, MA: D.C. Heath.

Karp, David, Gregory P. Stone, and William C. Yoels. 1991. *Being Urban: A Sociology of City Life.* New York: Praeger.

Kasarda, John, and Morris Janowitz. 1974. "Community Attachment in Mass Society." *American Sociology Review* 39:328–39.

Kasinitz, Philip. 1995. "Introduction to Part I, Modernity and the Urban Ethos." Pp. 7–20 in Philip Kasinitz (ed.), *Metropolis: Center and Symbol of our Times.* New York: New York University Press.

Kasson, John F. 1978. *Amusing the Million: Coney Island at the Turn of the Century.* New York: Hill and Wang.

Kasson, John F. 1990. *Rudeness & Civility: Manners in Nineteenth-Century Urban America.* New York: Hill and Wang.

Katz, Jonathan Ned. 1995. *The Invention of Heterosexuality.* New York: Dutton.

Katz, Peter. 1994. *The New Urbanism: Toward an Architecture of Community.* New York: McGraw-Hill.

Kelling, George L., and Catherine Coles. 1996. *Fixing Broken Windows: Crime and the Spiral of Decay in American Neighborhoods.* New York: Simon and Schuster.

Kendall, Diana. 2001. "Homeless Rights Versus Public Space." P. 150, Box 5.2: Sociology and Social Policy in Diana Kendall, *Sociology in Our Times,* 3rd ed. Belmont, CA: Wadsworth/Thomson Learning.

Kenyon, Kathleen May, Dame. 1970. *Archaeology in the Holy Land.* New York: Praeger.

Key, William H. 1961. "Rural urban differences and the family." *Sociological Quarterly* 2:49-56.

Kirsch, George B. 1983. "The Rise of Modern Sports: New Jersey Cricketeers, Baseball Players, and Clubs, 1845–60." *New Jersey History,* vol. 101:53–84.

Kirsch, George B. 1987. "Baseball Spectators, 1855–1870." *Baseball History* (Fall 1987): 4–20.

Klein, Naomi. 2005. "Power to the Victims of New Orleans: With the Poor Gone, Developers are Planning to Gentrify the City." *The Guardian* (September 9).

Kleniewski, Nancy. 2006. *Cities, Change, and Conflict: A Political Economy of Urban Life,* 3rd ed. Belmont, CA: Thompson Wadsworth.

Klinenberg, Eric. 2002. *Heat Wave: A Social Autopsy of Disaster in Chicago.* Chicago, IL: University of Chicago Press.

Kornblum, William, and Joseph Julian. 1998. *Social Problem. Ninth Edition.* Upper Saddle River, NJ: Prentice-Hall.

Kostof, Spiro. 1991. *The City Shaped: Urban Patterns and Meaning Through History.* Boston, MA: A Bullfinch Press Book; Little, Brown and Company.

Kostof, Spiro. 1992. *The City Assembled: The Elements of Urban Form Through History.* Boston, MA: A Bullfinch Press Book; Little, Brown and Company.

Kotkin, Joel. 2000. "Movers and Shakers: How Immigrants are Reviving Neighborhoods Given Up for Dead." *Reason Magazine* (December). http://reason.com/0012/fe.jk.movers.shtml

Kotkin, Joel. 2001. *The New Geography: How the Digital Revolution is Reshaping the American Landscape.* New York: Random House.

Kowinski, William Severini. 1985. *The Malling of America: An Inside Look at the Great Consumer Paradise.* New York: Morrow.

Kozol, Jonathan. 1988. *Rachel and Her Children: Homeless Families n America.* New York: Crown Publishers.

Kuklick, Bruce. 1991. *To Everything a Season: Shibe Park and Urban Philadelphia.* Princeton, NJ: Princeton University Press.

Kunstler, James Howard. 1993. *The Geography of Nowhere: The Rise and Decline of America's Man-Made Landscape.* New York: A Touchstone Book, Simon & Schuster.

Lampl, Paul. 1968. Cities *and Planning in the Ancient Near East.* New York: George Braziller.

Landau, Sarah Bradford, and Carl W. Condit. 1996. *Rise of the New York Skyscraper 1865–1913.* New Haven, CT: Yale University Press.

Landler, Mark. 2005a. "France Declares Emergency: Curfews to be Imposed." *The New York Times* (November 9):A12.

Landler, Mark. 2005b. "Flaming Cars: A Very French Message from the Disaffected." *The New York Times* (November 13):10.

Lang, Robert, and Patrick Simmons. 2001. "Boomburgs: The Emergence of Large, Fast-Growing Suburban Cities in the United States." *FannieMae Foundation Census Note 06* (June).

Lasch, Christopher. 1977a. *Haven in a Heartless World: The Family Besieged.* New York: Basic Books.

Lasch, Christopher. 1977b. "The Siege of the Family." *New York Review of Books* (November 24).

Latanè, Bibb, and John Darley. 1970. *The Unresponsive Bystander: Why Doesn't He Help.* New York: Appleton-Century-Croft.

Le Corbusier. 1947. *When the Cathedrals Were White.* Translated by Francis E. Hyslap, Jr. New York: Harcourt Brace and Company.

Le Corbusier. 1967. *The Radiant City.* London: Faber and Faber. Originally published in 1933.

Leas, Andrew. 1985. *Cities Perceived: Urban Society in European and American Thought, 1820–1940.* New York: Columbia University Press.

Lehman, David. 1996. "The World Trade Center." *Valentine Place.* New York: Scribner.

Lemann, Nicholas. 1991. *The Promised Land: The Great Black Migration and How it Changed America.* New York: Alfred A. Knopf.

Lerner, Daniel. 1958. *The Passing of Traditional Society: Modernizing the Middle East.* Glencoe, IL" The Free Press of Glencoe.

Levine, Peter. 1985. *A.G. Spalding and the Rise of Baseball.* New York: Oxford University Press.

Lewis, Michael. 2001. "Why You?" *The New York Times Magazine* (September 23, Section 8).

Ley, David. 1983. *A Social Geography of the City.* New York: Harper & Row.

Lindsey, Linda L. and Stephen Beach. 2004. *Sociology*. Third Ed. Upper Saddle River, NJ: Pearson Prentice Hall.

Litwak, Eugene. 1959–1960. "The Use of Extended Family Groups in the Achievement of Social Goals." *Social Problems*.

Litwak, Eugene.1960a. "Geographical Mobility and Extended Family Cohesion." *American Sociological Review* 25:385–94.

Litwak, Eugene. 1960b. "Occupational Mobility and Extended Family Cohesion." *American Sociological Review* 25:385–94.

Lofland, Lyn H. 1973. *A World of Strangers: Order and Action in Urban Public Space*. New York: Basic Books.

Lofland, Lyn H. 1976. "The 'Thereness' of Women." Pp. 144–70 in M. Millman and R.M. Kanter (eds.), *Another Voice: feminist Perspectives on Social Life and Social Science*. Garden City, NY: Anchor Books.

Lofland, Lyn H. 1983. "Understanding urban life: The Chicago School legacy." *Urban Life* 11(January):491–511.

Lofland, Lyn H.1998. *The Public Realm: Exploring the City's Quintessential Social Territory*. New York: Aldine de Gruyter.

Lofland, Lyn H. 2003. "Community and Urban Life." Chapter 39 in Larry T. Reynolds and Nancy Herman-Kinney (eds.), *Handbook of Symbolic Interaction*. Lanham, MD: Alta Mira Press.

Logan, John. 2006. "The Impact of Katrina: Race and Class in Storm-Damaged Neighborhoods." Paper from Office of Media Relations. Providence, RI: Brown University. Retrieved January 30, 2006. http://ww.brown.edu/Administration/News_Bureau/2005–06/05–068.html www.s4.brown.edu/Katrina/report.pdf

Logan, John, and Harvey Molotch. 1988. *Urban Fortunes: The Political Economy of Place*. Berkeley and Los Angeles: University of California Press.

Lubove, Roy (ed.). 1967. *The Urban Community: Housing and Planning in the Progressive Era*. Englewood Cliffs, NJ: Prentice-Hall.

Lynch, Kevin. 1960. *The Image of the City*. Cambridge, MA: MIT Press.

Macionis, John J. 2005. *Sociology*. Tenth Ed. Annotated Instructor's Edition. Upper Saddle River, NJ: Pearson Prentice Hall.

Macionis, John J., and Vincent N. Parrillo. 2004. *Cities and Urban Life*, 3rd ed. Upper Saddle River, NJ: Prentice-Hall.

Maine, Henry Sumner. 1960. *Ancient Law*. London: J.M. Dent & Sons. (Originailly published, 1862).

Makos, Donna L. 2005. "The Revitalization of Downtown Millville." Term paper for Suburban Studies, Spring 2005. Sociology Department, Rowan University. Glassboro, New Jersey.

Mangin, William. 1960. "Mental health and migration to cities." *Annals of the New York Academy of Sciences*. 84:911–917.

Mangin, William. 1968. "Tales from the barriadas." *Nickel Review,* September 25–October 8, 1968. Reprinted in William Mangin (ed.), 1970. *Peasants in Cities: Readings in the Anthropology of Urbanization* (pp.55–61). Boston: Houghton-Mifflin.

Marcus, Steven. 1973. "Reading the Illegible." Pp. 257–76 in H.J. Dyos and Michael Wolff (eds.), *The Victorian City: Images and Realities. Volume 1 Past and Present/Numbers of People*. Boston, MA: Routledge & Kegan Paul.

Marcus, Steven. 1974. *Engels, Manchester and the Working Class*. New York: Vintage Books.

Marx, Karl and Friedrich Engels. 1848. *The Communist Manifesto (Manifesto of the Communist Party)*. Authorized English edition translated, annotated and edited by Friedrich Engels. Reprinted 1948 by International Publishers, New York.

Marx, Leo. 1964. *The Machine in the Garden: Technology and the Pastoral Ideal in America*. New York: Oxford University Press.

Massey, Douglas S., and Nancy A. Denton. 1993. *American Apartheid: Segregation and the Making of the Underclass*. Cambridge, MA: Harvard University Press.

Mastrull, Diane. 2001. "Their own acre: Why 'walkable communities' don't fly here." *The Philadelphia Inquirer*. (May 6,7,8).

Mathis, Mike. 2005. "'Athens of South Jersey' Pushes Special Retail Mix." *Philadelphia Business Journal* February 28. http://philadelphia.bizjournals.com/philadelphia/stories/2005/02/28/focus2.html

Mayell, Hillary. 2004a. "Bead Find Proof Modern Thought Began in Africa?" *National Geographic News* (March 31).

Mayell. 2004b. "Oldest Jewelry? 'Beads' Discovered in African Cave." *National Geographic News* (April 24).Maykuth, Andrew. 2005. "Rebuilding: Who Returns May Determine What City Becomes." *The Philadelphia Inquirer* (September 8): A1,A15.

Maykuth, Andrew. 2005. "Rebuilding: Who returns may determine what city becomes." *The Philadelphia Inquirer*. (September 8):A1,A15.

McGarry, Molly, and Fred Wasserman. 1998. *Becoming Visible: An Illustrated History of Lesbian and Gay Life in Twentieth-Century America*. New York: Penguin Studios.

McKelvey, Blake. 1963. *The Urbanization of America (1860–1915)*. New Brunswick, New Jersey: Rutgers University Press.

McKenzie, E. 1994. *Privatopia: Homeowner Associations and the Rise of Residential Private Government*. New Haven, CT: Yale University Press.

McPhee, John. 2005. "Archives: The Sunken City." *The New Yorker*. (September 12):58–59. (Reprinted from "The Control of Nature: Atchafalya," in *The New Yorker*, February 23, 1987.)

Mead, George Herbert. 1934. *Mind, Self and Society*. Chicago: University of Chicago Press.

Mele, Christopher. 2000. *Selling the Lower East Side: Culture, Real Estate, and Resistance in New York, 1880–2000*. Minneapolis, MN: University of Minnesota Press.

Mellaart. 1967. *Catal Huyuk: A Neolithic Town in Anatolia*. New York: McGraw-Hill.

Milgram, Stanley. 1970. "The Experience of Living in Cities." *Science*, vol. 167 (March 13): 1461–68.

Milgram, Stanley. 1977a. "The Experience of Living in Cities." Pp. 24–41 in Stanley Milgram, 1977, *The Individual in a Social World: Essays and Experiments*. Reading, MA: Addison-Wesley Publishing Company. First published in *Science*, vol. 167 (March 13): 1461–68.

Milgram, Stanley. 1977b. "The Urban Bystander." Pp. 42–46 in Stanley Milgram, 1977, *The Individual in a Social World: Essays and Experiments*. Reading, MA: Addison-Wesley. This paper was written in collaboration with Paul Hollander and was first published under the title, "The Murder they Heard," *The Nation*, vol. 198, no. 25 (1964) pp. 602–4.

Miller, D.A. (Nd.). *Including the Arts will Improve the Local Economy*. Retrieved March 5, 2005 on the World Wide Web: http://njmayornet.com.

Miller, D.W. 2000. "The New Urban Studies." *Chronicle of Higher Education* (August 18).

Miller, DeMond Shondell and Jason David Rivera. 2006. "Guiding Principles: Rebuilding Trust in Government and Public Policy in the Aftermath of Hurricane Katrina." *Journal of Public Management & Social Policy*. (Spring): 37–47.

Mires, Charlene. 2002. *Independence Hall in American Memory*. Philadelphia: University of Pennsylvania Press.

Moe, Richard, and Carter Wilkie. 1997. *Changing Places: Rebuilding Community in the Age of Sprawl*. New York: Henry Holt.

Mogey, John. 1964. "Family and community in urban-industrial societies." Pp. 501–34 in Harold T. Christensen (ed.), *Handbook of Marriage and the Family*. Chicago: Rand McNally.

Mohl, Raymond A. 1985. *The New City: Urban America in the Industrial Age, 1860–1920*. Arlington Heights, IL: Harlan Davidson, Inc.

Molotch, Harvey. 1969. "The city as a growth machine." *American Journal of Sociology*. 82(2): 309–330.

Monaghan, Jennifer. 2004. "Commissioner Susan Bass Levin designates city of Millville to Main Street Program. NJ: Department of Community Affairs (DCA). Retrieved from Internet June 23, 2006. http://www.state.nj.us/dca/news/2004/pr092904.shtml

Montiel, Miguel. 1970. "The social science myth of the Mexican American family." *El Grito: A Journal of Contemporary Mexican American Thought* 3 (Summer):56–63.

Montiel, Miguel. 1973. "The Chicano family: A review of research." *Social Work* 18 (March):22–31.

Moore, Acel. 2005. "Response slowed by who victims are." *The Philadelphia Inquirer* (September 11): D7.

Moore, Joan and James Diego Vigil. 1993. "Barrios in transition." Pp. 27–49 in Joan Moore and Raquel Pinderhughes. (eds.). 1993. *In the Barrios: Latinos and the Underclass Debate*. New York: Russell Sage Foundation.

Moore, Joan and Raquel Pinderhughes. (eds.). 1993. *In the Barrios: Latinos and the Underclass Debate*. New York: Russell Sage Foundation.

Moore, Joan with Harry Pachon. 1976. *Mexican-Americans*. 2nd ed. Englewood Cliffs, NJ: Prentice Hall.

Moreno, Sylvia. 2005, "Flow of illegal immigrants to U.S. unabated. *Washington Post* (March 22): A02. Retrieved from the Internet June 23, 2006. http://www.washingtonpost.com/ac2/wp-dynA55202-2005Mar21?language=printer

Morris, A.E.J. 1979. *History of Urban Form: Before the Industrial Revolution*. New York: Halsted Press: John Wiley & Sons.

Muller, Peter O. 1981. *Contemporary Suburban America*. Englewood Cliffs, NJ: Prentice-Hall.

Mumford, Herbert. 1961. *The City in History: Its Origins, Its Transformations, and Its Prospects*. New York: Harcourt, Brace Jovanovich.

Mumford, Lewis. 1938. *The Culture of Cities*. New York: Harcourt, Brace.

Mumford, Lewis. 1975. *Architecture as a Home for Man. Essays for Architectural Record*, Jeanne M. Davern (ed.). New York: McGraw-Hill.

Mumford, Lewis. 1934/1963. *Technics and Civilizations*. New York: A Harbinger Book, Harcourt, Brace and World.

Murillo, Nathan. 1971. "The Mexican American family." Pp. 99–102 in Nathaniel N. Wagner and Marsha

J. Haug (eds.), *Chicanos: Social and Psychological Perspectives*. St. Louis: Mosby.

Murray, Stephen O. 1996. *American Gay*. Chicago, IL: University of Chicago Press.

Myers, John P. 2003. *Dominant-Minority Relations in America: Linking Personal History with the Convergence in the New World*. Boston: Allyn and Bacon.

New York City Surveillance Camera, NYCLU, mediaeater.com/cameras/breakdown/html, April 3, 1999 cited in Gary Gumpert and Susan J. Drucker. 2001. "Public Boundaries: Privacy and Surveillance in a Technological World." *Communication Quarterly*, vol. 49, no. 2 (Spring):115–29. Retrieved on 10/30/2003 from http://web5.silverplatter.com/webspirs/showFullRecordContent.

Nisbett, Robert A. 1966. *The Sociological Tradition*. New York: Basic Books.

Norquist, John O. 1998. *The Wealth of Cities: Revitalizing the Centers of American Life*. Reading, MA: Addison-Wesley.

Oakley, Ann. 1974. *Woman's Work: The Housewife, Past and Present*. New York: Pantheon Books.

Oldenburg, Roy. 1989. *The Great Good Place: Cafes, Coffee Shops, Community Centers, Beauty Parlors, General Stores, Bars, Hangouts, and How They Get you Through the Day*. New York: Paragon House.

Olsen, Donald J. 1986. *The City as a Work of Art: London, Paris, Vienna*. New Haven, CT: Yale University Press.

Oppenheim, A. Leo. 1964. *Ancient Mesopotamia: Portrait of a Dead Civilization*. Chicago: University of Chicago Press.

Page, Max. 1999. *The Creative Destruction of New York*. Chicago, IL: University of Chicago Press.

Palen, J. John. 1995. *The Suburbs*. New York: McGraw-Hill.

Palen, J. John. 2005. *The Urban World*. Seventh Edition. New York: McGraw-Hill.

Pardo, Mary. 2004. "Mexican American Women Grassroots Community Activists" 'Mothers of East Los Angeles'. Pp. 72–82 in Mark Hutter (ed.), *The Family Experience: A Reader in Cultural Diversity*, 4th ed. Boston, MA: Allyn & Bacon.

Park, Robert E. 1966/1916. "The city: Suggestions for the Investigation of Human Behavior in the Urban Environment." Pp. 1–46 in Robert E. Park, Ernest W. Burgess, and Roderick D. McKenzie, *The City*. Chicago: University of Chicago Press. (Originally published, 1925.)

Park, Robert. 1969. "The City: Suggestions for the Investigation of Human Behavior in the Urban Environment." In Richard Sennett (ed.), *Classic Essays on the Culture of Cities*. New York: Appleton-Century-Crofts. Originally appeared in *The American Journal of Sociology*, vol. XX.

Park, Robert E. 1922. *The Immigrant Press and its Control*. New York: Harper.

Park, Robert E. 1923/1967. "The Natural History of the Newspaper," *American Journal of Sociology*, 29 (November):273–89. Reprinted in Ralph H. Turner (ed.), *Robert E. Park: On Social Control and Collective Behavior*. Chicago: University of Chicago Press, Pp. 97–113.

Park, Robert E. 1925/1967. "The City: Suggestions for the Investigation of Human Behavior in the City Environment," in Robert E. Park et al (eds.), *The City*. Chicago: University of Chicago Press, Pp. 1–46.

Park, Robert E. and Ernest Burgess. 1970/1921. *Introduction to the Science of Sociology*. Chicago: University of Chicago Press.

Park, Robert E., Ernest W. Burgess and Roderick D. McKenzie, 1925. *The City*. Chicago: University of Chicago Press.

Park, Robert E. and Herbert A. Miller. 1925. *Old World Traits Transplanted*. Chicago: Society for Social Research. University of Chicago Press.

Parrillo, Vincent N. 1985. *Strangers to These Shores: Race and Ethnic Relations in the United States*. New York: John Wiley & Sons.

Parsons, Clare Olivia. 1997. "Reputation and Public Appearance: The De-eroticization of the Urban Street. Pp. 59–70 in Susan J. Drucker and Gary Gumpert (eds.), *Voices in the Street: Explorations in Gender, Media, and Public Space*.

Parsons, Talcott. 1943. "The kinship system of the contemporary United States." *American Anthropologist* 45:22–38.

Parsons, Talcott. 1955. "The American family: Its relation to personality and to the social structure." Pp. 3–33 in Talcott Parsons and Robert F. Bales (eds.), Family, *Socialization and Interaction Process*. New York: The Free Press.

Peach, Ceri. 2005. "The Ghetto and the Ethnic Enclave." Pp. 31–48 in David P. Varady, (ed.), *Desegregating the City: Ghettos, Enclaves, & Inequality*. Albany, NY: State University of New York Press.

Peiss, Kathy. 2001. *Cheap Amusements: Working Women and Leisure in Turn-of-the-Century New York*. Philadelphia, PA: Temple University Press.

Peretz, Henri. 2004. "The Making of *Black Metropolis*." *ANNALS, AAPSS*, 595, (September):168–75.

Perry, Wilhelmina E., James R. Abbott, and Mark Hutter. 1997. "The Symbolic Interaction Paradigm and Urban Sociology." *Research in Urban Sociology* 4:59–92. Jai Press.

Persons, Stow. 1987. *Ethnic Studies at Chicago 1905–45*. Urbana and Chicago, IL: University of Illinois Press.

Peterson, Karen S. 2003."'Urban Tribes' Build Bonds." *USA Today* October 6: 5D.

Population Reference Bureau. 2001. "What percent of the the world's people live in urban settings." June. http://www.prb.org/template.cfm?Secton=Quick-Facts.

Pritchard, James B. 1955. *Ancient Near East Texts*. Second edition. Princeton: Princeton University Press.

Putnam, Robert. 2000. *Bowling Alone: The Collapse and Revival of American Community*. New York: Simon & Schuster.

Putnam, Robert D. 1995. "Bowling alone: America's declining social capital." *Journal of Democracy* 6: 65–78.

Queen, Stuart A., Robert W. Habenstein, and Jill S. Quadagno. 1985. *The Family in Various Cultures*, 5th ed. New York: Harper & Row.

Rafferty, Kevin. 1990. *City On The Rocks: Hong Kong's Uncertain Future*. New York: Viking.

Rainwater, Lee. 1970. *Behind Ghetto Walls: Black Families in a Federal Slum*. Chicago: Aldine.

Rainwater Lee. 1966. "Crucibles of identity." Daedalus. 95:172–216.

Read, Piers Paul. 1995. *The Patriot: A Novel*. New York: Random House.

Reeder, Allan. 1998. "To see and be seen." The *Atlantic Monthly*; Volume 282 (July).

Reich, Robert B. 1991. *The Resurgent Liberal: and Other Unfashionable Prophecies*. New York: Vintage Books.

Reiss, Steven A. 1980. *Touching Base: Professional Baseball and American Culture in the Progressive Era*. Westport, Connecticut: Greewood Press.

Reiss, Steven A. 1989. *City Games: The Evolution of American Urban Society and the Rise of Sports*. Urbana and Chicago, Illinois: University of Illinois Press.

Reissman, Leonard. 1970. *The Urban Process: Cities in Industrial Society*. New York: The Free Press.

Relph, Edward. 1987. *The Modern Urban Landscape*. Baltimore, MD: Johns Hopkins University Press.

Retica, Aaron. 2005. "A Complex Complex." *The New York Times Magazine* May 15: back page.

Reynolds, Malvina. 1962. *"Little Boxes."* words and music. Schroeder Music, Co., ASCAP.

Riesman, David with Nathan Glazer and Reul Denney. 1950. *The Lonely Crowd: A Study of Changing American Character*. New Haven: Yale University Press.

Robertson, Campbell. 2005. "Coastal Cities of Mississippi in the Shadows." *The New York Times*. (September 12): A1,A16.

Rodman, Hyman. 1965. "Middle-class misconceptions about lower-class families." Pp. 219–30 in Hyman Rodman (ed.), *Marriage, Family, and Society: A Reader*. New York: Random House [Originally published in Arthur B. Shostak and William Gomberg (eds.), 1974, *Blue-Collar World: Studies of the* American Worker. Englewood Cliffs, N.J.: Prentice-Hall.]

Rodman, Hyman.1971. *Lower-Class Families: The Culture of Poverty in Negro Trinidad*. New York: Oxford University Press.

Rogers, Everett M. 1994. *A History of Communication Study: A Biographical Approach*. New York: The Free Press.

Rolland. K.L. 2004. *Arts District Invigorates Millville's Downtown*. A Community Development Publication Cascade. Retrieved March 7, 2005, on the World Wide Web: http://phil.frb.org.

Rosenzweig, Roy and Elizabeth Blackmar. 1992. *The Park and the People: A History of Central Park*. Ithaca, NY: Cornell University Press.

Rossi, Peter H. 1994. "Troubling families: Family homelessness in America." *American Behavioral Scientist* 37 (January) 3:342–395.

Rothman, S.M. 1978. *Women's Proper Place: A History of Changing Ideals and Practices, 1870 to the Present*. New York: Basic Books.

Rubin, Gayle. 1984. "Thinking Sex: Notes for a Radical Theory of the Politics of Sexuality." Pp. 267–319 in Carole S. Vance (ed.), *Pleasure and Danger: Exploring Female Sexuality*. Boston: Routledge & Kegan Paul.

Rubin, Trudy. 2005. "Tarnished image? Friends abroad say storm debacle could hurt America's influence." *The Philadelphia Inquirer*. (September 8): A17.

Ruderman, Wendy. 2005. "Towns Try a Singular Way to Save Old Homes." *The Philadelphia Inquirer* (May 3):A1, A21.

Ryan, Mary P. 1997. *Civic Wars: Democracy and Public Life in the American City during the Nineteenth Century*. Berkeley, CA: University of California Press.

Rybczynski, Witold. 1995. *City Life: Urban Expectations in a New World*. New York: Scribner.

Rykwert, Joseph. 1978. "The Street: The Use of its History." Pp.15–27 in *On Streets*, Stanford Anderson (ed.). Cambridge, MA: MIT Press.

Saffron, Inga. 2001. "Symbols of U.S. Capitalism Crumble." *The Philadelphia Inquirer* (September 12): A13.

Saffron, Inga. 2005. "Changing Skyline: Home on the Rails." *Philadelphia Inquirer* November 6.

Saffron, Inga. 2005. "Flaws and All, Edmund N. Bacon Molded a Modern Philadelphia." *The Philadelphia Inquirer*. Posted on Sunday, October 10. http://www.philly/12912032.htm?template=contentModules/printstory.jsp

Sagan, Carl 1977. *The Dragons of Eden: Speculations on the Evolution of Human Intelligence*. New York: Random House.

Salisbury, Stephan, and Leonard Boasberg. 2005. "Visionary Planner Behind City's Renaissance." *The Philadelphia Inquirer* (October 15):A1,A5.

Salisbury, Stephen. 2003. "A More Perfect Philadelphia Story." *The Philadelphia Inquirer* (December 21: C1, C3).

Salisbury, Stephen. 2004. "Slave Discovery Intensifies Park Controversy." *The Philadelphia Inquirer* (July 3): B1, B4).

Salisbury, Stephen. 2005. "Pioneer's Life is Dug up at Independence Hall." *The Philadelphia Inquirer* (June 12): B3).

Sampson, Pamela/Associated Press. 2003. "Heat wave toll tops 19,000." *detnews.com.* (September 26). http://www.detnews.com/2003/nation/0309/2 6/ao4–281883.htm

Sampson, Robert .J. and Stephen W. Raudenbush, 1999. "Systematic social observation of public spaces: A new look at disorder in urban neighborhoods." *American Journal of Sociology*, 105(3), 603–651.

Sampson, Robert J. and Stephen W. Raudenbush. 2004. The social structure of seeing disorder. *Social Psychology Quarterly.* 67(4), 319–342.

Sassen, Saskia. 1991. *The Global City: New York, Tokyo, London*. Princeton, NJ: Princeton University Press.

Sassen, Saskia. 1994. *Cities in a World Economy*. Thousand Oaks, CA: Pine Forge.

Satterthwaite, Ann. 2001. *Going Shopping: Consumer Choices and Community Consequences*. New Haven, CT: Yale University Press.

Scheper-Hughes, Nancy. 1992. *Death Without Weaping: The Violence of Everyday Life in Brazil*. Berkeley, CA: University of California Press.

Schuman, Tony, and Elliott Sclar. 1996. "The Impact of Ideology on American Town Planning." Pp. 428–48 in Mary Corbin Sies and Christopher Silver (eds.), *Planning the Twentieth-Century American City*. Baltimore, MD: Johns Hopkins University Press.

Scott, Janny. 1998. "New Respectability for Manners." *The New York Times* February 28:B9; B11.

Scott, Mel C. 1969. *American City Planning Since 1980*. Berkeley, CA: University of California Press.

Scully, Vincent. 1988. *American Architecture and Urbanism, New revised edition*. New York: Henry Holt and Company.

Seeley, John R., Alexander Sim, and E.W. Loosley. 1956. *Crestwood Heights: A Study of the Culture of Suburban Life*. Toronto: University of Toronto Press.

Seller, Maxine. 1977. *To Seek America: A History of Ethnic Life in the United States*. Englewood, NJ: J.S. Ozer.

Sennett, Richard. 1969. "An Introduction." Pp. 3–19 in Richard Sennett (ed.), *Classic Essays on the Culture of Cities*. New York: Appleton-Century-Crofts.

Sennett, Richard. 1970. *The Uses of Disorder: Personal Identity and City Life*. New York: Vintage Books.

Sennett, Richard. 1992. *The Uses of Disorder: Personal Identity and City Life,* Second Edition. New York: W. W. Norton.

Sennett, Richard. 1977. *The Fall of Public Man: On the Social Psychology of Capitalism*. New York: Alfred A. Knopf.

Sennett, Richard. 1990. *The Conscience of the Eye: The Design and Social Life of Cities*. New York: Knopf.

Seymour, Harold. 1960. *Baseball: The Early Years*. New York: Oxford University Press.

Seymour, Harold. 1971. *Baseball: The Golden Years*. New York: Oxford University Press.

Shapiro, Bruce. 2002. "Zero-Tolerance Gospel." *Index online.*

Shelley, Percy Bysshe. 1968. "Ozymandias." Pp. 411–12 in M.H. Andrews et al., (eds.), *The Norton Anthology of English Literature. Revised. Vol. 2*. New York: W.W. Norton. Originally published in 1817.

Shevky, Eshref and Wendell Bell. 1955. *Social Area Analysis*. Stanford Sociological Series #1. Stanford, CA: Stanford University Press.

Shibutani, Tamotsu. 1955. "Reference Groups as Perspectives," *American Journal of Sociology* LX: 562–69.

Shibutani, Tamotsu. 1961. *Society and Personality: An Interactionist Approach to Social Psychology*. Englewood Cliffs, N.J.: Prentice-Hall.

Shinn, Marybeth, J.R. Knickman, and B.C. Weitzman. 1991. "Social relations and vulnerability to becoming homeless among poor families." *American Psychologist* 46:1180–1187.

Shinn, Marybeth, and Beth C. Weitzman. 1994. "You can't eliminate homelessness without housing." *American Behavioral Scientist* 37 (January) 3:435–442.

Short, John Rennie. 1996. *The Urban Order: An Introduction to Cities, Culture, and Power*. Cambridge, MA: Blackwell.

Shorter, Edward. 1975. *The Making of the Modern Family*. New York: Basic Books.

Siegel, Fred. 1995. "Reclaiming Our Public Spaces." Pp. 369–83 in Philip Kasinitz (ed.), *Metropolis: Center and Symbol of our Times*. New York: New York University Press. First published in *The City Journal*, vol. 2, no. 2 (Spring 1992).

Siegel, Fred. 1997. *The Future Once Happened Here: New York, D.C., L.A., and the Fate of America's Big Cities*. New York: Free Press.

Siegel, Stephen J. 1998. "Chicago's Ambitious Plan." *Newsday* December 31: A21.

Simmel, Georg. 1995. "Metropolis and Mental Life." Pp. 30–45 in Philip Kasinitz (ed.), *Metropolis: Center and Symbol of Our Times.* New York: New York University Press. Reprinted from Georg Simmel, *On Individuality and Social Forms* (Donald Levine, ed.). Chicago: University of Chicago Press, 1971. Translated by Edward Shils. Originally published as "Die Grosstadte und das Geistesleben" in T. Petermann (ed.), Die Grasstadt. Dresden, 1903.

Simon, Bryant. 2004. *Boardwalk of Dreams: Atlantic City and the Fate of Urban America.* New York: Oxford University Press.

Sjoberg, Gideon. 1960. *The Preindustrial City: Past and Present.* New York: Free Press.

Skogan, Wesley G. 1992. *Disorder and Decline: Crime and the Spiral of Decay in American Neighborhoods.* Berkeley, CA: University of California Press.

Smelser, Neil. J. 1959. *Social Change in the Industrial Revolution.* Chicago: University of Chicago Press.

Smith, Carl. 1994. *Urban Disorder and the Shape of Belief: The Great Chicago Fire, The Haymarket Bomb, and the Model Town of Pullman.* Chicago: University of Chicago Press.

Smith, Craig S. 2005a. "Angry immigrants embroil France in wider riots. *The New York Times.* November 5:A1, A9.

Smith, Craig S. 2005b. " France has an underclass, But its roots are still shallow." *The New York Times.* November 6:WK3.

Smith, Craig S. 2005c. "10 officers shot as riots worsen in French cities." *The New York Times.* November 7:A1, A10.

Smith, Craig S. 2005d. "Inside French housing project: Feelings of being the outsider." *The New York Times.* November 9:A1, A12.

Smith, David A. 1996. *Third World Cities in Global Perspective.* Boulder, CO: Westview Press, Inc.

Smith, Joel, William H. Form, and Gregory P. Stone. 1954. "Local intimacy in a middle-sized city." *American Journal of Sociology* 60:276–283.

Smith, Michael Peter. 1988. *City, State, and Market.* New York: Basil Blackwell.

Smith, Neil. 1992. "New City, New Frontier: The Lower East Side as Wild, Wild West. Pp. 61–93 in Sorkin, Michael (ed.). 1992. *Variations on a Theme Park: The New American City and the End of Public Space.* New York: Hill and Wang, Noonday Press.

Smith, Neil and Peter Williams. 1991. "Gentrification of the City" quoted on page 148 in *If You Lived Here: The City in Art, Theory and Social Activism,* a project by Martha Rosler, Brian Wallis, ed. New York: Dia Foundation for the Arts.

Smith, Neil. 1996. "Gentrification, the Frontier, and the Restructuring of Urban Space." Pp. 338–58 in Susan Fainstein and Scott Campbell (eds.), *Readings in Urban Theory.* Cambridge, MA: Blackwell Publishers. First published in Neil Smith and Peter Williams (eds.), *Gentrification of the City.*

Smith, Neil. 1996. *The New Urban Frontier.* London: Routledge.

Smith, Neil. 1997. "Social Justice and the New American Urbanism: The Revanchist City." Pp. 117–36 in Andy Merrifield and Erik Swyngedouw (eds.), *The Urbanization of Injustice.* New York: New York University Press.

Smith, Robert. 1961. *Baseball in America.* New York: Holt, Rinehart and Winston.

Snow, David A. and Leon Anderson. 1993. *Down on Their Luck: A Study of Homeless Street People.* Berkeley, CA: University of California Press.

Snow, David A., and Susan G. Baker, Leon Anderson, and Michael Martin. 1986. "The myth of pervasive mental illness among the homeless." *Social Problems* 33 (June): 407–423.

Snyder, Robert W. 1995. "City in Transition." Pp. 29–57 in Rebecca Zurier, Robert W. Snyder, and Virginia M. Mecklenburg, *Metropolitan Lives: The Ashcan Artists and Their New York.* New York: National Museum of American Art in Association with W.W. Norton & Company.

Soja, Edward W. 1996. "Los Angeles 1965–1992: The Six Geographies of Urban Restructuring." Pp. 426–62 in A.J. Scott and E. Soja (eds.), *The City: Los Angeles & Urban Theory at the End of the Twentieth Century.* Berkeley, CA: University of California Press.

Soja, Edward W. 2002. "Taking Los Angeles Apart: Some Fragments of a Critical Human Geography." Pp. 150–61 in Michael J. Dear and Steven Flusty (eds.), *The Spaces of Postmodernity: Readings in Human Geography.* Malden, MA: Blackwell Publishers.

Solnit, Rebecca. 2002. *Hollow City: The Siege of San Francisco and the Crisis of American Urbanism.* Rebecca Solnit, text; Susan Schwartzenberg, photographs. London; New York: Verso.

Somers, Dale A. 1972. *The Rise of Sport in New Orleans, 1850–1900.* Baton Rouge, Louisiana: Louisiana University Press.

Sorkin, Michael (ed.). 1992. *Variations on a Theme Park: The New American City and the End of Public Space.* New York: Hill and Wang, Noonday Press.

Spalding, Albert G. 1911/1992. *America's National Game*. Reprinted from the original edition published in 1911 by the American Sports Publishing Company, New York by Lincoln, Nebraska: A Bison Book, University of Nebraska Press.

Spear, Alan. 1967. *Black Chicago*. Chicago, IL: University of Chicago Press.

Spirn, Ann Whiston. 1998. *The Language of Landscape*. New Haven, CT: Yale University Press.

Stack, Carol B. 1974. *All Our Kin*. New York: Harper & Row.

Staples, Carol B., and Alfredo Mirande. 1980. "Racial and cultural variations among American families: A decennial review of the literature on minority families." *Journal of Marriage and the Family* 42 (Nov.):157–73.

Staples, Robert. 1971. "Towards a Sociology of the Black Family: A Theoretical and Methodological assessment." *Journal of Marriage and the Family* 33:119–38.

Statistical Abstracts of the United States. 1997. Annual. Washington, D.C.: U.S. Bureau of the Census.

Stein, Maurice. 1964. *The Eclipse of Community*. New York: Harper (Torchbook).

Stern, Robert A.M. 1986. *Pride of Place: Building the American Dream*. Boston: Houghton Mifflin

Stern, Robert A.M. 2001. "To Rebuild or Not—Architects Respond." *The New York Times Magazine* September 23:81.

Stern, Robert A.M., Thomas Mellins, and David Fishman. 1995. *New York 1960*. New York: The Monacelli Press.

Stilwell, Eileen. 2005. "Price of success takes toll in Collingswood." *Courier Post*. April 20: 1B,2B).

Stoller, Paul. 2002. *Money Has No Smell: The Africanization of New York City*. Chicago, IL: University of Chicago Press.

Stone, Gregory P. 1954. "City Shoppers and Urban Identification: Observations on the Social Psychology of City Life." *American Journal of Sociology* (July):36–45.

Stone, Gregory P. 1968. "Urban Identification and the Sociology of Sport." Paper presented at the annual meeting of the American Association for the Advancement of Science.

Stone. Gregory P. 1973. "American Sports: Play and Display." In John T. Talamini and Charles H. Page (eds.), *Sports and Society: An Anthology*. Boston: Little, Brown. Pp. 65–85.

Stone, Gregory P. 1981. "Sport as a Community Representation, in Gunther R.F. Luschen and George H. Sage (eds.), *Handbook of Social Science and Sport*. Champaign, IL.: Stipes Publishing Co. Pp. 214–45.

Strasser, Susan. 1982. *Never Done: A History of American Housework*. New York: Pantheon.

Strauss, Anselm L. 1961. *Images of the American City*. New York: The Fress Press. Reprinted 1975. New Brunswick, New Jersey: Transaction Books.

Sudarkasa, Niara. 1988. "Interpreting the African Heritage in Afro-American Family Organization." Pp. 27–43 in Harriet P. McAdoo (ed.), *Black Families*. Newbury Park, CA: Sage.

Sussman, Marvin B. 1953. "The help pattern in the middle class family." *American Sociological Review* 18:22–28.

Sussman, Marvin B., 1959. "The isolated nuclear family 1959: Fact or fiction?" *Social Problems* 6:333–40.

Sussman, Marvin B., and Lee Burchinal. 1962. "Kin family network: Unheralded structure in current conceptualizations of family functioning." Marriage and family living 24:231–240.

Suttles, Gerald. 1968. *The Social Order of the Slum*. Chicago: University of Chicago Press.

Syrett, Harold Coffin. 1944. *The City of Brooklyn, 1865–1898*. New York: Columbia University Press.

Tannenbaum, Barbara. 2002. "Where Miles of Murals Preach a People's Gospel." *The New York Times on the Web*. www.nytimes.com.

Tagliabue, John. 2003. "Heat wave turned Pairs homes into ovens for elderly." *Toronto Star*. (August 21): New York Times. http://www.thestar.com/NASApp/cs/ContentServer?pagename=thestar/ Layout/Article_Print

Tallman, Irving, and Romona Morgner. 1970. "Life style differences among urban and suburban blue collar families." *Social Forces* (March): 334–48.

Tallman, Irving. 1969. "Working-class wives in suburbia: Fulfillment or crisis." *Journal of Marriage and the Family* 31:65–72.

Teaford, Jon C. 1986. *The Twentieth-Century American City: Problem, Promise and Reality*. Baltimore, MD: Johns Hopkins University Press.

The World Almanac. 2005. *The World Almanac and Book of Facts 2005*. New York: World Almanac Books.

Thomas, W. I. 1923. *The Unadjusted Girl*. Boston, MA: Little, Brown.

Thomas, W.I., and Dorothy S. 1928. *The Child in America*. New York: Knopf.

Thomas, William I. and Florian Znaniecki. 1918–1920. *The Polish Peasant in Europe and America*. Volumes 1 and 2 published by Chicago: University of Chicago Press; Volumes 3, 4, and 5 published by Boston: Badger Press.

Thompson, E.P. 1963. *The Making of the English Working Class*. London: Gollancz.

Time Almanac 2001. 2000. Boston, MA: Information Please.

Tönnies, Ferdinand. 1963. *Community and Society [emeinschaft und Gesellschaft].* Charles P. Loomis (trans. and ed.). New York: Harper (Torchbooks). (Originally published, 1887; original translation, 1957.)

Torrey, Barbara Boyle. 2004. "Urbanization: An Environmental Force to be Reckoned With." (April). *Population Reference Bureau.* http://www.prb.org/Template.cfm=PRB&template=/Content/ContentGroups/04_Artic

Trachtenberg, Alan. 1982. *The Incorporation of America.* New York: Hill and Wang.

Tremblay, Jason. 1999. *Mural Arts in Philadelphia.* "History of the Philadelphia Mural Arts Program. "http://www/courses.psu.edu/art/art122wilh18/student/tremblay/history.html

Tucker, William. 1997. "Unbroken Windows." *New York Press* (July 30-August 5, 1997): 36–37. Reprinted in *Annual Editions: Urban Society 9/e,* Fred Siegel and Jan Rosenberg (eds.). Guilford, CT: Dushkin/McGraw Hill: Sluice Dock. (1999: 186–89).

Turner, John F.C. 1969. "Uncontrolled urban settlement: Problems and policies." Pp. 507–534 in Gerald Breese (ed.), *The City in Newly Developing Countries: Readings on Urbanism and Urbanization.* Englewood Cliffs: NJ: Prentice-Hall.

Turner, John F.C. 1970. "Barriers and channels for housing development in modernizing countries." Pp. 1–19 in William Mangin (ed.), *Peasants in Cities: Readings in the Anthropology of Urbanization.* Boston: Houghton-Mifflin.

Uhlman, Marian. 2004. "Healthy Places." *The Philadelphia Inquirer* (March 1): D1, D3.

United Nations. 2004. *World Urbanization Prospects: The 2003 Revision.* New York: United Nations. Department of Economic and Social Affairs/Population Division.

U.S. Centers for Disease Control and Prevention. 1999. *Sexually Transmitted Disease Surveillance 1998.* Atlanta, GA: The Centers.

U.S. Conference of Mayors. 1996. *A Status Report on Hunger and Homelessness in America's Cities: 1996.* Washington, DC: Author

Vale, Lawrence J. and Thomas J. Campanella. 2005a. "Introduction: The cities rise again." Pp. 3–23 in Lawrence J. Vale and Thomas J. Campanella (eds.), *The Resilient City: How Modern Cities Recover from Disaster.* New York: Oxford University Press.

Vale, Lawrence J. and Thomas J. Campanella. 2005b "Conclusion: Axioms of resilience." Pp. 335–61 in Lawrence J. Vale and Thomas J. Campanella

(eds.), *The Resilient City: How Modern Cities Recover from Disaster.* New York: Oxford University Press.

Van Allen, Peter. 2004. "Haddonfield's Strategy Revs up Retail." *Philadelphia Business Journal* (November 15). http://philadelphia.bizjournals.com/philadelphia/stories/2004/11/15/story4.html

Vanderbilt, Amy. 1967. *New Complete Book of Etiquette: The Guide to Gracious Living.* Garden City, NY: Doubleday.

Vanderbilt, Amy. 1974. *Amy Vanderbilt's Everyday Etiquette.* Garden City, NY: Doubleday.

Vanderstaay, Steven. 1992. *Street Lives: An Oral History of Homeless Americans.* Philadelphia, PA: New Society Publishers.

Velez-Ibanez, Carlos. 1993. "U.S. Mexicans in the borderlands: Being poor without the underclass." Pp. 195–220 in Joan Moore and Raquel Pinderhughes. (eds.). 1993. *In the Barrios: Latinos and the Underclass Debate.* New York: Russell Sage Foundation.

Venkatesh, Sudhir Alladi. 2000. *American Project: The Rise and Fall of a Modern American Ghetto.* Cambridge, MA: Harvard University Press.

Vergara, Camilo Jose. 1995. *The New American Ghetto.* New Brunswick, NJ: Rutgers University Press.

Voigt, David Q. 1976. *America Through Baseball.* Chicago: Nelson-Hall.

Von Hagan, Victory W. 1961. *The Ancient Sun Kingdoms of the Americas: Aztec, Maya, Inca.* Cleveland and New York: World.

Wacquant, Loic J.D. 1995. "The Ghetto, the State, and the New Capitalistic Economy." Pp. 418–49 in Philip Kasinitz (ed.), *Metropolis: Center and Symbol of our Times.* New York: New York University Press. Reprinted from *Dissent* (Fall 1989).

Walkowitz, Judith. 1980. *Prostitution and Victorian Society.* Cambridge: Cambridge University Press.

Wallerstein, Immanuel. 1974. *The Modern World System.* New York: Academic Press.

Wallerstein, Immanuel. 1979. *The Capitalist World-Economy.* Cambridge, England: Cambridge University Press.

Wallerstein, Immanuel. 1984. *The Politics of the World-Economy.* Cambridge, England: Cambridge University Press

Walton, John. 1986. *Sociology and Critical Inquiry: The Work, Tradition, and Purpose.* Chicago, IL: Dorsey Press.

Walzer, Michael. 1995. "Pleasures and Costs of Urbanity." Pp. 320–30 in Philip Kasinitz (ed.),

Metropolis: Center and Symbol of our Times. New York: New York University Press. [Reprinted from *Dissent* (Fall 1986).]

Ward, Stephen V. 2002. *Planning the Twentieth-Century City: The Advanced Capitalist World*. Chichester, West Sussex, UK: John Wiley & Sons, LTD.

Warner, Jr., Sam Bass. 1984. "Slums and Skyscrapers: Urban Images, Symbols, and Ideology." Pp. 191–95 in Lloyd Rodwin and Robert M. Hollister (eds.), *Cities of the Mind: Images and Themes of the City in the Social Sciences*. New York: Plenum Press.

Warren, R. and Passel J. 1987. "A count of the uncountable: Estimates of undocumented aliens counted in the above 1980 United States Census." *Demography* 24:375–93.

Washington, Jr., Linn. 2002 "Park Service Burying a Shameful Fact." *The Philadelphia Tribune* (April 2).

Watson, William. 1961. "A Cycle of Cathay: China the civilization of a single people." Pp. 253–76 in Stuart Piggott (ed.), *The Dawn of Civilization: The First World Survey of Human Cultures in Early Times*. New York: McGraw Hill.

Watters, Ethan. 2003. *Urban Tribes: A Generation Redefines Friendship, Family, and Commitment*. New York: Bloomsbury.

Weber, Eugen. 1976. *Peasants into Frenchmen*. Stanford, CA: Stanford University Press.

Weber, Max. 1962. *The City*. Edited and translated by Don Martindale and Gertrud Neuwirth. New York: Free Press.

Weeks, John R. 1994. *Population: An Introduction to Concepts and Issues*. Update 5th ed. Belmont, CA: Wadsworth Publishing Company.

Weinberg, H. Barbara, Doreen Bolger, and David Park Curry. 1994. *American Impressionism and Realism: The Painting of Modern Life, 1885–1915*. New York: Harry N. Abrams, Inc.

Weitz, Rose. 2005. "Teaching about Hurricane Katrina: Resources for Faculty (and Students). http://www.public.asu.edu/~ymal14/Katrina.html

Wekerle, Gerda B. 1980. "Women in the Urban Environment." Pp. 185–211 in C.R. Simson, E. Dixler, M.J. Nelson, and K.B. Yatrakis (eds.), *Women and the American City*. Chicago: University of Chicago Press.

Wellman, Barry (ed.), 1999. *Networks in the Global Village: Life in Contemporary Communities*. Boulder, CO: Westview Publishers.

Wellman, Barry and Milena Gulia. 1999. "Net-surfers Don't Ride Alone. Virtual Communities as Communities." Pp. 331–66 in Barry Wellman (ed.), *Networks in the Global Village: Life in Contemporary Communities*. Boulder, CO: Westview Publishers.

Wellman, Barry and Keith N. Hampton. 2004. "Long Distance Community in the Network Society: Contact and Support Beyond Netville." Pp. 94–107 in Mark Hutter (ed.), *The Family Experience: A Reader in Cultural Diversity*. Fourth Edition. Boston: Allyn & Bacon. Originally appeared in *American Behavioral Scientist*, V 2001 Vol. 45, no. 3 (November) pp. 477–96.

Welter, Barbara. 1966. "The Cult of True Womanhood: 1820–1860." *American Quarterly* 18 (Summer): 151–74.

Welton, Jude. 1993. *Impressionism: Eyewitness Art*. New York: Dorling Kindersley.

Westenberg, Peter. 2001. "Metropolitan Representations." http://home.luna.nl/~westenberg/projects/ archis/Archis.html (first published in *Archis #5*)

Wheeler, Sir Mortimer. 1961. "Ancient India: The civilization of a subcontinent." Pp. 229–52 in Stuart Piggott (ed.), *The Dawn of Civilization: The First World Survey of Human Cultures in Early Times*. New York: McGraw-Hill.

Wheeler, Sir Mortimer. 1964. "The Indus Valley." Pp. 361–71 in Peter B. Hammond (ed.), *Physical Anthropology and Archaeology: Selected Readings*. New York: Macmillan.

Wheeler, Sir Mortimer. 1966. *Civilizations of the Indus Valley and Beyond*. London: Thames and Hudson.

White, Morton and Lucia. 1977. *The Intellectual Versus the City: From Thomas Jefferson to Frank Lloyd Wright*. New York: Oxford University Press. (First published in 1962.)

Whyte, William H. 1980. *Social Life of Small Urban Spaces*. Washington, DC: The Conservation Foundation.

Whyte, William H. 1988. *City: Rediscovering the Center*. New York: Doubleday.

Wilford, John Noble. 2005. "Ancient battle site is found: Discovery offers evidence of culture clash in Mesopotamia." (December 18) *The New York Times*.

Will, George F. 2001. "Drawn into the Fire." *New York Post* (September 12): 57.

Williams, Timothy. 2005. "In Bryant Park's rebirth, some chafe at growing corportate presence." *The New York Times*. (December 5): B1, B5.

Willing, Richard, and Jim Drinkard. 2001 "America's Descent into Madness: Attack Destroyed Lives, Landmarks and Nation's Sense of Security." *USA Today* (September 12): 3A.

Willmott, Peter, and Michael Young. 1960. *Family and Class in a London Suburb.* London: Routledge & Kegan Paul.

Willms, Johannes. 1997. *Paris Capital of Europe: From the Revolution to the Belle Epoque.* New York: Holmes & Meier.

Wilson, Elizabeth. 1991. *The Sphinx in the City: Urban Life, the Control of Disorder, and Women.* Berkeley, CA: University of California Press.

Wilson, James Q. 1975/1983. *Thinking About Crime,* Revised ed. New York: Vintage. Original edition published in 1975.

Wilson, James Q., and George L. Kelling. 1982. "Broken windows." *Atlantic Monthly,* vol. 249, no. 3 (March):29–36, 38.

Wilson, William H. 1989. *The City Beautiful Movement.* Baltimore, MD: Johns Hopkins University Press.

Wirth, Louis. 1929/1964. *The Ghetto.* Chicago: University of Chicago Press.

Wirth, Louis, 1927/1964. "The Ghetto." Pages 84–98 in *Louis Wirth On cities and Social Life; Selected Papers.* Edited and with an introduction by Albert J. Reiss, Jr. Chicago: University of Chicago Press. First published in the *American Journal of Sociology* XXXIII (July, 1927): 57–71.

Wirth, Louis. 1938a. "Urbanism as a Way of Life." *American Journal of Sociology,* vol. 44, no.1. Reprinted in Philip Kasinitz (ed.). 1995. Pp. 58–82 in *Metropolis: Center and Symbol of Our Time.* New York: New York University Press.

Wirth, Louis. 1995/1938b. "Urbanism as a Way of Life." Pages 58–82 in Philip Kasinitz (ed.), *Metropolis: Center and Symbol of Our Times.* New York: New York University Press. Pp. 58–82. Reprinted from *American Journal of Sociology,* vol. 44, no.1.

Wiseman, Carter. 1998. *Shaping a Nation: Twentieth Century American Architecture and its Makers.* New York: Norton.

Wiseman, Jacqueline. P.1979. "Close Encounters of the Quasi-Primary Kind: Sociability in Urban Second-Hand Clothing Stores." *Urban Life,* vol. 8, no. 1 (April): 23–51.

Wohl, R. Richard, and Anselm L. Strauss 1958. "Symbolic Representation and the Urban Milieu." *American Journal of Sociology* LXIII (March): 523–32.

Wolfe, Alan. 1998. *One Nation, After All: What Middle-Class Americans Really Think About God, Country, Family, Racism, Welfare, Immigration, Homosexuality, Work, the Right, the Left, and Each Other.* New York: Viking.

Wolfe, Gerard R. 2003. *New York, 15 Walking Tours: An Architectural Guide to the Metropolis.* 3rd ed. New York: McGraw-Hill.

Wolfe, Thomas. 1940. "Only the Dead Know Brooklyn." Pp. 123–138 in *Short Stories From the NEW YORKER.* New York: Simon and Schuster.

World Bank. 2003. *Sustainable Development in a Dynamic World.* Washington, DC: World Bank.

The World Almanac 2005. 2005. New York: World Almanac Books.

Worsnop, R. 1996. "Helping the homeless." *CQ Researcher.* (January 26).

Wright, Frank Lloyd Wright. 1938. *The Living City.* New York: Horizon Press.

Wright, Frank Lloyd. 1974. Quote from *The Chrome-Plated Nightmare (Televison Program, May 27, 1974)* quoted on page 264 in James A. Clapp (ed.), *The City: A Dictionary of Quotable Thoughts on Cities and Urban Life.* New Brunswick, NJ: Rutgers University Press.

Wright, Gwendolyn. 1981. *Building the Dream: A Social History of Housing in America.* New York: Pantheon Books.

Wright, Talmadge. 1997. *Out of Place: Homeless Mobilizations, Societies, and Contested Landscapes.* Albany, New York: SUNY Press.

Yancey, William L. 1973. "Architecture, Interaction and Social Control: The Case of a Large-Scale Public Housing Project." Pp. 107–22 in John Helmer and Neil A. Eddington (eds.), *Urbanman The Psychology of Urban Survival.* New York: The Free Press.

Yancey, William. L., Eugene P. Erickson, and Richard N. Juliani. 1976. "Emergent ethnicity: A review and reformulation." *American Sociological Review* 41 (June):391–402.

Yans-McLaughlin, Virginia. 1971. "Patterns of work and family organization." Pages 111–126 in Theodore K. Rabb and Robert L. Rotberg (eds.), *The Family in History: Interdisciplinary Essays.* New York: Harper (Torchbooks).

Ybarra, Lea. 1982. "When wives work: The impact on the Chicano family." *Journal of Marriage and the Family* 44 (Feb.):169–78.

Young, Michael, and Peter Willmott. 1957. *Family and Kinship in East London.* Baltimore: Penguin Books. (Rev. ed., 1963.)

Zorbaugh, Harvey W. 1929. *The Gold Coast and the Slum.* Chicago: University of Chicago Press.

Zuckerman, M.J. 2001. "Chances Are, Somebody's Watching You." *USA Today* (November 30) cited in Gary Gumpert and Susan J. Drucker. 2001. "Public Boundaries: Privacy and Surveillance in a Technological World." *Communication-Quarterly* vol. 49, no. 2 (Spring):115–29 retrieved on 10/30/2003 from http:/web5.silverplatter.com/webspirs/showFullRecordContent.

Zukin, Sharon. 1995. "Whose culture? Whose City." In Sharon Zukin. 1995. The Culture of Cities (pp. v–xiv; 1–47). Cambridge MA: Blackwell.

Zukin, Sharon. 1989. *Loft Living: Culture and Capital in Urban Change.* New Brunswick, NJ: Rutgers University Press. First published in 1982. Baltimore, MD: Johns Hopkins University Press.

Zukin, Sharon. 1995. *The Culture of Cities.* Cambridge, MA: Blackwell.

Zukin, Sharon. 1996. "Space and Symbols in an Age of Decline." Pp. 43–59 in Anthony King (ed.), *Re-Presenting the City.* London: Macmillan.

Zukin, Sharon. 2005. *Point of Purchase: How Shopping Changed American Culture.* New York: Routledge.

Zunz, Olivier. 1990. *Making America Corporate, 1870–1920.* Chicago: University of Chicago Press.

Zurier, Rebecca, and Robert W. Snyder. 1995. "Introduction." Pp. 13–27 in Rebecca Zurier, Robert W. Snyder, and Virginia M. Mecklenburg, *Metropolitan Lives: The Ashcan Artists and Their New York.* New York: National Museum of American Art in Association with W.W. Norton & Company.

Index

490

Photo Credits